Farewell, Revolution

Disputed Legacies, France, 1789/1989

Farewell, Revolution

DISPUTED LEGACIES

FRANCE, 1789/1989

Steven Laurence Kaplan

CORNELL UNIVERSITY PRESS

ITHACA AND LONDON

First published 1995 by Cornell University Press

Printed in the United States of America

♾ The paper in this book meets the minimum requirements
of the American National Standard for Information Sciences—
Permanence of Paper for Printed Library Materials, ANSI Z39.48-1984.

Library of Congress Cataloging-in-Publication Data

Kaplan, Steven L.
  Farewell, Revolution : disputed legacies : France, 1789/1989 / Steven Laurence Kaplan.
    p.   cm.
  Includes bibliographical references and index.
  ISBN 0-8014-2718-5
  1. Bicentenaire de la Révolution française, 1989. 2. France—History—Revolution, 1789–1799—
Centennial celebrations, etc.—Political aspects. 3. Historical reenactments—France. I. Title.
DC160.K35   1995
944.04—dc20   94-24107

For Nan E. Karwan Cutting
and James Cutting

Contents

Contents

BOOK THREE
THE BICENTENNIAL AND THE NATION

Acknowledgments

I am happy for the opportunity to express my deep gratitude to the many persons who proffered encouragement and assistance. My old friend Guy Sorman whispered "de l'audace" three times, talked issues out with me, and provided me with much help in making connections in all senses of the term. As Fellows at Cornell's Society for the Humanities, Colin Lucas and I shared a seminar and countless hours of exchange that enriched and clarified my thinking at the crucial early stages. We were occasionally joined in a mini-colloquium by Hans-Ulrich Thamer, who pressed me to think comparatively. I rebuffed the cautions of Maurice Aymard and Jacques Revel, but I profited from their insight on many questions that vexed me at the outset. The sage and exigent critic Claude Grignon sought more or less vainly to induce me to stretch beyond my limits.

At Editions Fayard, Claude Durand warmly welcomed my project, and Agnès Fontaine gently urged me on. At Cornell University Press, John Ackerman, a wonderfully cosmopolitan intellectual as well as a fine manager, helped me to resolve problems of substance as well as form. Managing editor Kay Scheuer and Joan Howard, the copyeditor, improved the book in countless ways. As usual, Eric Vigne, another gifted bookman, offered his special blend of hearty support and mordant suggestion. Normalien, geographer, and impassioned intellectual, André Charpentier died before he could complete the translation of this book into French, the language in which it first appeared. His many suggestions and refinements helped me to improve the American/English version substantially. In numerous subtle and therapeutic ways, my dear friends Eliane and Frank Simon impelled me to pursue my objectives.

With grace, wit, and solicitude, Jean-Noël Jeanneney, president of the Mission du Bicentenaire, guided me, opened countless doors, furnished documentation, and answered endless questions. His collaborator Claire Andrieu showed me infinite kindnesses, shared precious information, and challenged me to rethink certain problems. Another Mission agent, Christian de Montrichard, enlightened me on many subjects. François Baroin, son of the Mission's first president, generously evoked memories that surely pained him and opened up for me several new vistas on the bicentennial. Among the other members of the Mission who aided me were Thierry Collard, André de Margerie, Philippe Blondel, Angélique Oussedik, Jean-Pierre Cabouat, and Monique Sauvage. At a very early stage, Yann Gaillard, Edgar Faure's right-hand man, obliged me with an interview.

A number of historians permitted me to question them as actors on the commemorative stage. François Furet, who had helped me launch my doctoral research twenty-two years earlier, once again opened his door. My research itinerary led me to renew an old friendship with Jean Tulard and, I hope, to forge a new one with Michel Vovelle. Another new friend, Claude Mazauric, went to extraordinary lengths to arrange for me to plug into the network of the Vive 89 organization and to have access to its archives and its creations. Without any formalities, he allowed me to interrogate him vigorously, and he engaged me in tonic debate. Though he barely remembered me, Maurice Agulhon accorded me several hours of his time. Madeleine Rebérioux patiently fielded my questions. I hope Jean Favier will forgive me for thinking of him first of all as a historian. In addition to affording me his perspective on the commemoration, in his capacity as Director of the Archives de France he kindly authorized me to consult the Mission's papers, which were then being catalogued by an extremely considerate curator, Agnès Etienne-Magnien. At Poitiers, Jean-Marie Augustin received me cordially and Jacques Peret twice put himself at my disposition and lavished me with personal testimony and local publications.

Ingenious, efficient and irretrievably optimistic, France de Malval helped organize my field work, marshal documentation, and keep me out of trouble. Guy Rossi-Landi, a master political journalist, contributed useful data. With energy and devotion, Sylvie Le Moil took charge of my apprenticeship in the libraries of the Institut d'études politiques of the rue Saint-Guillaume. Around the corner, Daniel de Crozefon engaged me in a fecund dialogue on the forms (and *pièges*) of Parisian cultural expression. Two dear friends, Marie-Cécile and Philippe Desmarest, welcomed me back to Poitiers with touching warmth. A discreet and adroit diplomat, Philippe enabled me to enter into contact with dozens of persons who had played a local or regional role in the commemoration. With the same solicitude, Elisabeth and Jean-Michel Voge offered me hospitality in Paris and advice on iconography. Five comrades in the profession, Roger Chartier, Maurice Garden, Michael Kammen, Emmanuel Le Roy Ladurie, and Denis Woronoff, all distinguished historians, lent bibliographical guidance and procured key texts. Another member of this same category, Louis Bergeron, furnished me an office at the Centre de recherches historiques and chastened some of my extravagant thinking. At the Maison des sciences de l'homme, Clemens Heller and Maurice Aymard extended their support in both very concrete and impalpable ways, for the nth time.

Acknowledgments

For invaluable documentation and commentary, a host of strangers treated me with unwonted friendship: Christian Lescureux of the Amis de Robespierre pour le Bicentenaire de la Révolution at Arras; Roger Bourderon of Comité 89 en 93 (Seine–Saint-Denis); Gaston Mertz of Vive la Carmagnole at Thionville; Senator-Mayor Paul Souffrin of Thionville; Claudy Valin of the Société rochelaise de l'histoire moderne et contemporaine; Professors Guy Boisson and Raymond Huard, animators of the Vive 89 association of Montpellier; Jacques Blin of Mille Sète Cent Quatre-Vingt-Neuf; Marcel Alory of Vive 89 in Saint-Brieuc; Hubert Delport of Vive 89 at Nérac; Jean-Claude Mairal, president of the Amis de la Révolution française pour la célébration du Bicentenaire at Moulins; André Leroy of Vive 89 en Haute-Alsace; Jeanette Roquier of Vive 89 en Ille-et-Vilaine at Rennes; Jacques Demiot of the Fédération des oeuvres laïques at Poitiers; Christine Lazerges, deputy mayor of Montpellier; Colette Deblé and Ana Rosa Richardson, gifted artists who took a special interest in Robespierre; and Professor Maurice Moissonnier of Lyon.

In personal encounters many others donated time and precious testimony beyond the demands of simple courtesy: my friend Ladislas Poniatowski, deputy from the Eure (to whose father, Senator Michel Poniatowski, I am also indebted); Louis Mexandeau, former Socialist minister and party leader and current deputy from the Calvados; Chantal Grimaud, Mexandeau's solicitous parliamentary assistant; Roger Léron, deputy from the Drôme; Rector Robert Mallet of Paris; Robert Bordaz, lawyer, urbanist, and eminent *grand commis;* Christian Dupavillon of the Ministry of Culture; Françoise de Panafieu, deputy mayor of Paris; Thierry Aumonier, former top aide to Mayor Chirac; Msgr Claude Dagens, coadjutor bishop of Poitiers; Dr. Louis Fruchard, former president of the Conseil régional of the Poitou-Charentes; Claude Moreau, vice president of that Conseil; Jean-Marc Roger, the head of the Archives départementales of the Vienne; François Legriel, retired Poitevin business leader; Michel Morineau, one of the driving forces of the Ligue française de l'enseignement et de l'éducation permanente; his friend and counterpart at the Ligue des droits de l'homme, Bernard Wallon; Roger Le Coz, president of the Fédéderation des oeuvres laiques of the Manche; and Claire and Philippe Luxereau, civic leaders and neighborhood activists in Viroflay. I am sorry that I did not meet historian Patrick Garcia until my project was near completion. Our stimulating exchanges quickened my appetite to read his forthcoming thesis, which deals with the "aestheticization of politics" at several commemorative moments of the Revolution.

I am especially grateful to a group of scholars, most of them close friends, who took the trouble to read parts of the typescript and comment on it with great care and vigor. I profited enormously from their wisdom, their corrections, and their injunctions. I apologize to them for failing to defer to many admonitions and to attain certain levels of penetration and lucidity. Unable to embrace each of them before my readers, I list their names alphabetically: Haim Burstin (University of Siena), Roger Chartier (Ecole des hautes études en sciences sociales), Claude Grignon (Institut national de la recherche agronomique); Carla Hesse (University of California, Berkeley), Lynn Hunt (University of Pennsylvania), Christian Jouhaud (Centre national de la recherche scientifique), Darline G. S. Levy (New York University); Colin Lucas (University of Chicago); Philippe Minard (Institut d'histoire moderne); R. Laurence Moore (Cornell University); Gilles Postel-Vinay (INRA); Jacques Revel (EHESS); and John H. Weiss (Cornell).

At Cornell I benefited from the devoted and industrious help of my student assistant, Matt Jacobs, adept at both the poetry and the prose of the task, the challenging research assignments and the pedestrian work of proofing, photocopying, and office-keeping. Jennifer Gaffney ably succeeded him. With skill and celerity, Clare Crowston and Janine Lanza crafted the index. A local photographer, Andrew Meyn, availed me of his expert services. Over the phone from Atlanta, my son, Laurence, who earned his summer livelihood for many years as a computer consultant, patiently helped me to overcome hardware and software difficulties. Over the phone from Princeton, my daughter, Renée, in deference to the family fetish for sarcasm, impatiently queried: "Tu travailles toujours sur ce maudit bicentenaire?" My wife, Jane, supplied the counsel of good sense on several delicate matters.

My debt to Nan Karwan Cutting requires elaboration. When she was my undergraduate student at Cornell many years ago, she assisted me in preparing my first book for publication. Now an accomplished historian, she read every word of the present book more than once, discussed interpretations, pointed out errors and infelicities, and toiled selflessly to improve the final product. Her husband, James Cutting, intervened at crucial junctures to salvage text that I had lost in the computer and to provide wise advice on other matters. One could not hope for a team of more talented collaborators and faithful friends. With appreciation and affection, I dedicate this book to them.

S. L. K.

Paris
February 1993

Farewell, Revolution

Disputed Legacies, France, 1789/1989

General Introduction

My title is inspired by *Adieux à l'année 1789*, a work composed by Louis-Sébastien Mercier, one of the most prolific and versatile writers of the second half of the eighteenth century. *Adieux* is a text of enthusiasm and engagement, of a sort of preemptive nostalgia for the Revolution in its best days, the Revolution of emancipation, dignity, and heroism, the Revolution of grandiose symbols in deeds (the taking of the Bastille) and in words (the forging of the Declaration of the Rights of Man and Citizen). This is the Revolution with which the majority of the French bicentennial public felt comfortable, the Revolution of quasi consensus. Mercier enumerated the staggering achievements of this singular, beneficent, marvelous year, this period of profound change. It marked the end of "aristocratic despotism" and its multiple forms of enslavement, the ennobling of the people, the emergence of patriotism, the consecration of talent and enlightenment, and the inscription of liberty under the protection of the law beyond the capricious grasp of the prince.

All things considered, the relative restraint of the first year of the Revolution impressed the author of *Tableau de Paris*. At the same time Mercier stressed that year's deeply radical strain, and its potential for exponential explosiveness, for it was in 1789 that "the people" realized that they were "a power, and even the only power." A "regenerating year" was necessarily a "tumultuous year." The suddenness and depth of the transformation awed him: practically overnight, "the misfortunes and the extravagances of several centuries were rectified." Mercier oscillated between a yearning for closure (the people were already regenerated and "the government of dreadful memory" was irrevocably overthrown) and a sense that this was only the beginning, the dawn of liberty ("one must still fashion the dream of public happiness in order to build it into a truly durable edifice").

However 1789 would turn out, Mercier felt the need to bear witness to the lofty goals and especially to the indomitable spirit of voluntarism—about whose etiology and consequences historians continue to argue acerbically—that characterized the early Revolution, still blessed by a populist Providence: "but I'll write down at least *what I saw*, so that such events do not escape the memory of persons already born or those who will be born; so that they learn, in all times and in all places, that it is strictly up to their *arms* and to their *heads* to wipe out *every sort* of tyranny they encounter, that they need only *to will it*, and that God (who loves equally all his creatures kneaded of the same substance) manifestly protects all generous uprisings." Neither in its tone nor in its analysis did Mercier's *Adieux* suggest that he would never again see the stuff of '89. For once, this intransigent Parisian spoke the language of the south of France where adieu often meant both *bonjour* and *au revoir*. (The "farewell" of my title carries a similar ambiguity.)

It is tempting, in retrospect, to discern notes of contrapuntal irony in Mercier's euphoric overture. The author himself lived on to experience the buffeting trajectory of the period after '89. The unity of purpose he felt so intensely during the "incomparable year" did not last long. Despite some reservations, the revolutionary militant and journalist welcomed the advent of a republic in 1792 and was elected to its legislature, which also had the mission of drafting a constitution. He found the moderate stance taken by the Girondins on certain key issues—moderate by the standard of the unfolding Revolution, still extreme by the litmus of '89—more congenial than the burgeoning radicalism of the Jacobins rallied by Robespierre.

Anticipating the mood of his bicentennial descendants, Mercier voted against the execution of the king, whose guilt, he believed, could more usefully be punished by life detention. Not long after, he was jailed for protesting the purge of the Girondins from the Convention. After Thermidor he returned to the assembly and subsequently served in the legislative body called the Council of 500 during the Directory. Napoleon named him to the Institut, the empire's highest cultural honor. Mercier admired Napoléon's genius, but refused to forgive him for his overweening despotism. The spirit of '89 remained alive for him throughout the epoch, and he remained faithful to its verve and promise.

I admire Mercier's enthusiasm for '89, his effort to reconcile a regenerating idealism with a pragmatic liberalism, his capacity to survive. I don't know that I would have followed his precise Revolutionary itinerary. A moralist and a sociologist-voyeur, with a mercilessly penetrating and caustic eye for the human condition at its most exalted and its most abject, Mercier had already served me as a precious guide and companion during my long sojourns in Old Regime Paris. Surely I would have enjoyed his fellowship during the Revolution, and even afterward, when his critical regard became somewhat curmudgeonly and idiosyncratic. As I wrote this book about my '89, I tried to emulate Mercier's self-proclaimed vocation: "I want to stifle the race of stiflers."

Mercier's *Adieux* was meant to immobilize time. It constituted a pledge never to forget the momentous lessons of 1789. The text saluted not the end of the Revolution but the beginning of its sempiternal reign. It is now our turn to bid farewell (in the double sense of the word) to 1989. The agenda is not wholly different, though the stakes are no longer the same and the landscape has decisively changed. (I'd like to squire Mercier from the Pyramide du Louvre to the Arche de la Défense; or from the Centre Pompidou to the Tour Montparnasse; or from the Goutte d'Or to Chinatown in the thirteenth arrondissement.) Mercier used seventeen encomiums to characterize 1789 ("the most illustrious [year] of this century," "peerless in our History") and assorted adjectives, mostly superlatives, ("marvelous," "august," "very glorious"). Nineteen eighty-nine has no purchase on the dithyrambic register. Yet if the bicentennial year was not quite "rare and surprising," surely it was "memorable." It was memorable for the ways in which the French coped with their memory. It was memorable for the bitterness and the passion the commemoration provoked, and for the inertia and indifference that it failed to overcome. It was memorable for the festive energy and imagination it elicited. It was memorable for what it revealed about the French sense of self: certitudes, anxieties, ambitions, conflicts, ambiguities.

Farewell, Revolution is an effort to examine 1989 from many of the perspectives that made it memorable. It aspires to be a rigorous historical and ethnographic inquiry. But if it is decidedly not a *livre de circonstance*, it was born of very particular circumstances, the sort of astronomical convergence that often does not occur even once in a lifetime. The bicentennial effected a rare juncture between my "then" and my "now," both of which have been (trans)planted in French soil. France captivated me thirty years ago for reasons that I am still sorting out. France is always on my mind. I have the hubristic and unsettling sense that, somehow, everything that happens to France happens to me. I live two Frances, one as a professional and the other as an amateur, one in the past and the other in the present—as a sort of industrious *flâneur des deux rives*.

The first France, in which I am legitimately at home, practically a *regnicole*, is the Old Regime, particularly the eighteenth century. The second is the France of today, of my own time, in which I am alternately a direct and a vicarious participant-observer, depending upon the calendar. I must confess that I am no less interested in Poilâne's loaf than in the bread of Gonesse, in Laurent Fignon's Tour de France than in Agricol Perdiguier's (or Jacques-Louis Ménétra's), in the *petits juges* like Pascal and Jean-Pierre than in judicial dynasties of the Séguier and the Joly de Fleury, in Bernard Pivot than in Madame du Deffand, in the hip-hopping subway taggers than in the cemetery *convulsionnaires*, in the new banlieues than in the old faubourgs. Though I self-consciously try to correct for distortion on both ends, there is no doubt that my eighteenth century is refracted—and, if I am careful, perhaps also nourished—by my reading of the twentieth and vice versa. I have long mused about ways to confront the two epochs and the two identities without forcing the issue. When the bicentennial beckoned with just the requisite intersection of vectors, I ceded to the enticement.

The past, the present, and the future were inextricably commingled in the bicentennial experience. The eighteenth century received more public attention

(however lacking in depth) than perhaps at any time since the Revolution itself.
France strained to make sense of the Revolution and its legacy. The focus shifted
imperceptibly from the event itself to its heritage, from the history to the historiography, from the "then" to the "now." On the one hand, history constrained
what followed in myriad ways. On the other, what followed constrained the way in
which France surveyed its history. The weight of the present, with its claims and its
agenda, counterpoised and contested the weight of the past, with its permanent
demands for ransom. The French tried to figure out what they owed to the Revolution, and that for which they wanted to hold it accountable. They found it hard to
agree on what the Revolution was and why it came about, matters that briefly at
least seemed to have more than merely academic significance.

I ventured gingerly into the bicentennial arena with the hope that my combined
training as a historian and long immersion in contemporary French life would
enable me to see things that evaded other gazes. Since my own intellectual life had
long been a dialogue between the eighteenth and twentieth centuries, I felt a surge
of empathy with the burden that confronted the French as well as a familiarity with
the poles of exchange. I wagered that my own experience might equip me to
disentangle some of the interlocking threads, to unpack some of the densely
bundled baggage, and to work out some of the lived, remembered, and repressed
tensions and contradictions.

If in some ways I enjoyed privileged entrée, in others I remained an outsider. I
was after all not a Frenchman; worse, I had the arrogance frequently to forget this
handicap. Nor was I a breveted specialist of the Revolution, heavily invested in the
debate that had been accelerating for two decades, though I taught the subject year
after year and knew quite well a large portion of the literature. This double distance,
I hoped, would enhance my ability to apprehend and to decode.

While I constantly took stock of my subject situation as I collected data, reflected, and wrote, I consciously avoided interjecting myself overtly into the discussion. I do not pretend to have unmasked the bicentennial sub specie aeternitatis. I
have tried to present it from many different angles, even if I have not always been
able to sustain a precise symmetry of skepticism. I have sought not to truncate or
bowdlerize in unwitting or complicitous mimesis of certain of the characters in the
script. I wanted to engage, involve, and arm readers and thus not to foreclose
antagonistic readings or myriad forms of subversion. In some instances I have
juxtaposed and confronted rival claims, effecting my critique by using the words of
the adversaries to problematize their positions and expose what I perceive as their
respective weaknesses. In other cases I have subjected a given discourse to more or
less unmediated analysis.

Such an approach issues not in an implausible judicious neutrality but in a
certain number of distinctions and evaluations. While I have not written directly in
my voice, few readers will have difficulty in discerning my point of view. My aim is
never simply to *trancher* in the service of a hygienic intellectual robustness; at many
junctures, I'm not certain or I don't know. Nor do I propose full-blown alternatives

to positions I attack, sometimes because such scenarios would not be appropriate in the project as I conceived it, and more often because I do not have ready-made solutions.

Finally, I must not overlook a central objective of my enterprise: to tell a story, or a set of stories. These stories are not in some pristine sense devoid of my mark. But I have toiled to reconstruct, corroborate and relate them faithfully. Apart from the arguments I make, this study means to inform. It brings together a great deal of rich and disparate material about the many dimensions of bicentennial action. It is the beginning of a gigantic task that will go on for years to come. Much of this work will occur within the framework of the Institut d'histoire du temps présent, which has made the bicentennial one of its major research themes. Dozens of graduate students will produce monographs on specific aspects of the commemoration. Social scientists and critics of all stripes will venture more complex exegeses. Quite rightly, the IHTP aspires not only to write collectively the comprehensive history of the commemoration and its contextual linkages but to use the "long" and deep bicentennial moment as a window for exploring the problems that preoccupy and the attributes that characterize fin-de-siècle France.

It is perhaps inadequate to declare, in nebulous and self-protective terms, that this work does not pretend to be exhaustive. Let me specify a few of the more important things I foreswore. Non-French readers in particular should note that this book is about the bicentennial experience in France. The commemoration outside France was so substantial and enthusiastic, in scale and intensity, that it fed back into the Franco-French commemoration, powerfully reminding inhabitants of all persuasions of the continuing world-historical impact of *their* Revolution. In this sense the international story is arguably a part of the French one. I can merely plead that the domestic French undertaking was sufficiently daunting that I could not address the truly interesting and imaginative celebrations/commemorations that ranged from Kaplan, Louisiana (where 14 July has always been held sacred) to cities in Yemen, Uruguay, Senegal, Japan, and Russia.

This work is about the bicentennial in France, but it is obviously not about everything, every place, and everyone. From the bottom up, there are countless other strains to be incorprated into the saga. Further archival and oral-history research will doubtless also modify the picture from the center. Historians may rightly be vexed that I paid virtually no attention to the lush yield of scholarly production associated with the bicentennial (well over a thousand books of various sorts and many more articles and essays). Once again, I beg indulgence on grounds of my conception and means. I dealt with the historiographical debate that impinged directly on the public consciousness and the commemorative theatre. Surely it would be worth devoting an entire book to a thorough assessment of the areas of significant contribution as well as the zones of disappointment and barrenness.

I must call the reader's attention to one convention that I have employed throughout. When Revolution, or any derivative of the word, appears with a capital *R*, it expressly denotes the French Revolution that began in 1789. Rendered with a small *r*, revolution refers to generic insurrectionary experiences or ambitions or struggles. When I want to convey the double character of historical specificity and universality, I use the device of the slash: R/revolutionary. Thus a discussion of the R/revolutionary preoccupation with plots points both to a predisposition characteristic of the French Revolution and a propensity that seems common to most revolutionary movements.

The reader should also know about certain peculiarities in the nature of my sources. The bulk of them are quite conventional: a great range of published discourse of all manner. A substantial portion of this material is more or less ephemeral literature generated by ad hoc groups specifically for the bicentennial. Some of it was slickly produced; much of it bore the telltale artisanal marks of mimeographing or photocopying. The mode of diffusion varied as much as the format and method of production: some of it was widely available through public sale or subscription while a considerable part was distributed at specific public gatherings (meetings, lectures, festivals, and so on). I have amassed a sizable collection on my own. It is my hope that a very large portion of these publications have found their way to the national, departmental, or municipal archives, either as a result of local strategies of promotion or solicitation of patronage or as a consequence of aggressive entrepreneurship on the part of archivists.

I have used only a small fraction of the multifarious documents that constitute the bicentennial archives, in part because of their sprawling enormity and in part because the series was just being classified when I conducted my research. Thanks to the foresight and rigor of Jean-Noël Jeanneney and the skillful collaboration of the staff of the Archives Nationales, a vast quantity of the papers of the Mission du Bicentenaire is now available for public consultation. I was kindly permitted to work in them before they were fully catalogued. Thus in some cases I could not cite specific carton references; in others my citations may refer to provisional carton assignments. In yet other cases I used Mission material directly at the Mission offices, documentation that has presumably been integrated into the archival run. Similarly, in several departmental archives, I used records that had not yet been labeled and classified.

I draw frequently on an extensive correspondence that I conducted with various actors on the bicentennial stage, letters that remain for the moment in my possession. Finally, I conducted scores of interviews. The subjects varied enormously in disposition, depending on a host of factors, including the initial impression I made and the patronage that I could invoke, and their calculation of the extent to which I could serve or damage their causes and their interests. In virtually every case, my interlocutors stipulated which part of the conversation was "off the record," for discreet or oblique use as background information, and which sections could be cited and attributed. In almost two dozen instances, the parties I interviewed expressly requested that I not cite them by name or title, in order to spare them embarrassment or even professional sanction. I have scrupulously respected their wishes. I have utilized their "anonymous" testimonies only where I could independently corroborate the assertions they contained or where they were meant to exemplify a more or less notorious point of view. A number of witnesses in delicate positions courageously insisted on assuming public responsibility for their declarations, regardless of the possible consequences.

The French edition of this work appeared in 1993 (Paris: Editions Fayard) in a single volume entitled *Adieu 89*. Like that version, from which it differs somewhat in content and form, the English-language edition is divided into four quasi-autonomous "books" or sections, each built around a central organizing theme. Whereas in French the four sections composed a single volume, here they are presented in two volumes, subtitled respectively *Disputed Legacies, France, 1789/1989*, and *The Historians' Feud, France, 1789/1989*. The former contains the first three books dealing with the debate over the commemoration, the organization of the bicentennial itself, and commemorative practices in various parts of the nation. The latter is devoted to the battle among the leading historians. It must be emphasized that this presentation bespeaks merely a cleavage of convenience. While *The Historians' Feud* can easily be read on its own, it emerges directly from the global strategy and analysis of the whole project. It should not be construed as a free-standing exercise in historiographical criticism. Yet that volume obviously effects a shift in mood as well as in subject. Though it tells a story about the bicentennial, the major intellectual issues at stake both precede and transcend the anniversary of the Revolution. They are issues that will always matter deeply to historians and citizens of all times and places.

Entitled "Framing the Bicentennial," Book One explores the cultural and political climate in which the idea of the Bicentennial took form. The first chapter examines the debate concerning the possibility of commemoration, the moral necessity for it, the competing strategies for structuring it, and the leitmotifs available for articulating its objectives. I discuss different conceptions of memory, the tensions between history and commemoration, and the difficulties involved in attempting to commemorate a violent rupture. I confront two bicentennial recipes, one premised on the need to select or "shop" in the store of Revolutionary experience, the other predicated on the obligation to leave nothing out. A strong voice for a consensual approach made itself felt. Constructed around the great achievements in human rights, it was contested for different reasons by elements on the left and the right.

Chapters 2 and 3 deal with the powerful resurgence of the counterrevolutionary mood. Chapter 2 shows how the white lobby, operating on several different cultural levels, reached a wide audience, receptive in part because of the deepening horror of revolution, and its cortege of violence, which cut across the political landscape. Locating the roots of national identity deep in the Christian and monarchical past, the adversaries of the Revolution portrayed it as the source of France's long-term moral and economic decline and the matrix for the totalitarian virus that infected the modern world. Two quite different undertakings treated in Chapter 3 pointed to shifting attitudes regarding R/revolutionary tradition: a campaign to cleanse the *Marseillaise* of its bellicose gore, and a public retrial of Citizen Capet, Louis XVI. This chapter ends with a close examination of the tactics and rhetoric of the far right, which sought to launch a vast popular crusade against the godless, corrosively liberal modernity that the Revolution spawned.

Chapter 4 looks at the Vendée, trope and *idée-force* of the antirevolutionary campaign. It follows the itinerary of the politician and self-proclaimed moral tribune Philippe de Villiers, who fused his political ambitions with the quest for the rehabilitation/revenge of the Vendée. Claiming that the Revolution devised a "final solution" to extirpate the Vendée, Villiers and other counterrevolutionaries developed an argument in which Jacobins, Bolsheviks, and Nazis became interchangeable parts in a diabolical machine invented in 1789, and in which Furet's and Faurisson's revisionisms, of fundamentally antagonistic inspiration and method, cross paths. The Polish-Vendée connection, prominently staged in 1989, helped to cast into relief the themes of Christian victimization and Franco-French genocide, and incidentally to relativize, in the manner of the Polish stewardship of Auschwitz, the claims of the Shoah.

The church, once the militant institutional host of the Counterrevolution, is the subject of Chapter 5, which scrutinizes its controversial efforts to break out of the older paradigm. After pointing to the very mixed signals communicated by the church's official bicentennial program, I explore the strains in the church that the question of R/revolution crystallized. I suggest how onerous it was to stake out a middling position, based on a notion of (partial) reconciliation. Despite his self-proclaimed bicentennial centrism, Jean-Marie Cardinal Lustiger remained extremely wary of the Revolution, its legacy, and its highly dangerous Enlightenment origins. Though moved primarily by his rigorous and vigorous conception of the faith, the archbishop of Paris was not indifferent to the sentiments of the *intégriste* wings inside and outside the church. I consider their relation with the Revolution, which in some sense engendered them even as it poisoned their church. Then I turn to those Catholics, mostly but not exclusively on the left, who tendered a hand to the Revolution in a positive and sometimes even congenial spirit.

The next chapter deals with a different god, the lord of the château, François Mitterrand. He felt a deep attachment to the Revolutionary patrimony, but he was not indifferent to the problems that the commemoration posed. I trace the tensions in his analysis, and the evolution of his position. The president acknowledged that the Revolution committed crimes, not all of which benefited from the unction of mitigating circumstances, though he by no means repudiated the Terror. He criticized the inadequacies of the rights of '89 even as he celebrated them, and he tried to prove that liberty, the bulwark of any society, could not flourish without a substantial dose of equality. Beyond its unfulfilled promise, Mitterrand resonated in quasi-Gaullist tones with the sheer grandeur of the Revolution and its still vibrant influence throughout the world.

The last chapter in Book One treats the secular politics of commemoration played out in the political parties. Internal discord marked the governing and major opposition parties. Many Socialists scrambled to dilute their traditional R/revolutionary referents. The Jacobin line mobilized a spare minority. The civilized right navigated between degrees of rejection and appropriation. Many of its partisans enthusiastically endorsed the treasured human rights associated with the (early) Revolution. If they insisted more emphatically on the ways in which the Revolution trampled those very rights, this strategy bespoke in part their studied efforts to prevent the left from reaping the moral and political dividend that might seem automatically to accrue to the direct heirs of the Revolution. The far right both reviled the Revolution and tried to turn it against its exponents. Jean-Marie Le Pen's populist nationalism spoke a quasi-Revolutionary language and reached out to those who felt aggrandized by the emergence of the People as a real force on the historical scene in '89. Only the Communist party unequivocally welcomed the chance to celebrate the Revolution; and in light of their own internal disarray and the unraveling of sister parties throughout the world, even certain Communists complained about the unfortunate timing of the two hundredth anniversary of the Revolution.

Book Two shifts from theory to practice. Called "Producing the Bicentennial," it is a history of the bicentennial viewed from the center: the arduous effort to overcome various forms of inertia, obstruction, tragedy and dislocation in order to elaborate institutions, an ideology and a program for the commemoration. Chapter 1 chronicles the deflation of early Socialist exuberance as the project for an '89 world's fair proved stillborn. Curiously, it took the anomie of governmental cohabitation to rescue the state from its bicentennial torpor. Named the first president of the bicentennial Mission, Michel Baroin envisaged a commemoration inspired by the vision of the relation of state to society and the practice of social economy derived from his rich experience as a public servant, masonic leader, and highly successful businessman. The new project was barely off the ground when Baroin died in an African plane crash.

His successor, and onetime protector, Edgar Faure, is the subject of the next chapter, in which I assess the way the brilliant academician and adroit political survivor conceived of his task. Much like Baroin's, Faure's bicentennial would be future-oriented and articulated around the theme of universal fraternity and reconciliation, with special attention to youth, Europe, science, and ethics. Not without difficulty, the new Mission president put together a team that tried to compensate for a paucity of coherence and efficiency with a generous dose of enthusiasm. Its energetic efforts to forge a festive calendar and a system of national coordination and support were cruelly undermined by Faure's death.

The third chapter recounts the ascension of the third Mission president, Jean-Noël Jeanneney, a gifted historian from a celebrated political family, considerably younger than his predecessors, whose unusual career had taken him from the university to the presidency of Radio France, where he proved his capacity for management and indulged his passionate interest in the media and the nature of public opinion. He rapidly purged and audited the Mission and recast its organization, operation and discourse. Racing against the clock, he completed the program and reinvigorated the campaign of commemorative education and socialization, centered on an embrace of both the historical and mythological Revolutions and their ramifications in the past, present, and future.

Chapter 4 relates the opening and unfolding of the official bicentennial season, including the New Year's flight of the hot-air balloons, the springtime planting of liberty trees, and the historical reconstitution of the convocation of the States general at Versailles in May. I pursue in some detail the vain and embarrassing efforts of the Jeanneney Mission to establish a fixed center of national commemorative activity in the Tuileries gardens.

The protagonist of Chapter 5 is Jean-Paul Goude, a designer-artist-adman, creature and creator of ambiguity and liminality, whom the Ministry of Culture (and the Bicentennial) recruited to invent and realize the climactic bicentennial event on 14 July. The fact that the summit of the world's richest nations would occur at that very moment in Paris further magnified the stakes. After considering the strains between the ministry, Goude's protector, and the Mission, his administrative tutor, I focus on his background (in France, in America, in black reverie, in sexual and aesthetic fantasy, in cartoon expression, in music and kinetic communication), his official bicentennial charge (to fashion a genre of *Marseillaise* on the Champs-Elysées), and his working methods (the manipulation of stereotypes). The chapter ends with the antisummit, counterbicentennial demonstration organized by elements of the left and far left, the most visible spokesman for whom was Renaud, the iconoclastic-anarchist singer best known for his vernacularly fervent support of Mitterrand's election.

In Chapter 6 I marvel at the corner into which the Mission and the state had wedged themselves: the international reputation of the nation and the fate of the whole bicentennial enterprise now lay in the largely unknown hands of a puckish, professional image maker. After recounting the opera-ballet itself and suggesting different ways of reading it, I examine its triumphal reception, the anomalies of the populism in which it was cast, and the contrapuntal critique of its African and American excesses. I show how the Gouderie crystallized immediately into legend and became symbolically coterminous with the entire bicentennial campaign.

The final chapter of Book Two treats the anticlimactic events that followed *La Marseillaise*, intrinsically of genuine significance but diminished by the shadow of Goude. First, I visit the late-August celebration of the anniversary of the proclamation of the Declaration of the Rights of Man at the Arche de la Défense, featuring a speech by Mitterrand inaugurating the foundation for fraternity imagined by Edgar Faure, the presentation of an updated version of the Declaration forged by a youth assembly led by Baroin's son François, an exhibition dealing with the contemporary transgression of human rights, and a nighttime concert that both exalted human rights in universal abstraction and violated them in local practice.

The scene then shifts to Valmy, site of the grand Revolutionary victory in

September 1792 that ushered in the republic. Its bellicose and nationalistic inflections muted in deference to the spirit of European unity, Valmy stood alone as the unique event in the bicentennial calendar that explicitly commemorated the Revolution after 1789. The army collaborated in the creation of a series of Parisianized tableaux that it did not wholly fathom, and Mitterrand addressed the nation-in-arms.

Finally, the bicentennial year ends in the solemn precincts of the Panthéon on a fiercely gray early winter's day. The last chapter in this book explains how the government chose the trio of heroes to be immortalized. Representing the three estates, and thus in some sense the coalescing of the new nation, Grégoire the priest-reformer, Condorcet the aristocrat-philosophe, and Monge the commoner-mathematician more significantly symbolized the Mitterrand government's moral and political priorities: combatting exclusion and promoting education in the service of a future imbued with the best ideals of '89. I describe the solemn procession and ceremonial, largely constructed around the silent mediating figure of Mitterrand, who evinced a profound sense of communion with the nation's glories as he listened to an eloquent speech by his minister of culture, Jack Lang, and a short orchestral concert.

Book Three transports us to *la France profonde*, and the rendez-vous between the bicentennial and the nation. After explaining the relation between center and periphery, the protocols linking the Mission to the grass roots, I use the first chapter to investigate the staggering diversity of commemorative expression, featuring brief case studies of the Nord, Riom, and Montpellier. I accord a substantial place to the Comités Liberté, Egalité, Fraternité (CLEF 89), the joint creation of the Ligue des droits de l'homme and the Ligue de l'enseignement, one of only two national networks that inspired, nourished, and coordinated local initiatives in dozens of departments. Composed to a large extent of teachers at various levels, CLEF nevertheless failed to prod the Ministry of National Education to take a more interventionist role in the commemoration in the schools.

Chapter 2 ventures an anatomy of the bicentennial experience in the Poitou-Charentes, with special reference to the regional capital of Poitiers. I expose the quarrels, tensions, and hesitations that characterized the effort to craft a cohesive regional contribution in an area traversed by deep historical and persistent political cleavages. We discover actors present in many provincial cities: the Mission's correspondent (often chosen in a superficially functional manner, without regard for his or her interest in and attitude toward the Revolution), the delegate of the educational circumscription called the academy, the volunteer-militants of CLEF, the conciliators, the accommodationists, the Jacobins, the counter- and antirevolutionaries, the local citizens avid to learn about their past, the villagers thrilled by the visit of national dignitaries. I look at the major events of the Poitevin bicentennial season: historical exhibition, popular festival, Mitterrand's participation in the commemoration of the planting of the first liberty tree, lecture series, research and publications in local and regional history, and so on.

Chapter 3 is a study of the major effort made by the Communist party to implant itself at the core of local festive/commemorative activities throughout the country. After taking up the genesis, organization, and goals of Vive 89, as the national association was baptized, I inspect its major products: a colorful and engaging videocasette devised to inform and orient local commemorators in their choices and strategies, and a portable exhibition in seventeen tableaux, conceived by historian Claude Mazauric, the association's president, in collaboration with very talented graphic artists, that hundreds of groups all over France purchased or rented for multiple showings. Then I turn to a series of local studies of Vive 89 branches, in order to elicit the character of membership, the mobilizing tactics, the difficulties encountered, and the results obtained. The chapter concludes with a glance at the bicentennial action of labor unions and the initiatives undertaken at the workplace itself.

Chapter 4 deals with the commemoration staged by the city of Paris construed as a "local" enterprise. During the period of cohabitation, Mayor Jacques Chirac, who was simultaneously prime minister, encouraged close cooperation and in certain cases virtual fusion between national and municipal ventures. President Mitterrand's reelection and the return of the Socialists to power in 1988 changed everything. I examine how the municipality scaled down its bicentennial investment and distanced itself from the state's activities. The city deployed and enriched its Revolutionary cultural and artistic patrimony, broadly interpreted, and stimulated historical consciousness by promoting a search for descendants of Revolutionary figures of sundry levels. The city's most significant event, symbolically and financially, celebrated the centennial of the Eiffel Tower in a gala fête that barely evoked the Revolution.

The last chapter in Book Three peers into the bicentennial career of one of the Revolution's paramount icons, Maximilien Robespierre: for some the embodiment of honesty, humanitarianism, and progressive social reform, while for others the incarnation of despotism, cruelty, and vanity. Embroiled in controversy since the early years of the Revolution, Robespierre continued to elicit passionate fealty and antagonism. I sift through the efforts of several local and supralocal groups to rehabilitate him, and even to prepare him for the Panthéon. I track the protracted, bitter, and ultimately successful struggle to enshrine Robespierre in his hometown of Arras, though the citizenry remained divided over the gesture. I conclude with the spirited but abortive campaign to adopt and lionize him in Thionville, a leftist municipality with a Communist mayor.

BOOK ONE

FRAMING THE
BICENTENNIAL

Commemoration: Aporias, Dilemmas, and Opportunities

F or many weeks during the spring of 1989, *Les Nouvelles calédoniennes* devoted considerable attention to the bicentennial celebration. Its tone was positive, spirited, at times frankly boosterist, with no intimations of reservations inspired either by the history itself of the event commemorated or by the awkward relation of the colonial remnant to the emancipatory ideology embodied by the mother country's Revolution. The paper seemed to delight particularly in its patronage of a competition devised to select two hundred local children to attend the climactic moments of the fête in France. Brutally, its serene engagement seemed to be shaken by a poem composed by a youth, not quite twelve years old, to mark the departure of his comrades for their metropolitan bicentennial holiday. The child's verses depicted something resembling a class war in the waning years of the Old Regime. The author identified with the disinherited against the privileged, with the peasants spoliated by taxes and dues and more subtle persecutions that profited in particular the decadent and opulent aristocracy. "But the situation changed," the poet announced with satisfaction and a pristine sense of moral righteousness: "We killed some of them with our menacing tools," and the guillotine, in the name of social justice, did the rest.

On the eve of 14 July, this schoolboy lyric suddenly and poignantly recalled the dilemma—the traumatic dimension—of commemoration. The paper felt obliged to comment editorially, in a long parenthesis inserted after the poem. "What a shame that an eleven-and-a-half-year-old child got from the Revolution only its lethal and bloody side," was its first remark. Its second observation carried an implicit admission of guilt, an acknowledgment that perhaps the Caledonian community had not paid enough attention to the other side of the Revolution. It was still not too late to set the memory straight: "But it's true that we are celebrating today the bicentennial of what was also an immense slaughter."[1]

Commemoration and History, Forgetting and Remembering, Celebrating and Reflecting:
Penser le Bicentenaire

The specter that cast its rude shadow across the Caledonian festive firmament haunted French intellectuals and public figures for many years prior to the opening of the bicentennial season. Even as they quarreled acrimoniously over the worth and meaning of the Revolution, they began to reflect on the problem of publicly celebrating the anniversary of such a profoundly divisive, albeit momentous, event. The two questions were at once quite separate and inextricably intertwined. What was the relation between historical "objectivity" (about whose dearth, especially on the right, Elysée counselor and historian Claude Manceron complained) and commemoration? If it was true, as the critic Alain-Gérard Slama ruefully noted in *Le Figaro* in 1984, "that as our century comes to an end the Old Regime is not wholly liquidated, and our country is sinking, thanks both to its left and its right, into the archaic wars between the Revolution and the Counterrevolution," then how would it be possible to organize a national anniversary of the sort that in other countries, such as the United States and Australia, mobilized massive adherence? Would it be feasible in practice to find enough common ground to sustain a commemoration even if, intellectually, one could not resolve its aporias?[2]

On certain generic points there was concurrence: commemoration involved theatricalization, symbolic construction, the immobilization of time, the fixing of filiations, the hierarchization of significance, the allocation of roles, and so on. But discord was rampant on all matters of inflection if not on definition itself. When the historian Pierre Chaunu envisioned commemoration, he thought about a profoundly religious act akin to communion, a gesture exuding immense truth and solemnity. For sociologist Gérard Namer, commemoration was basically an artifice, devised to regulate, link, and manipulate conflicting memories and ambitions toward the imperious end of forging (provisional) unity.

Mona Ozouf, philosopher and historian, noted that "illusion," followed by painful disenchantment, was often the product of commemoration because of the fatal conflation habitually sealed between commemoration and history, a notion vaguely redolent of Pierre Nora's opposition between memory and history. History implied a certain distancing from the events, a problematization, a more or less pitiless scrutiny regardless of the consequences. Fundamentally different, commemoration demanded "an affective, emotional identification which let us recognize ourselves in the commemorated object." In fact, the risk of confusion was double. First, there was the folkloric temptation to collapse "lived history" and "recollected history." Thus Ozouf's somewhat condescending evocation of the venerable Ernest Labrousse, doyen of historians of revolution and honorary president of the bicentennial organizing committee of the Centre national de la recherche scientifique (CNRS), who could not help himself from exulting: "We are truly entering the prerevolutionary period."

Second, there was confusion between the historical task of chronicling the past, whose ethic of rigor and totality precluded any truncation or ideological concession ("What indeed would one think of a historian who would refuse to look at the Terror or the Vendée?"), and the business of marking an anniversary, which called for discrimination and selection. From Ozouf's analysis emerged at least one practical commemorative rule from which none of the bicentennial managers strayed: that the *mémoire savante* was alien to the popular festive spirit which needed to be created and sustained. Put into practice, this became the *lite* strategy that shaped the celebration of 14 July.[3]

The discourse of the Revolutionary festival makers themselves had long convinced Mona Ozouf that commemoration meant a subtle management of absence and presence. Close to her ideologically, lawyer-academician Jean-Denis Bredin agreed that commemoration was a complicated negotiation between remembering and forgetting. Others, however, on both the left and the right, rejected what they regarded as opportunism and compromise. "The cross of the commemoration," noted the moderate Catholic commentator Etienne Borne, "is that one has to shoulder it all, the rays of light and the shadows." Conservative Vendéen deputy Philippe de Villiers and fundamentalist Catholic-Lepéniste journalist François Brigneau demanded that nothing be left out, the only strategy, they believed, which would allow them to focus attention on the horrors of the Revolution. For symmetrically opposite reasons, the Communists denounced the idea of a centrist commemoration that would fail to highlight the struggle for social justice culminating in Year II. The philosopher and sometime presidential counselor Régis Debray tirelessly inveighed against an antiseptic version of the Revolution: the full truth was the only acceptable pedagogy.[4]

Did this mean an obligation to commemorate the Revolution en bloc? "We must have the courage to nuance the word or rather the famous paradox of Clemenceau," volunteered Claude Manceron, who may have discussed the question in the corridors of the Elysée with Debray. The Revolution was not a bloc "that one had to accept or reject in its entirety" but rather a kaleidoscope encompassing the whole range of human action, a Shakespearean drama combining heroism and pusillanimity, love and cruelty, grandeur and iniquity. But that ardent declaration did not inhibit Manceron from denouncing "the rigging and exaggerating of the number of September massacres, the victims of the Vendée, those guillotined by the revolutionary tribunal" which threatened to tarnish the bicentennial. Yet Jean-Baptiste Morvan, a journalist on the far right, would have been hard-pressed to castigate Manceron, for he took it as a given that commemorations were perforce impassioned: "One could hardly imagine an impartial and critical commemoration. To commemorate is more or less always to go on the quest for ancestors, for fatherhoods that bring us what we might call our justifications, our existential legitimacy."[5]

Unlike François Brigneau, who readily severed bicentennial commemoration (useful and necessary) from celebration (unthinkable and impious), Jean-Marc

Varaut, a lawyer on the self-styled liberal right, doubted that the two could in practice be uncoupled, and warned of the grave implications of sliding imperceptibly into approbation: "To celebrate a past event is to repeat it as an example for the present. A celebration is never neutral. One celebrates only what one approves."

"To commemorate is not to celebrate," averred the historian Madeleine Rebérioux from the Jacobin left. To be sure, commemoration bespoke attachment to "essential values," but it was above all an effort to "know and understand," perhaps even to "render justice." The legitimacy of this effort was assured by the critical and rigorous toil of history. Two other intellectuals on the left, Patrick Garcia and Pierre-André Taguieff, argued that it was in the very nature of commemoration itself to be tendentious. But they, too, implicitly contested Ozouf's claim that somehow the work of commemoration would be accomplished apart from—sequestered from—the work of history, which she invested with a surprisingly positivistic mission. Was doing history epistemologically estranged from the "active process during which the system of representations of the past and thus the perception of the present are modified," the process with which Garcia associated commemoration? For Taguieff commemoration necessitated rewriting history in order to construct a fictional time in which the past, present, and future could coexist.[6]

Edgar Morin, a philosopher and sociologist, and onetime Communist, defined commemoration as a regeneration of collective memory. That implied for him an act of national hygiene whose chief medicine would be a searching historical debate. In order to set the "founding grandeur" of the Revolution on healthier grounds, it had to be demythicized and desacralized. In this task history consisted neither in forging useful fictions nor in harvesting true facts. To see *chouans* or Jacobins as they really were required that "we stop construing the Revolution as a bloc, that we undertake our self-relativization, by recognizing that our point of view is influenced by the circumstances [in which we live]." Unlike Ozouf, Morin emphasized the intimate connection between the work of history and the fruit of commemoration. Historians were sometimes commemorators, and commemorators had to be historians. Even as they engaged "the critique, or the autocriticism, of the French Revolution," Morin insisted on the need for them to subject their own perspective to scrutiny, "to subject themselves to self-analysis in the light of their own historical situation."

Morin's propositions failed to appeal to Ozouf or to her collaborator, the historian François Furet. Both denounced the Labroussean axiom that one had to love the Revolution to understand it. (Furet: "One can perfectly well understand an event or an epoch without liking it"; Ozouf: "One must choose to love the Revolution or to come to know it.") Somehow "not loving" dispensed Furet and Ozouf from the (self-)analytical imperative, as if *not* loving were an unproblematic position. Nor did either feel impelled to worry about his or her subject position or to historicize and sociologize his or her intellectual and professional trajectory. They clung stubbornly to the Durkheimian banner unfurled in the ingenuous clubhouse idiom of the *Nouvel Observateur:* in 1889 the Revolution "was still politics. Today the Revolution is history."[7]

Family Feud: Ruptures, Cleavages, and Contradictions

Beyond the debate over the wisdom of commemoration loomed the specific problem of commemorating the French Revolution. Mona Ozouf conducted the most searching and influential inventory of the aporias and snags of commemoration. Her guiding axiom posited that "every commemoration draws its life from the obsessive affirmation of sameness." Put more simply, "Every commemoration is a family holiday." Yet there were several different Revolutionary families with antagonistic agendas. Even more troubling than the abyss between Revolutionaries and antirevolutionaries were the divisions within the Revolutionary camp, then and since. Thus the requirement for unity and sameness can be met neither among the actors in the event (those that we honor are not "the same [among themselves]") nor among the heirs to the legacy (we are not "all the same [among ourselves]," and we are not "still the same as in the past"). There were rival families because there were multiple revolutions in the Revolution. "To commemorate well," however, Ozouf remarks, "we need only one."

This lack of homogeneity precluded the enunciation of a single festive calendar or the codification of a heroic hagiography or even the crafting of a reassuring connective narrative of the Revolutionary experience. A further obstacle to commemoration was the lack of accord about whether the Revolution was really over. Commemoration could be a step toward closure (as certain festival makers in the 1790s had already imagined it to be) or an invitation to complete, or perfect, the Revolution. Given these deep contradictions, there was no possibility, Ozouf concluded, of fixing the "common interpretation" of the past that commemoration needed in order to do its work. Nor was the likelihood of the requisite "living together" enhanced by the general lack of familiarity with French history, the weakened sense of nation, which was partly the product of the heightened expression of individualism, and the demoralizing anguish over an amorphous and uncertain future.[8]

Its supporters no less than its detractors conceded that it was no easy matter to commemorate the French Revolution. "One does not undertake a national commemoration in order to divide the nation, to heat up a cold civil war," wrote Régis Debray, in statesmanlike mode, bespeaking the anxieties of the Elysée. "To obtain a unanimous view on any revolution whatever is, all the same, paradoxical: it means dedramatizing a drama, getting together to celebrate the beginning or the eruption of a cleavage." Debray could do no more than allow that it would require "an artist in the craft" to resolve this paradox.

"It is dreadfully hard to commemorate a breakup," acknowledged Jean-Noël Jeanneney, the third in the line of chief bicentennial artists. For Jeanneney the breach in some fundamental way defined modernity; it represented the crystallization of deep-seated political differences that, though attenuated over time as a result of a certain institutional reconciliation, still remained decisive. Unwilling to deny the continued reality and relevance of this rupture, Jeanneney tried to work around it and to canalize its energy.

While he agreed on the difficulty of commemoration, Maurice Agulhon preferred to emphasize the recent but widespread accord ("unanimity") on the basic principles of '89. For him commemoration foundered less on political rupture than on the malaise that Revolutionary memory provoked for modern sensibilities. The problem was to allay the turmoil of "the contemporary French person, humanitarian, sensitive, prudent, who has more dread than admiration for the revolutionary crises." Agulhon wanted to divert attention from the Revolution's horrors, many of which he felt were wildly exaggerated and wrenched from context, in order to free people's minds to focus on the positive achievements by which the Revolution constituted modern France.

"In a fête that is ideally imagined as a fête of Enlightenment," asked Mona Ozouf, paraphrasing the disabused reflection of Lecomte, a Revolutionary theorist of commemoration, "can one represent darkness and horror?" Without spelling out its prescription, the conservative *Quotidien de Paris* vaguely suggested that commemorative grounds could not be discovered so long as the blocists on both sides insisted on including everything. At the same time, however, the paper seemed to say that a truly fair-minded representation of the Revolution precluded a "moral rallying" because it led to the incongruous celebration of "a civil war." No wonder numerous French commentators looked wistfully to the allegedly placid origins of the United States and Australia, labeled "mythic" because these nations were believed to have come painlessly into the world by some sort of Lamazean originary magic.[9]

Precedents

Naturally, the eye of commemorators turned to the two previous grand anniversaries of the Revolution in search of points of reference and larger lessons. The general sentiment was that they were not "the same as in the past." Conditions, domestic and international, were so radically different that there was little analogical comfort or inspiration. In both 1889 and 1939 there were strong incentives to believe that the Revolution was not by any means over, that there were pressing issues to be settled requiring a marshaling of the Revolutionary spirit. Tyrannies cast portentous shadows on both horizons. On the eve of the centennial, Boulangism threatened the Revolutionary legacy. The commemoration became a proud and muscular affirmation of republican values and institutions.

The rise of facism marred and marked the sesquicentennial. Whereas the authoritarian peril had dampened some of the tensions on the left between radicals and opportunists in the late 1880s, in the wake of the withering of the Popular Front the left was deeply divided, with the Communists organizing their own celebration and the moderate left modulating its Revolutionary enthusiasm even more than usual in order to appeal to democratic solidarity on the other side of the Atlantic. Whereas Sadi Carnot incarnated the affective and biological connection between the centennialists and the Revolution, Edouard Herriot staked out a more distant and dispassionate kinship fifty years later. ("The Revolution is not a bloc," he asserted, and "the Revolution did not create everything in France.") Given the *ralliement* of the church and the political evolution of the country, the right was less hostile to the commemoration in 1939 than it had been in 1889. Still, heralding Vichy's brand of revolution, there was Léon Daudet brandishing the idea of the Revolution as a bloc, "but a bloc of garbage."

A few elements in these earlier commemorative moments may have appeared pertinent from the vantage point of 1989. Both centennial and sesquicentennial were squarely turned toward the future, especially the former with its world's fair, Eiffel Tower, and rhapsody to electricity. Each exalted the army in order to diffuse a sense of national prestige and assurance, and each honored the colonial empire as evidence of the vitality of its civilization. In both years the official celebration betrayed a muted, consensual style—a desire to emphasize cohesion and preempt ruinous debate, a lingering preference for Danton over Robespierre, an intuition that liberty merited more attention than equality.[10]

Going Shopping

Locating herself quite self-consciously on a middle road between maximalists and minimalists/negationists, Mona Ozouf proposed a selective and opportunistic mode of commemoration. It might be called the shopping strategy in deference to her contention that "not only can one go shopping, but one must do it." It was premised on her now familiar rigid distinction between commemoration and history, itself based on a functionalist conception of commemoration drawn perhaps from the protocols of the festival makers whose craft she had studied. Ozouf wants this discourse to pass for an incontrovertible social-scientific statement of fact: "Commemorative activity is a necessarily euphoric activity, in search of a reconciled collective actor." The evacuation of history allows the citizen a guilt-free trip to the memory store to buy whatever appeals to him or her with a guarantee of impunity for things left out.

Nothing obliges us to "take it all or leave it all" as if we were faced with a *prix fixe* menu, Ozouf assured her compatriots. Choosing was a right that every citizen had the liberty to exercise, and it was also a mark of intelligence, for how else could one hope to tame "the immense event" that was the French Revolution? Ozouf adroitly noted that such choices were rarely arbitrary. They tended to bespeak current needs and thus had a therapeutic logic. In this sense no choice could be a bad choice from an individual's cognitive point of view. Presumably, however, the potentially dangerous and fragmenting relativisim of this approach would be held in check by common integrating cues broadcast from above by opinion-making professionals. Following Ozouf's recipe, in 1989 the latter would be well advised to give expression to commemoration primarily through fête. Whether or not Ozouf was right to separate history from commemoration so severely, her admonition that memory, collective or individual, official or contestatory, was the product of constant triage could not be lightly dismissed. Nor could her exhortation to the Communists not to "confuse the fête with a thesis defense at the Sorbonne."[11]

Decried as an apology for the spoliation of "truncated" memory by many Jacobins/Marxists and counterrevolutionaries, the shopping strategy had considerable appeal in the center left, center, and parts of the right. Fellow historian and *Nouvel Observateur* collaborator Jacques Julliard rehearsed Ozouf's argument faithfully: "Well, then, still the bloc? Yes and no. As a historian I have the duty to take everything; as a citizen, I very well have the right to choose. Choose what? My references, my principles, why not my legends?"

Less elliptical than Ozouf, Julliard fleshed out his choice quite frankly. There was a great deal in the French Revolution—at least 50 percent of it, and not simply a malevolent 1793 in opposition to a beatific 1789—that he did not like, including its cult of the state, its deification of the nation, and its dependence on violence (he had absolutely no desire to "remake the Revolution, even metaphorically"). He preferred the American Revolution, whose "reality" corresponded to the soaring "myth" of the French Revolution, he claimed in an élan of febrile idealization of the sort he usually savaged in his *ideologizing* adversaries ("I beseech you," he importuned Régis Debray, "not to ideologize the Revolution," as if he, Julliard, somehow evaded the trap).[12]

On national television journalist Anne Sinclair put the shopping strategy in domestic terms for those who felt ambivalent about the Revolution: "To judge the Revolution one had to clean house, and keep only what was good." (Mona Ozouf had explained the triage mechanism in terms of "the grand rounds of spring and fall cleaning.") On the one hand, Jean-François Revel deplored the use of the Revolution "as a politico-ideological supermarket in which one freely selects from the shelves the materials destined to undergird one or another partisan contemporary position." Yet, on the other hand, he earnestly hoped that in the bicentennial year officials would for once choose "the good" and reject "the bad."

Writing in Revel's former organ, *L'Express,* Jean-Claude Casanova inveighed against the idea that "one had to take it all or leave it all." On television and in *Figaro-Magazine,* academician Jean d'Ormesson argued in favor of choice—choice as a moral imperative given the brutally sharp contrasts of which the Revolution consisted. In the same vein, according to another conservative thinker, the late Jean-Marie Benoist, it was the absolute "duty" of all ethically alert persons, on the left as well as on the right, "to make a selection" in order to sequester the "atrocities" ("the matrix of all the horrors that have bloodied our century") from the liberal heritage of '89. Even Jean-Noël Jeanneney, Jacobin sympathizer and fervent promoter of a coherent vision of the Revolution, seemed to endorse shopping and to absolve shoppers in advance of any commemorative sin: "Let everyone take what he wishes."[13]

Against Shopping

The shopping model elicited harsh strictures that did not always bear a robust political imprint. Deeply attached to his adopted city and profoundly imbued with the tragedy of Lyon's bloody experience in the Revolution, the political scientist Philippe Dujardin affords one such example. "One cannot select. One does not have the right to select" for purposes of historical scholarship or commemoration, he insisted. "To select is intellectually dishonest, and it's impossible." Triage from an institutional vantage point, Dujardin regarded as an act of usurpation; selection from above was ineluctably "arbitrary." His solution was to "celebrate at Lyon, while letting it be known that certain persons had good reasons not to celebrate at Lyon."

Of course the militant counterrevolutionary right had a deep political as well as moral interest in the public terms within which the bicentennial was inscribed. Vehement enemies of the Revolution such as Philippe de Villiers, deputy from the Vendée, and François Brigneau, editor of *L'Anti-89*, argued for the bloc in order to reclaim and concentrate on the parts that leftist historiography had obfuscated, diluted, or rationalized. As part of a project of aspersion and indictment, they were keenly interested in remembering and memorializing, but not in commemorating in the more or less positive sense that most French women and men ascribed to the word.

The moderate Catholic educator and writer Etienne Borne rejected shopping for its pedagogical and moral deficiencies, and for its failure to sustain the painful, illuminating, and perhaps cathartic debate between Revolution and Counterrevolution. Sociologist-philosopher Edgar Morin also wanted to conserve the deep tensions of the Revolution. He discountenanced equally a "selective commemoration" and a "frozen commemoration" because they drove out the "antagonisms" and the "contradictions" that articulated the Revolution. Morin wanted to construe it not as a bloc but as a "vortex, which allows us to see it all at once in its totality, its diversity, and its antagonisms, that it to say, in its complexity." The "vortex complex" flattened nothing. While it excluded the euphoric register, it nourished the dialectic between myth and history, between the lyric and the tragic, that opened the way to a rich double reading of the Revolution. But Morin's complex was not easily transposable into an instrument of public commemoration.[14]

The Jacobin left, for the most part Marxizing if not Marxist, acerbically criticized the timidity, the Tartuffery, and the shallowness of the shopping strategy. To embrace this appeal, for Régis Debray, was tantamount to capitulation, or at least to appeasement (a practice that bothered him more in the ideological theatre than it would later in the geopolitical arena). Preoccupied by electoral ambitions and a desire to project an image of hard-nosed modernity, the left succumbed to pressure to modulate the bicentennial tone. Its commemorative manner was apologetic rather than ardent; it chanted mea culpa instead of huzzah. In Debray's view the left had succumbed implicitly to the charges of the right and thus had internalized a sense of guilt by association for totalitarianism. "Holy Democracy, pardon us, we have committed a great sin; we made '93, and '93 was in '89, thus [we made] the Moscow trials also, and as a consequence Pol Pot as well."

While it reflected the resurgent authority of the right, this guilt complex, in Debray's reckoning, was in fact "an excessive tribute that the French left has once again paid to Leninism." Once again the Russian Revolution had interposed itself between the French Revolution and the French republic, this time in the name of revisionism rather than Marxism. This "psychological blackmail" prevented the left from commemorating "its eyes open and quite naturally." The bicentennial reminded us, however, argued Debray, that the cleavage which really mattered was between them (the counterrevolutionaries) and us (the fragmented tribe of the left). Though we are divided on many issues of interpretation concerning the French Revolution, "republican discipline" must galvanize us into a unified if not uniform commemorative front.[15]

Historian of Jean Jaurès and vice president of the Ligue des droits de l'homme Madeleine Rebérioux felt equally uncomfortable with the lukewarm and evasive official commemorative climate. The desire to "silence the Revolution," which emanated from the right but had infiltrated the left, had to be resisted. There was nothing cold about the Revolution-object for Rebérioux. She identified with it, it stirred her deeply, and she believed that it had as much to do with the future of France as with its past. The bicentennial, like the Revolution, was about the prospect for social change. Like the revolutionaries—Rebérioux meets Ozouf's "sameness" test—we the engaged commemorators must be prepared to encounter opposition: "Isn't this hostility inseparable from any grand political or social project?" Here was an embryonic and partial justification for the Terror, which grew directly out of the inimical environment that greeted the campaign for social justice and for national salvation in 1793.[16]

Rhetorically more cautious and stubbornly unwilling to risk passing for naive, Michel Vovelle, a Communist historian (with a noncanonical research itinerary) and the official coordinator of the "scientific" bicentennial, staked out a very similar position. A self-styled commemorative "maximalist," Vovelle wanted the bicentennial to embrace the entire course of the Revolution, from 1789 through 1799. In place of the obsolete ("historically dated") notion of a bloc he, too, proposed the idea of a "movement" or a "dynamic," replete with tensions as well as accomplishments, contradictions as well as coherences. Vovelle denounced the "hypocrisy" of confining the bicentennial to the palatable Revolution of '89 (one described as "carefully asepticized, beginning with a harmless common denominator")—as if '89 were not already mired in blood and as if it did not emphatically pose the problem of the legitimacy of R/revolutionary violence in its primal spasms of life.

Rather than an ironic ransom extorted by an incongruously renascent Leninist wraith, Vovelle hinted that the bicentennial flaccidity was a predictable function of the regnant conservative worldview. Those who wanted to confine the commemoration to the "fiction" of '89 were the same ones who feared the "anticipations" of

1989 as they trembled at those of 1793. They refused to acknowledge that the "hopes" of the Revolution still resonated with the aspirations of the oppressed two hundred years later. Vovelle believed that they "mutilated" the Revolution by cutting it into putatively "good" and "bad" pieces partly in order to stifle the demand for social change today. Operating from the left wing of the Socialist party, Max Gallo, a novelist, historian, and European deputy, made a similar case against the "illusion" of limiting the commemoration to '89. There was no solace for the left—or for any republican—in '89 on its own, for the attack on '93 would inevitably end up by engulfing and disqualifying '89. The defense of rudimentary Revolutionary values paradoxically began in '93, argued Gallo.[17]

Agulhon's Compromise

While historian Maurice Agulhon ceded to no one in his zeal for the Revolution, his bicentennial design combined the civic fervor of the Jacobins with the pragmatic poise of the shoppers. His argument turned on the double premise of an urgent imperative to commemorate in order to deepen the citizen's sense of identity and the concomitant need to reach as large a number of citizens as possible. Agulhon worried about the powerful forces that had gradually blunted one's sense of republican Frenchness: the leveling impact of an Americanized media, the ethic of "culturalism," fortified by the massive influx of immigrants, that celebrated differences to the detriment of common foundations (the prospect of a "Lebanonization" of France haunted the historian), the erosion of the history curriculum in the schools, the disintegrating impact of economic competition and other manifestations of acute individualism.

This burgeoning "absence of civic spirit" was aggravated by what Agulhon regarded as the cynical campaign of the antirevolutionaries (responsible for the "immense preemptive hostility" of the leading national media toward the bicentennial), which taught that the Revolution was essentially Jacobin and that Jacobinism was quintessentially hostile to liberty. This nefarious distortion elicited the intransigently combative side of the historian, who was tempted to posit a membership test in morally coercive terms that have a Jacobin timbre: "And those who refuse the bicentennial because they detest the Revolution must very well see that at the end of this logic they come to disdain everything that France has become during the past two centuries, [an evolution] which compromises patriotism itself."[18]

Agulhon's goal of reaching the widest possible audience constrained his choice of commemorative strategy. He sympathized with Madeleine Rebérioux's desire to move beyond the bourgeois individualism of '89 to the universal suffrage and the "anticipation of social laws" of '93. But the costs of this approach would be exorbitant. To force '93 in the current international conjuncture, in which liberty enjoyed primacy over the other basic rights, would be politically foolish for the left, which was historically the true source and vector of liberty. "If we proclaim our preference for 1793 too loudly and frequently," warned Agulhon, "we'll end up doing what we have already done numerous times on different occasions, that is leaving the flag of Liberty to our adversaries, who use it with virtuosity."

Moreover, to accentuate '93 was to militate against his ethic of *ouverture* by "privileging the right-left conflict." A consensus maximalist, Agulhon wanted to incorporate all republicans, on the nonfascist right as well as in the center and on the left. It was politically unwise to "drive the whole right into the camp of the Counterrevolution" by shifting the center of commemorative gravity toward the Terror and proclaiming that the left alone embodied the True Revolution (which, historically, it did in fact).[19] For most of the right subscribed to the core principles of '89, and they would be "in contradiction with themselves if they did not celebrate them as we do and with us." Here was an occasion to shift the fundamental line of division from right-left to right–extreme right.

For Maurice Agulhon was convinced that there was a "genuine consensus" around which one could build a strong commemorative majority. The consensus was the result of the political, ideological, and institutional evolution of the nation, especially since the centennial; in this regard, his analysis was not very different from François Furet's. Fewer and fewer people in France rejected "the grand principles," in particular the rule of law and the inviolability of liberty. This constituted "the essential of the heritage of 1789," and though it represented only part of the Revolution's patrimony, it was more than enough on which to lodge the commemoration. "I conclude, then, very firmly for the celebration of 1789 to be a great national undertaking, but reduced to the essential core precisely in the hope that it will be the object of the broadest consensus."

The commemoration must not be sectarian—at least not from an internal hexagonal point of view. It would not be "directed against the mayor of Paris but against the mullahs of Teheran." (The new totalitarianism that frightened Agulhon was religious rather than political.) Instead of preaching a "catechism," the commemoration would stress pride in France—a sort of Gaullist-republican nationalism that would appeal to (former premier Michel) Debré and Debray—and civic commitment. Nor were law and order the appanage of the right: "In order for political and civil society to remain livable, we must reinculcate the 'typically '89' idea that obedience to the law is the act of a free person and not a reactionary prejudice." To support his strategy, Agulhon counted on François Mitterrand, whom he esteemed to be "more liberal than Jacobin." Having adroitly ensnared the Communists in an "integrating trap," the president had already helped to remove one of the major obstacles to consensus making.[20]

Consensus

There was widespread agreement with Maurice Agulhon that a consensus existed, though not everyone welcomed it with equal enthusiasm. The middle-aged Marianne, icon of republican France, felt good inside the skin of "a soothed, humdrum republic, relieved of its passions," reported *Le Point*. The newsweekly detected blissfully "the signs of a new maturity" in the fact that France's institutions have "become consensual." Though lawyer-writer Jean-Denis Bredin doubted the capacity of the French to exploit their harmony, he nevertheless rejoiced at the consensus commanded by the R/revolutionary trinity. The "calming of the French passions" had engendered a diffuse attitude of "indifference," observed the historian Jean-Pierre Rioux—an apathy which could pass for consensus and which presaged stability.

Serge July, editor of *Libération*, marveled at how the combined timidity of the mainstream right and left reinforced the consensual disposition. For different, albeit complementary, reasons each feared the taint of debate over the Revolution, and thus both "prefer[ed] to practice abstention." The sociologist-philosopher François Ewald, writing pseudonymously as Condorcet, solicited by the bicentennial organizers to serve as symbol and deus ex machina of a moderate, apolitical, unanimist, '89-without-'93, civil-society-first commemoration, deplored the advent of the placid "age of consensus." Echoing Serge July, he declaimed: "On the left as on the right, there is no longer any notion of the Revolution. Everyone condemns the same thing—the Terror, Robespierre; everyone demands the same thing: the rights of man. . . . The Socialists—but does this term still have any meaning?—salute this blessed, terminated Revolution, which almost guarantees them, through the management of consensus, everlasting power." In the postrevolutionary, postpolitical, postmodern age of consensus, lamented Condorcet, "it is a matter of being rigorously conservative."[21]

The consensual strategy—"trick," "gadget," "manipulation," and so on— outraged important segments of the Jacobin and Marxist left. They saw it as futile, sterile, dangerous, dishonest, tragic. The philosopher Daniel Bensaïd, a militant in the Ligue communiste révolutionnaire, expressed disdain for those who sought to "commemorate in peace" by commemorating without the Revolution. This "consensual elixir" attracted and intoxicated "all the hypocrites and liars of the world." There was a pathetic irony in the effusively liberal discourse of consensus, suggested Bensaid, "for one finds unanimity only in totalitarian plebiscites, Stalinist congresses, and cabinet meetings."

It was in the very nature of the Revolution to be "a perpetual apple of discord." If "you contrive to change me into my contrary," wrote the philosopher in the voice of the indignant Revolution, if you want to transform me into "a nice little accommodating, conciliating, obliging girl," it will only serve the global project of ideological anaesthetization, social paralysis, "methodical depoliticization." The shoppers forced the recalcitrant Revolution into their procrustean shopping cart: "they refuse me en bloc, they take me retail . . . . they slice me up, amputate me, cut me like a sausage." The consensual butchers, the likes of Furet and Ozouf, were merely the servants of the prince, for whom Bensaïd reserved his warmest contempt—the prince who conquered and survived thanks to his cunning use of "consensus, cohabitation, opening—these lukewarm and melting words."[22]

Régis Debray deployed similar images and arguments. His "consensus drug that puts you to sleep" complemented Bensaïd's elixir. Like his Trotskyite counterpart, Debray interpreted consensus as exorcising the Revolution, rendering "the unacceptable acceptable," burying "a monster," lurching blithely toward entropy ("a consensual society is a dead society"). Like Bensaïd he inveighed against the shoppers and their *charcutiers* who treat "the Clemenceau bloc . . . like a salami." In his particular idiom, Debray described the abandonment, the renunciation, and the betrayal of the Revolution as another instance of the eclipse of republicanism by democracy, of equality by liberty, of the state by civil society, of justice by money, of the moral economy by the market economy, of fraternity by savage competition.

What scandalized both Bensaïd and Debray was that the *fauteurs* and the beneficiaries of consensus were as often on the left as on the right. In kindred manner, Max Gallo associated the apologists of consensus with the "money manipulators"—the true friends of totalitarianism—and the other subversives who undermined "the ethic of the republic," a "vision of the society" derived from the Revolution. Consensus was a frontal attack on "the French exception," which was the French equivalent of the Bible, the Revolution reified, Gallo's version of Debray's republican virtue.[23]

The Poll Bearers: Embalming the Consensus Alive

Sociologist Alain Touraine characterized his compatriots in a bicentennial interview as "profoundly antirevolutionary." While there are a number of discrete themes that one could embroider to sustain this judgment, the opinion polls of the late 1980s generally agreed that the French had come to digest and even approve their Revolution, within certain limits. Here were indicators that comforted the consensualists' claims to legitimacy and that encouraged the commemorators' conviction that their efforts would not go unrequited. The Revolution no longer sundered the nation. The public was inclined to view the Revolution as a heroic spasm of liberation, the womb of modern democracy, and the midwife of human rights. Even as many on the right overcame their reluctance to accept the Revolution, many on the left overcame their reluctance to criticize it.

To be sure, one must keep in mind the elusiveness and fragility of the notion of public opinion, and the infirmities of the techniques used to measure it. Public opinion is a constructed rather than a natural phenomenon, elicited by polls that are rarely of immaculate conception. Still, they are the only yardsticks of approximation we have, and in this case the different tests reveal striking convergences. Nor is there any discordance in the interpretation of the general trend: rightist and centrist commentators concurred with those on the left that the French now considered the Revolution "a good thing."[24]

An Ifop poll commissioned by the Communist weekly *Révolution* at the beginning of 1987 found that 73 percent of the respondents believed that the revolutionaries of 1789 "were right to want to change the political and social system of

France" and only 5 percent felt they were wrong to have done so. *Révolution* delected in the far more surprising—implausible?—answer to a second question ("In your opinion, will France experience the need once again to change its political and social regime?" to which 56 percent replied yes, 25 percent no), permitting it to conclude that 1789 had by no means resolved all the problems and to predict that the strategy of those who "heap praise on the Revolution of 1789 in order the better to preempt the revolution that France needs today" would fail. Sponsored by a periodical on the other side of the political spectrum, *L'Expansion,* a Sofres poll in August 1988 found that the word "revolution" evoked a negative image for 50 percent of respondents and a positive representation for only 38 percent. In both polls, the Communist electorate was massively on the side of revolution, Union pour la démocratie française–Rassemblement pour la République (UDF-RPR) voters strongly opposed, and Socialists divided.[25]

Several months later, working for the left-of-center *Nouvel Observateur,* Sofres learned that 66 percent of those queried believed that the Revolution "constituted a necessary stage in the process of changing French society." This group traversed all social classes and marshaled a majority of all political families, including the Front national. Only 23 percent considered it to be "a useless ordeal." When asked whether they would have actively participated in the Revolution or actively combatted it, 49 percent claim they would have engaged in its support and 6 percent would have struggled against it (almost a quarter would have stayed home). Communist electors (79 percent) surpassed Socialist voters (57 percent) in their enthusiasm for this engagement. Proportionally more supporters of Le Pen (40 percent) than exponents of the RPR (39 percent) and the UDF (37 percent) would have fought on the side of the Revolution. Citizens continued to differ in the zeal they felt for revolutionary action, though they agreed on the Revolution's essential merit. The vast majority of respondents construed the Terror as "rather a tragedy that stains the Revolution" than "a point of passage between the Old Regime and the republic"—the oblique formulation, particularly of the positive side, not investing the question with luminous clarity or precision. Citizens of all political persuasions converged on the negative side, over 70 percent on the right, 63 percent of the Socialists, even 47 percent of the Communists.

The classical binary lines of fracture no longer held firm on the eve of the bicentennial. Even among high school history teachers (only one among ten of whom identifies with the right), the Terror raises questions. Without apologizing for it, in a Sofres-*Express* poll 61 percent blamed it on the civil and foreign war waged against the Revolution. Yet when asked about the possible linkages between the Terror and Stalinist totalitarianism, 42 percent recognized that "there are differences, but it is a question of a phenomenon of the same order," while 49 percent rejected any comparison. In the same sense they rank Vovelle (15/20) higher than Furet (14/20), but the latter seemed to be closing fast.[26]

On the basis of a Sofres survey in early 1988, the rightist *Figaro-Magazine* found a clearcut "consensus" around the idea of the Revolution as a positive achievement regardless of age, gender, or political affiliation. Rejecting the bloc, 57 percent thought that there were several distinct revolutions in the Revolution. Only 16 percent of high school history teachers in a Sofres-*Express* study subscribed to the bloc; the vast majority conceived of several more or less distinct revolutions. Like several others, the *Figaro-Magazine* poll stresses the unambiguous predilection of respondents for the soft Revolution of '89 over against the rough and bloody experience of '93.

Equality was the core of ideological accord: for this public the most prized element in the Revolutionary legacy was equality before the law, followed by the "ideal" of "liberty-equality-fraternity" and the commitment to public education. Seventy-four percent of respondents esteemed that the Declaration was the best symbol of the Revolution (the Terror and the September massacres received only 6 percent). Overwhelmingly, they approved the abolition of the monarchy (75 percent) and the suppression of privileges (81 percent). They evinced a symmetrically robust distaste for violence: 68 percent judged the executions and repression of the Terror "abominable" (73 percent of the right and 64 percent of the left, not a huge disparity), while only 19 percent viewed them as a "necessity" (23 percent of the left—but 41 percent of the Communist voters—and 16 percent of the right).

To the chagrin of its clientele, *Figaro-Magazine* recounted that Counterrevolutionary resistance found relatively little favor—despite the rejection of Terror, perhaps in part because of the dislike for violence in general. Though the question was posed in tendentious terms that seemed geared to evoke a pro-Vendée stance, 38 percent of the respondents placed their sympathies with the blues rather than the whites, who obtained 30 percent, with almost a third venturing no opinion. Only 41 percent of the right preferred the Vendéens, while only 48 percent of the left favored the Revolutionary forces, another sign of the blunting of the old cleavages.

Allergic to wrenching conflict, the public in this poll seemed to yearn for a Revolution in linear terms, seized as a burst of (more or less sustained) unanimity rather than as a relentless, costly struggle. Nor did the juggernaut engineered by historian Pierre Chaunu to portray the Revolution as a consummate economic disaster seem to make much impression. Only 6 percent regarded "the impoverishment of France" as a significant issue. Proud of the prestige their Revolution enjoyed in the world, they believed that it generated more positive results than either the American or Russian Revolutions.[27]

Echoing these findings, an open-ended Ipsos questionnaire for *Le Monde* revealed a clear preference for the early Revolution marked by such positive accomplishments as the Declaration of Rights and a lack of interest in inquiring into the other, darker Revolution of deeply ambiguous yield. (*L'Express* reported that 83.8 percent of those interviewed regarded liberty-equality-fraternity rather than the guillotine as the appropriate symbol of the Revolution.) When asked, "What are for you the most important events of the French Revolution?", the Ipsos universe privileged the Bastille (37 percent) and the Declaration (16 percent); only 5 percent listed the guillotine and Terror, though 13 percent pointed to the execution of the king and queen. (Responding to the same question, participants in a Sofres–*Nouvel Observateur* poll enumerated by order of preference the Bastille, the night of 4 August/end of privileges, the Estates General, the execution of Louis XVI; the Terror obtained only 10 percent and the Vendée 5 percent.)

The violence of 14 July is left out or repressed or unknown. The emphasis on the Bastille as the liberation of the French is reinforced by the choice of de Gaulle, the protagonist of another liberation, as the "best continuer" of the Revolution among the major figures of French history (followed at a huge distance by Jaurès, Pompidou, and Mitterrand). The moderate inflection is confirmed by the substantial numbers who consider the king's execution as either excess and unmerited or as an error.[28]

The respondents selected Robespierre as the most important figure in the Revolution, though he was also the protagonist who drew the strongest hostile feelings. Lafayette headed the bicentennial hit parade, followed by Marie Antoinette, Mirabeau, Danton, Carnot, and Louis XVI. Unchallenged in first place for antipathy, the Incorruptible languished in last place for sympathy. Lafayette's popularity testified to the strength of consensus. He was the hero of America, site of the sage revolution; incarnation of the liberal Enlightenment, coauthor of the Declaration; protector of Paris and man of the cocarde; the embodiment of '89.[29]

A poll reported by *Pèlerin Magazine* underlines the preference for the concrete patrimony of '89 over the generic vocation of revolution. When asked of what they were most proud, 69 percent said the status of France as *the* country of human rights, while only 16 percent singled out France as "mother of revolutions" (a score barely more impressive than the 14 percent who elected France as "eldest daughter of the church"). Political analyst Olivier Duhamel argued cogently that the destitution of the Russian Revolution as a rival model fortified the potency of '89's magnestism.[30]

Despite polls published in their own press, there was still a widespread conviction on the right that the silent majority in France was hostile to the Revolution. They pointed to various antirevolutionary public meetings, to a lack of participation in commemorative activities, and to international trends that were somehow interpreted as indicators of a sweeping and irrevocable postrevolutionary tide. Though a habitué of *Figaro-Magazine*, the political commentator Guy Sorman did not allow its bicentennial poll to influence the analysis of his weekly newsletter. Positing a "spectacular" change in the French state of mind since 1981, his *Lettre politique et parlementaire* characterized it in 1989 as "more nostalgic for the Old Regime than for the ambiguous Revolution."

The far right adduced some evidence to back its claims, though it is very hard to assess its validity. After a televised debate between Jean-François Kahn, director of *L'Evénement du Jeudi*, and François Brigneau, creator of *L'Anti-89*, the host of the show, journalist Jean-Claude Bourret, invited viewers to respond by minitel to two questions. First: "Do you believe that the French people know what really happened under the Revolution?" to which 83 percent of the 2,380 respondents answered no. The unspoken text seemed to be that the truth was knowable and indeed known but that those in power did not want to diffuse it in order to protect the official version on which their legitimacy rested. Second: "In your view, was the Revolution a good or a bad thing?" For almost three quarters of the pool, it was a bad thing. Bourret explained the highly skewed results "by the mobilization of the Front national"; to which Brigneau retorted, with sprightly disingenuousness: "As if the Front national, a republican movement, ever declared itself hostile to '89." Why, wondered Brigneau, are we so reluctant to "recognize that the French Revolution is perhaps not as popular as is supposed"?[31]

The Right(s) Stuff

"Is it so loathsome to seek out consensus?" asked Mona Ozouf, in a tone that was at once plaintive and incredulous. The commemoration needed a "project." For her and the bulk of the shoppers and the consensualists, human rights were the right stuff in 1989. The choice of human rights as the core theme corresponded to the intellectual and political climate throughout much of the world. In the wake of the debacle of systems born of Bolshevism, more and more leaders and thinkers agreed that 1917 could no longer be cast as the future of 1989. On the contrary, 1789, the moment of the Declaration of the Rights of Man, had become the new future of 1917.

"The democratic idea has become the future of the socialist idea, and even that of the Communist world," observed François Furet. His great merit was the intuition that the "political" would displace the "social" on a stage far grander than the Left Bank of Paris or the historiography of the French Revolution. As a journalist for the *Quotidien de Paris* put it, "today it is liberty that is revolutionary in the world." Rights fit the consensus precisely because they were the rights of '89, privileging equality before the law and a vast freedom of endeavor. Liberty, as guaranteed in the Declaration, was now seen as both the gyroscope of society and the motor of economic well-being. More and more people, even some of the desperately poor of the Third World, came to see political rights as anterior to economic and social rights.

Not many voices on the left in 1989 would have contested Jean-François Revel's conclusion that "to venture to place equality before liberty is to annihilate them both." Certainly not that of Jean Daniel, editor-in-chief of the *Nouvel Observateur,* who wrote: "The great event of 1988 is that the Third World, conservative or revolutionary, the impoverished Third World whose empty stomach is not supposed to have ears, has discovered the importance of freedoms and of law regardless of the economic situation of the society." The admonition formulated by Mohamed Bedjaoui of the International Court of Justice in 1989 would have struck deaf ears just a few years earlier: "[Today's leaders must not be] tempted to postpone indefinitely political and civil rights by making their fulfillment dependent on the prior realization of economic rights." So powerful was the rights theme that it threatened to change the nature of the dialogue not only between left and right but also between East and West and between North and South.[32]

The rights theme had great appeal in France as the central bicentennial focus. After all, virtually everyone hailed them: Chaunu, Vovelle, and Furet among the historians (Furet taking pleasure in reminding a large portion of the left that it was a recent convert to the celebration of rights, having "rediscovered" their primacy after a long Marxist phase of contempt for their social inadequacy); President Mitterrand and former prime minister Jacques Chirac among the political titans; in the church no less a voice than the extremely prudent Cardinal Lustiger, who pronounced them intrinsically worthy and fully consonant with Christian doctrine (thus provoking the ire of leftist historian Claude Manceron, who reminded his countryman that before exercising "its marvelous faculty to recover, to 'baptize' in a sense everything it cannot resist," the church had long treated the rights of man as "coming under the rubric of mortal sin").

National hebdo, the Lepéniste organ, blasted the Revolution for transgressing the rights of man, but not for promulgating them. Gérard Longuet, a onetime student leader of the neofascist organization called Occident and former Chiraquian minister, detested the Revolution but worshipped "the religion of the rights of man, heir to the century of Enlightenment, precursor of liberal Europe." Horrified by the Revolution's violent disregard for the rights it declared, the philosopher Jean-Marie Benoist insisted on their nonrevolutionary origins: Judeo-Christian, Enlightenment, monarchical-reformist. If their collective momentum assured the "permanence" of the Declaration against the Revolution itself, Benoist conceded nevertheless that the Revolution decisively transformed this liberal text by casting it in boldly universal terms.[33]

The universalism of the rights theme flattered French amour propre and served the nation's diplomatic interests. A committee was formed to nominate François Mitterrand for a Nobel peace prize for fostering human rights. Another group proposed the Pantheonization of Lafayette as coauthor of the Declaration. The Académie des sciences morales et politiques announced that it would consecrate an entire year's reflection to the rights issue. Numerous universities, the Paris bar, and UNESCO, among others, organized colloquia around the rights theme. Pierre Bernis, leader of an association called Nouveaux Droits de l'homme, lobbied for an aggiornamento of the Declaration, based on new "cahiers de doléances" to be formulated at the grass roots and synthesized by the parliament, and for the creation of an Order of the Rights of Man, a pacific pendant to the Legion of Honor, of military genesis. The government's second bicentennial planner, Edgar Faure, anchored his commemoration around the creation of a foundation devoted to the rights of man.

The rights of man have become "the choice morsel of the Revolution, the roasting piece," noted the *Nouvel Observateur:* "Everyone takes seconds on the rights of man. Who is against the rights of man? Dogs perhaps. In any case, not man. Ninety-eight percent of dictators, according to Sofres, are for them (they simply have their conception of them), 115 percent of advertising executives, 300 percent of show-biz people."[34]

Contextually, the Wrong Stuff

The rights roast turned some stomachs, on the right, on the fringe, in particular, and on the left, somewhat more diffusely. Nostalgic for the time when Revolution was taken seriously—measured by the willingness to risk one's life, as exemplified by the heroes of Tiananmen—Condorcet/Ewald complained bitterly that "the rights of man have killed the Revolution." As domesticated for the commemoration, valorized for the consensus it galvanized rather than for its contents, the Declaration was "no longer in the service of liberty but of order, as a conservative, counterrevolutionary ideology." The perversion of the rights idea pained Condorcet. No wonder it inculcated "submission" instead of "resistance," conformity instead of iconoclasm, for outside the theatre of "combats" that gave birth to human rights—they were hardly the politely awaited, organic end product of Western history—they lost their meaning.

Playing on this genetic chord, the Communist writer Claudine Ducol protested against the beatific idea that our rights fell from the sky, a fable contrived to obscure the fierce "struggles" required to win them. We have been psychologically bludgeoned into forgetting, Ewald regretted, that the '89 rendition of the revolutionary rights doctrine was the "initial, provisional, and incomplete version." This was exactly what Daniel Bensaïd had in mind when he denounced "the truncated rights of man" in much the same spirit as that with which Philippe de Villiers condemned the "truncated memory." The Trotskyite militant derided this putatively "generous," "exemplary," "glorious" Declaration which was in fact egregiously flawed: witness its failure to deal with the problems of slavery, of women, and of the right to vote.

Socialist leader and minister Pierre Joxe, more stringently Marxizing in the mid-1980s when he was interviewed on this issue than he is today, fully endorsed Bensaïd's critique of the '89 Declaration, adding to the list of infirmities its narrow, individualistic conception of property and its indifference to the right to work. The writer Gilles Perrault, who in early 1991 would summon the troops to desert at about the same moment Joxe took over the Ministry of Defense in the war against Iraq, deplored the bicentennial burial of the Revolution "under the chrysanthemums" of a Declaration "purged of worrisome future convulsions." Careful not to attack the Declaration itself, Régis Debray assailed its abduction, its show-biz/video packaging, its prostitution to the vulgar ends of political integration. "Is it necessary today, in order to meet the approval of the public, to hide from it this duperie, this cowardliness, this thoughtlessness, this vanity, this fraud, this verbosity of the 'rights-of-Man' discourse, which has in common with 1789 only its name?"[35]

The rights fixation/consensus and its discourse (known familiarly as "droit-de-l'hommisme,"—"droidlomisme" in its rap mode) provoked criticism from more moderate quarters on the left. Hardly a radical, the sociologist Alain Touraine reproached public opinion for defending "human rights [so] ardently, to the point of casting into oblivion the whole French Revolution, keeping only the Declaration of the Rights of Man." By and large a consensualist, Jean-Denis Bredin neverthe-less complained about the narrow construction built on rights, "a shrunken but congenial conception of liberty." The "droidlom" were the rights of the comfort-able, the secure, the complacent. Though one of the bright stars in Furet's galaxy, Bredin seemed wistful for *le social* and sympathetic with the old Marxizing stric-tures against the formalistic limits of the right of liberty, to whose "real contents" the French public had become "inattentive."

The successor to Edgar Faure as president of the government's official bicen-tenial agency, Jean-Noël Jeanneney, quickly took his distance from the "dangerously consensual" rights ideology. Jeanneney disliked the way in which the rights mania foreclosed relations with the rest of the Revolution. Though he never really achieved the dialogue that he promised to open between '89 and '93, and though he went on to practice consensus even as he reviled it, on the rights issue Jeanneney's position was closer to Condorcet/Ewald's or Bensaid's than to Ozouf's: "under Edgar Faure's presidency, in the eyes of certain observers, the rights of man had served as a sort of envelope manifestly earmarked to conceal the ways in which the harsh side of the Revolution could still speak to our contempo-rary conflicts." To the deep chagrin of certain members of his executive team, the president of the Mission du Bicentenaire backed off from both the foundation launched by Faure and the multitude of social and humanitarian projects that had crystallized around the rights theme.[36]

Intrinsically, Pernicious Stuff

On the far right, many voices rose up not merely against the Revolution's ravag-ing of its own revolutionary doctrine but against that doctrine itself. Bespeaking a point of view shared by many antimodern, fundamentalist Catholics, the writer Jean Dumont railed against the liberalism with which Le Pen himself had occasionally flirted. Liberalism, codified in the Declaration of Rights, was godless, corrosive of social bonds, a leaven of decadence. Dumont linked the Declaration specifically with the "egotistical attitudes" which issue from "that excessive promotion of individual rights." Scrambling Alexis de Tocqueville, Hippolyte Taine and Au-gustin Cochin, Bernard Pascal, another editorialist of the extreme right, decried the Declaration for the very same quality for which Mona Ozouf hailed it: its abstract-ness. The "ideology of abstract liberty" was a "chimera" which resulted necessarily in "anarchy," in many cases in "crime." As for equality, it was an unreal notion with no possible concrete referent, for "everything is based on diversity and hierarchy."

A sly and accomplished polemist, François Brigneau discredited the Declaration of 1789 by associating it with the Terror through an oblique comparison with more recent events that fit into the same malevolent mold. Affixing his signature, he managed to tarnish the Declaration further by identifying it with what he viewed as that timeless and universal venom called Judaism. At the core of Brigneau's parable was René Cassin, an eminent jurist, an aide to de Gaulle during the war, and a Jewish community leader—to nourish the stereotype, Brigneau added: the brother of a businessman of dubious practices—who had recently received the ultimate national accolade of Pantheonization. "The perfect heir to 1789," Cassin was one of the authors of the Universal Declaration of Human Rights of 1948 and, symmetrically in Brigneau's eyes, "one of the organizers of the Terror of 1944."

The glissando from 1944 to 1789/93 was almost imperceptible. According to Brigneau, Cassin perverted the law in order to favor Gaullists and Communists ("the *Résistancialistes,* who profited from the *Epuration* as the purchasers of *biens nationaux* profited from the Revolution") at the expense of decent and patriotic Pétainists, who were judged "on the assembly line" and shot every day. The counterrevolutionary concluded: "M. René-Samuel Cassin is very much the descendant of Robespierre, who after having abolished the death penalty, had the guillotine erected in front of the prefectures of France."[37]

Rights Genealogy: Thatcherism and French Patriotism

One important consolation was available to rightist liberals, beyond the distinction they made between the abominable Revolution and the rights doctrine to which they subscribed. It found expression in their vigorous denial of the Revolution's claims to the paternity of the principles of human rights. This stance required of the rightist liberals, ordinarily given to nationalist braggadocio, a dose of abnegation that their pro-Revolutionary adversaries, in the climate of commemoration and in the glare of international limelight, regarded as *lèse-nation*. Philippe de Villiers put the case succinctly: "The rights of man were the old Christian values rectified by passing through Virginia." The lawyer Jean-Marc Varaut traced the genealogy back to the Greek fathers of the fourth century B.C.

Though neither paid homage to the English, perhaps in deference to the age-old distrust of Perfidious Albion that transcended all hexagonal cleavages, the position they staked out can perhaps most appositely be called bicentennial Thatcherism. For it was most fully, most publicly, and most churlishly articulated by the British prime minister in the midst of the climactic events marking the seven-nation summit and the French national celebration in Paris in July 1989. There was the Burkean high road to organic political maturity, and there was the vulgar and treacherous French carnival. "Human rights did not begin with the French Revolution," Mrs. Thatcher told the French press. "They go back to Judeo-Christian tradition . . . . then came the Magna Charta of 1215, and the Declaration of Rights of the seventeenth century, and our tranquil revolution of 1688 . . . . Incidentally, we celebrated this event last year, but discreetly." She was alleged to have repeated her argument in one of the final summit toasts.

Thatcher's ire was piqued not only by the French bicentennial swagger but by the risk of the bicentennial spirit infesting the work of the seven summit nations. (Perhaps there was also the lingering memory of Premier Rocard's recent evocation of "the tendency to social cruelty in Great Britain.") There was talk of a common declaration regarding European rights which would have a social and abstract cast and which would make a flattering reference to the French Revolution as the mother of all rights. Thatcher wanted to confine the summit gaze to the political and the concrete. As for 1789, the prime minister had recently told detractors in the Commons who reproached her with being out of step with the coming European revolution: "It took us so long to get rid of the effects of the French Revolution that we are not about to wish for another one!"[38]

Mrs. Thatcher was their dinner guest, and many of her French hosts were not pleased to see her "spit in the revolutionary soup." "Holy Maggie!" exclaimed the very sedate *Ouest France.* "She has no equal in uttering unpleasant things with a smile." The moderate *Tribune de l'expansion* was incensed by "this somewhat jealous animosity" which it contrasted to American sympathy. It sensed that Thatcher spoke not just for herself or her party but for a large share of British public opinion. What could be expected of such an arrogant and narcissistic nation, asked this representative of wounded French pride? "Great Britain is probably the most chauvinistic country on earth, and that does not date from 1789."

Thatcher did not lack press support back home. "No lessons from the French on issues of freedom," headlined the *Sunday Express,* which characterized the French Revolution as insurgent mobs that "found their counterparts over the centuries in Lenin, Mao, Hitler, and Iran's Khomeini." The British, boasted *L'Express,* had a very different tradition of liberty, "which has nothing to do with today's ambitious triumphalism of the French." "The bicentennial is finally over," sighed the *Sunday Telegraph* with relief, "we've had our fill of the French Revolution for the next hundred years." The correspondent of *Le Monde* in London was palpably irritated by the pervasive "mocking tone" of the English press. "Innumerable historical articles are devoted to the guillotine," he wrote, "which is by far what the British know best concerning the French Revolution."

The French public avenged itself on a small scale by booing Thatcher at the summit-bicentennial ceremonies in honor of human rights at the Trocadero on 13 July. According to the *Canard enchaîné,* Thatcher openly expressed dissatisfaction not only with French history but with the organization of summit protocol, Mitterrand's wearisome longiloquence, and the irreverent photographer who tried to take her picture as she walked up the steep staircase of the Pyramide du Louvre (revealing "Maggie's panties"). "The bicentennial is a success," French foreign minister Roland Dumas is alleged to have roared, "you have only to look at Mrs. Thatcher's face." Her countryman Robert Maxwell, Socialist, millionaire, and media baron—

not yet besmirched by financial scandal—whose long philanthropic/business arm touched several major bicentennial projects, tried single-handedly to atone for what he regarded as the scandalous conduct of his prime minister. "Mrs. Thatcher would have been better off to remain silent when she asserted that Great Britain had invented human rights," contended populist Captain Bob. "For the lords perhaps, but not for the people."[39]

But Mrs. Thatcher also attracted some vocal support in France. The British leader was "the sole official personage to refuse the imposture of the celebration" wrote Lepéniste Jean Madiran in *Présent*. "She says out loud what the French who know the True History think in silence." Despite the provocation and the political motivation, Joseph Rozier, bishop of Poitiers, granted Thatcher's point about the genesis of rights doctrine. "Of course Maggie did not choose her moment very well to play schoolteacher," concurred Jean-François Revel. But she had two strong points in her favor. First of all, she was right: "Whether we like it or not, it was Voltaire who wrote the *English Letters* and not Locke or Hume who wrote the 'French Letters.'" Secondly, there were extenuating circumstances for her lack of tact: "Let us not forget that for months we have been battering the whole world to death with our endless claims that France, and only France, brought liberty to the world."

In other circumstances, it is highly probable that the French left, along with the right, would have conceded Thatcher's point, at least in part. "Besides, we must be just, we French, and not claim for ourselves alone the exclusive credit for an immense transformation," declared Edouard Herriot, just before the outbreak of the Second World War when there was a burgeoning need for trans-Channel solidarity. "England preceded us on the road to liberty," he acknowledged.[40] Throughout his tenure, Jean-Noël Jeanneney, the official commemorative manager, dissociated himself from the haughty, Gallocentric spirit of the centennial, tirelessly admonishing his compatriots to "avoid chauvinistic bragging." To insist too emphatically on the French parentage of democracy and modernity was, first, a historical deformation, for it overlooked "everything that the Revolution . . . owes to foreign influences." In addition, it was a grave strategic error, a wholly counterproductive gesture, for the world in 1989 was naturally inclined to grant France credit without being solicited.[41]

East Winds Fan the Commemorative Flame

For many observers, ranging from the former minister of culture François Léotard on the right to Daniel Bensaïd on the left, the "real bicentennial" took place in the East—in the Orient and then in Eastern Europe. The hopes and the horrors of Tiananmen suddenly invested the commemoration with a cutting edge that it was unable to forge on its own. *Libération* overstated the case when it claimed that this event, "in its dramatic violence, saved in extremis a bicentennial that was lying dormant." But there is no doubt that the Chinese student uprising restituted a vivid sense of the enormity of the stakes involved in the struggle for human rights. Brandishing the symbols and words of 1789 and chanting the *Marseillaise*, the insurgents elicited the pride as well as the sympathy of the French. *Sud Ouest* hailed this lesson that reminded us "what a model our country represents for those who aspire to democracy."

Three Beijing images deeply moved François Mitterrand: "a Statue of Liberty, and four digits: 1789, and this young man, alone, standing in front of the tanks." It was "real revolution on the march," and it was inspired at least in part by the memory of the French Revolution. "Eh bien," the president told *L'Express* on Bastille Day, "I think that it's extraordinary, in a country as closed as China, and closed for such a long time, its youth educated, like the preceding generation, by a closed system, that the Statue of Liberty—the idea of Liberty—was able to traverse those thick barriers intact."

Neither the president nor the official commentators probed deeply into the analogies between the French Revolution and the Chinese insurrection. That might have led to embarrassing scenarios in which the students play counterrevolutionary victims vis-à-vis the juggernaut Terror of Deng and Li Peng (the tensions between "the aspirations of '89 and the persistent realities of '93," as a columnist of the pro-Mitterrand *Royaliste* nicely stated it). The important point seemed to be the "drawing power" of certain simple ideas most closely identified with the French historical trajectory. Jean-Paul Goude, the pageantmaker of 14 July, underlined the point by bringing the Spring of Peking to the Champs-Elysées.[42]

"The hope assassinated in the spring," wrote *Le Monde's* director, André Fontaine, "found new life in the autumn, where it was least expected: in proverbially disciplined East Germany." Gorbachev, who had paid homage to the principle of self-determination emerging from the French Revolution, made the critical decision not to dispatch the Terror of tanks to reclaim the German Democratic Republic or any of the other democratizing satellites. Though events did not accelerate in Eastern Europe until relatively late in the year, by the fall the connections between that struggle and the French Revolutionary legacy became a leitmotif of public discourse. "As in the grand hours of 1789, it was the people who made their clamor heard," Mitterrand told the European Parliament in October. Jeanneney characterized the ferment in Eastern Europe as "a revolution inspired by the ideals of 1789" and likened the dismantling of the Berlin Wall to the taking (down) of the Bastille. The minister of culture, Jack Lang, associated Soviet human rights advocate and Nobel laureate Andrey Sakharov and Czechoslovak playwright-president Vaclav Havel with the enshrinement of three (moderate/velvet) French Revolutionary heroes in the Panthéon to mark the close of the bicentennial season, reaffirming the identity between the (undifferentiated/unperiodized) French Revolution and the struggle for liberty in the East.

The unraveling of the Socialist universe in Eastern Europe left the French Communists in an embarrassing and disconcerting position. Instinctively, they wanted to appropriate the insurgency, identify with it, and avert their eyes from the enormous contradictions that it entailed both for the French Communist party (PCF) and the freedom fighters in the Communist bloc. Thus a group of Breton comrades mechanically hailed "the hour when Europe reconnects with the élan and the ideals of the revolutions" of 1789, 1848, and the twentieth century. For these Communists, there were many houses in the Revolutionary mansion. Privately, many communists agonized over the implications of the "implosions." How much solace could they extract from the strong identification of the East German rioters with the imagery of the French Revolution? Publicly, they clung to the increasingly dubious idea that the insurgents were groping for a '93 ("a socialism with a deliberately human face") rather than an '89.

Commentators from other perspectives imposed a different interpretation. Liberals and rightists contested the claim that the events in Eastern Europe vindicated the Jacobin position. On the contrary, these changes constituted a repudiation of part of '89 and of everything beyond '89, in other words, of Robespierro-Lenino-Stalinism; or, as *Le Point* put it the following year, they testified to "the victory of Tocqueville over Marx"—presumably then, too, of Raymond Aron over Sartre, liberty over equality, the political over the social. While ex-seminarian Léotard stressed the power of the marketplace as a wellspring of liberty, the archbishop of Paris focused on "the spiritual courage" of the believers of Eastern Europe.

Vendéen Philippe de Villiers courted the Poles, while the Socialists pressed the case of the Romanians. Ceausescu refused to permit several leading cultural figures to attend the 14 July ceremonies to which the French government invited them; two of them later became ministers in the post-Ceausescu regime, and a third the first ambassador to France. In the most febrile diplomatic gesture of the bicentennial year, redolent of Girondin cosmopolitanism, foreign minister Roland Dumas cried "aux armes!" He announced that France would support the formation of a volunteer brigade to fight alongside the prodemocratic forces, a proposal obviated by the collapse of the Romanian Old Regime. His purpose, according to the *New York Times*, was to dramatize "France's leadership in the fight for liberty, equality, and fraternity." "We are the same as they," one imagines Dumas muttering, commemoratively.[43]

Resurgent Counterrevolutionaries
and New Age Antirevolutionaries

From the early 1980s onward, observers on all sides were struck by the recrudescence of counterrevolutionary sentiment. Its immediate source was the conquest of power by the left in 1981. This first, chilling dose of political changeover terrified a part of the traditional right, which lapsed into masochistic fantasies of reprisal and social vengeance that bordered on hysteria. The advent of the Other—red, Marxist-Leninist, Robespierrist (by its own inadvertent admission at the Socialist party congress at Valence)—seemed to call for a rearticulation of the ideological arms needed to combat the menace.

This neorevolutionary spasm in France appeared all the more shocking because it eddied against the tide of things in the larger cultural and political universe. On the background of the denunciation of the gulag, the horror elicited by the efflorescence of Pol Pot's brand of (Sorbonne-refined) bloody Stalinism, the waning intellectual authority of marxism, the embourgeoisement effected by the years of postwar economic expansion (the *trente glorieuses*), and most recently the triumphant juggernaut of Reaganesque and Thatcherite "liberalism" predicated on the inseparability of free-market capitalism and freedom *tout court,* the revival of the left seemed aberrant. The right blamed its defeat in part on an ideological deficit, a failure to voice eloquently its values as well as a program.

The specter of the bicentennial on the horizon, an occasion that the left would surely attempt to exploit, gave further impetus to the counterrevolutionary revival, and to the crystallization of a more diffuse and frankly modern anti-Revolutionary movement. The early difficulties of the Socialists, marked by their agonizing "liberal" turn and by the disquieting silence of their intellectuals, nourished the hope that there would be an early Thermidor. Counter- and antirevolutionaries claimed some of the credit for the legislative victory of the right in 1986 and looked forward to the presidential election two years later with burgeoning confidence. The neoconservative mood that distinguished the new historiography—the revisionism associated in France with François Furet—comforted the growing intuition that the carnival was lurching to an end.[1]

The left appeared rather startled by the amplitude of the counter-and antirevolutionary currents. (Only the liminal left, hostage to Furet's imperative need to deny any truly significant fissures in the body politic over the Revolution, disparaged the seriousness of this resurgence; thus historian Michel Winock's stark affirmation that "all that has only museum interest.") "I wonder in truth whether we have not in recent times embraced a false idea," mused Régis Debray, "to wit, that the French right has *really* reconciled itself with the Revolution . . . . [We have] underestimated the persistence or the revival of the traditional rejection of the revolutionary gains (*acquis*), not only within the elites, but in the depths of 'the people of the right'." Had the increasingly jittery left, wondered Debray, internalized the rejuvenated stereotypes of classical rightist thinking, thereby intensifying its own R/revolutionary guilt complex?

Sociologically, politically, and culturally, the critics of the Revolution had very different itineraries and affiliations. They were sharply divided on many major issues concerning the nation's political institutions, the organization of the economy, the relation of religion to the state, the role of the individual in society, and so on. Adamantine counterrevolutionaries, formed in the Maistrean crucible, and more or less irretrievably alienated from the republic, and self-declared liberals with Enlightenment roots (among other sources of nurture) had little in common, except certain conclusions about the nature of the Revolution, frequently arrived at through quite different analytical strategies. Drawn together artifically by the bicentennial, these different "anti" and "counter" currents tended to avoid squabbling among themselves. They focused their fire on their common historical and ideological adversary.

Though the unregenerate counterrevolutionaries, most of whom gravitated around the far right, regarded the mainstream antirevolutionary current at best as timid and inconsistent, they drew heavily on its discourse and its momentum in order to enhance their own claims for credibility. For short-term polemical purposes, the implicit watchword of the mainstream seemed to be "no enemies on the right." But rather than endorsing classical counterrevolutionary doctrine, the antirevolutionaries reinvented many of those positions, grounding them on refurbished or new arguments and recasting them in less benighted and confessional language. Save during authoritarian regimes, full-blooded counterrevolutionaries had rarely enjoyed such generally favorable conditions. In order to advance (or regress), for once they were not reliant exclusively on their own energy. The antirevolutionaries had a more complicated task because most of them were not intransigent rejectionists. These critics detested much about the Revolution, but not everything. They had to discredit it, and expose its perils and defects, without, however, denying it certain positive accomplishments.[2]

The White Lobby

The success of the counterrevolutionary comeback was due in part to the methods deployed by the "white lobby," many of them in imitation of the tactics of the left. Linking the university, publishing houses, and the press, the antirevolutionary activists constituted a remarkably effective triangle of influence—and image making. The chief agent and emblem of this counterrevolutionary offensive was Pierre Chaunu, whose bicentennial role is assessed in *Farewell, Revolution: The Historians' Feud, France, 1789/1989.* "This Protestant historian, a respected professor," *Libération* noted colorfully, "has succumbed since 10 May [1981] to a curious syndrome of Koblenz, abandoning the thesis for the jeremiad and taking on the manner of a lecture-hall Cadoudal, the prosecutorial air of a Bonald, becoming Hersant's part-time journalist."

Chaunu gave the Counterrevolution a major foothold in the Sorbonne (Paris IV), in the publishing world (Presses Universitaires de France and Librairie Académique Perrin), and the daily national press (Hersant's *Le Figaro*). No one profited more opportunistically and deftly from Furet's destabilization of the Marxist camp. Chaunu was ubiquitous, glossing and/or epitomizing Furet in seminars and in his column, tirelessly execrating the commemorative impulse and the Jacobin line, shepherding and puffing the publication of such counterrevolutionary milestones as Reynald Secher's *Génocide franco-français* and René Sédillot's *Coût de la Révolution française*. Beyond the Hersant press empire, which included the widely diffused and rigorously conservative *Figaro-Magazine*, the counterrevolutionary stance elicited warm support in such newsweeklies as *L'Express* and *Le Point* and in the daily *Quotidien de Paris*. The far right had its own networks, including a daily and weekly press (*Présent, National hebdo, Minute*), a specialized bicentennial press (*L'Anti-89*), and the resources of the traditionalist Catholics, which included an anti-Revolutionary library for children published by Action familiale et scolaire.

Guardians of the left whined that the Counterrevolution had taken possession of the mass media, audiovisual as well as printed. Public debates that were ostensibly framed as fraternal left-left encounters, such as the controversy over Andrzej Wajda's film *Danton*, redounded to the signal advantage of the counterrevolutionary critique. So did the outspoken efforts of the Communist party to defend the Marxist interpretation and promote a maximalist Revolutionary commemoration. Edgar Faure's appointment to succeed Michel Baroin at the head of the bicentennial Mission appeared to be a conscious effort to mollify the counterrevolutionaries. "The bicentennial was shaping up to be as blue as [Revolutionary General] Hoche's tunic," reflected *Libération* in mid-1987, "[but] it suddenly paled in the fire of polemics." "Isn't the first paradox that the current commemoration of the French Revolution seems to be turning into a celebration of the Counterrevolution?" wondered historian Roger Dupuy at the beginning of 1988.[3]

Proliferating Doubts and Recast Judgments

After a long period of cautious reserve, the far right press sounded a triumphalist note by the end of 1987. "The movement of rejection of the Revolution . . . has become so strong," claimed *Aspects de la France,* "that it is no longer possible to glorify the Revolution globally." Given the bent of public opinion, observed *Le Choc du mois,* the theme of the bicentennial may turn out to be "the Revolution was good for nothing." *National hebdo* noted a "boomerang effect" produced by the commemorators themselves: "many people who confidently admired the French Revolution have suddenly seen revealed its excesses, its madness, and its atrocities."

Under the rubric "everyone questions the Revolution," both left and right invoked the case of the Jewish community, classified traditonally as enthusiasts of the Revolution, to which they were said to be deeply indebted for their emancipation. "Far from being a panacea," emancipation appeared to a growing number of Jewish skeptics, *Le Monde* reported with some surprise, as responsible for cutting Jews off from their community ties, exciting anti-Semitism, and even preparing the ground for the Holocaust. While Rabbi Josy Eisenberg insisted on the very positive relation between Jews and the Revolution, he admitted that some of its concrete consequences favored "de-Judaization." Lay leader and attorney Théo Klein regarded the "cultural homogenization" of Jacobinism as an unmitigated disaster for Jews. Patrice de Plunkett, one of the editors of *Figaro-Magazine,* wrote exuberantly about the work of the journalist-historian Patrick Girard, who showed that "the Revolution ended with the reduction of the Jews to the rank of second-level citizens," a view which fits nicely with Cardinal Lustiger's contention that the Enlightenment engendered modern racism. Nor was the weekly surprised when the Centre Rachi, a Jewish cultural association, rebuffed Robert Badinter's proposal to name their auditorium after the Abbé Henri Grégoire, artisan of a now suspect form of assimilation. Jews called upon in this context are seen as a vanguard and as a litmus group: their alienation from the Revolution is taken as proof of counter-revolutionary gains and prospects.[4]

Reactions to Robert Hossein's elaborate theatrical *La Liberté ou la mort* suggest a more subtle illustration of the redrawing of judgmental boundaries around the Revolution, or of the encroachment of antirevolutionary criteria. Christine Clerc, best known as the rightist columnist slapped by the irreverant comic Coluche, found far more to comfort the critics of the Revolution in this popular presentation, offered to tens of thousands of spectators at the Palais des Congrès, than she expected. It began with a withering parody of the trial of Louis XVI, condemned without being given the opportunity to defend himself; it gathered momentum with the "appalling farce" of the trial of Danton, condemned to death because he pled for clemency; and it ended with "a bloody farce," the trial of Robespierre, condemned without being allowed to open his mouth. From start to finish, "there are only cries of hatred, denunciations, summonses to murder, grasping faces," wrote Clerc, with only slight exaggeration.

Disinclined to feel tenderly about the Revolution, nevertheless Clerc claimed that she felt impelled to shout "Enough!" or "It's not true!" Upon examination, however, she reassured herself that everything was true, historically authentic (guaranteed by the fact that one of the coauthors, the historian-academician Alain Decaux, was a minister in the bicentennial Socialist government?). Though this was "the most cogently antirevolutionary show that one could imagine," remarked *Figaro-Magazine*'s star woman journalist, "it did not cause a scandal, it did not even provoke a big debate." Somehow it all seemed too easy. On the eve of the bicentennial, noted Clerc, the left not only failed to contain the counterrevolutionary offensive but did not even seem to care: "You recall, however, the tumult occasioned a year after the Congress of Valence by Wajda's film [*Danton*]? [Premier Pierre] Mauroy let it be known that he had a portrait of Camille Desmoulins in his office [Socialist party nabob Jean] Poperen—upset by the very mention of Marie Antoinette's name—rushed to the rescue of Robespierre. Today, no one cares about this any more. A bit shamefully." The *Nouvel Observateur* was one of several left or center-left organs of the press to recommend warmly *La Liberté ou la mort*.[5]

Hard-Core Animus

Hard-core counterrevolutionary discourse, only slightly inflected by the modernizers and mainstreamers, focused on the traditional themes of R/revolutionary animus. Its exponents expressed outrage at the idea of celebrating the Revolution, and they fired their anger by forging the myth, belied by almost every reasonable measure, of a "boisterous commemoration" or a "noisy bicentennial" or an "extravagant celebration" foisted on the public by the Socialist government. "To celebrate the bicentennial of the Revolution is as monstrous," wrote a reader to the editor of *National hebdo*, "as it would be if the Germans celebrated the anniversary of the creation of concentration camps and the Russians the creation of the gulag."

Beyond its sordid and horrifying nature, the Revolution did not merit celebration because it was not the decisive anniversary that its apologists made it out to be. Following the Capetian school, rejuvenated by Chaunu, counterrevolutionaries argued that France was not born in 1789. By stressing continuity across thousands of years, they tried to decenter the Revolution and thus both denigrate and domesticate its influence. This was a somewhat paradoxical stance for people who believed deeply—whatever antipathy the bicentennial-as-festival aroused—that all of modern history was dominated by the satanic corrosion unleashed by the Revolution and in incubation at least since the Reformation.[6]

Counterrevolutionary commentators such as Jean Dumont, author of the gospel of rejection, *Pourquoi nous ne célébrons pas 1789*, enumerated detailed explanations for their stand. The first reason he called the rubric of lies: the willful distortion of the history of the Revolution beginning with the taking of the Bastille, a pathetic nonevent bloated after the fact into a symbolic turning point. This made the bicentennial a double lie, a lie about lies. The itch to demystify the Bastille was the eczema of the counterrevolutionary imagination. The modern liberal anti-revolutionaries raged against "manipulators of opinion" as vehemently as the old guard. In an article in *Libéralia*, lawyer Jean-Marc Varaut set the scene in July 1789:

> There was no taking of the Bastille, because the governor of the prison opened its gates; nor any liberation of political prisoners, victims of arbitrary action, because there were none. The people of Paris were absent. Like the revolutionary leaders. German deserters and prowlers searching for ammunition are the authors of this modest combat and the lynching of the soldiers, who were invalids. A victory of the rabble over an empty prison, a violent and bloody impulse, that's the date chosen in 1880 to be our national holiday.

(After this highly charged, caricatural representation, in the next breath Varaut judiciously appealed for an end to tendentiousness and distortion in historiography and, mimicking Furet, proclaimed that "the French Revolution henceforth belongs to scientific scholarship.")

In his motion to the European Parliament seeking to anathematize the commemoration, Lepéniste–Catholic traditionalist (*intégriste*) Bernard Antony/ Romain Marie painted the same picture, barely modified by a slightly more articulated conspiratorial hue, of "the swindle of the legend of the taking of the Bastille, an empty and defenseless prison, invested by a drunken mob of thieves and bandits of all sorts paid by the duc d'Orléans, first grand master of the Grand Orient [Masonic lodge]." The true significance of the Bastille for him was that it marked— as early as 1789!—"the terrorist dawn." Gabriel Domenach of *Minute* gave the story a slightly more vulgar twist: "the drunken havoc of hatred, wine, and pillage" was radio-controlled by a demolition contractor named Palloy who did not even have the cachet of a Masonic membership to cover his greed. The Bastille mythology and the mandatory worship of the other "revolutionary conquests," *Le Choc du mois* emphasized, were imposed "by the guillotine first, then by a flood of falsified textbooks," two systems of terror combining antique and modern methods of brainwashing and purging.[7]

"The biggest lie" in Dumont's rubric of mendacity was "the dissimulation of the real project, which is anti-Christianism." No idea was more indubitable and more precious to old-school counterrevolutionaries. As it unfolded, they believed that the Revolution was not fundamentally antimonarchical and/or antiaristocratic. It was "by essence anti-Christian," claimed *Aspects de le France;* it was "anti-Catholic above all," *Rivarol* asserted. Its "only true essence," according to Dumont, was "totalitarian anti-Christianity." These traditionalists scoffed at the Christian-democratic fairy tale of an early honeymoon between Revolution and church interrupted by a fatal accident or unplanned deviation. Patiently prepared by diabolical forces for decades if not centuries, the Revolution was not only an attack on God but on the "identity of France," which was Christian before it was anything else.[8]

National Identity

Could one imagine a more propitious time to discuss national identity than during a period of officially sponsored commemorative reflections on the modern origins and character of the French nation? Conservative Paul Guilbert legitimately reproached President Mitterrand for failing to treat national identity in his Jeu de Paume speech inaugurating the bicentennial high season. Yet neither mainstream right nor mainstream left made a concerted bicentennial bid to reclaim the theme that the far right had monopolized in recent years. In the right-wing *Quotidien de Paris*, Frédéric Lazorthes deplored the missed opportunity to focus commemorative energy in an introspective gaze. This failure to probe bespoke the emptiness of the commemoration, its reduction to folklore, sound bites, and show-biz commodification. "The idealization of a consensual France marks in fact the crisis of the national community," Lazorthes concluded, "while the intoxicating reminder of the grand principles could not conceal the current fragility of our political identity." The conservative philosopher Jean-Marie Benoist hinted that collective identity was a Jacobin-Socialist issue. For in contrast to the Jacobin-Socialist tendency to reason in abstract categories englobing and classifying groups, those who appreciated the liberal legacy of the Revolution privileged the Judeo-Christian emphasis on the irreducible "singularity" of individuals.[9]

Patrolling the border between the civilized right and the extremists, Louis Pauwels of *Figaro-Magazine* implicitly censured the Socialists for *lèse-jacobinisme* rather than for Jacobin excesses. Abandoning the Jacobin homogenizing tendencies, the French left of the 1980s "promoted the ideal of a multicultural society and glorified 'the right to be different.'" Prodded by "the chador affair,'", the incident involving the wearing of the Islamic veil in public-school classrooms which shook the nation toward the end of the bicentennial year, Pauwels felt that this indifference to national identity undermined the process of integration, which in turn threatened the coherence of France's sense of self.[10]

The Lepénistes eagerly seized the veil episode in order to wax ironically on the left's abandonment of its basic tenets and to warn that this affair was yet another identity-crushing symptom of "the Islamization of France." But the Front national (FN) did not wait till the end of the year to press the identity issue. The erosion of French identity was coterminous in their reckoning with the decline of France in every other domain, a process detonated during the Enlightenment and accelerated drastically in 1789.[11] While *Présent* stressed that the Revolution struck at the very core of French identity by attacking Christianity, *National hebdo* accused the stewards of the Revolutionary tradition of abdicating their responsibility by allowing "foreign communities" to implant themselves on native soil, thus provoking "the breaking of national unity—which the revolutionaries had nevertheless affirmed as an absolute necessity." In the same vein, sympathizers of the 15 August/Anti-89 movement regarded the enunciation of rights doctrine as tantamount to "the annihilation of our identity," for rights meant the introduction of ideas corrosive of the

Truth. The bicentennial energized SOS-Identité, an organization close to the rightist Club de l'Horloge and the FN. "Does one have the right to exclude? The myth of exclusion, new expression of egalitarianism" was the title of one of its projected colloquia.[12]

Even as Le Pen castigated the politicians for wrenching their national identity from the French people, so Jean Dumont spelled out in a projective pseudohistory the connections between the Revolution's abjuration of French selfhood and today's allegedly ongoing national/cultural decomposition. He complained that the Revolution admitted foreigners "in unlimited numbers" into the clubs, the assemblies, the administration, the army, and the press. "As in the case of the aficionados of immigration today, all of that is the product neither of political accident nor of the simple opening of the heart." Like Furet, Dumont turned to Cochin's sociological insight to fathom this process: "Augustin Cochin emphasized it: docility toward the Jacobin political machine being more pronounced in the absence of any local or traditional attachments, the result was, during the Revolution, *this predilection for foreigners*, this haste to naturalize . . . . In [revolutionary] France, many foreigners were used; [Jean-Baptiste] Carrier [the organizer of the massacres at Nantes] had Germans do the drowning [of French priests]."

The immigration that undermined France's social and moral cohesion at the end of the eighteenth century produced in the late twentieth century an "internal Third-Worldization" which diluted national identity and weakened national strength. The two phenomena were linked because today's immigration was determined by a fatal ideological tropism: "it was celebrated and promoted according to the egalitarian, cosmopolitan, and allegedly fraternitarian phraseology spawned, in equal measure, by the Revolution." Dumont discerned a concomitant demographic connection between the Revolution and its twentieth-century behavioral legacy. As the chief source of "the rejection of life among the nations of the white race," the Revolution threatened the identity not only of France but of all Western civilization. It was midwife to the shift from a period of galloping demography to an age of permanently low fertility.[13]

At the end of the bicentennial year, the mainstream right still hesitated in its response to the identity issue. François Léotard acknowledged the presence of the "identity questioning," but he preferred to cast it—as did many communists albeit from a very different vantage point—in terms of the unfolding of the new Europe, "which is and remains our essential debate," rather than as a manifestation of domestic, inward-looking politics. In December the centrists asked the family of opposition parties not to use the (putatively) Lepéniste phrase "national identity" to baptize the second convocation of its Estates General. (The UDF advanced as a less worrisome program Fernand Braudel's title *L'Identité de la France*.)[14] For Guy Sorman, a leading, albeit idiosyncratic, conservative ideologue, the bicentennial had done nothing to clarify the problem of "the identity of France," which, he asserted provocatively, in any event ought not to be viewed as a real problem: "Those who have tried to define it have uttered only foolishness." But how many on the right were ready to endorse his debunking of the Frenchness myth? "The evidence suggests that it has been quite some time since it was indispensable to be Catholic and Gaulish in order to be French."[15]

Early in the new year, the unlikely team of opposition "renovators" consisting of the former RPR ministers Charles Pasqua and Philippe Séguin explained how they intended to "regenerate" their party and allied formations by emphasizing the identity issue, with which the popular echelons resonated. On the defensive, Alain Juppé, the general secretary of the RPR, recalled how recently Séguin, much more sensitive than Pasqua to the feelings of the centrists, had railed against "the formula of national identity, too Lepéniste-sounding for him." By the end of the year, Valéry Giscard d'Estaing frankly announced in *Figaro-Magazine* that "we have to get back to French identity." No less than the Balts or the Armenians or the reconnecting Germans could legitimately appeal to their national selfhood, "the French have a right to French identity."[16]

Identity claimed a marginal role in the bicentennial discourse of the left. Few were inclined to open what they viewed as a Pandora's box. They discussed the identity question obliquely, to the extent that they regarded the Revolutionary legacy as the nursery of national character and the foundation of contemporary French public and private life. But they did not reflect critically on the legitimacy of identity as an issue in terms of their political epistemology. They did not pose the problem of Frenchness in a political context that favored an emphasis on the universality of Revolutionary values. They did not probe the connections between memory and integration, between history and acculturation. Nor did they explore the Revolutionary legacy of tensions between the individual person and the national community (as nation? as nation-state? as society?) or between the diverse communities that inhabited the nation and the nation-as-a-single-community. By and large, there was more said about the state from above than about the society from below. Here, too, it was easier to deal with the character of political institutions than with that of social actors.

Unable or unwilling to construe identity in positive terms, the left avoided dealing with it because they did not want to taint the bicentennial celebration with its negativity. By a sort of self-fulfilling prophecy, it turned out that identity denoted that nether part of French consciousness, that embarrassing and volatile component which eddied against Revolutionary tradition. To talk about identity thus meant to talk about xenophobia, and that was not a pleasant subject. In the fraternal spirit of '89, no one was yet ready to call substantial numbers of ordinary Frenchmen *salauds* in anticipation of the risky and plucky manner of Bernard Tapie, who suggested in early 1992 in his campaign for the presidency of the Provence-Alpes-Côte d'Azur regional council that if Le Pen was indeed a *salaud*, so were his electors. While judicious outsiders such as the German historian Rudolf von Thadden insisted that fidelity to the Revolutionary tradition demanded that the question of the integration of immigrants figure high on the bicentennial agenda, only a minority of the French public, according to a poll taken in November 1989, felt that there was a connection between the ideals of the Revolution and the need "to offer a warm welcome to immigrants in France." Nor did this posture seem particularly embarrassing once "François Mitterrand bestowed letters of nobility to 'the threshhold of tolerance,'" as *Libération* put it, in reference to the president's late bicentennial acknowledgment that France could no longer absorb newcomers.[17]

The failure to address the identity issue squarely, and in particular to use the bicentennial as an instrument for collective self-analysis, probably fortified the seeds of pathology. Bertrand Renouvin, the Mitterrandian royalist, thoughtfully hinted that the lack of a grand project, which the bicentennial might very well have engendered, enhanced the fragility of French society (even as some celebrated its increased stability). "The unavowable reason for xenophobia is not the passion for one's country but a lack of faith in what it is," he argued. "When a culture is alive, it does not fear new contributions."[18]

Well-meaning commentators such as journalist Gérard Belloin paid lip service to the need to put identity at the center of commemorative preoccupations but did nothing to flesh out the theme. "One cannot have nothing to say about the Revolution," he said, "which leads me to say that the Revolution is truly constitutive of French identity." But where did this pious cliché take him? To the usual hortatory cul-de-sac, the bombast of nebulous and reassuring generalities: "The Revolution is not over, it is alive in the imaginary, it is integrated into French identity, and it is productive of ways of thinking and acting."[19]

Régis Debray opened a rich and stimulating debate on the relationship between democracy and republic. Indirectly, it was all about identity, but concretely, Debray did not use the occasion to seize the identity issue, in part because his categories transcended the particular experience of France, in part because they were too complex to be reduced to a transparent notion of identity. In other places, he alluded to the identity issue only in passing, emphatically yet perfunctorily. Thus the philosopher spoke vaguely of "commemorative vigilance" as "an obligation of identity." But in this context he seemed to be concerned with the collective identity of France vis-à-vis other nations, not the identity of French women and men vis-à-vis their larger community. While Debray groped for a just dose of nationalism that would not degenerate into *cocorico* excesses, the historian Suzanne Citron chastised the left for its bicentennial narcissism. "I have not seen a critical reading of French nationalism," she complained. This commemorative self-celebration contrasted rudely with, and implicitly contributed to, the outbreak of the end-of-the-year traumas: the chador debacle and the Lepéniste victory in the bielection at Dreux.[20]

Though the official commemorator Jean-Noël Jeanneney was deeply concerned about the question of exclusion, he did not press the linkages between the Revolutionary legacy, national identity, and the changing sociodemographic landscape of bicentennial France. "Jolted by successive migratory waves, the French are trying to locate their family roots," he noted, but he associated this experience with a genealogical fascination on an individual plane rather than with a collective preoccupation with identity. Max Gallo came closest to responding directly to Jean Dumont's portrayal of the Revolution as the source of a lethal mongrelization of French society, that is to say, to the annihilation of French identity. For the Socialist militant, the Revolution was "the point of departure of a French specificity and a national identity" precisely because it combatted the principles that the far right adored. He concurred with Dumont that the Revolution opened the floodgates— not to toxic substances but to a salubrious and generous notion of justice, to the hordes of excluded, to those who voluntarily embraced its values.

Welcoming this process, Gallo contended that the Revolution thus framed a dynamic concept of identity, an identity to be enriched constantly, an identity predicated on the synergy of the ideas of citizenship and universality. Alluding to the hotly debated code of nationality, the novelist-historian remarked that "in 1791 it was said that foreigners born in France were French citizens," a policy whose spirit he believed should infuse and shape French comportment today. Appropriating the voice of the Revolution, Daniel Bensaïd made the same point: "If you really, sincerely had the intention of celebrating me, this would perhaps be my first test and my first challenge: offer citizenship in my name to every immigrant who desires it, to every refugee who asks for it!" Having castigated François Furet for his Olympian estrangement from lived experience, the philosopher mimicked the historian, refusing to face up to the reality of the popular resistance to this sort of moralizing treatment of the identity question.[21]

For others on the left, the evocation of abstract Revolutionary values did not resolve the very concrete problems posed by immigration, in part because those values did not convey a univocal message. Long before the veil affair, Maurice Agulhon, armed with impeccable republican credentials, had warned against the disintegrating effect of a rampant multiculturalism. He contested the moral sanction that exponents of the "right to be different" extrapolated from the Revolution. For him the rights-of-man doctrine, "universalist in its essence," implied a single national community committed to the same defining principles. Very much in the same sense, Jean-Pierre Chevènement worried about the menace to identity which he did not define but which he conceived in holistic, national terms. He was unwilling to allow the Revolution to be tapped to provide comfort to subversive ends, centrifugal and atomizing. During a colloquium held in his Belfort fief in 1988, the minister of defense called attention to the perils of the "right to be different evoked by some to exalt particularisms, then shortly after by others to justify exclusions." For him the very notion of right connoted a universality that the idea of difference contravened. In the wake of the veil affair, Chevènement took an aggressively Jacobin position. "It was a matter of assuring that equality would prevail over 'the right to be different,' which everyone now knows, with the best intentions in the world, can lead to 'the apology of differences,' apartheid becoming paradoxically the supreme form of 'tolerance,'" declared the minister, in the hyperbolic idiom he favored when he wanted to underscore a point. Identity was something that the state fashioned, in the service of the nation's integrity and its survival.

The public schools were the crucibles that forged future citizens and bestowed on them an identity of Frenchness which would integrate them into the shared republic. In this perspective, he admonished weak-kneed *laïques* not to succumb to the parochial temptation to respect traditions of all sorts as if they were equally sacred in all times and places. "But tradition is not reason," the minister preached, "if not, out of respect for tradition, it would have been necessary to avoid undertaking the Revolution and to conserve serfdom."

Behind the so-called American model of cultural relativism Chevènement discerned the apocalyptic shadow of Beirut. The same specter haunted Maxime Rodinson, eminent Arabist and leftist. "Lebanonization" defined French national identity in the breach. "The stampede toward communitarianization" menaced the most cherished French values even as the bicentennial message tirelessly intoned them.[22]

The chador affair revealed significant fissures in the Socialist party (PS), which strained to remain faithful to its historical self-representation(s) and simultaneously to adjust to new realities. Writing in Chevènement's monthly, *Socialisme et République*, Pierre Guidoni, a national secretary of the party, noted that he and his friends had considered minister of education Lionel Jospin's "differentialism" to be perilous long before the incident in the high school. Republican values required a vigorous laicity. Rather than simple tolerance, laicity meant "the awakening through enlightenment and the apprenticeship of critical reason" that had constituted the mission of republican schools since the Revolution. Criticizing Jospin's "lukewarm" position, *Synthèse flash*, the vehicle of Jean Poperen's faction, deplored the party's failure to explore the connections between integration and "national identity" and ardently denied that "the disintegration of national identity" should be construed as a "progressivist phenomenon."

Rejecting the ultra-Jacobin line, more or less in Jospin's spirit, other Socialists tried to navigate between the hazards of *une-volonté-une*, or one, indivisible national will, and cultural/national fragmentation. Many of them spoke the syncretic, somewhat casuistical language later adopted by Gérard Le Gall, a national party leader, who invited his comrades to "put the emphasis, *within* the respect for particularisms, *on* that which brings us together." The weekly newspaper aimed at party officials throughout the nation insisted that differences existed and could not be denied. They had to be conceived, however, not as "a factor of segregation but as a source of enrichment." Geneviève Domenach-Chich, national secretary for "questions of society," admonished her comrades that, while "universalism" rightly claimed primacy, "the right to be different is a rampart against totalitarianism." Uneasy with the identity issue, like many fellow party members, she preferred tactical fire fighting to substantive ulceration: "we must dedramatize, relativize, talk, talk, talk."[23]

Nor was there a Gargantuan appetite to address the identity issue squarely among those who operated outside the PS but within the Elyséen orbit. Although troubled by Mitterrand's brutal proclamation of a threshold of tolerance, Harlem

Désir, the president's long-time protégé and leader of SOS-Racisme, vigorously denied that his organization was guilty of "differentialism." The SOS line "has always been a discourse of intermixing and integration around universal values."[24]

Jean-Noël Jeanneney was loath to see the commemoration end on such a sour note. Instead of seizing the issue to practice the sort of vigorous pedagogy he had espoused throughout the year, he retreated with a cautious and vague appraisal that was meant to be upbeat: "The Revolution inspires and fruitfully nurtures the debate on the veil, helping [us] reflect on the choice to make between the respect of differences and [the recognition of] values of universal significance." The following year the Carpentras affair, involving an obscene desecration of Jewish graves, immediately attributed by many to Lepéniste inspiration, further underlined, in *Le Monde*'s phrase, the left's "deficit" of national identity. And on the occasion of another commemoration, the 561st anniversary of the liberation of Orléans by Joan of Arc, Le Pen's favorite national icon, prime minister Michel Rocard, summoned the Socialists to resist the far right's efforts to confiscate the identity issue.[25]

The Declinists: Doomsday Discourse on the Downfall of France

In the eyes of counterrevolutionaries, the decline of France followed ineluctably from the assault on national identity effectuated by the French Revolution. Seventeen eighty-nine led straight to the crises of the twentieth century. For Jean Dumont, as we have seen, the lack of national renewal rendered France weak and vulnerable and obliged it to turn to immigrants who were difficult to assimilate. Citing a report of the European Community, he held "egotistical attitudes" responsible for this demographic stagnation: "Now, these attitudes, opposed to the family values of the old society, originated in the Revolution, this excessive promotion of individual rights . . . against the lived and sublimated duties of natural communities."

The ideology of liberalism was reinforced by such engines of destruction of national coherence and identity as laicity (desacralizing marriage and promoting divorce) and the Napoleonic Code (prescribing equality of inheritance and thus encouraging one-child families). "Sin—whether divorce, fornication, even abortion, or whether sacerdotal abdication or even apostasy—sin has become one of the Rights of Man (and of woman)," argued Dumont. An offspring of "the anti-Christian Enlightenment," the Revolution begot a "malignant inversion" that menaced the very capacity of the nation to reproduce itself culturally as well as biologically.[26]

The Revolution destroyed the economic as well as the biological and cultural capacity of France to reproduce itself. New Age laissez-faire antirevolutionaries concurred with traditionalist, antiliberal counterrevolutionaries that the Revolution was nothing short of an economic Armageddon. "No, 1789 did not mark the entry of France into [the realms] of liberty and prosperity," wrote Guy Millière in *Libéralia*, "but rather the beginning of a long, chaotic, and bloody economic, demographic, and political decline, which has since then never in fact been overcome." For these declinists, René Sédillot's *Coût de la Révolution* served as a "breviary." Initially released in a print run of five thousand, this catalogue of "the ravages" wrought by "the revolutionary frenzy" had reached the fifty thousand–copy mark by the end of March 1989. According to this scenario, Old-Regime France enjoyed a flourishing economy, buoyed by tonic demographic expansion, an exuberant international trade, and a growing industrial sector. *Grosso modo*, the French were more or less at the same level as the English, who would not have been able to trample their Gallic neighbors in the race to modernize without the critical contribution of the Revolution. The Revolution fostered deindustrialization, urban regression, commercial stagnation, the resuscitation of archaic landed interests, the enervation of entrepreneurial will, and so on.

Romain Marie, champion of an antiliberal populism, added an important and generally neglected theme that had been ardently espoused by the "social Catholics" of the late nineteenth century. Just as the Revolution mutilated the economy, so did it trample the rights of the working-class-in-the-making, noted Marie, delighted to cite Marx on "all the dearly acquired liberties [that] were mercilessly destroyed" by the Le Chapelier Law of 1791 prohibiting worker associations and by the nineteenth-century laws of social repression it inspired.

The declinists insisted that the handicap was not provisional. The Revolutionary "catastrophe" checkmated France permanently. The argument was also made by a specious retrospective analogy that acquired a prominent place in counterrevolutionary discourse. Just as everyone admits that, as Jean-Claude Casanova put it in *L'Express*, "without the Bolshevik revolution, Russia today would enjoy a larger population, greater prosperity, and more freedom," so France would have fared infinitely better without 1789 (inexorably solidary with 1793). Counterfactual reveries about what France might have been at the dawn of the third millennium had the Revolution not taken place (for example, had Louis XVI not read Fénélon, "he would perhaps have ordered his troops at the very outset to charge the rebels who threatened the gates of Versailles, and the face of the world would have been changed") led the declinists to idealize life during the Old Regime. "Who still believes today in the tyranny of the Old Regime?" asked André de la Fressange, an investment counselor writing in *Le Figaro*. Civilized, productive, and cohesive, the Old Regime had rough edges that could have been repaired and refined through reform conducted from above.

Finally, replicating and reinforcing in the political arena the damage it had done in the economic sphere, the Revolution endlessly poisoned French political life. In its overwrought way, *Le Choc du mois* made the case that Furet argued so eloquently: "Two centuries of useless slaughtering, of permanent instability, of civil discord, of endless arbitrariness and growing injustices, that can all the same cause one to stop and think." Following this cumulative logic, the Revolution was as thoroughly unnecessary as it was odious.[27]

The Right, the Totalitarian Matrix, and François Furet

Buoyed by the deepening disarray, and the searing self-critique, of the Soviets, the counterrevolutionaries insisted heavily on, and reviled, the totalitarian character of the Revolution. A favorite sophism inferred the Revolution's responsibility for modern horrors from the rhetoric of admiration it elicited. Thus, Romain Marie emphasized, "this bloody revolution has been exalted by all the dictators and massacrers of contemporary history"—as if one could impugn Christianity as a result of Franco's zeal for the church. Noting that "Lenin and Stalin referred continually to the Convention," Philippe de Villiers concluded that there was "in embryo" in the Convention "something resembling Stalinism." To underscore the paradigmatic role of the Revolution as the universal source of totalitarianism, Villiers summoned Khomeini, who apparently devoured Rousseau along with the Koran: "Robespierrism is a theocracy that, in its impatience, foreshadows the madness of Khomeini."

If the Revolution "fundamentally programmed totalitarianism," it was because it issued from and in turn spawned a "totalitarian logic." This was the quixotic logic of regeneration, of forging a new man, of building the heavenly city on earth without any supernatural referents, of social reconstruction according to the blueprints of abstract thought, of "omnipotence accorded to politics." The Revolution was "[philosophically] the ancestor of all modern totalitarianisms," argued jurist and Lepéniste Bruno Gollnisch, "because those who deny the natural order and the idea of a transcendent [power] independent of [human] will in the end come to worship their golden calves." Deeply invested in the idealism that shaped so much counterrevolutionary sentiment, he went on to caution that Robespierre, Marx, and Hitler were not merely connected by "an intellectual, wholly theoretical kinship, for the same moral causes produce the same social effects." Present in 1789 (the counterrevolutionaries varied in their appreciation of its early virulence), the totalitarian logic flowered by 1793 into "the matrix of the great terrors of the twentieth century." Some associated this logic with the "democratic idea" itself, while others, following Tocqueville refracted by Furet, differentiated between the salubrious democratic idea (linked to liberty) and the noxious "revolutionary idea" (linked with equality).[28]

To give credence and resonance to the totalitarian line, several commentators cited the prestigious anthropologist and academician Claude Lévi-Strauss, who wondered "if some contemporary catastrophes do not have their origin in the ideas and values of 1793." Others referred to guidance from Louis de Bonald, Joseph de Maistre, George Orwell, Charles Péguy, Charles Maurras, Aleksandr Solzhenitsyn,

Hannah Arendt, and latterly Jean-Marie Cardinal Lustiger. The Catholic writer René Pucheu cited a sesquicentennial text by Roger Labrousse entitled "The French Revolution as Ancestor of the Totalitarian Regimes." Not enough people gave credit to Jacob L. Talmon for his brilliant polemic and profession of faith, *The Origins of Totalitarian Democracy* (1952). But without the decisive contribution of François Furet, the claims of the counterrevolutionaries would have been worth little more than the spittle that Pierre Chaunu proudly deposited on the Lycée Carnot each time he passed the edifice. Furet gave the totalitarian connection an intellectual respectability, a scientific cachet and a political credibility that it otherwise would not have obtained. He won the confidence of the centrist and moderate-rightist press and public in a way that the counterrevolutionaries, even with the recent injection of liberal blood, could never have done. To the extent that his words infested the minds of millions of French men and women—apart from any question of authorial intention, in any case a dubious category on today's critical horizon—Furet was truly "king of the bicentennial." In a powerful formula that raises interesting questions about his conception of practicing the historian's craft, Furet wrote in 1978: "Today, the gulag leads [us] to reinterpret the Terror in light of a sameness in the [two] project[s]." "To go that far," castigated German specialist Alfred Grosser, "is to play into the hands of the furious surges of today's antirevolutionaries." A journalist in *Le Monde* put it slightly more gently: Furet's revision of the Revolutionary catechism provided the right with "a godsend" that they were not timid to exploit, a solid bridge to the mainland.[29]

A whole range of critics on the left chastised Furet for abetting *Le Mal:* either facilitating the counterrevolutionary offensive, legitimizing it, or frankly sympathizing with it. (From his usual place at the extreme, Jean-Edern Hallier simply reversed the terms of exchange: it was Furet who was indebted to the Counterrevolution, for "he owes everything" to the "prewar school of the far right," including Maurras, Daudet, Bainville, the Action française.) In the most common formulation—Madeleine Rebérioux made this case and it became a Communist party bromide— Furet is charged with opening the door to the revanchist columns of the Counterrevolution, furnishing them arms and then failing to decry their outrageous abuse of them. It was at once an invidious accusation and a more or less objective observation.

On the one hand, it was invidious because it assailed Furet not on the merits of his argument but on oblique grounds of imputed association. There was a vague yet distinctly unpleasant odor of a kind of McCarthyism in this effort to punish and discredit transgression. (To be sure, Furet was guilty of his own version of the smear in his hints that those who embraced '93 were crypto-Leninists giving comfort to the enemies of democracy.)

On the other hand, the charge that Furet's work served and encouraged the right is factually incontrovertible. The rightist press from *Figaro-Magazine* to *National hebdo* was rife with enthusiastic and grateful references to Furet. Commodified himself as a bicentennial product, Furet was abused as well as used by consumers with little interest in studying the recommended user's manual. Without Furet, Philippe de Villiers could not have gotten off the starting blocks—certainly not in the modern, technoscientific garb that he favors. In his *Lettre ouverte*, he invoked Furet repeatedly as his authority on the intimate connection between '89 and '93, on the French Revolution as the mother to the Russian, on the radical inadequacy of circumstances to account for the Terror begotten by the Revolution's very ideology, on the way in which "this omnipotence accorded to politics" opened the stage to regenerating fanaticism, on the concept of the people-king, on the fundamentally religious etiology of the Vendéen uprising, on the inexcusable failure to address the massacres and the extermination enterprise of the blues, and so on.[30]

That Furet was used by rightist Villiers or by ultrarightist Jean Dumont did not make him a counterrevolutionary any more than Robespierre's use of Rousseau made the philosophe a Terrorist or Pinochet's use of Milton Friedman made the economist a neofascist. The point is *not* that Furet is responsible for how his words and ideas are used. Rather, it is to understand the inspiration, the vectors, and the impact of the onslaught against the Revolution. Is there any doubt, for instance, to whom Claude Imbert, commentator for the moderate newsmagazine *Le Point*, is indebted? "With the passing years, the Robespierrist theory of violence was to become the avowed matrix of modern revolutions. In our time, the Stalinist massacres and the gulag led [us], step by step, to reconsider, with a less idolatrous eye, the political mechanism of the Terror. We won't go so far as to say that Stalin had Robespierre in his rearview mirror, but we discover between them the [shared] sameness of [their] revolutionary radicalism."[31]

François Furet can no more be held accountable for the way his friends enlisted him into service than for the way he was utilized by others. Still, it is interesting to see how the *Esprit-Nouvel Observateur* axis reflected and disseminated Furetian revisionism, and contributed in its own way to the counterrevolutionary revival. For Jean-Marie Domenach, philosopher and journalist, Furet is the historiographical authority for the totalitarian connection. Regarding a text on public education that Robespierre read to the Convention, Domenach commented: "Everything is said [there]: to regenerate the citizen, to remake a people. Stalin adopted this utopia as his own. Hitler, Mao Tse-tung, and Pol Pot as well. To reproach the French Revolution with being totalitarian is an anachronism, but it is true that 'the concept of the people-king was the matrix of totalitarianism' [Furet]."

Jacques Julliard, Furet's colleague at the Ecole des hautes études and the *Nouvel Observateur*, tried to have it both ways. No, he emphatically did not intend "to suggest, even on the sly, that the Revolution carries within it totalitarianism the way a thick cloud carries a storm." He rejected "the retroactivity of concepts" in history, and he denied that Robespierre was the ancestor of Stalin. After having established his card-carrying-leftist bona fides, Julliard the democrat succumbed suddenly to a paroxysm of existential guilt. A true democracy "has no right to unload its teratology [the monstrous degenerations from which the Revolution is indissociable] on its adversaries." Julliard then affirmed the connection that he had just denied, though in muffled terms of soft association rather than hard causality: "But total-itarianism would have been impossible without what I have indicated above: the accession of the people as the principal actor in politics."[32]

Extremely laconic vis-à-vis the counterrevolutionaries themselves, Furet was far more voluble in his reaction to those on the left who censured his alleged collabora-tion. He cast himself as a martyr to the truth in the manner of his alter historical ego Edgar Quinet, vilified by the Jacobin-republican left for "offering arms to his adversaries" by criticizing the Terror and contesting the indivisibility of the Revo-lution. Ever loath to relinquish his moral claim to a place on the left, Furet merged with his portrait of Quinet, "this persecuted [individual]," reviled for his "noncon-formity with the values of the revolutionary legacy," who suffered ostracism be-cause he was not "Jacobin enough to be a member of the family."

The Communists erected the traditional reticence of the left to criticize any part of the Revolution "for fear of offering ammunition to the right" into a canon of required conduct. The revisionist leader treated them with the same sardonic contempt that Augustin Cochin had reserved for the Jacobins. "The Communists tax me with having given arguments to [the forces of] 'reaction,'" Furet, the former Stalinist, remarked caustically, "always the same old song in order to impede freedom of thought." In a similar vein of outrage against the self-righteous thought police, Mona Ozouf rushed to Furet's defense against the charge of arming the right: "How much time, how many horrid examples are necessary in order to establish that a 'usable' remark, that is to say, one merrily exploited by the [forces of] reaction, does not as a result stop being sadly true?"[33]

More rarely, Furet complained—in moderate tones—about the misuse of his work by the right. Now that the right was flexing its muscles in the political arena everywhere, "my work is used to place into question the whole of the revolutionary process." This was "an absurdity," Furet maintained, for the Revolution remained "the great universal event of the history of France, the birth of democracy." Still, this superb sunrise was also a tragedy. It was as futile to contest the dark side as it was to claim that the Revolution was in some way superfluous. Clearly Furet did not want to get into a fight with the right—at least not at the expense of diluting his campaign against the left. He cast a pox on the houses of both the Jacobins and the counterrevolutionaries who "reinforce each other and keep us at a remove from the real historical task." More than a year after the end of the bicentennial, as if to distance himself from the ultraconservatives, Furet insisted that "the right is not kind with me; it gives me no breaks." The proof, framed with a blend of humor and regret: "I am not a member of the Institut."[34]

Furet would have a stronger argument against the suggestion that he objectively abetted the counterrevolutionary current had he been willing to criticize its extrav-agances as readily as he reproved those of the left and far left. Jean-Noël Jeanneney's polite vexation is understandable: "I sometimes regret that François Furet, through his interventions in the public debate, [and] in the mass-circulation press—when he himself crossed the line separating scholarship from politics—more often directed his fire against a dogmatic Marxism that is in utter ruin than against the theses of the right which benefit from a far louder and in my eyes more worrisome echo in the public and in the media."[35]

One of the leading candidates for the bicentennial prize for obfuscation is Pierre Nora, a former in-law of Furet, his colleague at the Ecole des hautes études, director of the bimonthly review *Le Débat*, and pillar of the venerable publishing house of Gallimard. He is quoted in the *New York Times* as referring to "an unanticipated return of the counterrevolutionary repressed." Could one of the best-informed and wiliest cultural professionals of the Left Bank truly have been surprised by the counterrevolutionary resurgence? Having himself helped to orchestrate Furet's ten-year campaign, could Nora have seriously believed that the torrent of resistance to the Revolution was "bizarre" and due to the political comeback of the extreme right?[36]

As for the totalitarian matrix idea in particular, François Furet responded on several registers. First, there is the unequivocal nominalist rejection of the filiation. "For me the Revolution is not totalitarian," Furet insisted, adding, "one cannot render it equivalent to the totalitarianisms of the twentieth century: the French Revolution is deeply anchored in juridical individualism." This is the high road that discountenances anachronism, reproves simplification (Jacob Talmon's reading of Rousseau), and calls for further research ("it would be necessary to undertake a methodical and complete analysis of the Bolshevik literature on Jacobinism . . . in order to apprehend clearly the exact nature of the fascination exercised by 1793 on the Russian revolutionaries"—as if this fascination, and the concomitant utilization of '93, could ultimately be taken as the telling measure of the Revolution's influence, and its nature).

Then there is the blurring of '89 and '93, the displacement of '93 into '89, the repeated suggestion that '93 is already present and that '93 anticipates and even shapes the ideological reflection and the constructivist ambitions of 1917 and beyond. If the despotic drift is not theoretically inevitable, the way Furet describes it is pragmatically inevitable. But the comparison with 1917 is merely the story of chickens coming home to roost: "It is an absolutely comical spectacle," wrote the historian, "to see the French Communists today, and their orchestra of accompaniment, complain about the shortcut practiced by the right between the Terror of Year II and the gulag: for it is they who invented and brandished this comparison like a diploma, before their adversaries turned it against them like a curse." (Note how Furet, in order to stigmatize and localize the reaction, subordinates the *orchestre d'accompagnement*—primarily a large chunk of the fellow-traveling Socialist party—to the moribund yet somehow still domineering Communists.) All the right had to do, according to Furet, was to "install themselves in the tracks that the [the Communists] had left."

But this, too, is a significant short cut. The counterrevolutionaries have tried to occupy that place vainly for more than a half century. It required an ex-Communist, anchored on the enlightened left, with impeccable academic credentials, and a redoubtable polemical agility, to realize the graft and prevent its rejection. François Furet used the comparison with 1917 repeatedly, yet since he was above the fray, he suggested, he was using it for the first time "seriously" and without partisan purpose. The comparison obsessed him as much as he claimed that it "obsessed" the Bolsheviks at every stage of their itinerary. Representing himself as the detached analyst who refuses to lend his talents to the crystallization of passions, Furet remarked that, in any event, the character of the audience has changed. In the new politico-ideological arena—he would say political culture—the French embrace the democratic idea more or less unanimously and as fervently as they rebuff the revolutionary idea. Thus the discourse that appears at first glance to be counter-revolutionary bespeaks in fact the new consensual view. As Furet told the *New York Times*, "It is not that French society has become counterrevolutionary. This is just the reaction of a pacified democratic society that doesn't think all this violence was necessary, that finds the protracted violence of French politics so strange." Rather than as broker of the counterrevolutionary resurgence, Furet projected himself as mentor to the postrevolutionary mellowing.[37]

While he was not ready openly to espouse the claim that twentieth-century totalitarianism originated in the Jacobin tradition, Furet affirmed unequivocally his belief that the R/revolutionary heritage "is not wholly compatible with the traditional values of liberalism." His point of departure, in emulation of Tocqueville and Quinet, remains both historically and philosophically of paramount importance: "Why is the democratic revolution bearer at once of a despotic potential and of a libertarian or liberal potential?" Since he himself framed the problem of R/revolution in long-run terms, Furet will have to face the question of its twentieth-century impact squarely and thoroughly, not by innuendo, glissando, or proxy.[38]

Revulsion for Revolution

It was not a great leap from the contention that the Revolution was totalitarian to the proposition that all revolutions were perforce totalitarian. Furet was as successful as he was in part because he understood that generically, revolution was *terminée* in the minds of most of his compatriots—finished as a fruitful and desirable way in which to alter the world. The counterrevolutionary current profited immensely from the deepening revulsion for revolution felt by millions of French citizens who did not adhere to the white cause. On a visceral plane, totalitarianism was identified with barbarity. It did not mean an abstract organigram of centralized control. It meant torture, inhumanity, murder. "No ideal justifies the murder of a person," affirmed the wife of Polish filmmaker Andrzej Wajda in an appreciation that seems as breathtakingly simplistic as it does morally irreproachable. "A murder is a murder," echoed the Polish-Swiss historian Bronislaw Baczko, for whom violence seemed to be the most profound expression of both totalitarianism and revolution. Blood sacrifice and purification had no appeal in the late twentieth century; there was little willingness to distinguish good from bad violence. Len Karpinski, a Soviet journalist with ties to the Kremlin, denounced the illusion of the redemptive virtue of violence as the only possible vehicle for social change. History showed that the inevitable sequence was revolution, despotism, beheading.[39]

Predicated on the illusion of radical, voluntaristic change, revolutions, according to this line of reasoning, were necessarily bloody, tyrannical, hypocritical, counterproductive. Focusing on the state's role as executor/executioner, historian Mona Ozouf gave the rejection of R/revolution a decidedly liberal cast, with immediate contemporary resonance. "The least widely shared belief in the France of today," she explained, parsing her collaborator Furet's pronouncement of the end of revolution, "is the belief that the state can organize collective happiness and that the latter consists of the unity of minds." The newsweekly Le Point found signs everywhere that "the revolutionary dream of a change of society is abandoned." Flora Lewis, foreign affairs specialist for the New York Times, put the matter in international context: "The word [revolution] may still be revered, but belief that it can deliver the promised land on earth has ebbed, not only in the Soviet Union, Eastern Europe and China, but in third world countries like Algeria, Mozambique, Burma and others with failed experiments."

Well before Timothy Garton Ash could report on the rather oxymoronic notion of the "almost complete lack of violence" in the revolutions of Eastern Europe ("the Marseillaise of 1989 said not 'aux armes, citoyens' but 'aux bougies, citoyens'"), the French public seemed to have opted for Edgar Faure's third-millennial vision of a technology-driven peaceful mutation, "a revolution of the astral type, a nonrevulsive revolution." Articles written by two authors usually at antipodes, journalist Georges Suffert and sociologist Alain Touraine, boasted the same revealing title: "The Revolution Is No Longer What It Used To Be." The revolutionary myth of liberating violence, noted Le Monde, "of the armed struggle against the enemies of the interior and the exterior, and of all the people against the tyrants and the oppressors is infinitely more alive in the sierras of Latin America or the African bush than in the low-rent housing projects of the Seine-Saint-Denis [a historically working-class department]." This change bespoke a "profound ideological evolution," in the view of Alfred Grosser: "Not long ago, the Terror, symbolized by the guillotine, was explained, excused and even glorified. What would a Revolution be that was not bloody? Moderates are necessarily latent counter-revolutionaries."

In 1989 blood was the mark of horror and failure rather than of grandeur. The Socialist premier himself, Michel Rocard, did not hesitate, publicly, to draw the lesson on the eve of the bicentennial "that revolution is dangerous and that it is better to do without it." The left oscillated between indignation and resignation. "In this year of the bicentennial, aren't we, simply and hypocritically, in the midst of celebrating the death of revolutions?" asked the leftist lawyer and writer Denis Langlois. The avowal of the failure of revolution will lead to "the return to that which requires no effort: economic liberalism, which means giving free reign to the most egotistical instincts." From geographer-sociologist Jacques Lévy's vantage point, "the concept of revolution seems clearly to have entered the phase of irreversible coma." The public approves changes *in* but not *of* society. Once they were well ensconced in power, the Socialists themselves proved that the idea of breaking with capitalism was no longer of interest. "The word 'revolution' remains associated with sudden violence and the pretension of the political to transform the whole society" and was thus abhorrent to the vast majority. Gracefully but not without lament, Lévy concluded: "Completing its own orbit, the term seems to have returned to its initial cosmic sense, which is hardly compatible with any conception of human development."

Régis Debray, quondam hands-on revolutionary, told a colloquium at the Sorbonne at the end of 1987 that "the Revolution is unwell in our heads; it is ideologically on the defensive." Later he elaborated in an article replete with disenchantment: "The characters of the Revolution, the acts and the words of this decade have quite obviously a deplorable look in our postmodern eyes. Not cool, not clean, not well-turned, these members of the Convention. Not neutral, not nice, not sympathetic. Corny, old-fashioned, kitsch. In the profile of a smooth and unbroken modernity, progress as we envision it excludes the passage via the revolutionary tearing apart." Increasingly pessimistic but remarkably lucid, Debray wrote in his book *Que vive la République* that "unbeknownst to ourselves, we have become counterrevolutionaries."[40]

Velvet Dreams and Satanic Nightmares
The Range of Bicentennial Rejectionism

Put Down Your Arms, Citizens!

Significantly, the *Marseillaise* itself came under bicentennial assault, not from the wry Serge Gainsbourg batallions, but from a diverse coalition of citizens who did not want to represent their nation in cutthroat terms. Michelet's gloss of it as the "hymn of fraternity" inspired at bottom by "a spirit of peace" no longer seemed wholly convincing. "On the occasion of the bicentennial of the Revolution," importuned the Abbé Pierre, a celebrated humanist and friend of the downtrodden, "let us change the words of hatred of the *Marseillaise* into a message of love." Among the signatories who supported his appeal were Danielle Mitterrand, publicity tycoon Jacques Séguéla (a *Marseillaise tranquille* after *la force tranquille*, Séguéla's winning slogan for the presidential campaign?), street-tough entrepreneur-politician Bernard Tapie, and radical-chic rights activist Harlem Désir. A committee planning bicentennial activities in the Aude envisioned "a competition for the rewriting of the words of the *Marseillaise*."

Another priest, Jean Toulat, an apostle of nonviolence, pleaded in *Le Monde* for a purge of the song's "words of hatred and vengeance," words inappropriate as a symbol of French moral authority and inimical to the new European union, whose members were not "bloody despots" or "merciless tigers." The text of the R/revolutionary anthem, concluded Toulat, was a "Bastille," and it was not "untakable." Defending the nationalist-Jacobin point of view, minister of defense Jean-Pierre Chevènement warmly defended the *Marseillaise*, whose "simultaneously patriotic and revolutionary energy" pleased him.

The debate over the hymn outlasted the bicentennial. After examining 175 national anthems from around the world, Armand Thuais, a retired Paris fireman, determined that "France is the only country in the world that uses violent, bellicose words, animated by a spirit of vengeance." He composed a substitute *Marseillaise de la fraternité*, redolent of Lamartine's *Marseillaise de la paix:*

> Ensemble Citoyens
> Marchons main dans la main
> Chantons, chantons
> Que nos chansons
> Fassent taire tous les canons

The very week that "Gainsbarre," singer-poet Serge Gainsbourg, the reggae-chanting blasphemer of the *Marseillaise,* died, in response to agitated inquiries from a centrist senator, the junior minister for veteran's affairs, André Méric, assured the nation that the hymn would remain inviolate. He honored it as the salutary emblem of a time when "France had to defend its independence and its liberty." The Socialist minister had the good taste not to remind anyone of the hymn's revolutionary vocation. The whole discussion horrified leftist pundit Max Gallo, who construed it as another component in the ongoing "'revision' of national history" and a denial of the identity that was peculiarly French.[1]

The Jacobino-Republicans Sound the Tocsin

"Reform having definitively won out over revolution, "wrote journalist Serge July, one of the left's head druids, "the left looks at the bicentennial the way one used to leaf through the Malet-Isaac high school history textbooks: with distance." While it is true that much of the left—the opportunists?—stayed out of the fray, a number of prominent voices rang out and tried to resist the counterrevolutionary rush. As early as July 1983 Max Gallo anxiously wondered whether "the left would abandon the battle of ideas." It was no ivory-tower matter in France "because in this country steeped in history, whose politics is composed of memory, recurrence, and symbols, everything that is played out on the terrain of ideas . . . directly influences social life." While the left licked its economic wounds and pondered its fragmentation, the right, unchallenged, flexed its antirevolutionary muscles, parading Charles Maurras, rediscovering Augustin Cochin, preparing to sabotage the bicentennial of the Revolution, "the founding murder of the French nation." The louder the right roared, the more deafening was the silence of the intellectuals of the left, simultaneously exhorted and excoriated by Gallo in his *Lettre ouverte à Maximilien Robespierre sur les nouveaux muscadins*, published in 1986.[2]

Max Gallo's open letter was a passionate defense of the Revolution of equality and of dreams, a rebuke of the spineless left, a denunciation of the moral and scientific pretensions of the Furetians, and a spirited counterattack on the Counterrevolution and its facilitators. Although they were not foppishly dressed, powdered, and perfumed in the manner of their lisping, bludgeon-wielding, counterrevolutionary namesakes and forebears, the new *muscadins* bashed Jacobins with the same vengeful zeal and rapture. They were ideological dandies who promoted "the most extreme theses of the counterrevolution." Despite their "wild excessiveness" and their "fanatical blindness," they enjoyed "an open field" because of the collaboration of Furetian scientific authority and the "embarrassed, indulgent, bemused, conniving, or prudent silence of almost all the press, specialists, and commentators."

The counterrevolutionaries had always been "the most powerful [force]" in the press, publishing, the theatre, and the Académie française. The new and ominous fact was their "conquering" entry into the university. With the Marxists on the run and the republicans cowed, the *muscadins* "invest[ed] the positions of power in the new Sorbonnes." From the new institutional bastions, they proposed a new catechism to replace the discredited Marxist version. Trained as a historian with a special interest in the Revolution, Gallo accepted important parts of the critique of the "bourgeois-revolution" interpretation. But he was not willing to trade it for a new vulgate based on a modernized and sociologized rendition of the old plot theory ascribing the Revolution to "a few declassed intellectuals . . . impelled by the resentment of failure" who manipulated an inert public opinion.

Gallo detested the *muscadins* because they were posturers who feigned historical evenhandedness in order to insinuate the most partisan revisions, even as they "r[o]de the wave in favor of human rights in order to sneak by their countreband goods." The *muscadins* had to be confronted on their own terrain with their own methods. Gallo took full advantage of the license to be unscrupulous. If the blues, or Revolutionary soldiers, were SS troops, then the *muscadins* were Vichyites, delighted to replace "Liberty, Equality, Fraternity" with "Work, Family, Fatherland." They felt comfortable with the foreign occupation, for such was the most cherished aim of Louis XVI and the noble commanders of the *chouans* at Quiberon who wore the English uniform. For them the Resistance was also a civil war, a provocation that generated a cycle of reprisals, and the prelude to the "crimes" of the Liberation. Second World War/Holocaust revisionism was implicitly *muscadin* revisionism, because the 1940s were the years of the "official triumph of the theses that they defend today." Gallo knew that he would be accused of "mixing together different notions, of sectarianism, of bad faith." Parodying the virile positivism of the counterrevolutionaries, he asked rhetorically, "But why should it be necessary to hush up what actually took place?" Wasn't it significant to take account of the way Vichy viewed the Revolution, of "that hatred that the Nazis had for our Revolution?"

Gallo believed that to put the Revolution on trial was to put the spirit and the values of the republic on trial. Thus, "it is time to take back the floor." It was important to contest the counterrevolutionaries because the stakes were enormous. Gallo scoffed at Furet's oft-repeated contention that the Revolution "no longer carries any real political stakes." This claim in itself was political in nature and partisan in substance. Gallo believed that the Revolution remained both a political litmus and a political lodestone. It identified the issues that were still crucial and controversial, it illuminated the principles that underlay them, and in so doing, it framed the choices that would determine the future of French society.

Though the counterrevolutionary camp was in fact politically heterogeneous, including many *intégristes* who reviled capitalism as well as socialism, and some secular neocorporatists who shared that perspective, Gallo tended to equate the new *muscadins* with Reagan-era liberals. The gravest threat to the Revolutionary heritage came from their social Darwinism, reified in the market model of social organization—an ideology that did not follow necessarily from the satanic exegesis of 1789/93. In other words, the liberals were the only truly dangerous Burkeans of the waning years of the twentieth century. The end of French exceptionalism would mean the end of a commitment to the goal of social as well as legal equality and to the belief in the capacity of the state to realize social justice. "The law of the fittest" would be the only law that mattered, and it would deal a double blow against French identity at home and French destiny in the world.[3]

Régis Debray shared many of Gallo's concerns. Favoring the ease of democracy over the rigors of republicanism, much of the left had forgotten about equality and sold out to liberalism. Debray preferred Chaunu, who had the merit of spitting directly in one's face, to the flaccid Socialists, who "bow at an angle, in fleeing." He marveled at the media, which accorded Furet, the "king of the bicentennial" who had smothered the Revolutionary tradition in "a shroud," an entire page at the very front, while Mitterrand, president of the republic, who explained why the Revolution was not over, got a few lines in a corner of an inside page. "It is he who 'makes opinion,' not you." Debray complained to Mitterrand.

Like Gallo, Debray believed that the political, cultural, and moral stakes of the Revolution were still huge. The Revolution served as political parable and oracle: "Tell me, Republic, what Revolution you commemorate, and I'll tell you what future you are preparing for us." Debray shared Gallo's refusal to renounce the old vulgate in order merely to make room for the (re)new(ed) one, and he added a relativist's contempt for the scientific pretensions of the (latest) replacement gospel.

> They were quite right to expose the naïveté and the incoherence of the "Leninist-populist vulgate"; but in so doing they did not destroy the collective need for a vulgate; their own denunciation served as the foundation for a new vulgate henceforth dominant, to be called, in their old Communist idiom, the "Tocquevillo-Aronian" vulgate. A vulgate of the right replaced a vulgate of the left because one does not replace a legend with a critique but with another legend. The one succeeds the other after upending it, and only the most recent is taken at its word, as objective and scientific, until the following one excommunicates it as ideological and polemical.

Finally, Debray agreed with Gallo that there was peril for the republic in the counterrevolutionary onslaught. Its legitimacy challenged, the republic was not defending itself with all its resources. Debray deplored in particular the demise of the passion for equality. Today's citizens do not resemble those of 1789 as described by the historian Georges Lefebvre: "For the French of 1789, liberty and equality were inseparable, two words to designate the same thing; but if they had had to choose, it is to equality that they would have clung above all."[4]

The imputation of a totalitarian vocation (and posterity) to the Revolution deeply rankled the left. It was the sort of charge/shibboleth that was likely to stick regardless of the refutation applied because it resonated so felicitously with contemporary events. For Max Gallo the Stalin = Robespierre equation was an "antihistorical equation" bespeaking "a totally ideological history, wholly detached from its causes." Régis Debray derided this "scientifically doubtful" practice of reading the present into the past and the past as providentially "radio-controlled" by the future, a procedure that mimicked the flawed logic of the "old communizing catechism" that Furet had so energetically assailed. Jean-Noël Jeanneney exposed the logical folly of allowing self-proclaimed "descendants" to determine the true character and intentions of their self-appropriated ancestors.[5]

No one addressed the totalitarian accusation more passionately than Maurice Agulhon, who resented it as a citizen as well as a historian. The historical claim was unfounded and undemonstrable. In discrediting the Enlightenment and the Revolution in this incendiary fashion, its main purpose was to portray their legacy as dangerous. Yet it was "a culture of the Left that had finally vaccinated French society . . . against the temptation of 'totalitarian democracy'!" The Revolution was the source and the refuge of liberty. The proof is epitomized in what might be called Agulhon's "bicentennial law": from the ninth of Thermidor (he does not try to salvage Robespierre) to the present, it was "the political regimes . . . that placed themselves in the direct line of the French Revolution which built, step by step, the liberties that we now enjoy," whereas "it was the regimes that detested the French Revolution which, on their own, placed into peril the liberties of our country." Fleeing Furet's abstractions, Agulhon begged the generic question of totalitarianism in order to draw up the concrete balance sheet: under the aegis of the Revolution, in the realm of freedom, France has done very well indeed.[6]

Violence

More than any other issue, the question of violence embarrassed the partisans of the Revolution. It was a trap: there was no way to come out clean, to respond without seeming to apologize for the unpardonable or to resort to dubious comparison or historicization. The public hygiene lesson, independently framed by Edgar Faure and Maurice Agulhon, depicting the guillotine as a humanitarian innovation, seemed, from the perspective of 1989, to be a ridiculous and implausible way to think about the problem, a derisory academic consolation. Nor did the reminder that Mitterrand's minions led the campaign for the abolition of the death penalty (against the very counterrevolutionaries who trembled at the mention of the guillotine) dull the memories of bloodthirsty revolutionary gods. (And as an inverted variant of the Robespierre = Stalin thesis, it had an ironic ring.)

The strongest argument of the defenders of the Revolution—a sort of retrospective anthropology of violence—was also the most difficult to make for a broad audience. Agulhon showed how deeply violence infiltrated the daily lives of the French in the eighteenth century—barbarity was "virtually normal"—and admonished against deploying twentieth-century sensibilities to judge Old Regime practices. Agulhon, Daniel Bensaïd, Michel Vovelle, Max Gallo, the Communist historian Antoine Casanova, and Arlette Laguiller of Lutte ouvrière, among others, reproduced the Thermidorean discourse that violence did not originate in the Revolution, that Revolutionary violence was a throwback to the Old Regime despotism and cruelty against which the nation had revolted. But violence was not reducible to one form of inhumanity, however extreme or definitive, nor was it the exclusive bailiwick of the semiprimitive or premodern. In a sort of postfunctionalist argument, Bensaïd recalled that "economic or moral, police or military, violence is an integral part of every conflictual society: it circulates within, sometimes diffuse, sometimes focused."

A historian of mentalities, Vovelle made the case for the responsibility of the "long run" in conditioning the practice of revolutionary violence, heir to a double tradition of street and market violence sparked by fear, want, and/or a collective sense of justice on the one hand and of the violence of the monarchical state on the other. Gallo also invoked the deeply rooted French "tradition of massacres," the early apogee of which was Saint-Barthélemy's. Vovelle and Claude Mazauric, another Communist historian, both called on the tormented alibi of Gracchus Babeuf, the proto-communist insurgent, who tried to explain the brutality of the early Revolution: "Our masters, instead of refining us, made us barbarous because they are that way themselves; they harvest and will harvest what they have sown."

Régis Debray joined Agulhon, Bensaïd, and Casanova to stigmatize the Counterrevolution for its violent provocation to violence. He decried the tendency to forget that the Counterrevolution had a record of violent acts from the very outset, as well as an ideology on which those acts were predicated. ("Those who refuse change, dismiss Necker, summon the king's troops to Paris, and soon foreign armies to France, they are exempted from having ideologies, the lucky ones!") The early Revolution was "humanist and humane," Agulhon pointed out; the violence arose from those who attacked it and relentlessly sought to stifle it. According to Casonova, it was the Counterrevolution which shed the first blood in the spring of 1789. The "selective indignation" of the counterrevolutionaries galled Max Gallo. If violence and crime are to be condemned, then none of the cutthroats should escape censure: "Do not denounce only the sansculottes and the blues but also the *muscadins*, the 'gilded youth,' the hired killers on the payroll of the nobility, the merciless *chouans*."

Ridiculing the right's knee-jerk historical method, Gallo asked, "Why aren't we told if this White Terror also heralds the gulag, unless it points instead to the regime of Franco or of Pinochet?" One hears a great deal about the human cost of revolutions, wrote Bensaïd. "When will we take into account the cost of counter-revolutions and nonrevolutions, the silent, daily price of resignation and capitulation?" The philosopher warned against taking too much moral altitude: "if one contemplates history from the vantage point of God and of eternity, one no longer perceives the relief, the contours, one no longer distinguishes the wrong side from the right side." Turning the Counterrevolution's victimization rhetoric in favor of the Revolutionaries, Bensaïd asked if the students of Tiananmen, whose peaceful demonstrations the world applauded, were to be held responsible for the violent repression that befell them? "Will one incriminate the victims?"[7]

At various moments strained, aggressive, mortified, and lyrical, this offensive-defensive treatment of violence did not please Mona Ozouf. It was not very revealing, in her view, to adduce case after case of the Other's violence in order to preempt, rebut, or mitigate the violence ascribed to one's own. This was a "a sinister game of tennis that tirelessly returned the ball of exaction to the opposite camp" to no useful or worthy end. But Ozouf posed the problem in terms that caricatured the intellectual claims of her adversaries. They did not propose a general theory of historical equilibrium based on a body count or endorse the morality of cumulative and/or delayed reprisals. Following Tocquevillean precepts that Ozouf honored in other contexts, they looked at long-run continuities (and discontinuities), at the long-term evolution of certain social, political, and cultural practices. In imitation of counterrevolutionary scruples, they protested the truncation of memory that resulted in serious distortions and an asymmtery of censure. The point was not to exact an eye for an eye, to play tit for tat, but to restitute some *historical* dimension to a debate that Ozouf cast in largely philosophical terms. She complained that the bidding war dulled one's sensitivity to injustice. But why was it healthier to be sensitive to one injustice rather than another? On what grounds did one determine the relative gravity of the injustice? Why was it so sterile to think about the sociogenesis of the injustices? Even if the ferocity of the Old Regime did not derive from the same "project" as the ferocity of the Revolution, why presume peremptorily that the one sheds no light on the other? For the purposes of historical understanding, are forward linkages (the gulag in which Furet recognized the Terror) inherently more legitimate and fruitful than backward ones (Gallo's religious massacres or Vovelle's jacqueries or Agulhon's everyday sociability)?[8]

In the course of its campaign against the brutality of the Revolution, the counter-revolutionary right did not want to be reminded of its historically ambivalent relation to the practice of violence. It preferred to label the violence with which it had been associated justice or patriotism or laissez-faire allocation of inputs and outputs or even divine retribution. While it frequently projected an image of muscled bravado or heroic vengefulness, during the delicate bicentennial season, with the world's gaze fixed on the hexagon, it cultivated an air of law-abiding serenity, identified with martyred victims, and pledged to turn the other cheek to acts of alleged Jacobin provocation. While the commemorators shamelessly paraded their life-size slaughterous guillotines (at La Ferté-sous-Jouarre, preceded by majorettes and followed by an ambulance; at Toctoucau in the Gironde, accompanied by actors playing Louis Capet and Marie Antoinette, along with the executioner, marching to the blasphemous beat of Serge Gainsbourg's *Marseillaise*), the counterrevolutionaries decorously read the *Journal des guillotinés*, which listed 17,500 victims in alphabetical order, reserving poignant comment for the most distinguished among them ("One out of twenty French people has an ancestor or someone close to an ancestor who was guillotined during the Revolution").[9]

Many of the partisans of the counterrevolutionary cause were thus deeply embarrassed by the vicious assault carried out by a royalist commando of between five and fifteen skinheads on the opera singer Hélène Delavault on the stage of the Bouffes du Nord theatre in early January 1989. She was in the midst of a show devoted to songs of or about the Revolutionary period; Jean-Noël Jeanneney was among the spectators that evening. While confederates guarded the exits and prevented access to the stage, others disoriented the singer with tear gas, knocked her down, covered her face with blue paint, and poured glue in her hair. Their aggression consummated, they left the theatre shouting "Long live the king!"

Five militants of the monarchist movement called Restauration nationale ("in other words, Action française," according to *Le Choc du mois*) were arrested; three were eventually convicted and sentenced to a year in prison, ten months of which was suspended in recognition of a lack of prior criminality. (After avowing their affection for violent confrontation, representatives of Restauration several years later regretted their bicentennial attack: "We made a big mistake three years ago in shampooing the singer Hélène Delavaut [*sic*] on stage. We looked at it as a baiting a little overdone, but it was perceived as a skinhead-type aggression.")

Horrified by these "ignoble acts of a small band of uneducated morons," the rightist *Quotidien de Paris* was even more shocked by the way in which the incident was allegedly used by the government and by the Communists to proclaim that the republic was imperiled: "No, Messieurs, France is not in the hands of a horde of fascists, it is not at the mercy of a few shaved heads . . . . what jeopardizes France today is more *affairisme* than fascism, the going astray of the morality of the state more than a group of young idiots." Associating Mitterrand with the same sort of "racketeer capitalism" that it detested in the Revolution, Restauration nationale was encouraged by the moral support that it elicited on the right, refused to condemn the attack on Delavault, and vaguely hinted that other bicentennial targets were at risk.

The son of the comte de Paris, scion of the Orleanist branch of pretenders to the throne, strongly denounced the attack—a welcome diversion from the bitter legal battle in which his family was engaged against the Legitimists over the use of the title duc d'Anjou, an important stake in the succession struggle. While the left/Mitterrand-oriented monarchists of the Nouvelle action royaliste insisted that "it is possible today to celebrate 1789 peacefully," the Garde blanche légitimiste envisaged "actions which would consist, for the most part, in defacing republican monuments." In fact, there were no other egregious acts of violence committed on the national stage during the bicentennial. Locally, counterrevolutionaries uprooted liberty trees and desecrated public spaces in a handful of towns but avoided serious confrontations.[10] Other counterrevolutionaries sublimated their propensity for violence in the rekindled cult of Charlotte Corday, object of expositions and impassioned discourses. For the right she was "the energetic figure, comparable to Joan of Arc," who richly merited "the glory of the nation" for having "wiped out the greatest of the assassins of the Revolution, Marat, and paid with her life for this gesture of vengeance for thousands of victims." In the estimation of Pierre Chaunu, Corday "is the purest heroine of the Revolution, the one whose statue could be substituted for the statue of Odéon that disfigures the exit of the Odéon subway station—this 'rotten idol,' following the just terms of Albert Mathiez."[11]

Undoing Revolutionary Violence: The Retrial of Citizen Capet as Bicentennial Augur

"Do the French people differ any longer on the issue of who would have decapitated or who would not have decapitated Louis XVI?" former Gaullist leader Michel Debré asked rhetorically in late 1983; "this is no longer of great interest."[12] Setting out to prove the onetime prime minister wrong, journalist-producer Yves Mourousi was one of the first figures in the public sphere to tap into the vein of bicentennial public opinion. His undertaking sparked sharp controversy not only over the significance of (crude) measures of attitude but also over the character and quality of the forthcoming commemoration. Mourousi planned a series of television trials reconstituting Revolutionary debates and inviting the television audience, by phone and minitel votes, to demonstrate how they would have judged the protagonists. Entitled "In the Name of the French People," the series was to begin with the trial of Louis XVI and subsequently deal with Danton and Robespierre.

As the date of the show approached, Mourousi encountered increasingly harsh criticism, largely but not exclusively from the left, and concrete difficulties that suddenly obstructed his way. The initial permission he obtained to use the Sorbonne's majestic grand amphitheatre as his stage was brusquely revoked. "There are people in university and judicial circles who do not wish to see the television viewers acquit Louis XVI," he complained angrily, openly accusing his adversaries of politicizing the affair. A cosponsor of the show, the extremely conservative *Figaro-Magazine*, was hyperexcited by the likely outcome. Its reporters admired Yves Mourousi, whom they considered "very much at home in the role of the nasty kid who is going to break the lovely bicentennial toy."

On the other side of the field, philosopher Alain Finkielkraut denounced the show both for its ridiculous pretensions ("What encounter could more fully satisfy the people than that between Mourousi and the Revolution?" read one of the show's press blurbs) and for its broader implications. Of the latter, two in particular concerned Finkielkraut: first, the ease with which the producer "falsified" history, mocked it, undermined the educational process by which the public should be invited to discover it; second, "the star system, *sans foi ni loi*." Instead of choosing players for their scholarly or moral authority, or artistic genius, Mourousi looked for big names, sacrificing excellence for notoriety. "In a word, we are no longer in democracy, we are in buffoonery," the philosopher concluded. "The French Revoluton is not over, it is canceled."[13]

The ninety-minute program was a hit with the television audience. TF1 obtained 19 percent of the spectators, the best score of the evening. Mourousi and the participants mixed relative authenticity and glaring anachronism. The judges and the defendant were garbed in eighteenth-century fashion; the lawyers—well-known professional defenders with a penchant for controversial cases—wore twentieth-century clothing. The professional actors, including the excellent Fabrice Lucchini as Robespierre, for whom there was a written script, were rather convincing. The personalities invited to improvise oscillated between pompous self-indulgence and mere travesty. Gilbert Collard, representing the victims of the king's alleged perfidies, accused the monarch of "crimes against humanity" and "failure to render assistance to people in danger." Drawn to revisionisms of all sorts, Jacques Vergès, Capet's attorney, evoked Watergate and *Canard enchaîné* "plumbers" (euphemism for domestic political spies) in relation to the opening of the king's secret iron wardrobe and compared the flight to Varennes to de Gaulle's furtive trip to Baden-Baden in 1968. The writer Jean-Edern Hallier, playing chief prosecutor Antoine Fouquier-Tinville, ventured to capture as much air time as possible with silly pastiche exhortations ("French men and women, make another effort, let us cut Capet") and even more insipid and hackneyed one-liners ("Capet, you're losing your head").

Over half the participating viewers judged the king innocent of the charges. If one adds to the 55 percent favoring acquittal the 17.5 percent who preferred a penalty of exile, one finds that almost three-fourths of the audience was hostile to the execution of Capet. *Figaro-Magazine* noted with satisfaction that this outcome represented a substantial shift in opinion in an enlightened direction, for in a survey conducted in July 1987 only 33 percent of respondents regarded the royal decapitation as "a crime." For the rightist periodical the verdict changed the very moral basis of the imminent commemoration: "Whatever the historians and the grand priests of the cult of the Revolution may think, a breach has been opened . . . . more efficiently than many history books, Mourousi has made the goddess Revolution wobble on her pedestal." Jean-Marie Le Pen rushed to claim the voices raised against the once invincible Revolutionary bloc: "The results of the recent televised trial of Louis XVI showed that the French people aspire not, as they once did, to play out the Revolution but to redo it, if not complete it."[14]

Beyond its contempt for the exercise, *Le Monde* cautioned the triumphant *Fig-Maggers* that the poll merely indicated that after two hundred years of the civilizing process, French women and men had a greater distaste for violence than their ancestors. The acquittal "does not signify that the French repudiate the Revolution." In the same vein, the historian Pierre Miquel noted that the English would not have sent Joan of Arc to the stake today either.[15]

The leftist press unanimously joined *Le Monde* in deploring this "Punch-and-Judy parody," this "tomfoolery." The matter would not be worth comment ("so, zap to another channel!") if television did not exercise such power, remarked a commentator in the *Nouvel Observateur:* "It remains true that, six months from now, if one asks the viewers of the [private] television channel TF1 who had been Louis XVI's lawyer in 1793, they will reply, Vergès." From deep in the provinces, the bicentennial bulletin of the departmental Fédération des oeuvres laïques entitled *Le Tribun de Loir-et-Cher* expressed shock that a "silly burlesque" treating so decisive a subject could appear on national television. It was tendentious in spirit, erroneous in the information it purveyed, and disdainful of history in its tone.[16]

For Mission president Jean-Noël Jeanneney, nothing could have augured less auspiciously for the mass-media opening of the bicentennial season. The trial show was a debraining, enterprise "a sort of absurd recapitulation of all the temptations of anachronism." He found some consolation in the fact that "this buffoonery" was rejected by the audience. He meant that TF1 canceled the programs that were supposed to follow, in his view because of audience antipathy but perhaps more significantly because of the negative publicity that the experience provoked.[17]

Mourousi's trial both reflected and elicited a great deal of interest in the monarch. The observance of the annual day of mourning marking Louis's execution took on a special intensity in the bicentennial year. Organizers of the traditionalist/counterrevolutionary mass at Saint-Nicolas du Chardonnet strained hard to unite the diverse and often contentious factions that made claims on the royal heritage, ranging from neo-Nazis to various stripes of royalists. Hatred for the Revolution formed the basis for consensus; from this nucleus ramified a throng of other passions, all in some way linked to the Revolutionary matrix, including the decline of religiosity, the Dreyfus affair, the permeation of noxious cosmopolitanism, the flood of immigrants, and so on.

In the rally at the Left Bank hall called the Mutualité that followed the religious service, speakers praised the king's courage, sober vision and faith, and pledged to "wipe out the deception of '89." While the people of 1989 hastened to acquit the king, the counterrevolutionaries continued to hold them partly responsible for his tragic end, the result obtained under the pressure of "the populace enlightened by red wine." The patriotism brandished by the people and their tribunes was obviously suspect. "The cocarde—this has never been told—but it's the yellow star of David inverted," remarked an ever fecund François Brigneau.[18]

Le Figaro seemed somewhat embarrassed to report that the mood of solemnity was seriously undercut by deep tensions which not only set rival princely families against each other but caused divisions within the competing lineages. Meanwhile, the antiroyalists did their best to sully and lampoon the day of remembrance. A hundred or so "blues," mobilized by the review *Digraphe,* sang a "hymn to the guillotine" on the place de la Concorde where it had once functioned. Manager of diverse bigotries, Jean-Edern Hallier recalled that "the loveliest pages of French history were written with the bloodstained tips of the pikes of the Revolution." Unperturbed by the problem of anachronism, a reader of *L'Evénement du Jeudi* vigorously reproached the left for supporting the execution of the king, given their strident opposition to the death penalty.[19]

The eldest son of the head of the Maison de France, the comte de Clermont, rehearsed the latest version of royalist revisionism. The monarch provided the ferment for the good and necessary (and limited) Revolution: "I think that Louis XVI was the true promoter of the rights of man and that the king always acted in the direction of a greater sphere of freedom." Not only was Capet enlightened and lucid, but he was brave and even tough, according to the actor Gérard Caillaud, who played the king in Antoine Rault's *La Première Tête,* presented at the Comédie de Paris. "In reading numerous documents, in talking with historians, I gradually came to see that the clichés which portrayed Louis XVI as a sort of flaccid lump, incapable of making decisions, were for the most part wholly unjust," insisted Caillaud. The good news announced by the leading man eager to play a role commensurate with his theatrical stature was that "in reality, Louis XVI was a true colossus who sometimes exploded in terrible fits of anger."

"When one reads simultaneously in the press about the bicentennial program and the bloody repression of the students in China, noted a votary of *Figaro-Magazine* keen on analogies suggested by current events, "it is difficult not to think of King Louis XVI." Backed by absolutely sure Swiss regiments, he could have put the Revolution down in its July infancy. "But, unlike Deng, he loved his people and did not wish to cause their blood to flow.[20]

The Far Right Organizes: The Genesis of Anti-89

In many ways the extreme right prepared itself more resolutely for the bicentennial than did the governing left. Its leaders began seriously to examine the question in the early days of governmental cohabitation. The prime movers were clerical militants of the *intégriste* church and sympathizers of the Front national. The first major public planning-cum-mobilization meeting took place at the Mutualité in mid-October 1987 under the aegis of the Abbés Aulagnier and Coache, the journalist-polemist François Brigneau, the writer André Figueras, the neofascist leader Pierre Sidos, and the Lepéniste politician Pierre Descaves. "Facing the Revolution, its crimes, its lies, its rejection of God and his law," the orators pledged in a single passionate voice to present the cleansing and vindicating truth to the nation and to the world.[21]

They envisaged not a campaign but a "crusade"; to serve as its principal vehicle, they created the Association du 15 août 1989. Narrowly construed, its vocation was to organize "a grandiose pilgrimage," "a gigantic rally" on the occasion of Assumption Day in the bicentennial year. Gathered to celebrate a solemn mass at the place de la Concorde—"in the place where the king of France dies a martyr"—hundreds of thousands, perhaps even millions of genuine French patriots would deliver a resounding double message: perfervid expiation to God for the horrors of R/revolutionary hubris and an equally febrile warning to Jacobins and fellow travelers everywhere that henceforth every inch of ideological, moral, and historical terrain would be contested. The broader objective was to profit from the bicentennial opportunity to reach a public much larger and more diverse than their familiar far-right/fundamentalist clientele in order to preach a destigmatized credo of counter-revolution acutely relevant to our times.[22]

To serve both ends, the Association endowed itself with a monthly newspaper. Confided to the talented and spleenful hands of François Brigneau, a seventy-year-old writer, born and raised in Brittany and formed in the Vichy militia, who made his political reputation at the far-right weekly *Minute* after two decades as a columnist for *Télémagazine*, *L'Anti-89* began publication in October 1987 and appeared regularly throughout the bicentennial season. An obscure parish curate in the Oise until the mid-1960s when his traditionalist views provoked the ire of the church hierarchy, Abbé Coache gave the journal its sacral cast. Its publisher, prophetically named François Triomphe, a former paratrooper and militant for Algérie française, assumed the presidency of the Association's patronage committee. Among its other members were the director of a slick far-right monthly magazine; a former leader of the OAS, the terrorist network that fought to preserve French colonialism; and two Front national deputies to the European Parliament, one of whom, Bernard Antony (a.k.a. Romain Marie), leader of a nonschismatic wing of the *intégriste* movement, was notorious for his sophisticated and scurrilous brand of anti-Semitism.[23]

Brigneau and Coache launched their anti-'89 appeal in terms redolent of the counterrevolutionary resistance movement at the time of the centennial. In June 1887, at a banquet-meeting of the Oeuvre des Cercles catholiques d'ouvriers, Albert de Mun had called on sympathizers "to prepare with us, for the year 1889, on the occasion of the centennial whose celebration is being organized, a great Christian demonstration, where we will proclaim together the rights of God in opposition to the rights of man."[24] While de Mun's corporatist politics evinced no interest in the Anti-89 camp, Brigneau and Coache emulated his efforts to reach down to the grass roots in order to elicit the "wishes of Christian France." They called on every reader to become a volunteer reporter ("become civil war correspondents on the front of History") for the purpose of unearthing documentation that would help "unveil the lie, denounce the imposture, demystify the mystification." Brigneau was especially avid to receive information on "mass executions, religious persecutions, the long hunt for and massacre of the nonjuring clergy who refused to swear an oath to the Revolution's civil constitution for the church, the pillage and destruction of Catholic France." Brigneau delected in the lists of sacked churches, vandalized statues of Notre Dame, and burned confessionals that he received.

The only effective way to combat the "adorers of Terror" was to organize a network of local groups throughout the country. It made little difference whether they were directly called to life by the Association du 15 août 1989 (Triomphe would later claim ninety local Association du 15 août committees in France and abroad) or whether they were existing entities subject to collaboration if not co-optation—diverse organizations with rather different missions and methods, but united by a steadfast counterrevolutionary engagement such as the Fédération bretonne légitimiste, Présence et priorité françaises, Action familiale et scolaire, the Association St.-Pierre, the Comité royalist et chrétien, Connaissance de Jeanne d'Arc, and the Cercle légitimiste de Touraine. The Association Vendée 89 in the Berry was a model of its kind. It set out to organize expositions, commemorate the murder of priests, collect narratives of atrocities, and provide case studies to illustrate the general theses formulated by Brigneau. The mother organization provided ideological guidelines—the equivalent of model *cahiers de doléances*—and hints about tactics for promotion and mobilization.

On 21 January 1989, after a somber service to commemorate the guillotining of Louis XVI on that day in 1793, the Association organized "a grand counterrevolutionary day" at the Mutualité. Speeches and display booths helped diffuse its ambitions and its suggestions. To raise money and, incidentally, advertise the cause, the Association entered into the business of bicentennial commercialization on a modest scale: counterrevolutionary agenda calendars vaunting "365 reasons not to celebrate 1789"; myriad pins, brooches, buttons, stickers, pens, lighters; cassettes featuring royal and liturgical music; a bicentennial *millésime* of counterrevolutionary wine embellished by a label bearing the Anti-89 logo, a cross striking out '89. In the eyes of the central leadership, the lobbying function of the local network was as crucial as its information and propaganda activities. The faithful were expected to place relentless pressure on their priests and bishops to take the right stand on the issues crystallized by the bicentennial—issues directly affecting the church as well as the state, the nation, and the society.[25]

The Satanic Line

The Anti-89 circle articulated the classical counterrevolutionary stance in its most unvarnished form. The French Revolution was of "satanic essence": everything else followed from this seminal premise. Driven by a diabolical mix of rationalism, atheism, hedonism, and materialism, the Revolutionary juggernaut traduced the "divine order." It was a "pure product of Evil." Superficial concessions to the contrary notwithstanding, it was primordially anti-Christian. In light of these convictions, devout counterrevolutionaries regarded as offensive and intolerable the distinction commonly made by the mainstream church between a positive Revolution that benefited mankind (1789) and a heinous, aberrant Revolution that betrayed man's humanity (Terror). The Revolution was nothing if not a "bloc," a

1789-1989
Va-t-on vraiment fêter cela?

Soutenez
l'ASSOCIATION 15 AOÛT 1989

Abonnez-vous à L'ANTI-89

40 F par an (12 numéros)
B.P. 125 - 92150 Suresnes cedex

Portraying the Revolution as a satanic and bloody horror, this poster of the Association of 15 August 1989 exhorted the French to boycott the commemoration of evil in favor of the celebration of the fundamentalist Catholic message.

unitary enterprise, carefully and patiently prepared and systematically executed according to plan.

Numerous contributors riveted the claim that the Terror began in 1789, that "to celebrate the Revolution is to celebrate the Terror." Brigneau sternly rebuked Charles Pasqua—the RPR baron was was then flirting with the far right—for erroneously affirming that 1789 was "a year in which there was no blood spilled," and thus worthy of national commemoration. The early Revolution was savage; it did not merely slay its antagonists, but in at least one instance it cut up the corpse and devoured it. What else could one expect of a mob composed, in the words of Romain Marie, following Edmund Burke and Gustave LeBon, of drunken "fish-wives, pickpockets, and bandits of all sorts, paid by the duc d'Orléans"?[26]

Violence begot deception on a grand scale. Thus the sham of the taking of the Bastille, a sordid attack on an empty and defenseless prison, portrayed in fulsomely heroic terms by apologists for ignominy. Nor were the victims of the Revolution-Terror all named de Launay or de Belzunce. Temperamentally and strategically populist, Brigneau took pleasure in reminding his readers that the Revolution had a predilection for killing the "little people of the people." Gushing with blood, the myriad tributaries of the Revolution converged in a torrent of "genocide," one of the critical terms of *L'Anti-89*'s cant glossary. To denounce this crime, Brigneau counseled an approach inspired by judo, elegant and economical: "One must make use of the adversary's strength, in this instance the power of the official ceremonies, and turn it in our favor by showing the terrible underside of the story that is said to be glorious; profit from the occasion by awakening a country that is ignorant or chloroformed." If we are to succeed, he concluded, we must remember that "the counterrevolution is also a bloc."[27]

Given the intense, uniformly pathogenic presence of the Revolution in their own world, the counterrevolutionaries of Anti-89 may have felt the indivisibility of their engagement even more sharply than the most zealous contemporary Jacobins. For the former, the modernity ushered in by the Revolution was monolithic in its malevolence. The Revolution inaugurated the decomposition, the decadence, the rotting that continued at an accelerating pace in the last years of the second millennium. The Revolution was so dangerous because "it is above all an idea, a principle"—a treacherously subversive idea that was very much alive today, in the official church itself as well as in the ambient society. The core of that idea is the rejection of "God and his Christ." For the Anti-89 group it was most powerfully expressed in the encyclical that Pius IX promulgated on 8 December 1866: "The Revolution is inspired by Satan himself, its goal is to destroy from top to bottom the edifice of Christianity, and to rebuild on these ruins the social order of paganism." The pagan order had in fact triumphed in many ways and in many places, thanks in part to the complicity of the church, which embraced its poisoned modernity.

Virtually everything that was wrong with the world today could be traced back to the Revolution. For Abbé Coache there was a clear causal connection between the crimes of the Terror and "the infinite and continual crime of abortion," between Masonic lies and Marxist lies, between dechristianization and laicity. As the Revolution continues its ravages, "France is sullied, France is degraded, and the true French people are covered with shame."

The champions of Anti-89 wagered on the readiness of these authentic French patriots to join the "spiritual combat" necessary to purge the Augean stable—not only of Marxists (they were after all, practically an endangered species) but also

Muslims, "whose Koran prescribes crime and violence against Christianity." The "immigrant invasion" seemed to be a direct consequence as well as the secondary cause of the widespread intellectual, moral, and physical decay of the French nation and of the deficit of godly virtue and healthy national sentiment. The demands of the fundamentalist counterrevolutionaries followed logically from this analysis: "we want the natural order to be respected, [preserved] against subversion, immorality, the ongoing rot; we want the freedom of the children of God in the public practice of our Holy religion as opposed to contemporary secularism and paganism; we want governments that serve God and France instead of playing the game of the godless and the idolaters of money and of occult powers."[28]

Against the Conciliar Church, Accomplice of the Revolution

Measured in terms of its starkest idiom, the spiritual combat of the Anti-89ers was directed as much against the conciliar church as against the Revolution and the shameful commemoration that they accused the church of endorsing. Indeed, the crusading tandem of Coache and Aulagnier portrayed the struggle as a war on a single front, the official church having sold out to "modern civilization." "May our Lord Jesus Christ and Our Lady," implored Aulagnier, "deliver our fatherland from both revolutionary principles and conciliar principles." According to Coache, instead of toiling to reinvigorate "the supernatural vocation" of France, "the cardinals, archbishops, and bishops relentlessly manifest their complicity with error and evil: support for revolutionary movements, approval of Socialism, praise of an unbridled liberalism, moral assistance to provocateurs." In a word, the hierarchy embraced all the vitiated currents emanating from the Revolution, right and left, and now stood ready to embellish this "treason" with an ostentatious bicentennial reverence.[29]

The *intégristes* were "shocked" by the desire of the church, affirmed at Lourdes in October 1988, to commemorate the Revolution, "being careful to avoid any resentment." This implicit repudiation of Pius's satanic version seemed irrefragable proof of the triumph of "the false revolutionary philosophy," of the "the new religion of modernism that rebuffs God and his rights in order to exalt sinful man." If the church was not quite guilty of treason in the eyes of a lay militant with a doctorate in history, its "ambiguous and singularly moderate attitude" was no less execrable. He was indignant that the hierarchy relied for scholarly advice on the Abbé Bernard Plongeron, a reputed leftist and a member of the Société des études Robespierristes, a group "peopled with Marxists and directed by the Communist historian Michel Vovelle."[30]

Brigneau construed the church's position on the Revolution—which he often glossed in truncated, tendentious terms—as the ultimate litmus of its integrity. "No conciliation is possible" between the church and the heretical Revolution, he asserted. "Either the church will kill the Revolution, or the Revolution will kill the church. It is a duel to the death." The appeasement of revolution followed the logic of Vatican II's "brigandage," its institution of a modern dogma "that chased out Christ." Today's church was in the hands of the "juring" clergy, direct descendants of the blaspheming apostates of 1789–91, "the new priests [who] removed the crucifixes from their meeting rooms, . . . the bishops [who] put all religions on the same level."

Brigneau took particular delight in vilifying Cardinal Lustiger ("Aaron"), who convoked the bishops in June 1989 allegedly "to sing the glory of the Revolution" in the cathedral of Notre-Dame, the scene of orgies of vandalism and perfidious abjuration. Lustiger's culpability was perhaps mitigated by the fact that his family was not born in France and was foreign to the traditions of the church ("I believe, moreover, that the opinions of your father were close to those of the Bolsheviks"). Having been denied the opportunity to learn of the crimes of the Revolution "at the age at which children's emotions are formed," Lustiger somehow managed to avoid the truth in seminary, which was perhaps already in the hands of collaborators. Brigneau exhorted the cardinal to remedy his lack of education by focusing on such Revolutionary derring-do as "the massacre of the convent of the Carmelites, [where] more than 150 ecclesiastics were the victims of the cutthroats."[31]

Brigneau held the church itself responsible for the monstrous historical cover-up of the barbarities of the Revolution. Once the church decided to make its peace with the republic at the time of Leon XIII, "it could not continue to denounce the Revolution." Unblushingly it suppressed the truth of the "Catholic genocide," of the Revolution's "will to exterminate." Determined to expose this wicked dissimulation, the members of the Anti-89 inner circle—its truth squad— undertook a selective Tour de France. Places they could not visit, they evoked in newspaper articles, informed by the documentation submitted by their reader-correspondents. The idea was to take the fight to the faithful at the diocesan level, to challenge the bishop to engage the debate, to submerge him in a sea of gory evidence, to force him to capitulate—or to avow that he was on the side of Satan.

At Marseille, where Msgr. Coffy, the archbishop, refused to furnish a meeting room, Brigneau burned to tell the story of "when God was put to death at Marseille," where the Terror dispatched over a thousand victims, many of whom were priests. There can be no doubt about the moral qualities of Msgr. Orchamp, bishop of Angers, who had recently denied access to one of the city's major churches to traditionalists yearning to celebrate the memory of their counterrevolutionary martyrs. Msgr. Marcus, bishop of Nantes, where the bestial Jean-Baptiste Carrier organized the systematic drowning of true believers, would certainly be invited to participate in the bicentennial saturnalia: "If Msgr. Marcus agrees to attend the fête, he will be not only justifying but honoring crimes against humanity and crimes against the church." "Everything permits us to believe," Brigneau apostrophized the bishop of Arras—birthplace of the tyrant Robespierre, in whose name local revolutionaries brutalized the church—"that you are going to be one of the big stars of the bicentennial. . . . What are you going to do?"

"So, Msgr. Bouchex," Brigneau interpellated the archbishop of Avignon, "are you going to forget the thirty-two martyred nuns of Orange?" As for the archbishop of Rennes, who announced his intention of "celebrating" the bicentennial, Brigneau was beside himself with rage. To celebrate signifies to honor: Is it conceivable for the prelate of a city where the guillotine was particularly active to "sing the praises of the Revolution, that is, of the *sole* French political regime which killed priests because they were priests, [and] Catholics because they were Catholics, and which finished up by outlawing the church?"

Numerous bishops rationalized their bicentennial engagement in terms of the putatively Christian character of the Declaration of the Rights of Man. But this document was irrevocably flawed, as Abbé Aulagnier put it, because "Our Lord Jesus Christ is not named. . . . He is rejected." It was time to affirm the rights of God: "It is neither a partisan question nor an optional question; for a Christian, Christ is everything." The rights of man, added Abbé Coache, "inaugurate the reign of the tyranny of the godless."[32]

Toward a Popular and Providential Vindication

The Anti-89ers were grave but happy, sanguine warriors. In the long term, they knew that they could not lose. In the short term, they buoyed themselves and their flock with an upbeat narrative detailing all the small daily victories and the harbingers of ultimate success. We are being heard, exulted Brigneau in October 1988. Jeanneney is worried about us, and said as much on national television. And if the rumor is true that a conscience-smitten Lustiger has appealed to Rome for the canonization of the butchered Carmelite priests, "we can think of it as a response to the systematic campaign beginning with the first issue [of *L'Anti-89*] to get the bishops to declare what they were planning to do in 1989."

Not only was God on their side, but so was *la France profonde,* the silent majority, if only it could be awakened, deprogrammed. Submerged, or involuntarily repressed, "rejection is very much alive in their hearts." The tautology was reassuring: either the tide was beginning to turn thanks in part to the "growing success" of *L'Anti-89,* or the crusade was succeeding as a result of a burgeoning, providential *prise de conscience.* The plebiscite-acquittal of Louis XVI in the mock trial conducted on national television was a sure sign of the new direction, and a welcome endorsement of "our historical revisionism," as Brigneau craftily put it, making allusion to and allying with the school of Faurisson via the unsuspecting school of Furet. The eleventh-hour efforts of the church, in the person of Max Clouet, secretary-general of Catholic Education, to fix the official prerevolutionary line in the minds of parochial school teachers as well as the lay public, was further reason to gloat: "The campaign to get the Catholic Church to recognize the Revolution is not moving ahead smoothly. It is encountering reticence, obstacles, blockages, refusals.[33]

Even as the Anti-89ers intoxicated themselves with visions of their manifest destiny, so did they puff themselves up in the eyes of the public at large with predictions of their climactic victory on Assumption Day. Taking quite consciously as their model the truly staggering magnitude of the march for *l'école libre*—private, predominantly Catholic schools—in 1984, they hoped for at least one million participants in their procession on 15 August. Brigneau and Coache repeatedly and passionately exhorted the faithful to be present and to marshal others. First they boasted and later they anguished that they would be judged by "the size of our crowd." The more they insisted on the critical significance of their numbers, the higher they bid the psychopolitical stakes. Of course, "it's not the number that will count, but our faith and our love," wrote Abbé Coache, in mitigation of the vulgarity and the risk of the wager. "And yet"—in the age of unforgiving medi-acracy, we must be realistic—"the number will help the prayer to ascend and the message to be delivered."

The closer they approached the day of reckoning, the more agitated the organizers became. "[We must] reinforce your convictions in this period of disaster for the church and for France," urged Coache, "and persuade you that your duty as a Christian and as a soldier of Christ is to do something." Many departments lacked organizing committees: "Two or three resolute persons suffice." The leaders made an effort to blunt the sharp *intégriste* thrust of the crusade in order to attract traditionalists who did not embrace the extremism of Msgr. Lefebvre. The pledge that the day's activities would be strictly "apolitical" was meant to overcome pro-fane as well as sacred cleavages among the potential constituency. In September Coache prudently downgraded the threshold of success to two hundred thousand, but Brigneau bravely camped at half a million during the following months: "500,000 crusaders and perhaps even more."[34]

Everything did not work out as the Association du 15 août 1989 would have liked. First, the prefect of police denied them authorization to hold their mass on the place de la Concorde, the bloody site where the *rasoir national* had accomplished its heinous mission. Denied to true Frenchmen, it was now reserved, Brigneau remarked sarcastically, "for Mr. Harlem Désir [leader of SOS-Racisme] and his rock dancers." (The rightist *Quotidien de Paris* denounced this act of government harassment, proof that the Anti-89ers were the party of healing reconciliation and the Socialists the party of "civil war" and "discord.")[35] Abbé Coache had expected that the authorities might try to stifle the embarrassing voice of truth and expiation, even through recourse to violent measures. Given to melodramatic affectation, he allowed that he was prepared to follow in the steps of the heroic nonjurors: "Person-ally, if I were impaled on this 15 August by a bullet fired by a regime hostile to Our Lord Jesus Christ, that would certainly be the most beautiful day of my life."

Coache survived to preside over the Assumption Day solemnities described by the center-right *Express* as "a failure" and by the moderate-left *Nouvel Observateur* as "a flop." Brigneau first warmed the disciplined and dignified assemblage, drawn substantially from the Vendée and *chouan* countries of the west, with one of his patented diatribes. As Coache celebrated the Latin mass in the large square opposite Saint-Germain-l'Auxerrois, other priests confessed the faithful, kneeling on the ground in the open air. After a picnic box lunch ("On a bouffé du laïc," reported *Le Monde),* the crowd began its march up the rue de Rivoli. Media estimates of attendance ranged from 7,000 (*La Croix,* television news) to 10,000 (unlikely consensus of *Le Quotidien de Paris* and *Libération*) to 50,000 *(Le Figaro).* The Anti-89ers themselves placed the figures at between 25,000 (the mass at the place du Louvre) and 50,000 (the procession stretching four kilometers).

If the Anti-89 gathering of 15 August was not precisely the Latinate Woodstock of the Counterrevolution, Brigneau nevertheless resented the television stereotyping of the movement's recruits, as if they were confined to "three old ladies of a particularly unattractive aspect." He insisted on the substantial presence of the young and the beautiful and the sunburned who willingly sacrificed several days' vacation "in order to say *NO* to the bicentennial." The enterprise was not a "flop," Brigneau contended spiritedly, because it caused the Establishment—Masonic, governmental, ecclesiastical—"an immense anxiety." Certain perspicacious observers on the left had warned that it would be wrong to dismiss the movement as merely "museographic" or "folkloric" or to judge its significance narrowly in terms of card-carrying initiates; and Jean-Noël Jeanneney emitted an audible sigh of relief when the crusade lurched to a mildly disenchanted denouement.

Mortified by the disappointing showing, one Breton militant invoked the triumph of Gideon, backed by a mere handful of men: "For faith is more powerful than we are." Brigneau owned up to hopes unrealized—but unrealized not for lack of human effort: "Certainly the definitive, unquestionable event of which we dreamed in our holy ardor apparently did not occur. The much awaited outburst of resuscitated Catholicity did not take place. . . . What can we say? That divine Providence, in her unique wisdom, probably did not want to respond in an inordinately striking fashion to our human expectation. 'Still a little more time,' she whispers to us."[36]

The Vendée
Trope and *Idée-Force*

The Vendée was and is the Counterrevolution incarnate. It did not begin that way in 1789, but for reasons that historians still debate, a large part of the population of this western province gravitated rather rapidly to an antirevolutionary posture. In the eyes of the Revolutionaries, the Vendéens were rebels and traitors, allies of France's enemies, mystified and/or willful apologists for old crimes and perpetrators of new ones, instruments of superstition and manipulation, fanatics, brutes, atavisms. The Vendéens, of course, represented themselves quite differently as Christian crusaders, royal warriors, defenders of genuinely French ideals, avengers of the people against an intrusive and overbearing state, defenders of local and regional interest and honor.

The Vendée as *idée-force* quickly outstripped the boundaries of the Vendée as place. Though the Counterrevolution can by no means be reduced to the Vendée, the more the province was battered and bloodied and spoliated, the more it came to stand for the Counterrevolution in action. It was the popular culture of the Counterrevolution, the lower part of its body in some ways but its spirit all the same, the source of its only spontaneity, the surrogate for the innocence it never had, the sometimes unwelcome reminder that the voice of the people could be interpreted as the voice of God. In its martyrdom, the Vendée became the soul of the movement, the trope of resistance, the metonym of a Revolution run amok, the symbol of irreconcilable differences.

In its affliction it consummated its own mythicization, rendering its sociology from below a permanent tension between populism and miserabilism, its social structure a tissue of highly functional and felicitous tribal reciprocities, its religiosity a mixture of virile earthiness and rarefied devotion. The Vendée's evangelical ardor imbued its hatred for the blues and reinforced its conviction that the heavenly city was not to be built here on earth. The Vendée drew its strength from the Christlike cast it took on, at once corporeal and impalpable, mortal and eternal, mutilated yet invincible.

This was a strategy of survival as well as an exercise in propaganda. The (post)Revolutionary Vendée (re)constructed itself even as it continued to hemorrhage. The Revolutionary legacy became the principal capital from which it lived, a kind of festering *rente* that nourished its pessimism and shaped its voting habits, the education it gave its children, and its relations with the rest of the nation. Only the church was commensurate with the task of representing and guiding the Vendée, mediating between past and present, guaranteeing cultural reproduction. Besides its primary vocation, each communion served as a memorial of collective suffering and a reminder of collective identity.

The Vendée modernized nevertheless, or was modernized. Market forces, the First World War, new technologies of communication, and pressure from the center all worked in favor of integration. Vendéens succumbed to the blandishments of the world, confiding the stewardship of their memory to the routine of the church and to small volunteer organizations of (not strictly folkloric) militants such as Souvenir vendéen, and confining the collective moments of intense recall of the past to a few specific calendar days a year. The *trente glorieuses* were corrosive of tradition—at least in the short run, while prosperity and consumption had an aspect of redemption and compensation. Beginning in the early 1980s however, there appeared signs of a resurgence of Vendée consciousness, signs doubtless magnified in retrospect by the bicentennial prism.

Renaissance

The rise to national prominence of Philippe de Villiers marked the beginning of a new militancy of both popular and elite cultures. Though his mother was a Catalan, her ancestor, Elisabeth de Montsorbier, was deeply anchored in Vendéen folklore as one of the "twelve Amazons of Charette," the military leader who played a leading role in the Vendéen insurrection. His father, a Norman, did not arrive in the Vendée until 1946. He founded an industrial laundry business, and immediately entered politics. The mayor of Boulogne from 1946 to 1983, the senior Villiers served as conseiller général from 1973 to 1987 and conseiller régional from 1979 to 1987.

Impelled by a similarly intense drive to participate in public life, Philippe de Villiers explored more modern paths to power in the service of ancestral and indeed transcendental goals. At the Ecole nationale d'administration, he learned the protocols of governance and made the requisite personal connections. Temperamentally, he was not suited for a career in public administration. Subprefectoral duties far from his native soil frustrated and alienated him. Rumor persists that he refused to reimburse the state for the cost of his education upon his resignation from the civil service, which he portrayed as a solemn protest against the advent of Red government. The Vendée was his passion and his springboard to prominence, the place and cause that would allow his ambition to masquerade cogently as altruism, and his evangelical authoritarianism as leadership.

Imaginative as well as overbearing, Villiers had ideas to accompany his appetite. With the help of his father's leverage and his own blend of charisma and technocratic adroitness, he overcame the skepticism of local mayors and a cruel penury of resources to create in 1978 the festival of Le Puy-du-Fou, an unlikely and surprisingly durable success that propelled him, along with the Vendéen story, into the national limelight even as it announced his conquest of the homeland. The Puy-du-Fou was a vast sound, light, water, and theatre/cinema spectacle of the region's heroic/traumatic past, mobilizing hundreds of zealous volunteers avid to steep themselves in their regional culture. With skill and passion, Villiers forged a veritable community of commitment, a sort of cultural confraternity, marked simultaneously by sharp hierarchical lines of leadership and an egalitarian ethos (all participants were "actors, not extras"). Set against an evocative castle, at once magnificent and partly in ruins, the show recounted the Vendéen saga in personalized, accessible, and moving terms to an audience that swelled to a quarter of a million per season, seated in specially constructed stadiumlike stands that presaged a very long run.

As creator of Le Puy-du-Fou, emblem of Vendéen sacrifice and resurrection, Villiers imperceptibly came to incarnate the Vendée no less powerfully than did his creation. Le Puy-du-Fou formally inaugurated the struggle against "national amnesia" that would culminate in the bicentennial. A "synthesis of 1793 and the laser," Le Puy-du-Fou betokened the design that was to inform Villier's entire public trajectory: the reconciliation of past and future, rural and high-tech, local and (inter)national, sacred and profane, aesthetic and political, socially heterogeneous and morally homogeneous.

A number of complementary enterprises helped to accelerate and reinforce the burgeoning momentum of Le Puy-du-Fou. Relatively early, Villiers began to think about expanding the attractions offered to tourists who came for the show. He envisioned a number of museum-monuments, including the reconstitution of a village-refuge where thousands of Vendéens had once taken shelter. Convinced that only a mastery of the media could enhance and perpetuate his influence, and assure his region of a public resurgence-cum-rehabilitation and a revival of regional patriotism, he endowed the Vendée with one of the first "free" (that is, independent and local) radio stations in the nation, France Alouette FM. To broaden the base of his project, shortly afterward he created a foundation for the arts and sciences of communication at Nantes.[1]

Despite these assiduous preparations, Villiers failed to win a legislative seat in the elections of March 1986. His growing notoriety, however, resulted in a compensatory prize. The new minister of culture, François Léotard, more discreet than Villiers in his practice of politics and piety, named him to a secretaryship of state in his department, on the recommendation of a mutual friend, Alain Madelin, the minister of industry, who resonated with Villier's emergent mix of Maurrasian liberalism. Rapidly Léotard and Villiers came to despise each other, largely as a consequence of the latter's aggressive contempt for, and jealousy of, the former. "That ministry was a bloody shambles! I was a flying goalkeeper who could never touch the ball," complained Villiers. Rarely constrained by personal or institutional loyalty, Villiers became known to the press for his delight in deriding his boss: "I lent Léo a book [but] he's not yet finished coloring it." This strained collaboration lasted barely a year.

In June 1987 he left the government in order to run for a legislative seat at home vacated by the death of the incumbent. He wrenched it from the hands of the infuriated RPR, whose government he had just served. He crowned this triumph two months later by winning a seat at the Conseil général, or departmental legislature. "Lord Villiers takes possession of his estates," announced *Le Monde*. A brief flirtation with Raymond Barre's presidential campaign confirmed his reputation as a wholly self-centered man unwilling to accept the rules of the game. An American might generously characterize him as a hardball player; for a close French observer, "this man has treason in his bones." But the only victims who mattered to Villiers were the mythic and historical ones who could further his career, not those contemporary ones who littered its trajectory. Thus he turned his attention to the somber Revolutionary past of the Vendée in the wake of two more smashing victories: reelection to the National Assembly with three-quarters of the vote in June 1988 and election to the presidency of the Conseil général of the Vendée a few months later.[2]

Another prod to regional reawakening was Pope John Paul's beatification of ninety-nine Angevin martyrs, killed during the Vendée war, in February 1984. This was vindication if not vengeance, the long-awaited assurance that the victim would turn out to be the victor. "The glory, the victory of triumphant Vendée," exuded the *Souvenir vendéen*, "despite the setbacks and the deaths." Thousands of Vendéen pilgrims, many wearing the red scarf of Cholet, including 480 direct descendants of the martyrs, flocked to Saint Peter's to hear the pope, himself intimately familiar with statist efforts to control a national church, condemn the totalitarian character of R/revolutionary religious oppression and praise the fidelity of those who gave then, and continue to give now, their lives for the faith. (The martyr image, incidentally, appealed to regionalists of green and red hues who were not counter-revolutionaries but who believed that this complex served to ground Vendée identity passionately and permanently.)[3]

The renewal of Vendée historiography was a spur to and perhaps also a product of the Vendée renaissance. For more than a century and a half, republican historiography neglected the Vendée, minimized its specificity, or obscured its suffering. Surely Vendée specialist Jean-Clément Martin is right that the very silence of republican historians accounted in large measure for the flowering of the association of the Revolution with totalitarian ideas and deeds. In the last two decades, however, enormous strides have been made in rectifying the errors and opening new avenues of research. "No one," insists Rennes-based historian François Lebrun, any longer denies the "abominable" and "atrocious" character of the repression. In the same vein, Jean-Clément Martin has shown that even the Marxists have recognized the complexity of the Counterrevolution/civil war, the autonomous character of the peasant movement, its cultural specificities. Among the wider intellectual causes of the revision of Vendée history, according to Claude Langlois, a historian of religion, are the decline of historical materialism as a dominant paradigm, the reinterpretation of the Enlightenment as a matrix of totalitarian state forms, the exaltation of oppressed national/regional/ethnic minorities, the rediscovery and lyrical advocacy of rural values, and the reevaluation of the impact of spiritual power, illustrated by the role of Catholicism as a vector of resistance, inter alia, for Poles and for Latin Americans.

Despite the surge of new scholarship, leading Vendéen and counterrevolutionary figures tend to focus on the old stereotypes that justify their rancor. They have effusively accorded their suffrage to only one historian, Reynald Secher, who himself is sharply criticized on central points of method and analysis by professional historians in France and abroad. His vision of the "Franco-French genocide" benefited from an orgy of prime-time and -space publicity: an appearance on *Apostrophes* in July 1986, four color pages in *Figaro-Magazine*, lengthy interviews on major radio programs.[4]

Premier des Vendéens

Drawing heavily on the work of Secher for the illustrative detail and of Furet for the general framework, Philippe de Villiers, self-proclaimed "premier des Vendéens," became the chief exponent of the Vendée cause in the public sphere. While remaining faithful to the traditional rhetoric of outrage and demonstration of atrocity perfected by the *Souvenir vendéen* (a catalogue of Revolutionary crimes broken down into rubrics according to mode of execution and nature of perversions including sadism and cannibalism, censuses of the numbers of victims of different socioprofessional groups), Villiers forged a more modern if not more moderate line marked less by self-commiseration than by an unrelenting assault on the adversary. His objective was not to reinforce a wounded (and largely futile) sense of difference but to make that difference matter, to exploit it for a return. That required a shift from inner- to outer-directedness, a *désenclavement* of Vendéen anger and anguish.

Villiers resolved to make the Vendée a household word before the end of the bicentennial season. In formulating his case, he stressed the profane rather than the sacred, the general as much as the particular, the whole rather than the parts. He no longer permitted the Vendée to be marginalized, by its friends or by its enemies, through some form of routinizing ritualization. The creator of Le Puy-du-Fou restored the Vendée to the central Revolutionary place it merited, for neither the Vendée nor the Revolution could be understood apart from each other (an approach for which J.-C. Martin provided the most cogent scholarly sanction).

Nor would the Vendée be the appanage of *intégristes* or royalists or descendants of the martyrs or of any other lobby. Villiers construed it as a national issue, at the core of French rather than regional identity. He did not portray the Vendéens as churlish outsiders who reviled the modernity engendered by the Revolution. He did not assail progress, materialism, greed, liberalism, capitalism—at least not directly. These were legitimate themes, but he would leave them to the likes of the Anti-89ers because they could not serve his interests. Though he subscribed to a quasi-satanic view of the Revolution, he refused to privilege this reading because it did not resonate positively with the mainstream instincts of the French people today. While remaining fervently committed to Christian principles, he tended to make his case in universal moral rather than exclusively confessional terms when-ever he could. And he linked his exegesis of the Revolution as tightly as possible with current preoccupations, so that it would earn an immediate political dividend.[5]

Because "we are all Vendéens," Villiers argued in his aspersive *Lettre ouverte* and in scores of bilious and sprightly interviews, it was a political, cultural, and moral imperative to shatter the silence that had stifled the story of the Vendée. The most significant "Bastille that remains to be taken" was the one he named "the truncated Memory," or "the mutilated Memory," or "the rigged, censured Memory." For partisan and ideological purposes, Villiers contended, republican historians have lied to the nation about the Terror and about the Counterrevolution. They have suppressed and distorted evidence. They have fabricated a history that excludes and insults a part of the citizenry. "One does not sift through and select one's his-tory. . . . One takes everything and forgets nothing."

It is interesting that Jacobin historians uttered the same complaint from the opposite point of view. "In 1989, when certain persons would like to efface our historical experiences from the collective memory," contended Communist sym-pathizer Louis Oury, "it is not morbid, but opportune, to reinject into that memory those fratricidal days of March 1793 in Machecoul, because it is out of these 'Catholic and royal' horrors of Machecoul that would develop the long and savage civil war which cast a tragic shadow over the young republic. The latter did credit to itself by punishing those who in its name (Carrier, Westermann, etc.) committed monstrous war crimes of reprisal."

Why not evoke the Vendée in the same breath as Valmy, the heroic battle which sealed the affirmation of the republic in September 1792 and which marked the finale of the bicentennial festive calendar? asked Philippe de Villiers. Vendée and Valmy, he advanced, were two facets of the Revolution: "Two very French manners of saying no; two very French ways of dying for freedom." In slavish mimicry of the most odious republican tradition, the "apostolic vicar of the commemoration," Jean-Noël Jeanneney (in whose boyish eyes the deputy of the Vendée discerned "hatred" when they faced each other on *Apostrophes*) continued the fraud, building Potemkin villages, "hiding" the real Revolution, celebrating what he had the effron-tery to call "the most positive." In an acerbic allusion to Le Pen's dismissal of the Holocaust, Villiers asked: "Must one definitively consider the Terror and the Vendée as 'points of detail' of the Revolution?"

The Vendéen polemist camped on the loftiest ground he could find: truth, accommodation, love, Socratic self-knowledge—the authentic ground of the republic, defiled and abandoned by its Jacobin trustees. Thus he posed as the legitimate herald of the rights of man, the first of which was, "the right to the truth; as the olive branch–bearing Henri IV, the most *franchouillard* of regal unifiers; as the republican teacher-*commissaire* who felt confident that "the republic can manufacture citizens if it is the republic of all memories"; as the confessor-psychoanalyst exhorting the leaders of the nation to believe in France, to love it, and thus to make it loved. Even as he oscillated between reconciliation and recrimination, so he navigated adeptly between past and present, excoriating the government for offering amnesty to political criminals instead of proffering conciliation to its own people, and juxtaposing the arrest of war criminal Paul Touvier, who hid in various traditonalist monasteries, to the impunity of Robespierre, who hid for two centuries in the Ministry of National Education.[6]

Villiers's diatribe and his call for recognition/reparation found considerable echo in the center as well as on the right. Virtually everyone looked to François Furet, given his scholarly credentials, his political itinerary, and his burgeoning media notoriety, as the source of legitimation for this campaign. Horrified by the massacres, to which the republican historiographical tradition had failed to own up, and persuaded of their significance, Furet considered it appropriate and even necessary for the right to raise the issue. Though Pierre Chaunu appreciated Furet's support, he did not await his cue before denouncing the "scandalous" exclusion of the Vendée from the bicentennial agenda, "the other aspect of 1789." But it ought to be pointed out that there were public-sphere intellectuals substantially to the left of Furet who openly called for an unequivocal acknowledgment of the trauma suffered by the Vendée. Claude Nicolet, guardian of republican rigor, expressed horror for the republic's treatment of the Vendéens: "They gave the order to kill women and children." While Jacobin Régis Debray rejected the application of the term "genocide," he declared that "we can be grateful to M. Reynald Secher, in the wake of others, for having pointed to a wound that was perhaps not causing us enough pain."

The conservative editor of *Libéralia* denounced the "dimension of falsification" in the Mathiez-Soboul-Vovelle line, enshrined in the republic's school books, and welcomed the immense gust of revisionist fresh air. Though he was not insensitive to bicentennial anguish in the Vendée, the charge that the republic had long orchestrated a plot to exclude the story of the Vendée from the schools enraged Jean-Noël Jeanneney. "I have had occasion, after a given debate with Philippe de Villiers or other less caricatural persons, to turn simply to my Malet-Isaac [the leading school text for several generations]: I had come to wonder whether truly we had not been told in school about the Vendée, the Terror, and the laws of Prairial," wrote the president of the Mission. "But of course we had been: with little partiality and much nuance."

Echoing Villiers's axiom of the indivisibility of memory, the *Lettre de la nation,* official organ of the RPR, held that "we must accept the soldiers of Year II who died for the republic, [and] for liberty, equality, [and] fraternity, but also the Vendéens who fell for God and the king." It reproached the Socialists, caught up in narcissistic revelry, with sacrificing statesmanship to politics by missing "the crucial opportunity to make of the bicentennial a symbolic act of unity." If the comte de Paris, pretender to the crown, accepted the idea, particularly onerous for a royalist, that "one must shoulder everything. . . . history is not divisible," wondered another observer, why couldn't the Socialist commemorators make the same concession? "The theorists of the 'principles of '89' should pay homage to the Vendée," wrote an irate reader—one of many—to the editor of *Figaro-Magazine,* "instead of effacing it from history as they have been trying to do for the past two centuries." The "ambiguity" of the Counterrevolution intrigued Catholic educator-writer Etienne Borne, who wrote in *La Croix* that its heroes and criminals had the same claims on commemoration as those of the Revolution.

In a voice at once sober and impassioned, Jean-Clément Martin agreed with Villiers that the bicentennial could not afford to overlook the traumatized and forgotten part of the nation. Intellectually, one could not pretend to fathom the Revolution without reflecting on the role of the Counterrevolution. Nor should public authorities make the mistake of identifying the Vendée narrowly with inveterate, practicing counterrevolutionaries. In civic terms, it would be catastrophic to forsake "a whole population [that], without itself being counterrevolutionary, will not be able to fit itself into the enterprise of commemoration." Like the deputy from the Vendée, though for rather different reasons, the historian of the Vendée wanted the bicentennial to be the catalyst for a comprehensive rethinking of the place of the Counterrevolution in French history: "So long as one continues to consider the Vendée as *the* land of *the* Counterrevolution, does one not continue to practice the political myopia of the deputies to the Convention, who refused to concede that there could be dissatisfied people, seeing only traitors and conspirators?"

"The commemoration of the bicentennial requires a deepening of our understanding of the Counterrevolution," wrote Roger Dupuy, another leading authority on western France. He also stressed the need to widen the perspective on hostility to the Revolution and to remember that the Revolution buffeted a society that was at least 80 percent peasant and still deeply Catholic. Villiers must have felt some ambivalence about the démarche of Martin and Dupuy, who insisted on the salience of the Vendée yet at the same time relativized its place in a larger context.[7]

The "Final Solution"

Historiographical recognition was a major step forward, but for Philippe de Villiers, at bottom, it was incommensurate with the nature and magnitude of the revolutionary evil. Historians could make partial amends for the long syncope that smothered the ravaged Vendée, but not for the ravager, the Revolution itself. (Like Soviet perestroikists, the deputy of the Vendée decried the black spots and the whiteouts, but for him as for them, they were symptoms of the disease, not its source.) Whatever nuance, refinement, or contextualization one might supply, for Villiers there was one central, overriding Vendéen fact next to which everything else paled: the "plan of extermination of an entire people." The Terror in the west was nothing short of a calculated "final solution." Even if Villiers preferred not to use the term "genocide," despite his conviction that it was objectively appropriate, in order to avoid the risk of devalorizing the ineffable singularity of the German concentration camps, the Nazi analogy was pervasive.

Republican repression was a "crime against humanity" according to the strict construction of Nuremberg criteria. The Committee of Public Safety anticipated the Nazi bureaucracy in organizing "human cargoes." Like the Nazi monsters who recycled human parts for various industrial and decorative purposes, the heinous blue executioners "established ateliers producing human skin as fabric so that the soldiers of the infernal columns could parade in leggings made of brigands' skin." The republican general Amey's bread ovens, stoked with human combustible— women and children—were nothing less than crematoria. At Lucs-sur-Boulogne, where Villiers planned to spend the morning of 14 July 1989 in prayer and mourning, the revolutionaries are said to have massacred 564 innocent persons, exclusively women, children, and old people. This was one of several Vendéen Oradours— Oradour being the site of one of the Nazis' most barbarous massacres in France. Villiers called this collective butchery "populicide," a word he derived from Gracchus Babeuf, whose politics ("the father of Communism"), in the eyes of the Vendéen, somehow guaranteed the unimpeachability of his testimony.[8]

Villiers conveyed a genuine sense of horror and bereavement, despite his rhetorical preening and his urge to turn tragedy and ignominy to political advantage. Other supporters of the Vendée emulated his position, often in a more strident and hyperbolic manner. In his *Pourquoi nous ne célébrons pas 1789,* Jean Dumont denounced the "thousands of Oradours" that littered the Vendée, related chilling stories of "units of children employed to finish off the exhausted and the wounded by bludgeoning them with stones," and exposed various Himmlers and Goerings in republican garb. The writer-historian Henri Amouroux, the deputy-political leader Philippe Mestre, and Catholic journalist Luc Baresta were among the dozens of observers who deployed the Oradour image. Though women were said to be the most alluring targets of the blue strategists who hoped to exterminate the "fertile sources" of the Counterrevolution, infants had no immunity from their bloodlust. Among other atrocities, a journalist at the *Midi libre* evoked the "officer of the blues" who specialized in the murder of babies. In one family massacre, the blues added the macabre touch of nailing the last-born, a one-year-old, to the door of the farm, according to the president of Souvenir vendéen.

"I am not truly neutral because I was born there," Reynald Secher conceded, "but I was all the same astonished by what I discovered." The republicans were the inventors of "genocide," not just of "political terror." According to Secher, they elaborated "a mechanism that heralds from far off and on a scale of three departments the methods of Pol Pot in Cambodia." While certain commentators stressed the Nazi filiation, others, such as *Rivarol*, emphasized the kinship with modern Communist practice. Summoning the Conseil régional of the Midi-Pyrénées on which he sat to cancel the bicentennial celebration in favor of a solemn commemoration of the hundreds of thousands of victims of totalitarian annihilation, Romain Marie/Bernard Antony characterized "the Bolshevik and Nazi revolutions" as the "monstrous children" of the French Revolution. (He also called attention to the Revolution's "strange innovations, such as the creation of foundries for human fat," another proof-by-analogy of the Vendéen genocide.) *Minute* described the revolutionaries as "the precursors of the doctrinaire and bloody tyrants of the twentieth century from Hitler and Stalin to Pol Pot." The secretary of Souvenir vendéen was buoyed by the unofficial assurance that under pressure from Chaunu and others, the Académie française would soon admit the phrase "génocide franco-français" into the national vocabulary. Quite justly she remarked that "there is no reason for a genocide to be automatically foreign."[9]

The Vendéens did not need to convince themselves of the barbarity of the blues. That belief had long ago acquired in their midst the unassailable status of legend— legend as the transmission of moral verities that were not falsifiable. The point now was to reach others, optimally to persuade them, minimally to disconcert them, by a double process of sensationalist *surenchère* and prosaic positivism. The two vectors often seemed in contradiction, for the one spoke in shrill terms, appealed to the passions, and assumed that the truth was blatantly self-evident, while the other spoke in a more studied voice, appealed to reason, and discussed evidence and sources. The first focused on the savage act itself, while the second tended to use the latter to work another, deeper logic of indictment. Partisans of the Revolution preferred the first approach, not only because it could be discredited for its sheer excesses but also because it rang more sincere than the second, which perhaps required refutation but whose argument reeked of casuistry. (They were also willing to accept the hypothesis of individual gruesome massacres, explained as aberrations or products of circumstances, rife during the Terror, but not the putatively intrinsic connection between the sadistic gesture and the very essence of the Revolution.) At sundry junctures, however, the two moods converged and strengthened each other, gore and (quasi-scientific) lore, both spawned by outrage.

The Vendéens refused to bow to the stern and quixotic wish of the commemorators that they calm down for the duration. That was far too much to ask of them in the name of a civic creed that struck them as elitist, remote, and cankered. The call to commemorate invited confrontation and implied the settling of scores. In this hot context, the problem of establishing viable equivalences—an eye for an eye, an epithet for an encomium—must have seemed like academic gamesmanship, a sort of extraneous and insoluble theodicy question. It was hard to imagine either side subscribing to an ethic of fair play. Even if exorbitance did not necessarily issue in a

Located in the Maine–et–Loire, the Chapelle des Martyrs at Yzernal was one of many solemn counterrevolutionary monuments that summoned the rest of the nation to recognize the martyrdom of those who resisted the Revolution and its repression. (Photo courtesy Professor J.-C. Martin of the Université de Nantes.)

healthy, functionalist discharge of anger, it probably constituted the only grounds for true-believer Vendéen participation in the bicentennial. If the commemorators offered very little to appease them, it is highly likely that, by the very nature of their commitment, they could not be mollified, at least not by measures the state deemed reasonable.

It was the Vendéen vocation to excoriate the Revolution; the bicentennial furnished the best opportunity they had had in half a century. It was their ambition to *change* the Revolution, retrospectively and prospectively. This was the prerequisite to any sort of reconciliation. To change the Revolution meant to alter the way in which it was represented, to freight it with new weight and responsibility, to rewrite its destiny as well as its daily life. Thus the violence of the *forcing:* the double-edged strategy of the pathological vignette and the archival reference preparing the way for the deployment of the ultimate weapon: genocide. In the hands of the twentieth-century Vendéens, genocide was the final solution to their two-hundred-year struggle for what they called justice.

Diabolical Trio: Jacobins, Bolsheviks, and Nazis

Identified in the first instance with the devastation of the Vendée, the idea of genocide and the Nazi analogies were appropriated by the broader Counterrevolution. In case the Vendée on its own failed to loom large enough in the consciousness of the public, the virulent critics of the Revolution wanted to saturate that public with the idea that the Vendée was neither an accident nor an isolated episode; that the Revolution meant genocide on all fronts, sooner or later; that the Revolution was not just the chronological forerunner but the moral and political progenitor of the twentieth-century genocides. It was important to those on the right, many of whom sympathized with the anti-Bolshevism of the Third Reich, to insist on the genocidal parity between concentration camp and gulag, on the symmetry of cruelty between the Gestapo and the KGB, on the kinship between all totalitarianisms. Yet, given the intensity and intimacy with which the French experienced the turmoil of World War II, the Nazi example remained in the forefront of their minds.

In this perspective, genocide sprang from a constructivist, voluntarist hubris, predicated on a total dependence on abstract and absolute reason as a guide, and channeled through the fabrication of a New Man and a New Order. "The archetypal script for genocide," professed the late philosopher Jean-Marie Benoist, "the archetypal script for this treatment of the tabula rasa in the Bolshevik, Chinese, Iranian, Cambodian, and Nazi revolutions—this script for the tabula rasa is indeed borrowed from the French Revolution." Benoist was drawn in particular to the deep, plutonian connection between the Revolution and the Nazis. Even as he had once told an audience at an elite American university that the head of the princess of Lamballe was worth no less than the lives of the inmates of Auschwitz, so he wrote on the eve of the bicentennial that "those who were sent in batches to the guillotine, in carts, are mysteriously the brothers of those whom the freight cars of *Nuit et brouillard* took to Auschwitz."

Cardinal Lustiger tried to dissipate the mystery that shrouded the link by recalling that "thought can be deadly," in this case the ideas of the eighteenth century. Cautiously oblique, he conveyed his analysis by citing a text of François Mauriac reminiscing on France's wartime experience fifteen years afterward: "The dream that Western man conceived in the eighteenth century—whose dawn he thought he glimpsed in 1789—this dream drew strength from the progress of the Enlightenment [and] the discoveries of science up until 2 August 1914. This dream shattered definitively for me in the face of the freight cars stuffed with little boys—and I was ten thousand miles from imagining that they were going to nourish the gas chamber and the crematorium." In Lustiger's view, Auschwitz could not be treated as "an aberration without precedent." Sharing a certain Heideggerian kinship, historian Ernest Nolte was merely the most visible of a growing number of West German conservatives who hinted aloud that the program of the Final Solution might have been implicit in the philosophy of the Enlightenment. Implicitly, Lustiger, the son of deported Jews, seems to mitigate the special stigma of Nazi crimes by making them, like the crimes of the Terror, the sins of Modern Man.

When Bruno Gollnisch, one of Le Pen's house intellectuals, observed that "the French Revolution prefigures the holocausts of the nineteenth and twentieth centuries," in his vocabulary the relation of prefiguration carried etiological weight. The "never again" galvanized by the recent trial of war criminal Klaus Barbie at Lyon, in the view of more than one observer, should refer as much to "the ignominy of the chopping blades of the Revolution" as to its Nazi legacy. Nor was the thesis of linkage exclusively a reflex of the right, sacred or profane. At a colloquium on the Revolution and the Jews held at Lille under the sponsorship of the International Council of Christians and Jews, "the most agonizing question was the following: was the Shoah merely an accident of history or did it germinate in the soil of the Revolution, considered by certain observers as the mother of totalitarianisms?"[10]

Other commentators emphasized that the analogy associating Revolutionaries and Nazis went far beyond superficial resemblance (for example, "on the horizon of the carts, the trains of the deported"). They pointed to allegedly common totalitarian motives for and methods of evisceration. Thus, counterrevolutionaries, like Jews, were arrested and executed for a "defect of birth" or a "crime of birth" (as if most victims and most counterrevolutionaries were of noble birth!). In the same vein, the "sort of anticlerical [and] anti-Christian racism" of the Revolutionaries was "very close to the anti-Jewish racism fashioned by the Nazis." The anti-Semitic caricature fashioned by the Nazis was "very similar" to the anti-Christian caricature of the Revolutionaries. The Revolutionary deportation of priests had much in common with the Nazi deportation of Jews: "At the end of 1792 the revolutionary Gestapo aroused its informers in the following manner: they will receive one hundred livres in bonus for every denunciation of a deportable priest." Like the Jews, the priests endured the torture of denial of food, sunlight, bedding, and so on.

Hitler's vision of purification was self-consciously inspired by the same spartan virtues that the Revolutionaries exalted.

In sum, the Terror was no less abominable than the Nazi oppression. On this basis François Brigneau spoke not only of a French Revolutionary genocide but of "the holocaust of French Catholics." With this same conviction of priority and perhaps magnitude of suffering, an officer of the Souvenir vendéen compared the death artisanship of the blues and the Nazis (decorously omitting to mention the identity of the Nazi victims): "One speaks of lampshades made by the Nazis; I prefer a lampshade to a *culotte* [made of Vendéen skin]." At bottom the question then becomes, Are French Catholics of the eighteenth century to be denied what European Jews are opulently accorded in the twentieth century? A journalist in *Rivarol* joined the issue crudely: the Revolutionary crimes against humanity were not punished because "the victims were not Jewish but Catholics." Since it was by definition the vocation of the Jews, "refusing to recognize the Messiah in the prophet Jesus," in the words of the Lepéniste newspaper *Présent*, to consider Christ as "a blasphemer and an imposter," and since in this sense anti-Semitism expressed "the very essence, the supernatural essence of Catholicism," it was only a small step to apprehend why the Jews once again refused to recognize the sacrificial status of Catholic martyrs. The new-old Vendéen genocide was as abominable to them as had been the "new Israel" galvanized by Jesus.

More subtle, Villiers made this point several ways, playing at once on the historical antagonism and jealousy and on the unintended solidarity between (French) Catholics and Jews. Were the Terror and the Vendée to be reduced to mere "points of detail," an ignominious status that Jews and their protectors furiously rejected for their Shoah? Didn't the denial of the one genocide jeopardize the other? Weren't the Vendée skeptics, after all, "a couple of Faurisson types who deny through an odious process of editing and arrangement the facts documented by archival evidence?" Pilloried by the right as a leftist Faurisson, Max Gallo riposted that the negation of one genocide, the Shoah, was the instrumental precondition to the birth and consolidation of another, the Vendéen.[11]

From One Revisionism to Another

The revisionist theme, which Villiers rejected yet which he milked for leverage and points, tempted others, likely and unlikely users of this line. In the latter category, stood Pierre Chaunu, the eminent historian known for his generosity as well as his febrile transports, who wrote: "While we never had the written order of Hitler concerning the Jewish genocide, we possess those of Barère and Carnot relative to the Vendée." Here it is not merely priority that is claimed for the Vendée genocide but a sort of historical irrefragability and thus legitimacy at the expense of the Shoah, built on a more fragile foundation.

On the side of predictability one finds the stalwart François Brigneau, who proudly identified his brand of Revolutionary "revisionism" with Faurisson's: they were fighting the same battle. "Beneath the deformations, the lies, the fabrications of the imagination and of propaganda," Faurisson sought to uncover the truth about the deportation, which meant to expose "a historical falsification without precedent." David against the Goliath of "colossal interests, both financial and political," Faurisson found himself, in a society otherwise boastful of its tolerance and liberalism, denied access to the media, denied even rooms in which to hold meetings. "Making due allowances," ventured Brigneau, "my enterprise is not different. Beneath the lies, manipulations, fabrications of Masonic and Marxist ideology, I try to show the true face of the Revolution. Since the interests threatened by this revisionism are of small importance compared to the interests threatened by the first revisionism, I am tolerated."

Shrewdly, Brigneau tried to associate all revisionism with Faurisson revisionism, all criticism of Jacobin dogma with this crusade against the Historical Lie in all its avatars (Jewish, Masonic, Marxist, conciliar Catholic, and so on). Thus he chided the historian Elisabeth Badinter, notoriously linked, personally and through her husband, with Socialism and Judaism, for being simultaneously for and against the death penalty, a penalty recently abolished in France in no small part through her husband's efforts. She was against it when it was to be applied against a child murderer, Patrick Henry. But she was in favor of it when the criminal was named Louis XVI. Brigneau referred to the nationally televised mock trial in which the French public massively favored the king's retrospective acquittal. "This is Faurisson," Badinter is said to have scoffed. In a way she is right, Brigneau bigheartedly conceded: "There is no doubt that in trying to reestablish the historical truth in opposition to the official history, the authors of this trial of Louis XVI, and the televiewers who followed them, behaved like *revisionists.*"

Louis Pauwels, director of *Figaro-Magazine* and plausible spiritual director of Philippe de Villiers's future campaign for the Elysée, protested sharply against what he claimed was the left's irresponsible use of the Faurisson bogey to smear those who rebuffed the Jacobin vulgate. According to this quasi-official Manichaean bigotry, "whoever sees in the affair of the Vendée what it [really] was, that is, the organization of a genocide, considers the gas chambers a lie and denies the Jewish martyrdom." It is true that many on the left deeply resented what appeared to be a calculated attempt to manipulate the Vendée in order to diminish the significance and even question the reality of the concentration-camp horrors. But it was the right rather than the left that repeatedly linked Vendée and Shoah. Having publicly taken his distance from Le Pen, in part over the genocide issue, Pauwels should have known better than anyone that it was a commonplace in Lepéniste circles to question the veracity of the Shoah while simultaneously affirming the incontrovertibility of the Vendéen genocide.

That same right made the connection in the other sense as well. Thus, in a piece on the Vendée that rapidly slid into a discussion of the "imposture" of Nuremberg and the way in which the victors confiscated control of the past, Pierre de Salagnac remarked that "those who sanctify the Revolution are the same as those who punish crimes against humanity." As for Le Pen himself, he preferred the macrocosm, where unremittingly in their everyday life "the French people are victim of a political genocide," to the pitfalls of the bicentennial microcosm. In passing he remarked that if after two hundred years there are still enormous differences in estimations over the numbers killed in the Vendée (from fifty thousand to five hundred thousand), then it is reasonable to think that it would take time and cooperation among historians of all persuasions in order to count the real number of victims of "the Jewish genocide."[12]

The use of the word and the concept "genocide" provoked serious and sometimes indignant criticism from historians and intellectuals, situated mostly but not exclusively on the left. They challenged the comparability of the Vendée massacres (as an expression of the French Revolution) and the Jewish extermination, both of which suffered distortion at the hands of the analogy, and they questioned the intentions of those who undertook the comparison.

The ordinarily tranquil historian François Lebrun, Old Regime expert with a special interest in western France, administered a stinging rebuke to Pierre Chaunu on the honest way to do history. He posited certain canons for historical practice that were neither without ambiguity (the distinction between a necessary "serenity" and a probably unattainable "objectivity") nor likely to win unanimous corporate endorsement (the historian, obligatorily "neutral," had to abstain from "judging"). Still, Lebrun's reproaches were powerful and pertinent. Chaunu presented the world through a narrow ideological grid in starkly binary and partisan terms that undermined the open-minded quest to uncover and understand. "To establish a parallel between the repression in the Vendée and the Holocaust is the very example of an antihistorical endeavor," charged Lebrun, because it obscured the specificity of the events that France experienced in 1793–94. By sullying the Revolution with the genocide blot, Chaunu sought to assimilate the work of the Convention to the most awful totalitarian systems of the twentieth century. Lebrun saw the appropriation of the word "genocide" as a critical element in a larger campaign, politically driven, to discredit the Revolution on the eve of the bicentennial. He called for a genuine scholarly enterprise in order to fathom how and why the Vendéen insurrection developed, how and why the Convention reacted, how many victims the war and repression left in their wake.

François Bédarida, a historian of the twentieth century, echoed Lebrun's admonition against anachronism and his plea for historical specificity. He deplored the "strange blends and sensationalist gestures" by which the term "genocide" was dangerously banalized and abusively applied. For genocide to take place, there had to be a deliberate program to exterminate systematically an entire ethnic group, the technological and organizational power of a modern bureaucratic state, and the capacity to conceal the operations. None of these conditions obtained in the Vendée: "the Final Solution clearly remains without equivalent in history."

J.-M. Montremy reiterated the point that the Vendée did not constitute a race or ethnic group and that the Convention struck out against it "as a political enemy." "There was nothing racial in this tragedy triggered by the murder of the republican delegates on 11 March 1793 in the little village of Machecoul in the Loire-Atlantique," noted the writer Henri Guillemin. "Rather than a totalitarian will of extermination," wrote Roger Dupuy, one of the leading scholars of the Vendée, "I discern an archaic manner of reprisal—a repressive spiral."

While he readily admitted that the Jacobins and patriots perpetrated "Oradours" in the Vendée, republican historian Maurice Agulhon considered it "inadmissible" to call this genocide—from , the perspective of both the Revolution and the Holocaust. If one described "massacres" as genocide, "then one must find another word to designate the specificity of the Hitlerian program—for lack of which this program will be half exonerated by this reduction of the phenomenon to the status of the commonplace." In its rigorous etymological sense, genocide was meant "for Auschwitz, an extermination camp destined to wipe out the entire Jewish population." The Nazis were also responsible for Oradour, Agulhon hastened to add, "an abominable cruelty, but alas, much more classic." Louis XIV "Oradourized" the German palatinate and Simon de Montfort did the same in Languedoc, without prompting the charge of genocide. Nor can one brand genocide the eradication of Camisard villages, added Alfred Grosser, a historian of Germany, to which the Protestant Pierre Chaunu should be especially sensitive.

While Grosser accused François Furet of opening the gate to the "furious surging tide of today's antirevolutionaries," the latter unequivocally rejected the use of the term "genocide" as inappropriate and anachronistic. Senior modern historian and colleague of Chaunu, Jean Meyer dismissed such objections as vain "sophisms." Genocide meant massive extermination. In the Vendée, "there was clearly a will for genocide, a will to extirpate the people of the cities and the countryside." Usually the first to remind readers that words were not the mere labels of things, philosopher-journalist Jean-François Revel jauntily endorsed the use of the genocide term. He was unperturbed by the implications of the analogy, and the banalization it wrought. It was no different from any other of the many anachronisms commonly employed, such as "inflation" under Diocletian. In addition to positing criteria for a loose construction of genocide, Revel predicated the argument for the Vendéen instance on historical grounds—a premeditated extermination of the whole population—that most specialists vigorously contested.

Given the "monstrous" nature of the crimes against the Vendée, Claude Nicolet, the robust republican, was willing to concede the word, though he pointed out some of its difficulties: "Genocide perhaps, but it did not apply strictly to a certain race and it did not touch mass concentrations." However "atrocious" it was, the Vendée was a civil war, not a Holocaust, maintained Claude Mazauric, a veteran historian of the Revolution and Communist militant. "It seems as if an imaginary genocide had as its function to obscure a very real one." Mazauric suspected the revisionists of both the Chaunu and the Faurisson-Roques schools of marching to the beat of the same sinister drum, with the goal "of excusing the greatest genocide in history, the one perpetrated against the Jewish people by the Hitlerians."[13]

Beyond the more or less objective question of whether a genocide occurred in the Vendée, it is not clear to what extent Villiers and the others pondered the implications of their call for genocidal recognition. What sort of burden would France have to assume if "it" had been guilty of genocide—indeed, of having invented genocide? To be sure, the Jacobin and Nazi experiences were very different, but would the "work" of memory be completed (as Villiers seemed to hint) once the crimes were formally recognized—or would it just be beginning? Did the Vendéen lobby understand that comparisons have consequences (even as the rightist relativization/historicization of Nazism in Germany had consequences)? Just as Ernst Nolte suggested that not to be alone among societies perpetrating genocide dissolved a whole set of interlinked chains of inhibition for Germany, so did parts of the French right appear to think that not being included in the genocidal genealogy deprived the nation of an important part of its identity. But, then, what would it mean for the collective sense of self to imprint the genocidal mark on the republican matrix? It does not appear that the Vendée exponents looked beyond the short-term partisan gains and the satisfaction of a certain ideological vindication to the longer-run political and psychological significance for a nation increasingly worried about its identity and its roots.

The ready use of the Nazi analogy in France, not only in connection with the Revolution but throughout the political and cultural domains, merits a thorough study. For our purposes, let us note that the Nazi comparison was not the monopoly of the right and far right. It emerged occasionally on the left, especially among the Communists, for whom the Resistance remained extremely vital, even incandescent. Few put it as bluntly as Louis Oury, for whom the triumph of the Vendée would have prefigured the Nazification of France:

> I would remind you first of all that if our forefathers had not been able to subdue the Vendéens, it is evident that we would not be commemorating the bicentennial of our Revolution. That is why, at a time when certain people are attempting to lay guilt on the republicans by evoking the crimes committed by Carrier, Turreau, and others, it is important to note, without thereby approving it, that this vanquishing of the Vendée was militarily as necessary as were, a century and a half later, the crushing of Dresden by the British flying fortresses, of Berlin by Stalin's juggernaut, and of Hiroshima by the American atomic bomb. Because it was an early genre of Nazism that our forefathers had to defeat.[14]

The Polish Connection

The Polish-Vendéen affiliation nourished the Vendée's sense of exceptional martyrdom and indirectly reinforced the region's claim to genocidal standing. "We are all in some way Polish," Philippe de Villiers averred time and again. The Vendée was "a little Poland" in its afflictions, its heroic and costly resistance to tyranny, its unyielding fidelity to the church, its "rejection of the unacceptable." Jacques Cathelineau had fought and died for the same rights as Jerzy Popiélusko. The pope's nationality made the Polish affinity even more salient for the Vendée. No one knew better than he the onus of religious persecution by the state. It was John Paul II who had recently ordered the beatification of the Angevin martyrs and who had paid solemn deference to the collective victimization of the Vendée. A delegation of Polish clergy had visited the region on the occasion of the beatification in 1984.

In early July 1989 Philippe de Villiers invited Cardinal Glemp, primate of Poland, along with Polish political leaders, intellectuals, and representatives of Solidarity, to the château of Puy-du-Fou to sign an accord by which several French provinces would provide various forms of assistance to the dissidents. Surely it was an appropriate bicentennial gesture to proffer moral and material support to a people struggling to reconquer its liberty—and to publicize that gesture. At the same time Villiers orchestrated the encounter as a conscious bicentennial counterpoint, a kind of rightist pendant to rock and roll bard Renaud's demonstration/concert at the Bastille.

Cardinal Glemp did his part in the homily he pronounced after the mass. Sisters in agony, Poland and the Vendée were also partners in spiritual victory, for they had embraced the side of truth. Subjected to different but equally monstrous "forms of Terror," in both places "the people of God sustained their deep religious intuition; here and there, God triumphed." Glemp praised the Vendée as a universal symbol of courage and pointedly emphasized that in sanctifying the beatified martyrs, the church honored "hundreds of thousands of victims of bloody Terror." In the primate's view, the French Revolution was inherently flawed and destined to go berserk because it espoused the "illusion of creating a new and beautiful world . . . that did not require salvation and thus had no need of God, of a moral order, or of the Church of Christ."[15]

The Conservative Club of Lodz further embroidered the satanic view of the Revolution in a mimeographed brochure drafted in French as an appeal against the bicentennial commemoration. The club called on Christians, conservatives, nationalists, and friends of order everywhere to "organize counterdemonstrations opposed to this impious and anticultural glorification of the Revolution." From above it identified itself with Edmund Burke, who foresaw that 1789 would become 1917, the embodiment of revolution with which the Poles were most intimately familiar, and from below with the "salubrious force" of the Vendéen peasants, who sagely revolted against the Revolution in the name of the eternal values of God and king.

During this year, 1989, the enemies of Latin and Christian civilization celebrated the assault on the Bastille, the event that detonated, two centuries ago, the process of the degeneration of Europe which gave birth to the New Barbarism. The scale of the cult that surrounds this lugubrious bicentennial testifies to the depths of the moral fall of modernity and its immense disdain for the truth. The secularization of public and private life points to the degree of this depth. The crimes of the sansculottes and the Jacobins provided the source for totalitarian ideologies and criminal systems, such as Socialism, Communism, and Nazism. We must thus oppose this prorevolutionary mystification with all of our strength.

Not all Poles agreed with the satano-Burkean interpretation and the Vendéen kinship. Bronislaw Geremek, a historian and counselor to Lech Walesa, declined the invitation to Le Puy-du-Fou, and Solidarnosc made it clear that its members attended only in their personal capacity. Even as *Le Figaro* headlined "Poland-Vendée: Same Battle," *Gazeta*, the Solidarnosc daily, countered with "The Bastille or the Vendée," suggesting that the Poles chose the wrong camp. Yet even so-called progressive Poles had trouble digesting the Revolution. "Rationally I want to sing the praises of the French Revolution, for all it contributed to the rights of the individual and the sovereignty of nations," confided Krzysztof Sliwinski, deputy director of *Gazeta*. "But in the bottom of my heart, I have much sympathy for the Vendée." Though Sliwinski was now a Socialist, the Vendée remained for him a "mythical country," as it had been portrayed to be in an essay-novel by Pawel Jasienica that marked a whole generation of students in the late 1960s. Evoking the Vendée during the Terror was Sliwinski's oblique way of depicting the Polish resistance and instilling the youth of Poland with hope.[16]

Several days after Glemp appeared at Le Puy-du-Fou, a group of Jewish Americans climbed over a fence separating Auschwitz from the property of a Carmelite convent to demonstrate against its continued presence overlooking the death camp. In language the newsweekly *Time* characterized as "inflammatory misrepresentation," Glemp later hinted that the demonstrators had intended to murder the nuns. Installed since the mid-1980s in a large building that had once stored Zyclon B gas, the convent, with its towering cross, deeply offended a large part of the Jewish community, which viewed its establishment as a further effort to de-Judaize the Holocaust. Already Polish authorities had done everything they could to obscure the specificity of Jewish extermination at Auschwitz. Now it seemed that the Carmelites, whose founder had Jewish roots and whose most recent saint was a Jewish convert, wanted to convert Jewish souls.

Despite an accord, engineered in part by Cardinals Decourtray and Lustiger, that called for the transfer of the convent from the camp to the town, the Polish church stalled, and encouraged public opinion to manifest hostility to this infringement of Polish sovereignty, this transgression of Polish memory, and this affront to Catholic practice. In a shockingly vitriolic homily delivered in late August at Poland's most sacred holy place, Cardinal Glemp raged against Jewish arrogance and international control of the media, and he suggested that whatever anti-Semitism thrived in Poland resulted directly from the propagation of anti-Polish sentiment. "Poland sees itself as the Christ of nations," commented American historian Lucy S.

Dawidowicz. "There is a sense among the Poles that Jews are usurping Polish suffering." The Polish appropriation of Auschwitz was the pendant to the Vendéen appropriation of the genocide. Glemp's presence at Le Puy-du-Fou symbolically reaffirmed Polish custodianship of Hitlerian martyrdom and conveyed legitimacy of title and usufruct to the Vendée. If the revisionists of both the Faurisson and Chaunu schools were right, then both the Polish and Vendéen cases would be dramatically fortified.[17]

The Vendée-Auschwitz connection did not escape the perspicacious eye of François Brigneau. Like Glemp, the editor of *L'Anti-89* believed that "the causes of anti-Semitism have always resided in Israel itself"—words cynically cited from a nineteenth-century Jewish writer. Historically the Jewish vocation was to undermine the structures of the Christian social order. Brigneau used the occasion to show how Jews and Masons combined to prepare the way for the French Revolution. After having helped disestablish the church, the Jews took the lead in selling its relics and property.

National hebdo portentously announced that "the quarrel over the Carmelite convent at Auschwitz could be the final battle, the Armageddon of the metaphysical and metapolitical war that Judaism and Christianity have been waging against each other for the last two thousand years." The weakened conciliar church recently granted the Jews what generations had been clamoring for: "to see themselves cleansed of the imputation of being a deicidal people guilty for all time for having put to death the Son of God." Notoriously extortionate and impossible to satisfy, the Jews showed their true colors at the Auschwitz showdown with the Carmelites: "Because the same people who, yesterday, demanded to be absolved of the crime demand today that the victim be forgotten."

The Jews objected strenuously to the thirty-foot cross ("the supreme horror," ironized *Rivarol,* reminder of another martyrdom that the Jews could not abide). "There we are," seethed *National hebdo,* "the bare shadow of the victim has become an affront to those who were for two thousand years considered to be the artisans of his execution." The Jews tried to substitute themselves, through their Final Solution, for the death of the Messiah: "At bottom, the Extermination furnishes an argument to those who contend that Jesus of Nazareth was not the Messiah announced in the Scriptures but at best a visionary, at worst an impostor, and that the role which devolved upon the Messiah is in fact played by the Jewish people themselves."

This was not far from what Msgr. Lustiger believed, *National hebdo* added maliciously. The archbishop of Paris was of course implicated in this debate on multiple levels: as the Jewish-born son of Nazi deportees; as one of the official negotiators on the Carmelite issue; and as an influential moralist and theologian. Lustiger, too, made the connection between Auschwitz and the Revolution, not to besmirch the Jews in Brigneau's manner, but to discredit the Revolution. He contended that the same vice engendered Auschwitz and the Revolution, not Jewish perfidy, but human deviation, the rejection of transcendental references in favor of a

Rebuilt as a result of a campaign organized by the Association Souvenir Vendéen, the Chapelle du Mont des Allouettes in the Vendée stood as one of many reminders of unhealed wounds and persistent hostility to both the Revolution and its legacy. (Photo courtesy Professor J.-C. Martin of the Université de Nantes.)

vision of autonomous human perfectibility. As victims of this excess of rationality, Jews and Vendéens had much in common, regardless of the scale and the mode of their devastation.[18]

Pro Victis

"I speak in the name of an assassinated people," Philippe de Villiers told a national television audience in mid–bicentennial year. In the name of the victims, he formulated a set of demands—*doléances*, or grievances, in the spirit of the Revolution—addressed to President Mitterrand. If they were granted, they would mark the beginning of the full restitution of the national memory, the historical resurrection of the Vendée, and its reunification with the rest of the nation. Once the enormous issue of their past was settled, the Vendéens could join with other Frenchmen in "a common vision of their common future." First, Villiers called for the recasting of the historical image of the Vendée to bring it in line with the research of the last decade. That meant not so much a full-scale adoption of Chaunuean revisionism, which Villiers recognized was beyond his immediate reach, as a searching reappraisal on all levels of the character and lived experience of the Vendée insurrection. Concretely, from an administrative point of view, this revision made it incumbent on the Ministry of National Education to purge the school texts "impregnated with Jacobin and Marxist ideology" and commission genuinely scholarly accounts that did not mask the massacres.

Second, Villiers quite rightly argued that a reassessment of the Vendée implied necessarily a reevaluation of "the Revolution taken as a whole." Scientifically imperative, this task, he believed, would also prove fruitful in civic terms, for the rights of man, no longer encumbered—at least not in the same way—by the harrowing moral lien of the Vendée, "would emerge enhanced." Villiers's third grievance focused on the visceral needs of his constituency. He had to wrest symbolic reparations on a fairly grand scale. His requirements were at once specific and nebulous. Beyond the official expiatory gesture and the sepulchral mien that would frame it, it is not clear what would be involved in "the classification of the Vendée as a national cemetery." Nor is it easy to imagine how one could achieve by fiat "the total discrediting of the authors of crimes against humanity—Robespierre, Carrier, Turreau." After all, there were not many Robespierre statutes to vandalize; and the minister of the interior could hardly be expected to dissolve the rather sedate Société des études Robespierristes as a subversive association. For Turreau's sacking, Villiers prescribed a simple recipe: as a "war criminal" for his spoliation of the Vendée at the head of the infernal columns, his name was to be obliterated from the Arc de Triomphe where the republic had treacherously honored him.

Villiers couched his final demand in terms that transcended the Vendée in order to reach the diverse strains of the anti- and counterrevolutionary heritage. In an ambiguous formulation that seemed to reduce the Terror to mere wanton bloodshed, he asked Mitterrand himself for "an official gesture in order to render homage to the victims of the massacres of the Terror." In fact, the president made a number of rhetorical signs, including the well-publicized speech at Roanne in which he evoked the "crimes" of the Revolution and wondered whether they could not have been avoided. To judge from the reactions that reached the press, however, those of counterrevolutionary inclination either did not listen to him or regarded his discourse as insufficient or insincere and thus unacceptable.[19]

To Villiers, it would have been "paradoxical" for the French to celebrate their Revolution with great unthinking pomp while everywhere else—Poland was only one of many cases—the disenchanted and often involuntary heirs of Rousseau, Robespierre, and Babeuf contested the Revolutionary heritage. At the grass roots in the Vendée, and in other parts of the West, there was in fact little bicentennial festivity. Jean-Noël Jeanneney's appeal to Vendéens to "to take into account the luminous side of the Revolution" fell on deaf ears. Much to his credit, he rejected the temptation to play to his audience when he visited the west. If on the one hand he assured them that "commemorating the Revolution never meant rejoicing in the bloodshed," on the other he vigorously attacked the analogy linking blues and Nazis: "Turreau is guilty of war crimes, not crimes against humanity."

La Roche-sur-Yon, a town with fifty thousand inhabitants and a Socialist municipality, was one of the rare sites of bicentennial commemoration. The city council allotted three hundred thousand francs to sponsor the reconstitution of an eighteenth-century café to serve as the setting in which a dozen professional actors would discuss the unfolding Revolution with passersby invited to stop for a drink. ("And why not pay for some guillotines?" shouted a furious critic during the debate over the appropriation.) Three times the municipality had to replant the liberty tree next to the city hall because of nocturnal vandalism. Counterrevolutionaries complained of counter-vandalism in the Maine-et-Loire where a Vendéen war sanctuary was desecrated and statues of Jean Stofflet and Jacques Cathelineau decapitated. A schoolteacher near Nantes was ostracized by the local historical association for agreeing to serve as the prefect's correspondent for the commemoration in the Vendée.

At Nantes, also in Socialist hands, counterrevolutionary sympathizers bitterly criticized the municipality for shamefully celebrating the bicentennial on the very hillside where Carrier sent "tens of thousands of innocent Nantais" to their death. Many Vendéen villages, such as Chambretaud, had obstinately refused to celebrate 14 July until the mid-1980s. Gilbert de Guerry de Beauregard, mayor of Chavagnes-en-Oailliers, resisted the national holiday with the same ardor he devoted to opposing the opening of a public school in his commune. The old cemetery grounds are marked by a plaque erected by the Souvenir vendéen dedicated "to our dead, 1793–1796, let us be faithful to them." A recent issue of the Association's magazine described in vindictive verse the proper attitude for the Vendée to take vis-à-vis the bicentennial:

> I will not celebrate your Revolution
> Theft, rape, and crime are not to be hailed
> But I will mourn our poor victims   .
> They alone are entitled to my veneration.

It would be "indecent" to commemorate events that decimated 60 percent of the local population, insisted Louis Fruchard, mayor of Mauléon in the Deux-Sèvres. At Lucs-sur-Boulogne, site of one of the most horrible massacres, there would be a simple fireworks display on the eve of the fourteenth in honor of the Declaration of the Rights of Man. "The people really want me to organize something in 1993," related the mayor, Paul Bazin, who added, "one cannot be on the left here." As early as 1986 the Conseil général of the Vendée had envisaged a major effort in 1993, for which purpose it created the "Center for the Study of the Counterrevolution in the West [of France]" (not to be confused with the "Center for Counterrevolutionary Studies" that *intégristes* set up at the Institut Saint-Pie). According to *Libération*, Philippe de Villiers worked hard to keep the Vendéen passions in check during the bicentennial. He is said to have feared that ostentatious antirepublican demonstrations would tarnish the "democratic" image that he wanted to cultivate. But he entertained grandiose plans for 1993.[20]

A Seigneur's Epilogue

In the wake of the bicentennial, Philippe de Villiers "felt arise within himself a soul of Robespierre dressed in a monk's robe," as *Le Monde* playfully put it. Avid to capitalize on his polemical successes, and increasingly frustrated with the timidity of the opposition family, vis-à-vis both the Socialists and the Lepénistes, he scouted for the opportunity to establish his own direct line to the nation, the millions of Vendéens beyond the Vendée. He found his calling without having to strain. It followed more or less coherently from his "doctrinal training" with the young monarchists of the movement called Restauration nationale in the 1970s, from his irresistible fascination with the Revolution's perilous quest for Virtue, from his resentment of the Front national's shrewd efforts to corner morality in the public sphere, and from his desire to profit from the thickening accumulation of scandals that gravely tarnished the image of Mitterrand's party.

He would battle corruption in all its avatars, the Vendéen decided in 1990, deploying as his chief arm the media rather than the guillotine. He would mobilize the nation in a "Combat for Values" campaign. In the spirit of Jerry Falwell, Villiers groped to constitute the moral majority. He invoked "a mystical strategy" that would transform his past struggles into a religious crusade. He launched a monthly newsletter (Fr 150 a year), which he claimed to diffuse at a rate of twenty thousand, and he commenced what would become an endless *tour de France* to propagate the good word, and to lay the groundwork for a future institutional structure.[21]

Villiers sharpened the vehemence of his attack against "l'Etat-Ripoux" as more information surfaced concerning the illicit financing of Mitterrand's campaign and of the Socialist organization at every level. He depicted Socialism as "a sin against the spirit." It hardly appeared accidental to the Vendée's Mr. Clean that he received, in November 1990, notification from the tax department of the finance ministry of a huge claim against the Association du Puy-du-Fou for allegedly seeking and accumulating illicit profits. ("For the Socialists, an association only seems truly cultural if it piles up deficits," ironized *Figaro-Magazine,* one of Villiers's most fervent supporters.) "I will break you," the puckish and merciless minister of the budget, Michel Charasse, a cigar-smoking Saint-Just, is alleged to have ejaculated when he encountered Villiers after a vote of censure against the government took place at the National Assembly.

"I will continue to fight, and I'll go to the very end," retorted the deputy from the Vendée, indignant when the other side took up his hardball style. "In the current climate, with the proliferation of 'affairs,' to announce in this fashion that the internal revenue service takes a political personality in its sights, is to suggest to the general public that this personality is hiding something," complained the crusader who knew so well the damage that deft mudslinging could do. "Even if the file is really empty, the effect is produced, and that's the only thing which matters to the manipulators."

Not only would Le Puy live on and the Combat for Values continue, pledged Villiers, but the nation would hear from the Vendée during *its* bicentennial in 1993. The announcement of this program was one way in which Villiers riposted to his critics. What more appropriate vehicle for him than the commemoration of 1793, "the uprising of the conscience"? Insisting that he sought to promote concord rather than division, and that he recognized that the Vendée, now and then, was not monolithic in its ideology, "le premier des Vendéens" nevertheless vowed to honor those who "who revolted for their religion." He opened a national subscription to construct a monument "to the glory of all the Vendéens of 1793" at Lucs-sur-Boulogne, where Turreau's infernal columns shot and bayoneted 564 persons, including 110 children. In addition to the monument, to be erected on the road leading to La Roche-sur-Yon and thus to serve as a reminder and "signal" to the thousands of motorists who would pass by, the Conseil général planned a second building near the chapel, "a miniature memorial, very modern, with two or three very striking rooms."

At the château de la Chabotterie, where the insurgent military leader François Charette was wounded and arrested, the decidedly prepostmodern Villiers planned "a museum of the third type." He planned a film on the uprisings coproduced with TF1, and an international colloquium titled "Terror and Liberty," starring the conservative trio of François Furet, Emmanuel Le Roy Ladurie, and Pierre Chaunu—on the morrow of what is certain to be a crushing victory of the right over the left in the legislative elections— backed by a large cast of extras consisting of "all the victims of terror worldwide." Finally, Philippe de Villiers announced that a group of lawyers would work out a petition asking the United Nations to recognize the "Vendéen populicide as a crime against humanity." Hardly fashioned to honor his pledge to avoid reopening deep wounds, this procedure would enable the world community, if not the state, "to [condemn] for complicity those who deny this populicide," thus consecrating the moral symmetry with the Holocaust that Villiers craved.[22]

1993

Philippe de Villiers enjoyed his richest hour of commemorative satisfaction, and vindication, four years after the end of the official bicentennial year. At the end of September 1993 he welcomed Aleksandr Solzhenitsyn to the Vendée. The great Russian writer visited the Puy-du-Fou and inaugurated a memorial to the martyrs of Lucs-sur-Boulogne. "The bicentennial of the Terror would more or less have passed unnoticed were it not for the presence of Aleksandr Solzhenitsyn," observed *Le Monde*. In some ways there could have been no more fitting closure to the protracted anniversary of the Revolution in its successive avatars. Even as the writer had jolted a substantial part of the left into a searching reassessment of their attitude toward the Communist experience in the 1970s with his *Gulag Archipelago*, he had also indirectly initiated a sweeping revision of the historiography of the French Revolution in France. François Furet acknowledged his inspirational debt to Solzhenitsyn in the book that made his reputation and launched his crusade, *Penser la Révolution française.*

It seemed perfectly reasonable for Villiers to characterize the Vendée as a quasi-necessary stopping point on the Nobel laureate's long road home. Though the Russian thinker hardly required comparison with an ideological adversary to enhance his moral authority, it also seems an appropriate reminder of the new balance of things that at the very moment he made his pilgrimage to the Vendée, the singer-actor Renaud, celebrated for having campaigned passionately for Mitterrand and then for having led the charge against the president's insufficiently sansculottic bicentennial, toured the country preaching the virtues of the R/revolutionary heritage in his role as Lantier in the film *Germinal* ("He's no match for his opponent," announced the journalist Christine Clerc, with her usual perspicacity.)

Nor did Solzhenitsyn really need the stage provided by Lucs according to Villiers's *mise-en-scène:* a ghastly slaughter in a church; an Oradour that prepared the ground for Nazism with which it seemed so consonant; not an accident but the ineluctable product of a R/revolutionary logic that went on to ravage the twentieth century. The Russian expatriate rose at Lucs to embroider the attack on "the Jacobins of yesterday and today" that he had already articulated in the *Gulag.* His soul resonated with the spirit of the Vendée, universal model for resistance to totalitarianism and emblem of the power of relentless spirituality. Fusing past and future into a timeless web of absolute truth, he spoke about the dire peril of attempting to build the heavenly city here on earth (or, rather, "the happiness of the people," in the idiom proper to the Enlightenment). Stirring as prophecy, his speech was feeble as historical analysis.

Solzhenitsyn predicated his argument on the conviction "that all revolutions unleash in man the instincts of the most elementary barbarism." Redolent of Burke, Maistre, and Chaunu, the speech denounced revolution for "destroy[ing] the organic character of society," wiping out "the best elements of the population and allowing free run to the worst," and engendering an extensive pauperization. It was also vain to imagine for a moment that "revolution could regenerate human nature": the tragic outcome of this enterprise could be readily seen first in eighteenth-century France and later in twentieth-century Russia—the latter revolution permitting one clearly to take the monstrous measure of the earlier, paradigmatic one.

In Solzhenitsyn's view, the French Revolution foundered on the contradictions symbolized by its trinitarian slogan "Liberty, Equality, Fraternity." Liberty and equality were "mutually antagonistic," for it was the role of liberty to extirpate social equality. As for fraternity, its only true realization was "of spiritual order." Without explaining how it would come about, the writer admonished that the only way to obtain "the social effect so ardently desired" was through a so-called normal evolutionary development. "Progress," watchword of the eighteenth century, led directly to the horrors of the twentieth century, "a century of terror." The Russian

Revolution (later followed by similar abominations in China, Cambodia, and Vietnam) mimicked the French, improving on its "cruel procedures" only through superior organization, not conceptual innovation. The result was foreordained: Russia experienced its genocides and its Vendées.

Philippe de Villiers hailed Solzhenitsyn's oration as the ultimate step in the unmasking and desacralization of the French Revolution. Fellow rightist Alain Griotteray provided a crude translation of the Russian's lesson: those who continued to admire the French Revolution were the same as those who had for so long "propagated the idea that communism is certain progress." Hardly any of the intellectuals targeted by this attack responded publicly. No one relished taking on the monumental Russian writer, one of the rare persons who could get away with pronouncing such erroneous assertions and such egregiously stylized cant. Through their silence they hoped to make the commemoration of the Counterrevolution a non-event. Some of the most indignant reactions came from citizens who resonated with Solzhenitsyn's Christianity and his condemnation of revolutionary barbarity, but questioned his interpretation of the French Revolution (especially his apparent indifference to its enunciation of human rights) and his amalgamation of the French and Russian Revolutions. One letter to *Le Monde* regretted the asymmetry of the writer's skepticism. By failing to examine critically the enthusiastic claims of Communists that the Revolution of October 1917 was "the crowning" of the Revolution of July 1789, Solzhenitsyn ceded "curiously to a typically Bolshevik deception."[23]

The Church

N ext to the state, the church was the most significant institutional actor in the bicentennial drama. It was not an easy role to play. The historical and liturgical repository of counterrevolutionary hurt and rancor, the church could not be expected to vibrate with joyous nostalgia for the conquests of the Revolution. Yet the church had changed over the years. It was no longer a single-minded redoubt of unregenerate antirepublicanism and antimodernism. On the national and international levels the church had new interests and fresh strategies. It had developed more wholesome and fruitful relations with the state, with other religions, with society at large. It had attained a compelling moral credibility, consonant with its redefined ambitions and its irenic outreach policy, that it was highly motivated to protect. The bicentennial would be widely perceived as a test of the earnestness of the church's commitment to aggiornamento, to dialogue, and to growth, spiritual and social.

But if the church's performance would bear heavily on the future influence it could wield *outside* its own house, it would have perhaps even more serious implications for its capacity to govern within its own realm. For the bicentennial would test the church's internal cohesion. Different constituencies articulated very different expectations. The church had to worry about the enhanced appeal that the bicentennial might enable schismatic *intégristes* to exercise over their more docile traditionalist brethren. It could not afford to neglect the still festering wounds of the mobilized and susceptible Vendée-*chouan* populations, most of whom had no incentive to flirt with excommunication. Nor could it scorn the acute sensibilities of the reformist/leftist post/-Vatican II branch of the Catholic family. It had also to think about the silent majority inside and on the perimeters of the church whose precise feelings were not known, and who looked to it for their cues in stressful and complicated situations. The church leadership had to worry not only about its flock(s) but also about its shepherds. For the parish-level clergy itself was seriously divided on many of the issues crystallized by the bicentennial. Nor could the issue be framed in reassuringly binary terms opposing a marginal, albeit vociferous, extreme right to a more or less harmonious mainstream. Jean-Noël Jeanneney correctly noted that the debate over the Revolution "did not oppose . . . the fundamentalist-traditionalist wing to the rest of the faithful but cut through the very center of the institution."[1] Opportunity? Trap? Challenge? The bicentennial was all of these to the church, which greeted it with even less relish than did the political parties.

The Bicentennial Church

Though their appreciations of the transformation vary substantially, virtually all commentators concur that the bicentennial church differs radically from its centennial forebear. In 1889 the church hurled anathema on a Revolution represented as satanic incarnation, "the origin of all our misfortunes."[2] A hundred years later one of France's most distinguished Catholic historians diagnoses a "*reversal*—the word is not too strong—in the judgment that Catholics make of the Revolution." Once overwhelmingly dominant, the counterrevolutionary position had become a minority current. Without necessarily agreeing on the weight to accord to each, experts attribute this "conversion" to a host of exogenous and endogenous factors, some of which required long gestation. The experience of the two world wars induced Catholics to "relativize" their historical gaze, to venture comparisons that enabled them to apprehend the connections between the "two humanisms," one engendered by Christianity, the other by the Enlightenment-Revolution, both of which were vilified by the totalitarian and fascist regimes born between 1917 and 1933. Vichy's national revolution deeply besmirched the counterrevolutionary ideology, even as the Resistance drew into common cause devout and unbeliever. Corrosive of authority and submission, the idea and practice of resistance became intimately associated with the struggle for justice, an engagement made more urgent by the church's gradual "discovery" of misery and injustice and reinforced by the galvanization of a reformist will.

Even as Catholics discarded their normative lenses and began to see the world as it was, so too did they move toward a new anthropology in which the accent shifted from man crushed by sin to the grandeur of man created in God's image. Fundamental to all the rest was a sea change in the church's ecclesiology: "a renewed vision of the church, of its nature and its mission," a new conception of the relation between religion and politics and between church and society. No longer an intransigent model for a "perfect society," nor a power rival to the state, the church adjusted to the notion of laicity as rule of law rather than plan for extirpation. With a deepened sense of humility, it focused on the task of serving humanity. The final step in its forward march was the most difficult: ratifying, if not quite embracing, a pluralism based on freedom of conscience and expression.

Pressed by Pope John XXIII, the church's evolution culminated in the principle enunciated by the Council of Vatican II that "the right to religious liberty has its foundation in the dignity of the human person as it has been made known by the word of God and by human reason." In the most optimistic perspective, this properly theological foundation, in the context of a quasi-linear development, bespeaks neither "repudiation" nor "infidelity" but profound reflection, which "made possible the reconcilation of the descendants of the martyrs with the sons of 1789." A more cautious reading of the church's course points to persistent contradictions and counterpoints (for example, the fierce affirmation of pontifical authority; the ongoing rehabilitation of Pius VI; the hesitations attendant on the arrest of Paul Touvier, a major figure of Vichy collaboration whose flight from justice certain elements of the church had facilitated), to the unresolved burden of the painful conflictual past, and to the continued hesitation of the church today "to give clear approval to the values of 1789, to wit: liberal individualism and the laicization of the state."[3]

The Commemorative Gesture

In stark contrast to their bitter hostility in 1889, the bishops of 1989, writes historian René Rémond, invited Catholics "to associate themselves with the commemoration and to join in it." In many ways, however, the official position of the church was more reticent than he suggests. The church announced its intention to mark the occasion of the second centenary in a declaration adopted by a plenary session of the bishops of France at Lourdes in October 1988. But that statement was carefully hedged to appease various clienteles and blunt any unambiguous exegesis. Though the Revolution was "a great ordeal for the Church of France"—some would say precisely because it was such—Catholics must not turn their backs on the bicentennial, for they were all stewards as well as products of the memory of *everything* that forged them. That memory was richly positive to the extent that it concerned the efforts of 1789, emblematized by the Declaration of the Rights of Man and Citizen, to build a "responsible society," an objective Christians hold dear today. Even in this relatively felicitous moment, however, many acts and words were "unjust" and too many protagonists ceded to the temptation to "sacralize" and to "absolutize" their ideological engagement while peremptorily impugning their adversaries. Because the "positive" part of the legacy, over the long run, has shaped the development of France far more decisively than the negative, and has helped make the nation a universal model, this should be the focus of the church's bicentennial regard.

Significantly, the bishops evinced no interest in collaborating directly with the commemoration projects of the state, or of civil society. Instead they committed the church to a single moment of institutional involvement, a service to be held at the beginning of the bicentennial summer at Notre-Dame de Paris specifically to mark the transformation of the Estates General into the National Assembly, a process by which "a people expressed their consent to live together" and in which many clerics actively participated. To the extent that memory was a seamless aggregate, the Revolution had to be experienced or remembered as a bloc. To the extent that it was not fruitful to become mired in controversy, the bishops would "commemorate"— the episcopal declaration employed this term—in a highly selective manner. But as a gage proferred to those who wanted to privilege the "failures, errors, crimes," they suggested that they would not forget anything while at the same time, by Christian duty, refusing "any resentment" and seeking divine pardon for everyone.[4]

More than thirty bishops joined the French primate, Albert Cardinal Decourtray, at Notre-Dame on 20 June 1989, the anniversary of the day that the majority of the clergy joined ranks with the Third Estate to inaugurate together a new era in French history. By their tone and their discourse, the bishops demonstrated that they were not ready to open a new era in the relations between the church and the Revolution. In some ways they were even more guarded than they had been at Lourdes. The aim of the ceremony was now cast in more diffuse and evasive terms: a mass "for justice and peace destined to commemorate in prayer the last two centuries of the history of France." Instead of consciously marking the advent of modern democratic society, in this piously vague formulation the bishops obfuscated the profound political significance of the event.

Jean-Marie Cardinal Lustiger had warned in advance that the mass should not be construed as a "celebration" of the Revolution, or even part of it. If the church could discern traces of "evangelical values" in the achievements of the halcyon days of enthusiasm and hope, its attention, even on the anniversary of 1789, turned inexorably to the "countless victims" of the Terror. A defensive chord pervaded Decourtray's homily. Following the lead of his Parisian counterpart, who renounced "commemorate" [*commémorer*] in favor of the prudentially Fauriste "recall" [*remémorer*], the archbishop of Lyon excavated the somewhat arcane affectation "commémoraison," "oraison" being the French word for prayer—transparent to clerics perhaps, but obscure to the faithful and pregnant with another kind of meaning to the skeptical. Looking both left and right, he urged his hearers not to read into the service "a provocation" of any sort, the exhortation betraying the magnitude of his anxiety, and perhaps producing the effect he sought to avoid.

About the origins of the Revolution, and the question of the church's responsibility as partner, beneficiary, and protector of absolutism, Decourtray had nothing to say. He readily allowed that the Revolution began propitiously, its as yet unentailed contingency (if not innocence) symbolized (if not guaranteed) by the grand procession of the Holy Sacrament that accompanied the opening of the Estates General in May. Yet if the primate made the crucial distinction between 1789 and the ensuing years, the unforeseeable "horrors" he presently evoked dramatically undercut the early accomplishments. The detestable Civil Constitution of the

Clergy, the violent abolition of the monarchy, the persecutions and executions, and the cult of reason that defiled the very cathedral from which he spoke seemed to tip the balance far in the other direction. Manifesting no hint of sympathy for the juring clergy whose profound fidelity to Christian values many church liberals have recently stressed, Decourtray hailed the martyrs who refused to allow the Catholic voice to be muzzled and who preferred death to the idolatry erected into the unique measure of Revolutionary purity. The right of God for which they fought was also a right of man.

Without specifying which rights might be covered by this double covenant, the president of the episcopal conference suggested that the Declaration bore the mark of "the spiritual victory of Christ" even as it simultaneously reflected a rationalism sharply hostile to revealed religion. He contended that it sealed the inseparability if not precisely the oneness of the rights of man and those of Providence. The cardinal called upon Frenchmen to love their country and be good citizens as Christ prescribed. But he clearly demarcated the limits of civic fidelity—limits which seemed to reproduce the frontier between the (ephemerally) good and the (predominantly) bad Revolution—by enjoining Catholics "never to let themselves be subjugated by the power in place or led by ideologies in fashion."

Reactions to the church's bicentennial gesture were predictably mixed. *Figaro-Magazine* and *Rivarol* were much happier with it than *La Croix* or *Libération*. In an op-ed piece for *Le Monde,* the Jesuit Paul Valadier regretted the church's extreme timorousness, which he attributed largely to "the pressure of the tradionalists, whose influence has remained ever steadfast in the Church of France." Dominique Julia, a Catholic historian on the left, echoed and enlarged this critique. Motivated by such strategic needs as maintaining episcopal unity and churchly distance from the state, the episcopal bicentennial was at bottom

> an act of piety that aims to mask a rift. But is not this rift first of all internal to Catholicism itself before becoming a division of the nation? One may wonder whether indeed . . . the care taken to develop a purely "spiritual" reading of the event does not lead to casting into the dark conflicts and dissolution within the church itself as well as the long history of the church's rejection during the nineteenth century of that which was making the "modern" world.[5]

The Middle: Fluid and Agonizing

Before and after the official church ceremonies, debate among Catholics concerning the Revolution and its commemoration remained brisk. The most commonly expressed opinion mirrored (and perhaps shaped as much as it reflected) the institutional line. It was a more or less centrist position that covered a wide range of ideological space and bespoke a serious malaise vis-à-vis issues acknowledged to be legitimately contentious and difficult. The agonizing made ostensibly small matters loom large. Thus René Rémond reassures the tremulous that commemoration "is not necessarily a celebration" while another Catholic commentator insists that "whoever says commemoration says public celebration of an anniversary."

If their posture was equivocal, self-styled "liberal" Catholics maintained it was because the Revolutionary heritage was itself "profoundly ambiguous." They articulated their view in a way that hardly differed (and surely drew solace) from François Furet's: "The fundamental ambiguity of our Revolution issues from the fact that it contains simultaneously the makings of a modern state founded on the rule of law and the makings of a regime of Terror." The dilemma is heightened by the fact that "from the beginning, the best was burdened by the worst." The only solution, contended *France catholique,* was to "shoulder" both the lofty and the somber, to "reflect" rather than to "celebrate." But as the veteran Catholic commentator Etienne Borne remarked, "the terrifying infidelity of the Revolution to its own principles" made it difficult to take heart in "the lovely moments." One's critical spirit—not merely one's tropistic fideism—worked against a rehabilitation of the Revolution.[6]

A middling position, then, was not intellectually or morally easy to attain, these centrists avowed, some, in particular the prelates, more emphatically than others. The bishop of Poitiers, Joseph Rozier, solemnly warned enthusiasts that "in the work of the Revolution everything does not deserve the same exaltation, even in behalf of the bicentennial." Yet fidelity to the deeper past and the unchartable future called for a positive approach. Given the fact that the Revolutionary trinity bespoke values that took root far earlier than 1789, in Christian soil, and would continue to flourish long after 1989, Rozier was ready "to *celebrate* the moment when the aspirations called 'liberty, equality, fraternity' began to be translated into political reality."

Viewed by the faithful as more conservative than his episcopal colleague, Claude Dagens, coadjutor bishop of Poitiers, did not strike a pose geared to make it easy for Catholics, right or left. Intense, quietly charismatic, and deeply learned, this graduate of the Ecole normale supérieure and doctor of both theology and letters, refused to spare believers, or nonbelievers, the burden of working through an extremely complex social, political, and moral experience. Simplistic formulas, of the genre "the Revolution is over," he considered incommensurate with the gravity of the issues that had to be faced. The fact that the bicentennial occurred in a period of "relative serenity" in church-state relations as opposed to the "context of crisis" that had marked earlier anniversaries augured positively for the requisite task of reflection.

Dagens noted that Catholics today were very much different from their centennial forebears. The Counterrevolution no longer framed and pervaded their cognitive universe. They lived in a "pluralistic, splintered, uncertain society." To be sure, the counterrevolutionary tradition persisted and in some quarters flourished, but it was no longer monolithic and without nuance. Almost symmetrically, the Revolutionary tradition manifested itself in enormous diversity. Between the two traditions there were points of contact today that had not previously existed. Nor was the nascent dialogue strictly an exchange between elements in the two more or less antagonistic camps. Dagens also construed it as an internal dialogue within each Catholic, and perhaps within every person, between "the diverse currents that coexist within each of us." Each French woman and man was "the bearer of a double tradition" that the bishop preferred to label Catholic and laic rather than Revolutionary and counterrevolutionary. The tensions the two currents generated could be profoundly enriching as well as potentially deleterious. In any case, "we must spare a person from having to repudiate himself," even within the church.

How did Msgr. Dagens construe the bicentennial responsibility of the church? It did not seem to him necessary or wise for the church to expect the faithful to express themselves in a single voice: "it is up to each person to make good use of anniversaries." But for "the work of memory" to advance, it was important for Catholics to be lucid—that is, at once tolerant and exigent—in their attitude toward the past and the present. Since Catholics and nonbelievers lived together, it was imperative that they come to know each other better. The bishop reminded them that the church "is no longer to be mixed in with the camp of the defenders of the Old Regime." He intimated that the pope's recognition that the "ideals of the French Revolution" possessed "Christian roots" had acquired quasi-doctrinal status. But neither Catholics nor nonbelievers should be asked to "hide their wounds, . . . otherwise the repressed returns."

Msgr. Dagens invited the faithful to see the Revolution as a purifying "ordeal," as a positive, fruitful force that taught Catholics "new ways to profess [their] faith" in terribly stressful, even agonizing circumstances. Moreover, a willingness to die for one's cause produced martyrs on both sides of the Revolution, each contributing to the foundation of a new society. In spiritual terms, concluded Dagens, the basis for such a new departure is "the pardon extended to executioners, following the example of Jesus." Reconciliation, then, was the historically and religiously mandated message of the bicentennial. But reconciliation was not an exclusively Catholic internal affair, and moderation did not imply a paucity of confessional ardor. Dagens asked that the whole nation "respect us as believers, members of the people of God in the midst of the people of France," and he summoned critics "to renounce definitively the suspicion, uttered in the name of the so-called Enlightenment, that the Catholic faith, received from the apostles, is an alienation of the human spirit."[7]

Staking out the ground of realism and reason, the archbishop of Rennes, Msgr. Jacques Jullien, predicated his argument on an incontrovertible fact that adversaries and partisans of the Revolution had no choice but to acknowledge: it was a turning point in the history of the nation and the world, and it shaped people's lives in myriad ways. In this sense, "whether we like it or not, we are all in a certain sense the sons [of the Revolution]." It was naive to think that we could "ignore" it, or pretend that its anniversary had no significance; or, perhaps worse, honor the Manichaean reflex by taking refuge in the "image d'Epinal," or oversimplified image, that portrayed its significance as exclusively evil. The archbishop demanded of the citizens of his diocese a more serious effort at apprehension and comprehension: the exercise of "a critical memory."

Jullien strained to problematize the Revolution, and its representation, in a balanced fashion. Thus it was not only necessary to face up to the terrible paradox that in three short years the spokesmen for the Revolution's great principles became "executioners," but also to account for "the long allergy of the church to the values of liberty and equality, Christian in their essence." Jullien had the courage to throw down the gauntlet to the *intégristes* by affirming that whatever happened later, the Revolution was not "antireligious at its outset." But what happened later was so chilling and troubling that its very enumeration eddied against the archbishop's educational aspirations: the diocese "does not forget the guillotine or the drownings, the horrors of civil war and repression."[8]

Like Jullien, Bishop Jean-Charles Thomas of Versailles, an extremely conservative diocese, yearned to break out of the crippling procrustean mold that divided France into "two cultural blocs." Like it or not, all French men and women were heirs of the Revolution, bearers of "the best and the worst" of a tumultuous decade that proved to be the "determinate phase" of modern history, legatees of "an immense reform" that produced the basic institutions that continued to govern French life. Neither mindless execration nor encomium would help to explain this complex past. As did his colleague from Rennes, Thomas urged Catholics to seize the occasion to "look at [the Revolution] face to face, without hatred and without fear," in order "to enlighten" and "to analyze." Yet if the bicentennial was a compelling opportunity, it was also "a trap."

The anniversary worried Thomas because of the enormous risk that it would "reactivate the cleavages and large divisions among the French." He sensed that the deepening of understanding which he espoused would inevitably generate, at least in the short term, an intolerable aggravation of tensions. How, for example, could he avoid arousing passions when he subjected the Declaration of the Rights of Man to searching scrutiny? In contravention of his own lucidity, somehow Thomas wanted a "clarification" that would be soothingly "peace making," a soft analysis that would privilege a "transcendence over our resentments" to a genuine grappling with the thorny issues.[9]

Cardinal Decourtray elaborated on his version of the middling position in an interview with *Le Monde*. In light of the "essential ambiguity" of the Revolution, "one can neither reject nor accept everything en bloc." Prepared to court the risk of appearing indecisive—which made him an easy target for sentinels right and left—the primate refused the "all or nothing" game of extremists on both sides who sought to turn the difficult bicentennial issues to partisan advantage. To attain "a true knowledge" of the Revolution required "an open and constructive memory," an approach somewhat more selective and less comparative and rigorous in method than the ideal of "critical memory" proposed by Jullien. As Decourtray conceived it, his memory was probably more important for what it rejected than for what it fostered: it was adamantly "opposed to the memory that cultivates resentment."

Yet resentment was extremely difficult to circumscribe and disarm. It seemed implicit and irresistible in the host of "crimes" that the Revolution committed "in the name of liberty" which "the truth obliged" the cardinal to rehearse. He had in mind crimes that desecrated Notre-Dame in Paris and Saint-Jean in Lyon, but in particular the atrocities that struck "the Christian population of the west, especially in the Vendée," whose interests the church did not want to abandon to the stewardship of the irredentist *intégristes*. Like other centrists, Decourtray posited a potentially good (or positive) Revolution that issued in a heinous Revolution which, in the cardinal's studiedly oblique language, "deformed the initial revolutionary message." Though he left unexplored the genesis of the Revolution, his discussion bespeaks a desire to quarantine that good Revolution, if not appropriate it under churchly auspices.

The cardinal of Lyon denounced "a certain rationalism" as one of the primary engines that drove the Revolution to Terror. Presumably, then, the early message was not tainted with that rationalism, the fruit of the Enlightenment. Was the early Revolution, in some elliptical but important way, the product of underlying evangelical values, consonant with the pope's celebrated identification of Christianity and the Revolutionary/republican trinity at Le Bourget in 1980? In any event, now that the church had "recognized itself" in the Revolution, it was time for the lay community, state and civil society, to acknowledge that rights not founded on transcendent principles were flawed and fragile—at risk of being "disfigured and betrayed"—as they had been so frequently in the past two hundred years, including in very recent time. According to this reasoning, the ball was no longer in the church's court, where it had lingered for an embarrassingly long period of time. To position the church even more decisively on the offensive, where it could breathe fresher, unencumbered air, Decourtray urged that the debate be shifted to a new, more relevant arena.

Following Edgar Faure, the primate contended that the surest ground for national reconciliation lay in the challenge of the future. Like the late president of the bicentennial Mission, the cardinal caressed the impression that the commemoration had been "turned toward the past," a direction that was ultimately sterile and immediately perilous. Instead, the nation should focus on the third millennium in a post-1992 context: "If the commemoration serves to draw up the inventory of the Bastilles that remain to be taken or to contribute to the emergence of new collective values, then it will not have been in vain." Even as the rights of man were inseparable from (and inconceivable without) the rights of God, so, concluded Decourtray, did the European world of the future have to be founded on "the spiritual values"—presumably the updated values of the "initial revolutionary message."[10]

Lustigerism

"God is not conservative," François Cardinal Marty once remarked. But Jean-Marie Lustiger is, more or less in the image of Pope John Paul II. Biographers may be inclined to trace his particular ideological framework to his Jewish roots and his conversion to Catholicism. Within the church, however, conservatism is a highly relative notion. As chaplain to the students at the Sorbonne, Lustiger often seemed to be out of touch with their sensibility. May 1968 found him, as *Le Monde* delightfully put it, "standing up on the brakes." Posted the following year to a parish in the sixteenth arrondissement, he found himself in a strange world where the mass still had a Latin patina, Vatican II had only small purchase, denunciations tinged with anti-Semitism emanated from certain parishioners, and the conservative priest found himself suspected of Communism! That experience did not make him any more hospitable to the social and Third World gospels that had been practiced by his predecessor when he was named ten years later to the bishopric of Orléans. For Lustiger, "it's faith, faith, [and more] faith."

Nor did he conform to the regnant practices when he took the episcopal seat of Paris in 1981. He governed the diocese in an authoritarian manner, enjoyed strained relations with a portion of his clergy, denounced the seminaries for sacrificing the teaching of the faith to the pedagogy of the human sciences, and lobbied for a catechism taught *inside* the public schools. As he fought in every quarter to advance the claims of the church, he anguished over the deepening decadence of modern man, whose intelligence and moral fiber were sapped by television, ambient violence, and attacks on the integrity of life through abortion and genetic engineering. He remained torn between gloom and hope, commented *Le Monde*, "as if there were within him an interminable clash between the image of the cross, which haunts him, and the hope of resurrection."[11]

The most powerful prelate in the French church, Cardinal Lustiger, archbishop of Paris, represented himself as a bicentennial centrist. But he imbued his discourse with a canonical inflection of extreme wariness and misgiving. The press depicted him as extremely uncomfortable with the Revolution/commemoration issue, in part because he was temperamentally uneasy with middle-of-the-road positions. Although convinced, on the one hand, that "evil forces would like to silence Catholics," according to *L'Express*, the archbishop of Paris would have liked, on the other hand, "to be able to remain silent on the question of the Revolution—but on this question alone." At bottom, for him what mattered deeply was less the church's attitude toward the Revolution than the revolutionary legatees' treatment of the church: "When, then, will the republicans finish with their problem vis-à-vis the Catholics?"[12]

Still, Lustiger had no illusions that he could remain on the sidelines. He prepared himself in his characteristically thorough manner, meeting with historians, organizing a study group, reading widely. By demonstrating how far mainstream historiography had come in reassessing and taking its distance from the Revolution and its shibboleths, François Furet gently prodded him to help move the church in an analogously revisionist direction. Lustiger contended that the church's position on the Revolution was both less rigid and less monolithic than often supposed. (There had always been, for instance, a liberal current.) He blamed "aggressive anticlericalism" for delaying the Catholic embrace of the republican heritage, which did not move decisively ahead until after the Second World War. Yet he intimated that however far reconciliation might proceed, there would always be a contrapuntal "Catholic memory."

Constitutive of the Catholic personality, this memory also composed part of the national patrimony. Despite the bicentennial incentive, the cardinal was not prepared to consign the old antagonisms that alimented the Catholic memory to the domain of the archaic, the museum of lost and/or anachronistic causes. On the contrary, they expressed "differences that were still pertinent." There was no question of Lustiger following Decourtray's flight into the future: one had to muster "the courage to look [these differences] in the face." With an ardor that would have pleased Vendéens and traditionalists, the archbishop of Paris disdained the idea that the price of admission to modern democratic society was the abandonment of even a part of the Catholic memory: "Does the republican state consider itself obliged to obliterate this segment of memory and pursue in this way the unification of the nation? Or has it finally become capable of admitting, within the unity of the French nation, the totality of the French people with their historical diversities?" The "recomposition" or, in a more spiritually compelling idiom, the "purification" of the national memory, to which Lustiger attached the highest importance, meant cleansing the memory of the Revolution by rectifying error and incorporating an apparently unexamined, intact, and untouchable—sacred?— Catholic memory. Once anathema to the church, the pluralism in the name of which the cardinal called for this brand of purification was now a matter of institutional survival. How could the left, save in its most obdurately Jacobin incarnation, be unmoved by an appeal based on one's right to difference? Unification and commemoration both passed not through the melting pot but through the proud affirmation of diversity. Did this mean the Revolution en bloc? While Catholics could never accept the Revolution en bloc, the state had to take it on those globalizing terms. To fulfill this "duty," the state had to apologize to the excluded and offended part of the nation, the wounded part, the neglected part. It must retrospectively confess the sins of the originary act, the founding matrix.

This was the minimal condition of commemorative legitimacy, and Lustiger's price for participating: "The legitimate republican authority can and must evoke the successes of the great Revolution in order to take them into account; it must also recognize and regret the excesses and the crimes linked to an event whose political significance is, today, irreversibly established." Like the die-hard revolutionaries, the martyrs were entitled to their due: tit for tat, "this step must be taken in both directions." Only this exchange would render the commemoration "acceptable et fecund."

The people of the faithful can agree to acknowledge in Abbé Grégoire a great figure only if the clergy and the Catholics with whom the constitutional bishop clashed are equally recognized for their share of human, Catholic, and French truth. In order for the commemoration to be a true reconciliation and for it not to be confined to a partially amnesiac consensus, fatally precarious and vain, the memory of these men that the Catholic Church beatified as 'martyrs' more than sixty years ago must also be honored.[13]

In unison with the Le Bourget orientation, Lustiger argued for "the continuity of Christian values in the Revolution." This was not, he insisted, "to venture an eleventh-hour takeover," though this tack suggested that most if not all that was positive and beneficent in the (very early) Revolution bore a Christian pedigree. By rejecting the claim that the Revolution was from its very beginning quintessentially antireligious, the archbishop of Paris distanced himself from the *intégriste* counter-revolutionaries. Yet his estrangement from them, at least in this context, was tantalizingly abbreviated, for the Revolution "quickly became *violently anti-religious.*" How does Lustiger account for this stunning turn of events? Was it unforeseeable, a function of some sort of *dérapage* (as Decourtray and the early Furet suggest)? Or was it always in the cards, a function of the very nature of the Revolution (in line with classical counterrevolutionary doctrine and the more re-cent Furet)?

Lustiger inveighed against the clean "political interpretation" that ascribed the brutalization of the church and its agents to their attachment to the Old Regime. Priests were first assailed and then murdered for their Christianity. There are strong indications that in his view, the accident (or surprise) was that the early Revolution was not immediately antireligious, given the dominant ideology that drove it. For whatever its Christian component, it was not nearly enough to resist the treacherous and toxic strain of the Enlightenment virus. The error and sin of the Enlightenment was the rational pretension to grasp the meaning of life, to proclaim absolute truths without reference to the Absolute, to render reasoning man fully autonomous. (Staunchly defending the Enlightenment project, "relying on the support of human reason," to found a just and progressive society based on universal precepts, Jean-Noël Jeanneney assailed "certain followers of revealed religions who esteem that only they have the right to the Absolute.")

Lustiger considered the Enlightenment, in its overweening arrogance, to be an immense illusion and a fatal usurpation. Paradoxically, by divinizing man, it diminished him, stripped him of his true dignity, and incited him to run amok. The Shoah, very much on the collective bicentennial mind, seemed to echo the Terror as proof of the limits, and the ghastly potential, of reason on its own. Is Lustiger's analysis, asks Dominique Julia, "so removed, then, from the catastrophism of Catholic fundamentalism?"[14]

Cardinal Lustiger asked the advice of François Furet, among other historians, on how a prelate should look at the Revolution two hundred years after the fact. Furet insisted on the futility of pursuing a counterrevolutionary line, but saw no warrant for portraying it as a decidedly good thing. It is not likely that Lustiger needed Furet in order to reach this conclusion. But he shared Furet's horror of the bloated state and the depredations of political voluntarism. Whether it represented an oligarchy or incarnated the people, when the state substituted for God—Lustiger's analogue to Furet's regeneration—it practiced "lying" and "fraud." For the cardinal, totalitarianism began when the state pretended to incarnate the Absolute. Millions of dead bodies across two centuries testified to this mad hubris.[15]

Relentlessly suspicious of the Revolution and unwilling to see it as fully coterminous with the course of modernity, Lustiger tilted the middling position to the right. Yet he was careful to publicize the points on which the church had shown some movement, and to present himself as a tireless man of dialogue. L'Express reported that President Mitterrand himself engaged the archbishop of Paris in a series of secret discussions in July and August 1989 in the hope of moving toward the "national reconciliation" for which the chief of state had publicly appealed. According to the newsweekly, the serious difficulties that the church had recently encountered in the public sphere, quite apart from its bicentennial "embarrassments"—its peremptory "execution" of Martin Scorsese for The Last Temptation of Christ, a film the censors did not even bother to screen, the strident debate over contraception rekindled by the RU 486 pill, the bitter controversy over the Carmelite convent at Auschwitz, the stifling of independent ecclesiastical voices such as that of Jesuit Father Paul Valadier, and the episcopacy's assiduous courtship of the intégristes who had not followed Msgr. Lefebvre out of the church—inclined Lustiger toward some accommodation that would enhance its image. The protagonists allegedly struck a bargain. Mitterrand vigorously reproved and regretted the "persecutions and massacres" that the church had suffered in a major interview published on Bastille Day. In exchange Lustiger attended the ceremony held a day earlier at the Trocadero to commemorate the Declaration of the Rights of Man and Citizen ("Obviously, he's not there by chance").[16]

Perhaps excessively enthralled by its own scoop, L'Express suggested that the two leaders might very well jointly preside over the Pantheonization of the strong-willed Jacobin prelate-reformer Abbé Grégoire. In an earlier interview published by Le Débat, Lustiger had hinted fuzzily that Grégoire might prove to be a totem of state-church symbiosis. Subsequently, having calculated that the internal cost of its participation was prohibitive, the church, with Lustiger in the lead, turned its back on Grégoire—and on Mitterrand. By the end of the year, Lustiger himself, perhaps merely reverting to type, sounded increasingly pessimistic. The bicentennial may very well have been a unique opportunity for the task of recomposing the national memory. But the commemoration so heightened the horrors of the Revolution, which constituted en bloc so abominable a memory, that it inhibited this work, as much the work of conscience as of science. Ironically, the cardinal concluded that it would not be possible to fulfill the mission of the bicentennial until the bicentennial was over and filed away. Rapidly reburied without a religious ceremony, the corpse would have to wait patiently for the results of an autopsy that could take years to complete.[17]

The Mother Church and the Mother of Revolutions

If the Revolution were a purely national/domestic affair, objectified in and confined to a single event that occurred long ago, it might have been easier for the church to deal with the bicentennial. But the Revolution proclaimed itself the mother of all revolutions, and during the two hundred years that followed its eruption, it served countless times as inspiration if not paradigm for violent upheavals and profound mutations. Whatever small concessions the Church of France might make to *its* 1789, on the generic issue of revolution the church's position remained adamantine. Though Pierre Eyt, archbishop of Bordeaux, took pains to argue recently that the church opposed revolution not from a conservative but from a socially progressive position, it nevertheless feared and reviled recourse to turbulent insurrection. From its earliest encounter with sociopolitical revolution, the church associated it with "pagan violence," in contrast to the "revolution of the gospel" that is Christ's example and love. The church felt even more deeply threatened by the virtual confiscation of the concept and dream of revolution by Marxist ideology, an ideology predicated on the idea of class struggle as the motor of history; this was simply another form of systematic violence in the ecclesiastical purview.

Sacralized and then scientized, revolution pretended to achieve man's regeneration according to an earthbound eschatology that rejected the potency and necessity of God's grace. "In the name of Christ the liberator and the redeemer, in the name of a witness and an action in favor of other paths of social change," the church rejected both the "demonic reality" and the "globalizing and simplifying myth" of revolution. This deeply anchored analysis made it very difficult cognitively to separate revolution from the Revolution. How could the church endorse an interpretation of exceptionalism so radically out of step with its worldview? The latter powerfully favored the counterrevolutionary posture, historicized into a long-run perspective. This made the middling position harder to reach and defend. Indeed, in many cases the centrist discourse seems to be informed by the fiction that the Revolution was sui generis, and could be treated as such, disconnected from its partly unwilled posterity.[18]

The Temperate Right

Within the Catholic bicentennial compass, some on the right took their cue in part from the doctrine of the generic defect of revolution. On the one hand, these Catholics found the middling position too foreign, too parlous, too much at odds with their instincts and their instruction. On the other, they saw themselves as reasonable and moderate, and were allergic to the excesses of the hard-core traditionalist refuseniks. This stance required some intellectual acrobatics: for example,

Maurice Schumann's strained appropriation of the *Syllabus* (1864) for the liberal camp. An elder statesman and academician, Schumann contended that this document, perhaps the Vatican's most important codification of counterrevolutionary dogma, was not a condemnation of liberty but "of the excesses of freedom or of freedom left to itself, of freedom gone mad." A writer in *Le Figaro* tried similarly to stake out liberal ground for a moderate Catholic right, portraying Pius VI, a reputed reactionary, as a clairvoyant political analyst who clearly saw the totalitarian implications of the Civil Constitution and the state sacralized as absolute.

Certain Catholics in this category seemed less concerned with theology and history than with the immediate political lessons thrust into relief by the bicentennial. Even as the insurgency of the students in Tiananmen Square moved them, they were repulsed by the quasi-ubiquitous specter of the guillotine, whose presence, *grandeur nature,* in numerous local celebrations, reminded them of the depth of their horror. Thus the syllogistic amalgamation that assimilated First Republic Jacobins to Fifth Republic Socialists; those who refused the death penalty for rape of children and recidivist killers (Socialists) to practitioners and apologists of the Revolutionary guillotine (Jacobins); and fans of the guillotine (bicentennialists) to Chinese repressors.[19]

The Hard Right

The right-wing Catholic bicentennial position was frankly, stridently, exuberantly occupied by the *intégristes,* not only those who followed Msgr. Lefebvre out of the Roman church but those who remained within its orthodox midst. The *intégristes* lived in a strangely intimate relationship with the Revolution. If the latter did not quite beget *intégrisme,* it nevertheless imparted to it its particular form and tone. Emerging, crystallized, from the revolutionary experience, vis-à-vis which they defined themselves, the *intégristes* were understandably keenly interested in the bicentennial. As the sole trustee of the exclusive truth, the church had nothing to learn from the world, no need for aggiornamento or rejuvenation. It is in this sense that René Rémond views *intégrisme* as "the refusal of history," still wedded to steadfast Maistrean dogma.[20]

Yet the *intégristes* historicized their Other, their diabolical enemy, for the Revolution grew out of a multi-secular campaign to destroy religion and it issued in two hundred years of accelerating decadence and tragedy. The Revolution was no less alive today than it had been in 1789/93. "The Revolution has entered the church," the schismatic Msgr. Lefebvre observed with disgust. "We are still in the Revolution; we are still subject to its influence," affirmed Saint-Nicolas du Chardonnet's Abbé Philippe Lauguérie, a priest with close ties to Lefebvre. More orthodox traditionalists shared this perspective, though they did not necessarily agree that the way out—if there was any exit—was through "restoring the church." The Abbé Julien Bacon, an editorial writer for a traditionalist review that sympathized with Lefebvre's lifelong mission but criticized his departure from the church, noted bitterly that after two hundred years, "it is still the spirit of '89 that reigns," and argued that the R/revolutionary onslaught continued today: "thus the school, the family, life itself is attacked; moral doctrine disappears, replaced by the law."

For Lauguérie, the Revolution was in the church as well as the world. The perfect society had fallen prey to the devil: "Vatican II, that's '89 in the church." For the less extreme traditionalists, it was almost as bad: though not yet overrun, the church was besieged. The *intégristes* were reluctant to acknowledge any discontinuity between sacred and profane preoccupations. For them more than for other Catholics, the bicentennial implied a struggle on all fronts, an all-azimuth war. Lauguérie's vision was theocratic—in some ways redolent of a certain Jacobin discourse in Year II: "The state must not be neutral."[21]

A violent, sustained mutiny against God's plan, the Revolution, as the right-wing Catholic writer Jean Madiran put it, "cast original sin into the plural." To the extent that Adam ventured to make his own law against the law of God, he was the ancestor of the rights-of-man renegades, and the ultimate author of the "diabolical consequences" that have accumulated ever since, a capital of perfidy and ruin replenished by compound interest.[22] The rhetoric of catastrophism, the signature refrain of *intégrisme* from its infancy, took on a more studied, concrete specificity during the bicentennial, thanks in part to the nagging polemics of Pierre Chaunu and the exaltation of René Sédillot's single-minded reductionist pastiche *Le Coût de la Révolution française*. Thus France, a flourishing eighteenth-century superpower with a hegemonic culture, a vibrant demography, and an innovative and productive economy, was drastically, irreversibly destabilized by the Revolution.

Apart from the sacrilege a celebration of the Revolution implied, Abbé Bacon marveled at the inappropriateness of glorifying "the greatest catastrophe in our history." Bacon ascribed this perversity partly to a masochistic penchant in the national character. But it was equally the fruit of two hundred years of state-sponsored mystification and mythicization of the Revolution that ineluctably corrupted the understanding even of right-thinking Catholics. Ernest Lavisse along with Isaac and Malet was responsible for forging "a truncated history." If the "first genocide" went unrecognized for so long it was because of the profusion of "lies" that constituted the official cover-up.

For Catholic fundamentalists, Georges Clemenceau seems to have been the only public figure to utter a single truth about the Revolution: that it was a "bloc." Their commentators hammered the point that the Revolution was a seamless web, that it was "fundamentally antireligious if not anti-Catholic" from its earliest moment, and that it contained the seeds of its worst horrors from the moment it took root. "Thus '89 had to beget '93," remarked Bacon, scoffing at the idea of *dérapage*, "it was in the logic of things, it could not unfold any other way." Certain orthodox *intégristes* did not dismiss out of hand the once liberal/iconoclastic, now quasi-official thesis that the Revolution had "Christian roots." But they viewed them as "remote origins," linked to the notion of liberation through Christ. Heretical in every way, the Revolution took place outside this Christian framework, which would have endowed it with a radically different destiny.

Hard-liners such as Jean Dumont and Romain Marie saw the shared-Christian-causality line as part of an enterprise of so-called reconciliation ("very close to a capitulation") engineered by "modernist" clerics such as Abbé Plongeron, a highly regarded professional historian of the Revolution, who shamelessly labored to "heap praise on the constitutional priests," and the bishop of Cambrai, who appeared on television alongside Jeanneney to hail the church's betrothal to the Revolution. The Revolution stood the world on its head, wrote Abbé Bacon, and the carnivalization spilled over into today's world. For the real *intégristes*, in the pejorative sense of the term that the enemies of religion have cultivated to discredit true believers, were the Jacobins and their descendants. They were the real "fanatics," practitioners of a dangerous system of democratic laicity that sought quixotically to found "a new man . . . without theistic religious reference." For Catholic fundamentalists the bicentennial was the celebration of the R/revolutionary *intégrisme* with which they were locked in a life-or-death struggle.[23]

The Catholics Who Tender a Hand

On the other side of the church's ideological universe were Catholics who, for various reasons, welcomed the bicentennial. They are more difficult to evoke than the *intégristes* because they are more heterogeneous, they have fewer translocal institutional poles of action and sociability, and they disagree about many matters, spiritual and profane. One is tempted to baptize them "left" in contradistinction to the decidedly right wing of traditionalism, but this label unfairly blends and stereotypes them. These Catholics ranged in opinion from those who were virtually enthusiastic about the Revolution and its anniversary to those who merely felt that it was right, salutary, and opportune to associate the church with the bicentennial commemoration.

The first posture is embodied, in its extreme, by the bishop of Evreux, Jacques Gaillot, a marginal but vocal figure in the episcopacy notorious for his "progressive" record of resistance to church policy. Stigmatized the "Red bishop" by the Lepéniste newsweekly *National hebdo*, Gaillot earned the title by denouncing the ideas of the Front national as "incompatible with the Gospel," boycotting the massive church-sponsored demonstrations of the spring of 1984 in favor of parochial school education on the grounds that they were political in character, warmly supporting homosexual causes, espousing the ordination of married men and the use of prophylactics, and approving Scorsese's *Last Temptation of Christ*, among other impieties. It is easy to imagine that the church would have preferred to see him during the bicentennial in one of the Third World countries he liked to frequent. Instead he was in the spotlight, alongside the anarcho-Socialist singer-poet Renaud at the concert and march protesting Mitterrand's Northocentrist neglect of the world's Third Estate in the South or at a grassroots festivity marking the Revolution's achievements (as well as its inadequacies).

For Gaillot the French Revolution was "the most important [event] since Jesus Christ." The church was not prepared for the seismic shock. "It was not a simple matter to admit democracy, laicity, freedom of conscience," noted the prelate, with jolting understatement. While the church suffered enormously, "it was liberated." The church has not yet come to grips with the significance of that liberation. The bicentennial was a real chance that must to be seized: "[The church] must not refuse to deal with it, but must define the role it wants to play, its place in a state that is laic, pluralistic, and democratic."

Good citizenship and good Catholicism went hand in hand for Gaillot. Both required social as well as spiritual commitment. Thus, he told the *Nouvel Observateur,* "To commemorate the Revolution, for me, is not sufficient. It must be continued, and not folklorized. It is not tolerable to allow the gap between rich and poor to get wider and deeper." Like Decourtray, with a different and more militant Third Estate, Third World agenda, Gaillot proclaimed that "there are still Bastilles to be taken." And if, like the *intégristes,* he was repelled by "the pomp of the official ceremonies of the bicentennial," it was not because they honored the Revolution but because they betrayed it.

The fact that there were vociferous clerics manifestly to the left of the bishop of Evreux did not console the church hierarchy. Joseph Comblin, a Belgian priest based in Latin America, discerned little to celebrate in a Revolution made by and for the bourgeoisie. Democracy and the rights of man would remain cruel "fictions" unless the Revolution was revived and radicalized to bring justice to the mass of people, victims of the capitalist system codified by the men of 1789.[24]

Other voices, Christian and civic, characteristically unburdened by the weight of protracted dissidence, called on the church to abandon its "vengeful narcissism" and come to grips with the Revolution. The veteran scholar of the Revolution Abbé Plongeron was not a man of the left, either in the church or in the commissions of the Centre national de la recherche scientifique where he has sat. His fervent Gallicanism probably explains his enthusiasm for Abbé Grégoire and his nuanced attitude toward the Civil Constitution of the Clergy. This Gallicanism along with his intimate knowledge of the Revolutionary period impelled him urge Catholics to reject the reductionist minefield of fideist historiography. The Revolution was not a "bloc." There was no evidence of a "satanic intelligence" distilled in the Enlightenment and culminating in a coherent Revolutionary policy on religion. The Revolution was an inordinately complex event that required critical scrutiny rather than sweeping animadversion. It was time for the church to move beyond a mechanistic exaltation of its martyrs, which delivered an unmistakable, negative political message, to a full-fledged effort of "reconciliation between the Gospel and the Revolution."[25]

Another scholar, Jean Marensin, made the case that from the vantage point of Pope Pius VI, "the Revolution was not a bloc." The pope did not question the legitimacy of the National Assembly's powers and he did not take action against the Revolution until the promulgation of the Civil Constitution, which, Marensin insists, did not emerge necessarily and logically from the principles of '89. To which Dominique Julia adds, in an effort to mitigate the onus of the juring clergy, that the two papal briefs condemning the Constitution did not begin to be known in France until April-May 1791—thus after the bulk of the priestly oaths had been taken.

It is in this spirit that the Jesuit Paul Valadier, recently deposed as editor of *Etudes*, asked the church fathers to undertake a "positive rehabilitation of *all* the sons of the church carried off by the revolutionary torment." In his view, the example of the Grégoires—who were not unfaithful to the church, who wanted to invent a new relation between church and society, and who worked for "a poorer church, [a church] with a freer hand to deal with the [various] despotisms"—was more relevant to the concerns of Catholics today than the views of those honored with the title of martyr. "I am delighted that the bicentennial is to be celebrated," commented Father Max Clouet, secretary-general of L'Enseignement catholique. It was time to overcome "certain sterile quarrels" concerning church-state relations that have needlessly poisoned the atmosphere. Catholics, beginning with school-children and their teachers, must learn that the Revolution was not undertaken against the church. If on the one hand one cannot deny the Terror, "on the other one can no longer place in doubt the integrity of the initial revolutionary ideas."[26]

The moderate Catholic popular press and one major Catholic organization echoed these views. Unequivocally repudiating the satanic anchor of the traditionalist historiographical vessel, Pierre Pierrard, writing in *La Croix*, summoned the church to "take the stand to associate itself, lucidly and courageously, with the bicentennial ceremonies." "The Christians of France," observed another journalist in the same paper, "today wonder by what aberration it should have taken so many years to recognize that these three words [liberty, equality, fraternity] participate in the ideal that they have claimed as their own for the last two thousand years." In *Témoignage chrétien*, Roger Tréfon evoked those Catholics who believed that "the Revolution of 1789 remains still to be done over," following the Colluchean axiom: "the problem is that certain people are more equal than others." Discontent with the church hierarchy "paralyzed by its traditonalist wing," the Mouvement rural de la jeunesse chrétienne—ten thousand strong for its Estates General held at Nantes in July 1989—openly embraced the celebration of the bicentennial. They looked at the Revolution "positively" because it addressed their interests on both the universal and corporatist levels: first "its human and social achievements, the liberation of mankind, so dear to Abbé Grégoire," and then the fact that "for the first time it gave the peasant the right to speak out."[27]

A No-Win Situation for the Church?

In the end, though the debate may have been healthy and cathartic, the church hierarchy's handling of the bicentennial satisfied hardly anyone. The fact that two public figures as different (and as rhetorically gifted) as Jean-Noël Jeanneney and François Brigneau mercilessly pressed the episcopacy to take a strong and unequivocal position made such an outcome virtually impossible. Reputed and admired for his cool, muted style, on this issue Jeanneney evinced passionate feelings. As a historian he was intimately familiar with the church's long and bitter war against the Revolutionary legacy and the mixed feelings with which it finally embraced the republic, the separation of church and state, and the culture of laicity. As a citizen politically engaged on the left, he regarded the church's position as a kind of subversion that did not serve the commonweal, and as ideologically gratuitous and obsolescent within the confines of the church's own conciliar evolution. To the extent that the internal affairs of the church had an effect on the public sphere, in particular on the functioning of democratic society, the president of the bicentennial Mission felt authorized to address them. ("As a person exercising a public office, I consider that it has not been our business, since 1905, to involve ourselves in the decisions of the Catholic Church[;] but there is in this instance, for the sake of our understanding of today's society, for the sake of reflection on its moral sensibility, there is here an object of analysis that merits our full attention.")

Jeanneney missed no opportunity, from the Mission bully pulpit, to challenge the church to make the right choice: to recognize the positive contributions of the Revolution (without abjuring its wounded memory) and to join with state and society in commemoration of the seminal Revolutionary moment. He chided the bishops for their timidity. The Lourdes declaration was "vague," albeit conciliatory, in tone—"more conservative than dynamic." Though Jeanneney himself took the right-wing fringe very seriously, he scolded the church fathers for their myopic preoccupation with the most vehement *intégristes*. "By its malaise, its silence, its absence," the church would broadcast the impression that it subscribed to the traditionalist cause. Did the church fear that the bicentennial would oblige it to deepen its internal debate not only on the way it should see the world but on how it should govern itself?

While old reflexes persisted in many quarters, Jeanneney did not want to allow the Catholic leaders to forget how far the church had come since the days of a hegemonic satanic exegesis. Yet he himself seemed to harbor doubts about how much fundamental difference this progressive turn could be expected to make. Profoundly tolerant by temperament and conviction, the Mission leader nevertheless wondered aloud about the compatibility of "a revealed religion, persuaded to have the truth," and the exigencies of liberty of conscience, indeed of liberty *itself*. Was the ex-archbishop of Dakar, Msgr. Lefebvre, the only prelate who believed that "only the truth has rights, error has no rights at all, that is the teaching of the church"? "At the very moment that the affairs of Martin Scorsese's *Last Temptation of Christ* and Salman Rushdie's *Satanic Verses* move [public] opinion," commented Jeanneney's monthly *Lettre*, it was incumbent on all persons of good will to think about the republican roots and the sanctity of liberty of expression. Khomeini and Lustiger dispatched in the same sack?

The Pantheonization of Grégoire offered the church a last bicentennial chance to redeem itself for what the Mission regarded as its failure of nerve. Jeanneney exhorted Lustiger to join in the ceremonies "in order to testify that the Revolution was—and remains—a source of moral and civic liberation." The church's refusal to participate disappointed and perhaps even angered Jeanneney. From its reiterative "reticences," expressed with particular "vivacity" by the archbishop of Paris, he drew the lesson again that the French Revolution was by no means over, that the putative "cold heritage" still burned to the quick.

Etienne Borne's mordant riposte to Jeanneney's critique sought to put the Mission leader on the moral and intellectual defensive. What was "astonishing" was not Catholic hesitation to embrace fully the Revolution but the absence, on the part of the official commemorators, of "a symmetrical hesitation to embrace fully the whole Revolution." Borne invoked Jeanneney's hero, Grégoire, to make the point that "the problem is posed in exactly the same terms for the Christian memory and for the republican memory: there is in the Revolution [both] the worst and the best." Taking leave of his flock in the Loir-et-Cher, the abbé/constitutional bishop noted sadly that "The National Convention, majestic when it founded the republic, abandoned its scepter to the hands of crime." Still, as judicious a Catholic commentator as Dominique Julia offered Jeanneney indirect comfort by questioning whether "the intellectual system proposed [by the church leaders] to interpret the Revolution" had changed at all.[28]

The Catholic far right, in the person of François Brigneau, judged the "silence" of the church to be as "striking" as did Jeanneney. "Everyone is talking about nothing but that [the bicentennial] . . . everyone, that is, except the Church of France." Hesitations, tergiversations, placatory gestures satisfied the animator of *L'Anti-89* no more than they had the president of the Mission. Brigneau waged a vigorous campaign to shame the church into taking the right position: anathematization of the Revolution as the diabolical source of the world's ills. Brigneau's organ interpellated bishop after bishop on "the reasons for their silence . . . for this scandalous silence." How could the church be faithful to itself and fulfill its mission without loudly denouncing the horrors, the ineffable barbarities of the Revolution, in its principles and in its acts? "It's a pretty balance sheet. But who remembers [it]? What bishop? Msgr. Decourtray, who shows himself so horrified by the positions taken by Jean-Marie Le Pen defending Catholic France against the invasion of Islam, did not utter a word, not so much to condemn as to ask a bit of moderation and decency of those who wish to be the heirs of the Grand Ancestors, slaughterers of the Carmelites and drowners of the priests of Nantes."[29]

Despite their extravagance, and their now marginal position in Catholicism, the Anti-89ers and other *intégristes* had strong spiritual claims on the church. To make this case, they had as unlikely an advocate as Dominique Julia, who solemnly enjoined kindred left-liberal spirits not to "ignore this victim-focused dimension which puts the emphasis on persecution and martyrdom" because "it is an integral part of a religion that is founded on the memorial of the original sacrifice of Christ." Another Catholic intellectual, the Jesuit Jean-Yves Calvez, urged the hierarchy and its traditionalist critics to enter into a dialogue of reconciliation based on a frank, dispassionate discussion of the Revolution: "Their unity as a church remains precarious as long as such questions are [considered] so burning that one prefers to avoid them."

The bishop of Versailles, hardly a radical, implored the *intégristes* to reread and rethink the Revolutionary experience: "To decide to make this effort is not tantamount to the beginnings of a betrayal of the rights of God: I believe, rather, that our Unique Lord and Master Jesus summons us to do so through the whole of his Gospel and especially his Beatitudes and his commandment of universal love." Yet the envenomed climate of the bicentennial did not prove to be an auspicious opening for exchange mediated by unfettered love.[30]

The Presidential Mode
of Commemoration

F or historical, political, and symbolic reasons, François Mitterrand cared deeply about the bicentennial. Frustrated in his early attempt to mount a grandiose celebration in the guise of a world's fair, he had reacted by somewhat petulantly distancing himself from the commemorative horizon.[1] Preoccupied shortly after with the traumatizing shift to austerity, and subsequently with the experiment in governmental cohabitation, the president appears not to have truly reembraced the bicentennial project until the middle of 1987, perhaps in anticipation of his decision to run for a second term.[2]

Mitterrand and the Bicentennial:
From a Destiny to a Strategy

Foreseeing an irresistible story, the press announced that 14 July 1989 would mark "the apogee" of Mitterrand's "brilliant and long career." For political analyst Alain Duhamel, writing in *Le Point*, Mitterrand's reluctance to "leave to anyone else the embodiment of the republic on that day" had significantly influenced his decision to stand for the presidency a fourth time in 1988. Given his fascination for and knowledge of the Revolution, his intellectual capacity to venture a global reading of its impact, and his taste for "grand, epic frescoes," Duhamel predicted that Mitterrand would monopolize the stage on the fourteenth in order to "intone the greatest speech of his life."[3]

The president proved to be shrewder still, and less clumsily vain, than the commentator imagined. He wisely avoided the trap of administering a world-historical lesson on world-wide television. But throughout the bicentennial year he manifested his passion for the Revolution and his revivified commitment to commemoration. While he made important concessions to diverse camps during the year, at bottom he continued to gravitate between Jaurès's social rationalism and Michelet's social romanticism.

Mitterrand's personal bicentennial strategy was to intervene infrequently but potently. He made remarkably few public speeches and he gave only a handful of interviews. He forged several parallel discourses—or perhaps it would be fairer to say a capacious discourse with several inflections and emphases—that were geared to appeal to different clienteles and/or constituents. Surely he was conscious of the ambiguities he projected, and he exploited the room for maneuver that they accorded him. Thus, on the one hand, he stressed a Furetian line of reconciliation around principles that virtually everyone had come to espouse. On the other hand, his most important address of the year, at the Tennis Court Oath commemoration in June, seemed to herald a resurgence of left-republican Revolutionary ardor.[4]

Mitterrand did not spend a great deal of time justifying the commemorative gesture: the rationale and the imperative seemed self-evident in his mind. In January at the Sorbonne and in June at the Tennis Court, he warned that "a people without a memory is no longer a free people." Obliviousness was tantamount to civic abdication: "a republic that forgets its origins will not be long in repudiating them." Memory was a powerful preventive of tyranny, for it fostered a comparative and critical perspective and served as a permanent baseline marker of dreams and of reality against which to measure everything that ensued. It was no accident, Mitterrand observed, that "dictators begin by wiping out the history of the facts that encumber them, by barring access to the past, and, believing themselves masters of the avenues to the future, [that they] muzzle any mutinous thoughts or words." This Orwellian specter was not foreign to the French experience, in the nineteenth or the twentieth centuries, Mitterrand suggested, betraying his own commitment to Jaurès's, and more recently Maurice Agulhon's, intensely republican brand of memory: "Remember. Each time that one tried to blur the mark of the Revolution here in France, our liberties were threatened." Possessed of a double vocation, lyric and pragmatic, memory crafted and reinforced bonds, it integrated, and it exalted.

The real focus of memory was the future, not the past. Citing Hugo, Mitterrand said: "To celebrate great anniversaries is to prepare for great events." Memory was a leaven kneaded into the living substance in order to energize and renew it, to expand, to open its eyes to fresh ways of viewing yesterday, today, and tomorrow. "To commemorate," promised the president, "is to rejuvenate." One's relation to the past is always complicated. One should not try to reduce memory to a simple prescription for action or an enumeration of unpaid debts and unfulfilled pledges. Yet the past had to explain to us something about our trajectory, about the embattled origins of the vision that still sustained the nation. "We do not ask the France of 1789 to hold up to us a mirror, but we ask it to remind us from what dreams, from what combats, from what joys did contemporary France emerge, [and] on what values was the republic which is ours founded."[5]

The Presidential Doctrine of *Ni-Ni*

Once Mitterrand articulated the argument in favor of commemoration in general and commemoration of the Revolution in particular, could there be any doubt about the tone he would wish to impart to the anniversary of 1989? Certainly not in the minds of his political adversaries, who began to pillory him for sectarianism even before he had made any public declarations regarding his intentions. His speech at the Sorbonne, on the eve of the presidential election campaign, gave some credence to this point of view. After all, he did not leave much room for honorable dissent when he argued that "to put the Revolution on trial" was very often "the authorized form for putting democracy in the dock. Disdain for the former contributes, sooner or later, we can be sure of it, to contempt for the latter."

Yet Mitterrand's official commemorative doctrine was a paean to prudence, a variation of the famous nationalization-privatization *ni-ni,* or neither-nor—"neither anathema nor approving liturgy." This public pronouncement seemed to confirm what he had told numerous interlocutors in private: that he did not want a "hard bicentennial," a sulfurous and partisan festival which could only discredit the commemorators and the event they commemorated. Rather than shocking or offending public opinion, the president wanted to (re)educate it—surely an apposite strategy on the eve of the election. Somehow he hoped to use the bicentennial to attenuate instead of exacerbating the "natural divisions of the French." Quite genuinely, Mitterrand groped for a year of broad-based, national *rassemblement.*[6]

If he aimed at a certain moderation, however, Mitterrand never construed the happy medium as a charter for a course of historical and ideological evasiveness. Thus it is hard to believe that Edgar Faure conveyed the president's position faithfully when he told reporters that Mitterrand aimed to "avoid useless polemics concerning whether it was good or bad to undertake the Revolution." Polemics over a question as fundamental as that could hardly be futile for a man as deeply engrossed in history as Mitterrand, for whom, in any case, the Revolution was surely both good and necessary. The president counted more on an appeal to lucidity and a certain balance rather than on an unlikely and factitious consensus.[7]

Mitterrand affirmed categorically that his compatriots could not celebrate the anniversary with a single voice because two hundred years was too short a buffer for wounds to heal fully and for profound differences in view to evaporate ("That the Vendée, which suffered so much—even if it also caused others to suffer—feels on its own in the celebration of the bicentennial is not surprising"). Yet there were realistic grounds for convergence, which the president, perhaps overoptimistically, believed did not require an implausible degree of abstraction or rationalization. "But an immense majority recognizes itself in the Revolution," he reasoned, "because it recognizes itself in the republic, and because the republic is the offspring of the Revolution and of the principles that engendered it: liberty, equality, fraternity, sovereignty of the people."

The logic of this derivation, however, was neither simple nor as evident as the president supposed—unless he merely meant that the bulk of French citizens embraced the Revolution the way Monsieur Jourdain practiced prose, unaware that they were doing so. He himself betrayed some of the difficulty by unselfconsciously turning to Jaurèsian categories—"conservatives and people of progress"—to describe the "vast common domain" that millions of French women and men had somehow managed to acknowledge as joint conquest. To grasp their common patrimony, Mitterrand urged his fellow citizens to look at the Revolution in the long term. (He traced its origins to the lethal reign of Louis XIV and subsequently to the Enlightenment.)

To say the least, the president's program was strained. First, he reiterated, there would be no "veil of mourning" contrived to obscure or exorcise "the historical reality of a period replete with contradictions." Second, we will agree that we may disagree on the interpretation of the Revolution (but not on the validity of the fundamental rights which it restituted to mankind). Third, as if to remove the febrile short-run fluctuations so as to reveal the trend line, we must move beyond the "grave crises," the "civil war," the "bloody and useless acts" in order to apprehend "the general direction of the history of a country." This was a whiggish recipe for using moving averages to elicit progress, a recipe with the vague odor of ends justifying means: "We must decide whether we appreciate what 'after' means in the birth of French democracy and in the establishment of a few simple principles which continue to dwell in those who think that progress by democracy is a reality, even if it was often wrenched from pain, tears, and blood." The common bond was not the Revolution but its heritage—the two were not coterminous, though intimately linked. But Mitterrand knew very well that he could not really separate the two without denying a historicity in which he deeply believed, a dialectic that he had cultivated all his life. His problem was not how to avoid throwing out the baby with the bathwater but how to conserve (most of) the bathwater along with the offspring.[8]

In concrete terms, the president was deeply troubled by the public debate, in the mass media as well as in the more arcane periodicals, which threatened to favor those who doubted or hated the Revolution's accomplishments. At the same time, he was increasingly frustrated by the apparent temporizing and tergiversations of the Faure Mission.[9] The reception he offered in honor of the Mission's scientific committee had, at least momentarily, the makings of a *séance de flagellation:*

We can discuss it. I talked it over with M. Baroin. Edgar Faure kindly came to see me on diverse occasions. I read many articles on this subject. A whole series of debates must not be allowed to strike from memory the essential [fact]: there was a French Revolution beginning in 1789, it had sufficiently momentous consequences that we should not celebrate it, we should not commemorate it as a small local event but as a decisive part of France in the evolution of the world and of human society. That merits, therefore, much attention and much care.

This is the core of the question, the president concluded, in a tone that was both tough and hortatory: "If you don't intend to do that, or if you intend to do the contrary—but that is not your attitude, of course—it would be better for you to change immediately your way of doing things."[10]

On Mitterrand's Bloc

Still, Mitterrand continued to struggle with the aporias of R/revolutionary commemoration. His dilemma was reflected in the somewhat tormented way in which he treated the—partly conceptual but powerfully symbolic—issue of the Revolution as a bloc. Here was another bicentennial trap: commentators of all stripes eagerly waited for the president to ensnare himself. In December 1987 he is said to have fed *Izvestia* what appeared to be the full Clemenceau dish: "one must either take everything or refuse everything"; then, an agonistic gloss on the purchase en bloc: "Must one say, like Clemenceau, 'the Revolution en bloc'? I would be so inclined." But then one would have to accept everything or reject everything, a mercilessly binary divide that did not favor discernment.

Mitterrand proposed an alternative formulation that retained the bloc essence but allowed some latitude for relativizing and evaluating: "Should not one say, rather: the Revolution is a whole, a complex whole, like life itself, where there is, at every instant, in 1789 as in 1795, in the year of the Bastille as in the year of Thermidor, enthusiasm and the unacceptable, hope and fear, elite and crowd, violence and fraternity?" Still, this deep imbrication did not facilitate a genuine sedimentation of the elements: "How can we not distinguish them in our judgment, but how can we separate them in the reality of things?" Finally, Mitterrand effected a shift from the Revolution (all of whose actions, exalting and debasing, he assumed in passing) to its consequences, in a formulation more reminiscent of Edgar Faure than Jean Jaurès: "Without the Revolution, France would not be the country of the Rights of Man; . . . values outlast behavior."

In January of the bicentennial year, on his trip to Bulgaria, Mitterrand gave the bloc an articulation that the political analyst Jean-Claude Casanova hoped was "definitive." The "indissociable bloc" was not the Revolution itself but its heritage, that is to say, an amalgam of national sovereignty, human rights, and democratic practice. "Let us admire the shrewdness of the shift," remarked Casanova, who may have rushed prematurely to judgment, "he retains the word 'bloc' so as not to give the impression that he has recanted, but the formula takes on a meaning precisely opposite to the one in Clemenceau's phrase."[11]

Of course "bloc" meant different things to different interpreters—regardless of what Clemenceau had wanted to suggest. In the context of the bicentennial, it seemed commonly to be reduced to the question of what would be included under the umbrella of memory and celebration. Even as many Socialists seemed to move away from the bloc concept to avoid stigmatization by the Terror, many conservatives insisted on retaining it in order to extract some form of acknowledgment for the depredations committed by the Revolutionaries. To deny the bloc became a double offense, to embrace it a double risk. At about the same time that Mitterrand visited Bulgaria, the *Nouvel Observateur* reported that when asked "if he admired the Revolution 'en bloc' or if he omitted certain episodes," the president replied: "I am rather on the side of the bloc. I have regrets for the second period. There were excesses that I do not approve. But it's a succession of linked events in which nothing can be omitted." In his Tennis Court address, Mitterrand vigorously affirmed this rejection of Mona Ozouf's shopping strategy: "In the collective adventure of 1789, we should not flatten out the harsh relief, cut out that which might displease us, retain only that which fits our needs. We would have nothing to gain in so doing.[12]

But what were the implications of this engagement? Certainly it was not an endorsement of Terror, as certain commentators claimed with respect to Clemenceau. Mitterrand explicitly deplored the "inexcusable excesses," but not without regard for the context, as we shall see. Dominique Julia interpreted Mitterrand's version of the bloc not as a strident reassertion of venerable neo-Jacobin claims but, rather, as a therapeutic innovation because "he rejected any manipulation of the past." The bloc was not all or nothing for the sake of a political line but for the sake of the whole nation, its battered as well as its triumphant components. The president thus moved toward reconciliation, Julia contended, sympathetically, by integrating "the uncommemorable—that is to say, the ripped tissue—into the heart of the commemoration." Once divisive and partisan, the bloc was transmogrified into a national healing elixir.

Deeper into the bicentennial season, Mitterrand slightly modified his rhetoric, but not his posture. "It is not a bloc," said the president concerning the Revolution, in an interview with *L'Express* on 14 July, but "a continuous movement." It was marked by harsh combats at home and abroad, and by inordinate passions on all sides. The appraisal had to be equilibrated. If on the one hand "one cannot present as exemplary men who let themslves go to needless violence"—all violence was not of the same moral significance for Mitterrand—on the other hand "we must also understand the logic of the situations." In the last analysis what mattered was the overwhelmingly redemptive end: "And to think that the French Revolution changed the face of the globe." Mitterrand embroidered on the same theme at the Arche de la Défense in late August. The Revolution had to be assumed in its globality; the horrors of the Revolution must not cause us to renounce its heritage; "from this painful gestation . . . there emerged an enhanced project of democracy."[13]

If Mitterrand's Revolution was bloclike, and if he took retrospective responsibility for it all, he wanted to make it clear that there were still some parts that he liked better than others, some actions he admired more than others. This was his way of responding to the shrill demands (of Villiers, for instance), as well as to the more discreet lobbying-negotiating (Lustiger) for something resembling an acknowledgment of, if not an apology for, the Revolution's crimes. Mitterrand did not make a penitent's pilgrimage to the site of the Carmelites' house in the heart of mainstream Catholic Paris. Nor did he entirely abandon claims for circumstantial justification and mitigating conditions with regard to Revolutionary events.

Crime and Circumstances

It would be, however, a serious error to fail to see the important concessions made by the Jaurèsian chief of state to alienated constituents, counterrevolutionary or merely moderate in sensibility. Philippe Boucher of *Le Monde* read the Tennis Court speech as an unequivocal recognition of "the errors, the excesses, and the crimes" and an equally irrefragable rejection of "the discourse of the excuse." Solemnly and eloquently, the president evoked the "atrocious images of Nantes, of the Carmelites, of the prisons of September. The list is long." Mitterrand pointed out, however, that the story had at least two sides. "Blood ran in each camp."

The motivations of the revolutionaries were neither trivial nor pathological. "Let us not forget the war abroad, the war at home, the perils incurred by the country, the Nation in danger." Don't forget what Agulhon called the *history* of the Terror, what Furet derided as the mindless and indulgent thesis of circumstances. All things weighed, including the crimes and the errors, Mitterrand's choice was transparent: "let us try to understand why, in the complex movement of the Revolution, at an equal level of courage and conviction, all choices are not equally valid." While claiming to understand those who did not share his point of view, Mitterrand remained true to himself. Paul Guilbert of *Le Figaro* had some reason to wonder still whether the president considered the Terror "a necessity or a contradiction of the Revolution."[14]

Later that summer Mitterrand placed more stress on the horrors and backed off somewhat from the thesis of circumstances. On 14 July he made his final offer to the archbishop of Paris in terms that were devoid of any ambiguity: "One must admit, after all, that the terror which struck priests guilty only of having professed their fidelity to the church—I already cited, in this respect, the massacre of the Carmelites—revolts the conscience and contradicts one of the most sacred principles of human rights." Once applied nearly exclusively to the counterrevolutionary right, the word "fanaticism," recently rehabilitated by Furet's galaxy as a scientifically valid epithet, entered the president's vocabulary to describe and stigmatize certain R/revolutionary propensities.

While he privileged his standard legacy argument, in his August address in honor of the Declaration of the Rights of Man, Mitterrand did not avoid prominent mention of "deviations, oppressions, and later derelictions." Nor did he shrink from using the highly charged word "exterminate" to refer to the killing of the Carmelites, whose sole crime, he reiterated, was to have served their faith. Still tempted to historicize the crime, Mitterrand warned that it was unjust to wreak vengeance on the priests in retribution for the iniquities of the Old Regime (with which they were implicitly solidary?). But the balance in this speech was manifestly against any significant attenuation of responsibility. The massacres spoke the language of panic stampede, not that of progressive revolutionary action. In September and later in Year II, they "belied in horror the hopes of the previous day." If the nation-in-danger still accounted for much of the Terror, Mitterrand retreated to the nineteenth-century liberal-left position on the chronological limits of this argument: "after the victories of the armies of the republic, the Terror was no longer in a position to appeal to the necessities of public safety. It had become a system of government."

The president never admitted to a pernicious logic intrinsic in '89 that burst forth in '93. (He could not fully overcome his disposition to relativize: the fleeting months of Terror seemed less singularly imposing when juxtaposed to the previous centuries of brutality and intolerance.) The *dérapage* had more to do with human nature, whose dark side flourished under stress and in response to the prod of memory as well as fear. In the end, however awful and inexcusable the excesses were, what mattered most to Mitterrand was that the commitment to human rights and democracy (re)emerged somehow fortified if not purified.[15]

From Positivism to Relativism

The president's interpretive trajectory appeared to reflect a shift in his thinking about the historiographical process. Speaking in honor of the Pergamon archival project at the Sorbonne in January 1988—perhaps in deference to the sheer power of the documents whose diffusion he saluted—Mitterrand took a positivist-scientist line, predicated on the optimistic assumption that diligent research would (eventually?) cause the truth to burst forth. His mood seemed quite different, however, when he returned to the Sorbonne eighteen months later to greet hundreds of historians from the world over. Though he warned against the perils of a teleological and narcissistic history based exclusively on the "obsessions of the present," he categorically rejected "the myth of the historian's objectivity." One could not reasonably expect to "detach oneself from one's own approach" or from the preoccupations of one's time."

If the president did not follow his sometime counselor Régis Debray in reducing everything to "ideology," nevertheless he did not venture to argue that if one line of interpretation was right, its contrary was necessarily wrong. For Mitterrand, "history" could not be erected into a putatively neutral and sapient arbiter. It could propose protocols of honesty and rigor that narrowed the range of possibilities and held the antagonists to high ("scientific") standards. But it could never bring tranquil closure to the debate about the past. The best one could hope for was that the multiplication of investigations and the salutary clash of ideas would provisionally generate "a dominant interpretation that will inspire our successors." Here was one sphere where the president seemed willing to rely on the workings of the marketplace, provided it was genuinely free.[16]

In evoking his personal Revolutionary heroes, the president again showed evidence of his *relative* moderation in the debate over the Terror, closer in this context to Alphonse Aulard's republicanism than to Jaurès-Mathiez's class struggle–oriented social revolutionism. He would never put Robespierre in the Panthéon, despite his crucial historical role: "he has his grandeur, but he inspired too many bloody events." Mitterrand understood that it would be a political error as well as an affront to many of his fellow citizens to honor bloodletting. Yet there is no doubt that the president believed that much of the bloodletting, however tragic, was legitimate and unavoidable. When the nation was endangered during Year II (Mitterrand spoke almost interchangeably of "the war against the Revolution" and "the war against France"), patriots could not recoil from taking the harsh measures required.

Focusing exclusively on the criterion of war, Mitterrand chose Danton and Carnot as the best embodiments of the Revolutionary and the republican spirits. Each was part of the Terror, but each in his own way, sooner or later, came to oppose it as it was conceived and practiced by Robespierre. Danton was the hero who had always resonated with the sensibility of ordinary citizens, who identified with his bravado, his passion for life, and his patriotic ardor. Pierre Chaunu rightly reminded the president that Danton's hands were venal as well as bloodstained, but neither mark was potent enough to dislodge him from his popular pedestal. Pantheonized in 1889, Carnot remained the organizer of victory and the man of republican measure, despite his decisive part in the crushing of the Vendée.[17]

Rights: Mitterrand I versus Mitterrand II

While Mitterrand viewed the Declaration of the Rights of Man as the incarnation of the best of the Revolution, he was keenly aware of both its fragility and its imperfection.[18] Given the nature of things, the so-called *acquis*, or Revolutionary accomplishments, were never irrevocably won. The heritage was permanently "in uncertainty and always threatened." To justify his pessimism and the vigilance it demanded, the president pointed to the relatively recent experience of Vichy, a year after the sesquicentennial of the French Revolution, when "the motto 'Work, Family, Fatherland' very officially replaced 'Liberty, Equality, Fraternity.'" Though much of the world in the late 1980s seemed to be turning passionately to liberty, Mitterrand called on true believers to be relentlessly "on the alert, . . . I will go so far as to say even more today than yesterday."[19]

It was not enough, however, to fight merely to protect the Declaration of the Rights of Man. It was necessary—and logical—to fight to extend and enrich them. For as worthy as it was, the Declaration was flawed by "the absence of a social doctrine" that left the poor, women, blacks, and servants outside the realm of democratic practice. Now, Mitterrand was very much aware that if there was something resembling a consensus in French civic life, it pivoted on liberty, not on equality, on the political, not the social. But he rejected the new Tocquevillism that posited a sempiternal struggle between liberty and equality and found vindication in the rampant rejection of generic socialism, particularly in its Leninist-Stalinist expression, the world over. The president did not for an instant question the paramount place accorded to liberty. Nor did he traffic in the Marxist game of disdaining the political as a purely formal (and thus in some way inferior) domain to the social. Rather, he argued that liberty was inconceivable without and indissociable from equality, that legal rights had to have a "real" dimension, that the political emerged from and implied the social.

As we celebrate the victory of the Revolution-republic, "one must not forget, however, that liberty does not end with political rights." Without worrying overmuch about the exact derivation, Mitterrand insisted that "it also contains social, economic, [and] cultural rights" (much in the way that certain revisionists, emulating many counterrevolutionaries, contended that '89 contained the seeds of '93). Mitterrand refused to stake the legitimacy of equality—of the social doctrine—on '93, on Ernest Labrousse's famous "anticipations," on the Marxizing emphasis on the social audacity of the Terror. (Yet in one address at the very end of the bicentennial year he alluded to the "sacred debt" that the Convention believed the state owed to the poor, the current form of which was the president's RMI, the *revenu minimum d'insertion*.) Without the predicate/promise of equality, '89 could not be '89, for "inequality violates liberty."

The social had *voiced claims that could not be ignored* from the beginning of the Revolution. Far from being anatagonists, as the Tocquevilleans maintain, liberty and equality were mutually dependent and deeply solidary. Far from undermining liberty, equality nourished it and made it credible and responsible. Both were "existential" needs that impelled men and women to strive and struggle for their realization. "Nothing better defines modern democracy than the synthesis, always to be reinvented, between liberty and equality," Mitterrand told a bicentennial audience at New York University. These principles had to be "enshrined in fact," not just underwritten rhetorically.

"But economic liberty necessarily produces inequality," objected an interviewer for *L'Express*. Apparently this was the question meant to tangle the president in contradiction; or, as the *Lettre politique et parlementaire* put it, to force Mitterrand I (whose discourse stressed social justice) to come to terms with Mitterrand II ("who swears henceforth only by the market economy . . . [and] no longer envisions pursuing the Revolution but, rather, [foresees] burying it for good"). The president answered *L'Express* forthrightly: "You are right." Laissez-faire admittedly generated inequality. It was a mixed blessing and thus required a mixed response. Here, first, is Mitterrand II, for whom the break with capitalism was a Gracchean relic of a lost world: "To facilitate as much as possible creation, and thus initiative; to promote quality, to vanquish the competition because we are the best, [all that is] very good. Create goods, exchange them, sell them, manage the profit derived from these transactions, [all this] requires no comment, it is normal and even necessary."

A panegyric of lucidity rather than enthusiasm, this endorsement of the free market constituted the keystone in the fin-de siècle social-democratic arch. But it was hedged and buttressed by an age-old doctrine that was hard to calibrate precisely. Speaking in the voice of Rousseau, of Diderot castigating the Physiocrats in defense of Galiani, of Attorney General Séguier upbraiding Turgot, of Robespierre warning solemnly against the lethal destabilizing influence of great excesses of wealth and poverty, of the moral economy over against the market economy, Mitterrand I invoked the necessity of limits. Unbridled liberty led to what Old Regime moralists (including radical utopians as well as reactionary apologists of the Great Chain of Being) called libertinage. "Any form of liberty imposes constraints," Mitterrand I affirmed, in a sort of Newtonian law of social dynamics.

"Why should the economic sphere be spared?" The problem of course was, as always, one of timing, dosage, and method, and Mitterrand I proffered few precise details. "But there comes a time when a common consciousness of a common interest must emerge, in order [for us] to escape the law of the jungle." (Its avid embrace of the law of the jungle, Mitterrand would later remark, was the major reason why "liberalism is exhausted," symmetrically in the same posture of bankruptcy as Communism, which had its own varieties of jungle life.) Even as there were judges and gendarmes "to protect liberty in general," so there had to be "guardrails" in order to guarantee that economic liberty would operate "in a healthy fashion." That task devolved on the state: "the elected officials of the people are there for that purpose."

Not to worry, Mitterrand I/II assured the private sector: "Don't confuse this duty with an abusive centralized power that puts its hand on everything, which is called dirigisme, [a governmental strategy] constantly practiced in France during periods called liberal." In lieu of an efficacious "invisible hand" devoted to attaining a fruitful equilibrium between liberty and equality, market and moral economy, the political and the social, the president proposed in extremely vague terms rules whose vocation would be to "protect the liberty of everyone, by rectifying, as much as possible, the inequalities."

While declaring himself "for a complete political liberalism," Mitterrand believed that, given the enormous power of money, the historical tilt had patently favored liberty over equality. Economic liberalism "masks too much arbitrariness, too much injustice . . . . it usurps the name that it assigns itself." He enthusiastically applauded the Chinese who wanted laws now that they had finally obtained enough food on which to survive. Yet he seemed even more sensitive to the problem closer to home of the Western democracies where "free men can die of hunger." (In a television program in early 1990, citing the example of fifty million poor in the United States, and sections of New York—a "splendid city" in an "admirable country"—that resembled "a disinherited place in the Third World," he denounced "the excessive distinction between a rich society and a society of the poor.")

Refusing Exclusion

Thus, for Mitterrand, the great *task* of the bicentennial and the years to come was the redressing of the social balance of power through what the president called "the rejection of exclusions." Certain persons or groups were excluded from the practice, pleasure, and profit of liberty as the result of an inadequate allowance of equality. Vagrants spattering the social space, potential sources of combustibility as well as emblems of collective shame, these outcasts suffered a double handicap because they could not function in the political arena or in the arena of political economy: "The republic needs to take stock of its world: those excluded from work, those excluded from knowledge, those excluded from well-being, those excluded from dignity, those excluded from health, those excluded from housing, those excluded from culture must dispose of all their rights. Equality demands this, [and] so does liberty."

Racism, sexism, and ignorance all had economic roots and conditioners and amplifiers, in Mitterrand's view. In the subtler forms of social tyranny of the late twentieth century, the outcasts were not incarcerated in Bastilles (or even in general hospitals) that had to be taken. Rather, they were more insidiously hidden behind a multitude of "Berlin Walls, small and invisible, which loomed almost everywhere in our social body." To overcome these walls of money—of sometimes "insolent" fortunes—which continued to swell "the gap between the richest and the poorest," Mitterrand called for the application "of social means, of fiscal means," just as he had pressed in the same spirit for the European Community's "social charter," so ardently resisted by Prime Minister Thatcher. The negative tax and the tax on large fortunes were small steps in this sense toward "the major objective: to make sharing our law" in a synthesis of liberty and equality.

Was such a synthesis really feasible? Was it possible to "redistribute wealth without falling into exaggerated excesses?" Centrists and technicians regarded the vision as utopian; many on the right continued to see it as a specter of Terror, of the "agrarian law" cast in deceptively liberal terms; and many on the left regarded it as a sellout to Grand Capital despite its (mystifying) social discourse. The president deeply resented the suggestion that somehow this logic bespoke totalitarianism. On the contrary, it was the sole guarantor of democracy. "Everything is in the synthesis," he repeated. Just as "the countries that toppled to the side of dictatorship fell short of Socialism because they fell short of liberty"—liberty and equality are perforce solidary—so did the socioeconomic underdevelopment of democracies new and old threaten their capacity to sustain liberty. Mitterrand's shibboleth remained: '89, '93, it's all the same battle.[20]

Grandeur and Revolution: The Mittero-Gaullist Vision

Numerous commentators, right and left, warned Mitterrand against the perils of a commemoration flooded in nostalgia for the grandeur of yore, when France had moments of quasi-hegemonic influence and a model to offer or impose. Aware of the risk of appearing ridiculous or bloated, the president nevertheless was not prepared to abjure totally the practice of a certain "messianism" (Debray) and of giving "lessons to the world" (Pierre Billard). His strategy was not to pretend that France today was what it used to be but, rather, to insist on the extraordinary durability and continual relevance of the peculiar historical mission and of the tradition that it still embodied. Mitterrand himself seemed surprised and inspired by the obstinately powerful resonance of the French Revolution throughout the world. Reports not only of the homage of bicentennial celebrations but of the appropriation of the rhetoric and symbols of the French Revolution in actual contemporary political practice seemed to demonstrate that the dream of 1789 had aged better than he could have hoped in the most favorable scenario. Here was another proof that the Revolution was not over, that it was "alive," and that it was needed. With Jaurèsian relish, Mitterrand concluded that "it is still feared, which inclines me rather to rejoice." This sentiment, among others, estranged the president from his bicentennial prime minister.

While the Revolution had become "the common inheritance of humanity," it was proper for the French to take pride in the fact that they were the first to articulate this "immense hope" in genuinely universal terms. Even as Mitterrand toiled to sustain a Gaullist credibility for French leadership in East-West, North-South, G–7, and European Community relations, without self-indulgent hubris but with a clear sense of purpose and measure, so did he invite his fellow citizens to view the bicentennial as a mark not of French historical regression but of continued efflorescence.

"Ladies and gentlemen," he told the nation at the Tennis Court ceremony, "if the French sometimes doubt themselves, let them listen to the murmuring that rises from the four corners of the earth. All over the world where one fights for the right of a people to determine its own destiny, for the accession of poor nations to a sharing of the wealth, for freedom of thought, for equality of rights, it is the message of the French Revolution that one hears, and everyone in the world follows it." To countrymen like Renaud, whose "good reflex" (to oppose the bicentennial summit conference of the world's richest powers in the name of the Third Estates of the world) was triggered by "bad information," and whose acerbic critique had pained him, the president observed that if the French Revolution exercised such attraction today, it was at least in part because French policies today reflected and buttressed its inexorable passion for justice.[21]

The bicentennial turned out to be a triumphant experience for Mitterrand. He had just completed a vigorous phase as chief of the European Community. Gorbachev's visit in early July reinforced his stature as an authentic world leader. The G–7 summit was judged a success, though, like most such meetings, it achieved remarkably little in concrete terms. The ultimate credit for the spectacular celebration on the fourteenth of July redounded to the president. During the previous year he had taken risks and he had played his cards brilliantly; now he relished, for himself and for France, the long (Warholian) moment at the center of the world stage. The general verdict was that he had managed the commemorative discourse with tact and aplomb. He had been true to himself—to his evolving self—yet he had tried to accommodate the feelings of French men and women with different orientations. A self-styled republican rather than a Jacobin, he had nevertheless made a passionate case for the "social" in tandem with the "political."

The president who believed that the Revolution occurred in part because the Old Regime king "isolated himself from the people" used the bicentennial, in the words of the *Dépêche du Midi*, to "tighten the links of affectionate complicity with the country." In the eyes of his critics, his revolutionary posture was merely a domesticated attribute of a new, more durable and cunning kingship. The final paradox of a career of contradictions was that Mitterrand had become "the most monarchical of our presidents," "the constitutional monarch." For certain commentators this evolution had institutional roots: "it is the result of the nature of the power, the excessive length of the term of office and, from now on, the absence of electoral sanction." For others, it was the result of deep-seated popular needs: "our people need a chief who is looked upon as a supreme recourse and arbiter, as the guarantor of the rights of all and of national interests." For still others, it was peculiarly a product of Mitterrand's grasping, Oriental temperament: Jean-Edern Hallier's "tricolor Buddha," "Mitterrandescu," or simply "emperor."[22]

The Political Parties
Managing Memory in the Microcosm
and the Macrocosm

The bicentennial posed thorny problems for most of the political parties. An immensely complex and multivocal event, the Revolution did not lend itself readily to a brutally reductive litmus test—at least not any longer, not after the *ralliement* of the church and the gradual republicanization of the right. A large part of the right could no longer comfortably excoriate the Revolution en bloc any more than a considerable part of the left could eulogize it indiscriminately. Chirac's Rassemblement pour la République (RPR) adopted the Phrygian cap (classical emblem of republican freedom appropriated by the sansculottes) as part of its logo, betraying both its ideological evolution and its continued ambivalence. Meanwhile, on the left, moderate elements felt increasingly ill at ease with a Revolutionary heritage refracted through a Marxist-Leninist prism. It was never easy for politicians to be at once coherent and nuanced; navigating the treacherous shoals of the Revolution made the task even more difficult. Few politicians enjoyed the idea of being pressed, being interpellated by the inquisitorial specter of the Revolution. Each had to worry not only about how his or her adversaries would use the commemoration but about how his or her own colleagues would define themselves vis-à-vis the Revolution. All the politicians had to be concerned about both shaping and responding to the needs of their diverse clienteles.

The Socialists and the Revolutionary Reference

Revolutionary reference surged to the forefront of Socialist discourse with the party's ascension to power in 1981. Wildly celebrated at the place de la Bastille, the tenth of May 1981 was hailed as "the new taking of the Bastille." The new president identified his victory with the R/revolutionary triumph of the people—the bone and sinew of France who were historically excluded from power save in the moments marked by the "brief and glorious fractures of our society." Jack Lang, among others, spoke in classical trope of the daylight (liberty) following the dark shadows (oppression) in mimetic reenactment of the Enlightenment followed hard by Revolution. President Giscard's "monarchy," cankered and sapped from within, fell to the democratic warriors of the popular left, according to the Socialist script.

In anticipation of their new perspectives and intentions, Socialists associated themselves with the idea of rupture that seemed to be at the core of the Revolution. Pierre Mauroy, the new prime minister, played a bowdlerized but boisterously populist Père Duchesne, the demagogic Revolutionary journalist, admonishing the "folks in the castle," excoriating the "émigrés of Koblenz" (the uncivic businessmen who rushed to export their capital), and pledging that "the people will have its word." Mauroy's message was that the social would displace and reshape the political in the coming years. The party echoed this theme in October at its congress at Valence, whose rhetorical flourishes, in the advanced R/revolutionary idiom, would return to haunt the party for many years to come. Orators linked the right with the (quasi-permanent) aristocratic reaction, stressed the need for rapid action leading toward a transformation of society, and exhibited the voluntaristic determination of '89/'93. Party notable and minister Paul Quilès, dubbed Robespaul, adduced the need to see heads roll in order to accelerate the purge of the Augean stable, at least according to certain press reports, denounced by the Socialists as distortions.[1]

The Waning of Revolutionary Ardor

The Socialists spent the next few years learning how difficult it was to manage public affairs while cultivating the aim of rupture. As they were increasingly constrained to revise their political economy, and their politics *itself*, they imperceptibly became more reticent and circumspect about the R/revolutionary reference. They began to nourish the distinction between a progressive republican legitimacy and the henceforth obsolete idea of deep social discontinuity. If the left intended to stay in power, it became more and more patent that it would have to break with the notion of R/revolutionary rupture, and a fortiori, with any vision of utopia. The idea was now to connect the Revolution's "positive achievements," as minister Yvette Roudy put it, with the Herculean task of renewal undertaken by the PS in power.[2] Forced to renounce the project for an international exposition, the Socialists became painfully conscious of "handling an object that was still burning hot." In the four years following this relinquishment, the Socialist government did virtually nothing to prepare the bicentennial, "another sign of . . . malaise," noted *Le Monde*.

The release of Andrzej Wajda's film *Danton* called forth another measure of Socialist disarray concerning the Revolution. Many were bitterly disappointed that it did not provide the same encouragement that Jean Renoir's *Marseillaise* had for the left of the Popular Front. Several party leaders were said to have walked out of a premiere screening complaining "he's heaping ridicule on us." Instead of balancing the "horrible" with the "magnificent," and revealing the immense burden of the circumstances of foreign invasion, civil war, hoarding, profiteering, and plotting, Wajda depicted a city terrorized by a totalitarian power of Stalinist inflection sprung from the Revolutionary message itself. While many Socialists bitterly denounced the film for its bias, distortion, and injustice, others sensed that its enormous impact bespoke important changes in the way French men and women, on the left as well as on the right, were inclined to see the French Revolution. Mitterrand's own more moderate reaction may have signaled the need for a new look. Wajda's nasty stigmatization of Robespierre accelerated the harrowing process of the Socialist descent from the Mountain.[3]

During the 1988 presidential campaign, very few Socialists dared invoke the revolutionary blessing. Hardly anyone resonated to Louis Mexandeau's soulful summons to the blue: "If François Mitterrand is not reelected, we will be swamped in *chouans* and in Puy-du-Fou." (Several years later, this disenchanted Socialist leader ascribed the party's dearth of R/revolutionary ardor to "the assault of pessimism" that accompanied the exercise of power and that led the PS "to doubt its capacity to organize the *Fête populaire*," that is to say, to assume the historical vocation of the party of the people.) By 1989 what had earlier been a calumny in the mouth of journalist-ideologue Guy Sorman became a profound insight in that of his confrere Serge July: "After having nourished itself for almost two centuries on this identity/reference, the left has ceased defining itself in terms of the unfinished nature of the French Revolution." Now that reform had "definitively" replaced revolution as modus operandi, continued July, "the left looks at the bicentennial of the Revolution the way one used to leaf through the [high school history text by] Malet-Isaac—with distance." The Revolution was over for the PS as it was for others in France. "The Socialist party has broken loose without a warning from its moorings in its historical tradition," July concluded, in his characteristic acid-polemical fashion. "This fact already amounts to one of the outstanding traits of this bicentennial."[4]

"The Revolution is not over," party chief Pierre Mauroy vehemently protested. Objectively, it was not over, and cognitively it could not be over, he hinted, because the Socialists still needed the idea of R/revolution in order to identify and recognize themselves. The Revolution was a precious Socialist resource, and the Socialists intended to "perpetuate" the idea of the Revolution (and presumably of revolution). The rank and file followed Mauroy's lead with greatly varying degrees of enthusiasm. Between the party congresses of Valence and Rennes, the Revolution acquired its "currents" too. It seemed doubtful that the claim of Michel Charzat, a representative of the left wing of the party (ex-Ceres), still held true as the bicentennial season opened: "The left accepts the Revolution en bloc. Therefore what distinguishes the left from the right is that it accepts all the Revolution, and in particular 1793."

The Range of Socialist Opinion

In the mid-1980s the Marxist reading of the bourgeois character of the Revolution still commanded a substantial Socialist following. The class struggle was the core of the Revolutionary experience for Véronique Neiertz and Pierre Joxe, two outspoken ministers. Jean Gatel, a junior minister of the same generation, made the sort of distinction in 1983 between "formal" and "real" liberties that caused many of his party colleagues to cringe in 1989. Lionel Jospin, who led the party for much of the decade, adumbrated a more supple stand. While he agreed with Charzat and Joxe that the Terror had a heroic and strictly necessary dimension, at the same time he admitted that the violence was frightening and that the vision of the Revolution devouring its own children was troubling. Allowing for its usual vulpine partisanship in formulating the issues, the right-wing *Quotidien de Paris* was basically correct when it wrote that "the left fears to see itself invested with responsibility for the Terror and, in consequence, for the founding act of modern totalitarianism."[5]

While committed to the "social," the bicentennial Socialists had no intention of allowing the right an uncontested takeover of liberty. Significantly, the association that the Socialist party created to orchestrate its commemorative efforts adopted the name "Vive la Liberté." Former premier Laurent Fabius insisted on "Equality" as the chief objective of Socialists: "more social and economic democracy." But Fabius, like his mentor Mitterrand, viewed equality not as the earthy antagonist of an ethereal liberty but as its necessary complement in daily life. A society that was "more egalitarian" would perforce be "freer." It was clear that those in the party who had not yet accomplished their personal Bad Godesberg—a renunciation of Marxist premise of action—and installed themselves in a frankly social-democratic perspective had little in common with those who longed for a break with capitalism nebulously foreshadowed in Year II.[6]

Edwige Avice, another minister, cast the Revolutionary legacy in decidedly unbloody, modern, quasi-clinical, and fully international terms. As rigid ideological systems collapsed throughout the world, democracy struck her as the grand fin-de-siècle question. If Edgar Morin was right to claim that the Revolutionary trinity was still "the star of the future" two hundred years later, it was on condition, argued Avice, that "equality means first of all development; liberty, the rights of man; and fraternity, disarmament." Jack Lang took a step in the same general direction by avowing that revolutions were cauldrons of contradiction, desperately hard to manage and domesticate. (His view seemed little different from neoconservative thinker Jean-François Revel's characterization of revolutions as "complex, unstable, double-edged phenomena.")[7]

Roger Léron, a rank-and-file deputy from Valence with a passionate commitment to social justice and a keen sense of economic realities, spoke for many colleagues when he categorically affirmed that the Revolution was over. Society had changed profoundly; the old slogans and nostrums were no longer applicable. Léron sensed that the old mythologies confined the Socialists, arrested their intellectual and political development. With a new sociology that made it a petty-bourgeois party and a new legitimacy conferred by years of surprisingly effective management in spheres where they were supposed to be weak such as the economy, it was time for the Socialists to change their paradigm. For Léron that meant not abandoning liberty, equality, and fraternity but redefining them in the new context, with new tools, linguistic and social.[8]

No Socialist went as far as Michel Rocard, the bicentennial prime minister himself. Sternly criticized by many of his own flock for a "social deficit" during his watch, this exponent of realism and compassion ("tempered capitalism") averred on national radio that "in the multiple consequences of the great Revolution, there is one that is important: the one that convinced a great many people that revolution is dangerous and that it is just as well if one can do without it." One imagines the satisfaction of his interviewer on this *Journal inattendu de RTL*, François Furet. *L'Humanité* reacted with irony and ire: "Now there is a lovely statement that is not likely to weigh heavily on the nights of the richest property owners . . . . one has to reach deeply into one's memory to recall that we are dealing with the same political figure who criticized the Communists in 1968 for failing to trigger the revolution within twenty-four hours."[9]

The party press on virtually all levels was piercingly silent on the bicentennial. It was as if the global division of labor spared the party the need to get involved. The organization of the commemoration was the business of the government and its Mission; and meditation on the heritage of the Revolution was the business of the intellectuals. The standard formula in the party publications during 1989 was hardly more than a solemn and evanescent reference to the commemorative moment, sometimes followed by carping and moralizing comments on the inadequacies of the *official* bicentennial action. It was, after all, easy—and potentially useful, for those who wanted to hedge their bets—to denigrate the bicentennial as a "humdrum routine of gadgets" (*L'Ours*) or "a gigantic American-style show from which history will record only that it was a stellar commercial success" (*Renouveau socialiste*, André Laignel's organ). Fortunately, unprogrammed world-historical vicissitudes offered the Socialists (and a large part of the civilized right) a more or less graceful way out. For who could resist the high drama played out in China, Poland and the Soviet Union, sites of "the true commemoration of the bicentennial" (*PS Info*)?[10]

Still, the latter publication, entrusted with the task of cuing party regulars on what action to take each week, worried, at least in passing, about the perils of the ultralow profile. The risk was that the field would be left open to the right, which, buoyed by the revisonists ("theorists of neoliberalism, in the line of R. Reagan"), would continue to propagate "a totally negative vision of the Revolution." If Agulhon and Mitterrand were right that the attack on the Revolution was often nothing less than "the authorized form of putting democracy on trial," then the PS had a much larger and more complicated stake in the bicentennial than many of its militants were prepared to admit. *PS Info* urged them to present the Revolution as the "founding act of democracy." Instead of dwelling on the past, however, they should shift the focus to the present and future by addressing the problems that the Revolution confronted but did not resolve: education above all, equality of opportunity, and the reinforcement of basic liberties about which one could never afford to become complacent.[11]

The PS In Action

L'Evénement du Jeudi, left-leaning yet staunchly independent, esteemed that the PS was "totally inexistent" during the glorious commemorative moments. "The rose-colored encephalogram was as flat as the wallet of a mimimum-wage worker." The Socialists were too busy scavenging petits fours and making careers, a double *grande bouffe* at which they made themselves valiantly felt. Though less harshly cynical in their appreciation, the militants of Section XIe (Charonne) of the PS in the capital made the same basic point. In the bicentennial the party leadership failed the party, and the party failed the nation: "May we express here our regret over the extreme timidity and the absence of initiative shown by our party concerning the bicentennial? The Mission headed by Jean-Noël Jeanneney having focused all its energy on garnering the widest possible consensus on this commemoration, there was a political space that our party should naturally have occupied. The opportunity was not seized. What a shame!"[12]

While it would be unfair to say that the PS was inert, its record for bicentennial vitality was hardly dazzling. Whatever successes could be claimed took place at the grassroots level, thanks to the work of groups of militants acting on their own initiative. The somewhat disenchanted Section XIe of Paris furnished one example. Its members created "Vive la Nation," an association that aimed to reach out to the citizenry and involve them in debates, lectures, exhibitions, and discussions of republican values and the rights of man. The Section of the thirteenth arrondissement named a commission to organize events, including a gala soirée on 7 July. In many places, such as the Corrèze, the annual *fête de la rose* served as a vehicle for bicentennial celebration (very much in the manner of the annual fêtes of the Communist party in 1989). In two days of commemoration, the citizens of Chambouline were invited to several "rustic repasts," to a liberty tree–planting ceremony, to concerts and a popular ball, and to a speech by Henri Emmanuelli, future president of the National Assembly. In retrospect, the party could claim credit for huge popular festivals in a number of cities. Yet in some of these—Poitiers is a case to be examined below—the Socialist dignitaries kept at a safe political distance. Arguably the "people on the go" program put on by the socialist municipality of Saint-Priest (near Lyon) typified the party's bicentennial posture. Focusing on the very safe value of liberty, it avoided any evocation of conflictual issues or personalities: no sansculottes, no wistfulness for '93, no ode to equality.[13]

In cooperation with the Fédération nationale des élus socialistes et républicains, in November 1987 the PS created an organization specifically charged with the task of promoting commemoration and celebration. Lushly dubbed Vive la Liberté and headed by veteran deputy and minister Louis Mexandeau, who possessed the advantage, or burden, of having been trained as a historian, it was far less active than its Communist counterpart. It defined its goals partly in a defensive and reactive idiom: "urgently to rekindle memories" in order to parry the "falsifications of history" engineered by the right and the extreme right. Its positive message was sober and risk-free: to remind the nation how France, thanks to the Revolution, became "the homeland of human rights."

The departmental/local implantation of Vive la Liberté was quite uneven. Some federations proved to be "more imbued with memory," as Mexandeau put it, than others, and not always in predictable fashion, Vive la Liberté faring better in the Loire-Atlantique bordering the Vendée than in the red-pink Nord (but how much of this differential is attributable to the play of faction and jealousy within an always turbulent PS?). Beyond the question of internal party (dis)harmony, much depended on the local vitality of other left-republican institutions. The federation secretary responsible for the bicentennial in the Hérault, Jean-Claude Gegot, had considerable success in launching Vive la Liberté owing to the cooperation of the Ligue des droits de l'homme (LDH), the Fédération des oeuvres laïques (FOL), the Fédération d'éducation nationale (FEN), and the Fédération Léo Lagrange (FLL)—often comprised of the same interlocking directorates. Branches that came into existence at the very end of 1988, such as the Vive la Liberté of the Essonne, barely had time to put together a minimal program, sometimes little more than a paper profession of faith. The Socialist mayor of puny Chanteloup-en-Brie did more with this very modest commune's Vive la Liberté than certain of the larger PS federations achieved with their far more robust associations.

Presided over by a historian from the University of Grenoble, assisted by local and regional politicians and members of the FOL, the LDH, and the FLL, the Vive la Liberté of the Dauphinée took a relatively audacious ideological line "in order to restore a meaning to this bicentennial." The Revolution was "far from over," proclaimed the Socialist celebrants, because its concerns are still the preoccupations of French citizens today. The Dauphinois association rejected a commemoration circumspectly confined to 1789, a "truncated and fallacious vision" of the Revolution. In addition to spreading the right historical and moral word, this Vive la Liberté undertook a coordinating and publicizing role throughout the region, distributing a newsletter, organizing lectures and historical visits, sponsoring exhibitions, concerts, plays and film screenings, and compiling bibliographies and documentation kits for schools and employee groups. Less self-consciously ideological, interested in promoting a familiarity with the experience of the Revolution in the towns and villages of the Gironde, the Vive la Liberté based at Bordeaux offered a similarly rich menu of activities and support services: periodical bulletin and calendar, pedagogical packages (containing casettes, illustrations, slides, scripts), itinerant shows and exhibitions, fraternal banquets, a night-time march to pay hommage to the abolition of privilege in August 1789, and tree plantings. The association of the Gironde benefited, too, from the guiding hand of an intellectual and teacher and the collaboration of the Cercle Condorcet (originally an emanation of the Ligue d'enseignement) and the FLL.

With very little staff support, Mexandeau coordinated—or, more nearly, thankfully blessed—the activities undertaken at the grass roots. In October 1988 he convoked a two-day meeting of representatives of the various Vive la Liberté associations in Paris, but time to devise strategy and modify calendars was running out, and in any case attendance was sparse. The national committee—in practice, Mexandeau himself—accorded its patronage ("parrainage") to a host of projects (plays, film scenarios, colloquia, commemorative happenings) which hoped to profit from this label in order to attract financial backing and elicit local demand. Mexandeau tried to inform the federations of potentially interesting enterprises ready for immediate use, but it does not appear that the promised "Catalogue of Sponsored Projects" ever saw the light of day.

Vive la Liberté put together an exposition on political posters, organized or participated in several colloquia, and sponsored a number of public meetings. Its scientific committee, which included Maurice Agulhon and Michel Vovelle, does not appear to have been heavily solicited. Perhaps Georges Ferre, codirector of the association, consulted these scholars, for he wanted the (Socialist) world to recall what *really* happened during the Revolution. Accorded a weekly page in *Vendredi*, the party magazine, he treated such themes as the *Marseillaise*, the causes of the Revolution, the metric system, suffrage, divorce, bread riots, the Phrygian bonnet, the emancipation of women, and education.

The theme and action Mexandeau chose to denote commemoration at the hands of Vive la Liberté was treeplanting, a campaign superseded and overshadowed several months later by the Mission's arborial endeavors ("On s'est planté," mused one Socialist wag). Mexandeau justified this obvious and compelling choice of symbols in an elaborate and somewhat strained manner. He portrayed the year 1788 as crystallizing all the discontents and all the aspirations of the frustrated and oppressed Old Regime society. Food and tax riots buffeted the kingdom that year: "these uprisings often came to an end with the planting of a tree on which was placed a sign reading 'to Liberty.'" Thus an old tradition, known to the Greeks and the Gauls, acquired new urgency and signification on the eve of the French Revolution. In 1988, Mexandeau concluded, part of the world (including part of French society) was still fighting for liberty—liberty construed in a broad sense to mean the struggle against misery, unemployment, and exclusion as well as the exercise of political rights. Vive la Liberté furnished associations and municipalities detailed instructions on how to choose a tree and prepare it for planting. The climactic moment in Vive's botanico-evangelical efforts occurred on 8 April 1989 with the dedication of a "vineyard of fraternity" by children of different nationalities at Ferrals-les-Corbières in the Aude.

Reporting to the party at the beginning of 1990, Ferre and Mexandeau regretted "that the imperatives of the calendar and the lack of certain support did not allow the party and kindred associations to realize the project of a grand popular fête in which the citizens would have been the actors." They esteemed that this sort of mobilization was all the more urgent in the wake of Jean-Paul Goude's extravaganza, a parade of quality that nevertheless reduced the citizenry to the status of spectators. Such a self-serving reflection, whatever its intrinsic merit, seems particularly unseemly given the party's desultory engagement in the bicentennial public sphere.[14]

The Communists

The Communist party approached the bicentennial with an agenda very different from the Socialists', despite the fact that they were historically and historiographically linked in many ways. The Communists suffered neither the advantage nor the burden of being in power. On the contrary, they had to face the dramatic problem of their continuing decline and proliferating internal disarray. The bicentennial furnished the party leadership with an extremely attractive opportunity to mobilize the submissive faithful, as well as the internal critics of the regnant orthodoxy, around the banner of R/revolutionary glory.

Few issues commanded more consensus in the party than the passion for the Revolutionary origins of the republic. French Communist national identity was built around the Revolutionary experience. If the Revolution did not precisely constitute a script for future action, it served both as anchor and as telos for the working out of proletarian destiny. The Communists wanted to seize the bicentennial occasion to mark their deep differences not so much vis-à-vis the right—they were conspicuous and familiar—but vis-à-vis the Socialists, whose commemorative malaise both angered and served their comrades on the left.

The Communists saw the bicentennial as a decisive struggle over memory, a struggle with immensely significant political and cultural implications. The French Revolution had been very important in the Communist management of memory even when the prestige of 1917 was reasonably untarnished. (Note, for instance, the representation of the Resistance as Jacobin continuity, with Maurice Thorez as Robespierre and the people opposed to the generals.)[15] Now that 1917 has come into serious question—in the Soviet Union and throughout Eastern Europe as well as in large segments of the Western left, including the Italian Communist party— 1789/93 loomed as more crucial than ever before. While the French Communists could no longer hope to frame the national memory with the striking institutional success they had enjoyed for much of the twentieth century, they were determined to chart out their claims and to challenge the Socialists to acknowledge them, or own up to some sort of *lèse-social*. Indeed, the Communists tended to view themselves as the sole legitimate guardians of the authentic R/revolutionary legacy. This testamentary entail endowed them with special rights and obligations that they meant to exercise in the bicentennial spotlight.[16]

For the Communists, the French Revolution served as an immensely powerful clarifier. It provided a probing and reliable test that enabled the party to articulate its position clearly because of its putatively unproblematic relation to the R/revolutionary past. Writing in *L'Humanité*, the historian and party militant Claude Mazauric depicted the commemorative stakes in Manichaean terms: "Ideological and even philosophical stakes: progressivism or reaction? Conservatism or demands for transformation? Political stakes: yes or no, does a people have the right and is it in its interest to change its 'constitution' if things lead, as they are now doing, toward ruin and national degeneration?"

An Un-common Program for the Bicentennial: Popular, Social, and Anticonsensual

In 1937 the Communist central committee, preparing the 150th anniversary celebration, invited the entire nation to undertake "a new French Revolution." Fifty years later it entertained goals that were more modest and more sectarian. Instead of calling for a united front in defense of the Revolution, the party depicted itself as exclusive heir. Contemptuous of what historian Patrick Garcia described as the "cohabitationist marsh symbolized by the duet of F. Mitterrand/E. Faure, accused of turning its back on the true message of the Revolution," the party set out to demonstrate its singular fealty to the R/revolutionary ideal and to the Jacobino-Marxist exegesis. For the Communists the defense of the Revolutionary legacy implied the conviction that the heritage was hot, not cold; that it was universally pertinent, not obsolete; that it was meant to issue into action, not merely into reflection. Some parts of that heritage belonged to all French women and men. But because of its blood sacrifice and endless toil, the working class had a particularly powerful claim to the stewardship of the whole thing, and a historical and moral obligation to continue the struggle begun in '89/'93. "If the proletariat gave up claiming this heritage, it would lose its most solid cultural base," wrote Louis Viannet, one of the chiefs of the Confédération générale du travail (CGT), who drew on the authority of Jean Jaurès. The protection of the heritage could not be entrusted to the hands of the ruling classes, for their tyrannical self-regard would impel them to stifle its two most decisive and subversive dimensions, the popular and the social.

The French Revolution was of course a bourgeois revolution, conceded André Lajoinie, a prebicentennial candidate for the presidency. But unlike the American and English revolutions, "it was deeply marked by popular and democratic struggles, asserting in the eyes of the world the right of a people to construct its own future." Citing Robespierre, a worker-dominated social-and-cultural affairs commission (comité d'établissement) in a Renault plant in Normandy carried the argument one step further: "Everything the Revolution produced that was wise and sublime was the work of the people." The people operated in the social arena through class struggle. Many Communists feared that the bicentennial would be turned into some sort of Bad Godesberg in order to make the world forget this quintessential fact. "But the French Revolution is richly relevant to our concerns today," boasted *L'Ami du peuple,* "the bicentennial bulletin of a communist group at Montluçon wedded to the hard-line Marxist view of the world. "It was wholly the product of class confrontation."

Georges Séguy, former head of the CGT, complained of the burgeoning "inclination to mimimize the class character of the confrontation of '89" and the "determinant role of the people." Now as then the bourgeoisie denied the people its autonomy and its own future. Séguy called on the people to combat the ruling-class effort to "strip" all the great moments of French history—the Revolution, the Popular Front, the Resistance, and May 1968—of "their social content." Begot by incessant struggle, that social content in its fullest expression was a reified utopia, the dream of the people of '89/'93 and of the working people of the end of the second millennium "that the state assure the happiness of everyone." This was the political overinvestment, the febrile voluntarism denounced by the Furetians and myriad liberals as the wellspring of despotism. In the Communist view, it was the means and ends of democracy.

The people assumed control of their destiny by becoming the state, by making it speak in their name for their good. The state was the agency of the transformation symbolized by popular intervention. Both the image of a hypertrophic state and of an insurgent people speaking for itself were abhorrent to the bicentennial ruling class. "It is absolutely necessary for them to succeed in concealing that essential lesson," wrote Georges Marchais, "that the people are the authors of their own history." The bourgeoisie fully understood that the living memory of the Revolution incarnated in the flesh-and-blood people "constitutes an obstacle of some magnitude to the designs of the forces of capital today." It was in the character of the bourgeoisie to deal. The deal it offered the people today was to efface itself in the fabric of bicentennial consensus, to forget that it was historically the vector of a vast and victorious liberation movement. To succumb to these blandishments was to abjure the hope and need (and threat) of radical social transformation. The historian Antoine Casanova called on the people to cede nothing in their demands and aspirations and to join staunchly "the struggle without compromise against the right and the financial aristocracy."[17]

Echoing politburo member Guy Hermier's hint of a right-Socialist plot to "impoverish and disarm" the forces of movement by impugning and diminishing the R/revolutionary heritage, Georges Marchais, in his keynote address at the party's major bicentennial gathering, affirmed that "the French Communist party was the only party that celebrated the French Revolution." A few months earlier, the secretary-general had questioned the moral right and the cognitive capacity of the bourgeoisie to identify with the very Revolution that the Marxists label bourgeois but onto which they graft a postbourgeois, "popular" penumbra: "How could it celebrate the abolition of privileges, [this bourgeoisie] whose system is based on privileges that grow more and more intolerable?"[18]

Shamefaced bourgeois, the Socialists predicated the bicentennial on a consensual vision, according to their Communist critics, that evacuated the Revolutionary essence and made a mockery of the commemorative gesture. They supposed, and in some sense tried to create, "a spectator people, divested of all critical expression, having lost even the memory of the acts that founded it and for whom the Bastille would be no more than an opera or a subway station." Folklorization was at the center of the consensual strategy: reducing the Revolution to a museum piece, eviscerating its progressive core, denying its burning relevance "in today's struggles for justice, freedom, and peace." The "area of consensus" was contrived by those who want to prevent change at all costs as "a convenient alibi to camouflage the great misfortunes that threaten the civilization of mankind." The Communists saw the consensus pitch as truly insidious, more subtle "in deep continuity with the propositions of the *antirevolution*." The Socialist strategy was to separate the people from their Revolution, to distance them ideologically through a process of "jamming" and mystification, and to distance them physically by obstructing their access to the festive occasions.[19]

The Socialist "maquillage" began not with 1793 but already with 1789. The Communists did not confine their characterization of '89, following a cherished Marxist line, to the denigration of the sordid triumph of possessive individualism. Like the far right, they emphasized the radicality of '89, the "fantastic upsurge" of popular feeling, thought, and action, which they claimed the bicentennial consensualists tried to obscure. ("One would have us believe that 1789 [was] the year of unanimity, of the French people awakening as the embodiment of all the orders reunited.") On the contrary, it was a year of violence, of class violence, of social confrontation, of cascades of plots and panics.

The treason of the Socialists—their "sliding away" from the common program positions of bygone times—mimicked the betrayals that the masses would suffer throughout the Revolution at the hands of their bourgeois mentors. Preaching the superfluity of the Revolution (and a fortiori of revolution), Rocard embodied the perfidy of consensus, of the plan, in Mazauric's words, to "rally around a middling heritage that, in the last analysis, would be the foundation of social liberalism," or "of moderate republicanism of the social-democratic sort." Again echoing the far right, the Communists charged that the Socialists, in the name of consensus, were trying to clean up the Revolution by abridging it and purging it of its passions and its strife and its soaring ambitions.[20]

The maverick *Evénement du Jeudi*, by no means a spokesman for the PS, reacted savagely to the PCF's attack on the alleged bicentennial consensus. In their tone and content, its remarks testified to the deterioration of left-left relations, exacerbated by the commemorative prod:

In exactly the same terms as Le Pen, Pasqua, Léotard, *Le Figaro*, Krivine, and Arlette Laguiller, the chiefs of the sect denounced the "soft consensus" that is said to have shaped the organization of the [bicentennial] ceremonies. Who can say to what extent this all-purpose expression, flat and mechanical, has become a sort of invisible ink meant to hide the zero degree of collective reflection? . . . But at least the PC knows what it is talking about. When it denounces the soft consensus, we know that it is thinking regretfully of the good old days of harsh purges. If the PC demands the rehabilitation of Robespierre, it is because in its opinion this exemplary prosecutor would not have hesitated to have Pierre Juquin or Marcel Rigout beheaded: in those days the party line resembled the razor's edge [of the guillotine]; [it was] a time of dreams.[21]

Undaunted, as ever, by the irony or the evidence of its adversaries, the PCF lost few opportunities to hector and embarrass the PS around bicentennial issues. In the national arena of the parliament, Communist deputies called into question the Socialist determination to celebrate the Revolutionary heritage. In late 1988, for example, Paul Lombard, a Communist deputy from the Bouches-du-Rhône, asked maliciously whether the government had decided to "strike from the agenda the bicentennial of the French Revolution?" (To which Catherine Tasca, the junior minister of culture, replied fiercely: "No effort will be spared to make of 1989 a year worthy of the events of two centuries ago.") Georges Marchais and other party leaders missed no opportunity to deplore the "tepidness" of the state's commemorative will. At the local level, Communists were not as willing to cooperate with Socialists in joint civic and commemorative projects as they claimed to be, especially when they calculated that little or no advantage would redound to them.[22]

Occupying the Social Terrain and Embarrassing the President

Once the bicentennial year opened, the Communists directed the brunt of their fire directly at the president of the republic, whom they continued to regard primordially as the head of his party. "Emmerder Mitterrand" is how one member of the central committee privately described the party line. No longer a mass party with a genuine capacity of mobilization, thanks in part to Mitterrand's cunning, the PCF was reduced to the vengeful business of using every device to spoil "Mitterrand's celebration" [*la fête à Tonton*]. Thus its unwonted haste to join the Trotskyite-inspired antisummit and its attempt to expose the president's "antisocial" nature in the affair of the "Renault Ten," in support of whom the CGT, their union, contemplated a subway strike for Bastille Day. The summit, *L'Humanité* contended, represented a "confiscation" of the Revolution, another blow against the little people of the world. "We must extol the people who took charge of its history," the fatidic connection between the third estate *and* the Third World, not the recurrent triumph of the builders of the world's Bastilles.[23]

From Renaud to Renault: the CGT and the PCF occupied the "social terrain" in the weeks preceding the bicentennial climax. Ten CGT militants, including a son-in-law of Georges Marchais, had been dismissed by the Renault management in 1986 for a "serious offense" [*faute lourde*], including the sequestration of executives and vandalizing of the premises. For years the union, backed by the party, fought for their reinstatement under the banner of "union liberties." Renault, still owned by the government, embodied for the Communists the marriage of grand capital and its protector-state. The Régie, as the car-maker's management was called, was one of the Bastilles that the party wanted to take in the spirit of the bicentennial.

On the grounds that a "serious offense" could not be so pardoned, in early July, the Conseil constitutionnel, France's highest authority of judicial review, rejected the reintegration of the Ten in application of the wide-ranging amnesty law recently passed by the National Assembly. A chastening blow to legislative arrogance, the Conseil's decision was bitterly denounced by the Communists as bearing the "stamp of class" and forsaking the fundamental principles of democracy engendered in 1789. (Almost at the same time, François Furet, among others, invoked the operation of the Conseil as proof of the stabilization and normalization of institutional and political life in the Fifth Republic.) According to *L'Humanité*, it was no wonder the court, composed of Mitterrand's cronies, rendered a judgment that served the interests of the right. The judicial system, the PCF organ pointedly noted, paid little attention to insider trading, illicit arms dealing, and fiscal fraud, evils wholly compatible with the capitalist ethic.

After having participated in Renaud's concert on 8 July, the Communists joined the CGT four days later in a protest march that they hoped to conduct as close as possible to Mitterrand's private (rue de Bièvre) and public (Elysée) domiciles. The "mass riposte," according to *Le Monde*, was a derisory spasm that did not transcend "the boundaries of a PC in decline." "Fewer people marched for the 'Renault Ten,'" commented *L'Evénement du Jeudi*, "than for the sales at the Samaritaine department store." *L'Humanité* painted a far more heroic picture: "thousands of demonstrators, marching to the shouts of 'Amnesty, Liberty,' reinstilled an inspirational force into the spirit of the Revolution, of the sansculottes, of the conquerors of the Bastille."[24]

Rectifying Their Aim: The PCF on Rights

"Liberty" was a critical slogan in the Communist bicentennial vocabulary. In predictably mechanical fashion, Georges Marchais proclaimed the social interpretation according to the Marxist gospel of the place du Colonel-Fabien: it was a bourgeois revolution ("but democratic and popular") forged by "the rising class of the time, the bourgeoisie, which developed in the midst of feudal society, and which in the eighteenth century took charge of commerce, nascent industry, and finance." But he was careful not to repeat the error for which he openly reproached himself and his comrades. "In the first part of our history—our own and that of other

Communist parties," Marchais reasoned with exquisite casuistry, "our clearheaded-ness about the incapacity of capitalism to achieve equality and fraternity lead us to fail to give to liberty the primordial place which it must have in every project for and every construction of a socialist state."

The fruit of internal party requirements as well as fraternal foreign influence (in retrospect, perhaps Marchais realized that he had visited Romania far too often) and scholarly scrutiny, this "clearheadedness" issued in what the Communist leader called a "strange paradox." While no other political party had done more for liberty and human rights than the Communist party in its struggle for the claims and the dignity of workers, in its battle against fascism and the Nazi occupation, in its campaign against colonialism, and in its critique of excessive excecutive power, "we ourselves for a long time qualified as 'bourgeois' the liberties that we see today trampled by the bouregoisie."

We corrected that error at our twenty-second congress in 1976, Marchais empha-sized: We set as our goal a socialism built by and for liberty, and each of our acts is infused by it." (One is tempted to shout as one reads these lines in the wake of the twenty-seventh congress: "Tell it to the renovators, the reconstructors, the re-founders, the so-called liquidators," the critics who could not be heard or published in the name of democratic centralism—not to mention the francs-tireurs like Pierre Juquin who were already expelled.) Gorbachev's perestroika and the developments in Eastern Europe ("the socialist countries") reinforce our conviction, Marchais concluded, that we returned to history and to science when we embraced liberty, "that the indissoluble link which we have instituted between liberty and socialism corresponds to historical necessity."[25]

Yet Marchais, like Mitterrand, tended to fuse liberty and equality, to define the former in terms of the latter, to argue that one could not exist—save formally—without the other. (Each in his own way, the president and the secretary-general were both sufficiently *enragé* to share the contention of the Revolutionary priest Jacques Roux that "without equality, liberty is no more than a vain phantom.") The political without the social was a charade; the liberty to exploit was as unjust as the liberty to suffer want was intolerable. "For those who do not know of what their tomorrow will consist, for those who are deprived of everything, for those who are confronted with insecurity," contended Marchais, there was no liberty. Once prop-erty was declared absolute, argued *Révolution* on the two hundredth anniversary of the night of 4–5 August, it transformed "the equality that [the Revolution] pro-claims into a formal element, all the while assuring the longevity of material inequality." "For the Communists," that same periodical averred, "liberty is only a vain appearance so long as inequality affirms itself."

At bottom, the error the Communists committed, their exponents intimated, was not so much to have deprecated liberty as to have failed to make greater demands on it. The Communists refused to allow the Tocquevilleans and their Socialist allies to set liberty over against equality as they had pitted the masses against the elites. The PCF denounced the hierarchy that placed the noble rights ("civil and political rights") above the minor ones ("economic, social, and cultural rights"). This distinction enabled the powerful "to hold up to ridicule day after day the grand precepts" of the French and the Universal Declarations of Rights, and it framed for the Communists the "the political and ideological battle" of the bicentennial.[26]

Despite the official aggiornamento, many Communists remained conflicted over the relation between liberty and equality, between what many used to contrast as the formal and the real rights. "But what are liberty and equality, what are these proclaimed rights," asked Jean-Claude Gayssot, a Communist deputy, and Georges Valbon, president of the Conseil général of the Communist bastion in the Seine-Saint-Denis, "if each man, each woman does not have the possibility of exercising them really?" That department's bicentennial newsletter, 89 en 93, edited by the historian Roger Bourderon, was deeply galled by philosopher-historian Marcel Gauchet's suggestion that it was dangerous to attempt to translate rights into a practical reality: "If we understand correctly, [the message is, be] careful; there is danger as soon as one ventures to establish in society the exercise of real rights recognized by the most solemn texts." Could one have real confidence in rights declared with rhetorical flourish but without social bite? A Communist-led commemorative group in Brittany worried about "abstract principles often contradicted in reality." Claude Mazauric considered "this idea that the conquest of real rights for the dominated [classes] implies the suppression of formal freedoms" to be a "Stalinist" aberration. Yet he attacked the Ozoufian reading of the rights engendered by the Revolution, a reading that "reinforces the abstract, formal dimension of the Declaration of 1789" at the expense of "the concrete implications." Nor was this concern confined to the PCF. In the ghettos and the *quart monde* of rich nations like France, noted a brochure produced under the label of the Ligue des droits de l'homme, "economic, social, and cultural rights are unevenly respected and the exercise of democracy reveals itself to be sometimes more formal than real."[27]

The Communists and the Terror

The reclamation of liberty—but of a liberty planted firmly in the soil of the social—did not lead the party to a sweeping reevaluation of its position on the Terror. The Communists did not flee from it with the panicked celerity of certain Socialists. Yet it was no longer in the forefront of their discourse. The party members of the Seine-Saint-Denis formed the "Comité 89 en 93," the 93 representing both their departmental number in the national administrative taxonomy and the beginning of the Terror. No group flaunted '93 as unabashedly as they. But even these militants evoked it in rather general and more or less anodyne terms as "a source of references, of continuity, and of renewal." It was a time of "anticipations" of future social legislation as well as a time of "revolutionary conquests."

That was also the theme that appealed to Jean Combastel, a Communist deputy and the mayor of Tulle. While he conceded that the Terror was a time of errors, he saw in Robespierre the actor who attempted to go beyond his time in search of a more just world. André Lajoinie, the Communist candidate for the presidency in 1988, camped on a traditional Jacobin position: "the Terror was an arm of the nation defending itself." Yet there were small signs of a certain anxiety, and perhaps of a ferment of change, from both orthodox and heretical quarters. Addressing the central committee in a stilted manner, Guy Hermier referred to "the legitimate questions that the practices of the period called the Terror raise."

From the ranks of the reformers, former minister Charles Fiterman, once Marchais' right-hand man, described the "*dérapage* toward a monstrous aberration" that followed the Revolution of October 1917 in terms very similar to the early revisionist/rightist view of the French experience after 1793. Not even the orthodox were inclined to venture openly an analogy with 1917. Still, they continued to hint that the Terror conserved the fundamental and positive achievements of the Revolution, that somehow without it France would not have been spared the decline that their adversaries claimed the Revolution in fact guaranteed.[28]

The Central Committee Sets the Party Line

The central committee of the PCF devoted a session in April 1987 to the preparation of the bicentennial. Guy Hermier drafted a report rehearsing the party's analysis of the issues at stake in 1989 and sketched out a series of recommendations to govern militant action. The framing theme was that unlike the other political entities in the nation, the PCF remained "a revolutionary party." As such, it had an infinitely greater interest and responsibility in dealing with the R/revolutionary past.

The party had not always been comfortable with the French Revolution. A "vast process of critical reappropriation of national history, of the revolutionary heritage" began during the Popular Front and gained momentum as the party lived through the rout of republican Spain and the rise of fascism. Hermier suggested that the Resistance really began in 1939 when party leader Maurice Thorez exalted the Revolution against the evil designs of Hitler before sixty thousand people at the Buffalo Stadium. Resistance remained the watchword of the Communists in 1989. The party had to resist the onslaught of revisionist historiography and the treason of the PS, which "embraces the theses of François Furet." "Our people," declared Hermier, in a proprietary tone that had a bourgeois ring, got out of the crisis of the Old Regime; and it was once again up to them to get the nation out of the deep crisis of the end of the twentieth century. The new revolution would not necessarily have to be violent. But it would necessarily result in a radical transformation in a peculiarly French style consonant with national values and habits.[29]

Hermier reviewed the party's concrete plans for commemoration. It would rely on the talent and commitment of its many historians and "creators," its press, and its publishing house to forge and convey the message of the R/revolutionary legacy. The idea for Vive 89 had not fully matured, but the party envisaged a vast network of propaganda, education, and participation. The commemoration had to reach into the neighborhoods and the workplaces as well as into the associative fabric. The bicentennial had to be an epitomized mimesis of the Revolution itself, a mobilization of the people, not only in order to fulfill the party's ideological/normative requirements of self-identity but also in order to give it a realistic chance to make some difference: "today it is a rallying of our people that we envision to blaze the path toward a new French Revolution." He urged the militants in the cells and the federations to plan their tactics both for independent local organization, including an effort to recruit non-Communist sympathizers, and for infiltration of the official commemorative apparatus. The central committee wanted to examine various plans as rapidly as possible.

The Party's Celebration

The decline of the PCF was reflected in the modest way in which it corporatively celebrated the bicentennial. The rumors that filtered down to the grass roots of "initiatives planned for 1989 in the same style as Thorez at the Buffalo stadium" in 1939 were pathetically unfounded.[30] Weakened and on the defensive—and, to be sure, situated in a very different international context—the Communist party of 1989 undertook nothing comparable to its impressive mobilization for the sesquicentennial. To assure a "dynamic and popular" celebration of the bicentennial, the party, seconded by the CGT and diverse prominent "personalities," founded an association called Vive 89 whose tactics and activities will be scrutinized below in Book Three.[31]

Billing itself as "the only party to celebrate the French Revolution," the PCF organized the first major bicentennial event at the annual fête sponsored by *L'Humanité*, christened "Fête de la Révolution." But the mammoth popular homage to the Revolution that Gaston Plissonnier, secretary of the central committee, had promised did not materialize. Children paraded in Phrygian caps. Visitors inscribed grievances in notebooks opened at the stands of the party federations. The injustice of the monthly minimum wage (the SMIC), the ravages of growing unemployment, and the militarization of France were among the issues that aroused concern. Exhibitions illustrated "the birth of a nation," science and technology during the Revolution, and the press during the Revolution. The Association Vive 89 advertised the range of services with which it could provide affiliated local commemorative organizations.

A major display focused on books dealing with the Revolution. While Michel Vovelle struggled in the real world to convince scholars that a new and fresher

Marxist historiography was slowly on the rise, in the Communist microcosm Editions Messidor, the press of the PCF, casually brushed off the revisionist assault ("working for the rightward shift of our society," and thus perforce flawed historical analysis) and announced that "the Marxist tradition . . . is doing quite well." The mood was decidedly upbeat if not downright surreal, for *L'Humanité* hailed the signs of a party comeback. All this was made easier to digest by a savant mix of music of contrasting styles: engaged (Léo Ferré), sentimental (Charles Aznavour), and youth-oriented (Garçons Bouchers, Négresses Vertes).[32]

The PCF put on its biggest gathering of the bicentennial season proper in April 1989 under a tent opposite the château de Vincennes, a sort of Bastille II where Rousseau once visited his imprisoned friend Diderot. About eight thousand people participated, including writers, scientists, historians (Vovelle, Mazauric, Casanova), at least one of the Renault Ten, and figures of international revolutionary prestige (Angela Davis and Miriam Makeba). They watched a ballet and excerpt from Renoir's Popular Front *Marseillaise,* which remains one of the most stirring and interesting films devoted to the Revolution. They listened to actors reading Revolutionary texts, and scholars praising them. They heard entertainers sing lines of melancholic tenacity such as the following stanza, unlikely to be etched eternally into the memory of progressive militancy:

> Y'a deux cents ans j'étais sans-culottes [*sic*].
> Aujourd'hui j'ai d'jeans[,] j'ai des bottes.
> On pourrait croire que ça a changé. Mais ça
> rame toujours du même côté.
> [Two hundred years ago I was a sansculotte.
> Today I have jeans and boots.
> You might think that things have changed.
> But we're still breaking our backs in the same way.]

Georges Marchais delivered the keynote address, stressing the continuity between today's struggles and the "emancipating monument" of the Revolution. On the one hand, he pointed to the vigor of perestroika as a sign of the capacity of socialism to modernize and adjust to the demands of tomorrow ("socialism revolutionizes itself in order to develop its potentialities for progress, efficiency, and democracy"). On the other hand, he insisted on the peculiarly French path that socialist construction had to take at home. Without explicitly acknowledging the need for a domestic perestroika—that would have conceded too much to renovators and other internal critics—and without denying the international logic of Communist engagement, Marchais played the national card in a context of increasing concern with national identity.

The secretary-general adumbrated a sort of essential and legitimate French exceptionalism that would respond to national requirements without entirely ignoring global historical necessities. In the name of its R/revolutionary heritage, France had to resist integration into a new Europe whose official program bespoke "a dizzying social regression, the stifling of social rights, a dictatorship aggravated by business scandals (*affairisme*), the overarmament of our continent, the continued pillage of the Third World, the end of the sovereignty of France." For the secretary-general, '93 had a double meaning from the perspective of '89. *Le Monde* noted in passing that Marchais invoked Barnave, Babeuf, Jaurès, and even Tocqueville but failed to mention Robespierre, "to whom French Communists generally refer." At the site of their annual fête the following September, there does not appear to have been a major thoroughfare named for him to complement the avenues of Marat, Saint-Just, and the sansculottes.[33]

The "Civilized" Right

The mainstream right, including large elements of the two main vehicles of the opposition, the RPR and the UDF, had no coherent bicentennial strategy. Members disagreed quite sharply among themselves on the nature and meaning of the Revolution. Some identified more or less passionately with the patriotic/nationalist or statist/centralist or humanist/lyrical dimensions of the Revolution, while others reviled the legacy of Jacobinism in all its avatars. Among the latter were the RPR's Jean Foyer, who lost a nonjuring Angevin clerical ancestor to the guillotine, and for whom the Revolution connoted "millions" of deaths," "inexpiable" hatreds, and a Chaunuean economic catastrophe that fatally handicapped France; and the RPR's Gilles de Robien, a descendant of émigrés, who regretted the baleful legacy of a France permanently "cut into two."

Some were willing to subscribe to a diluted consensualism, while others thirsted for fierce public purging of the Revolution's patrimony of toxic guilt. Some were very much concerned about the bicentennial's impact on the image of France abroad, while others focused strictly on domestic objectives. No one ignored the potential political stakes of the bicentennial season, though they did not agree on the specific advantages or costs of commemorative engagement or repudiation. Eschewing any national doctrine, the party leaderships left it up to individuals to forge their own line vis-à-vis their consciences and their constituents.

Bereft of a clear policy of their own, opposition leaders compensated by relentlessly attacking the Socialists for their putatively diabolical one. They accused their adversaries of a sort of commemorative hijacking—of diverting the festive current to their partisan mill. The right fed its own anxiety, for its failure to articulate a positive bicentennial program encouraged the left to concede no ground and led many opposition politicians into a tautological cul-de-sac in which they (mis)took the slightest sign of bicentennial fervor for a trophy of Socialist aggrandizement.

The president of the RPR, Jacques Chirac, complained bitterly of the confiscation of the celebration by the Elysée and the Ministry of Culture. "I discern something like a will to politicize this commemoration," he said, "by privileging certain historical aspects to the detriment of consensus." His protégé Alain Juppé, secretary-general of the party, gravitated between a splenetic resentment of the Socialists' misbegotten "monopoly of the revolutionary heritage" (after all, we are the *republican* opposition, our think tank is called the Club 89, and the Declaration of the Rights of Man is our credo) and a conviction that to embrace a consensus was to fall into a terrible trap, that celebration was perforce Socialist "political profiteer-ing." A tough infighter, Juppé hinted that the "attempt to capture the heritage of 1789" was personally engineered by the president himself, for it served the insatia-ble needs of his "megalomania." In the same vein, Pierre-André Wiltzer, a deputy of the UDF, detected "a slight odor of the Cult of the Supreme Being," by which he meant not Providence but God-the-President.

La Lettre de la nation, the official voice of the RPR, contended that, in Socialist hands, the bicentennial relinquished its national and civic status and became "a politician's base maneuver." Unable to resist the partisan temptation, "the Social-ists seek to accredit the idea that the heritage of the Revolution belongs to them, that they are the institutional heirs, the wardens of sequestration." Intoxicated by revolutionary fantasies, concluded the RPR's organ, the Socialists regressed to their most sectarian habits and resurrected "those old demons which, in 1981, made them say that light was supplanting darkness." But if the PS was so readily able to lay quasi-exclusive claim to the republican-origin narrative, it was at least in part because of the opposition's failure to insist vigorously, following the example of one of their most prestigious historic chieftains, Michel Debré, that "today the Revolu-tion is part of the inheritance of all the French."[34]

The Right Reclaims the Revolution—Desultorily

"In this commemoration the republican right," lamented the historian Michel Winock, "could have taken easy advantage of the situation" because it had a power-ful genetic title to the rank of "the true heirs" of 1789.[35] In fact, somewhat belatedly and fragmentarily, the opposition tried to reassert its proper place in the originary line of descent. Etienne Pinte, a renovator in the RPR, encouraged supporters of the opposition to embrace the bicentennial, provided it was understood that "1789 was not 1793." Stick the Socialists with the dirty and bloody Revolution, and reclaim the glorious one as our own, recommended rightist commentators. Geared to forging "a new man" and "a perfect society," the Revolution of the Socialists led directly to "all the totalitarianisms of the twentieth century," according to Bernard Pons, Juppé's equally vitriolic predecessor. The left's deeply hewn Robespierrism—its fascination for "a virtuous power"—accounted for its "initial infatuation" for Khomeini, *Le Figaro* reminded its readers. The Terror was the quintessential Socialist revolution, and it betrayed "the founding ideals" of 1789, argued *Le Quotidien de Paris.*

"Seventeen eighty-nine is not the ideological source of Socialism," lectured Juppé the pedagogue-*normalien*. "In reality, 1789 is the product of the philosophy of the Enlightenment, that is to say, a personalist, humanist, and liberal conception of society which is our reference, not that of Socialism." François Léotard and Philippe Mestre, two of the leading voices of the UDF, preferred the English, evolutionary trajectory. If one focused on the great liberating themes, it was not too farfetched to see 1789 as a sort of English Year. Although liberals celebrated '89, Léotard avowed, they were "pessimists of the Revolution," for they could not at any moment forget that "it is pregnant with perversions." Though extremely conservative, former Giscardian minister Michel Poniatowski rejected the claim that the Revolution was an utterly superfluous happening in the best of all possible worlds (the Old Regime was direly crippled, in large part as a result of the "egotisms of the privileged orders") and argued for accepting it en bloc ("Every French person is *indivisibly* its heir.")[36]

Chirac: Between Paris and Koblenz

Of all the opposition leaders, only Jacques Chirac, given his public responsibilities, found himself in a position where his attitude toward the bicentennial impinged concretely on the official plans for celebration. The Socialists were by no means the only ones who believed that Chirac's veto of the world's fair project, as mayor of Paris, was much less the product of finances than of politics. As cohabitation prime minister, Chirac claimed to have energetically seconded the work of the Mission, confided first to Michel Baroin, "a very close friend," and then to Edgar Faure, a longtime political associate for whom he obtained the designation of the roof of the Arche de la Défense as the site of a projected human rights foundation and of a primary bicentennial monument.

Once he left Matignon for the Hôtel de Ville, Chirac insisted that he did all he could to assure a "harmonization" between the efforts of the Mission and those of the city. From Jeanneney's perspective, the cooperation was less perfect than Chirac claimed it to be. The mayor frankly warned the Mission's last president that he would fall flat on his face, and relations between the two men remained strained. Beyond his charge of commemorative "politicization," the former prime minister was irritated by the brutal elimination of his friend Jean-Michel Jarre and by Jack Lang's attempt to take control of the *bals populaires* of 14 July as well as by his lukewarm attitude toward the mayor's human-rights monument on the Champs-de-Mars (dubbed Phallus-sur-Seine by the *Canard enchaîné*). The government was angered by the Chiraquian outcry against the summit-cum-Gouderie on the abject grounds—given the historical and international context—of public inconvenience and fiscal rigor.

Chirac's decision to boycott the climactic events of the fourteenth proved to be a serious political error, and lent retrospective credibility to the charge that he truly wanted the celebration to fail. The left and moderate press vilified him for his "desertion," his "emigration," and his myopia. "The opposition, with the mayor of Paris in the forefront, must be kicking itself for having refused to have anything to do with the grandest and most successful fête that the capital has known for a very long time," observed André Fontaine, "all the more so, for never has a commemoration of the Revolution been less revolutionary." The nation and the capital were shamed and dishonored, asserted *L'Evénement du Jeudi*, which marveled at the poor judgment of the president of the RPR: "When one is mayor of a capital that is more beautiful, more radiant than ever before, one does not sulk in estrangement, one does not hide . . . and one does not offer such a naive gift, four days running, to Mitterrand."[37]

The Far Right and Le Pen

Serving as the intellectual bridge between the extreme right and the conservative wing of the mainstream right, the Club de l'Horloge also disputed the left's exclusive claims to the Revolution. The left perverted the true sense of '89 by casting the Declaration of Rights in universalist terms and denying its historical specificity and cultural rootedness. For the Horlogistes, rights were inconceivable outside the context of national identity. By wrenching "human rights from their civic and community arenas," abolishing "the distinction between citizen and foreigner," and transforming "kindness for one's neighbor into a veritable cult of otherness," the Socialists had sold out 1789. Forged in large part by Yvon Blot, a former RPR militant who had joined Jean-Marie Le Pen's governing ranks, the Horloge line could be read either as a cynically oblique way of travestying and thus discrediting the Revolution or an adroit strategy of partial reappropriation.

Blot took pains to contest the Socialist claim to direct filiation with the republic. The republican ideal was founded "on the two key values of Nation and Liberty." Everything for which the Socialists stood was antagonistic to those values, Blot contended. He tried to turn the history of the Revolution itself against the Marxist line, which he associated intimately with all socialisms, commingling the PS and PCF. The "surpassings" that Albert Soboul and his Jacobin friends extolled, Hébertisme and Babouvisme, movements to enhance the political and social power of working people, were combatted in the first case by Danton and Robespierre together and in the second by Carnot. The "principles of hatred and egalitarian dictatorship" shared by Hébertisme and Babouvisme subverted the very foundations of republicanism, which drew its life force from the idea of the Nation, of unity and *rassemblement*.

Heirs to social division and totalitarianism, the Socialists today were protectors of "a host of feudalisms" meant to protect their clienteles, a honeycomb of privileges that transgressed the Revolutionary principle of liberty. Though he drew radically different lessons, like Mitterrand and Marchais, Blot identified liberty with equality, or more precisely, equality with liberty. Equality did not signify the redistribution of riches to endow liberty with a concrete meaning; this was the new feudalism. Rather, Blot's equality was "the end of privileges and the advent of a society founded on individual merit (and thus on liberty)." He called on the entire right to resist the Socialo-Communist effort, on the eve of the bicentennial, "to unearth some republican ancestors so as not to frighten off the majority of electors."

Though it had among its constituents a frankly counterrevolutionary clientele, in this instance the Club de l'Horloge appealed to Le Pen's "national-populist" stance. As Pierre-André Taguieff points out, while the traditional counterrevolutionaries globally reject the Revolution and its aftermath, Le Pen and certain, though by no means all, of his followers "shoulder the entire past of France," as their leader phrased it, including the two centuries of the republic. Still, the Front national accepted the Revolution without enthusiasm as a very modest part of a very long national history that stretched back between twenty and forty centuries. Distinguishing the authentically "national" from the ominously "foreign" elements of the Revolution, the Lepéniste prism refracted out everything that did not resonate with its vision of the construction of national identity.[38]

François Furet is probably correct in placing Le Pen closer to Pierre Poujade than to Charles Maurras. But if "he does not define himself in relation to the Revolution and against the ideas of 1789," there is certainly a great deal in that legacy that he despised and combatted. Again under Blot's tutelage, Le Pen assailed the core of Furet's Revolution, but in terms that were meant to draw succor from the vernacularized version of Furet's analysis. On the anniversary of the Declaration of the Rights of Man, Le Pen denounced this text as the carrier of the germ of totalitarianism. In the name of their war against exclusion, the Socialists set about destroying all the institutional bulwarks that guaranteed liberty. This "totalitarian egalitarianism," warned Le Pen and Blot, would lead France ineluctably to injustice and inefficiency, even as it had in the past issued in bloody terrors every time it had been implemented.

At the first colloquium of the Front national's scientific committee ("and if 1789 were to be done all over again?"), numerous orators developed the argument that the Revolution and the rights of man were nothing more than a myth created and sustained by "pseudohistorians and pseudophilosophers" in the service of socialo-Marxist dominion. Jurist Bruno Gollnisch challenged an idea to which Le Pen himself had appeared to subscribe, that the Revolution deserved credit as a catalyst of national unity. Other speakers portrayed the Revolution as essentially a "bloody event," more or less reducible to the Terror, and the rights doctrine as inimical to a healthy social development alimented by "religious faith, that is to say, Catholicism," and inoculated against the peril of "cosmopolitanism," which could only lead to "uprootedness," "egotism," and regression to the state of nature.

One of the FN's key national leaders, Bruno Mégret, closed the day with a scathing attack on the Socialist confiscation of the revolutionary mythology, not, as the mainstream right complained, because the Socialists excluded the rest of the nation from its rightful claim on the revolutionary-republican patrimony, but because they used that mythology for vicious ends. Unlike Blot, Mégret did not reject equality as an unnatural and perverse metaphysical contrivance. Rather, he construed it in the Socialists' own terms and accused them of flouting it "while maintaining privileges and feudal fiefs for the benefit of the unions, the media, and the administration," even as they scorned the principle of national sovereignty "to the profit of the immigrants." Like the Chiraquians, Mégret did not want to allow the Socialists the "imposture" of magnifying the significance of the Revolution while discreetly suppressing its "totalitarian dimension." In a discourse redolent of Bernard Pons's, Le Pen himself showed how the Revolutionary "new man" led directly to Hitler and Pol Pot.[39]

Populism and the Right to Resist(ance)

If the Revolutionary idiom was always a part of Le Pen's rhetorical baggage, it became especially prominent in the bicentennial season. It was tempting to use the anniversary to demonstrate that the France of 1989 was suffering from a legitimacy crisis as grave as the one that ushered in 1789. In a rollicking populist appeal for a new revolution that he published in *Le Figaro*, Le Pen contended that "the grand priests of the religion of '89 have become merchants of the temple." Just as the eighteenth-century public had denounced the king for speculating on grain instead of distributing bread, Le Pen portrayed the Socialists as hoarders, profiteers, and usurpers who impoverished instead of nourishing the people. From his palace, Mitterrand "wishes himself king and even god." His minions call my electors riffraff, gloated Le Pen, just as the aristocrats of the Old Regime had stigmatized the laboring poor. "In the Pantheon of their values, the people are missing."

Without the people, exclaimed Le Pen, there was no fraternity. Nor was there liberty, for the government restricted access to public communication and refused recourse to referendum (the people want the death penalty—even though they were prepared to spare Louis XVI) and protected the unions which crushed freedom of work. Nor was there equality, because the Socialists trafficked in privileges of all sorts in order to perpetuate their rule and denied representation to the FN, despite its substantial electoral following. Proliferating crime, especially against women and old people, proved that there was as little security as in the waning days of the Old Regime when authority was utterly corroded. "The French know which are the Bastilles to be conquered," Le Pen concluded with a flourish. His accolytes appropriated the same imagery. "The Bastille, today," clamored Bruno Mégret, is "the politician [*sic*] class and the lobbies that support it."[40]

In language more reminiscent of the Vichyssois revolutionaries than of those of '89, Le Pen even called for the convocation of the "Estates General of the French people of 1989." Two hundred years after the Revolution, "the French no longer enjoy the advantages of the monarchy, [and] they suffer all the disadvantages of the republic." As the only political leader untainted by scandal and unimplicated in responsibility for the "decline of the nation," and as the beneficiary of 4.5 million votes registered in the name of a national renaissance, he demanded, "as did Lafayette in 1787, the meeting of the Estates General of the provinces and the trades" so that the people could express their grievances and their will. "Down with the Fifth Republic, dishonored, decrepit, destabilized, discredited, exhausted."[41]

The burgeoning discredit of the political class, and the scandals leading to the amnesty law—all in the penumbra of the bicentennial—served mightily the interests of the FN. A sort of Robespierre-Cromwell-Robin Hood on a white horse, crusading against political corruption and abuses of power, Le Pen called for the creation of "committees of public health [*salubrité*]." Contrasting his own purity with the sloth of the old (Socialist) regime, he indignantly denounced contemptible efforts to sully him (yet with a certain Robespierrist inflection of righteousness and allergy-to-calumny) and thus destabilize his cause. Pilloried for repeated (calculated?) outbursts of anti-Semitism, indicted in the courts, and convicted in the media, Le Pen reacted with outrage: "Nor do I accept subjection to either the dictatorship or the persecution of a certain number of extremist Jews of the left." The press, where Jews swarmed out of proportion to their numbers in the general population, erected itself into "a revolutionary tribunal." "You believe that you are living under the French Revolution," fulminated Citizen Le Pen. Scorned as a matrix of totalitarianism, the Rights of Man became a source of precious recourse to the head of the FN when he felt threatened. He warned that he would invoke the right of "resistance to oppression," one of the "four essential human rights," if the rumored plan ("a totalitarian idea") to penalize those convicted of racist crimes with a suspension of their civic and political rights came to fruition. In promising a relentless campaign of "national resistance," his reference, naturally, was not to the Communists in 1941 but to the Vendéens in 1793.[42]

BOOK TWO

PRODUCING THE
BICENTENNIAL

Toward a Bicentennial Project
From the World's Fair to the Grand Orient

Among the many reasons Socialists had to exult in François Mitterrand's ascension to the presidency was the opportunity it appeared to give them to prepare a lavish bicentennial celebration that would underline the intimate connections they perceived between the fin-de-siècle revolutionary ambitions of the eighteenth and twentieth centuries. To be sure, they would have to win the presidency a second time to assure control over the orchestration of the solemn and festive events of 1989. But if they could set planning in motion rapidly, in some sense they would, in effect, hold a mortgage on the commemoration that would be impossible to ignore. In September 1981 the government announced its intention to organize a world's fair—or, more precisely, an international exposition—in 1989. The eyes of the whole world would then focus on the living patrimony of the Revolution and on the particular genius of France as the economic, cultural, social, and moral pacesetter for the next century. Though it was structured separately from the centennial commemoration, the international exposition of 1889, whose most striking emblem was the Eiffel Tower, loomed as an obvious source of inspiration.

Wholly apart from possible bicentennial connections, the celebrated airplane builder and idiosyncratic rightist legislator Marcel Dassault had articulated the idea of an international exposition on several occasions. In 1979 he urged a benignly indifferent National Assembly to sponsor an exposition in order to stimulate economic development and diversification, attract tens of millions of buyers to France, and buoy the youth of the nation with a climate both festive and educational. A year later, President Giscard d'Estaing evoked the possibility of a world's fair to mark the year 2000. Ever purposeful and perseverant, Dassault returned to his theme in the inaugural address he delivered as doyen of the Socialist-dominated Assembly in July 1981.[1]

177

Announced two months later, the government's bicentennial project elicited an initially favorable response in most quarters. The "state of grace" encouraged cooperation; and, in concrete terms, the proposal promised attractive benefits to the entire nation, left and right, Paris and provinces. In November 1981 Mitterrand named the lawyer, urbanist, and distinguished civil servant Robert Bordaz to conduct a preliminary·study. Close to the RPR, Bordaz had achieved a reputation for nonpartisan competence during his tenure as manager of the Pompidou Center construction project and as French commissioner at several world's fairs. With the accord of the city of Paris, in December France submitted its candidacy as host nation for a world's fair to the assembly of the Bureau International des Expositions.

Consulting widely among public figures and historians (including Albert Soboul and Jean Favier) in search of framing themes, Bordaz developed a vision of the Revolution as both a specifically French emancipation from a regime of "unbearable inequalities" and the beginning of an epoch of human rights and scientific progress that belonged to the entire world. Encouraged by the president, Bordaz planned to focus on the latter aspects rather than the former, privileging the relation of the Revolutionary legacy to the future rather than to the past, in a geyser of pre-postmodern civic and technological optimism. Meanwhile a "workshop of urbanism and creation" (including Renzo Piano, Antoine Grumbach, and Pontus Hulten) explored potential sites and imagined bold design scenarios playing off the Seine, featuring a floating boulevard leading to an exhibition cluster in the old Citröen space in the west and a whole new urban district to be built on the eastern side of the capital at Tolbiac-Bercy. Between these poles heralding the twenty-first century, the project marshaled the great historical monuments and sites of the capital in a celebration of liberty, solidarity, and science.[2]

Stillborn

By February 1983 Bordaz presented a scale model of the exposition project. Both Mitterrand and Chirac scrutinized it. The following month the government named Gilbert Trigano, the highly successful head of the Club Méditerranée tourism-vacation empire, to organize the Commissariat Général that would manage the entire operation. But the grand design began to unravel in the spring. Even as the parliament worked on a law needed to beget and frame the exposition, the opposition leaders, who controlled the municipal and regional governments, suggested shifting the site of the exposition to Marne-la-Vallée, later to be crowned the home of EuroDisneyland, or at least splitting it between Paris and this eastern suburb. The Chiraquian "Fronde" culminated in the publication of a formal declaration in early July in which the city of Paris and the region of Ile-de-France contested the wisdom of holding an international exposition in the capital on the grounds that it would be onerous for the taxpayers and deleterious to the interests of city and hinterland. Mitterrand reacted sharply and swiftly with a curt statement announcing the definitive abandonment of the exposition project. Given the government's commitment to decentralization, reasoned the president, it would be inconceivable to proceed without the approbation and collaboration of local and regional leaders.[3]

This brutal rupture generated an acerbic polemic. Chirac's supporters hailed his good sense, juxtaposing it to the irresponsible and profligate reveries of the Elysee. The exposition was merely another of the left's "castles in Spain," the symbol of a failed ideology "which is built on the postulate of culture and which denies the economic realities in order to privilege the political imperatives." This critique implicitly assimilated the Socialists to the Jacobins, who had sought to regenerate mankind at the cost of ruining the economy. The right pressed the claim that at bottom Mitterrand was relieved to free himself of the bicentennial millstone. According to this view, it was purely cynical and hypocritical—an elliptical accolade to the president's tactical acumen—to blame the "sabotage" on Chirac and the opposition.[4]

The Socialists interpreted the affair as an example of quintessential Chirac: opportunism, treachery, self-serving political machination. One minister, Paul Quilès, speculated that Chirac's ulterior motive was to win the Olympic Games on his own for Paris in 1992. His colleague Jack Lang put the matter in a broader psychopolitical and biographical context. Chirac's career consisted of weather-vane changes dictated by the direction of the wind at the moment, betrayals of persons and causes to further self-interest. "It is grave," read Lang's indictment, "for a national leader, as a result of his lack of commitment to his given word, to undermine the international credit of his country." It is interesting to note that in 1981–82 Lang and Bordaz were ready to settle for a Marne-la-Vallée exposition, a notion vetoed by Mitterrand, who felt that a non-Parisian site would "diminish" the commemorative impact as well as the image of France in the world (Paris being "the flower of France" and "the heart" of the Revolution). Nor did the Socialists concede that the exposition project was an economic "chimera." On the contrary, in bottom-line terms it would have been a highly profitable undertaking, stimulating the economy and creating jobs, even as it restituted to Paris the title of artistic and intellectual capital of the world.

The Communist party echoed these accusations. Paul Laurent of *L'Humanité* solemnly denounced Chirac's behavior as contrary to the national interest. Other Communist leaders vigorously pursued a line that the Socialists (even this early in the game) tended to avoid, making a crucial connection between Chirac's attitude toward the French Revolution and his renunciation of the international exposition. A member of the "international elite," the incarnation of a right "more and more Versaillaislike and seditious," Chirac "certainly has no appetite to honor our ancestors of 1789." Nor did the critique of the abandonment follow a rigidly partisan left-right fault line. Though he saw the fiscal dimension as a genuine problem, Jean Favier, a conservative, regretted the unique opportunity to show the entire world the positive side of the Revolutionary patrimony, one of the major sources of the genius of France. He feared that, without a grand project, the bicentennial risked dissolving into "the fragmentary."[5]

Whether the project would truly have been prohibitively expensive, noted *Le Monde* prudently, "no one will ever know." Could one cavalierly dismiss the calculations of Bordaz, who was no political friend of the Socialists? He foresaw an unequivocally positive balance, both in fiscal terms and as a function of the longer-term benefits for infrastructure (transportation, communications, and housing), for industry, and for culture. What about the figures of Trigano, notorious for his good sense in business? For a "dispersed" exposition, leaner than the grand Bordaz project, located simultaneously at many different intramural sites, he estimated costs at Fr 11.4 billion, a sum offset by rapid returns of Fr 10 billion in building contracts and Fr 4 billion in expenditures by visitors, a positive balance to be amplified further by worldwide purchases of French technology, for which the exposition would provide a unique "showcase." Yet can partisanship alone account for the Senate's calculation that the real costs would be closer to Fr 40 billion? While appreciating the lyrical and historical tenor of Mitterrand's vision, *Le Monde* reproached him for failing to do his homework on the economics of the enterprise before broadcasting the idea publicly. Times of austerity where politics was reduced to demoralizing "management" were especially perilous moments "for the killing of symbols." Thus the newspaper's chastening conclusion: "To stifle hopes is a serious thing; it is better not to give rise to them in the first place." In the same breath it taxed Chirac for narrow, self-serving electoral motives that induced him to forget with unseemly celerity the passion with which he had espoused the Paris candidacy before the Bureau International des Expositions not long before. *Libération* cast a pox on both houses, scolding the mayor for political machination and bad faith and the president for his dreamy, slipshod approach to a grandiose undertaking.[6]

Mitterrand's apparent abjuration not merely of the exposition but of the whole bicentennial dossier is still hard to explain. "How are we to view the renunciation of all substitute projects?" asked *Le Monde*. "Is it a fit of bad temper, a reaction of relief, or the result of a calculation?" In an increasingly morose political context, did the bicentennial horizon suddenly seem too remote, beyond ordinary hubris? The failure to address the issue squarely until the slippery and bewildering days of governmental cohabitation jeopardized the prospect of realizing a celebration commensurate with France's sense of self.

Toward a Low-Key Bicentennial: Rector Mallet

There was, however, a last spasm of preelection bicentennial planning in the fall of 1985. Worried about the absence of the necessary institutions at a relatively advanced date and fearful that the forthcoming legislative elections threatened further delay, a number of Mitterrand's own counselors argued strenuously for immediate action. A decision was made to offer the post of bicentennial coordinator to Robert Mallet, a former rector of the Academy of Paris, France's most prestigious educational jurisdiction. That decision seems a priori to suggest that the Elysée was opting for a relatively low-profile, bureaucratic undertaking. Save in a highly circumscribed universe of professors and educational administrators, Mallet was utterly unknown. A specialist in modern French literature, but not a renowned scholar, Mallet had no cultural following in the intellectual milieu. After a brief period at Aix-en-Provence, he moved to Madagascar where he helped create a university. Upon his return to metropolitan France, he participated in the creation of the university at Amiens, where he became rector.

In the wake of May 1968, de Gaulle (Mallet takes pleasure in emphasizing) named him to the critical rectorate of Paris, a position he exercised for eleven years. Reduced to a simple professor by Alice Saunier-Séité, Giscard's aggressive minister of education, who sought to "punish" him for unspecified sins, Mallet claimed to have declined the invitation of Mitterrand's first minister of education, Alain Savary, to return to the rectorate when the left took power in 1981. Still, he accepted the charge of vice president of the Conseil supérieur d'éducation nationale presided over by the minister and usually reserved to the Paris rector, a sort of indemnification for his unwarranted disgrace.

Beyond his record as an able administrator, Mallet boasted one modest claim to experience in practicing commemoration. Serving as vice president of the national commission for the celebration of the Capetian Millennium, he reports that Mitterrand playfully noted when they met that he would be shifting from the Capetian "cradle" to their "coffin." Called to the Elysée several months before parliamentary · elections for an hour-long meeting with the president, Mallet relates that they were in "full agreement" for a soft, ecumenical bicentennial. Dazzled by Mitterrand's "serenity," his "enormous culture," and "his liberal spirit," the rector recalls a president determined not to exacerbate divisions or rekindle conflict: "no blood." In their discussion not only did the president repudiate the Revolution-as-bloc, but he endorsed the Ozoufian idea of remembering the "better" rather than the "worst." Mallet also contended that the president summoned him to stress the future in preference to the past, a line that seems inconsonant with Mitterrand's celebrated passion for history.

Mitterrand's irenic posture appealed to Mallet's deepest instincts: toleration, concord, engagement in "the party of ideas" rather than "ideas of the parties." As part of a strategy of "reconciliation," the rector (who acknowledged absolutely no political or ideological attachment) obtained authorization to "reintegrate" the Vendée into the commemorative campaign. The only firm project that Mallet appears to have formulated reflected his temperament: a huge "fête de la qualité de l'homme" at St.-Florent-le-Vieil, a tiny town near Cholet, where human values had triumphed at least briefly over barbarous inclinations in an incident of compassion joining blues and whites during the Vendée insurgency. Perhaps inspired by a segment in Philippe de Villiers's scenario at Le Puy-du-Fou, the allegory evinces the rector's sensibility and the style of commemoration that he intended to pursue.

Direly wounded in October 1793 by the republican forces, General Charles Bonchamps ordered his retreating army to spare the lives of several thousand blues whom they had captured. Carried before his soldiers, who had massed cannon and guns before the abbey in which the republican soldiers had taken refuge, Bonchamps, "in a dying voice," is reported to have exclaimed: "Christian soldiers, remember your God; royalists, remember your king: Mercy! Mercy for the prisoners! I ask for it, I order it." Descendants on both sides kept the memory of the episode alive, some to stress the sense of honor and chivalry that marked the losing cause (in a manner redolent of post–Civil War American Southerners wistful for heroic Dixie), others to cast into relief the underlying humanity that bound all men who believed in their cause (again in anticipation of a prominent American theme of gray-blue reconciliation). In 1827 a funerary monument was dedicated to the memory of the general. The statue, in a lachrymose classical style, depicted Bonchamps rising from his stretcher, his bare chest draped in bloodied robes, to order mercy for the prisoners. The artist was David d'Angers, whose father had been among the blues saved by Bonchamps. All his life he had yearned to "acquit his debt of gratitude toward the man called 'a hero as generous as he was brave.'" The deeply moving ceremony, marshaling scores of veterans, did not fully purge the emotion felt by the latter. During the two days that followed "the virile faces of the old peasant soldiers passed in review before the sculptor, 'who recorded with the same pencil their testimonies and their features.'"[7]

From here the story of the rector's destiny lapses into a certain fuzziness. Mallet maintains that his nomination decree was ready the very day that he visited the presidential palace. Yet it was the supremely apolitical rector who urged the very political Elysée to postpone its promulgation until after the elections. Ostensibly more lucid than his interlocutors, the rector felt that it would be inappropriate to act before the democratic process of readjustment.

Mallet appears to have been neither surprised nor alarmed by the right's victory. He felt that he had been on good terms with Chirac during his rectorate, which he owed after all to the Gaullist benediction. Matignon, the prime minister's office, called him as soon as Chirac was installed in order to convey the new government's approbation of his appointment. Mallet departed confidently for a July vacation only to learn on his return that, "regretfully," Matignon had changed its mind. A discreet, self-possessed man, the rector allowed that this volte-face was "a little much." He attributed it to political calculation: Chirac stood to gain not a single vote in naming Mallet, but the Masonic-mutualist networks of a Michel Baroin, the new nominee, could be of precious succor. Mitterrand communicated his "consternation" to the rector, who showed dignity in his effacement. Deeply civic-minded—he depicted his own inclination as "close to the Masons"—Mallet gracefully assumed the modest task of president of the bicentennial committee of Picardy, where he toiled inconspicuously for a sober yet festive commemoration.[8]

Masonic Cop: Baroin to the Rescue

With François Mitterrand's concurrence, in August 1986 Premier Jacques Chirac named Michel Baroin, a prominent fifty-five-year-old businessman and former civil servant, to direct the newly created "mission of commemoration of the bicentennial of the French Revolution and of the Declaration of the Rights of Man and Citizen."[9] Baroin seemed tailor-made to fit into the procrustean bed of cohabitation. If the rightist *Quotidien de Paris* characterized him as "a well-pedigreed liberal close to the RPR," the left-leaning *Le Monde* stressed his good personal relationship with Mitterrand. Classmates at the Institut d'études politiques de Paris, Chirac and Baroin had remained in close touch over the years and had consulted frequently when the former was minister of the interior and the latter a member of the prefectoral corps. The connection with the president was more oblique, but it involved the sort of personal-patronage mediation that still governed relations in the provinces: Mitterrand had been conseiller général in a canton of the Morvan inhabited by Baroin's uncle, a fervent supporter. By and large this appointment was well-received, save on the far right, where Baroin's Masonic ties made him deeply suspect, and in certain fractions of the left, where he was stigmatized as a man of the right. Leftist historian Madeleine Rebérioux was particularly ferocious: he was a mystical reactionary whose belief that "all men are brothers" struck an "insufferable" Orwellian chord for her.[10]

Baroin's personal, professional, and cultural trajectory, which seemed to mark him as a "federator of human ambitions," made him an attractive and interesting choice. His biography reads like a Horatio Alger tale with a slightly Rousseauian hue (the Rousseau of the *Polish Constitution* rather than *Emile*). His working parents, of peasant stock, raised him in a "modest" household. A war orphan, his mother worked for the postal service. His father abandoned the land for a career with the police. Both toiled for the Resistance, apparently with a characteristic lack of ostentation. The "mutualist ethic" that shaped Baroin's ideology took root in a rural society built on reciprocity and solidarity and in a family that swore by hard work, disdained advancement save by merit, and inculcated a hardy "moral rigor." After completing studies in public policy and administration and obtaining a doctorate in law, Baroin followed his father's footsteps into the police, joining the Sûreté nationale, with which he allegedly remained in discreet touch all his life. Infused with a Platonic vision of the police-in-the-polis that reminds one, in the hexagonal context, of the totalizing and scientific ambitions of the eighteenth-century Paris police officials Delamare and Lemaire, Baroin regarded this phase as "one of the most beautiful periods of my existence."

Though he was not indifferent to the macho mystique of the heroic cop, prevention rather than repression commanded his attention. "There is nothing more noble than this task," he contended, because the guarantee of one's security was the precondition to collective life, comity, and civic virtue, and because "nonviolence is one of the first human rights." Long before the bicentennial Baroin subscribed to a philosophy of consensus consisting of a somewhat unwholesome blend of paternalism and mutualism. From the metacop's vantage point, the bad news that flooded the press and the airwaves not only demoralized the citizenry but in some sense became reified as a material force of social disintegration. In the name of civic order and harmony, Baroin called on the media to stop emphasizing violence and catastrophe, to "cease putting the accent on that which divides in order to favor once and for all that which binds people together and makes them solidary." Even with the help of word professionals, Baroin never overcame his inability to express his idealism in terms devoid of a lingering sanctimoniousness.[11]

Beginning in 1964 Baroin served as subprefect for five years at Nogent-sur-Seine, a task that was conceptually for him still very much in the grand tradition of the police of the commonweal. There followed a two-year stint as secretary-general of the department of the Aube at Troyes, a crucially located post of observation and mediation. Baroin unabashedly lived the cult of the state because the state was the guarantor of peace through the rule of law. Thus his determination as a state servant, in his stilted phrase, "to maintain an absolute independence with regard to what is called political power." Yet Baroin was keenly interested in politics because he knew that politics was the practical language of civic action from below and of policy-making from above.

At Troyes Baroin became known, in the best sense, as a fixer. When local politicians of all colors needed to get something done rapidly, they turned to the secretary-general, a man admired for his back-channel network and his problem-solving efficacy. Even as he practiced politics while admonishing against its contamination, so too did he hesitate between a steadfast commitment to "apply the law" as the supreme virtue of the state servant and a moralizing/civilizing discourse that seemed elliptically to question the sapience if not the legitimacy of certain official ways of doing things. This tension between positive law and a higher law, between rival claims on his obedience, marked his entire career in the private as well as the public sector.[12]

From the periphery Baroin returned to the very center in 1971 for two years of apprenticeship in national politics as a staff aide to the presidency of the National Assembly. Helping to make the legislative process work, "I knew the entire political class," Baroin confided. He spent much of his time shaking hands and making deals as he had done at Troyes, but with far greater stakes in a much headier environment. Edgar Faure, the second of the parliamentary presidents whom he served and for whom he developed enduring esteem, taught him lessons that clashed starkly with his childhood ethic and the conception of duty that he brandished publicly: "In politics, my dear Baroin, the way to reach the goal is never the straight line, [but] it is always the broken line."

It is not impossible that this counsel influenced Baroin's decision to stand for the mayoralty of Nogent in response to the appeal of the two previous officeholders, who sought a candidate capable of blocking the Communists in a city almost evenly divided between left and right. As usual when he faced deep cleavages, Baroin opted for a third way, the quest for pragmatic reconciliation embodied by a unity list vaunting its selfless devotion to "the promotion" of the "real" interests of Nogent, including a program for the construction of a nuclear power plant that was well under way but still hotly contested. Contravening all the established customs of local politics, Baroin obtained almost two-thirds of the vote, and ran the city with the support of "a unanimous city council," he claimed, including the votes of the Communists. In 1973 Baroin repeated his coup in the cantonal elections, wresting a seat in the Conseil général with 66 percent of the vote.[13]

The next year Baroin ventured once again into terra incognita, the business world, though the insurance company of which he became chief executive officer, given its mutualist character, was not quite like all other enterprises in the private sector in its ethos. Nor was it like the best of the others in its results, for it was a listless operation, occupying a comfortable terrain with a quasi-captive clientele but unmoved by a vigorous appetite to improve and compete. Baroin transformed the Garantie mutuelle des fonctionnaires (GMF) into a dynamic, pugnacious, but socially conscious enterprise. A decade after he took over, it became one of Europe's leaders in its field with 2.5 million members, almost twice as many policy subscriptions, thirty-seven hundred employees, and two hundred offices. It diversified into banking and into the burgeoning market of culture and leisure (FNAC); as a trophy of its vitality and grasp, it even acquired an American insurance company.

Baroin's house hagiographer depicted him as a sort of righteous and squeaky-clean Midas: "There is a side to Michel Baroin that is a little bit magical: he transforms rather quickly everything he touches into gold." But Baroin surely did not view himself as merely another talented and rapacious entrepreneur transfixed by the bottom line. Just as he had been a moving force in the international police community in efforts to forge a charter of ethical conduct, so as a capitalist did he labore to diffuse the spirit of "the social economy," a conception that subordinated profit to higher humanitarian concerns—or, more precisely, argued for their long-term synergy and mutual dependence.[14]

Given Baroin's philosophical preoccupations and his temperament, it is hardly surprising that he became a devoted Mason, though his adversaries continue to allege that he joined the order as part of a long-term intelligence mission ordered by the upper echelons of his first professional confraternity, the police. (An observer close to the Baroin family notes that Baroin joined the Masons *before* he entered the Renseignements généraux, the internal intelligence-gathering service, and denounces rumors concerning his putative infiltration as a smear campaign orchestrated from the Elysée.) He traced his Masonic engagement in part to his life-long passion for the Declaration of the Rights of Man, galvanized by a high school teacher who made it the core of his curriculum during the Occupation. "I admit that this memory still moves me," remarked Baroin, "to study a text of this kind in such circumstances!" Later he defined the Masons as "the pilgrims of human rights." In 1978 he assumed the highest dignity of France's leading order, grand master of the Grand Orient. During two years he presided over 398 meetings throughout the land, in the style of the *missi dominici* who had once woven the administrative bonds that constituted the nation's tissue. "This experience enabled me to come to know France well," he told an interviewer.

Philosophy and Pragmatism: The Third Way

Ideologically, Baroin seems to have been foreordained to be the man of the ecumenical bicentennial. His abiding ambition had always been to be "one of the artisans of a greater social harmony." It is easy for intellectuals to scoff at his worn pieties and for political commentators, themselves the products and clients of the left–right manichaeanism they routinely assail, to dismiss him as an archaic and/or opportunistic anomaly. But it is impossible to gainsay Baroin's talent and his tenacity, and it is worth noting that his quixotic discourse is deeply rooted in post-Revolutionary history and gives voice to a utopian dream which many of his compatriots still find enthralling. His brand of Masonic humanism combined nicely with his vision of the social economy and his memories of Morvan communitarianism. Science has proven Darwin wrong, Baroin believed. The savage aggressiveness that had marked much of human experience, especially in the economic arena since the industrial revolution, was a mere chance mishap. Through intelligence and goodwill, men and women could avoid mutual destruction.

This tough cop hated violence in all its forms, a visceral allergy that never permitted him to embrace the French Revolution despite his Masonic ardor for the Enlightenment. Discursive brutality to the contrary notwithstanding, Baroin believed that "divisions are most often artificial. They do not correspond to the deep reality of the country. They serve only the good fortune and the careers of our politicians." Tolerance, "the respect of differences," education, and a commitment to "the common good" were the remedies, the vectors of unification. "I am not afraid of this worn term: Fraternity," avowed Baroin before he was called to bicentennial responsibilities. This value, known also as love, corresponded to humankind's deepest instinct; liberated from the oppressive structures that stifled or mystified it, it could become the paramount ordering principle of every level of social organization, from the family to the world community.

As a businessman and as a civil servant, Baroin knew that consensus had to be the objective of workplace as well as civic relations in order to generate the right blend of growth and stability. He boasted that in his enterprise he practiced the Auroux Laws (democratizing the workplace, formulated by a Socialist minister) long before they were passed, in a constant effort to "verify that consensus exists between the wage earners and management." Whether the personnel shared his optimistic appreciation of relations remains to be seen. Baroin's immense admiration for the role of consensus in Japanese society and enterprise raises questions about both the means and the ends that he had in mind. Yet his declarations of humanism appeared to bely the worst authoritarian features of the Japanese model.

Rejecting both the bureaucratic planification of a Socialist system and the untamed jungle of classical liberalism, Baroin called for liberty with security, which he translated concretely as "to have more in order to be more." He was a rugged individualist ("one must be in charge of oneself") who believed at the same time in the necessity of solidarity among individuals. Despite his call for balance, however, parts of his political testament have the ring of evangelical liberalism: "Every time that man preferred security over freedom, he accepted a logic of decline and led civilization toward its ruin. . . . this is just what we are doing now." Given his dislike of the intrusive state (he called this his "anarcholibertarian" strain), it is not clear how he envisaged the allocation of fiscality and the practice of transfers and redistribution that fraternity-solidarity seemed to require. The Masonic evocation of the mellifluous encyclopedist message—"mankind, reason, nature, progress, happiness"—was unlikely to reassure the Third or the Fourth Worlds.

Since the Masonic itinerary resonated so well with the bicentennial charge, most observers focused on it in assessing Baroin's worldview. To commentators on the extreme right, such as François Brigneau, for whom the Masons were key players in the conspiracy that made the Revolution, it seemed logical, even fateful that a Michel Baroin would organize the commemoration. The *Quotidien de Paris* cast the picture in metaphorical terms: the three poles of Baroin's brilliant career—security, business sense, philosophical dimension—epitomized "the Masonic triangle." Beyond its commitment to Enlightenment rationalism, the Masonic shibboleth-goal, "to bring together that which is scattered," seemed particularly appropriate in the relentlessly rancorous arena of Revolutionary debate.[15]

Fraternity and the Logic of Love

Baroin's notion was to divert attention from the Revolution's negative passions by shifting the focus radically away from the patrimony's divisive potential. This was the strategic leitmotif of Baroin's "charter" for the Mission, a strange, albeit in many ways sympathetic, manifesto—frenetic, hyperbolic, intense. It begins with a bloated discussion of the state of the universe, which is depicted as "destabilized" in every domain—economically, demographically, socially, spiritually, and so on. This context of uncertainty, runs the first of several conclusory non sequiturs, makes it imperative that the rights of man be at the core of our efforts to build the third millennium. In this new age only parts of the Revolutionary heritage are germane and useful, those aspects that are genuinely "universal" and "humanistic." The most urgent and relevant Revolutionary/rights theme for the third millennium is fraternity, the third and often neglected component of the celebrated trinity.

While the leading voices in the public sphere maintained that liberty was the predicate without which nothing else could be achieved, Baroin inverted their equation. Fraternity should replace liberty as the first element in the national motto, "for it is patent," Baroin proclaimed in his inaugural speech to the Mission, "that if this Fraternity is not practiced here and elsewhere, liberty will disappear." In his conception of "universal fraternity," Baroin privileged a line that Mitterrand would make the nucleus of his bicentennial message, and which would become sharply controversial in the immediate postbicentennial sociopolitical conjuncture: "It is possible to live united in the respect of [our] differences."

To achieve this sociopsychological nirvana, Baroin counted vaguely on a mix of science (technology and education) and love (generosity and understanding). The gravest threat to science and love—and to "the survival of man"—is violence, by allusion to which Baroin obliquely hinted at his distaste for revolution as much as for war. He would not allow history to get in the way of his higher objectives. The integrity of the past mattered infinitely less than the good health of the future. To the extent that commemoration required a historical regard, he would focus on what the Revolution brought "that was promising, powerful, evolutionary, and humanistic, instead of recalling that which divides and which does not seem to us to speak to the general interest of the people in this particular moment of their history." To the chilling side of this exorcism, its heavy-handed paternalism, he did not seem to be alert. If he could not avoid reference to the past, he would at least succeed in decentering it.

It is only fair to note that elsewhere, outside the commemorative context, Baroin betrayed a greater deference toward history. He pleaded for the restitution of its centrality in the schools, for "to sell off history is to insult the future, to advance blindly toward it." A nation had to live in harmony with "its originating myths," by which he seemed to mean its dominant historiography. As for the Revolution, he conceded that it was not "pointless" in light of its vigorous promotion of meritocracy through education and the extirpation of privileges that frustrated talent and hard work. Yet he seemed persuaded that the Enlightenment—"the triumph of reason"—invented "the new idea of happiness" and prepared the conditions for its realization without the need to revert to violence.

Like his successors at the Mission, with Micheletian zeal, Baroin was determined to mobilize the people, providential incarnation of the nation and its wisdom. To marshal "a true popular movement," he believed he needed to limit historicization to the narrow band of the "consensual spirit" of 1789. Reciprocally, to protect this consensus, he had to lodge it within a popular movement.

Did Baroin betray a certain lack of confidence in the reliability and self-discipline of the people, and incidentally in the resilience of consensus, by proposing a new declarationn based on that of August 1789, that would stipulate *duties* as well as *rights*? The answer is not clear. In his own thinking, Baroin could not envisage rights without responsibilities. They were dialectically linked and mutually dependent. The only way of guaranteeing to the practice of solidarity the primacy that Baroin wished to bestow on it seemed to be by making justice an obligation and not simply a prerogative. He earnestly believed that this was one way to render it morally and perhaps even juridically untenable for opulence to coexist comfortably with hunger, and for bigotry to cohabit with equality. In addition to placating moralists and *intégristes*, the marriage of duties and rights, in Baroin's view, would further reduce the pretext for the state to intervene as mediator—in the worst case as "confiscator"—of fundamnetal values.

AD 89, the association of youth assigned the task of producing a new declaration for 26 August 1989 consonant with the problems and prospects of a world infinitely more complex than that of 1789, was fully cognizant of the historiographical significance and the polemical potential of this emendation-cum-rectification. Indeed, in the vigorous *Manifesto for 89*, it defended its position thoughtfully, even if it did not always sustain a philosophically coherent position. The fact that Baroin embraced the ambition of this organization of several hundred young people, the doyen of whose drafting commission was barely twenty-seven years of age, bespeaks a genuine openness and a sort of entrepreneurial humanism in the best sense of the term.

The intimate involvement of Baroin's two children in the project strengthened his instinctive affinity for this aggiornamento which directly confronted the social as well as the existential human condition and placed ethics at the core of the practice of both technology and power. The tragic death of his daughter just as the work began to accelerate further deepened his attachment to it and his fervent belief in the ancient logic of love as the driving force of human relations in the age of genetic manipulation and artificial intelligence. In sum, the watchwords of Baroin's bicentennial charter were evolution, universality, humanism, solidarity, populism, circumspection, democracy (mediated by the primacy of the law), transcendence (of the Revolutionary legacy of cleavage and acrimony), and the prestige of the nation today (France as cultural lighthouse and moral conscience to the world).[16]

Administration and Imagination:
Running the Bicentennial Shop

A leader of initiative, Baroin launched the Mission even before it obtained the status conferred by a budget, housing it in his own headquarters and drawing largely on volunteer help. (An audit later conducted by the general inspectorate of the Ministry of Culture suggested that one of the prime reasons Chirac designated the president of GMF to head up the Mission was precisely for the business infrastructure that would give him a flying start.) Despite the urgent exhortation to rush to his aid that Baroin addressed to the interministerial committee named by the government to facilitate (and monitor) his work, he found himself largely abandoned to his own devices. This proud graduate of the public sector, ambivalent in his attitude toward the state's role in society but unequivocally certain of the duty that public service imposed on those who operated in its name, found himself rebuffed by politicized bureaucrats who were reluctant to venture into what they feared would be a minefield. In any event, Baroin drew his management model from the private sector: he would run the Mission as "a big company." Running government as if it were a business, the classical American standard of competence, was now very much a part of the French liberal climate.

No less than his successors, Baroin felt a real sense of urgency. For an undertaking of the magnitude required by a major national commemoration, the start was already quite late in 1986. "We must make up the lost time," he reminded his collaborators and interlocutors every day. Seconded by his company staff, by January 1987 he had rented a vast array of offices (that even his bon vivant successor Edgar Faure later found too costly) and began to recruit personnel beyond his in-house collaborators. A freshly hired member of his team worried about the Jacobin impulses Baroin carried over from his prefectoral days: he seemed reluctant to allow much initiative to departmental committees. A future member of the scholarly advisory committee (comité scientifique) anguished about another sort of Jacobinism—the imperative of "the search for harmony" imposed by Baroin, which would constrain the discussion and evaluation of projects.[17]

But everyone was struck by the energy that Baroin invested in the Mission. In fact, he achieved a great deal in the short time he presided; bitter complaints from those close to him that his real contribution was never fairly acknowledged by the Mission's ultimate steward, Jean-Noël Jeanneney, appear to have some merit. He established the festive calendar to which his successors more or less adhered (5 May, 17 and 23 June, 14 July, 4 and 26 August). He envisioned four great events: a festival of "universal fraternity" and one of "life," a revised declaration of rights for the new century with its focus on youth, and an international congress of "spiritual and scientific families" to deal with the sort of problem that preoccupied a Mason of the third millennium: how to fashion "an ethics" for this world of constant mutation and innovation. Jacques Chirac, mayor of the capital as well as prime minister, pledged his support for the idea of bringing all the heads of the communes of France as well as mayors from towns throughout Europe and delegations from the other nations of the world to Paris to sign the "pact of fraterntiy" on Bastille Day. Baroin proposed the responsibility for organizing the grand gala of the fourteenth to the talented musician Jean-Michel Jarre, he initiated discussion with producer-journalist Yves Mourousi to plan a number of major shows, and he began making contact with foreign television companies.[18]

Foreseeing a tourist boom, Baroin organized a group to coordinate promotion. Another committee reflected on the allocation of economic benefits induced by the bicentennial in other domains (manufacturing, distribution, and so on). Though it was too late to envision a bicentennial monument commensurate with the centennial legacy, the Mission planned a competition for a massive sculpture celebrating human rights. From a number of proposals, Baroin chose a logo that failed to charm his successor: "1789" written twice, once in the graphic style of the Old Regime and a second time in modern guise, the two representations superimposed on a tricolor stalk of wheat—"a symbol of union and continuity" evoking "life in its evolution and its progressiveness."[19]

According to a specialized business periodical, Baroin was prepared to raise virtually all the money needed to commemorate and celebrate from the private sector: "He has the business world at his feet; the arts world is at his service. With all the confidence in the world he envisages raising several hundreds of millions of francs through these contacts." The extravagance of this portrait to the contrary notwithstanding, it is true that Baroin had no illusions about governmental largesse. Beyond the cloud of uncertainty cast by cohabitation, the president of the Mission confronted the determined resistance of the powerful finance minister, Edouard Balladur. Whether or not this elegant and influential adviser to Chirac was, as a member of Baroin's entourage claimed, "a royalist at heart," he barely concealed his contempt for the *franchouillard* aspects of what he imagined could only be a vulgar and boisterous celebration.

Soundings with political party leaders, left and right, convinced the president of the Mission that they were wholly preoccupied with election maneuvering and unwilling to mobilize their clienteles to support the year of the fête. Baroin turned to his business colleagues, arguing for their mobilization on grounds of both lofty principle and self-interest. According to his son, Baroin had realistic hopes of eliciting a half-billion francs from his newly formed Club de mécènes and other connections in the business community. If he could have realized such a Gargantuan fund-raising operation, it would have been owing largely to his personal credit and charisma. For as skilled a manager as Jacques Friedmann, the former head of Air France who chaired the businessmen's group for the bicentennial in the aftermath of the Baroin regime, was barely able to raise 2 percent of the sum envisaged by the president of GMF.[20]

Through his dense international network, Baroin began to develop contacts with institutions and individuals of other nations who were interested in promoting bicentennial activities. One such connection proved extremely controversial and embarrassing. It involved Dr. Daisaku Ikeda, leader of the Soka Gakkai, a Buddhist sect founded in the 1930s that boasted ten million members around the world, including a burgeoning contingent in France. The sect owned its own daily newspaper in the Japanese capital and controlled a large group of deputies (the "Clean Government party") in the lower legislative house. A cultivated and enterprising man, Ikeda offered to organize and subsidize a major bicentennial exposition at the Fuji Museum in Tokyo, which the Soka Gakkai owned. Baroin promised Ikeda the Mission label, a pledge of approbation renewed by his successor, Edgar Faure, who also visited the sect's headquarters in Japan. *Le Point* recently claimed that Baroin had envisaged associating Ikeda in the drafting of a new declaration of rights for the third millennium. Ikeda's humanist discourse, which conveyed certain Masonic overtones, appealed to the Mission president.

The story becomes complicated when one looks more closely at the sect and at its manipulative leader. Ikeda's rightist inclinations disqualified him, in the eyes of some critics, from any bicentennial role. Others suggested that he wanted to use the bicentennial to help refurbish an image tarnished by spectacular financial and political scandals. The French counterespionage service worried about Ikeda's motive in purchasing several châteaux located next to French nuclear plants and laboratories. Other investigations revealed that Ikeda had visited Manuel Noriega shortly before his capture and that he had abandoned a safe containing a million dollars in strange circumstances.

Whatever induced Baroin to associate the Mission with the Soka Gakkai, he was in good company. Ikeda managed to meet and have himself photographed with many of the world's leaders, including Bush, Gorbachev, and Mitterrand (as well as such leading French political figures as Chirac and Senate president Alain Poher). He donated money to France Libertés, the foundation presided over by Danielle Mitterrand, for whose benefit he organized a bicentennial concert in Tokyo. Still, it seems curious that an ex-police and intelligence official and generally prudent businessman would not have scrutinized more closely the reputation of the sect and reflected on the implications of the relation. There is a wildly implausible note of naïveté in the recommendation formulated by one of Baroin's collaborators, shortly after the death of the first Mission president, urging Michel Vovelle, a Marxist and Jacobin, to nourish links with the Soka Gakkai as part of his worldwide scientific strategy.[21]

Though he was a cosmopolitan man, Baroin was no intellectual. He was surely at a disadvantage when invited to discuss history or literature in spontaneous critical colloquy. One of his new aides was aghast at his "astonishing lack of culture," doubtless a panicky exaggeration, yet an assessment not drastically at odds with the view of his admirers in the intelligentsia. Nor did Baroin have any illusions about his capacity to judge matters pertaining to scholarship. A firm believer in a functional division of labor, he never hesitated to call on specialists. To help him navigate the bicentennial shoals, he asked Jean Favier to preside over the scholarly advisory committee, heroically dubbed by the Masonic leader the "Chamber of the Sages." He did it in the decisive style for which he was known, dispatching a chauffeur to the airport to deliver a message to the unsuspecting Favier who was returning from a business trip. The two men had a passing acquaintance and mutual esteem. Baroin wanted a person of stature and diplomatic skills; and he wanted to name the president rather than propose him for election, in order to avoid the divisiveness that an election among a highly disparate group of intellectuals would surely entail.

Apparently Mitterrand and Chirac agreed on Baroin's choice. With some rectifications—additions rather than deletions—they also approved the list of names submitted by Baroin on Favier's recommendation ("quite well balanced") to make up the scholarly advisory committee. Baroin expected that Chirac would announce Favier's selection at the official installation of the committee at Matignon. For some reason, that did not occur. Baroin assured the director of the Archives de France the following week that he himself would make public the decision ("an open secret") if the prime minister did not do it within a week. Several days later Baroin embarked on a trip abroad from which he never returned, and the question of the governance of the advisory committee was left in abeyance.[22]

In Memoriam: The Mission Orphaned

Thus the Baroin Mission ended tragically even as his staff was gearing up to deal with the practical issues of program and organization. Its chief died in February in an airplane crash in Africa. The last word on this grievous end has not yet been written. Like most powerful and controversial figures, Baroin remains, even in death, the object of countless rumors. The most troubling, emanating from adversaries as well as partisans, was that he did not die accidentally. All sorts of grounds are invoked: perilous, subterranean business dealings; his appetite to devour TF1; his political ambition; his Masonic connections; involvement with religious sects; alleged treasons in the eyes of both left and right; a settlement of police scores, and so on. These are matters best left to an investigative reporter or an oracle.

Clearly Baroin's ambition had proved disconcerting. It is quite extraordinary how ambivalent the French public remains even today about ambition, whose social legitimacy was (theoretically) conferred by the Revolution. That ambition seems tolerable so long as it remains compartmentalized. When a Jean-Jacques Servan-Schreiber or a Bernard Tapie or a Michel Baroin ventures to move from civil society into the so-called political class—a step considered part of the normal and normative itinerary in other Western democracies such as the United States—there is a sense of transgression, a revulsion for the hubris implicit in the act. Typical of this attitude, and its wistfulness for the taxonomical rigidities of the Old Regime, is the following description of Baroin in a recent issue of *Le Nouvel Observateur:* "a huge megalomaniac who had transformed an insurance mutual into a financial group in order to establish a base for his political ambitions, this former cop wanted to become president of the republic."

Baroin's demise dealt a cruel blow to the bicentennial undertaking. He had enjoyed virtually no contact with the public. He was still groping for a concrete style of commemoration consonant with his temperament, with the exigencies of cohabitation, and with the intrinsic importance of the anniversary. François Baroin recalls the enthusiasm that Mitterrand evinced for his father's ideas in the course of frequent meetings during the Mission president's short tenure. A year and a half later Mitterrand is said to have confided to a not wholly disinterested witness that Baroin's conception of the commemoration had made no sense to him at all ("It's a mishmash fit for pet food"). A more immediate and verifiable disgrace to Baroin's memory was committed in the weeks after his death when his successor as chief executive officer of GMF, J.-L. Pétriat, refused peremptorily to furnish any further assistance to the bicentennial organization.[23]

A Man for All Seasons
Edgar Faure as Bicentennial Missionary

Exactly a month after Baroin's demise, the government named Edgar Faure to the presidency of the Mission—according to several sources, on Faure's own recommendation. But his talent was commensurate with his narcissism: for a number of reasons, his was a compelling appointment. A brilliant lawyer and professor of law, an academician, historian, musician, novelist, former prime minister, frequent minister, and one-time president of the National Assembly, Faure boasted an astonishing record of achievement. Politically and temperamentally, he was also well suited for the climate of cohabitation. According to *Libération*, he was appointed precisely for "his legendary sense of compromise." Though a prominent leader of the center-right, his "radical-socialist" background meant that he cultivated many friends on the left. He was the uncontested master, in the evocative words of *Le Monde*, "of tightrope-walking artifices and marriages between water and fire," which endowed him with "a natural vocation to manage, from above, this enormous enterprise of compromise [that of the Mission] relegated to the politico-ideological slalom course from the outset."

Faure's nomination also bespoke a conscious desire for continuity, though in practical terms this was not, alas, an issue of consequence. Edgar Faure had been the president of the National Assembly on whose staff Baroin had served, and since then the two men had maintained close ties, including a regular monthly luncheon. They shared intellectual affinities, Masonic sympathies, and certain political appreciations. Shortly before Baroin's death, the two men had discussed a collaborative bicentennial undertaking dealing with the rights of man, Faure's terrain of predilection even before he came to the Mission.[1]

Faure's assertion that there were "no divergences" between him and Baroin on how to engage the bicentennial was not purely complaisant exaggeration. Faure deployed his own genre of Gongorism, but in the service of many of the same ideals:

consensus (pushed therapeutically much further than Baroin dared); the allergy to "useless" polemic; the primacy of fraternity as the paramount objective and vehicle of mobilization and pedagogy, and the concomitant rejection of exclusionary policies; the resolute inflection toward the future; the centrality of science—at the frontier of science fiction—as the revolutionizing agent of the last years of the twentieth century; a fascination for the ethical and juridical dilemmas posed by (post)modern progress; a distaste for violence and for revolution (though Faure did not shrink from historicizing the problem and viewing it in contingent terms).

Still, significant differences separated the two men. Baroin was a moralist in style and, on many issues, also in substance. Although Faure knew how to deploy right-thinking sentiments, in most matters if not all, he was an utter relativist. Baroin's moralizing estranged him from politics, without dulling his appetite for power. Politics implied a certain level of contestation and conflict. Baroin gravitated toward apolitics, in which union if not unanimity emerged from the embrace of common values. At best, Baroin was an idealist; at worst, in the vivid and harsh image of one critic, a sort of postwar Pétainist. A political animal with an instinctive talent for dealing with diverse interests, Faure did not shrink from confrontation even if he preferred compromise; and, while not precisely a Parsonsian, he had no illusion that social life could be (or should be) purged of strife.

While fascinated by the future, Faure could not successfully extricate himself from his thick historical culture. He administered to himself a sort of intellectual Valium therapy. As one of the collaborators put it, however, he suffered "historical anxieties" of the sort that never perturbed Baroin. The one-time premier worried about the connections between past and present, and the capacity of the present to liberate itself from the past. History meant cleavages of all sorts as well as points of concord, and in this way informed and paralleled politics. In his own mind, Faure was never sure whether the golden mean was attainable or sustainable. If he pursued Baroin's line grosso modo, he did it with less conviction and more trepidation, suspending his own incredulity for the sake of the higher cause.

To combat what he regarded as dangerous doctrinal rigidities potent enough to poison the bicentennial atmosphere, Faure embraced the dogma antidote of consensus, whose necessity he tirelessly preached with evangelical fervor. "Not only must the bicentennial not be a subject of division," he said and wrote over and over again, "rather, it is duty bound to be an agent of harmony, reconciliation, and unanimity." "One must bring together that which is scattered about," he wrote, in emulation of the Masonic apothegm.[2] Injecting a megadose of Baroin's love into the body politic, Faure wanted to provoke a national embrace, the sort of mythopoeic exorcism solicited by American healers on the morrow of the Civil War.

The idea was to avert one's eyes from the issues and instead focus on the common human dimension of passionate combat. On the part of North and South, it was a good, hard fight, and both sides deserve great credit for their courage and conviction; now it is time for all American brothers to return to their common family.[3] Slightly more sophisticated, Faure's version of "a grand national reconciliation" was not fundamentally different in hortatory spirit or less reductive in nature: "It is time now for the descendants of the Vendéens and those of the combatants of Valmy to recognize that they were both men of sacrifice, men representing the national interest, men of human interest. It is now time to bridge the gap, to arrive at this reconciliation in almost theological terms, to come to the idea of being done with the right-left opposition, which transforms France into two blocks that seem impermeable."[4]

This consensus could not be forged; in some sense, it had to come about of its own inclination. But Faure had some strategic suggestions to hasten its crystallization. The first required the historian-philosopher to defer to the men of politics. There was no point in bringing to bear a "moral judgment on a historical event." Indeed, it was unwise to delve too deeply into the past, a past rife with minefields.

As a practical matter for dealing with the past, Faure proposed a crucial distinction between what he called "the movement of ideas" (always unblemished, positive, irresistible) and "the clash of behaviors that followed or accompanied the ideas" (often tainted, negative, repulsive). In his own way Faure considered "circumstances" to be as "feeble" as François Furet said they were. In any event, they were not sufficiently convincing to do the work of reconciliation. But unlike Furet, whose logic was to condemn vociferously the ideas he held responsible for certain behavior, Faure invited everyone to a sort of pious causal restraint: regardless of their possible (unintended? perverted?) consequences, let us honor the intrinsically good-natured ideas of 1789. Let us not allow the ugliness and violence that we all— including most of the partisans of the Revolution—deplore to cast a disqualifying penumbra over the great achievements of those turbulent years, especially in the domain of rights and institutions.[5]

Before his advisory committee, Faure puzzled and agonized over the disparity between the concern for rights, a concern widely shared by the public, and the increasingly shrill debate over the general theme of revolution that was spilling over from the arcane scholarly reviews to the mass media: "There does not exist for the word 'revolution' a consensus analogous to the one that obviously covers the formula which epitomizes its core: the trilogy Liberty, Equality, Fraternity." Instead of merely circumventing the Revolution, Faure tried gamely to disarm or preempt the usual categories of execration. First of all, none of the true friends of the Revolution celebrated the massacres performed in its name. Second, the Revolution as it unfolded in 1789 was probably inevitable, given the stalemate of "closed" French society, which Faure believed that he had objectively established in his study of end-of-the-Old-Regime reform, *La Disgrâce de Turgot*. Faure preferred not to conflate or contaminate the "rational" early stages with the violence that followed. But he did concede that the question of whether recourse to violence was necessary was intellectually futile and morally deleterious since "this question is not subject to a scientifically demonstrable response."

Faure felt absolutely sure, by contrast, that it could be scientifically proven that the next revolutions could not be successfully realized through violence of any sort.

The good news was that revolution, old-style, was fully obsolescent and no longer conceptually pertinent. The speech was replete with the sort of ambiguities, pirouettes, and bombast for which Faure was renowned—along with a fund of erudition and a leaven of imagination that helped temper the irritation if not untangle the confusion of many of the distinguished figures, mostly scholars, who made up his committee. Delivered in late May, the address revealed a Mission president still groping to set his commemorative agenda even as he was still straining to recruit a stable staff and extract an adequate budget. For the moment, the reactions to his discourse merely confirmed his worst fears: that he would be dismissed by the left as a *muscadin* and suspected by the right of being a closet Jacobin.[6]

The Rights of Man: Priority to Fraternity

Faure's one gilt-edged property was the rights theme. It was particularly attractive to him both because he believed in it and because it gave him enormous, low-cost mileage. In the public sphere, no one failed to pay homage to the rights of man. Profoundly anchored in history, rights were also of urgent, immediate concern in today's world and, in Faure's mind, perhaps of even more pressing future consequence, given his conviction that the third millennium would fundamentally alter our manner of living and of living together. Following Baroin's formula, for which he unearthed more elegant and esoteric authority, Faure historicized the three primary categories of rights into three "generations": the political focus (liberty) of the late eighteenth and early nineteenth centuries; the socioeconomic focus (equality) of the nineteenth and twentieth centuries; and the human focus (fraternity) of the late twentieth and twenty-first centuries. To be sure, the generations overlapped, their chronology varied from culture to culture, and Faure did not believe that the questions of the earlier generations were now irrelevant. But they involved contentious issues that he did not want to address in his role as bicentennial master of ceremonies.

Faure was more comfortable with fraternity in part because it was inherently nebulous, protean, elusive; it had no specific agenda of entitlement. Since it had been largely ignored since the days of the Revolution, it could now be conceptualized in terms of "rights responding to new problems," problems with a foggy social content but with a strikingly universal resonance ("peace," "development"). Fraternity bespoke statesmanship on a heroic scale. It transcended the political microcosm and the social stock exchange, superseding questions articulated around the increasingly anachronistic relation between individual and state in favor of the rarefied air of the "universal collectivity." Even as his liberal friends, left and right, argued that liberty mattered above all to all peoples regardless of their level of development, Faure reminded them that as early as 1950, in his capacity as a junior minister, he had told the Chamber of Deputies that "there are in the world populations so mired in misery that liberty just doesn't interest them." The truth, he suggested, was that liberty and equality were not nearly as "accessible" as fraternity, because fraternity derived from nature as much as from culture, from the heart and the genes as much as from social experience.[7]

Fraternity was soft and it passed easily. Just as important from Faure's bicentennial perspective, it was subject to a sort of commemorative reification—that is, it could be readily translated or transformed into a monumental message that immobilized time as it reached into the next millennium. Faure's preoccupation with "perpetuation" was the mirror image of his passion for the future. He wanted the bicentennial to leave a legacy of its own, apart from the dower of the Revolution that it transmitted, even as the centennial had done in 1889.

Faure found the Eiffel Tower that he quite consciously sought in the Arche de la Défense, Johann Otto von Spreckelsen's imposing futurist building at the western end of the Bastille-Louvre-Concorde-Etoile vista. The claims of equivalency posed no dilemma for him: "It is a technological achievement as remarkable as that of the Eiffel Tower." At the summit of this soaring building, rebaptized the Arch of Fraternity, Faure planned to establish the International Foundation of Human Rights and Human Sciences. According to its statutes, it would be neither a university in the canonical sense nor an institutional voice for a self-proclaimed moral authority. Rather Faure saw it as a grand arena for debate and reflection of the most critical and wide-ranging sort.

The Arch Foundation was the major concrete initiative, literally and figuratively, that Faure wanted the bicentennial to bequeath to the next century. Based on "the consensual and universal message of the French Revolution," the Foundation adapted that message to the needs of our time. Better than the Eiffel Tower, it reached inward as well as upward. It provided the occasion for a legitimate *cocorico*, for the Foundation masterfully exemplified the genius for which the nation was renowned, France being "the country that is always in the vanguard of thought and action on the big questions on which the future of humanity hinges."[8]

The Foundation embodied Faure's determination to avoid the pitfalls of Revolutionary commemoration by illuminating the future rather than by exploring the past. Commemoration—Faure, like the cardinals of Paris and Lyon, felt uneasy with its liturgical aspect and its affective overtones—would yield imperceptibly to *remémoration* [recollection], a somewhat abstruse term (its abstruseness itself being a virtue) that favored Faure's irenic flight by shifting the burden from past to future: "it is an expression that engages not only memory but the lesson of the memory and therefore its promise." The most salient "relevance" of the Revolution was to be found in what he called "the new Bastilles to be struck down."

Faure emphasized the latter even at the cost of depreciating the civic interest of scrutinizing the past. The new challenges were "more relevant than the forced labor requisitions [*corvées*], the salt tax [*gabelle*], the status of the commoner, and feudal rights." Among the "new Bastilles" Faure cited drugs, the handicapped, the situation of immigrants, disease, and unemployment in the French context and illiteracy, famine, disease, and the rights of man in a worldwide compass. Faure also cast

The Arch at La Défense, Edgar Faure's monument to Fraternity and the Bicentennial's counterpart of the Eiffel Tower, dedicated in 1889. (Photo by J. Cutting.)

the struggle in more politically assimilable terms as a campaign "against all forms of exclusion"—but he located the problems of exclusion largely outside France, primarily in the Third World, accessorily in Eastern Europe.

Though resolutely internationalist, Faure felt especially warm about the European dimension, in light of his historical culture and his exuberance over the union of 1993. He stressed "the profoundly European character" of the Enlightenment and of the ensuing "mutations," mutations that constituted as much a "European revolution" as one strictly French in inspiration and ambition. What more propitious moment than the bicentennial to reaffirm the role of Paris: capital of Europe in the eighteenth century, capital of a unifying Europe at the end of the twentieth? "I see 1989 as the Year of Europe," he wrote, "of all the Europes . . . the whole continent: if it pleases God, a hundred years after the birth of General de Gaulle, Europe from the Atlantic to the Urals." Through the Foundation, Faure proposed the solicitation of *cahiers de doléances* on a European scale, and vaguely dreamed of an "académie de l'Europe de la conscience" to help resolve conflicts arising over issues of interest and sovereignty. The European veneer, like the millennial perspective, further obscured what was peculiarly French and Revolutionary in the bicentennial showcase.[9]

Faure's Bicentennial Program

Faure insisted that it was not the Mission's role "to define an official manner of celebrating these important events—the French Revolution and the Declaration of the Rights of Man." Yet in fact he had defined a way of celebrating—palatable, graceful, enriching. Faure put this definition into practice by promoting bicentennial projects that embodied it. These included films, theatrical spectacles, and concerts illustrating and celebrating the rights of man (and, in a few instances, specifically of woman); a "revolutionary" expedition to Mount Everest; numerous scholarly colloquia; a European rights-of-man train. Faure retained the project of the AD 89 group that was so dear to Baroin, though the idea of presenting what amounted to a replacement declaration taxed even his sense of audacity and perhaps shocked the agrégé's notion of juridical modesty. "The question of a new declaration has been raised," he told his advisory committee. "It is an exalting idea, but I prefer to speak of a working paper, or a text which would not necessarily be a new declaration per se." Still, he welcomed the collaboration of Baroin's son François with genuine affection and eagerness, and he vigorously endorsed the idea that the task of thinking about the rendezvous of the human rights of past and future should be the bailiwick "of youthful minds, at the beginning of life, whose sensibility is not yet worn down like ours."

In the spirit of his father, young Baroin hoped that the "faith" and "enthusiasm" of the world's future adults would engender "a new revolution, shorn this time of any violence." Its midwife would be fraternity, the practice of which Baroin did not want to remain "exclusively the possession of priests and Masons." The analysis of Baroin and his friends drew on vestigial sentiments from May 1968 and their renascent contemporary echo, a critique of the withdrawal from the civic agora, of "individualism, egotism, and hedonistic behavior in all respects." Their self-conscious ultramodernism concealed from them the extent to which they framed the issue as one of moral regeneration in terms redolent of the violent Revolution of '89 and '93. They might have deepened their insight into the problem by taking a greater interest in history, beginning with the Revolution, particularly in the relentless and cruel struggle between liberty and equality that stunted the growth of fraternity.[10]

Intuitively Edgar Faure preferred undertakings that would endure and perpetuate: sculptural and musical monuments and ambitious publishing ventures, including a plan to complete the massive source publications launched shortly after the centennial by Alphonse Aulard, first occupant of the chair of the History of the

French Revolution at the Sorbonne. He wrote to all the parliamentary deputies to solicit recommendations for contributions in the scientific and cultural domains, accentuating his desire to stimulate "creation" and to reach and "sensitize" that elusive and ubiquitous entity called "le grand public," the general public. He asked the political scientist Olivier Duhamel to help devise methods, through *cahiers* or other means, to elicit the feelings and aspirations of the public(s). Faure presided over the opening of the competition called "Invent 1989," which he hoped would generate other lasting artistic homages to the bicentennial. He approved a scheme to bring together all the manifestations of bicentennial creativity in a vast exposition scheduled to be held at La Villette in the spring of 1988.[11]

Faure did not, however, ignore the ephemeral, the one-shot designs that would mobilize the masses, domestic and planetary, through television. Sharing his predecessor's conviction that no one was better equipped to reach an international audience in an exciting fashion, he renewed Jean-Michel Jarre's charge to devise a gigantic concert for 14 July. In an expanded scenario, the concert would be the culmination of twenty-four or perhaps even forty-eight hours of a nonstop festival of sound, light, and street theatre, with events dispersed throughout the capital at the grand squares and monuments. In ways that were not fully clarified, the Barnumesque Yves Mourousi was also to be involved in what was dubbed "the longest day."

Its evocation before a plenary session of the advisory committee issued in one of those scholastic debates that Faure seemed to relish. What were the hidden implications of this modification of the calendar? Were historicity and festivity compatible? Scenting a scheme to decenter the taking of the Bastille and its symbolic specificity, Michel Vovelle wondered whether one should not extend the period to encompass the (short) week between 12 and 17 July that galvanized the people of Paris and accelerated the confrontation with both the monarchy and the privileged orders. He obtained oblique comfort from Madeleine Rebérioux, for whom the twelfth marked a portentous moment. Such a restructuring, Mona Ozouf riposted, did violence to the republican tradition that contracted into a single day the celebration of the Bastille and, with an added dose of fervor, the Festival of the Federation. Envisaging the utilization of sites at the Bastille and the Champs de Mars to represent the two commemorative poles, François Furet supported Ozouf's rigorously positivist argument.

For reasons that were not merely historical, this conflation of the violent, liberating, popular Bastille and the orchestrated, hierarchical, harmonious Federation troubled Vovelle: "I am among those who hope that we are going to continue to celebrate the French Revolution and that we will do something for the fourteenth of July 1990." Exposing himself to a devastating counterpunch, the holder of the Sorbonne's chair in the French Revolution complained that the amalgamation of Bastille and Federation was an affair of 1889, and that 1989 need not march to the centennial drumbeat. "It's 1880, Michel," corrected Ozouf, jovially, referring to the creation of a national holiday.[12]

A shrewd promoter, Mourousi hedged his bets. He proposed a whole series of "bombshells of great prestige" that seduced the president of the Mission. For the sumptuous and aristocratic cadre of Versailles, the producer imagined an international horse show and an exposition of luxury arts and crafts. For Paris his plans were only slightly more plebeian: a festival of the music of the world at the Bastille, a big variety show on the Champs de Mars on 26 August, a theatrical production by Robert Hossein or Ariane Mnouchkine for the cour carrée of the Louvre, a Maurice Béjart spectacle of dance, and an exposition of the Revolution's high tech on the Champs Elysées' high chic. Among other promised "merriments," Mourousi spoke vaguely of a "night of the army." Show business would not entirely obscure civic business in Faure's grand scenario. With Chirac's city-hall sponsorship and the help of the Association des maires de France, Faure fancied an immense gathering of all the elected officials of France and a republican banquet that would dwarf the glorious mayoral repast of 1889.[13]

Faure as Manager

Faure's patronage was not always very convincing, because he disposed of astonishingly little money (some of which he spent embellishing his expensive quarters on the rue Talleyrand), and because he was prodigal in his enthusiasms. Nor did he elaborate a bureaucratic structure capable of discreetly correcting his excesses and/or indulgences and effectively implementing the informed decisions that he made. He resisted efforts to organize rationally, to adopt rules of procedure, and to institute certain checks and balances. By temperament and experience Faure was a man of ministerial cabinets and their Byzantine mores. He relished holding court, making people wait hours to see him, rewarding friends and clients of various ilks. This casual managerial style resulted in some embarrassing incidents, including the revelation that the "expert in cultural engineering" who contested the powerful Federation of National Education for the concession of the "rights" train was the fiancé of one of Faure's granddaughters and that the company which received a lucrative minitel contract from the Mission was a well-known connection of the RPR.

According to one close collaborator, Faure forgot that, unlike a minister who was supported by a vast administration, he had "nothing at all to back him up." Though Faure sometimes seemed reckless in his willingness to take local risks, cohabitation rendered him even more cautious than he was instinctively in the public sphere, and as a consequence he took no political initiatives to mobilize grassroots collaboration on the governmental level or in civil society. Because he did not establish a rigorous calendar (eighteen months before the climactic fourteenth of July he esteemed that it was "too early" to announce the festive program), he drew criticism for moving too slowly at the same time that he was chided for his bicentennial bulimia.

In retrospect, Yann Gaillard, a prominent senior civil servant who worked closely with Faure, regarded their late start as a near fatal handicap. He admired his mentor's kinetic energy and imagination: "he soared to the roof of the Grande Arche de la Défense, which at that moment existed only in his dreams," just as he had committed himself to building ten universities in a single summer when he had served as education minister in the wake of May 1968. Gaillard realized after the fact, however, that a major celebration had become nothing less than "a huge worldwide industry" requiring long preparation, a substantial budget, a highly competent and ample staff, a massive effort of national mobilization (the government should have declared the bicentennial "a grand national cause"), and a truly coherent commemorative vision and strategy ("How can one do without an official doctrine when it is a matter of an official ceremony?")—none of which conditions obtained under Faure's aegis.[14]

The transition from the Baroin regime proved more difficult and costly in time and money than it ought to have been. Given the boorishness of the new president of GMF, Faure found himself deprived of a locale and a key part of the Mission staff. At first the Mission nucleus worked out of Faure's own home, then from the borrowed quarters of Faure's Contrat social, a club for intellectual and political reflection, and finally in the Maison de Franche-Comté, the office maintained in Paris by Faure's region. Once offices were rented on the rue Talleyrand in the seventh arrondissement near the National Assembly, there were further delays for rather elaborate renovations and refurbishings. Despite its austere veneer, it is a wagering quarter, and the smart money on the rue de l'Université and in the ministerial mansions said that Faure would fall on his face.

This ambient pessimism made it hard to recruit a first-rate staff rapidly. Clients as well as protégés declined offers to join him. To many of them it seemed "a rotten affair," "a dangerous business," "a trap." In any case, "you don't have the means to succeed." His old collaborator Rector Gérard Antoine reemerged to counsel and encourage him, as he convoked an endless series of roundtables in March and April to discuss possible modes of celebration and/or commemoration. After many weeks, Antoine finally unearthed a secretary-general, the number-two man of the Mission, an obscure figure named Alain Marais whom he had known in the Lorraine. In the vernacular, Marais was known as a professional "sociocul," who had started as an animator of an inconspicuous rural activities center and ended up in the office of the Direction régionale des affaires culturelles. Probably because he was ill-suited to undertake a task that was so ill-defined, he was never able to establish himself.[15]

Marais was replaced at the beginning of the summer by Ambassador Jean-Pierre Cabouat, an experienced senior diplomat with useful credentials: an impressive record in the Resistance, political experience and an affiliation on the left, and considerable charm and cultivation. His partisans admired his ascension from modest origins, his signal quality of perseverance, and his taste for rules and order but contrasted his sometimes lordly style vis-à-vis the subaltern personnel with his permanent posture of submission vis-à-vis interlocutors of authority.

Cabouat's inadequacies emerged most graphically after Faure's death, when he ran the Mission on his own for an extended period, making financial decisions of dubious merit and failing to advance substantially in terms of program preparation. Even while Faure presided in name, however, he was frequently absent, depending on Cabouat to mind the shop. Omnivorous, Faure remained deeply involved in a wide array of public activities and private interests that made immense demands on his time. At seventy-nine years of age, he chaired the Senate hearings dealing with the Nucci scandal (concerning the management of funds destined for French "cooperation" programs primarily in Africa), he was active in multiple European organizations, he was preparing for various elections, and as usual he was writing. He counted on Cabouat to improvise in his place, but that was not the style in which the diplomat had been trained.

A memo Cabouat drafted in December 1987, presumably addressed to the Mission staff, shows him at his best and at his worst. Without changing inflection, he rebuked staff members for slovenly discipline and deficiencies in the exchange of information and he summoned them to fuse in a spirit of selfless and cohesive teamwork, which he referred to as the "commando" rather than the administrative style. Reminding them that work began at 9:00 A.M., he remarked that "nothing is more appalling than the outside calls which go unanswered till 9:30, 10:00 A.M. I had several opportunities, unfortunately, to observe and deplore the absence of the supervisors until an advanced hour of the morning."[16]

Gradually the other crucial staff positions were filled. A Mason and a fellow agrégé in law whom Faure had known for a number of years, Pierre Lunel, arrived from the University of Limoges. Philosophical affinity complemented their common juridical background; in almost literal terms, as a colleague discerned, "they spoke the same language." Congenial and effusive in the manner of certain southerners, intellectually stimulating but often diffuse and disorganized, Lunel implausibly served as deputy secretary-general. Dubbed Rastignac (after Balzac's arriviste) by certain colleagues, he was widely perceived as intriguing and ambitious.

Even as he cultivated his self-regarding interests, it was widely believed at the Mission that Lunel accomplished useful work in the "rights" sector. He established links with numerous unions and voluntary associations that shared his passion for the rights question. He worked to give a concrete character to Faure's visions of fraternity. Lunel made the case elegantly for the continuities between old and new Bastilles. He also helped craft general policy declarations in the fustian style to which both he and the Mission president were attached.

Surely the least popular and most sinister figure at the Mission was Faure's chef de cabinet, Olivier Passelecq. Though a municipal counselor in the sixth arrondissement, he showed no sign of political sense. A specialist in labor and social law, he did not bring the normative lessons of this discipline to the job.

Christian de Montrichard, who enjoyed old ties with Faure from the late 1960s, assumed responsibility for dealing with local, departmental, and regional institutions. Trained as an agricultural engineer, he had served as mayor of a small commune in the Mitterrandian penumbra of the Nièvre, and he had been active in Socialist-party politics after experiencing the futility of old-style radicalism. Both experiences, working the land and participating in grassroots politics, afforded him a precious capital on which to draw during the next several years. Wily, well informed, and charming, in the best traditon of democratic sociability, he tended to promise more than he could deliver. His friends praised his capacity to see both the trees and the forest. He felt keenly the lack of conceptual coherence that he believed prevented the crystallization of a genuinely collaborative approach to the commemoration. He toiled to establish networks of exchange and reciprocity within the Mission. At the risk of being labeled officious, he was probably the member of the Mission who knew the most about everyone else's sector. His critics suspected his conviviality and complained that he was evasive and pretentious.

Recruited by Baroin, Elie Schulman initially was responsible for virtually the entire "cultural" rubric, excepting the audiovisual. After a brief term on contract for the Quai d'Orsay in New York, he had held a number of positions involving cultural animation. As the division of labor at the Mission became more sharply articulated, Schulman focused on theatre, dance, music, and artistic expositions. He enjoyed excellent contacts in the artistic milieux. People were his forte, not ideas. "He got nothing off the ground on his own, but he put the players in touch," explained one colleague. Others described him ambiguously as "an original," known for both his hard work and his frenetic effort to cultivate personal relations and anticipate the cruelly whimsical *mode de Paris*. Warm and amiable, he was one of the few old hands who succeeded in forging close ties with Faure's successor.

Endowed with a very different profile, Marie-Christine Wellhoff, a graduate of the Ecole nationale d'administration who had made her career in the Ministry of Culture, took charge of the audiovisual domain beginning in the Baroin phase. Clearheaded and resolute, she launched her film projects rapidly and always seemed to be far ahead of her colleagues as the bicentennial clock ticked its countdown. Some of them suspected that she cast such an efficient image because she circumspectly chose the "path of least resistance."

Marais recruited Didier Hamon, a magistrate who had worked in the Ministry of Culture. He became Cabouat's de facto assistant, given his tested administrative capacities. But as a self-styled man of action, he preferred the creative freedom that his title of "director of programs" gave him. Avid for recognition, he was "a man of great drive" who generated "too many ideas at once." His major achievement was the organization of the first major bicentennial encounter with the public, 89 Avant-Première. Designed to showcase projects that required sponsorship and to sensitize the nation to the commemorative spirit, this bicentennial salon attracted considerable attention. Hamon was assisted by Dominique Ferniot, a vigorous and talented woman, with some experience in the organization of expositions, who managed the salon on the ground and felt that she received inadequate credit for her efforts.

Thierry Collard also worked with Hamon. Interested in paragovernmental public service, before coming to the Mission he worked in the philanthropic department branch of the Caisse des Dépôts, and after leaving it he joined Madame Mitterrand's foundation, France Libertés. In addition to working on the Avant-Première, he monitored the project for assembling the world's greatest sailing vessels and helped to coordinate relations between the Mission and the city of Paris.

To serve as historical/historiographical counselor, Faure hired Claire Andrieu, a young historian of contemporary France with a thesis in gestation who was happy to take a respite from teaching in the lycée. Her father, scion of a family of the grande bourgeoisie, was in the upper reaches of the civil service (inspection des finances) who served briefly as a minister. Her mother, daughter of a physician, had more modest provincial middle-class roots. Militant Resistance fighters from the earliest hour of the Occupation, Andrieu's parents imbued her with a passion for human rights that ultimately found expression in her bicentennial commitment. Their experience also oriented her scholarly career. Formed in Paris public schools, after passing the agrégation in history in 1974, she wrote a book about the ideology of the Resistance and participated in a number of collective projects dealing with wartime history. Published in 1990, her thesis, *La Banque sous l'occupation: Paradoxes de l'histoire d'une profession, 1936–1946*, won a prestigious prize awarded by the National Assembly.

Cautious and self-effacing, with none of the airs of an *héritière*, Andrieu had a perspicacious eye, a graceful pen, and a plucky will. She dealt with one of the most delicate and far-reaching of all the Mission dossiers: the definition of a historical line and the management of the historical and allied professions that claimed a vested interest in the bicentennial. She was much admired for her ability to reconcile passion and diplomacy, combativeness and sobriety of judgment. She knew how to salvage impossible situations created by Faure's impulsive gaffes and how to deal with eminent and sometimes overbearing intellectuals many years her senior. As one colleague put it, "she [was] constantly indispensable."

Jean-Jacques Lubrina was surely less loathsome than his book about his experience at the Mission suggests. Among the staff, he did not have an odious reputation. Working on rights issues, he was close to François Baroin, with whom he shared a certain idealism and a conviction that the commemoration should focus on the social issues of today and tomorrow. Others at the Mission qualified Lubrina as awkward and plodding but diligent and serious. A self-made man with a rich and versatile life experience, he was rendered sympathetic by his background. His book is strangely inconsistent with the picture that friends such as Baroin painted of him. It is cruel and cowardly in its thinly veiled allegorical mode. (It seems astonishing that the man who joined the cabinet of the secretary of state charged with humanitarian action at the end of the bicentennial year could so callously fix on the flawed physical characteristics of colleagues, whatever their moral infirmities, in order to burlesque them.) The author strains pathetically to be clever but rarely surpasses the level of commonplace malice. A tone of righteous self-satisfaction pervades the book.[17]

The Advisory Committee

The legislation creating the Mission had simultaneously established two ancillary committees. Perhaps because he felt so comfortable in dealing with the diverse ministries, Faure manifested little interest in the interministerial committee, to whose occasional needs Cabouat admirably tended. Given its very title—in French, "comité scientifique"—and its many eminent members, the Mission president could not be indifferent to the advisory committee, though he was patently less in need of "sages" than Baroin had been. He had several different ideas about how to make it useful and/or limit its nuisance capacity. Shortly after he took office, he convoked Jean Favier, whom he had known for many years, and announced somewhat brutally that he really had no need of a entourage of scholarly advisers. Since it was mandated and in fact existed, he, Faure, would preside himself, and he would convene it rarely. What caused Favier to bristle was less the slight of disgrace than the oblique means Faure subsequently used to try to pick his brain.

Faure held a number of plenary sessions that lasted several hours each, treating the group as a sort of assembly of notables whose support he coveted morally though he did not require it juridically. "It is your committee that constitutes, strictly speaking, the essential and singular organ of the Mission," he proclaimed. He even seemed to relish the opportunity to declaim before men (and a few women) whom he regarded as his intellectual peers.

Certainly he delivered his fullest expositions of the problems as well as the prospects of the Mission to the plenary sessions of the sages. His rhetoric was invariably hard to read, not only on the level of content but also on the level of intent. Listening to him, certain members suspected manipulation, others ingenuously marveled at the intellectual pyrotechnics, while still others wondered whether he was not more than a bit loony. In reflecting on the human condition within its bicentennial context, what was one to make of "l'homme du quatrième cerveau venant après le reptilien, le limbique, et le néo-cortex" or of the "hypothèse de chronotomie," marked by the three ages: "la machinerie, le machinisme dynamo-cinique, la technologie cérébro-semeiolotique"? Numerous members stayed away after the initial plenary session—indeed, some even left in the middle of it. These faultfinders felt that Faure was not in command of his dossiers, and they resented the waste of time involved.

One of the most memorable meetings took place in early January 1988, when one of the committee's most distinguished delegates, the scientist-physician-academician Jean Hamburger, uttered words that must have resonated familiarly in the ears of certain colleagues: "I'm not quite sure what I'm doing here." After a year of exchanges he was compelled to ask, "What is the role of biology in all this?" Faure handled this mutiny of anomic modesty with aplomb: what a question, *cher confrère*, "you are the philosopher of human destiny." Did he not recall that genetics and bioethics were to be at the nucleus of the concerns of the Arche Foundation?

There followed a protracted and rich dialogue touching on such diverse issues as migratory birds, infanticide, and the ethics of cats. (Six months later Hamburger resigned; Faure's successor as Mission chief evinced little interest in "the very big colloquium on the state of the world two hundred years after the French Revolution" that had been promised him.)[18]

With almost fifty official members, and several dei ex machina placed on stage by the president of the Mission, the advisory committee was an unwieldy body. For purposes of sustained, probing reflection on specific issues and for the appraisal of projects and ideas, Faure divided it into three subsections, each of which would meet according to its own needs: a section devoted to human rights, Faure's flagship issue; a second concerned with historical questions; and a third dealing with the whole range of cultural activities that sought Mission sponsorship in one form or another. (Deferring to the emphatic advice of his staff, Faure abandoned the plan to forge still two other subunits, one treating the "sciences of the human element" and the other, in honor of Baroin, exploring "communication and cooperation between the spiritual and scientific communities.")

It is hard to say whether this division of labor generated useful results. There was considerable absenteeism from these subgroup meetings. Staff counselors themselves felt that they were often consulting the sages on relatively petty matters and that even on affairs of moderate significance, they could be polled without obliging them to attend a meeting. The human rights unit discussed the possibility of convening all the Nobel laureates of the world to a "festival of freedoms" in May 1989 and the prospect of organizing a "a fortnight of the human element" to explore the ethical and "rights" dimensions of the impact of technology. It considered the wisdom of offering a doctorate through the Foundation, a prospect to which Faure was increasingly attached. Scoffed one critic at the idea of dispensing doctorates "ès-fraternité," in the field of fraternity, one could embrace Abbé Pierre without awarding him an advanced diploma. The group on cultural activities scrutinized numerous projects concerning music, theatre, and the plastic arts.[19]

To assist him in coordinating the whole enterprise, Faure briefly envisaged a sort of kitchen cabinet/Sanhedrin on whose members he would bestow the title of counselor-consultant-chargé de mission. The project never came to fruition, in part because of recruitment problems. "You're going to help me," he enjoined François Furet, anointing him with this special title and promising him the chance to shape policy. Furet had worked with Faure in the post–May 1968 Ministry of National Education and had advised him on his historical studies; he knew him reasonably well and respected him. But he backed off quickly, partly for reasons of self-regard ("This is not my job. . . . I have my books to tend to") and partly because he saw that it could not work—that they would not have a real liberty of action. Furet detected "an enormous bureaucratic battle around Faure." Convinced that the Elysée, through the intermediary of his bête noire, Régis Debray, did not want Faure to succumb to the influence of the revisionist historian, Furet judged it pointless to persist.[20]

The history subgroup—and more broadly the historians acting within the plenary committee—proved the most difficult to manage. Ideological cleavages were most sharply marked among the historians, who collectively seemed to claim a sort of right of eminent domain—*retrait féodal*, also known evocatively as *clameur* in Normandy, is perhaps a more apposite image—over the bicentennial space whose precise boundaries were being defined. It is not at all clear that they were inherently more "political" than the other members. Rather, it was their inability to separate their political affiliations, and even their sense of civic identity, from their "scientific" responsibilities as they were framed by the charge of the Mission that delineated them. (It was for this reason that Claire Andrieu, the Mission's central liaison officer with the advisory committee, regarded its very creation as an "institutional error," perhaps necessary for Baroin, given his lack of command of the historical field, but superfluous and even perilous for Edgar Faure.)

Though Chirac's Matignon appointed the committee members, the right (Jean Tulard) protested bitterly that the body was dominated by the left, and the left (Maurice Agulhon), more plausibly, argued the contrary.[21] Among their peers, if one deploys the crude traditional antinomy, and if one (wistfully) counts Furet and Ozouf with the left, the historians seem almost evenly divided. The volubility and the fervor of certain representatives of the left, Vovelle and Rebérioux in particular, may have demoralized the right and created a momentum or an ambience that seemed inimical to them.[22]

Tulard, Vovelle's conservative counterpart at the University of Paris IV— another staircase of the Sorbonne—claimed that the cabalistic confessional left blocked "all serious propositions," by which he meant "scientific" projects submitted by his own clan. He was especially incensed by the committe's refusal to fund the republication of the *Moniteur*, Panckoucke's famous Revolutionary newspaper. Certain historians in the adversary camp contested the authenticity of parts of the nineteenth-century edition from which the reprint would have been drawn; and the Mission staff was surprised by the casual and undocumented formulation of the request for subvention.

The right formalized its "Fronde" in a letter of 3 December 1987 addressed to President Faure and signed by twelve members, including Jean Favier (whom the Mission staff considered the éminence grise of the group), Pierre Chaunu, François Caron, Bruno Foucart, Jean de Viguerie, Jean-Pierre Poussou, and Tulard. They criticized the lack of periodicity of meetings, yet they announced that they would not attend the next meeting, scheduled imminently, for which they demanded a delay. They questioned the wisdom of the committee's tripartite division of labor, judged "somewhat hastily wrought." Most significant, they solemnly protested against numerous actions of the committee—gestures of sanctification of various sorts—the thrust of which was "to privilege certain authors and certain schools of opinion."

Beyond the conflict over the *Moniteur*, several specific incidents sparked their anger. The Mission had organized receptions to celebrate the publications of the books of two historians notoriously situated on the left. In cooperation with the publisher Bordas, it sponsored an elaborate ceremony at the Musée Carnavalet in honor of Georges Soria, a one-time Communist who authored a vigorously written, multivolume narrative history of the Revolution conceived in the Jacobin tradition and intended for the general public. In light of his densely charged calendar, Faure's presence added a special luster to the occasion.

The second reception, a less elaborate affair held in the salon of the Mission, honored the Elyséen counselor Claude Manceron, whom Tulard regarded as the evil genius of the committee because he was the direct conduit from Mitterrand. Then, in its first issue, the bulletin of the Mission, a slick publication called *Bicentenaire 89*, featured both an article by Michel Vovelle, Monsieur Marxism-Leninism-Communism for the right, and an interview with the omnipresent Manceron, only slightly less Red in their eyes. Produced by a friend of Faure's, Sibille Ionesco, hired as a communications specialist but unschooled in the public relations problems peculiar to this particular commemoration, the newsletter mixed historical digest, program notes, and hortatory publicity.[23]

President Faure responded promptly and drily. There were no compelling reasons to postpone the meeting. In the future he pledged monthly assemblies. In the light of the protestors' ardor for regular meetings, he found their request for cancellation of the forthcoming meeting "bizarre." Perhaps in order to avoid further dramatizing the clash, he did not directly address the intimation of systematic favoritism, which, he confided to one of his staff, he regarded as nothing less than a "blow" struck against his honor.

Apparently acting independently, another member of the advisory committee, Jacques Chailley, president of the Académie du disque, expressed astonishment in a letter to Faure over the exaggerated homage offered Manceron, whose opinions thus "enjoy a sort of official unction as a result of the presentation in the *Bulletin,* despite the fact that they seem far from being shared by all of us." In any event, continued Chailley, implicitly recalling Faure to his duty, they seem "hardly favorable to the national consensus that you have quite rightly made one of our goals."

A fellow melomaniac, Faure replied pianissimo to what could only be interpreted as a rebuke. The Mission was wholly committed to a "pluralistic" policy and betrayed no trace of "partisan spirit." The Mission would afford the same warm support to other committee members who had books to launch (Favier, it was rumored, was about to beget, and Chaunu was perpetually pregnant). Moreover, Faure reassured Chailley that as a careful reader, he had found nothing in Manceron's corpus "that could upset me intellectually."[24]

Claire Andrieu viewed the whole affair as unfortunate and unnecessary. It was naive to have imagined that the concentration of attention on the left would not affront and indeed incense the right. Though her own sensibilities were decidedly on the left, she believed it was a matter of both intelligence and responsibility to "reestablish a proper balance." Andrieu worked hard to quiet the furor and avoid the splintering of the committee. She was assisted by an unexpected conciliator,

Chirac's counselor for bicentennial affairs, Jean Boutinard-Ruelle, who reasoned with Tulard and Favier, and with their friend and colleague Michel Fleury, an influential antirevolutionary historian and administrator who operated outside the committee. Tulard was sufficiently soothed to accept an invitation to be the beneficiary of a reception to mark his forthcoming dictionary/historiography of the Revolution.

In the post-Faure period, Andrieu did nothing to salvage the advisory committee. On Cabouat's suggestion, Jean Favier reclaimed the presidency for the first meeting after Faure's demise. Rector Hélène Ahrweiler, who perhaps felt that the chancellor of the Paris Universities ought to have precedence over the director of the French archival system, confronted him sharply. This noxious climate, and the absence of any constructive debate, afforded Faure's successor the occasion to allow the committee to die of inanition.[25]

The Elysée and the Mission

The issue of Elysée influence was not simply a red herring of the right, however much the latter deployed it for polemical points. Cohabitation did not mean presidential abdication. In retrospect, it appears that the closer Mitterrand came to a firm decision to run again, the more his interest in the bicentennial rekindled. The Elysée was never, for a moment, disconnected from the Mission. A series of presidential counselors of diverse profiles and efficiencies conducted what was variously perceived as dialogue, surveillance, and meddling.

Claude Manceron bombarded Baroin with advice. A number of his ideas, including the planting of liberty trees and the posting of the Universal Declaration of Human Rights in all classrooms and public places, were either implemented or very seriously entertained. The Faure Mission was less receptive to Manceron, especially to demands that appeared to imply an institutional or political character. "The deep passion that M. Manceron has developed for the Mission," wrote a staff member in a sprightly and ironic confidential memo, in early 1987 "has led him to ask for the use of an office in our suite and for the use of the title 'special historical counselor.'" Our work spaces are so exiguous, suggested another staff member, "let's tell him simply that there is no office commensurate with his status." Manceron never infiltrated the rue Talleyrand, nor did he succeed in obtaining the appointment or election of Maurice Agulhon as vice president of the advisory committee.

From the fall through Christmas in 1987, a graduate of the elite Ecole normale of the rue d'Ulm named Jean-Michel Gaillard took over official liaison responsibilities as Mitterrand's bicentennial man. The staff found him well disposed and responsive, a good listener who had some worthwhile ideas. Gaillard later went on to far greater challenges, serving a brief and inglorious term as president of the major public television station, Antenne 2. The staff found his succcessor, Régis Debray, as intrusive as Gaillard had been discreet. It was his nth return to the Elyséen fold—can anyone affirm it to have been the last, even after the recent betrayals?—and he arrived as usual with both an ideological and a personal agenda.

Debray recounts his arrival in modest terms: "During the period of cohabitation, the president asked me to take a look at what Edgar Faure was preparing for the bicentennial. Given the context, I had no decision-making power, only the capacity to gather information and to discuss." His initial auscultation, which implied soundings in the body public as well as the body missionary, worried him deeply: "Very quickly I became aware of a major sense of predicament, of an uneasiness not only concerning what was to be commemorated—the old debate opposing the years 1789 and 1793—but over the very act of commemoration itself. More than an uneasiness, there was a a real awkwardness, a feeling of shame." Debray pressed his brand of republican virtue as an alternative to Babbittlike (and in his idiom, democratic) consensus. At the Mission he was said to have taken on the airs of a "second president." He "heard" its representatives, whom he would convoke to Monday luncheons at the presidential palace. When it came time to replace Edgar Faure, it is rumored that he lobbied for his own candidacy.

Cynics at the Mission were glad to see him replaced by an unrenowned woman named Françoise Fugier, today a subprefect, described as a protégée of Mitterrand from his political home country in the Nièvre. She rendered the Mission considerable service in her first few months by winning Elysée patronage for quite a few projects. Her swelling amour propre, however, soon alienated the Mission staff; Faure's successor completely short-circuited her at the end by dealing with the deputy chief of the staff of the Elysée, Christian Sauter, whenever the Mission required a presidential contact.[26]

Mitterrand himself received Faure frequently during the course of 1987. Faure needed to be reassured, and the president of the republic in any event wanted to make clear his desire to see the concrete shape of commemorative plans. At an early meeting Faure boasted that he had managed to obtain from France Télécom a telephone number for the Mission ending in "1789." Mitterrand is said to have replied cuttingly: "I take note that President Faure is not short of ambition." Increasingly impatient with Faure's tentativeness—"You must get going! I want to see [results]," he allegedly told the Mission president—he openly displayed his irritation at the reception he offered the advisory committee on 24 June 1987.

Mitterrand feared that Faure was paralyzed by uncertainties of an ideological, managerial, political, and temperamental nature. Faure ventured forthrightly into areas that the president deemed a bit marginal, despite their intellectual allure. A quasi university/think tank on the roof of the Arche was "a lovely and commendable idea." But Mitterrand wondered whether Faure's penchant for "seeing things from on high" had not led him to lose track of the commemorative object: the Revolution.

The bicentennial would utterly miss the mark if it failed to celebrate the birth of French democracy, without denying the tears and the blood of the delivery. This was Mitterrand's way of responding to the all-out media assault on the Revolution and on the idea of commemoration itself. The choice was not starkly, as some would frame it, between rights and Terror. Rather, the charge was "nothing but the Revolution, but all the Revolution." Mitterrand's goal was to shock the Mission into action, to push it off dead center.

"Troubled" by Mitterrand's comments, Faure nevertheless read the message clearly. Without missing a beat, he spoke out more forthrightly than ever before against those "would seek to put the Revolutiuon on trial," an enterprise, he suggested in surprisingly trenchant terms, that bespoke a disaffection for democracy itself. The impact of Mitterrand's foray is hard to measure precisely. A number of staff members felt that it clearly accelerated the pace of business. One of the sages remarked ironically to Faure himself that as prime minister he had been able to free Morocco in one day but that as head Missionary it took him months to organize a colloquium.[27]

Faure as Financier

Like business everywhere else, the Mission's business depended in considerable part on its finances. Edgar Faure was severely criticized not only for the way in which he used the sums he had on hand but also for failing to obtain substantially more. When he evoked money—it was not his preferred theme—he affected the insouciant tone of the grand seigneur who above all wanted to reassure his clients: "Of course there will be a problem of funding," he informed the advisory committee, "which can be examined by the Club des partenaires [private-sector supporters], and which can probably also be dealt with through licensing fees and royalties." In retrospect his serene optimism seems extravagant if not irresponsible.

With far more political experience and leverage than Baroin, Faure obtained a fifty-million-franc commitment from Finance Minister Edouard Balladur. His defenders regarded this as a veritable triumph, given Balladur's antipathy for the commemoration. His critics decried the deal as a capitulation. A member of his own staff, Jean-Jacques Lubrina, reproached him for failing to "to put his foot down" at Matignon during the budget process. Consumed by the goal of obtaining the roof of the Arche de la Défense for his Foundation for the symbolic price of one franc, Faure "did not fight for his budget." The president of the Mission was not lamely satisfied with "small potatoes," retorted Christian de Montrichard, another of his advisers. He had to navigate the murky waters of cohabitation with cunning; at the very end of his tenure, according to Montrichard, Faure expected to extract between Fr 120 and 150 million in supplementary allocations.

Yet Faure, like his predecessor, counted primarily on the private sector, where he had much less familiarity and clout. "The celebration of a grand national event as many-sided as the bicentennial of 1789," the wishful rationale proclaimed, "cannot today be confined to an exclusive reliance on the support of the public sector:

participation in the social and cultural life of our country has expanded too markedly during the past decade for that to be conceivable." Since the commemoration focused on the notion of individual rights "to which the entire economic world subscribes," it seemed reasonable to call on business to tithe for its liberty.

Faure farmed out the task of dealing with the private sector to Yann Gaillard, his longtime collaborator, who served as president of the association created by the Mission to facilitate its financial transactions, and to Jacques Friedmann of Air France, who agreed to try to marshal "partners" in what seemed to be an increasingly negative conjuncture in terms of the image of the bicentennial. From the outset Gaillard seems not to have shared his mentor's sanguine expectations, a state of mind that did not enhance his effectiveness. Friedmann appears to have encountered a tide of resistance, which may have demoralized him in turn. Only three other companies besides his own agreed to serve as "benefactor-members" of his Association d'entreprises pour le Bicentenaire.[28]

The financial management of the Faure Mission fell prey to slashing criticism from the Ministry of Culture's Inspection générale de l'administration (IGA), which conducted a full-scale audit at the end of Faure's tenure, with the Socialists back in power. From the perspective of his successor, Jean-Noël Jeanneney, it was a prudent and necessary requirement, wholly neutral in intent, the sine qua non of a clean transition. From the vantage point of Jeanneney's critics and the guardians of Faure's memory, the call for an audit and the manner in which it was articulated bespoke not merely a desire for an unencumbered takeoff but an appetite to discount and even besmirch the legacy.

According to this view, Jeanneney sought not merely a tabula rasa in financial terms, a business precaution hard to contest, but an officially authenticated claim to a more sweeping tabula rasa, the idea that Faure (and a fortiori Baroin) had bequeathed very little in terms of useful achievement. Understandably these accusations aggrieved Jeanneney, who steadfastly denied any nefarious intent. This is the sort of meta–domestic quarrel, alimented by many different strains of fidelity and animosity, that is unlikely ever to enjoy closure. Whatever the motivations, however, there is no doubt that the verdict of the audit was in many ways devastating.

The style and tone of the audit are as significant as its findings. A sinister undercurrent of irony marks the entire exposition, endowing it with a sort of énarquo-Libé voice. Grave charges are followed by halfhearted allowances of mitigation; patently bad judgment is pardoned or relativized in an unconvincing Old Testament lilt. According to the audit, Faure took a risk in turning to the "association" model for managing fiscal affairs. "This procedure, always criticized by the Cour des comptes but more and more utilized by the Public Administration," wrote the examiners, "is surely a guarantee of efficiency but can also present the risk of being a source of squandering resources."

The rationale is simple and alluring, especially if one is pressed to move quickly. By creating an association, transferring one's subsidies to it, and authorizing it to finance activities approved by the "mother" administration, one can circumvent the miles of red tape, the mandatory procedures, and the listless cadence of the public sector. Freer to disburse funds, an association also has the latitude to raise monies (sponsorship, philanthropy, subcontracting, and so on) on its own in ways denied to the administration itself. Administration watchdogs dislike associations because of their capacity to conceal, maneuver, divert, and generally escape systematic scrutiny and accountability.

Named president of the Bicentennial Association by Faure, Yann Gaillard, himself an inspecteur des finances, betrayed questionable judgment in the way he handled business. Loath to allow around Fr 5 million in state subsidies to lie dormant while the Mission decided how to allocate its resources, Gaillard invested the funds in various types of short-term paper. On the whole, he made a modest profit, losing in one category but more than compensating for these losses in another. "The principal was preserved despite the stock-market crash of 1987," observed the auditors.

But should Gaillard have taken any such risk? And wasn't he guilty of an egregious conflict of interest by consigning the portfolio to the Société centrale de banque, where he had previously been a senior executive? With insidious playfulness, the auditors concluded that all's well that ends well, the ends justifying the means: "But the experience of the president of the Association turned out to be beneficial in the last analysis, because the Association did not suffer penalties for its investments during an especially unfavorable cycle in the stock market."

The auditors concluded that the Mission's money—the state's revenues, the taxpayers' earnings—was frequently not well spent. Thanks to the association model, the Mission was able to arrange for the renovations of its future headquarters on the rue Talleyrand without having a public architect named, obtaining administrative design approval, formalizing the bidding for contracts, and so on. But "this work was expensive." Indulgently, the report allowed that "it was normal for the Mission to install itself in conditions of comfort (if not luxury) in order to be able to work efficiently." There was, however, more than a hint of sarcasm in its comment that "it was also very fitting for the public image of the Mission to be as positive as possible in the eyes of all those who would have occasion to visit its headquarters. It is well known that the public"—the sansculottes of the third millennium—"is sensitive to the setting in which the administration receives them."

The auditors could not swallow the "most extravagant" of the refurbishings: woodwork costing over a quarter of a million francs and painting amounting to almost six hundred thousand francs. In light of their short stay in this building— but that could not be foreseen—these expenditures appear "seriously overdrawn." Defenders of Faure regarded these reproaches of prodigality as so many calumnies. Prior to the Mission's arrival, the locale was filthy and decrepit. The renovations produced only one luxurious salon; the rest was nothing more than banal, and crowded, office space.

The examiners wondered about the elaborate equipment purchased for the kitchen/dining room: ten thousand francs for cookware, ten thousand for glassware from Christophle, twenty thousand for silverware. These acquisitions seemed "truly needless" in light, first, of the rigid constraints of Faure's agenda (he had time to host a meal at the Mission only once during his regime) and, second, "when one takes note of the level of expenses in Parisian restaurants that the Association had to reimburse." Once again the condescending benefit of doubt, the unctuous and sardonic declaration of professional empathy: "Business lunches, it is well known"—the diabolical *on le sait*, the auditor's scud missile—"are the best means of propelling forward one's projects." In 1987 the Association reimbursed almost a hundred and fifty thousand francs in restaurant meals, and in the first half of 1988, almost ninety thousand (these sums considered apart from over a quarter of a million for diverse travel costs). Then the withering commentary, the mutilating moral of the story: "The facility provided by the Association's checkbook was thus very useful for the Mission. It is understandable that this instrument was highly utilized. Yet one is justifiably astonished that so many opportunities for contact yielded by June 1988 only [a handful of] undistinguished projects."

None of the financial strictures would have had much weight if the auditors had been obliged to concede that the Mission had been truly productive. On the contrary, they took pleasure in stressing "the indigence of the operations chosen through June 1988." Their harsh balance sheet read as follows:

Among the sixty activities funded by the Association d'entreprises pour le Bicentenaire, what does one in fact find? Seven film/television projects of minor interest, seven publications of serious colloquia, three feasibility studies (whose conclusions did not augur well for the chances of bringing the proposals to life), three exhibitions which will enjoy extremely limited resonance, three documentary research projects, seven miscellaneous events unlikely to bear fruit, ten payments of bills for publicity in behalf of the Mission (that is, for the promotion of the Mission itself, not the bicentennial).

Some of the six million francs expended by Gaillard—only twenty-seven projects were fully funded before his departure—seemed especially dubious. The Association accorded a quarter million francs to the Chambre syndicale des céramistes et métiers d'art for a competition that in any event they ran annually to promote creativity. They planned this year to award a grand prize to recompense "an object celebrating the bicentennial." The competition failed to attract the level of quality anticipated. Two projects were crowned, a watch ("which vaunted nothing revolutionary") and "confettis that were not even in the tricolor pattern to which the Revolution gave notoriety." The Association paid a rare book dealer a hundred and eighty thousand francs for a first edition of Diderot's *Encyclopédie* that Faure planned to make part of a permanent Revolutionary collection. The project was stillborn, and the Association lost ninety thousand on the resale at auction. Finally, the auditors praised the decision of the government, through the financial auditor assigned to the Mission, to intervene to block the expenditure of about eight million francs on a billboard campaign that they judged ill-conceived and exorbitantly priced. Despite their panoply of reproaches, the IGA informed the Mission's new president at the beginning of 1989 that it saw no reason not to accord a formal discharge to the previous regime.[29]

Auditing the Audit

What kind of bicentennial would have occurred had Edgar Faure survived remains an open question. A counterfactual projection would have to take into account a host of variables, not the least of which was the new political situation created by Mitterrand's reelection and the new urgency it imparted to the commemorative operation. The audit does not demonstrate that Faure would necessarily have failed, though he would surely have faced one of the major challenges of a career rich in trying tests. Nor does it establish that Jeanneney was nothing less than a providential savior, though his leadership certainly proved decisive in the end.

While many of the IGA's strictures on financial management seem cogent, its dismissal of the substantive accomplishments of the Faure Mission is quite unfair. Partial in both senses of the word, its coverage simply does not do justice to the unheralded staff work or to the particular virtues of Faure's own febrility. Its judgments on program development were frequently summary and superficial. Focusing on finished product in a strained and often reductive way, the auditors allowed little evaluative space for the nonquantifiable conditions and actions: the inherent difficulty of the task given the political and ideological climate, in France and beyond; the enormous, albeit fragmented, investment in preliminary exploration and reconnaissance; the elaboration of structures of information and coordination; the myriad and burdensome transaction costs (in time and energy rather than cash) involved in the process of generating projects and negotiating their execution; the genuine quality of many of the ideas that surfaced, once stripped of their turgidity; and the ripening of projects of relatively long gestation, credit for which would redound to the successor regime.

It would be absurd—and unseemly—for example, to presume because the bulk of Faure's fantasies for the Foundation did not come about that the discussions themselves were not fruitful, that their ventilation did not shape the unfolding sense of the possible and the desirable, and that their failure was total and irreversible. What is true about Faure's passion for the "rights" theme is equally true of his interest in historiography: aside from the hundreds of colloquia for which his regime can claim only indirect responsibility, is he to be blamed for the failure of his successor to realize a number of the excellent ideas for Aulard-style primary-source publications? If the rights theme, for both good and bad reasons, withered a bit in the post-Faure period, his campaign against exclusion in all its forms—to be sure, less frenzied, more focused—reached its apogee in 1989. Nor is it to his discredit that a throng of interesting projects mobilizing the community of youth were diluted or abandoned after his demise. Faure's adviser Lunel made this case somewhat more perversely, in the mode of the intellocrat's paradox: "It is to the honor of the Mission and its advisory committee to have managed to give top priority to 'the unpresentable' and 'the unpackageable [*l'inmédiatisable*].'"

The festive calendar bequeathed by the Faure Mission was strewn with uncertainties. But it obviously shaped the physiognomy of the definitive calendar at several critical points, and it proposed certain activities that warranted execution. Faure's agenda included the hot-air balloons to mark the inauguration of the bicentennial season, a re-creation of the procession of the three estates at Versailles on 4 May, a reconstitution of the unity march of the national guardsmen called *fédérés* to Paris in June, some sort of commemoration of the end of privileges on the night of 4 August, a "rights" fête on 26 August, and a ceremony marking the foundation of the republic on 21 September. Beyond the Jarre show scheduled for 13–15 July, the Mission staff candidly avowed in March 1988 that its "plan for grand public events . . . remains insufficiently developed [or] structured in relation to the objectives of the celebration, and incomplete in many areas."

The protocol for the attribution of the Mission label was drafted. The plans for television and cinema retrospectives were wholly worthwhile. Moreover, the projects for new television shows around bicentennial themes were not as mediocre as the IGA conveyed. The Faure Mission also deserves credit for the "Avant-Premiere" at La Villette, the "festival marketplace" that assembled in a single time and space hundreds of individual and institutional, private- and public-sector sellers and buyers—those with projects requiring support and those interested in sponsoring projects, along with a general public avid to get a taste of the commemorative menu and the media whose coverage would help make or break the entire year.[30]

A word must also be said about the impact of the cohabitation experience on the life of the Mission. The staff toiled in a climate of burgeoning demoralization. Even before the president took ill, there was a growing mood of futility, a sense that things were unraveling instead of congealing. Chirac's government seemed frankly hostile to the whole commemorative notion. Beyond larger ideological antipathies, there was the frank political calculation that it would be unwise to invest significantly in a project that had an inherently leftish aspect and that could be wholly recovered and exploited by the Socialist party in case Chirac failed to take the presidency.

"No gifts for the left," muttered one of the chief advisers at Matignon. When the interministerial committee met in October 1987, it was presided not by Chirac but by one of his counselors, Boutinard-Ruelle. The Mission staff interpreted this as an unequivocal message: "You do not exist." (The relief loomed sharper in retrospect because at the beginning of the next political year the new premier, Michel Rocard, personally conducted the interministerial session for an hour; and its members were not the highly political cabinet appointees but the "institutionnels," career civil servants including the directors of the ministries, who assured better administrative mastery and continuity.)

The Mission was jolted and confused by the shrill antileft ambience of the end of the year. Once Faure left the scene for medical reasons, the staff felt that they had lost their final rampart. There was virtually no money left; Cabouat's leadership was neither inspiring nor effective; there was much internal maneuvering for position, described euphemistically by one staff member as "desolidarization" and more vividly by another as "decomposition."[31]

"Still, and Now Once Again, We Lived in the Funerary Mode"

Edgar Faure started too late and ended too soon. After a protracted illness, which kept him away from the Mission for several months, he died in March 1988, less than a year from the opening of the bicentennial season. The *Canard enchaîné* published a cartoon of Mitterrand phoning Chirac, his opponent in the forthcoming presidential elections—to propose to him the ill-starred presidency of the Mission. The far right ironized and delected over the hapless commemoration. François Brigneau reminded his flock that the series of disasters did not begin with Baroin, for even before he was selected, the government had proposed the Mission to the head of Renault, Georges Besse, who was assassinated by the terrorist group Action directe before he had had a chance to respond. The message seemed clear to counterrevolutionary zealots: the bicentennial was not meant to be. In point of fact, the entire apparatus of the Mission was paralyzed, and the celebration once again placed in doubt.[32]

Alle Guten Dinge Sind Drei
Jean-Noël Jeanneney and the Mission Impossible

A s the *Canard enchaîné* put it, in May 1988 France "perpetuated on his throne Tonton, who had become God, according him a second triumphal lease, which blocked in its tracks the Chiraquian Counterrevolution." Certain now that they would preside over the anniversary, Mitterrand and his new Socialist government manifested a fresh determination to reinvigorate the commemorative enterprise. On 25 May the Council of Ministers named Jean-Noël Jeanneney to replace Faure. The president is said to have chosen him from a list of five (or ten) candidates supplied by Régis Debray (among the names bruited: Françoise Giroud, Léopold Senghor, Georges Kiejman). Rumor has it that Jack Lang pressed for the creation of a secretary-of-stateship for bicentennial affairs, under the aegis of his Ministry of Culture, to be offered to Pierre Nora, a historian of memory, Furetian, and mamamouchi of historical and social-science publishing.

"Le Plus Ane des Trois N'est Pas Celui Qu'on Pense" (La Fontaine)

The new head of the Mission could boast neither Faure's mastery of pork-barrel politics and clientage networks nor Baroin's command of the business world and his range of Masono-economic contacts. Unlike his predecessors, Jeanneney was a professional intellectual, professor at the Institut d'études politiques of Paris specializing in twentieth-century history. Yet, unlike most intellectuals, he had acquired management skills at the highest levels, serving as chief executive officer of Radio France from 1982 to 1986, and he was intimately familiar and comfortable with the media, as a result of both his practical experience and his scholarly

220

interests in communications, public opinion, the press, and all manner of audiovisual expression.

Nor was Jeanneney handicapped by his family origins. In the words of one of his colleagues, he was the "bearer of a grand name." His grandfather Jules Jeanneney was minister under the Third Republic and president of the Senate, while his father was several times minister under the Fifth Republic. He drew his deeply republican and laic values from his family experience. Rooted in eastern France, his grandfather came from peasant stock and had a provincial's lifelong fascination with Paris as a site of beauty, mystery, and power. It is hard to find traces of the grandfather's Restivian instincts in the very proper and polished manner of the grandson. One cannot imagine Jean-Noël promenading on the grands boulevards at dawn, in the footsteps of the young lawyer Jules at the turn of the century, rhapsodizing on the magic of the city and taking immense pleasure in the freedom to urinate "in the open air."

Jean-Noël's father, Jules's only child, obtained his agrégation in political economy and taught at the University of Grenoble. Named to de Gaulle's committee of economic experts, he subsequently served three times as a minister. His most celebrated political campaign pitted him against Pierre Mendès-France—whom his son came to admire—at Grenoble in 1968. President of the Conseil général of the Haute-Saône, he voted for Mitterrand in the second round in 1974 after having voted for Jacques Chaban-Delmas in the first. He later served Mitterrand as a sherpa to the Ottawa economic summit and as a negotiator with Algeria. Jean-Noël owes his Augustinian strain to his mother's family, scions of the BSP (the *bonne société protestante* as opposed to the *haute société protestante* of which Couve de Murville is a memorable exemplar). Her father was a physician and her mother a budding historian, one of the first women to attempt the agrégation in history, and an ardent Dreyfusard.

Born to a family with an immense respect for diplomas, Jean-Noël followed the classical elitist trajectory in the public school system, winning a coveted place in the Ecole normale supérieure of the rue d'Ulm, but finding time to do a year of law school before the final preparation for the Ulm competition and to attend the Institut d'études politiques while he worked toward the agrégation in history. Before he completed his doctorate, a scholarship enabled him to travel around the world. Five months in the Orient following political campaigns in Japan, Laos, and elsewhere induced him to write his first book, *Le Riz et le rouge*. Though deeply impressed by de Gaulle's historic role in the war and in the decolonizing process, the young graduate of the Ecole normale of the rue d'Ulm, whose classmates remember him as a conservative, refused offers to enter several ministerial cabinets in the late 1960s because he found the government "too far to the right."

On the margins of the practice of politics, Jeanneney made politics the center of his intellectual life. Even as Mitterrand was attempting to regroup the left, he wrote a study of the failure of the cartel of 1924–26, which he meant not merely as a piece of learning but as "history lessons for a left in power." Another of his influential books treated the relations between political power and the business community, a classical preoccupation of the left. Even as he assumed a professorship at the Institut d'études politiques of Paris in 1977, he knew that he would not remain permanently a spectator of political life. Policy differences concerning, inter alia, the place of capitalism, the institutions of the Fifth Republic, and the French nuclear capacity separated him from the Socialist party. But he would have run for the parliament against the right in 1981 had the PS been willing to back non–party members.

"My family education had taught me very early what the reality of power was," he confided to an interviewer, "it remained for me to discover its harshness." He had his first taste at Radio France at age forty. Though he had served for several years on the Haut Conseil de l'Audiovisuel and had begun to focus some of his research on media issues, he was still, in his own words, "a little prof," with no credibility as a leader in either the public or private sector. The idea of exercising authority appealed to him; and it was by using his authority decisively and some-times mercilessly that he imposed himself, at the cost of earning "some solid enmities," by no means the last of his career. In particular, his success in organizing a complex program of decentralization and his toughness with the unions im-pressed many informed observers on the right and on the left who had questioned the wisdom of his appointment.

His independence irritated both sides, though by the time he had to confront Philippe de Villiers, the rightist junior minister for communications in the cohabitation government, he probably felt some nostalgia for his tutelary nemesis on the left, former minister of communications Georges Fillioud. *Panurge*, "a book of combat," recounts Jeanneney's efforts to save as many local public radio stations as possible against Villiers's campaign of extermination. Though the appeal of the library had not wholly abated, the "political brawl" captivated Jeanneney. "To do battle, to have it out in order to clarify things"—he enjoyed this give and take. A luncheon with Mitterrand—was it to console him for his dismissal from Radio France in 1986?—confirmed his appetite for politics even if it elicited no concrete promises for the future. His second marriage, to Annie-Lou Cot, a historian like him but also a member of the same dynastic elite and the sister of a prominent Socialist leader, marked another avenue into the world of politics. His next major assignment, as the head of the official commemoration, placed him at the intersec-tion of high politics, high administration, and high intellectualizing, and tested him severely on all three fronts.[1]

From the outset Jeanneney had no illusion about the glamor of the task. He was being asked to "manage the unmanageable." He accepted the job because he felt flattered and challenged and obliged. The call to public service at a difficult and important juncture by a president for whom he had voted in the name of principles in which he believed could not leave him indifferent. Even as ideological affinity and civic duty impelled him, so did the idea of commemoration and the work of collective representation and memory stimulate his "historian's gourmandise." The fact that he was not a specialist in the history of the Revolution he construed as a real advantage, for it meant that he owed no "allegiance to this or that school" and that he had "a free hand" to deal with the intellectual and university milieux. His rich experience "as a player and as a researcher" in the audiovisual domain hastened his conviction that he could handle the responsibilities of the Mission "so clear was it that the bicentennial would succeed or would fail, to a very large degree, on this very terrain."

If he ulcerated, however, during the night that the government gave him to decide whether to accept his nomination, it was not over his capacity. He was talented and proven, and he believed in himself, without swagger but unflinchingly. His anxiety crystallized on the constraints of the charge. Prime Minister Rocard had acknowledged that the Mission was in bad shape, and that it would not dispose of opulent means to facilitate its recovery. The most daunting factor was time: once he moved beyond the inherited disarray, he would have barely six months to invent and organize the ceremonies. During his night of reflection, Jeanneney recalls that he stumbled on the page dealing with the preparation for the first major Revolutionary celebration, the Festival of the Federation (14 July 1790), when he haphazardly opened Mona Ozouf's important book on the nature and orchestration of Revolutionary festivals. Jeanneney recounts his reactions:

> The author relates that, around the tenth of July 1790, in the midst of preparations for the celebration of the first anniversary of the taking of the Bastille, a citizen had written: "How late we are!" Indeed, they were significantly behind schedule, but the collective effort would overcome this handicap. Everyone joined in, night and day, to build the necessary installations. . . . And finally the festival took place. To put it another way, in certain special cases, when one has little time to accomplish a task, one realizes it in less time than required. That gave me confidence and courage.[2]

Beginning the morning he took office, Jeanneney tirelessly repeated this upbeat message that the press and public needed so urgently to hear: "We have little time, but having little time is a stimulant" and "I am going . . . to recoup the lost time." He had inherited a cumulatively bad press. The least worrisome strictures—at least for the moment—were the ideological ones. As early as January 1983 François Furet had sounded the tocsin against the prospect of a Communist-driven bicentennial—an ineluctable prospect ("by the force of things") if the Communists were still participants in a Socialist government in 1989—that would engender a very "unitary" commemoration "around a highly unified French Revolution, without a gulf between '89 and '93." Though subsequent events spared Furet this nightmare, critics on the right continued to echo this reproach-admonition as if a fiery red outcome were inevitable in any commemorative enterprise regardless of the hue of the sponsoring government. Pointing to an Association des amis du Bicentenaire guided by prominent Communist advisers, in the fall of 1986, *Le Figaro* denounced the Jacobin "cultural monopoly" practiced by the left in preparation for "the grand revolutionary mass." The fact that the Mission was starved for means at that time did not prevent Pierre Chaunu from condemning "Socialo-Communist governors" for having crammed it with funds "as one does gooses from the Périgord."

But the more telling criticism focused on the substantive failures of the commemorators, on their torpor, their tardiness, their dishevelment. Mitterrand himself had warned Faure that the lead time was "already too short." "If things continue like this, we will celebrate '89 in '92!" railed Yves Mourousi, eager candidate for several major bicentennial roles. "After having botched the International Exposition and the Olympic Games," he added, "we will end up by missing our great rendezvous with History." Lacking "impetus or scope," the bicentennial "will probably not be the international event to which we were in a position to aspire," *Le Quotidien de Paris* predicted. *Le Canard enchaîné* summed up the situation on the eve of Jeanneney's arrival as follows: "The Revolution of 1989 is turning out badly. The dossiers of Edgar Faure are empty. So is the cash register."

The day before Jeanneney's nomination, under a headline reading "State of Emergency for 1989," *Le Monde* published a probing critique of the drift toward commemorative entropy. "Launched tardily, slowed down or arrested in its movement by very constraining human and/or political circumstances," the bicentennial machine "is once again broken down." Once an insuperable obstacle, the uncertainty over the presidency had now been resolved. But the government was still paralyzed by its failure to articulate clearly its goals ("What exactly is sought for the bicentennial of 1789?") and by the increasingly plausible fear that the celebration could never be ready in time. *Le Monde* found only faint consolation in the multitude of small projects that were ready to leap off the drawing boards. The "critical big events" had not yet been delineated and, above all, "the general orientation which could structure and possibly carry the whole has remained in abeyance."[3]

If Jeanneney's selection was not hailed as a one-stroke antidote to all the morosity, it was generally welcomed as an important first step toward clarification and acceleration. Only the far right grumbled and indulged its crabbed black humor. "But he is not a moderate," *Aspects de la France* complained, not without reason, "which suggests that we will have a tumultuous bicentennial." Though Jeanneney's brazenly youthful appearance—he looked ten years younger than his forty-six years—seemed geared to symbolize the extraordinary youthfulness of the Revolution, the extreme right took pleasure in reminding this "'purebred' Jacobin" of the "elevated rate of mortality in the position." Withdraw, warned "Meursius," resign while there is still time: "The charnelhouses take revenge, Jean-Noël! The tons and tons of human flesh accumulated on the territory of the realm as a consequence of the guillotines, the fields of execution, the rivers of Nantes, the bread ovens of the Vendée cried out in this vast unknown that surrounds us a warning of mysterious disturbances which we endure still today." Resolutely unsuperstitious, the Mission's new president survived all the maledictions and bad vibrations, though not without the jarring receipt of anonymous letters threatening dire punishment.

Death threats apparently emanating from "royalist milieux" led authorities to assign him bodyguards.[4]

Autopsy and Reorganization

Autopsy, if not death, was the order of the day. Jeanneney subjected his predecessor's administration to a searching postmortem in order to determine what changes to make. The "deficit of esteem that afflicted this Mission" was intolerable. It was only partly the reflection of objective failure. Though he did not underestimate the gravity of certain errors and gaps, he recognized that the Mission had in fact moved forward on many fronts—in establishing networks across the departments, in developing an audiovisual program, in soliciting scores of institutional and individual initiatives. To a considerable extent, the Mission's "negative image" was the result of poor image making. One priority was thus "to institute very quickly a new policy of public relations and comunications."

Concerning the quality of the personnel and the organization of their work, what others called "havoc" or "an amiable shambles," Jeanneney characterized as disorientation. Insufficient in size and talent, the staff was coherent neither in its recruitment nor in its internal division of labor and lines of accountability (inter alia, there were too many "of President Faure's friends and counselors with nebulous functions and responsibilities"). The lack of sustained leadership had caused crippling uncertainty, hesitation, and confusion. There seemed to be no unifying conceptual logic, no global strategy of organization and operation. The great events of the festive calendar had not been fleshed out. Faure had settled for a drastically insufficient budget, and then he had utilized an excessively large proportion of it for administrative purposes. Jeanneney strenuously objected to "the prodigal contracts" that his predecessor had signed with promotional and publicity agencies (including the RSCG group, one of whose principals was close to Mitterrand). Important opportunities were missed in the sectors of commercialization and tourism.[5]

"It was urgent," concluded Jeanneney, "to reforge the staff, to rearticulate its goals, and first of all to give it the financial and material means to work efficiently." Housecleaning began with the departure of ten members of the old staff—"resignations demanded or encouraged"—the recasting of assignments and the elaboration of new work procedures, and the recruitment of fresh, full-time collaborators. The new president could not abide the suffocating "locus of intrigues" that the Mission had become during the Faure period. He immediately liquidated the feminine court that attended his predecessor. Its untitled first lady had been Marie-Edith Legendre, an ambassador's wife, who controlled the inner space of the Mission, used a Mission car, and organized important events ranging from intimate luncheons between Faure and critical interlocutors to the cocktail party for Manceron, her ideological antithesis, that helped to provoke the storm on the right in the advisory committee. Dispatched with her were Dominique Besse, a member of the advisory committee who had become a quasi-permanent fixture at the rue Talleyrand, and Louisa Maurin, an employee without compelling credentials.

Nor did Jeanneney require the counsel of Faure's old collaborator, Rector Antoine, who had also exercised an informal but critical role in the Faure system. Even had he not refused to lend the new president his official automobile, one of the petty but revealing episodes in the hectic transitional period, Olivier Passelecq would surely have been dismissed for the demoralization he had wrought. Sibille Ionesco, who had worked in communications with mixed results, was disgraced. Didier Hamon had already left to join Lang. A later *fournée* saw the departure of Yves Marek, a young graduate of the Ecole nationale d'administration (*énarque*) from the Quai d'Orsay who had worked for Jean-Pierre Cabouat. Much to the surprise of the staff, the latter stayed on, but in a radically reduced role. Still, the international sector, whose superintendence he received and where he was most at home, swelled into a very substantial undertaking. Sensing negative vibrations, Pierre Lunel left the Mission of his own volition.[6]

At its zenith, the new staff consisted of fewer than sixty persons, double the size of the Faure regime, but, as Jeanneney liked to boast, barely a fifth the magnitude of the Australian centennial organization. (Before it was over, Jeanneney would owe a lot to those remote, sparse, and festive Australians, whose availability for comparison proved very reassuring.) Fifteen persons exercised executive responsibilities of one sort or another (finances, communications, public relations, international relations, and sectorial responsibilities such as project coordination, liaison with local government, historiography, rights of men and women, audiovisual and theatrical activities, and so on), ten of whom carried over from the previous administration.

To fill the critical positions closest to him, Jeanneney convinced several key collaborators from his days at Radio France to rejoin him. First came Monique Sauvage, an audiovisual professional, who directed his cabinet with authority and vigor. She deployed strength rather than sensitivity, implacable logic rather than intuition or sentiment. In contrast with her sometimes volcanic temperament, André de Margerie exuded an unflappable sangfroid. He shared a sort of sociogenetic bond with Jeanneney. Their families were part of "the grand administrative dynasties"—analogous to the famous two hundred families denounced by the PCF in the 1930s—"which gave France corteges of ambassadors, ministers, and high officials." A thoughtful and discreet man trained in economics and urbanism, de Margerie served as Jeanneney's chief counselor and alter ego. Old-boy ties in both the public and private sectors made him especially valuable for gathering intelligence and making discreet contacts. A third person from the Radio France period was Angélique Oussedik, a persuasive and enterprising woman, who took over press relations. Though trained as an educator, she had achieved great success in public relations. She seemed to know everyone who mattered, in the press and in the relevant ministries. Self-confident and upbeat, with a precious talent for improvisation and rapid problem solving, her arrival buoyed the morale of the Mission.

She encroached on the "communications" sector, still nominally in the hands of Jacques Banaszuck, who had come to the Mission after years of marketing the Parisian subway. To judge by the "Communications Plan, October 1988–March 1989," he had not crafted a compelling strategy. Written in quasi-technical terms apparently meant to convey a high level of professionalism, it was often cryptic and pervasively vague, and it failed to develop clear lines of attack. It belabored the difficulties of a consensual strategy ("federating concept") that would require a "Mourousian event" in order to succeed. It recommended a billboarding campaign despite the disaster of the previous summer. It suggested getting the Mission president on television, preferably with zealous variety host Michel Drucker. It ulcerated over the lack of public esteem for the Mission "as a social body." While the Mission desperately needed to conquer public opinion, the report argued, "only three themes are mobilizing: the sacred, sports, show business." Unfortunately, none really applied to the Mission. Nevertheless, without explaining how these projects would redound to the Mission's reputation, the author proposed an illumination of Notre-Dame from the inside and a soccer tournament.

Jeanneney made a halfhearted effort to retain François Baroin: it would have been inconceivable to dismiss him. He placed him before an impossible choice: he would have to choose between working for the Mission where he evaluated competing projects in the youth and rights areas, and working with AD 89, the association that he and his late sister helped to engender, since it would not be proper, Jeanneney reasoned, for him to be both judge and party. Baroin opted unhesitatingly for his friends, though he would have liked to continue to lobby for his father's ideas within the Mission and felt that Jeanneney, had he not been hostile to many of those ideas, could have found a solution of accommodation.

Christian de Montrichard continued to work the local/regional liaison, a snowballing task that threatened to overwhelm the Mission. Under the direct gaze of the president, a fellow professional, who found her sociologically as well as intellectually congenial, Claire Andrieu persisted in the task of trying to manage history and historians. Neither she nor her boss believed it was useful to convene the advisory committee frequently, either as a whole or in working groups. Under the new regime the committee receded into marginal significance. Marie-Christine Wellhoff introduced Jeanneney to segments of the media world that he had not yet discovered, and Elie Schulman took him to the theatre.

An able diplomat and protégé of Jeanneney's brother-in-law Jean-Pierre Cot, Jean Mendelson, joined the Mission. As a former student of Albert Soboul, he probably knew more about the Revolution to begin with than any other staff member. He described himself puckishly as the Mission's "token Marxist." Under his theoretical tutelage, Jean-Jacques Lubrina continued to toil in the rights and "social" sectors. He did not make a positive impression on Jeanneney, in part because of his slow and drudging style of expression, and an oblique manner of dealing with people and issues that caused one colleague to remark, "he likes to operate in the dark." Apparently to satisfy this appetite, he was posted to work not in the central Mission office but in a small room across the street. Symbolically, this exile seemed to mark the estrangement of the Jeanneney Mission from the Baroin-Faure legacy.[7]

Within a few weeks Jeanneney moved the Mission from Faure's exiguous and stately seat to quarters that were larger but far cheaper and more austere, a practical and symbolic affirmation of his intention to spend as little as possible on operating expenses. Jeanneney equipped the new quarters with computers and multiplied the phone lines, but the offices remained both overcrowded and understaffed until the end.

Relations between Jeanneney and His Staff

As a boss and as a leader, the president received mixed reviews. His inner circle worshiped him. They appreciated his rigor, admired his alert and agile mind, marveled at his cultivation and refinement, and took pride in their opportunity to be his accomplices. Some of his "new" collaborators were much less enthusiastic. A portion of the bad feelings issued almost organically from the change of regimes and the circumstances that occasioned it. The staff carryovers were in mourning on a number of different levels, some for the second time. Professionally and emotionally, none had fully resolved her or his sense of loss. The consummate insider, Jeanneney was *their* outsider, a sort of interloper. He was in a hurry, and he showed little deference for the Baroin-Faure joint legacies. (Several Mission counselors were shocked and mortified that Jeanneney and especially Monique Sauvage publicly denigrated the Mission's past as part of what seemed like a tawdry, self-aggrandizing mise-en-scène rather than a fair-minded and lucid new beginning.) Jeanneney's prudence regarding the inheritance was understandable and even necessary. But his insensitivity was inadmissible, and over the course of time it seemed, in the eyes of his critics, to bespeak a real character flaw rather than a circumstantial reflex.

Some of the hostility to Jeanneney had to do with the way he represented himself and with the way he treated others, the two forms of address being inextricably intertwined. He himself admitted that he was "a little bit of a spoiled child." Jeanneney projected a superciliousness and a patrician condescension that offended a number of his collaborators. The tribal snobbery into which he had been socialized, he could neither overcome nor conceal. Surely there was an important element of jealousy and of revolt against authority in the reactions of Mission employees. The new president was exigent in a way that few of his staff members had yet encountered. Moreover, he seemed too young, too handsome, too well garbed, too successful, too sure of himself (though his perceived arrogance could very well have concealed a certain timorousness). One departing counselor imagined Jeanneney, Boy Wonder, proclaiming: "France is thinking of me for a grand, universal mission."

For all these reasons, however, his distance and his manner seemed all the more galling. He did not seem to be an attentive listener. He did not delegate responsibility in a fashion that fortified morale. Even his gestures of solicitude lacked conviction. At the Mission's end, for instance, he made institutional arrangements to help place his personnel, but he seemed to take little personal interest in their fate. "He is closed off," commented one staff member, scandalized that he barely knew half of the Mission's forty employees. In terms of warmth and passion, given his discreet nature, Jeanneney suffered in comparison with the demonstrative and kinetic Edgar Faure. Jeanneney's remarkable sense of self-control—one senses his maternal grandmother here—may also have unfairly enhanced the impression of haughtiness. Whether the strictures against him are well founded or not, however, there is no doubt that they affected the mood at the workplace.

In more concrete terms, Jeanneney was reproved for lacking "team spirit" and for failing to develop both a sense of shared objectives and a useful hierarchical structure. (Nor did Sauvage know how to compensate.) He was said to lack interest in the prosaic but fundamental work of the Mission, though in a caviling spirit he might just as readily have been rebuked for miring himself excessively in detail had he been more involved in day-to-day business. According to one staff member, he seemed to be elsewhere during sessions devoted to the award of the Mission's approbation, or label, to projects and products, a fastidious but crucial part of the Mission's business: "Jeanneney endured that wearily." Another collaborator extrapolated from his snobbery—"he does not like the people"—a policy shortcoming, a failure to make adequate connection with the "the world of unions" and the "milieu of associations."

Still another echoed charges made by hostile voices on the right, including at least one on the rue St.-Guillaume, that the president of the Mission was supinely "at the beck and call of Mitterrand." Situating himself squarely on the left, this critic reproached Jeanneney with failing to resist Socialist and Elyséen pressure— "the rackateers of the left"—when the facts of the case morally required rejection. Given the Mission's own rules, he claimed, Socialist leader Jean Auroux, mayor of Roanne, ought not to have received one hundred thousand francs to purchase a Revolutionary ceramic collection and another fifty thousand to celebrate the arts of the table; the leftist municipality of Valence should not have been accorded one hundred thousand francs in an eleventh-hour request to sponsor a mammoth bicentennial soirée; and finally a Madame Ivelda, boasting a putative family connection to the Mitterrands, should not have obtained fifty thousand francs to organize some sort of musical competition. These subventions, it was charged, hardly flatter Jeanneney's self-styled image as Mr. Lean and Clean. And they bespeak a lack of procedural rigor that demoralized part of the staff.

Dissension of a substantive character rarely came to the surface in staff meetings. An eruption of criticism marked a meeting held in mid-December 1988. Much of the sharpest discussion seems to have taken place while the president of the Mission was absent from the room in order to conduct an interview. Christian de

Montrichard opened the assault. Intellectually and culturally, the Mission was not succeeding in delivering its message, even though it was announcing hundreds of events and a handful of spectacular initiatives. Leaving the terrain to our adversaries and failing to contextualize our various undertakings, Montrichard contended, "we are falling into the void." Vainly struggling from the margin to salvage the Baroin-Faure focus on human rights, Jean-Jacques Lubrina blamed the situation on the lack of a convincing "mooring of the French Revolution in contemporary society." He made the objects of his nostalgia and his reproach patently clear: "With President Faure, the anchor was the rights of man. In abandoning them, the Mission deprived itself of its message." Implicitly, Lubrina accused the Mission—Jeanneney—of succumbing to anti-Revolutionary pressure whose goal was to make "the notion of human rights . . . too shameful to mention."

At this juncture, Jeanneney appears to have returned and to have apprised himself of the tenor of the debate. He rehearsed the three themes around which he was forging the Mission's engagement: the fundamental Revolutionary gains, the core of which were presumably human rights, which remained threatened around the world; contemporary problems dealing with such issues as education and equality, the role of the army in the republic, and the treatment of immigrants and immigration; and finally the linkage between past and future in the commemorative discourse. By and large, these rubrics were in fact the preoccupations of the first two Mission presidents, despite differences in language and inflection.

Curiously unaware of the extent to which Faure subscribed to the revisionist theses, Lubrina rejoined that "the fact that the media turn toward F. Furet reveals a weakness that the Mission must overcome." (Montrichard had earlier invoked the need to respond to Furet.) Jean Mendelson sought to defuse the quarrel with a not very cunning argument that the very debate over Furet was tantamount to his undoing, for it undermined his claim that the Revolution was over.

Claire Andrieu demonstrated, however, that Mendelson's complacency was perilous. Perhaps "the media effect will dissipate," she allowed, but lest our vigilance diminish, she noted that "certain teachers gave up the idea of doing educational projects [PAEs, or Projets d'action éducative] devoted to the French Revolution once they became familiar with the theses of François Furet." The Mission formed the bridge between "the projects" and "the message." If it is true, in the opportunistic spirit of Mona Ozouf, "that everyone has his/her Revolution," it was equally certain "that a common denominator [was] necessary" to galvanize the patrimony of "the party of movement" and to clarify the relationship between the interpretation of the Revolution and the Revolution's relevance to contemporary concerns.

In closing the session, Jeanneney promised to reflect on these ideas and to reconsider the whole question at the next meeting. In fact, such a discussion never took place again. Yet it would be unjust, despite a counselor's caustic reproach that "he is afraid of the object," to overlook Jeanneney's reiterated critique of Furetian revisionism and his vigorous defense of a Jacobin—albeit a soft Jacobin—reading of the Revolution. And though no debate transpired, the president took the occasion of a meeting with a human rights group led by the conservative (but nonconformist) politician J.-F. Deniau to reassure his staff on 20 December: "There is no question, as certain feared during our last meeting, of abandoning this strong bicentennial theme." The interview he gave to the magazine for high schoolers, *Phosphore*, was typical of his public position on the place of the rights theme in the commemoration: "The first message [of the Revolution] is obviously the Declaration of the Rights of Man, which remains the charter of all the movements of generosity and protest in the world." Jeanneney also went to considerable symbolic heights to publicize the rights message by sponsoring group ascensions to some of the highest peaks in the world to place there plaques celebrating the declarations of 1789 and 1948.[8]

In his book on the Mission experience, Lubrina developed the theme of betrayal that he evoked in the staff meeting. He accused the "Lilliputian" president of fleeing the great challenge represented by the human rights issue. It was not that Jeanneney neglected the *historical* dimension of the rights question, and its centrality in the Revolution. Like Baroin, Lubrina did not care much for the past, unless its accumulated capital was invested fully in the humanist agenda of the present and the future. Jeanneney was "neither revolutionary nor reformist nor progressive," because he did not sustain the Baroin-Faure effort to make the assault on the new Bastilles the centerpiece of the Mission's mission. Before Jeanneney brutally decapitated the program, the (old) Mission had gathered 140 associations of various kinds (humanitarian, syndicalist, and so on) around this idea. Lubrina hated him for abandoning this cause, for forcing his friend François Baroin to renounce his ambitious program for involving the youth of France in public life and mobilizing the youth of Europe in common projects, and for repudiating stewardship of Faure's dearest bicentennial dream, the foundation for human rights, "a sort of humanist brain for Europe."[9]

Jeanneney detested exclusion genuinely, despite Lubrina's self-regarding left-left fantasy that noblesse oblige was the highest level of moral consciousness to which offsprings of the elite could attain. He repeatedly and vociferously denounced the new Bastilles in the framework of his larger bicentennial discourse. But he contended that the function of the Mission was not to plan a campaign for their eradication. It was not a grand social ministry ("a ministry of social derelicts," he was heard to say in a moment of exasperation). It lacked the resources and the mandate for such a vast undertaking.

The job of the Mission, as its president construed it, was to commemorate the Revolution, to educate the citizenry about the nation's past, to stimulate civic consciousness and pride, and to develop connections between the past and the present/future. In his view, that task required a blend of pedagogy and festivity, of old-fashioned preaching and newfangled media communications. If the Mission succeeded in reaching a large part of the nation, then the nation would in the next stage of its collective life seize the initiative to strike at the new Bastilles. It may be that the Mission president "was afraid of the people." It is certain that he had a horror of disorder, imprecision, and wishful scenarios. In his eyes Lubrina's sector was a "shambles," a cacophony of half-baked notions about hunger, homelessness, drugs, and a thousand other terrible ills that were beyond bicentennial reach.[10]

Jeanneney Defends His Turf

Notoriously circumspect ("prudent as a Sioux," chanted the satirists of *L'Oreille en coin*), Jeanneney was nevertheless stubbornly independent and willing to take risks. He was cowed by neither ministerial bluster nor bureaucratic ponderousness. Even as he defended his newly staked-out turf, he aggressively tested the system by improvising ways to rationalize and quicken decision making and implementation.

Jeanneney's honeymoon period was abruptly cut short by a nasty clash with Jack Lang, the voracious and powerful minister of culture, who had the title "minister of the bicentennial" added to his attributions in late June. Jeanneney was infuriated ("disconcerted," said he in polite public language) by what he interpreted as an attempt at appropriation and domestication. He adamantly refused to see his liberty of action curtailed and the frontiers of responsibility blurred. He might very well have left his post had not the prime minister immediately reassured him that the Mission remained "interministerial" in character and under Matignon's "direct authority." The official rationale for Lang's surveillance was that it would strengthen the Mission's claims in the Council of Ministers, where the minister of culture would battle personally for more funds and other support.[11]

Jeanneney's worst fear was that Lang would constitute a parallel bicentennial organization within his ministry that would compete with and undercut the Mission. This did not happen, though the Ministry of Culture, through the intermediary of Christian Dupavillon, an architect and Lang's longtime collaborator in the theatre and in government, cast a permanent shadow over the Mission's activities. Dupavillon's "negativism" and his indiscreet carping nettled and demoralized the entire staff. He took a special interest in the preparations for the climactic festivities of 14 July, and most outsiders regarded the show as his thing. Lang's accomplice conceded that he and Monique Sauvage "yelled at each other" frequently concerning this operation, but he respected her as a hard and able worker.

Christian de Montrichard described a climate of incessant "guerrilla warfare" between the Mission and the ministry led by Dupavillon, who seemed to take pleasure "in contesting" Jeanneney. In his view, Lang did not expect Jeanneney to resist as fiercely as he did and to aspire to play the role of "a heavyweight on the national level." The minister betrayed an authoritarian and petty side to his nature by referring to Jeanneney in his correspondence not as the president of the national commemorative agency but as "Responsable de la Mission interministérielle du Bicentenaire."

The only overtly nasty confrontation between Lang and Jeanneney occurred in

November over the planning of the exposition-theme park in the Tuileries gardens. As a member of the jury that selected the conceptual/architectural project, Dupavillon opposed the winning entry on the grounds that "the problem was not well posed," a reproach with which he would probably have tainted most of the other proposals. De Margerie esteemed that Dupavillon's "negative reactions" seriously damaged the Tuileries enterprise and helped transform it into "a taboo subject, a political subject."[12]

Another center of power, with which the Mission had far less warm relations, was the Parisian municipality. Chirac's entourage decried Jeanneney's appointment as exemplary of the bicentennial's "political drift." Jeanneney's decision to abandon the megaconcert that Baroin and then Faure had commissioned from Jean-Michel Jarre, a Chirac protégé, further envenomed relations. Vengefully, the mayor predicted openly that the Mission president would fail in his task. Another unsuccessful candidate for a glamorous bicentennial assignment, Yves Mourousi, contended that these frictions jeopardized the entire celebration: "The real problem was the general muddle of the decision makers. The city of Paris gave its accord for one thing; the Mission did not follow along; or the Mission gave the green light, and the city or the government did not endorse the proposal. [It was] an incredible system of mixing jurisdictions, which ended up in a succession of rescue efforts because one had to do something, after all."

Mourousi's complaint should not be peremptorily dismissed as an expression of personal bitterness. These tensions and rivalries, reflecting larger and more or less permanent political, ideological, and institutional struggles, surely hampered both planning and execution. In the afterglow of the resounding success of 14 July, Jeanneney wrote serenely of his troubles with Chirac as mere nuisance: "Chirac desired to play his part separately, and he never let us peek at his script over his shoulder. These shenanigans appeared to us sometimes as a bit childish. But the mayor's public criticism of our projects was held in check by his fear of appearing to wish the failure of a celebration of national significance. Thus his posture could not become a major handicap for us, and we even collaborated with the city of Paris on some points of detail." If the Mission had failed miserably, Jeanneney conceded, the president of the RPR could have made of it significant political capital, "but since that was not the case. . . ."[13]

Finances: The New Deal

Without governmental pledges of serious financial support, Jeanneney would never have accepted his post. The Mission's budget—"literally a pittance in relation to the magnitude of the task to be accomplished"—had been fixed at Fr 45 million, Fr 15 million a year beginning in 1987. By the time Jeanneney took office in May, the budget for 1988 had already been exhausted (save for staff salaries). On 10 June the Mission received an emergency injection of Fr 50 million, which would enable it to discharge existing obligations (subventions and contracts that had been postponed) but would not permit any significant new ventures. Three weeks later the definitive "ordinary" budget for the three-year term was increased to a total of Fr 125 million, "ordinary" denoting the exclusion of expenses for the great events—the *temps forts*—which had not yet been conceptualized or priced.

In October, once Jeanneney had submitted rough plans and estimates, the government allocated another Fr 200 million under the "extraordinary" rubric ("reserved for the very big events"), including a guarantee of up to Fr 45 million in case of a deficit in the project for the Tuileries gardens. Bracketing the guarantee and allowing for adjustments, the Mission had a definitive allocation of Fr 282 million, which Jeanneney, with sansculottic frugality and rigor, personally pledged to the prime minister not to overspend "by a penny." The ministry placed ceilings on operating expenses (Fr 37.2 million) and communications (Fr 23.9 million), leaving Fr 220.9 million for direct project support. Regarding intervention strategy, it proposed a number of recommendations that the Mission followed: in the spirit of decentralization, leave the financing of "local projects" to municipalities, departments, and regions; make a special effort to assist celebrations abroad; concentrate the bulk of resources on the big, national projects.[14]

The government encouraged the Mission to seek supplementary funding in the private sector. Thierry Collard, who dealt with "sponsoring" in his capacity as projects coordinator, hoped for between Fr 50 and 100 million, between an eighth and a fourth of the annual pool of cultural philanthropy in all of France (and Navarre). For various reasons the results proved very disappointing. Of course, the instability of leadership compromised the whole effort. But was it really too late to educate the business community, to show them why it was in their interest to support the commemoration? "The Mission," Collard admitted, "committed the error of believing that businesses would come forward on their own with fully packaged projects." In fact, businesses did not take the initiative—why should they have?—and, when they were willing to consider sponsoring, expected the Mission to provide the appropriate vehicles. In addition to the handicaps of a late start, inadequate manpower, and a crippling lack of experience, the Mission was not able to present "the global design of things and the great commemorative events until quite late in the calendar. "Why invest money in a nonexistent undertaking?" numerous executives asked. It is not clear to what extent their hesitation masked a fear of espousing an inherently controversial theme that was certain to alienate some of their customers.

Almost Fr 31 million was raised directly by the Mission, with the assistance of professional fund-raisers, the bulk of it (Fr 25 million) linked to Jean-Paul Goude's show. The Mission proposed a package of sponsoring opportunities (television plugs, billboard mentions, blocks of seats, and so on) for Fr 5 million to about thirty big companies. Only four, all of them nationalized enterprises, accepted the complete deal; four others negotiated a partial sponsorship; while two companies offered simple donations. Nor were the results of the Association d'entreprises pour le Bicentenaire brilliant, despite the devoted efforts of its president, Jacques Friedmann, who headed Air France when Edgar Faure asked him to undertake this assignment. Only four firms agreed to participate as founding members at six hundred thousand francs apiece (including his own company and another nationalized giant). Twenty-one others adhered as "active" members at three hundred thousand francs each. The Association contributed Fr 8.5 million to twenty-five projects proposed by the Mission.[15]

To deal with the new resources, Jeanneney introduced new structures of governance and control. (For Ambassador Cabouat, a carryover from the early days of the Mission, this implied a veritable sea change from a "protoplasmic jumble" into a differentiated organization.) In order to insulate and distance himself from money matters, Faure had created a dyarchic system: on one side was the Mission, whose vocation was to create, and on the other a nonprofit corporation—an association under the law of 1901—whose function was to finance. Such a discontinuity struck Jeanneney as both inefficient and perilous. By becoming president of the corporation, he effectively merged it with the Mission, whose new secretary-general, Philippe Blondel, became its treasurer.

An engineer with fourteen years' experience as a middle-range civil servant specializing in highway safety and a frustrated dream of entering the elite world of the *énarchie*, Blondel was ready for a professional change. He became Jeanneney's financial watchdog, a chain-smoking, shirtsleeved technocrat awash in a sea of computer output that did not dampen his enthusiasm for calculating long series of figures by hand. His familiarity with the tortuous working of the administration made him an excellent point man; and his mastery of the dossiers along with a mixture of intense job pride, patriotism, and protectiveness vis-à-vis the Mission and its chief made him an excellent safety monitor.

Jeanneney tried to leave nothing to chance. An audit of the Fauriste heritage reassured him, in Blondel's words, that "there were not any grave problems." He arranged for several levels of institutional checks that would guarantee integrity without hindering rapid action or obstructing shortcuts. A financial auditor (*contrôleur financier*) named by the ministry of the budget took part in all the association's executive sessions; first an accounting firm and then a public accountant (*commissaire aux comptes*) scrutinized all financial transactions; an oversight board (*comité d'engagement*) composed of representatives of several ministries was named to review all major commitments "in order to protect us from the risks of skidding out of control as a result of the haste with which we had to act, while sparing us the ponderousness of the public administration." Understandably, Jeanneney wanted to emerge from the bicentennial experience with the double reputation for rigor and thrift. He would spend four times less than the Australians (or, a somewhat wry alternative comparison, one and a half times less than the cost of Hirohito's funeral!), and he would spend it in the finest tradition of Jacobin transparence.[16]

Commodification

Another money-raising opportunity involved the commercialization of products anointed with the Mission's unction. First developed by Faure and his financial counselor Yann Gaillard, for whom the prospect of levying Fr 7 or 8 million to complement a meager budget of Fr 15 million was quite compelling, the idea elicited less enthusiasm from Jeanneney. He was less pressed for funds than his predecessor had been, he was vaguely worried that the "merchants of the temple" (as Elysée adviser Claude Manceron had stigmatized them) would contaminate the civic message, and it was very late in terms of commercial lead time for the development and promotion of merchandise created especially for the bicentennial (the marketing salons of 1988 had already been booked and/or held). In Blondel's words, Jeanneney did not invest the Mission with "a genuine philosophy of commercialization." Instead he relied on the Faure-Gaillard plan to adopt a wide range of products by granting them the exclusive right, in return for royalty fees, to display the official logo, Folon's trinity of tricolor birds. Commercialization was subcontracted to licensing agents who had a vested interest in ringing up as many billings as possible, though the Mission itself decided whether or not to approve each proposal.

The Mission awarded the label to 80 percent of the candidates (a "severe selection"?), privileging, said Jeanneney, "objects of quality, useful in daily life" and eliminating "the objects that hold up the French Revolution to ridicule" (for example, the miniature guillotine or the three versions of the tricolor condom: one with the Revolutionary motto on a white background, another featuring the guillotine on a red backdrop, and, for those who made love on the regal right, an image of Louis XVI cast on a blue setting). Concessionaires were to pay a good-faith cash advance on fees that would amount to between 5 and 10 percent of their sales. For a total sum of approximately Fr 8 million, the Mission authorized ninety-five companies to market three hundred articles with the official bicentennial label—"a line of merchandise somewhat lacking in harmony," as Jeanneney's final report euphemistically phrased it. They included prestige goods as well as common merchandise: candy, soaps (a tricolor bar whose colors did not mix upon use required Fr 2.5 million and three years to develop: "a veritable technological innovation," according to its bubbly inventor), umbrellas, hats, scarves, watches, lighters, apparel, rum, perfumes ("Marianne"), toys, art supplies, wine (Yvon Mau's Bordeaux), pewter objects, model figurines.[17]

For the business community, the results seem to have been mixed. "We are here to help French businesses develop and export," affirmed the Mission's Danièle Langellier, "the label is an excellent springboard." In March 1989 the *Nouvel Observateur* cited Canard-Duchêne champagne as "the loveliest success." Heretofore unable to penetrate Japan, Canard was now in touch with three major Japanese distributors thanks to the bicentennial label, with a view toward fruitful long-terms contract, "not counting the Fr 55 million that the bottles labeled 1789

An 112-year-old firm advertises a "bicentennial" product, hand-painted artificial flowers, boasting the Mission's endorsement, its logo–imprimatur, a trio of tricolor birds. (Photo: Bicentennial Mission.)

should bring in." Three and a half months later *Figaro-Magazine*, after a nebulous and derisive account of a quasi debacle in Japan ("In Tokyo, the exhibition of bicentennial products was relegated to the corner of a room, unknown even to the attendants"), reported: "Certain of having suffered a serious loss, Canard-Duchêne champagne bitterly regrets the imprint of the bicentennial logo on its bottles ('at a cost of two million'), which the customer identifies with a fanciful bubbly wine [rather than with authentic champagne]." The company president protested furiously when he learned that not only was Canard-Duchêne not the official champagne of Tuileries 89, the major commemorative site in the capital, but that it was not served at all whereas rival Moet was readily available. A toy manufacturer was equally disappointed ("We are far from having taken the Bastille of exportation"), and several companies faced judicial liquidation. According to Blondel, the vast majority of logo purchasers praised the benefits of the bicentennial cachet.[18]

Folon's tranquil birds flew into one particularly ugly maelstrom, propelled by Jean Veillon, a man ingenuously described by Blondel as "an American-style boss." In early May 1989 Veillon, president of Waterman, a firm best known for the power of its pens, published a vicious diatribe against the Mission in Le Quotidien de Paris. He complained acerbically that the logo which he had purchased dearly was virtually unknown to consumers as a result of the incompetence of the Jeanneney team. "The organization of the bicentennial is totally worthless, and everything is going to the dogs," he railed. "At no time were we able to obtain—it seems to be the least of things—the program for media events and information on the projected follow-up operations." Burdened with inventory, Veillon claimed "that at this moment we are taking a serious loss as a result of having been misled." Not only did he refuse to remit any royalty payments, but he threatened to demand "indemnification" if he did not obtain "satisfaction"—whatever that meant—before Bastille Day.

Jeanneney called his bluff. Invoking a clause in their contract that permitted the Mission to examine the sales records of the client company, he dispatched an accountant who discovered that Waterman's sales for the previous five months totaled a hefty Fr 17 million and that Waterman owed the Mission not Fr 150,000, as everyone had estimated, but one million. Jeanneney summoned Veillon to honor his engagements and upon his refusal initiated legal action before the Tribunal de commerce in July. A few days before the judgment was to be announced, "given the Mission president's refusal to agree to any compromise solution," Waterman paid in full. (Subsequently, Blondel remarked with a puckish grin, they became "our best concessionaires.") Jeanneney found nothing amusing in this "small-minded operation," which he read as a politically motivated assault by a well-known enemy of the Socialists.[19]

Given the magnitude of public interest that the bicentennial elicited and the manipulative appetite of business, the Revolution would have been commodified with or without the Mission's blessing. In most cases, the historical and/or ideological referents were blunted or obscured by the luster or wit or vulgarity of the object that putatively embodied them, or by the sheer banality of the commercial nexus. It is doubtful that one's stomach was convulsed with horror by the deliciously sweet candy shaped in the form of the heads of guillotine victims. Did one experience a vicarious twinge of sadistic glee or grieved compassionate or existential culpability each time one sliced one's block of opulent foie gras with a slicing device in the form of a guillotine? Did one separate the good guys/objects from the bad in the soup garnished with Valfleuri's bicentennial noodles shaped to represent guillotines, execution wagons, sansculottes, liberty caps, and Bastilles? (Did they sell as well as the Smurf noodles of the previous year?)

The night-light in the form of the horrific Bastille, nightmare of the Old Regime, was supposed to soothe and reassure children in the middle of the night. (Called "the true *prise* of the Bastille," it played on the French word for electric outlet, *prise*, also used to denote the "taking" of the fortress-prison.) The board game "Guillotine," devised by a sly *énarque*, "is marvelously faithful to the turbulent history of the Convention," in the ironic words of the counterrevolutionary *Choc du mois*, "by casting into relief the massacres and denunciations." By ingesting a *homard Thermidor* did one incorporate oneself into the checkered world of post-Robespierrist ambiguity, self-indulgence, and revenge? (The lobster dish was proposed as the mainstay of a Revolutionary repast, offered at the once illustrious Grand Véfour, a.k.a. Café de Chartres, for nine hundred francs, or catered at home on a half hour's notice by Jacques Hesse for Fr 305.) "No one seems to have yet thought of tricolor suppositories, but that will come soon," predicted *L'Evénement du Jeudi.*

There were many bicentennial products at reasonable prices, especially those that did not boast the logo (T-shirts for forty or fifty francs, liberty caps for thirty francs, assorted key chains, scarves, boxer shorts, aprons, sweatshirts, toilet water, and so on, at similarly accessible prices). But the prices on so-called luxury or prestige items must have jolted present-day sansculottes with an acute case of cognitive dissonance: a Balenciaga T-shirt for twelve hundred francs topped by a Hermès rival for fourteen hundred, a Dior-created "Marianne" plate for Fr 580, a Nina Ricci belt for Fr 545, a Saint-Just porcelain doll for twenty-five hundred francs, a Dupont lighter inscribed with the logo for thirty-three hundred francs. One item specifically targeted Americans in the hope of exploiting "the persistently lively sentiment of gratitude" that they were supposed to feel toward Lafayette. It was a tiny plot of land (a square of thirty-two centimeters) from his home village of Chavagnac. For one hundred dollars the grateful buyer would receive a notarial deed dated 14 July 1989. Over a million lots were to be offered, making the hectare of the impoverished land of the Haute-Loire one of France's most expensive. Accustomed to merchandising the faith (as evidenced by the booths set up after evangelical sessions at the Mutualité), the counterrevolutionaries did not drive the merchants from their temple. Constrained by a narrower market, they nevertheless managed to offer jewelry, lighters, T-shirts, and a *cuvée royale anti-89*.[20]

Scores of merchants who did not have products susceptible to an expeditious bicentennial appropriation nevertheless made use of the Revolutionary idiom and helped to flood public consciousness with revolutionary images. Surely more people encountered the (perfunctory but cumulatively influential) signs of the bicentennial season in advertising campaigns than in more sophisticated and less accessible instruments of education and propaganda. Some of the publicity had the nonchalant charm of the absurd. Thus:

Louis XVI: "Is it a revolt?"

Distinguished courtier: "No, sire, it's a Volkswagen."

("Non, sire, c'est une révolution" is the stock answer, one supposed to have begun the process of disabusing the perplexed monarch.) "Take up books, citizens," exhorted FNAC, the megabookstore. The Paris subway and railroad system, under the aegis of the RATP, whose tickets bore Folon's signature, played on the theme that today "the price to pay for liberty" was much less onerous than it had been two hundred years earlier. To calm one's cough the wily pundits of Valgorge proposed "the taking of the pastille." Always grave in their battle for consumer rights, the Leclerc supermarkets viewed 1789 nostalgically as "the good old days" because then "there was only one Bastille to be taken."

Other marketers appealed slightly more obliquely to values associated with the Revolution. AEG promoted a car telephone as "the instrument of your liberties." Pro-Kennex boasted a tennis racket forged by technologies "that liberate your ambitions." Easy-to-prepare Maggi soups promised "a summer of liberty." A sun-products company preached "the right to tan" while an insurance firm insisted on "the right to total security." Cartier jewelers fashioned a declaration of rights for yuppies of the left and right with an indulgently liberal inflection: "Men are born free and equal in rights . . . (but nothing stops them from being different)." Putting a positive gloss on the darker side of the Revolution, Nicostep characterized its antismoking product as "the guillotine of nicotine." Hundreds of retailers promised "guillotined" or "reduced" or merely "revolutionary" prices. Lancôme paraded its "revolutionary" colors, while L'Oréal puffed its "revolutionary" antiaging discoveries and Hammerite emphasized its "revolutionary" antirust agent.[21]

Jeanneney Repudiates Faure's Soft Consensus

Even before Jeanneney had the money in hand, he began to articulate the tone with which he wanted to imbue the bicentennial.[22] Though he ended up using more of the Mission heritage than he anticipated, from the outset he vigorously took his distance from what he regarded as Edgar Faure's "shivery line" of commemoration. Centrist, evolutionist, allergic to tumult, and wedded to the notion that there was always room for a negotiated settlement, Faure evinced "a real repugnance for the revolutionary fact." Jeanneney liked to cite Faure's bon mot, which bespoke his conviction that the Revolution was both regrettable and unnecessary: "There were two men who might have been able to avert the Revolution— Turgot, who died before it broke out, and myself, who was not yet born." (Indeed, in his sprightly *Disgrâce de Turgot*, Faure waxed counterfactual over a reformist blueprint that allegedly could have thrust France into the modern democratic orbit at low cost.)

Faure wanted to flee the Revolution, in Jeanneney's eyes, by organizing a commemoration (a word he mistrusted) at a quantum remove from the real spirit of

1789–94 (or even 1789–1800) by putting "the emphasis on what brought people together while avoiding very prudently what was capable of dividing them." According to Jeanneney, this organized escapism—"falling back"—forsook the civic objectives without which the bicentennial was merely another fête. Nor did the exciting opportunities to orchestrate a truly memorable fête interest Faure: otherwise he would never have accepted "the pitifully small budget that the government of Jacques Chirac had allocated to him." Faure took refuge from the would-be crowd in his imposing Arche-fortress, in the Foundation of Human Rights, the presidency of which Jeanneney declined precisely to distinguish his own démarche.[23]

Jeanneney categorically rejected a commemoration built around "an artificial consensus," "a soft consensus." To him consensus signified first appeasement and then capitulation. His ambition was not to apply a mystifying analgesic, to stake out a healing middle ground that would blunt or deny the true "virulence" of the revolutionary message. Consensus made sense to Faure because he believed either that the Revolution was over or that it needed to be over. Comfortably anchored in the left, Jeanneney believed that the Revolution still had a calling today and that "the Revolution is still a burning issue and its legacy is heavy with menace on many accounts and for many people." This was the spirit in which he adopted as the Mission's manifesto Victor Hugo's phrase "There is in what the Revolution gave us still more promised land than conquered territory."

Jeanneney the astute political historian clearly recognized that there were objective grounds for consensus in 1989. Many on the right and in the church had gravitated to the republic even as the rude trials of the twentieth century had chastened the left's utopian optimism. Yet Jeanneney betrayed an ambivalent attitude toward the implications, and perhaps the real depth, of this rapprochement. At the very moment when he told one periodical, in terms redolent of Faure, that, in contrast to 1889, "there exists today a certain national consensus on the values of 89," he expressed to another grave doubts that "these values inherited from 1789 are the object of a consensus in the France of 1989." He did not believe that "all the French today recognize themselves in the Revolution of 1789 and relate to its values, for example, the values of nonexclusion and fraternity." There was disquieting evidence that "the ideals of the French Revolution are still threatened in France," despite the placid assurances of the theorists of the republic of the center. On the right Jeanneney detected "underlying reticences that have not yet openly expressed themselves but are not far from springing to the surface."

Elsewhere he put it more starkly, evoking "the rejection of the French Revolution by a part of moderate opinion" and suggesting that within the church the cleavage did not neatly oppose the *intégristes* to the bulk of the faithful but "cut through the very center of the institution." For these very reasons it was unthinkable to "fall back on the lowest common denominator of a possible agreement on the French Revolution while denying the existence of anything that might introduce discord." Precisely because this heritage was still urgently needed today, the "strong brew" could not be reduced to a "soft watery beverage." Repeatedly Jeanneney warned that "I have no intention whatever to cool down the message in order to win over I don't know what imaginable current of opposition to the Revolution or even the republic."[24]

Without entirely abandoning the Fauriste clientele ("what should be celebrated is what the Revolution brought in the way of *reforms*"), Jeanneney paraded his pugnacity, and that of the Revolution whose stewardship he had quite consciously assumed ("We simply want to recall how very strong the Revolution was"). No one must be allowed to doubt the Mission's newfound zeal. If it was "timid," "lukewarm," or flaccid in any form, it was not Jeanneney. Under no circumstances would he "smooth down the sharp angles," "seek to temper the sharp edges" or "to weaken the message."

At times this muscular discourse took on a patina of moral and political radicalism in a voice of aggressive defiance. The president of the Mission intended not merely to put into relief "everything that might still be troublesome for the established order in the revolutionary message" but to nourish and then unleash "all its jolting power, its force of generosity against all the conservatism, feebleness, cowardice." The Front national was Jeanneney's target at a colloquium at Belfort—an occasion to demonstrate the pertinence of the Revolution ("we still have very much need of it") and his determination to utilize the bicentennial moment for healthy civicopolitical ends. "I guarantee that we will not put on a flaccid celebration," he pledged, "neither concerning the question of nationality nor with regard to the question of citizenship."

In retrospect, Jeanneney's Jacobino–chauvinist language sometimes seems strained and affected. At the time, however, he felt an urgent need to (re)mobilize his troops, to reinject a large dose of passion into the commemorative mix, and to dramatize the political resonance between certain Revolutionary values and certain contemporary problems. In addition, he had a particular interest in reaching the often badly informed and blasé youth of France to alert them both to the historic price of the rights they took for granted and to the power of their Revolutionary patrimony. Jeanneney's rhetorical pugnacity was perhaps also meant to compensate for his own demeanor, which was habitually mild, reasonable, and gracious. Psychologically and politically, the relentless exorcism-excoriation of consensus enabled him to lapse discreetly into moderation and compromise in practice—for example, in the articulation of the calendar and content of the commemorative events—without worrying overmuch about jeopardizing the heroism of his line.[25]

The "Living Message" and the "Versant Lumineux"

Toughness and fervor did not license the Mission to operate "a Ministry of the Truth." Repeatedly, Jeanneney promised to eschew "a state didactic," the inculcation of an official exegesis and canon that would have done violence to "the complexity of the revolutionary events" and offended the "liberty of opinion of the citizens." Yet he was not at all bashful about broadcasting a strong "civic message based on the republican motto." He construed the bicentennial as a "civic weapon," and he was determined that it would be socially "useful." Thus his vaguely Robespierrist desire to promote "civic virtue" in part through the encouragement of "a civic reflection."

That approach did not imply focusing on "the founding act" itself. Although he wanted his fellow citizens to appreciate the struggle out of which their democratic system was born, he sensed that there was less interest in history for its own sake than in its direct relevance to today's concerns. His goal was to "adapt the message to the problems of our epoch." Instead of celebrating the principles that had been incorporated into law and practice, the established gains, or "acquis"—one of the bicentennial's chief household terms—Jeanneney wanted to shift the focus to the unfinished business of the Revolutionary heritage. Glossing Hugo, he wrote that "the principles of 1789 must be celebrated less as an assured attribute [*acquis*] than as the prod toward an incomplete conquest."

What Jeanneney styled civic, however, clearly moved beyond a sense of the responsibilities and duties of the citizen. In demarcating "everything that remained to be done," he adumbrated a veritable political program in the service of liberty, equality, and fraternity in the context of the end of the twentieth century. He identified his cause with the forces of progress: "It is a matter of putting into relief everything that in the aspirations of 1789 could still be, in the France of 1989, a stimulus to 'the party of movement.'" Among the specific issues he had in mind that responded to the hopes of the Revolution were justice ("whose practical application is so negatively judged by public opinion"), education (which had to be better deployed to reduce "inequality of opportunity"), and the struggle against all forms of exclusion.

As both a citizen and a political actor, Jeanneney was worried about the sinister portents in the world around him: the resurgence in the 1980s of "the temptations of xenophobia, of racism, of the refusal of the Other"; the 10 to 15 percent of voters that Le Pen seemed able to marshal; the victories of the neo-Nazi "Reps" in West Germany; the persecution of Salman Rushdie (whom he compared to his hero Grégoire); the atrophy of laicity (which he denounced well before the chador affair); the offensive of diverse religious fundamentalisms. "As long as there subsist situations of profound injustice and profound inequality," Jeanneney affirmed, the basic gains of the Revolution would not be able to flourish in France or the rest of the world. Embracing "the faith of the revolutionaries according to which one could do better," he hoped that the bicentennial experience would not merely raise consciousness but concretely teach French women and men to "live better together."[26]

Though it is hard to imagine a more vigorous civicopolitical discourse, it was not always easy to translate the message into collectively shared bicentennial experiences. There was a real incongruity between Jeanneney's intense and exigent evangelism and the motley character of the key festive events. Because the latter tended to eclipse the former, Jeanneney found himself the target of rebuke from the left for sins of civic deficit even as he was assailed by the right for crimes of civic overkill. In the leftist bastion of the Cercle Condorcet, member Roger Fayolle faced the president of the Mission at the end of his mandate:

> I would like to ask Jean-Noël Jeanneney if he does not regret—my question is deliberately provocative—for fear of appearing to favor a state pedagogy, having voluntarily abandoned any pedagogy at all by giving all manner of forms to the fête, which on the national plane and in the treatment by the media remained a spectacle before which everyone stood passively. Perhaps a pedagogical initiative, in a true republican tradition, would have contributed to stimulating this citizenly spirit which we are not at all sure how to revive.

Despite certain reproaches regarding the Mission president's Mitterrandist fidelity, author Gilles Perrault, who had tried so hard to steer the commemoration leftward, in the last analysis absolved Jeanneney and ruefully incriminated the general culture. The lack of civism? "That's France today."[27]

While Jeanneney defined his task politically as the "defense" of the Revolution "against those who disparage it," he felt that he had no proper role to take in the swirling historiographical controversies amplified by the bicentennial. It was a delicate distinction to sustain. "It would have been disastrous to allow the impression," he asserted, "that we tried to utilize scholarly research in the service of the civic conviction which we espoused." But this was an ambiguous abnegation. Of course Jeanneney drew on the latest research to fortify his own perspective; and in his civic discourse he implicitly favored one point of view, and sometimes even one method, over another. When he said that "I could not stand for the idea that the state would choose between this and that historiographical doctrine," he affirmed the principle of academic freedom to which he was deeply committed. Concretely, that meant that the Mission would not "award the [Mission's] label to books, because it is not up to our state agencies to make distinctions between one family of interpretation and another." More diffusely, that signified that the Mission pledged "to impose no sectarian and/or univocal reading of the facts and to respect the liberty which everyone has to give primacy to one aspect of the heritage rather than another."

Yet if this constituted neutrality, it was an armed and interested neutrality. Jeanneney's zealous articulation of the "living message" entailed choices that implied a certain interpretive framework. It was impossible to insist so passionately on the "versant lumineux"—not another Latin American guerrilla faction but Jeanneney's somewhat stilted term to denote the Revolution's exhilarating and substantial positive dimension—without betraying both ideological and historiographical commitments. (It was his militant insistence on this "luminosity," and his failure adequately to problematize its relation to political theory and practice in the nineteenth and especially the twentieth centuries, that later prompted strictures from two leading figures of Furet's galaxy, Mona Ozouf and Marcel Gauchet.) "Balance" was his watchword, but it was hard to ask him to take an evenhanded position between pro- and anti-Revolutionary postures, or even between the revisionist school (which he reproached for excessive flirtation with certain counterrevolutionary claims and for inordinate contempt for "the history of social struggles and of economic forces") and the Marxist cause (whose Jacobinism was as congenial as its materialism/reductionism was repugnant). Whereas the Mission dispensed more or less equal patronage to Furet and Vovelle, it did not hesitate to deny its label to a handful of projects animated by "a patent hostility to the principles of 1789."[28]

The chief palliative that Jeanneney offered the adversaries of the Revolution was his promise neither to "rejoice in the blood spilled nor to forget it." But in the name of balance, he systematically relativized "the most tragic aspects and excesses," much to the chagrin of critics such as Jean-Marie Benoist, who believed that barbarism was exclusively on the side of the Revolution. "Shared responsibilities" was the refrain of Jeanneney's analysis. Thus, he averred, "at no moment did we hide the violations of the principles behind the principles themselves"; to which he immediately added, "any more than we concealed the fact that those who, from the very beginning of the process, totally and profoundly rejected these principles bear also a weighty part of the responsibility for the bloody aberrations which ensued." While calling attention to the "horrors" and the "dérapages," one must "avoid the converse errors, which would involve exaggerating the dramas—for instance, evoking genocide when it is sufficient to speak of crimes."

Although Jeanneney defended Clemenceau's notion of a "bloc" in the context of the antirepublican challenge of the late nineteenth century, he readily admitted that the conjuncture had changed. Today "we are civically free to nuance, to cease considering the Revolution as a bloc, and thus to pose the big question of the Terror." But it was no more appropriate or illuminating to curse the Terror than to celebrate it. One had to reflect on it, to seize its contradictions, to fathom its genesis. If, "for some"—Furet's galaxy and the counterrevolutionaries—"the Terror is intrinsically linked to the Revolution," for others, diverse Jacobins and Marxists, "it is the attitude of the king and the Counterrevolution that created a string of events leading to civil war." Though he criticized the thesis of circumstances as incommensurate with the phenomena it sought to explain (and was berated for so doing by *L'Humanité*), he did not by any means deny the significance of circumstances as part of a larger model. Jeanneney was struck by both the psychological fatigue of the Revolutionary leaders and the treason of Louis XVI: "Think of the obsessional fever engendered by the war, of the way in which the peaceful dreams of the members of the Constituent Assembly might have taken form if the king, instead of setting in motion the tragic seesaw of repression and counterrevolution, had been capable . . . of accepting the new order of things."

In the name not of a bloc but of balance, Jeanneney also argued that the commemoration had to cover not just 1789 but the subsequent events at least through the fall of Robespierre. There had been outbursts of violence in '89, "and even in 1794 [elsewhere he cited 1792–93], there were very grand things done, very grand things said, which also merit being honored." Jeanneney was no Berlusconi "to cut the Revolution into slices." In practice, however, the Mission made little effort to "celebrate all the Revolution" as Jeanneney had promised, perhaps because he sensed how little appetite there was for this ambition.[29]

The Opening of the
Bicentennial Season

The festive calendar elaborated by Jeanneney did not differ significantly from Baroin's. Fittingly, January would signal "takeoff," to be marked by a massive hot-air balloon launching throughout France. March represented "rootedness," symbolized by tree plantings. May called on "the memory," to be incarnated by the re-creation of the convocation of the Estates General at Versailles. June bridged fraternity and elections, both of which were meant to find expression in the anniversary of the birth of the National Assembly, the instrument of democratic modernization. July meant the Bastille, the visceral commencement of the Revolution and the embodiment of the popular Revolution, and the Federation, a time of unity and assembled national will. It would be the locus of the bicentennial's paramount fête-happening ("Unique in the world, this show will be the apotheosis of the bicentennial").

Jeanneney very much wanted to mark the dramatic night of 4–5 August, the renunciation of privileges and the adumbration of a new social structure. The public television stations turned a deaf ear to his plea for "a reconstitution in real time of the night of the abolition of privileges," which would have reached vacationers otherwise unavailable for a grand public event. The right had anticipated a major exploitation of this moment by the Socialist government ("Can you imagine them not taking advantage of the night of 4 August?" asked *Le Quotidien de Paris* back in September 1988). It was, after all, according to a Sofres poll, the second most important moment in the Revolution, after the Bastille, in the eyes of the public. The puckish left, in the voice of *Libération*, chided the government and its Mission for their superb obliviousness: "No firecracker, no event of major magnitude, no official discourse will occur that night to salute one of the paramount events of the Revolution." But the paper did not puzzle over the paradox of this "consensual silence" smothering the most euphoric moment of consensus in the entire Revolution—at least in the entire Revolution from above.

So August was dedicated to the rights of man, to be celebrated on the anniversary of the promulgation of the Declaration by the inauguration of the Foundation of Human Rights in the Arche de la Défense. September augured the rest of the Revolution: the birth of the republic in 1792, whose fragile existence was preserved by the victory at Valmy, site of the penultimate great commemorative event. The bicentennial year would end in December with a triple Pantheonization, one that would further seek to direct reflection beyond 1789, through the lives and work of Condorcet, Grégoire, and Monge.[1]

A Wintry Takeoff

Eighty-two of the ninety-six departmental capitals participated in the launching on the first of the year. The bulk of them sent hot-air balloons aloft simultaneously. The ceremony evoked the fruitful connections between science and the Revolution, and the territorial and administrative reorganization of France, one of the great reforms of 1789–90. To the sound of music played by the Garde républicaine, Parisians witnessed the flight of replicas of the original montgolfiers of the 1780s. At Le Puy a tricolor hot-air balloon called the Marquis de La Fayette and bearing the image of the hero of two worlds inaugurated the bicentennial. From the air it showered spectators with copies of the Declaration of the Rights of Man. Actors or local dignitaries read the Declaration in every capital (complemented in Paris by Sylvia Montfort's rendering of Olympe de Gouges's "Declaration of the Rights of Woman").

Special post offices sold 625,000 stamps bearing Folon's logo, ten times the previous record for first-day issues. Volunteer stamp clubs also sold souvenir envelopes celebrating the rights of man ("Mortals are all equal, it is not birth [but] only virtue that makes the difference"). The proceeds of these sales would be donated to the Fondation de France for use in international human rights projects, providing another opportunity for Jeanneney to rivet the world-civic theme that "much remains to be done." The official Mission historian summed up the significance of the takeoff day in a (f)rigid didactic lesson more chilling than the brisk winter air: "The flight of the balloons symbolizes liberty, while equality is represented by their simultaneous takeoff in all the departments; fraternity is . . . the work in common of different people with diverse outlooks."[2]

A Sylvan Spring

Just before Christmas 1986 Claude Manceron, a historian and Elysée counselor, proposed to Michel Baroin a national commemorative project that was likely to have widespread appeal. "Since everyone agrees that the word 'liberty' should be one of the key words of the bicentennial," he wrote, "one could perhaps envision a vast planting of liberty trees across the land." On 21 March 1989, the first day of spring, the Mission organized a massive tree planting throughout the nation. The tree had irresistible symbolic allure. By no means an exclusively Revolutionary marker, the tree nevertheless rapidly became associated with the triumph of liberty. According to Abbé Grégoire, whose path Jeanneney crossed as often as possible, the first liberty tree was planted by a republican curate near his church at Saint-Gaudent in the Vienne in May 1790. "At the foot of this tree," he told his fellow citizens, "you will remember that you are French and, in your old age, you will recall for your children the memorable time when you planted it."

Several years later Grégoire summoned the Convention to prescribe a replanting of liberty trees in all communes where the trees had perished. The bicentennial spurred healthy local historical emulation. Saint-Gaudent barely affirmed its claim before the Breton hamlet of Gahard unearthed municipal minutes evoking the plantation of "an oak of liberty" four months earlier. Thanks to the prestige of Grégoire, however, the Bretons proved unable to dislodge their rivals from the Poitou as arboreal standardbearers of the bicentennial.[3]

With the help of two ministries (Environment and Agriculture-Forests) and the Bull computer company whose logo propitiously boasted a tree ("the liberty tree is also the mark of entrepreneurial freedom"), the Mission enabled people all over the country to plant thousands of trees on the same day. Providing information kits and material incentives, the Mission encouraged the municipalities, partly in commemoration of their foundation in 1789, to take the initiative at the grass roots, in coordination with schools, business, and civic and cultural associations, and to embroider the tree plantings with other festive activities (exhibitions, drama, music, repasts, and so on). It avoided any odor of politicization by casting the ritual in terms of the reaffirmation of consensual values, the reassuring but unnamed "founding values of democracy."

For the education of municipalities, the consortium of sponsors produced a pamphlet entitled *36,000 Arbres pour la liberté* that sketched the historical context and offered practical advice on planting the trees and on organizing civic and festive activities. To underline continuities between the past and the future, it proposed a drawing contest for children on the theme "Imagine your liberty tree in the year 2089." Other ideas included a public "fresco space" for encouraging spontaneous artistic expression, cooperative methods for making and distributing Revolutionary costumes for the children, collective research projects on local life, theatrical representations of local history, tree decorating ceremonies, human chains of solidarity linking the tree of one village to that of a neighboring commune, and songfests around the tree. For distribution to the public, the Mission furnished a splendid thirty-two-page color guide in pocket format to the history, iconography, and music of tree-planting ceremonies, printing eighty-five-thousand in an initial run and another twenty-five thousand in response to intense local demand. The magnitude

Marrying twentieth-century ecology with a multi-secular symbol of freedom, the Mission, in conjunction with several ministries, organized a massive planting of liberty trees in which several million children and adults
took part in fifteen thousand communes throughout the land. (Photo: Bicentennial Mission.)

of the tree operation heavily taxed the Mission's capacity. Indeed, a large part of the
logistical/communications burden was farmed out to private-sector specialists. A
number of municipalities complained that they did not receive the information
packets and instructions until after the scheduled day of the event.

Though the Mission did not attain its goal of thirty-six thousand plantings—one
in each commune—it nevertheless mobilized two to three million adults and as

many children. Fifteen thousand communes participated, a respectable figure that would have swelled even larger had the ceremonies not been preceded by a hectic and divisive campaign for municipal elections. In numerous communes where the leaders chose not to take part, sometimes for ideological reasons, plantings were held in schoolyards. Twelve thousand schools participated in a "Bicentennial Day" organized by the Ministry of National Education to coincide with the plantings. Hundreds of thousands of students planned commemorative projects and discussed "the founding values of our democracy" in addition to planting trees. For compelling horticultural reasons, the green revolutionaries were forced to traduce the populist heritage by planting lindens or other hardy species instead of poplars.

Certain parts of the country did not wait for the Mission's signal, or could not follow its calendar. Thus in the Drôme, over fifty communes consecrated trees to liberty during other moments of the year. On its own initiative, the Conseil général of the Hérault distributed trees to all the communes that desired them. At Vailhauquès, near Montpellier, the citizenry planted a second tree after the first was cut down by vandals presumed to have counterrevolutionary motivations. Christian de Montrichard may not have exaggerated much in claiming that almost one of two communes turned to the liberty-tree theme sometime during the year.[4]

To underline the importance of the event, President Mitterrand made the pilgrimage to Saint-Gaudent, where he reenacted the original liberty-tree planting and delivered a speech linking the quest for liberty to the pursuit of education, and the triumph of liberty to the attenuation of inequality. On the local level ceremonies varied widely in style and ideological inflection. While they all reaffirmed Grégoire's airy vision of the tree as emblem of liberty because it embodied "living and protecting nature, which grows strong and shares its benefits," some grafted messages that burdened the common trunk of civism while others opted for a sagely consensual approach. At Montreuil, one of the strongholds of the PCF, the tree represented "memory," linking the Revolution of '89 to the other revolutions within the Revolution and to the forest of Berbeyrolle, one of the first maquis of anti-Nazi resistance. The elegant simplicity of the tree image was rather sapped by a fustian text:

> From the beginning of time, man has experienced the tree as the ideogram of the cosmos, as the central object of rituals and symbols through which he had access to the totality of the universe, to its genesis as well as to its immensity. That this tree was summoned by the Revolution to be its very image says a great deal about the historical, cosmological, [and] universal aspiration of which the revolutionaries wanted to be the bearers. In linking itself to the tree of all origins, the Revolution affirmed its will to be a founding event.

After planting four linden trees at Mondeville in the Calvados, speakers recalled the burning of liberty trees by counterrevolutionaries and drew a moral of mobilizing vigilance: "nothing can be taken for granted as definitively acquired." That evening the citizens gathered again at the Maison du Peuple to listen to a reading of the Declaration and a performance by the town chorale. Bedecked in tricolor ribbons, organizers of the tree planting at Fresville in the Manche made the same point. Begotten in suffering, "liberty is never won in advance." At Riom in the Auvergne, the outgoing Socialist mayor, historian Jean Ehrard, in one of his last official acts, chose a residential quarter of mixed rooted and immigrant population as the site of the planting, which was accompanied by dancing, singing, and the distribution of souvenir tricolor ribbons. Rehearsing a theme with both immediate, local and timeless, universal significance, the mayor argued for the indivisibility of the three dimensions of the Revolutionary trinity. "A symbol of protection," the tree "illustrates the solidarity without which liberty does not exist." In the courtyard of a secondary school not far away at Clermont-Ferrand, another Socialist leader, Senator-Mayor Roger Quilliot, depicted the red oak he planted, despite its proverbial sturdiness, as the symbol of the fragility of liberty, "the most delicate thing to sustain."

In Strasbourg yet another Socialist mayor, Catherine Trautmann, opted for discretion. In place of a speech, she asked the rector, historian Pierre Deyon, to read from Condorcet in the courtyard of the Fustel de Coulanges lycée, whose students had put together an elaborate exposition on the city's Revolutionary experience on the basis of research conducted in the departmental and municipal archives. Barely 150 kilometers to the south at Delle in the Belfort Territory, where hortatory moralization appears to be a regional mania, the mayor told an audience of high school students gathered around an American red oak: "You are born to a society of leisure and consumption, but you are the youth of tomorrow's France, a country that guarantees all freedoms while certain others are still at the stage of slavery and torture. It is up to you to become citizens in the fullest sense and adults." Still in the east but on the other side of the Vosges in the village of Ville-en Blaisois (population circa two hundred), a number of citizens complained that the municipality had planted a tree more or less surreptitiously, without inviting the public to a ceremony.

The mayor of Tourlaville, a Norman coastal town, decentered the Revolution and the mixed signals it emitted by inserting the tree-planting rite into a multisecular perspective that dated at least from the Middle Ages. Though he quoted from Hugo, the principal of a high school in the port city of Honfleur, surrounded by children in sansculotte attire, gave the Revolution a moderate spin: "It is above all the Declaration of the Rights of Man." Equilibrium marked the all-day commemoration at the hamlet of Le Hommet-d'Arthenay, in the Manche. Slides illustrating the Revolution featured the *chouans* as well as Danton. Officials read the local *cahiers de doléances* and planted a weeping willow, aided by children costumed in Revolutionary garb. Much of the day was structured around a relay run that took place across the country through the network of agricultural high schools. An innocent ceremony in the Norman town of Saint-Hilaire-du-Harcouët would several months later take on a fatidic air. Mr. Wang, the scientific counselor from the

Chinese embassy, made the detour from Paris in order to plant the liberty linden in honor of the departure of twenty-nine Chinese young people who had successfully completed a traineeship.

In Arles the crowd sang Revolutionary airs as they planted the trees, while in Rennes representatives of 130 agricultural lycées took part in a relay race. Gathered around their tree, the lycéens of Villefranche-de-Rouergue listened to extracts from the *cahiers* of the Third Estate (the grievances addressed to the king in 1789) and a text in which Condorcet emphasized the intimate connection between education and the practice of liberty. Like thousands of others, the students of the elementary school of Pasteur de Lambersart in the Nord donned Revolutionary garb that they had helped confect and danced the carmagnole around the linden.[5]

Bon Chic Bon Genre: Versailles's Muted Revolution

In epitome, the organization of the reconstitution of the inaugural procession of the Estates General at Versailles on 4 May rehearsed many of the difficulties involved in the bicentennial task. A large part of the Versailles of the 1980s did not feel at ease with the Revolution. (No more, Jack Lang might have added, than it had felt in 1871 when it served as a base for the crushing of the Paris Commune.) If the city was not the caricatural redoubt of old people and commuters that it was often depicted to be, it still had a very high rate of religious practice and a solid block of conservative opinion in its midst. In 1984 Versailles was at the heart of the massive uprising against the government's plans to curtail private education. The Versaillais who marched in support of private, predominantly Catholic schools were the true revolutionaries, according to the *Bulletin municipal,* for they prevented the state from exercising "an absolute power over the children."

For the centrist mayor André Damien, the Revolution was a "skeleton in the closet." On the one hand, he believed that "'89 is essentially an event of Versailles" and thus that Versailles had to participate in some way in the anniversary. On the other hand, he would venture nothing that might "wound the sensibilities of certain of our inhabitants." The emergence of the Front national in the wake of the presidential election probably reinforced his prudential conviction. In fact, the way to deal with the bicentennial became one of the issues in the municipal election campaigns of the late winter.

Damien's position was founded on the sharp distinction he drew between celebration, in which he refused to engage, and commemoration, which struck him as a relatively antiseptic and fully legitimate undertaking. He would forge a usable, palatable past with which most citizens could live. To the left, who accused him of harboring an "antirepublican bias," he made clear the limits of his engagement: the evocation of "the happy period of the royal Revolution" when things could have turned in a very different direction. To those on the right who could not help glimpsing the specter of the wildcat procession of the angry women of Paris on 6

October in the interstices of the decorous procession of 4 May, the mayor firmly said he would pay no teleological blackmail: "No anachronisms. The fourth of May precedes the earliest massacres. Robespierre was still a monarchist and the guillotine did not yet exist."

So Versailles launched a hot-air balloon to mark the advent of the bicentennial year, planted liberty trees, listened to the recitation of the Declaration, and attended performances of *Le mariage de Figaro.* At the same time, to reassure the right thinkers, the *Bulletin municipal* told the story of a pervasive Enlightenment, a universal commitment to reform, and a modernizing/technocratic royal Revolution—all of which implicitly called into question the necessity of what came after '89.

Without an extreme courtesy on each side, it is doubtful whether the marriage of convenience between Mayor Damien and the president of the Mission could have taken place. Perhaps because he was a historian, Jeanneney manifested a certain allergy for historical reconstitutions, to which he preferred "popular fêtes," which he regarded as more or less incompatible with the rigor and distance demanded by historical re-creations. With Damien, however, the Mission conceived of the Versailles commemoration as both, as "a popular fête, a festive reconstitution of what the day of 4 May was—the real beginning of the Revolution." The rightist press interpreted this as a triumph for the mayor: Jeanneney "had to give in," noted *Valeurs actuelles.*

While Jeanneney strains one's credulity in reducing his differences with Damien to mere "nuances" in his official report, he felt obliged in their common press conference presenting the project in April to remark: "This exemplary collaboration nevertheless does not signify that we are ready to decompose the Revolution into slices and oppose 1789 to the years that followed." Jeanneney remained genuinely torn between a civic and intellectual unitarianism on the one side and a liberal respect for diversity and (consumer if not civic) choice on the other. Presumably he was not privy to the issue of Versailles's *Bulletin municipal*—which, it is true, appeared only a short time after Jeanneney's nomination—that contrasted the sureness of Damien's approach to the Revolution and the bicentennial with "the wavering and the uncertainties" at the national level.

More than two thousand players participated in the parade, conceived by popular historian Arthur Conte. From the Church of Notre-Dame to the Cathedral of Saint-Louis marched bewigged aristocrats, tonsured monks, and black-garbed bourgeois carrying candles. While Marie Antoinette, dressed in a dazzling white satin gown, elicited the most applause, surprisingly few spectators greeted Louis XVI, with praise ("Long live the king!") or malediction ("To the gallows!"). The reporter for *Le Monde* was struck by the apathy of the crowd of over three hundred thousand dispersed along two kilometers, just desserts for a spectacle that lacked "warmth" despite the magnificence of the costumes, the carriages, and the arms.

Jeanneney discreetly noted "the limits of the genre" in his report. Television constraints deprived the spectators of loudspeaker commentary and the sort of spontaneity that might have engaged them. They had a long wait and then little time to admire each passing group. The current began to pass at the very end when the actors mixed with the spectators in street concerts and animations. That evening smaller numbers witnessed a living reconstitution of David's celebrated Tennis Court Oath and a light-and-sound show featuring the history of the chateau. As if to underline Damien's own sense of how the royal Revolution should have turned out in June the mayor's office sponsored an exhibition entirely consecrated to Louis XVII.[6]

The Genesis of the Tuileries Debacle

The Mission itself launched one massive project in Paris, a sort of compact Revolutionary theme park in the Tuileries gardens that was meant to serve as a semipermanent counterpoise to the occasional and ephemeral great commemorative events. It would prove to be the least fortunate chapter in Jeanneney's tenure, in terms of both the experience itself and his reaction to it. It was the story of how an excellent idea, handicapped by inadequate gestation, expertise, and financing, failed to live up to its promise. The plan was to endow the bicentennial with a home base, a fixed site in a powerfully evocative ambience that would serve as a symbol of the ongoing commemoration-celebration, provide the surest source of information on festive activities throughout the world, and offer a colorful and educational voyage back to the years of Revolutionary exhilaration and tumult. Perhaps the press later idealized the founding ambition in order to sharpen the chiaroscuro of failure, calling the project "in some sense the very soul of the commemoration" or "something sumptuous where everyone can come in order to renew his heart in the fountains of '89." But Jeanneney himself clearly wanted the Tuileries to be his centerpiece—at least until it actually opened. Convinced that it would attract numerous visitors from the provinces and abroad, the tourism lobby warmly supported the idea.[7]

The project did not enjoy a smooth takeoff. The government refused to involve itself either directly or fully in the financing of the operation. It pledged a maximum of Fr 45 million as a sponge to absorb an eventual deficit incurred by the sponsors. This decision had grave managerial implications, which may not have been fully digested by the Mission at the outset. "This 'distanced' position of the state," Jeanneney wrote later, "will weigh on the project and weaken the authority that the Mission will be able to exercise over it." In late July the Mission opened a competition for designs for creating a bicentennial space in a five thousand-square-meter section of the Tuileries. The directive was extremely general, even nebulous: the program had to evoke "the events that transpired during the Revolution" and put into relief "the progress of parliamentary democracy." All entries had to be submitted by 9 September. Jeanneney presided over a jury of seven, including Christian Dupavillon, an ex-architect and Jack Lang's right-hand man; Jean Tulard, a rightist historian and professor at Paris IV representing the city of Paris; Madeleine Rebérioux, a leftist historian and human rights activist; and Patrick Bouchain, the architect to be charged with the task of organizing the Valmy commemoration in September 1989.

Though the "consultation" period was extremely short, there were a substantial number of entries. Many of the projects were imaginativly conceived and elaborately presented. Some were reincarnations or modifications of designs that their architect-creators had crafted for the "Invent 1989" competition announced in the spring of 1987 and unveiled to the public at the "Avant-Première" in June 1989. At least one group, Exposium, had proposed a full-blown amusement-park concept to Edgar Faure in the fall of 1987. Dubbed "Révoparc," in one of its earliest forms it was to be located in a tunnel seven hundred meters long and cost between Fr 150 and 200 million. Indeed, the president of Exposium, F. Bauer, and its chief architect, Georges Alexandroff, complained bitterly about the conditions in which the competition took place and the constraints that governed it. After months of "temporizing, disappointments, hesitations, [and] . . . paralyzing political turbulence," the competition was hurriedly launched at the worst possible moment, in the middle of the summer "at the height of the period of national inactivity." Bauer regretted that "the consultation, instead of expressing with force, power, and generosity a grand national will to make of the celebration of the bicentennial a prestigious event worthy of France, is above all the reflection of inexplicable reticences and excessive precautions on the part of the various branches of administration."[8]

Apparently Alexandroff manifested a more bilious and aggressive tone, for Jeanneney made it clear in his response how little he appreciated his manner of communication. The architect was furious that the competition rules specifically excluded the use of the central mall of the Tuileries, around which his entire project had been fashioned. The president reminded him that when he took office at the end of May, "no site had been selected to house any sort of evocation of the revolutionary period." He succeeded "in less than a month" in obtaining the Tuileries—apparently a stunning victory for an outsider to achieve on the French administrative battleground—but the Tuileries minus the major alley, a bargain struck "at the highest levels of the state" for reasons he did not specify. Alexandroff appears to have taken the recourse to a competition as a slap in the face, since several projects including his own had been on the table for many months prior to Jeanneney's arrival.

Jeanneney assured him that "the competition is not at all directed against your work." First, it was necessary because no existing project other than his own, "which has the defect of occupying that part of the site that must be avoided," fulfilled the thematic requirement, "a full evocation of the revolutionary period." Second, it was necessary because a major investment by the state involving the concession of certain privileges to the private sector demanded "a call for a modicum of competition." Given its "spontaneously" auspicious beginnings, anticipating the thematic objectives of the Mission, Jeanneney urged the Révoparc group to revise their project in light of the site guidelines so that it could "in the end be squarely and fairly compared with other projects" in the competition.[9]

The project called "Révoscope" drafted by Bauer and Alexandroff may very well be the wished-for revision. It proposed the reconstitution "in trompe l'oeil" of the facade of the Tuileries palace, a historical walk through the Revolution that included the re-creation of the décor of a typical Parisian quarter in the eighteenth century, and a commercial gallery. Sound and light as well as other dramatic and technical vehicles would be used to instill a sense of the Revolutionary era. Exposium asked for a May opening, a six-month run, and a single admission fee for the entire space. It evaluated the price tag at between Fr 190 and 255 million. Architect Jean-Jacques Fernier presented a considerably less expensive project called "Dimensions 89." It included a Galerie des Lumières, a museum, a series of "Pyramides-Spectacles" containing large movie theatres, and an Arche de la Liberté. Companies such as Perrier would sponsor spaces for relaxation and play.

With I. M. Pei in the air, another group (Thomassin-Robin-Duc) proposed a Pyramide de la Liberté, reaching almost one hundred meters high, 184 meters long and forty-six meters wide, constructed in extremely light material that could be rapidly built and dismantled. It would contain a welcome and information center, projection rooms, three floors devoted to an evocation of major Revolutionary themes (political life, the movement of ideas, the advance of science) through various pedagogical and amusement modalities, and the studios of the premier French television production company, the SPF. Two smaller structures would contain theatres and meeting spaces. The total cost would be over Fr 160 million, more than 10 percent of which went to the cost of financing.

In a conception that seemed more attuned to the Baroin-Faure spirit than to the Jeanneney line, architect Jean-Claude Montias tendered "the Paths of Fraternity." The plan envisioned the convocation of an "Estates General of the World," to which each of some 159 countries would present a list of grievances in the style of the Old Regime called a *cahier de doléances*. This meeting would occur in the context of a "National Exposition" focusing on the history and legacy of the Revolution and a "Universal Festival of Culture and Human Rights." The exposition would occur in two pavilions containing reconstitutions of the Salle du Jeu de Paume of Versailles, where the deputies of the Third Estate declared themselves a National Assembly, and the Salle des Menus Plaisirs where the National Assembly debated the Declaration, as well as an exhibition hall and several movie theatres. The festival would take place on the grand terrace of the Tuileries, where a huge stage containing giant screens would be erected (to represent world communication) along with a number of light buildings to house displays of culture from diverse parts of the world. Near the rue de Rivoli shops and cafés would take form, and kiosques in the gardens would be dedicated to the philosophes. Commensurate with the monumentality of the design, the price tag was Fr 460 million. On the basis of ten million paying entries (with double fees for general admission and admission to the shows) and collateral revenue from television and commerce, Montias affirmed that "this project is therefore comfortably in the black," though it would require a government financial guarantee to get off the ground.

R. C. Sportes and J.-R. Gomart proposed three thematically less articulated pavilions to illustrate the unfolding of the Revolution month by month from 1789 through 1799, with an emphasis on the drafting of the Declaration and its consequences. The central building, on the vista from the Pyramid du Louvre, would contain an auditorium of three thousand seats and would serve as an information and conference center as well as a space for festivities. Rising next to the Seine, the "media" pavilion would contain information tools enabling one to explore historical questions as well as communications facilities. A floating platform, marked by a tower with a torchlight flame symbolizing the Revolutionary trinity, and bearing a café and restaurant, would permit access from the river. Across the gardens on the Rivoli side the "revolution-of-the-world" pavilion profiled the decisive changes that had shaped the world since the end of the eighteenth century with particular reference to the struggles for rights. The vista between the media and revolution-of-the-world pavilions, baptized "Revolutionary axis," would be lined with restaurants, shops, and meeting halls and would be fitted with an audiovisual system that would rehearse Revolutionary themes. The perspective linking the central pavilion and the Louvre, called the "the Rights of Man axis," would offer a similar audiovisual show. Constructed largely of steel and cloth, the structures could be built and disassembled rapidly and at reasonable, albeit unspecified, cost.[10]

From Jury to Construction Site

On 27 September, one week later than announced, the jury awarded first prize to a project signed Hennin and Normier, the same couple that had proposed the "Paths of Liberty" at La Villette. The manner in which the jury made its choice provoked a miniscandal that disrupted the procedure without tainting it. "The consultation organized by the bicentennial Mission in order to pick the creators and investors who were to take charge of the temporary transformation of a part of the Tuileries gardens has ended in confusion," Le Monde somberly reported. Two days after the jury's decision, Jean-Claude Montias, one of the losing candidates, filed a suit that raised questions about the fairness of the selection in light of the week's delay. The Mission did not help its public relations by making more or less contradictory statements to the press about the rigor of the protocol followed by the jury in making its award, which, it turned out, was construed as a concession to a private individual rather than a public contract per se.

Even as the Tribunal administratif appointed an expert to check on the state of the different projects at the time of submission, another losing team led by Jean-Jacques Fernier prepared a suit to learn whether any of the projects were submitted late and/or withdrawn for modification after the submission deadline. Jeanneney retorted firmly that the jury toiled "in the most total transparence." Although nothing came of the accusations and suspicions, the affair embarrassed the Mission. Later on there were other acrimonious episodes with ancillary project designers who believed that they had been mistreated. Commissioned to create a Revolutionary café, the Groupe de recherches art, histoire, architecture et littérature (GRAHAL) was astonished and angry over its sudden eviction at the turn of the year in favor of another café builder. Apothéose, creators of an animated spectacle, expressed similar, even more vehement sentiments when it discovered that it no longer held a contract. It suggested that its rivals pirated its concepts, hinting darkly that the Mission may have facilitated this treachery and denouncing Jeanneney's sovereign disregard for the "rules of professional ethics."[11]

It was not long before Hennin and Normier discovered that their victory had a pyrrhic aftertaste. The winning design was an immense *galerie des glaces* that stretched in a gently descending slope on piles eight meters off the ground across the entire width of the Tuileries for four hundred meters from the rue de Rivoli to the Seine. Evoking the site of the Tuileries palace, destroyed after the Commune, the galery was complemented by two pavilions, soaring thirty-five meters, baptized towers of liberty and equality. Numerous sophisticated high-tech exhibitions, including animations and films, were to furnish this vast space. According to the press, the cost of the project was estimated at between Fr 230 and 250 million. Even before Jeanneney had squarely addressed the issue of financing, on 19 September he wrote to the architects to request certain modifications in their blueprint, ostensibly in response to strictures expressed by the jury and others consulted by the Mission. He invited them to rethink the massiveness and monotony of the grand gallery, which in fact they later abandoned. The design of the towers now seemed insufficiently precise. Nor were the descriptions of the historical and cultural animations that would inhabit the structures sufficiently spelled out. Finally, noted Jeanneney candidly, "the project as a whole appears to lack the allure necessary to entice large numbers of people to visit." Given its multiple flaws, one wonders how the jury could have endorsed the Hennin-Normier project on grounds other than default.[12]

A powerful financial institution, the Caisse des dépôts et des consignations (CDC), the Mission's major potential source of financing for the Tuileries, commissioned a feasibility study by its subsidiary, SCIC-AMO, which had some experience with amusement parks. In light of its pessimistic conclusions on the prospects for a profitable operation, the CDC demanded a state guarantee of Fr 70 million—almost twice what the government had allocated—and the use of the Tuileries for either eighteen months or two years of exploitation, three times the concession period envisaged. The Ministry of Culture esteemed that the public would tire of the bicentennial project much more rapidly than its promoters imagined. In any event, it had programmed a renovation for the Tuileries gardens that supposedly could not be postponed. In his final report, Jeanneney noted drily: "These two conditons are exorbitant for both the ministries concerned, Finance and Culture."

From the beginning, however, the crucial variable seems to have been Lang's distaste for the project and perhaps his resentment of Jeanneney's independence.

As a member of the jury, Dupavillon had voted against all the projects, seconded by fellow architect Patrick Bouchain, also of the Lang orbit. Practicing a "negative neutrality," in the words of one Mission executive, the Ministry of Culture's conduct proved to be "quite subversive." Jeanneney's advisers had no doubt that Lang could easily have overcome in-house objections to the time frame and perhaps even marshaled more money—or at least moved the affair toward some sort of compromise.[13]

In light of these apparently insuperable blockages, the president of the Mission coolly drew the logical conclusion, issuing a press release (on 25 October, indicated *Le Monde;* on 11 November, according to Jeanneney's final accounting) that summarily announced that "the idea is abandoned and the competition is ruled fruitless." On 26 October Jeanneney told his staff that he could have appealed over Lang's head to Rocard or Mitterrand but that such a step "would have created a climate of hostility between the Mission and the Ministry of Culture" which the press would have exploited at the expense of the commemoration. (Jeanneney's strategy was right, but his choice of language is implausible: a climate of hostility between the two institutions already existed.) The minister of culture and of the bicentennial was furious, for the responsibility for failure seemed to redound to him. He claimed never to have said that the Tuileries idea was moribund.

On 1 November thirteen persons, including the two architects who had contested the integrity of the Mission's procedures and several others who had exposed at the Avant-Première, cosigned a rather pompous and self-regarding op-ed piece in *Le Monde* that assailed the Mission's incapacity to forge a "coherent project" and its preoccupation with a "commercial quest." The French nation would not be satisfied with a few July fireworks, and the rest of the world was shocked by "the absence of a program, with the exception of regional initiatives." In light of the regnant "confusion" and the rapidly ebbing time left before the start of the bicentennial year, the signatories leagued together to propose a collective solution for the Tuileries, "installations with a cultural content, an authentic historical trajectory over two centuries." These commemorators proposed "the erection, for the period covering July through September, of an ensemble of buildings, designed to be ephemeral and inexpensive, consisting of a dominant gallery of light structures occupying the historical axis of the Tuileries leading to a large scenic space at the octagonal pond, a big multipurpose room fitted with an arch that serves as a signpost, and auditorium-theatres located at various places in the gardens."

It is not clear whether there was any relation between this diatribe-prospectus and the report in *Le Canard enchaîné* that on 4 November the president of the Mission threatened to resign if the Ministry of Culture did not facilitate some sort of positive denouement for the Tuileries. ("Lang has only to threaten to resign in his turn in order to obtain Jeanneney's head," *Le Canard* beneficently advised.) There is no question that Jeanneney wanted the Tuileries very badly. He resented Lang's arrival on the scene and his haughty, possessive attitude toward the organization of the Big Bicentennial. Jeanneney feared that Lang had effectively confiscated the fourteenth of July from the Mission. He wanted a major project—as the publicists later touted it, "the largest and longest activity of the bicentennial"—under the signature and nurture of the Mission. Given the magnificent and central nature of the site, he was convinced it would be a winner.[14]

Not long afterward, probably as a result of discreet collaboration between the Lang and Jeanneney cabinets—and perhaps with the counsel of Gilbert Trigano of the Club Méditerranée, who knew a great deal about managing collective entertainment activities—the architects, the executives of SCIC-AMO, and the originators of several educational amusements presented a new project geared for a six-month run. Hennin and Normier scaled their design down to the two towers, light structures composed of metal and canvas cresting over two small buildings erected on the Louvre-Concorde axis. "Liberty" was to serve as the Mission's center of information and, without deliberate irony, "Equality" was to be used for paid receptions organized by businesses. The buildings, barely eight meters in height, would house a theatre, two cinemas, and an exposition hall. Between the towers and the pond would be placed several dozen shops interspersed with a number of open-air stages and two small bars. Two large cafés and a restaurant were to be set on the Concorde side of the pond.

Within a month all the authorizations were obtained and a company called "Tuileries 89" was formed, galvanized into existence by a loan of Fr 130 million from the CDC. Although the Mission was careful to point out that it was linked to Tuileries 89 by a mere "tacit understanding" which invested it with quality control—Jeanneney's pendant to the distance taken by the state from the project—its full moral responsibility was utterly undiminished. Four civic and/or cultural associations concerned with the Paris environment and landscape unsuccessfully sued early in the new year to halt construction on the grounds that alteration of the Tuileries was tantamount to a spoliation of the national and natural patrimony. (After all, they had said a hundred years earlier that the Eiffel Tower would only stand for the duration of the world's fair.) Writing in *Le Monde*, in mid-February, two architects deplored the gratuitous "vandalization" of the Tuileries gardens and savaged the Mission for engendering a "dwarf bicentennial," marked by a derisory central project wholly incommensurate with the significance of the occasion. Much to everyone's surprise and delight, a crash building effort enabled the park to open at the beginning of May, barely four months after construction began.[15]

An Exuberant Grand Opening

Enormously relieved, the Mission staff instinctively felt that the worst was now behind them. Jeanneney took a tone that sounded almost triumphalist in his monthly *Lettre*. Evoking the "felicitous alchemy" of "a bold and modern architecture" and "entertainment of quality," he allowed that the arduous toil had been well worth it. One suspects that he is not ordinarily a betting man: "I wager that people will find there a combination of seduction and rigor." Part of this discourse was surely self-conscious hype, from the exuberance-as-contagion school of publicity. In the same boosterist spirit, kits prepared for the press portrayed Tuileries 89 as the very "base of the commemoration." Folon, step aside: "at the edge of a dream-world," the Hennin-Normier towers "aspire to become the very symbol of the bicentennial." Although conceived and edified in barely six months, "the architecture was duty bound to present a grandiose spectacle," and the six hectares of rich and varied activities constituted "a grand, total fête inviting one to learn, to laugh, to dance, and to be moved." The Mission, the press was informed, had won "a formidable bet." Presiding over the inauguration ceremonies, Prime Minister Rocard shared this wagering optimism: "With Tuileries 89, the bicentennial resolutely enters into reality, at the desired level of quality, and I bet that the public will respond with enthusiasm to this event."

Enthusiasm lapsed into imprudence when the Mission began to predict just how popular—that is, how successful, defined in terms of its own bottom-line obsession—Tuileries 89 would be. The Mission first set the global attendance figure at two million; later it was quoted by *L'Humanité* at three million and by *Le Monde* (three times) and *Figaro-Magazine* at three and a half million. In retrospect these estimates take on a bit of the pathos and desperation of François Brigneau's predictions for the mass mobilization of the Anti-89 movement on Assumption Day. For within a few weeks of the opening, Tuileries 89 was pronounced a "flop" and a "fiasco" by the press. Jeanneney had said "from now on it's up to the public to judge," and the public voted massively with its feet, staying away in record numbers. The managers of the enterprise, the CDC, and the Mission joined together in ringing "the alarm bell."[16]

The visitors of those early days encountered a staff more preoccupied with security than with welcome. It was hard to learn exactly what awaited one behind the forbidding fences that separated the bicentennial citadel from the rest of the gardens. Rather brusque and disinclined to answer questions, the personnel at the gates did not generate a warm feeling of fraternity and anticipation. Merely to traverse the threshold of Tuileries 89, one had to pay twenty francs (thirty-five francs after 6:00 P.M.), and thereafter ten francs for each of the three major exhibitions.

"1789, Promenade in Paris" used computer-generated images and cartoon animation projected onto a huge screen to create a brief but engaging and lifelike walk through Revolutionary Paris. One of the first historical films forged in three dimensions, "Promenade" achieved a stunning street realism with its sense of texture, its attention to detail, and its fidelity to the architecture and mood of the neighborhood. The public visited buildings that no longer existed, such as the Bastille and the Grand Châtelet, as well as extant monuments and quarters, it took off in a hot-air balloon, and it boated on the Seine.

"Les Androides" was a less successful and more strident high-tech show, featuring screeching robots with the faces, bodies, and voices of real men and women incarnating important figures in the Revolution. ("Sort of the Return of Robes-tein," noted *Libération*, "in which one sees [Antoine] Fouquier-Tinville as a robot screaming before a guillotine illuminated by a laser, Abbé Grégoire in a ball gown, or Théroigne de Méricourt as Miss Bicentennial.") The fruit of fifty-five thousand hours of work, "The Spirit of the Revolution," as the show was entitled, cost Fr 9 million and was replayed every ten minutes. Finally, "The Long Memory, or the Revolutionary Heritage" proposed a more sober itinerary through the Revolution's major achievements in the form of a series of diaramas bathed in sound and light. Articulated around the theme of the birth of democracy, it took the visitor from the razing of the old Bastille to the need to conquer new ones, from the causes of the Revolution to its short- and long-term consequences.

It was extremely difficult for the unprivileged visitor to obtain access to the towers, symbols, the official program emphasized, of "the rise of freedom." In the vast open spaces in the central axis, one encountered actors in eighteenth-century garb, playing simple citizens or grand protagonists such as Marat, Robespierre, and Madame Roland, some of whom performed sketches from the two open-air stages. Acrobats, tumblers, and dancers moved both in the alleys and on the two stages, where a troop of thirty-two actors performed "The Newspaper of the Year 1789," ten scenes of twelve minutes each depicting such decisive moments as the drafting of the *cahiers*, the meeting of the Estates General, the Tennis Court Oath, the taking of the Bastille, the night of 4 August, and the October march on Versailles. In addition to scheduled concerts of a formal nature, musicians played intermittently in various modes, from baroque harpsichord to light heavy metal. In forty small shops, vaguely camouflaged as old-fashioned marketplace booths, the visitor could purchase a vast range of largely forgettable bicentennial souvenirs—T-shirts, shorts, umbrellas, posters, postcards, pens, lighters, pins, scarves, perfumes, and so on. For refresh-ments, the visitors had a choice of several cafés and a large restaurant.

The overall visual impact of Tuileries 89 was disappointing. Though not without a certain stimulating elegance, the towers seemed strangely pointless. The authors of the project did not succeed in capitalizing on the magnificent site, in summoning up the monarchical vestiges, in evoking the absent Manège (on the rue de Rivoli side) where the Revolutionary assemblies had met, in playing off against the recon-structed pavillons de Flore and de Marsan where the two great committees of the Terror had sat. It was the hollow and halfhearted historicization rather than the innocuous and inevitable commercial vulgarity that might have justified *Libération's* "good republicans" to conclude that "one would have done better to take the children to the Foire du Trône," an amusement park fair held annually in the bois de Vincennes. (At the other end of the cultural spectrum, there was a nearby alternative: "For considerably less money, it is preferable to go to the nearby Louvre, where at least one knows what to expect," recommended *Le Quotidien de Paris*.) [17]

Harsh Strictures and Rapid Readjustments

Tuileries 89 drew harsh criticism from every direction. Christian Clément, a communications specialist, put it tersely in the business idiom: "a product that was badly launched because it was badly defined." Treating the overall conception with special emphasis on the architecture, Frédéric Edelmann of *Le Monde* deeply regretted "this accumulation which smacks of the marriage of the carp and the rabbit—without wishing to give offense to the society for the protection of animals." Even allowing for the pressures of time and the political handicaps of cohabitation, he believed that the organizers—the leaders—could have done better: "A bit of reflection all the same, a bit of cohesion would have enabled [them] to forge a symbolic dimension, as one could have hoped for in this sort of undertaking." This failure struck at the very essence of Jeanneney's civic objective, because it trivialized the bicentennial. The lack of seriousness of Tuileries 89 will not surprise foreigners who see the French in stereotypical terms of "frivolity." But it "will not encourage them, any more than the French, to ponder the real meaning of these festivities."

Much of the press agreed that the program suffered from "a dizzying conceptual vacuum." The leitmotif of the reproaches was "the mediocrity of the performance offered to the public." The cost was unacceptably onerous, "especially in light of the quality proposed." Even if the content had been better, the failure to explain it more clearly to the visitors at the site and to promote it more vigorously to the rest of the public would have flawed the operation.

The merchant-concessionaires themselves contested *L'Humanité*'s charge that "commerce dominates the entire enterprise." The lack of attendance led them to panic or revolt; some of them claimed that they were doing no more than Fr 350 worth of business a day, hardly enough to amortize the rent of Fr 120,000 a shop. Even as the Galeries Lafayette closed its doors the others signed a petition demanding free entry to the grounds and condemning the managers for failing to keep their promises about promotional activities such as daily concerts. As if the Mission did not have enough tribulation with the merchants on the spot, it received a furious protest from one of its royalty-paying official sponsors, the Canard-Duchêne company. The latter was "shocked" to discover that the Tuileries cafés served Moët and other champagnes instead of their bicentennial brand. It would be wholly unfair to dismiss the judgment of *Le Quotidien de Paris* as a purely partisan jeremiad: "In fact, the responsibility for this failure [the failure of Tuileries 89] belongs in large measure to the Mission, which delegates its powers to private investors without charting out a clearcut line of conduct and specific requirements for an operation portrayed as the permanent star attraction of the whole bicentennial."[18]

In the first weeks, André de Margerie, who monitored the enterprise on a day-to-day basis for the Mission, did not seem to apprehend the gravity of the situation. If there was a problem, it was not intrinsic to the park, in whose "great quality" (Cabouat's phrase) he continued to believe: "The visitors are satisfied with the different shows, but by and large the public is not familiar with 'Tuileries 89.'" In a meeting at the end of May the oversight panel (on which, among others, sat de Margerie and Michel Zulberty, the chief of the company operating the park) discussed a wide range of issues including attendance, ticketing, programming, and technical problems. They consoled themselves with a reminder of just how difficult the wager had been, a veritable mission impossible to imagine the whole park in two months and build it in six. The conviction continued to prevail that "Tuileries 89 is a good, quality production, but insufficiently known." A survey of visitors comforted another firmly held notion that seems astonishing in retrospect, that "the flat price (forty-five or fifty-five francs) is not an element that generates discontent, on the contrary." (Blinded by our self-protective complacency, admitted one Mission staff member after the fact, "we took people to be dumb asses.")[19]

By early June, however, it was no longer possible to deny the ambient reality. The performing and technical personnel of the park added their voice of mutiny to the chorus of commercial and journalistic strictures. They deplored the absence of the public, which they attributed to indifferent conditions of reception, poor communications, a dearth of comfort, and a global failure of festive imagination. In growing disarray, Tuileries 89 turned to Denis Fortin of BGF, a management-consulting firm specialized in "business strategy," to assess the situation. Fortin diagnosed serious weaknesses in the "readability" of a park of enormously diverse attractions, in the organization and manner in which the public was welcomed, and in the lack of an effective system of publicity.

Fortin in turn called on experts in "active business communications" and publicity; collectively they recommended lowering the price of admission (it hardly required three high-priced consultants to formulate this dazzling insight), investing heavily in an advertising campaign, improving procedures for orienting the public, modifying the use of space within the park, and strengthening the program of attractions. After having considered and rejected two other plans—closing down the entire operation on 14 July or opening the whole show to everyone without charge—the Mission, the management company, the CDC, and the interested ministries agreed to follow Fortin's counsels.

Rebaptized *Oh! Tuileries,* the bicentennial referent exorcised from the title ("An 'in' formula, with its ad-copy taste of orange pulp," noted one journalist), the park could now be entered for five francs, with the price of the three exhibitions remaining the same. The new animators enjoined all the personnel, clerical as well as artistic, to help create a more festive ambience through a conscious effort at projecting affability if not jubilation. The emphasis was to be on all-out fun; any civic edification or learning would be a welcome but incidental increment. Big-name musicians and singers would now headline daily and nightly shows; presumably, after the passage of the Lionel Hamptons, the Cab Calloways, and the Chick Correas, it would be easier to argue that 1789 (Oh!) was the matrix of jazz as well as of Terror.

Toward the salvaging goal, the Mission itself poured in cash—3 million for a high-powered, dense radio advertising campaign, and substantial sums to finance "apéritif" concerts and other attractions, including a two-week visit by the "Elephant of Memory," the magnificent bicentennial creation realized by the Conseil général du Nord. These changes resulted in a dramatic improvement in attendance, with crowds increasing from an average of around a thousand to three thousand a day and from about three thousand to between six and ten thousand on weekends. This partial recovery enabled the CDC to escape with a loss of Fr 80 million, a little more than half of which would be absorbed by the state. Jeanneney calculated that the state's contribution of Fr 45 million represented a per capita subvention of fifty-six francs for each of the eight hundred thousand spectators, a sum he considered not unreasonsable.[20]

Jeanneney and the Press

Mortified by the Tuileries experience, the Mission understandably took the criticism rather badly. Blended in with the plethora of generic vituperation, most of it ideologically motivated, the Tuileries critique may have been hard to distinguish from the rest, especially from the wounded perspective of the recipients. Yet the Tuileries was an egregious failure, even after its second wind. If there were journalistic low blows—for instance, dispatching a camera crew to film the park when no one was there—there were also searching evaluations, overwhelmingly negative, by observers without any prior animus, including many who believed deeply in the bicentennial ethos. Writing after Goude's providential global absolution of the Mission's work, Jeanneney could easily impute the attacks on the Tuileries to a general *muscadin* climate wherein "it was good form to 'shoot on sight' against most of the initiatives of the commemoration." But it was wrong and unjust to assimilate most of the criticism to "a political attack."

On the defensive, deserted by his usual judiciousness and sangfroid, the president of the Mission impugned his critics instead of owning up unequivocally to error. His uncharacteristically tortured prose, however, testifies to his own malaise: "It remains that the success of this undertaking—which we continue to think was necessary—remained, during the whole period of activity, clearly beneath the level fixed at the outset, and that should make us ponder." "Success" obstinately remained the framework for everything the Mission undertook; and most of its deficiencies, in particular those concerning the Tuileries, were said to have resulted from a lack of time. At the end of the Tuileries section in his official report, Jeanneney was still fleeing responsibility, invoking "the juridical nature of the operation and the limited proportion of public money invested" which did not always allow the Mission to "control as it would have liked the evolution of the operation."[21]

Jeanneney was particularly hard hit by this debacle precisely because "the 'flop' of Tuileries 89 seems to symbolize the flop of the entire bicentennial," as *Figaro-*

Magazine gloatingly put it. If the image of failure became widely associated with the bicentennial undertaking—wags already began to talk of the "Flopcentennial," or "Bidecentenaire"—it would be extremely hard to overcome the momentum of discredit. A student of the different vectors of opinion in a democracy, Jeanneney knew better than anyone how easily press-driven opinion (which alternately led and followed, depending on the opportunity cost at the moment) could destabilize an operation or ruin an ambition, of whatever magnitude. In the first six months of his regime, he had not succeeded in reversing the negative tide of the press, despite Angélique Oussedik's prodigious efforts (she saw herself as a "commando") to provide more and better information, to establish personal contacts with the key players in the press corps, to make the president of the Mission maximally available (he gave something like two hundred interviews during the year).

In his first few months, in the view of the moderate Catholic daily *La Croix*, Jeanneney did not put an end to "the evident confusion concerning the contents and the meaning of the projected events." Four months later the same paper still reproached the Mission with failing to "see big enough." The Communists of *Révolution* shared the diagnosis of the rightists of *Figaro-Magazine*: "The big projects have fallen by the wayside," the commemorative organization is paralyzed by "inertia" and stagnated "in woolly vagueness." Whether or not its motivation was political, the judgment of the Communist daily, *L'Humanité*, might have appeared in any newspaper in the fall of 1988: "The two hundredth anniversary of the French Revolution looks worse with each passing day."

Even in the provinces, Jeanneney's preferred terrain, given its distance from Parisian cynicism and lordliness, there were expressions of disappointment.[22] The year of the bicentennial has opened without sparkle and seems destined to continue at the same cadence," commented the *Nouvelles républicaines du Centre-Ouest*, taking note of the absence of a "central project" and the lack of a moral and political climate hospitable to fervor. Rehearsing the latter theme, a human rights activist who condemned the "saddening poverty" of the bicentennial projects in a stinging article in *Le Monde* did not hold Jeanneney or any of his predecessors responsible; rather, "it's the force of things." On the eve of the opening of Tuileries 89, *Libération* designated the party of the lifeless bicentennial the RUY: the "Republican Union in the Yawn." "We thought that 1989 would be the apogee of the revolutionary mythology," observed the conservative editor-poet Louis Pauwels, "we observe its decline," paradoxically under the aegis of the left. Nor did the attitude of the press change dramatically after the Tuileries was given a second life. Remarking that "the commemoration does not seem to catch on," the editor of *Historama* was not wide of the mark when he suggested that 14 July was the last best hope.[23]

Jeanneney's relations with the press, especially the so-called national press based in Paris, remained strained at least until the events of 14 July impelled many publications to modify their bicentennial line. He resented their impatience to deprecate, and the glib, self-satisfied manner in which they dismissed commemorative initiatives. More broadly, he detested "the wall of skepticism and mockery" of large segments of the Paris cultural and socioeconomic elites, though he took some solace in his historian's knowledge that this pose was a chronic anniversary syndrome in the French past. (Oussedik had a particularly low regard for the rarefied snobbery of André Glucksmann and Alain Finkielkraut.) In classical populist fashion, though with lots of class, Jeanneney, the *grand bourgeois*, Ulm graduate, and Jacobin, appealed to *la France profonde* (and Girondist?), which he believed had a lively moral capacity and appetite for bicentennial fervor. (He avowed that, even while president of Radio France, he had never taken the full measure of "the problem of this breach between the capital and the regions.")

Jeanneney took the pulse of French—that is, provincial—opinion regularly, making scores of trips to every corner of the country. The press in Paris tended to ignore this middle France (the France beyond the beltway, to extend a Washingtonian metaphor). The president of the Mission reproached its members for their lack of professionalism as well as their hostility. He cited the press's grossly inadequate coverage of genuinely important national events marshaling millions of citizens such as the liberty-tree planting in March and, more generally, its drastic underestimation of the "social demand" for commemoration throughout France. A recurrent, splenetic theme in staff meetings, this irritation with the press was not merely a product of Jeanneney's blemished self-esteem; it was one of the few issues on which the Mission counselors were unflinchingly unanimous and solidary.

Jeanneney would have preferred, and indeed felt entitled to, a much warmer reception on the left. From the earliest days of the Mission, the attitude of *Le Monde*, "master thinker of those in power," in the words of one collaborator, had galled the staff. They judged the articles of journalist Michel Kajman, the prime bicentennial reporter for the prestigious daily, as systematically negative and biased. A historian of *Le Monde* and a member of one of the paper's multiple governing councils, Jeanneney pressed one of its chief editors, Claude Sales, whom he had known at Radio France, to give the Mission and the bicentennial a fairer hearing. While it is hard to imagine *Le Monde* caving in to such pressure, for whatever reasons, a change was made. Yves Agnès replaced Kajman. He evinced a keen interest in the commemoration, especially in the provinces, and the Mission welcomed his pieces as better researched and more evenhanded. As Jeanneney put it, gratefully, *Le Monde* shifted from an extremely critical posture to "a scrupulous and balanced sympathy." Predictably unpredictable, *Libération* remained rather whimsical until mid-July.

"As for the right," declared the president of the Mission, "I often thought of de Gaulle's jeering reference to 'Messrs.-it-must-fail.'" Jeanneney denounced rightists' "deliberate political utilization of doubt and criticism: by announcing that we would fail, they expected to contribute to our failure." *Le Quotidien de Paris*, relentlessly truculent and scornful, exercised an influence, especially among the elites, wholly disproportionate to its "very small circulation." In the service of its ideological crusade, it did not hesitate, according to Jeanneney, to deform the facts ("shamelessly"). The Hersant press, *Le Figaro* and *France-Soir*, reached millions and had nothing kind to say, Jeanneney contended, until its readers forced it to change its mind after the night of 14 July.

As for television coverage, the Mission president felt that the bicentennial was much more favorably treated by the private-sector channels, TF1 and channel 5, than by the leading voice of the public service sector, Antenne 2, which was "distinctly more hostile and ironic." It was a mark of the volatility of what is called Parisian opinion (and of the treacherously surreal brand of psychopositivism used to measure it) that the Mission staff attributed a deep change in attitude toward the bicentennial to a ten-minute appearance by Jeanneney on TF1 in June. The show, *Ciel mon mardi*, was more often than not an occasion for the abrasive host, Christophe Dechavannes, to liquidate one or more adversary-guests. Instead of assuming a sacrificial stance consonant with the Tuileries humiliation, Jeanneney was vigorous and mordant, projecting an image of strength and confidence. Oussedik had been worried that Jeanneney might come across as "too refined, too delicate, too much a professor."

Her Mission colleagues shared her relief and elation. Independent reaction corroborated the Mission's more or less ecstatic reading and consecrated Jeanneney's appearance as a mythomomentous turning point in the Sisyphean struggle to beat/ win over the media, a process somewhat temerariously equated with gaining *true* public favor. "I saw you the other night on *Ciel mon mardi*," Guy Philip of Radio France-Isère wrote to Jeanneney, "the questions were aggressive, the animators hostile, [but] you succeeded in communicating your enthusiasm even as you remained serene." Ever an extravagant cheerleader and a devoted press agent, Oussedik calculated a change in Parisian opinion of "at least 180 degrees." She rapidly negotiated for the Mission president to make appearances on the fast-paced, satiric radio show *L'Oreille en coin*, where she might have hesitated to send him before, and on the cultural Zion of *Apostrophes*.[24]

Preparing the Climax
From Jungle Fever to Summit Fever

When the planning for the celebration of 14 July first began in 1986, no one imagined that it alone would determine the fate of the entire bicentennial enterprise. The fourteenth was to be the high point, given its privileged position in French festive life, but it would be preceded and followed by other great commemorative events, and there was no reason to dramatize in particular its status or its burden. The stakes increased spectacularly, however, first as a result of a wholly exogenous factor, and later, as we have seen, as a result of a deficit of dynamic commemorative momentum. The external variable was the announcement, diffused not long after Jeanneney's appointment, that France would host the annual summit of the seven most industrialized countries (the so-called G-7 nations) to correspond with the celebration of 14 July. Thus the cameras of the entire world would be focused on Paris, including many that might not otherwise have paid more than casual deference to the bicentennial alone. The show planned as a homage to the fourteenth now required a more self-consciously international inflection in order not only to gratify the primary audience at home but also to reach the tens of millions of foreigners for whom France and her people did not project a particularly warm and sympathetic image, despite their revolutionary heritage.

Preparing 14 July: A Jarre-ing Musical Note

Jean-Michel Jarre, the noted musician, was the first sacrificial victim of these new circumstances, or so it appears. Famous for his highly publicized mass concerts in London, Houston, and Lyon, Jarre was asked first by Michel Baroin, who was impressed by his international resonance, and then by Edgar Faure to assume creative responsibility for the 14 July centerpiece. Though without a binding contract, he invested a great deal of energy into preparing the task. He spoke thoughtfully about the Revolutionary experience and legacy and, under Faure's tutelage, agreed on a project "to move beyond the historical framework of the tricolor fair in order to turn toward the future." Jarre saw himself as a bridge between popular culture and high tech. While respecting the popular traditions of local balls and fireworks, he would thrust the bicentennial consciousness into the future with his lasers, his computer-regulated music and light, and his lyrical sensibility. Even without the prod of the summit conference, Jarre instinctively saw things in terms of satellite transmission and a worldwide audience, to whom he wished to convey "a cultural image of France with its specificities and its technologies."

By the spring of 1988, Jarre had a concrete program, informed, he boasted, by "a conceptual unity" and a festive exuberance. The official commemorators would launch it with a ceremony in midafternoon on the thirteenth. At 4:00 P.M. an inaugural concert would take place on the Champs-Elysées. At 5:30 thirty-six thousand children—"the Children of the Bicentennial"—representing each of the communes of France and symbolizing the passage of the civic flame to the new generations, would march from the Etoile to the Arche. That evening on the steps of the Arche a "Recital of the Revolution" would present the whole range of late-eighteenth-century song and music. A huge fireworks display would announce the start of the *bals populaires* in all the quarters of the capital.

After the traditional military parade the following morning, Jarre's program would begin with a "nautical ballet," a water-borne "Homage of the World to the French Revolution." Initially the idea was to restrict the selection to those nations most intimately associated with the development and dissemination of human rights. Apparently such a criterion proved embarrassingly Malthusian and socio-centric, excluding much of the world. In any event, each of the countries elected would decorate a barge with its colors and put on a show reflecting its national talents and its dialogue with the Revolutionary legacy and legend. In the late afternoon a concert would be offered at the Trocadéro, followed by the unveiling of a "fresco of the world" painted by artists of many different cultures. That evening Jarre would cap the celebration with a spectacular concert, featuring his own music composed for the occasion, as well as a panoply of sounds from around the world. Giant screens and special effects and lighting would be set up to accommodate hundreds of thousands of spectators at eleven central sites, five along the Arche-Bastille axis, and a number of others each in the northern and southern sectors of the capital.

Initially, Jeanneney seemed quite favorable to the idea, in his public statements as well as his conversations with Jarre. After an attentive examination of Jarre's artistic corpus, however, Jack Lang and his brain trust, for their part, were less enthusiastic. That a significant part of the press savaged the London Docklands concert ("facile effects . . . without dramatic art, . . . simplistic symbolism; . . . technolyrical music bursts out in confusion") did not help his case. There was a sense that Jarre had a tendency to repeat himself time and again, depending on increased magnitude rather than fresh inspiration to differentiate one show from the next. (Or, as Christian Dupavillon, the acerbic artistic arbiter, reportedly said, "Jarre is not a creator.") His reputation as "a costly artist," in the words of one Mission counselor, aroused anxiety. Though Jarre confidently predicted that he could raise at least half of his budget from sponsors and television contracts, his price tag of Fr 80 million seemed staggering in the early days of the Jeanneney period.

Shortly after the announcement of the summit, its chief organizer and Mitterrand's universal Sherpa, Jacques Attali, convoked Jarre to an in-house summit with Lang, Dupavillon, and Jeanneney. The draconian security constraints imposed by the presence of the world's key leaders, the Elysée counselor gravely informed Jarre, would make it impossible for him organize a Gargantuan concert on a fixed center-city site on the fourteenth. In the pithy phrase of a Mission counselor, Jarre was "kicked out like an unsavory person." Another Mission staff member, who also sympathized with the musician, felt some consolation that Attali and not Dupavillon conducted the meeting, sparing him a far more brutal "you are not new enough, you are not beautiful enough."

In fact, Attali offered a consolation prize: a show to be put on the evening of the sixteenth after the summit had dispersed. In the heat of the moment, Jarre did not reject the proposition out of hand. The city of Paris reacted angrily to this development. Though it had pledged a large sum for the Jarre concert, it had been excluded from this crucial meeting and the discussions that preceded it. Regarding this decision as a casus belli, Chirac withdrew the pledge of municipal funds and advised Jarre to rebuff the poisoned gift, a counsel the musician followed.

From *L'Humanité* to *Le Quotidien de Paris*, a large part of the press was acutely skeptical of the contention that Jarre's purge was necessitated by logistical imperatives. A more plausible explanation seemed to reside in Jack Lang's distaste for the sort of "aesthetic" represented by Jarre. One reproach, which rings ironic and improbable given the choice made subsequently, was that Jarre would not be capable of injecting meaningful "content" into his pyrotechnics. Another hypothesis argued that Jarre's sort of concert was somehow not well suited for television, despite the fact that the musician was a careful student of that medium. It was suggested that Jarre's cordial relations with Chirac contributed to his inglorious displacement.

It is interesting that the musician situated himself on the cultural left and interpreted his disgrace as punishment for a populist desire to make a magnificent party for the people instead of "the fête of a political consensus." The pro-Communist members of the Breton bicentennial association Vive 89 defended Jarre as a friend of the sansculottes sacrificed with the rest of the humble to "the privileged" in the orbit of the G-7 summit powers. Inelegant and on many grounds unwarranted, Jarre's dismissal revealed one significant fact: whatever faults of character Lang may have harbored, he was not risk averse. Instead of settling for an almost certain success with Jarre's more or less familiar style, he opted for something more iconoclastic and potentially more striking.[1]

Christian Dupavillon, Bicentennial Talent Scout

On at least one count the skeptics were absolutely on the mark: Mitterrand had no intention to "let pass by such a date and in such circumstances without seeking to dazzle his guests and the whole planet." Lang immediately set his accomplice Christian Dupavillon on the scent of a fresh candidate. The Mission reported that thoughts turned first to the realm of the cinema in search of a figure who was at once creator and organizer (Milos Forman was one of the "image men" envisaged), but Dupavillon insisted that from the beginning he wanted an advertising genius (which presumably implied advertising impresario as well). Described by a collaborator as "a man replete with ideas, but with an awful characater, . . . more a traveling acrobat than a surveyor," the architect and public servant Dupavillon was nevertheless the man who had adeptly organized some of the major public ceremonies of the Socialist regime, in particular Mitterrand's excursions to the Panthéon. It is no wonder that an architect, habituated to detailed blueprints, who emphasizes "how much I like precision," was not enthralled by the bicentennial assignment, in part because of the late start, in part because of what he considered the inherently "disorderly" [bordélique] nature of such a massive undertaking.

Dupavillon enjoyed both Lang's total confidence (he characterized their relations as "antique") and an intimate familiarity with the liminal reaches of the art world, broadly construed. In his search for an idea that would surprise and move France and the world, it seemed perfectly natural to Dupavillon to turn to advertising, the métier best situated to fathom the magnitude and object of the task and to attack it swiftly and imaginatively. It was especially appropriate in light of the conviction militantly shared by all the decision makers that they must avoid at all costs a historical reconstitution or any ponderously didactical approach. "I adore history," Dupavillon reassured the historian who interviewed him, but he maintained knowingly that too unvarnished a dose of history "would have turned off the public." This was the untested predicate of official thinking at the highest levels, along with the tendency to reduce the "historical" model to a necessarily static as well as a boring reconstitution—thus Jeanneney's frequent and misleading reference to Williamsburg, Virginia, as negative proof of the hypothesis.

For Dupavillon, it was not merely the difficulty of making the great themes into a spirited, colorful, made-for-television show ("Go ahead and stage human rights," he challenged; "what can one say about the Revolution to a million spectators and 200 million television viewers?"). It was the sagely perceived need for a certain discretion, for avoiding a posture of zealous moralizing or lecturing on right Revolutionary behavior to the rest of the world. Who better than an adman, Dupavillon asked rhetorically, could deliver "a moment of true collective happiness with things never before seen?" What better way to underline the modernity of the ministry charged with the custodianship of national treasures—Dupavillon himself would soon become the director of the vast department of cultural preservation and aggrandizement within Lang's empire called the Patrimoine—and to mark the community and the dialogue between the values of the Revolution and those of the end of the twentieth century? It made him "sick when he heard people say that creators of advertising are less great than other creators." A sixth artistic sense ought to have sufficed, but Dupavillon, like the painter David, his predecessor, understood that culture was politics by other means, and thus he invoked public opinion polls, the philosopher's stone of the French public sphere, to justify his choice. Unspecified surveys allegedly showed that the French yearned for "a modern show including forms of contemporary art, imagery, [and] advertising."[2]

Dupavillon hesitated among three candidates—Jean-Paul Goude, Etienne Chatilliez and Jean-Baptiste Modino—all notorious in the advertising milieu and unknown to the public at large. In the end he opted for Goude, a man of the stage, "because his advertising conceptions are very theatrical." Goude's capacity to tell a complete story in thirty seconds, "something never seen anywhere else," impressed him. The graphic artist-adman filled two other basic criteria: he was comfortable with television ("the fête must be above all made for television") and by temperament he could only treat the theme, as Dupavillon wished, "in a totally contemporary manner." To reassure himself—the phrase might affront a man who claims never to ulcerate about his decisions—he visited Goude on a film set for an ad for Bas Dim, the hosiery maker, and he found exactly what he was seeking.

In response to Dupavillon's soundings about whether the bicentennial might interest him, according to one version, Goude replied with a characteristically jaunty yet anxious "Why not?" When interviewed subsequently, however, Goude recalled that he had been much more diffident. "A priori I was not swept off my feet, but I found this man sympathetic, with a wonderful sense of humor," he told *Le Figaro*. "For me this is primordial: I function to a great extent according to my feelings."[3]

Red, Black, and Goude

Forty-nine years old, with a slight, wiry build, Goude was a comic-strip character, aptly described by *Le Monde* as a man-child, forever garbed in a baseball cap and sweatpants, who "resembles the images he designs."[4] This costume, like almost everything else in Goude's life from the time he was a boy, was not merely a matter of convenience or happenstance. "I have always been interested in the image I project," Goude admitted, in this instance in relation to his rejection at age twelve of traditional Boy Scout garb in favor of a more fashionable and original outfit. Goude explained that he embraced the baggy look relatively early, as a compensation for his small physical stature (baggy pants "make me look taller") and his lack of what he called classical good looks.

Appearance, style, and movement, and their portrayal, became the chief themes of his life—to some extent, if we are to believe Goude's obviously dramatized, self-aggrandizing self representation, the product of his heredity. He described his paternal grandfather as a "famous French designer" who died at age twenty-nine from "overwork," thereby casting his son, Goude's father, into a public orphanage that shaved his head, taught him nothing of life, and discarded him as soon as he turned fourteen. He grew up to become "better looking than Charles Boyer," enjoying some success as a model. His crucial life decision was to try his hand in the United States, where he met his future wife, Goude's mother, at a Broadway show in which she was a lead dancer, an occupation she concealed from her father, a religious fanatic who lived in Queens and regarded Manhattan as Babylon. Al Jolson, the celebrated white entertainer who characteristically sang in blackface, "had the hots for my mother," boasted Goude years later, "but she couldn't stand him."

The play of black and white—more generally of dark and white—decisively influenced Goude's cognitive development. As a child, he told stories through his drawings. "As early as I can remember, I drew Indians and black people." He preferred the Indians to the cowboys—the allure of the underdog? of the exotic?— and he tended to draw them with blackface. His favorite figure at the sideshow of the fair was the savage of Borneo with the ring through his nose. He was cruelly disenchanted when his father revealed that the savage was merely a white man painted for the role. His father "never liked colored people," Goude confessed, perhaps because a black American had once stolen his wallet. But his mother shared Goude's "particular feeling about blacks," a feeling that would shape his life and mark his bicentennial creation. As a child he "would have given anything to be Sabu," the second-level star of many jungle-based adventure movies. He identified with Sabu because "he was short like me," and because "he was brown and savage-looking, which was my dream."

When Goude was an art student, his drawing remained "negroid." Black struck him as more beautiful, especially the "thick lips and flat nose." (Whites were burdened with "ridiculous" woodpecker noses.) Later, Goude enlarged his appreciation of blacks. He admired what he considered their natural grace, their genius in dance improvisation, their magnificent physical features. "It is the somber [color] that inspires me." This darkness meant rhythm, a quality he associated particularly with American blacks. "Their walk seems to be choreographed, sometimes almost comic as a result of their flat feet and their highly perched rear ends." When Goude was young, he tried "desperately" but vainly to imitate the black walk. The more intellectual side of blackness never galvanized him, perhaps never penetrated. The politics of black power did not interest him, in part because it made him feel "left out." Their "comic-book rhetoric" left him cold. "My enthusiasm was aesthetic." Africa, mediated largely through America, became his lifelong passion, a passion both personal and professional.

Flashes of dark color illuminated an otherwise drab childhood existence in Saint-Mandé, "a predictable, gray, middle-class community" that Goude found "boringly normal." Avid to escape from this "nowhere," Goude discovered that the route to outbound and upward mobility was not to be the public school system, in which his performance was "lousy." He knew that he had "no future there," all the more so because his parents had "no money." Money would be a lifelong obsession for

Goude, along with art and blackness. He resented his father's lack of material success, and he became, in his own words, a "rich kids' hanger-on." His parents managed nevertheless to send him to dance and art schools. His mother's conviction that he had "a natural sense of rhythm"—a phrase that he often used to describe blacks—encouraged and motivated him, though he eventually understood that he would never make it in ballet—for the same reasons that spawned feelings of inadequacy in other spheres of his life: his legs were too short and he lacked a noble visage.

His real talent for drawing did not save him from expulsion from art school for missing too many classes in his second year. Still, this talent brought him his first success: an opportunity to paint frescoes on the walls of the Printemps department store when he was about twenty years old. Thereafter his drawings began to sell. The first thing he did when he marshaled enough money was to buy a secondhand Rolls Royce. "I paraded in my neighborhood without any sense of shame. You should have seen the neighbors' faces. Now, people will say to me: 'Ah, Negroes, they like things that shine. They like to show off.' Why not? I say, if you've never had much in your life, it's a tremendous thrill to sit your ass in a flashy car and just drive around."

Jungle Fever

Goude crafted an autobiographical album-text aptly entitled *Jungle Fever*. According to the critic of the *Los Angeles Times*, it was "surely the worst book of the season." *Punch* found the text amusing "in a sub–Norman Mailer manner." Black intellectuals, among others, read the book as evidence of Goude's racism.[5] *Jungle Fever* is to a great extent periodized in terms of the black women he encountered, colonized, and transformed. His relationshop with these women and with their Africanness seems profoundly ambivalent. Goude detects neither pathology nor exploitation. He recounts a lubricious Horatio Alger tale of an alchemist who turned black into gold, who not only realized many of his fantasies but also made money on them. Only in America? Perhaps, for that was where Goude found the action, succeeding brilliantly in the 1970s as photographer, artist, and then artistic director of the chic New York men's monthly *Esquire*.

But Paris apparently was the site of his first fully articulated fascination with Gargantuan black women. There he encountered Judith Jamison, an Alvin Ailey dancer: "She was so *huge*. I'd never seen a dancer so huge." She danced with "a little Puerto Rican boy" whose frail appearance contrasted starkly with her raw power. "For me it was a thrill to see a little guy my own size manipulate a six-foot-two-inch woman. It gave me hope; . . . he manipulated her with such machismo, such authority, it was incredible." In this epiphanous moment, Goude discovered or reaffirmed something resembling a vocation. He went on to manipulate a series of black women, to alter them, to make them larger than life, to play creatively, and perhaps sometimes maliciously, with physical, racial, and cultural stereotypes.

Sylvia, another Ailey dancer, was Goude's "first black girl," and the first person to tease him about what she called his "jungle fever," what he knew to be his Sabu self. On one level, Goude understood this fever as peculiar to his particular familial and cultural trajectory. On another, however, he seemed to phrase it as a symptom of a universal white man's obsession/dream that very few had the opportunity to live out. In bed with black women, Goude-Sabu freqently worried whether "my sexual performance was adequate and whether my partner would not be more fulfilled by a big black man." He interpreted this inquietude as illustrating "the jealousy that white men may have for the virility of blacks."

Goude had a Wonder Woman outfit made for Sylvia. "A black Wonder Woman! But it wasn't enough and I began to do other things to her." She was distressingly small, and Goude was determined to repair certain features, particularly her nose, that he found out of proportion. But the "very famous plastic surgeon" to whom he took her, it turned out upon inspection of his watercolors, had no artistic talent. "And since he couldn't draw, he couldn't sculpt, much less with flesh than with clay. So we skipped it."

His second black girlfriend was Radiah, whose Southern origins evoked for Goude his youthful discovery of James Brown—"You'd never hear James Brown on the French radio, it was too busy pushing our national stars"—at a small club in Montparnasse frequented by black American servicemen where he learned to love "funky black music, soulful dancing, ribs, fried chicken. . . . it was heaven." For Radiah, "a country girl" from Mobile, Alabama, Goude "devised the complete African look, with removable scars. This made the papers." But he wanted to "improve on her" even more. He decided to make her look seven feet tall, utilizing her giant Afro hairdo and elevator shoes hidden under a skintight dress made to match the color of her skin. Goude reveled in the juxtaposition of his smallness to her enormity. "With me at her side, looking like a midget, we'd go from party to party." "Do you love me?" he queried Radiah one day. "As much as I can love a white man," she replied, much to his gratification.

Next came Toukie, an androgynous nineteen-year-old beauty with a "pretty-boy's face, very short hair, and a voluptuous woman's body." Though she was not "that tall," happily for Goude she "*looked*" tall." He was enchanted with her "huge, long, long legs, big buttocks, powerful thighs, small calves." Since she was "a masterpiece of nature," Goude "naturally set about to see what I could do to improve her." Much of it he did vicariously, taking pictures of her, chopping them up, and reconstituting an image that "made her buns even bigger and exaggerated her proportions." He did the same with a life-size cast of her that he reduced to twelve-inch models and then reworked to endow her with a backside like a racehorse. "The real Toukie was a step in the right direction, but she was not quite like my drawings." Toukie found the role of "primitive voluptuous girl-horse" uncomfortable, obliging Goude to reforge his "dream" elsewhere. Goude later complained that he was denounced for racism when he expressed his fascination for the horselike behinds of black women. "But a racehorse is beautiful," he protested. What could cleanse him more spotlessly of the charge of bigotry than his conviction that "many white women would love to be thus compared"?

The last chapter of *Jungle Fever* is called "Grace." (Was the liturgical side of the image lost on the author?) The album section begins with an *imagined* photograph of Grace Jones, age seven, exposing her genitals on the porch of a shanty in Jamaica. ("Why not?" asks Goude, with a taste of vengeful acrimony after their split. "I show her as the natural exhibitionist she probably was. Certainly she has become one since.") It ends with a startling photograph of a masculinized Grace with blue-black skin, a black man's blazer or tuxedo, extremely broad shoulders, a partially bared, muscular chest, a flattop haircut, and a cigarette dangling from sensuous red lips. Though he "didn't realize it at the time," when he first saw Grace Jones, "I had already decided to work with her. She was exactly what I had been looking for all these years."

Grace Jones embodied the right mix of African regality, animality, and androgyny. That first encounter occurred in a "room full of shrieking gay [male] bobby-soxers," wildly energized by her rendition of "I Need a Man." The ambiguity of her act, Goude noted, "was that she herself *looked* like a man, a man singing I Need a Man to a bunch of men." Black, shiny, bare-chested, she oscillated in Goude's mind between the magnificent ("the great African beauty") and the grotesque ("the organ-grinder's monkey"). "Strangely, it was almost as though I had already drawn her before I met her," he later mused. "So when she did come along, she was the best expression of what I had been trying to draw. She was the true representation of all the attractiveness and beauties of the black women I had ever known. They all came together in Grace."

Goude seems to have had the same sort of relationship with Jones that he had with his earlier companions, though it appears to have been more intense, more public, and more professionally rewarding. Part of the allure of blackness to Goude seems to have been its cultural and psychological susceptibility to manipulation; its "primitive African" nature seems to have elicited his instrumentral-colonial response. "Grace let me make her over completely, use any effect I could find to turn her into what I wanted her to be." She proved to be "an ideal vehicle for my work," Goude related in one place; when she left him, he noted in another, "I [had] to find a new vehicle." Candidly narcissistic, in the end he was "no longer sure what I fell in love with, Grace or my idea of what Grace should be." He reworked the "African mask" of her face, darkening and sharpening her blackness, making it more threatening and more exotic. He focused on the raw and visceral parts of her mind and body, portraying her as liminally placed between savagery and civilization, unpredictable, protean, dangerous. In one act Jones, bedecked as a tiger, sang and snarled to a live tiger in a cage. Brusquely the lights went off, a tape played the sounds of two tigers engaged in violent battle. Then the lights and music returned, and Jones was singing and chewing on a slab of meat in the tiger cage.

In part animality was a form of aggrandizement; Goude remained preoccupiued with size. Onstage he crafted her as "a menacing eight-foot black silhouette." To his friends he confided, "I couldn't help exaggerating, making her appear bigger than life in every way." He was a cartoonist as well as a sculptor, and he was irresistibly drawn to the terrain between caricature and naturalism. But nothing seemed to move Goude more deeply than Jones's androgyny. He resonated with this special plastic beauty that "transcended" the gender of her sex. She gravitated between poles, conflating and combining them. Dressed conventionally as a woman, Goude discovered, she looked masculine. But when she dressed in male attire, her femininity was not merely restituted but enhanced. Onstage, and perhaps off as well, he made Grace "the threatening, blue-black, male-female, erotic menace I wanted her to be." One of the most striking photographs in his album is an imagined protrait of Grace Jones and a nonexistent twin brother, naked in front of a window overlooking the Eiffel Tower, exactly alike save for genitalia, body configuration, and lips, a male and a female version of the same person.

Sexuality is so salient in Goude's life and work that it would be obtuse to avoid speculation on its dynamic. An ambiguous sense of self and a bisexual flavor pervade his discourse. He appears to have an ambivalent attitude toward homosexuals. To a certain extent they worry and threaten him, surely in part because he sees his reflection in their midst. Connoisseur and exploiter of stereotypes, he was keenly aware that his professional and creative milieux were traditional loci of homosexuality. "I thought all dancers back then were gay," wrote Goude, in reference to a youthful stint as a student with the Joffrey Ballet, "so me, I talked about pussy all the time to discourage whoever I thought might be interested in me." He made allusion to "fruit bars," but the derision that such an ostensibly contemptuous phrase ought to have connoted lacked conviction.

Goude was of course quite conscious that he projected an ambiguous air. He styled himself a "heterosexual sissy." (In French the term conveys a sharper binary image: "tapette [fag] hétérosexuelle.") "I'm a special kind of person," he remarked, "I like androgynous women." The androgyny could take different forms, among them a more or less straightforward blurring of gender identity and masculinization through the exaggeration of size and other features. Each seems to afford the possibility of being in a homosexual relationship while remaining genitally in a heterosexual one. Goude's description of himself also invites speculation about masochistic fantasies, enacting childish impulses, and fleeing from parental reprimand. In a very different register, Goude's self-representation raises questions about the cultural legacy of French contact with Africa and Africans as well as about the French encounter with Americanized Africanness. These matters, and Goude's biographical trajectory in general, are worth looking at because of the light they shed on Goude's bicentennial creation. For the restless kid from Saint-Mandé became, for a short time, the most important person in France and the object of the whole world's attention.[6]

Making Images in France

After the *Esquire*–Grace Jones period, Goude apparently shifted much of his professional attention back to France. He became a major player in the French advertising business, imagining brilliant spots featuring strange, albeit sympathetic, gnomes in striped outfits and pointed caps, among other creations, for such prestigious clients as Kodak, Orangina, and Lee Cooper. "The grand image maker of consumer society," Goude found his medium in the frugal, impish, and insidious clip, thirty seconds in its long version, eight seconds in the short, which could be repeated thousands of times without tiring the viewer. Advertising professionals were struck by the volubility of his rapid-fire images, their capacity to tell a story. "If [Charles] Perrault were to return today, he would be called Jean-Paul Goude," declared *la force tranquille* of French advertising, Jacques Séguéla, known for his phrase-making talent.

Nothing impressed his peers more than his audacity, his innovative use of familiar techniques and his anticipation of new ones. By the mid-1980s he had become "the Annapurna of the most expensive advertising film directors, thus those most heavily in demand." Though he succeeded brilliantly in advertising, and found its mores and rhythms consonant with his temperament and taste, he fiercely resisted being pigeonholed. Art, after all, not selling, was his vocation: "I was not born in advertising; I am above all a commmercial artist who plays with illusions." Goude identified himself with Jean Cocteau and Andy Warhol, with the enormous rush of transient power, with magical transformation, with a carefully ordained blend of humor and frenzy, with ultramodern technology, with self-dramatization, with mundane success and moderate defiance.[7]

To pull it off, commented Charles Gassot, the film producer hired by the Mission to work with Goude, "we needed a mad man." But, as *Libération* put it, the man described "as a manic person, a clone of the little shaken-up characters who people his commercials, is in reality quite remote from this image." He was a serious businessman, Tintin in an invisible gray flannel suit, a scrupulous professional who knew how to plan and execute as well as erupt. His friends depicted him as a pragmatic visionary, a doer and shaker who knew how to modify his "fantastic ideas" in order to meet clients' objections. He was indeed an artist ("It is to the *artiste* that one turned," journalist Olivier Salvatori plaintively noted), but an artist who knew how to play the artist's card to advance his interests.

Approached in September 1988, he responded less rapidly and less rhapsodically than certain observers reported. "I have not yet signed," Goude told *Figaro-Magazine* at the end of October. Once he signed, he revealed himself to be astonishingly inept in presenting—selling?—his product to the press, whose skepticism for the bicentennial he was supposed to overcome swiftly. Before the regional press in a chic mansion in the sixteenth arrondissement, his cryptic talk of "tribes" and his emphasis on African themes provoked disarray. At a huge press conference at the Palais-Royal in June, alongside Lang and Jeanneney, Goude proved incapable of articulating his ambitions: "Here are my notes."

Even as he explored the creative horizon, he negotiated adeptly to obtain the sort of freedom and insulation—not to mention the huge remuneration—he needed. Avowedly mesmerized by money, he refused to reveal the sum he would make, the equivalent of what he could earn during a year of advertising work. "I am not Americanized enough for that," he remarked, betraying the limits of a double cultural identity. The artist was acutely jealous of his creative prowess, which was less the expression of the "authentic megalomania" ascribed to him by the *Nouvel Observateur* than of the temperament of the "spoiled child" detected by Monique Sauvage. Goude was furious when Chirac's Eiffel Tower show on 17 June 1989 borrowed ("filched," he cried) elements from the design that the Mission had shown to the mayor and his entourage earlier in the year. (Just how much responsibility did Goude wish to claim? Dupavillon, taste maker supreme, dismissed Chirac's show as "a pure horror.") The mayor's staff indignantly turned the reproach back against Goude, who allegedly had "borrowed" from the stillborn but grandiose plans of Jean-Michel Jarre.[8]

Goude's Instructions

Dupavillon narrowed the government's conditions to three imperatives: extol the *Marseillaise*, which celebrated a bellicosity that metamorphosed into an irenic summons to fraternity; represent the participation of all the provinces of France (and, by extension, the rest of the world) in the Revolutionary experience, with or without explicit reference to the Festival of the Federation (14 July 1790) that the national holiday is supposed to commemorate, and do it all on the Champs-Elysées. "The project is too serious to allow me to be smug," Goude declared to *Communication et business*, "this is going to make me read the history of France." But once he accepted the assignment, it is not likely that he spent an inordinate amount of time reviewing the elements of Revolutionary history (texts) and historiography (interpretations) with which Dupavillon and Jeanneney provided him. It was not that he was allergic to learning. (His repeated assertion, "I'm not an educated person," though not entirely false, was largely a ploy to disarm and manipulate; Dupavillon, given to adman's hyperbole, gushed over Goude's "formidable cultivation"). Rather, he knew himself and he knew how he worked; or, as he expressed it, "one can only do what one is."

Quite rapidly, he seems to have decided what he would do. His method was simple: "When I was a kid in Saint-Mandé, I began by drawing, then I imagined the story. I do not proceed any differently today." Mona Ozouf, the leading expert in the field of Revolutionary festivals, who herself believed in the futility of rigorous historicization in the service of commemoration, absolved Goude of the need to study the past when he called on her for advice: "Above all don't force the poor man to undergo a thesis defense!" Surely because he knew it so poorly and encountered it habitually in its most commodified and etiolated forms, Goude was suspicious of history. As a spectator on the scene in New York, he recalled the centennial show for the Statue of Liberty as "pitiful," with hordes of anomic ciphers "dressed in period clothing, with the wig on crooked." One wonders if he anticipated how perfectly his determination "to avoid all the *cocardises, jacobineries, guillotineries*" would gratify his tutors.[9]

Had Jean-Noël Jeanneney been a more rigorously conventional intellectual, he might have had real difficulty with Dupavillon's inclinations. After all, if advertising was the leading idiom of modern public discourse, its ethics were hardly a model for the practice of civism in the public sphere: truth is what sells. (Or as philosopher Alain Finkielkraut mordantly put it, "it must be clearly understood that the consecration of advertising is necessarily tantamount to the destitution of the professors"—Jeanneney's tribe, after all.) Now the president of the Mission did not endorse the truth = sales aphorism as Weltanschauung, but he accepted it as a fundamental fact of the sociocultural and economic landscape.

Nothing seemed more important to Jeanneney than to reach as many people as possible on 14 July, and to draw as many celebrants as possible to the Champs-Elysées ("two or three million people"). He was virtually obsessed with the idea of making the fourteenth a "grand popular fête," an objective that he voiced repeatedly. "We must put on a fête," he told a national television audience; he sermonized the print media on "the necessity of making this commemoration into a true popular fête"; "the crucial thing is to put on a very beautiful fête," he confided on national radio. If the size of the crowd was the primordial criterion of the fête's "popularity," certain conditions had to obtain in order to guarantee its festiveness and its festive populism. It had to elicit joviality, joy, even jubilation in a sort of dialogic exchange between public and spectacle. (Given the difficulty of actively engaging two to three million persons, this must have been the sense in which Jeanneney declared: "My greatest concern in this matter is to avoid putting on a show that will be presented to a wholly passive audience; rather, [I want] to get the public to participate.")[10]

In order to achieve this goal, the festival makers had to refrain from making excessive pedagogical demands on the public. Echoing Ozouf and Dupavillon, Jeanneney asserted that "the fête must not be a lesson in history or civics." The rejection of "any form of historical reconstitution" was an article of faith from the beginning for the Mission. It was less a question of Ozouf's concern with the central commemorative aporia than of the master of ceremonies' fear of boring the expectant crowd and provoking yawns and the zapping reflex in televiewers. The assumption underlying the rejection of history as incompatible with fête seems puzzling in a nation that knows better than any other how to make history exciting, even breathtaking. There was a touch of condescension in the idea that the masses could not resonate with historical cues. There was perhaps also a loss of nerve on the part of Jeanneney the historian, himself a masterful writer and brilliant lecturer capable of astonishing transports of imagination, who was tired of reading in the press that "nourished on history, we always think like professors: speeches and sermons."

The custodians of elite culture are always uneasy about their relation to popular culture and are especially susceptible to something resembling mystification when they attempt to stage popular culture for the masses. The cult of popular culture often turns out to be mere cant. The president of the Mission quite correctly criticized the Debrayists for a somewhat overbearing and austere vision of merrymaking by didactic gavage. But was a dish of bicentennial "lite" (or was it rather commemorative junk food masquerading as health food?) the sole palatable alternative? Jeanneney was right to upbraid "the supercilious attitude of such and such an intellectual affecting disdain for" the festive pleasures. But the reproach seemed again to be premised on the notion that true festiveness was necessarily a mindless excursion.

Yet Jeanneney was certainly not a proponent of empty calories. As if to conjure the demon, he warned time and again against the peril of "gratuitousness—fête for the sake of fête." After having invested so heavily in civic schooling, however, it does not seem unreasonable for Jeanneney to have wanted a climactic moment of light-hearted and convivial fun and to have wanted to frame it in terms of a "contemporary sensibility," a language of ultramodernity that would make people alert to the connections between past and present, especially the young people, whom Jeanneney believed had a deep affinity for "the art of advertising."[11]

In an informal but fundamentally political sense, Dupavillon remained Goude's boss even as he had been his recruiter. Lang's collaborator described himself as an ideal patron and protector. His strategy was disarmingly simple; though it conveys a self-serving air in retrospect, given Dupavillon's artistic temperament and experience, it is quite plausible. Once he selected Goude, he gave him his "entire confidence." He believed in him so manifestly, recounts Dupavillon himself, that "[Goude] was always astonished that I said yes" to his most adventurous ideas. They shared certain ambitions that proved impossible to realize, such as the plan to evoke the Federation spirit by having corteges of musicians from the various regions arrive on foot carrying instruments and perhaps bearing grievances. On delicate matters, it was almost always Dupavillon to whom Goude turned. This privileged relation with Dupavillon(-Lang) pained and embarrassed Jeanneney, to whom Goude felt accountable only in a platonic way. Jeanneney's inability to exercise effective artistic or administrative control left him exposed and vulnerable. Goude enraged him, for example, when he allowed *Libération* to publish some of his parade plans as an exclusive scoop without obtaining the authorization of the Mission president. Goude had ventilated the matter with Dupavillon.

Dupavillon treated Goude as a sort of personalized neoclassical market: "I let things go their own way"; and Goude "corrected his own course" as he went along. Dupavillon protected *l'artiste* from administrative harassment, this being how

Goude construed the need to seek administrative authorization or to practice constant accountability. Unblinking but not imprudent, Dupavillon obtained daily intelligence reports on Goude's activities, and he conferred with him about once a week. While virtually everyone else quivered more or less frantically, Dupavillon insists that the Goude project inspired "not a single fear." He claims that he was much more worried about the prefect's sepulchral prediction—a kind of sociohygienic projection—that at least sixteen people were likely to die in the crowd on the night of the show.[12]

The ordinary task of channeling and monitoring Goude's art fell to the Mission. It served as producer of the show, with administrative responsibility for its content, preparation, finances, and so on. As "executive producer," it subcontracted the day-to-day operational command to Charles Gassot, head of the Téléma production company, who had recently won accolades for his film *La Vie est un long fleuve tranquille*, a masterful piece of bittersweet ethnography and burlesque. An experienced show maker, Gassot understood the imperatives of accountability, celerity, and efficiency, and he had worked with Goude before—one of his collaborators, Pascal Ortéga, knew Goude well and was assigned as his liaison—thus enhancing the chances of harmonious collaboration with *l'artiste*. Téléma helped assess the feasibility of Goude's notions and provided ongoing evaluations of the cost of realization.

Determined not to exceed his budget by a sou, Jeanneney used his cunning to expand the resource base by obtaining the massive logistic support of the armed forces, transportation assistance from the Parisian subway and national railroad companies, and supplementary cash for the production from commercial/institutional sponsors and donors. Though agreed upon in principle, the big television contracts required arduous negotiations, and were not signed till 11:00 P.M. one night in late June 1989.

Meanwhile, Goude had begun to draw, and he regularly submitted his sketchbook to Jeanneney and his senior staff for their opinion. Monique Sauvage was very much taken with his "poetry," and his lyric talent for converting ideas into images, though she did worry at the beginning about the problem of translating those images into some form of theatrical reality. Confronted with endless sketches of big women and little men, Goude's fantasy predilection, Jeanneney must have had to strive hard to resist the temptation to subject them to therapeutic analysis. Though Goude fixed upon a number of the critical leitmotifs from the outset, notably the ethnic pluralism and the gallimaufry of rhythms, he went through six scenarios until the definitive version was agreed on in mid-March.[13]

Scenarios and Clichés of Fraternity

The physical setting rather than the theme dictated the genre of entertainment that Goude appropriated. The imposing site of the Champs-Elysées, an immense arena (2.3 kilometers in length, affording a stage of seventy-two thousand square meters) that would be lined by hundreds of thousands of spectators, required some sort of moving theatre. Goude envisioned not merely an elaborate procession, but an ambulatory variety show combining music, vaudeville, opera, dance, allegory, pictorial and cinematic image, sketch. It was to be both more and less than a parade.[14] It would have the elaborate orchestration, ornamentation, and ostentation of a parade, but not its pompousness. Like the burlesque *parade* of the Old Regime fairs, it would have a dimension of farce, but not of the authentically coarse grade. It would be ludic and mirthful in spirit rather than ceremonial and solemn. It would beguile by fantasy rather than flummery.

The parade genre generated its own restrictions in terms of complexity, engineering, timing, acoustics, viewability, magnitude of participation, and so on. Goude had only two hours, the endless time of hundreds of clips painstakingly prepared in studio conditions but the terrifyingly fleeting time of a live show involving thousands of inadequately trained elements. He was constrained by the security requirements of the summit, he had to defer to the imperatives of television, and he had to showcase the singing of the *Marseillaise*. And if he did everything else right, short of obtaining the intercession of Sainte Geneviève, the patron of Paris specialized in meteorological affairs, he could not be sure that rain would not ruin the whole evening.

The problem of decoding and recoding, or incorporating, the governing theme was clearly secondary to the choice of genre. Understandably, Goude was somewhat daunted by the Revolution. It was not a part of his culture, intellectual or political. He did little to overcome his estrangement from it. He recognized it as a momentous event, and he felt instinctively that its ramifications continued to affect the world. "For me, it's first of all human rights," he allowed, demonstrating that he was fully in tune with the average Frenchman. "The rest is only a memory." But he does not seem to have pondered deeply the significance of the Revolution. When he discussed it, he used a stilted, formalistic language that betrayed his malaise (for example, "I cannot really evoke the French Revolution and its sufferings, it's too far away").

It is interesting to note in passing that Goude may indeed have acquired a visceral sense of the meaning of the generic phenomenon of revolution when he was in China, in the midst of preparing his bicentennial show, at the moment of Tiananmen. That experience probably informed his work in subtle ways. Plainly, however, he was relieved when his patron-clients acquitted him of any historicizing responsibility at the very outset. Whatever it may have meant, "the Revolution, narrowly viewed in performance-showbiz terms," observed Goude, "is a very hard thing to put on." Aside from the fact that historical reconstitution "was not my turf," Goude esteemed that with six months rather than two years to mount his spectacle, it would have been folly not do do what he did best.[15]

What Goude did best was to rework clichés and stereotypes, as he did in his ad-making shop, in a metaphorical strategy of *décalage*. He took images that were familiar to him or that appealed to him, and he endowed them with the task of evocation, of echo, of tantalizing, but rarely in a transparent or one-dimensional manner. *Décalage* implied displacement and distancing, a playing out of a theme indirectly, obliquely, paradoxically, at a remove in time and space. It was a way of achieving concordance through discordance, a high-risk cognitive technique that depended utterly on the power of its aesthetic to be compelling. *Décalage* was the device that linked past and present, that imperceptibly became the metaphor for a powerful, corrosive but constructive force resembling the idea of progress, reified unevenly across time and space. This was the way in which Goude could forge the single-world identity without didactic bludgeoning and without sacrificing the medley of national/cultural differences. This was what provided the license for "world music" ("For me," said Goude, "the true Revolution is the birth of a world sound"), the chief vector of fraternity, especially among the young people of the end of the twentieth century. This was the Revolution of Goude's generation, and of the MTV generation: "The Phrygian cap and the guillotine, thank you, no. I celebrate the Revolution of modern times. Thus the crossbreeding of cultures."

Because it was something Goude felt and believed in, because it was a simple yet grand idea that incarnated gentle, consensual revolution ("which got everyone to agree"), he made "the fraternity among people" the unifying theme of his show. "There is a boy-scout side to my personality, colored with a rather simple kind of militancy," he avowed; "all men are equal, despite ethnic and cultural differences, and they must be able to get along."[16] The adept manipulation of stereotypes, each marching to its own music but "to the same beat," produced the United Colors of Goude. One man's Benetton/Baden Powell was another man's Revolutionary Aesop. Thus Jeanneney read the moral of the project with earnest satisfaction as "the diversity of the reception elicited by the revolutionary message, which gave it all its power and its influence."[17]

The play of stereotypes proved a parlous game for Goude. On the one hand, he felt comfortable with them to the extent that they obeyed a logic of irony. Irony rescued them from mere banality, and redeemed Goude intellectually inasmuch as it proved that he was not the dupe of his own images. In presenting his project to his Soviet collaborators, for instance, Goude expressly disavowed "a *traditional* revolutionary reconstitution"—the formula was interesting, perhaps consciously paradoxical, meant to convey the anachronism and decadence of certain commemorative practices in a postperestroika world—in favor of a "ballet" of revolutionary elements drawn from many countries "with a kind of irony." When a Soviet choreographer indignantly objected that Goude's suggestion of marrying a comely woman dancer to a goose-stepping soldier was a violation of the rules, "a parody" of graceful movement, Goude exploded jovially: "But of course! But of course! It's a parody, that's the whole idea." In the name of *décalage*, he did not want a *real* revolutionary walk; this was contrary to the Gorbachevian spirit, he noted wittily. Otherwise, we might just as well have a straightforward military march.[18]

On the other hand, the play of stereotypes could give offense; Lang and Jeanneney repeatedly admonished Goude to avoid the peril of "derision." In lieu of ominous irony the artist embraced reassuring benignity. "It's the tender application of stereotypes that I was seeking," affirmed Goude in retrospect. So, for example, his use of the peasant clog, the *sabot*, which he sought to "ennoble, just as the parade was ennobled by Cocteau and Balanchine." He did not view the *sabot* as "synonymous with mud, with an outdated and comic peasantry," but "as a beautiful object that produces a beautiful sound when it strikes the paving stones, and it's that which I wanted to emphasize." The same principle applied to his version of folkloric clothing, to which many of the French musicians strenuously objected ("he is ridiculing our music and our traditions"). It was "their sublimation that I wanted to obtain."

The flight from "derision" led him "on several occasions to come close to preciosity as a result of all the adjustments." As a case in point he cited his giant dark-skinned waltzing women. They were supposed to be Islamic women, Maghrébines, but the paucity of willing "young Arab women with a theatrical streak" forced him into a double *décalage*. Antillean dancers and an African American model replaced them. ("In any event there are millions of black Muslims; as far as the message is concerned, the dancers remain Muslim waltzing women as I revised them.") Each woman, fitted in a giant black gown set on a motorized float, was paired in an ingenuously erotic embrace with a young boy dressed to represent one of the world's many cultures (for example, a lad in a red Canadian Mountie's uniform). But in the name of gentle, offsetting stereotypes, the two protagonists among the children were an Israeli and a Palestinian—"which I was able to do thanks to the agreement of Jacques Attali, because people on my staff were afraid of the complications that this could cause." Goude alluded to the summit and the diplomatic sensibilities of the G-7 and Third World leaders, and incidentally testified to the rigor with which he was monitored.[19]

Goude's gyroscope was intuition, not critical sociology. For him, stereotypes were innocent and in some sense socially natural and legitimate: "If they exist, it's because they have a reason for existing and they say something." Goude acknowledged, however, that his valorisation of stereotypes had caused him some problems, notably in the United States. Fascinated by music, rhythms, and images, he was especially taken with the culture of black America. But his enthusiasm was not always well received, for reasons that he still does not appear fully to appreciate: "But, if I speak to an overly conventional black American intellectual about my admiration for the sense of rhythm of black people, he calls me a racist, reminding me of the accomplishments of blacks in the fields of medecine and the sciences. These are domains about which I know nothing; after all, I can't organize a parade of surgeons! Even done respectfully, the utilization of stereotypes gets you accused of racism."

There is an echo of Goude's attitude in the way French citizens visiting Harlem for the first time used to behave. Their Frenchness gave them a right of entry that white Americans could never claim, for France was a renowned place of refuge for black American musicians, writers, and artists, or so the logic credibly went. But its unspoken corollary is much more problematic: that French people somehow are not susceptible to the sorts of racist thinking that shape American views. Many French people of Goude's generation, among others, seem curiously oblivious to the African colonial experience of France and to the shadowy black presence with which it invested French life on many planes.

In an extraordinarily blasé and naive declaration, a revealing non sequitur, Goude affirmed that: "My conception [of blackness] is free of all social connotations because I am European." Then he continued, with gradually increasing plausibility, to pose some of the dilemmas of black-white relations and white-white relations concerning blacks, regardless of the particular cultural/national context:

> Americans cannot dissociate themselves from the social implications of their artistic evalution of black people. Liberals [the American left] are afraid of being mistaken for flippant, superficial, or frivolous in this kind of artistic evaluation. As for conservatives, of course their artistic evaluation is nil to begin with. . . . So I really find myself in a strange situation, because, on the one hand, liberals are embarrassed by my attitude, while racists ironically misinterpret me as one of them.

"And the blacks?" Goude finally asks, almost as an afterthought. He answers with disarming frankness and circumspection: "I'm not sure; I think that my conception may appeal to some with a sensibility similar to mine. I'm not sure." Even as it gained him entrée, his Frenchness, and its particular hubris, may have foreclosed his gaze and occluded his understanding about certain crucial aspects of African American life, and about the play between dominant and ambiguously insurgent cultures. Goude seems very French indeed in his failure to grasp the social violence of much hip-hop inspiration, and the combustible imbrication of race and class. He embraced the good-natured facet of hip-hop, in the same sense in which his protector Jack Lang associated rap with the commedia dell'arte.[20]

The theme, then, of Goude's show was fraternity understood in a number of more or less complementary ways under the universalist title of "the fête of the planetary tribes." Though remote from French bicentennial consciousness, motley, hybridized Brazil was in many ways the perfect metaphor and instrument of his conception: "Brazil is the ideal for my project, neither African nor Indian nor Portuguese but all of them at the same time." To counterpoise this extremely general and often exotic inflection, which seemed to evacuate the specificity of the Revolutionary commemoration, Goude accorded a major role to the countries identified as having a particularly significant "revolutionary past," England, the United States, the USSR, and China, in addition to France. The pervasive African presence, representing the rest of the world—especially the Third World—can be construed in a number of ways. On the one hand, the Africans were victims of the colonization of Europeans who spoke the language of the rights of man, Europeans against whose oppression they fought in the name of revolutionary values first articulated in the so-called mother countries. On the other hand, Goude viewed (generic) Africans as victors rather than victims, colonizers of the colonizers: "however great were the tribulations of the peoples of African origin throughout the world in the social sphere, it is beyond question that in the musical sphere negritude permeated the entire surface of the planet."

Apart from the West, which it had infiltrated and conquered in part through black-American mediation, the African influence extended around the globe. Rebuffed on a trip to India by "a great Indian woman dancer" who rejected out of hand the idea of compromising the purity of national traditions, Goude encountered the timid beginnings of "fusion" in the music he heard that same night in his hotel. In the Russian heartland, Goude spent the day listening to the music of monastery bells while at night, even in this remote zone, he watched Soviet youth on the dance floor of a disco in his hotel trying "somewhat awkwardly to reproduce African body movements on a background of Michael Jackson's music."

In Goude's discourse, however, it is not clear whether Africa captured the West or the West appropriated Africa through a kind of cultural strip-mining. In discussing, for example, the marriage of break dancing and traditional Chinese dance forms, Goude describes "eternal China self-consciously associating itself with the influence of the West," a museum and studio of African rhythms. Goude supposes a sort of perfect harmony or fit between African and Western cultures in the musical sphere. There is no relief in his topography, no ambiguity, no tension. This serenity is startling and wholly implausible, save perhaps on the level of cliché. Equally unsettling is the calculus Goude used to measure the influence of African-based music in its home away from home, the United States. Proving himself more American than he was inclined to admit, he observed: "Their music has greater impact than their political rhetoric: the multimillionaires in the United States are Quincy Jones [and] Michael Jackson. Not Jesse Jackson."

In any event, "a subtheme in this parade," which Goude claims he avoided emphasizing publicly—yet how could one miss it?—was "African rhythmics." For Goude there was no doubt that it was the appropriate leaven in the bicentennial ferment: "To have groups of French traditional musicians play a symphony written by a composer of African origin [Wally Badarou of Benin] who synthesizes Western and African rhythms, now that's revolutionary." For a world audience—the artist tended to look beyond the confines of the bicentennial homeland—what could be more suitable than world music?

One wonders whether Goude recognized in the drum not only the African signature but also the sound of revolution. The drum evokes the crowd in its differential intensity, in its oscillation between urgency and patience, its tension between passion and reason, its negotiation between disorder and order, war and peace, mourning and celebration. For Goude, however, it was the mood picture and not the ideation and its historical referents that mattered. Despite his expressed disdain for a show of stars (the vulgar model of which for this unevenly Americanized French artist was the quintessentially American Macy's Thanksgiving Day parade with its covey of gaping stars vapidly planted in the passing floats), Goude's bicentennial "summum," he avowed, would have been a gyrating Tina Turner astride a Brazilian drum.[21]

Around the World with Goude: Genius, Resistance, Accommodation

Even before his definitive scenario was ready, Goude began the task of mobilizing the thousands of artists he would need to play their music and dance and march down the Champs-Elysées. Pascal Ortéga set up a recruitment network in the French provinces, using classified advertisements, newspaper articles and interviews, and institutional connections. Auditions, and later rehearsals, were held in gymnasiums and festival halls throughout the country. Wally Badarou, the principal composer for the show, worked in Paris with the leaders of the provincial groups. The twelve hundred amateur musicians came together for the first time at Parthenay in the Deux-Sèvres in early May. Deeply moved by the way in which the players coalesced and by the effects of the traditional instruments playing Badarou's march, Monique Sauvage felt sure, for the first time, that it would all work in July. Goude was a taskmaster who wanted to leave nothing to chance. He had some difficulty conveying his carnavalesque vision of attaining creative disorder through regimented order. "It's bizarre, but in our country order = fascism," he complained. "Yet order brings out the striking qualities of creative frenzy. If one merely adds frenzy to frenzy, the two cancel each other out." The Goude team, some fifty strong, set up its technical headquarters in the vast space of the then abandoned Musée du Jeu de Paume in the Tuileries. Computers sat next to sewing machines, planners toiled alongside seamstresses, maps and designs posted on the walls marked the itinerary. Meanwhile Goude traveled around the world, looking for talent and personnel to match his ideas, seeking inspiration for creation, negotiating with various political and artistic authorities in order to win cooperation. He did not always have an easy time in establishing fruitful working relations. He elicited, according to his own reports, a certain incredulity. In appearance and manner, apparently he did not correspond to what his interlocutors expected, and he had to strain to overcome their unwillingness to take him seriously.[22]

The Soviets were particularly skeptical and recalcitrant. "I always had the impression that they never really believed in our thing," lamented Goude. He made five separate trips to the Soviet Union in an effort to obtain what he wanted. "They tried to pass off on us third-rate groups of folk performers." Goude hoped to organize the Soviet parade around the goose-stepping drill of the guards at Lenin's Tomb, what he called "the Kremlin step that I consider a magnificent dance—I see it as a dance and not as a military march."

The Soviets seemed to suspect a caricatural trap, and they evinced little enthusiasm. Goude felt insulted and scandalized when they offered him a "a middle-aged troop, some with little bulging bellies, others bald-headed," to perform this virile dancing march. How could the nation with the world's greatest athletes and dancers allow its youth to be represented so shabbily? In Goude's estimation, it was the Soviets who were guilty of caricature, a position he was able to communicate only after the intervention of Lang, and the wives of both Mitterrand and Gorbachev, thanks to whom the Soviet army agreed to supply the heroic types he coveted. Even then the Soviets took umbrage at the costume proposed, which seemed to evoke the czarist rather than the revolutionary past.

For another part of the Soviet tableau, Goude imagined a homage to the artistic movement called constructivism, the futurist cult of the machine born on the morrow of the Russian Revolution with the goal of overcoming the artist's isolation from society. The kinetic and dynamic elements employed by the constructivsts to express the true nature of time resonated with Goude's own aesthetic inclinations. More concretely, a London encounter with a young Soviet designer and a television performance by a Soviet rock group testified to the renascent influence of constructivism in the contemporary artistic world.

Though a Soviet minister expressed interest in the project, Goude could not obtain the choreographer he sought. He was sent to talk with Boris Heffman, director of an important Soviet dance company on tour in Zurich. While Heffman was very much taken with Olivier Bloch-Lainé's musical mélange of Stravinsky and machine-tool sounds on a background of African rhythm, he did not seem really convinced. When Goude asked one of the Soviet choreographer's dancers to try the constructivist costume that he had conceived, "she became red with shame, believing this grotesque costume to be an invention of the decadent French!" In retrospect Goude declared that "we could have recruited phoney Russians, but we wanted to do things according to the rules." In fact, in the end he had to use several dancers from the Lido, for Heffman showed up in Paris only two days before the show without his company, and he improvised a constructivist choreography on the avenue Foch.[23]

With the English Goude encountered problems not with conception but with execution. His framing cliché was the notorious cross-Channel weather, for which the choreographer, Lea Anderson, fashioned a ballet on the theme of the head cold. Every forty-five seconds, the dancers, mostly whites with several Jamaicans, emphatically sneezed, "which punctuated the funky beat infused with Indian songs, accompanying twenty other dancers, all Indians, in order to make it clear that London is not peopled exclusively by Cockneys." Unseasonably cold weather wrought a disaster at the grand rehearsal, which ended at six o'clock in the morning. Soaked by the constant flow of artificial rain, chilled to the bone, and exhausted, ten members of the troop ended up in the hospital, and the others revolted, refusing to march and dance in the rain, "which deprived the choreography of a large measure of its meaning."

As if in solidarity with the English insurgents, the male elephant, rented from an English circus, became ill. Without his leadership, the other pachyderms could not march, and Goude was deprived of an important element in his pageant. Few of his animal fantasies came true. He had to renounce the plan to accompany his Provençal musicians with one thousand sheep, primarily because these beasts had fragile hearts, and experts predicted that at least fifty would collapse on the Champs-Elysées.[24]

Nor were frictions limited to the foreign companies. Goude faced what he rightly called "a 'Frondish' mood among a part of the French musical contingent." Antimilitarism led some to protest the martial marching step. Many took offense at the costumes: flaring Bermudas, striped socks, desert boots, and a helmet that carried a lamp to illuminate the musician. "Forget tradition. Have faith in me. We're going to astonish the whole world," the pageant maker exhorted and promised them. But they remained suspicious of the adman, the Parisian, perhaps also the cosmopolitan. What struck them as callous burlesque that wounded their sense of regional and artistic pride and violated their idea of authenticity, Goude regarded as his signature: "I cannot conceive them otherwise, for that's my mark." Here he drew the line: he would not tolerate interference with "my creative work." In his *tour de France*, Goude experienced some of the same frustration that certain *représentants en mission* encountered during the Terror: "In each little village, we had our quasi-official critic."

Considerations of time and money constrained Goude to abandon another idea that probably would have provoked resistance and reproach. He would have liked to insert a film clip during the descent of the Florida A & M Marching Band on 14 July (clearly the television shaped much of his creative thinking) showing a jailhouse interview with James Brown—"certainly the most influential musician, the most imitated in the whole popular musical world"—followed by a rendition in front of the prison by David Byrne of the Talking Heads ("Always preoccupied with balance, I had in mind white America in turning to David Byrne"), accompanied by the entire Florida A & M band, of his hit song "Mister Jones," transmogrified for the occasion into "Mister James." Goude's self-evaluation was perfectly lucid: "That could have turned out moving or comical, in any event at the limits of bad taste."[25]

The director of the Florida A & M Marching Band, a skilled musician and conductor named William P. Foster, regarded Goude as a "true genius." In this instance and in others, Goude had trouble historicizing himself rigorously and consistently. As long as Quincy Jones, one of his major idols, was supposed to "serve as grand patron" of the entire musical dimension of the parade, Goude credited him with proposing the marching band and introducing him to his friend Foster. Later Goude preferred to attribute the connection to his own memory of an American television show a decade earlier. In any case, he paid two visits to the Florida campus to prepare the band's bicentennial role. He spent little time in historical acculturation. After a summary evocation of Bastille Day—one wonders about the intellectual and psychological transition from the joy-in-liberating-violence of 14 July 1789 to the jubilation-in-peaceful-fraternity that Goude wished to illustrate—Goude turned primarily to the requirements of pageantry. "He wanted us to put on a great show," recalls Dr. Foster, "that's what he stressed."

Impressed by his "amazing high energy," the Floridians had no clear idea about Goude's global strategy, or what Foster called the "inside implications," until their arrival in Paris. These black Americans were stunned to discover the centrality of the African motif and presence in the whole spectacle. Goude himself was responsible for the choreography of the Florida marching band, and he collaborated on the orchestration of their pieces. Foster, the black American educator-musician, remains indebted to black-on-white Goude for introducing him to "the magic of James Brown's riffs." Goude demonstrated his delight with the Floridians, whose rehearsals electrified the Parisian onlookers, by shifting them from seventh to last position in the parade, where they were charged with the honor of effecting a torrential finale.[26]

The China story was the most exciting and the most poignant episode in Goude's odyssey. He visited China in February to ferret out the youthful Chinese break-dancers about whom he had heard. Captivated by the traditional choreography of the Peking Opera, his imagination rushed toward "a fusion between the ancestral body movements of the opera and the contribution of the break dance." Assured of the cooperation of the director of one of the Peking operas, whose dancers secretly practiced African American break steps, Goude put together "a revolutionary ballet glorifying the Long March to an Afro-Chinese beat."

When he returned for rehearsals, he found Tiananmen occupied and the city in effervescence. Some of the acrobats assigned to the show by the army came from the regiment that would later have prime responsibility for the repression. Goude moved ahead full steam, overcoming the ethical and aesthetic objections of a colonel ("the army accepted the funky rhythm") and persuading the male dancers to don military garb and the female dancers to combine fan-dance with martial-arts steps. The choreography was powerful and sensual, witty and grave, ferociously expressionistic and subtly understated, a stunning marriage of Harlem and Peking. For Goude "it was the most ambitious part of the show, the part that took the most time."

The bloody crushing of the democratic movement put a stark end to the Chinese bicentennial role. "As a matter of decency," averred Goude, "my first reaction had been to eliminate any reference to China." Jack Lang convinced him that this idea was ill founded, that the Chinese should not feel forgotten, "that the moment had to be marked." The minister of culture instinctively understood that in a gruesomely perverse way, the horrors of Tiananmen were a stroke of luck for the bicentennial commemorators. As a reporter for *Libération* noted, "It was the Chinese students, intoning the *Marseillaise* on Tiananmen Square, who restituted to the memory of the great Revolution its dimension of emotion and tragedy." It would have been foolish not to surf on this emotional wave; or, to put it less crudely, not to echo and thereby honor the courage of the Chinese demonstrators. Thus the decision to have scores of Chinese students in France descend the Champs-Elysées pushing bicycles representing their absent comrades, preceded by flag lancers whose chests were inscribed with the Chinese characters for "Liberty-Equality-Fraternity," the same words that adorned the T-shirts worn by the Chinese dancers during their rehearsals in Peking. "I wanted to avoid a sentimental evocation of the Revolution," commented Goude. "And all of a sudden I inherited a tragedy."[27]

In some ways the most exotic recruitment for Goude's show took place right at home, and illustrated incidentally some of the Bastilles that remained to be conquered in the multiracial, multicultural France of the late twentieth century. Apparently it would have been prohibitively costly to transport to Paris 386 genuine natives to play the roles of the "Senegalese skirmishers" who had fought in the French army. Instead Goude's crew sought to hire African surrogates in seventeen specialized dormitory-houses for foreign workers in the capital and its environs. Sylla Samba, an unemployed driver representing thirty-seven Malian immigrants from a worker-dormitory in the nineteenth arrondissement, went to the Jeu de Paume in search of a statement in writing that would enable his compatriots to absent themselves from their work in order to participate in the show.

In certain houses, the immigrant workers asked for a period of reflection before deciding whether to participate, apparently because they feared some sort of administrative trap that might deprive them of their right of sojourn or livelihood. In the sansculottic tradition (which in fact long preceded the Revolution) of reasonable and prudent paranoia in a world governed by conspiracies, one group of Malians, when they learned that they would be taken for a rehearsal to the military airport of Villacoublay, worried that they would suffer "the trick of the Charter-for-Mali," that is, the tactic of sudden, peremptory deportation that Chirac's government had used in the past. The first rehearsals were difficult for the subway workers and janitors and dishwashers who were given a crash lesson in military drill in order to make convincing skirmishers. According to Le Monde, "Jean-Paul Goude agreed to dress them in a sable jacket because they found it somewhat degrading to march bare-chested."[28]

A prodigious amount of labor went into the preparations for the show, which in turn caused enormous logistical and technical problems. Approximately seven thousand costumes had to be manufactured, along with fifteen hundred flags, thousands of special lamps, and other accessories. Not universally averse to reconstitution, Goude had built a twenty-seven-meter replica of the locomotive of Zola's eponymous bête humaine, belching smoke and blaring its whistle, the symbol of another sort of revolution. The pyramid for the Guinean drummers was 8.5 meters in height, slightly taller than the desolate Chinese drum. The parade also required some thirty other floats, ten mobile stages, and fifteen motorized devices for the fifteen waltzing gowns.

One evening in mid-June around 9:00 P.M. Monique Sauvage phoned Philippe Blondel in a panic: "We're screwed!" She had just learned that the biggest floats could not make it through the immense decorative iron gates of the Tuileries gardens. If the parade were to be held, it was the only way out, the Pont de la Concorde having been closed for security reasons. (The historian's mind flashes back to the terrible disaster that occurred in 1770, on the occasion of the mass celebration of the marriage of Marie Antoinette to the dauphin, when at least 130 people were crushed or trampled to death on the rue Royale between the future Concorde and the *grands boulevards,* in part because the gates of the Tuileries were closed.) Sauvage had determined that the floats were too big to be accommodated by a ramp, and she was certain that the stewards of the national patrimony at the Ministry of Culture would not allow the uprooting of this national monument, lodged six meters into the ground in lead and cement mountings. But Sauvage underestimated Lang's investment in Goude. Three days later the gates were removed, and the garden path was reinforced to sustain the weight of the vehicles.

The rehearsals during the last ten days required an enormous infrastructure to lodge, nourish, dress, makeup, transport, and guide the seven thousand participants. Expelled from the Villacoublay airport by the armed forces preparing for their own parade on the fourteenth, and denied access to the streets of Paris for security reasons dictated by the summit, the Mission had to rent in extremis the Auteuil racetrack and a part of Le Bourget airport—and seven hundred buses. Goude had to rush from site to site; the participants and the crew worked virtually around the clock. Only at the last minute did the prefecture authorize one grand rehearsal on the Champs-Elysées the night of the twelfth and another on the Concorde the night of the thirteenth. These and other eleventh-hour costs added Fr 7 million to the budget, which Jeanneney had to raise from sponsors and television contracts.[29]

Northern Aristos and Southern Sansculottes

If the summit hampered Goude's preparations, it generated a far more vexing problem for the government and its commemorators. Critics, most of them on the left, many of them ordinarily sympathetic with Mitterrand's policies, questioned the wisdom of linking the French Revolution with the meeting of the world's richest nations. A "false good idea," suggested sometime presidential adviser Régis Debray, who found it incongruous to remember the outburst of popular insurgency with "the festival of power." For historian-columnist Jacques Julliard, "this procession of carriages to celebrate the taking of the Bastille" was "a surreal idea." To preempt or defuse these objections, the government had decided to invite a substantial number of Third World leaders, not to the summit, the bulk of whose participants did not want to transform this annual institution into a North-South rendezvous, but to the bicentennial celebration, where they would have ample occasion to meet informally with the world's economic leaders.

Jacques Attali, presidential majordomo and summit sherpa, hoped that their presence would symbolically reinject "the spirit of the sansculottes" into the ambience and remind the world that France, the only power among the G-7 governed on the left, was the leading voice for North-South dialogue in general and for debt readjustment in particular. Debray would have preferred to see the bicentennial Mitterrand "surrounded by the heads of state of the seven poorest nations of the planet." Ever seeking to navigate between symbolic and pragmatic exigencies, Attali argued forcefully that the leaders of the poor nations were less interested in chatting among themselves in commiseration than in making their case directly to their creditors. It would be unseemly, he added, to exclude from the Revolutionary commemoration "the representatives of the countries where the ideals and rules of democracy were born."[30]

Nor was it a simple matter to organize the visit once the principle of Third World participation had been ratified. Drawing up the guest list was a difficult task. The government embraced the fiction that no one was invited: "those who wished to attended." In fact, the Quai d'Orsay prompted certain countries, especially the poorest and, where possible, those with passable human rights records, to manifest their desire to attend. On the eve of the convocation, Attali boasted that the Third World would be represented in Paris by four Latin American presidents, fifteen African heads of state, and five Asian leaders. Certain of these poor countries, according to an indignant *Le Canard enchaîné*, would be spoken for by "superrich potentates and looters, corrupted and corruptors." It was thinking in particular of President Mobutu of Zaire, who apparently invited himself, and whose personal fortune allegedly was large enough to cover his country's immense national debt. The parti républicain's Gérard Longuet, an ex-right-wing commando converted to liberalism, complained that a number of Third World nations practiced policies of internal social and political control that were radically out of harmony with the Declaration of the Rights of Man, the grand bicentennial emblem.

Still others protested that the Northern aristocrats and the little people of the South would be treated unequally and thus ignominiously during the bicentennial ceremonies ("Grandeur and Misery of the Bicentennial," headlined *El Pais*). Attali pledged that "from the twelfth of July at 3:00 P.M. until the fourteenth of July at 3:00 P.M. all the heads of state of the North and of the South [would] be together, eat lunch and dinner together, and participate in all the ceremonies together." The Elysée even abandoned the plan to have them dine in two separate places on the evening of the fourteenth. They would all have the same menu in the Hôtel de la Marine, though Mitterrand would host the G-7 in one room and Rocard would welcome the Third World nations in another, after which they would watch the Gouderie together, as *Le Nouvel Observateur* noted, "sheltered from bullets by a special protective window equally resistant in all details."[31]

God's Prodigal Nephew

All the king's horses and all the king's men, however, could not save Mitterrand from an embarrassing counterbicentennial demonstration and a second summit.

The Ligue communiste révolutionnaire, a fringe party on the left with moral pretensions that outstripped its numbers, took the lead at its annual congress in January 1989. It proposed a meeting of the poorest countries of the world, "today's Third Estate," to intensify the struggle against apartheid and colonialism and to demand the abrogation of Third World debt, "the slavery of peoples." As *Le Figaro* observed, "all this would have been buried in one of those sempiternal meetings at the Mutualité where the memory of Trotskyism is preserved" if the issue had not possessed an intrinsically powerful appeal that transcended the sectarian concerns of a single chapel.

Others on the left who agreed that the combined bicentennial-summit was "an insult to the rights established by '89 and to the poor" signed the manifesto drawn up by Alain Krivine's party: author Gilles Perrault, ecologist René Dumont, Bishop Jacques Gaillot, cartoonists Wolinski, Loup, and Siné, former Communist minister Jack Ralite, members of a number of leading labor unions (CFDT, CGT, SNES) and, to conjure the specter of utter marginalization, a number of prominent Socialists, including Jean-Christophe Cambadélis, deputy of Paris, and Jean-Luc Mélenchon, senator from the Essonne. (From the heights of Zion, these two montagnards declared that "the bicentennial must not confine itself to popular dances, blaring noise, the sentimentalism of the celebration of 1789 that forbids the evocation of 1792 and 1793.")

There were some contacts between the protest organizers and the Mission. The moderate fractions among the former explored the possibility of some kind of official sanction, perhaps even a subvention from the Mission, that would seal some sort of contract of mutual forbearance. The Mission staff discussed the developing situation with growing anxiety. It delegated Monique Sauvage to meet with the antisummit representatives, but nothing came of those exchanges.

The most important adherent, in terms of political symbolism and the capacity to mobilize (youthful) public opinion, was the singer Renaud, an anarcho-Wobbly version of Bruce Springsteen, more poetry and charisma than music. This troubadour of the people had been a favorite of the Elysée, for he had vigorously supported Mitterrand's reelection ("Tonton laisse pas béton"). Now he considered that the president had committed "a historical blunder." Renaud pledged to organize a mammoth free concert to make the case not against Mitterrand, he insisted, but for a bicentennial that consecrated the cause of social justice in the world. Commenting ironically on the intersection of base capitalist preoccupations and grand causes, the right-wing *Quotidien de Paris* claimed that the concert, paid for by Virgin Records, was "above all geared to promote the sales of Renaud's records." The company admitted that he was not then in an ascendant career phase.[32]

Attali tried energetically to woo the Socialists back into the fold and to disabuse Renaud of his misconceptions. A number of Socialists found Perrault's fiery rhetoric unacceptable. Comfortable with the notion of debt abrogation—Mitterrand, after all, was the first to press in this direction—representatives of the party tried to fashion a text that was "less incendiary." In the end only a handful remained publicly associated with Krivine, Perrault, and Renaud, including Mélenchon and Julien Dray, a deputy with historic ties to SOS-Racisme, whom center-current socialists were delighted to expose as leftists at heart. Renaud resisted Attali's charm and his reasoning in a tête-à-tête luncheon at the château, as the presidential palace was known. "You betray the president by attacking the summit," the Sherpa is said to have told the minstrel. "Not at all; it is he who is betraying the spirit of '89," the latter allegedly replied.

Scandalized that "one can celebrate at the same time the sansculottes and the masters of the world," Renaud noted that it was not only the poor of the Third World who were excluded from the bicentennial. The little people of France were also excluded, kept on the other side of the "statist, policified, and gadgetized" commemorative wall, reduced to the passive status of "spectators instead of actors in the fête." The far left shared with the right an allergy to a commemoration that was, in the singer's words, "bloated, pompous, grandiloquent, and megalomaniacal." Strictures such as Renaud's surely incited the masters of commemoration to emphasize in fulsome terms the quintessentially "popular" nature of the Gouderie.

Though he was inclined to spare Tonton, who exercised an avuncular attraction over him, Renaud clearly identified the Socialists with the profiteering, spoliating bourgeoisie in power, the bourgeoisie that was the primary client and supporter of the G-7 monsters "who oppress three-quarters of the planet by their economic imperialism." Maintaining his right to "criticize with as much honesty and ardor my friends as I do my enemies," Renaud reiterated that the demonstration and concert planned for 8 July would not constitute "an anti-Elysée maneuver."

For certain of his supporters, however, in particular the Communist party, that was precisely the objective. The bicentennial-summit was proof, the Communists contended, that Mitterrand was not a sincere proponent of the Revolutionary trinity. "Equality will truly take root only once the sons and daughters of the sansculottes, the immense army of society's rejects of the North and the South, abolish privileges inherited through wealth and the possession of land and of the means of production," wrote *Rouge*. That cannot happen, explained *L'Humanité*, as long as the president of the republic "confiscates" the Revolution and defends the privileged.

Nor was Renaud's *journée révolutionnaire* a narrowly Parisian affair. A civic extension of the PCF and its "progressive friends," the Association Vive 89 of the Ille-et-Vilaine vibrated joyously to Renaud's "true retaking of the Bastille." The Bretons endorsed the view that the G-7 nations "pillage, ransom, and exploit the peoples who are merely there to do their masters' bidding." It was less this relatively futile political recuperation of Renaud's rally-concert that Attali feared than the broader public impact of an inverted massacre of the Champ-de-Mars in which, for the first time, the people shot at the stewards of Revolutionary order, the left organized a mass demonstration against Mitterrand.[33]

The Antisummit

On the afternoon of 8 July, under the banner "Debt, Apartheid, Colonies, Enough Is Enough," between fifteen and twenty thousand people marched from the Bastille through the place de la République to the stock exchange, from the seat of the popular Revolution to the citadel of speculation and capitalist aggrandizement. The organizing committee, dominated by Krivine's group, claimed that "400 Personalities" led the procession, representing the cream, of the "left of the left." Maxime Gremetz of the politburo of the Communist party walked shoulder to shoulder with Krivine. who was flanked by Msgr. Gaillot (attired in "chaplain's sportswear"). In addition to the standard institutional presences such as the labor unions, there were delegations from less mighty organizations such as the Committee of Support for the Tibetan People, the Committee of the Badly Housed (with women in African garb beating out a rhythm on jerry cans), SCALP (the Section carrément anti–Le Pen, an anti–Le Pen lobby), the Anarchist Federation, and groups speaking for the Basques, the Kurds, and the Palestinians ("Vive the Intifada").

They marched in what one journalist called an "amiable disorder," and they sang songs that bespoke a familial rather than a militant ambience ("Alouette" outdid the "International"). Some youngsters sported Mitterrand and Thatcher masks, and others wore Tiananmen headbands or carried photographs of renascent and new heroes, Che Guevara and Nelson Mandela. The slogans on the banners, T-shirts. and badges were usually witty and sometimes searing: "Bicentennial, my ass!"; "*Seigneurs* [lords] of the world, *Saigneurs* [bloodletters] of the Third World"; "In 1789, the bourgeoisie takes power, in 1989 it still has it"; "Arms sales, famines, thanks Tonton [Mitterrand], thanks G-7" (one of "only" three slogans overtly hostile to the president). Extremely heterogeneous in composition—in social and cultural terms the delegation from the Essonne lobbying for the cancellation of Third World debt had virtually nothing in common with the Third World French residents struggling for adequate housing—these marchers were the people who had learned the civics lesson that Jeanneney had toiled so valiantly to inculcate. They admired the Revolution, they identified with it, but they wanted it to speak to their diverse needs, to do what was morally right regardless of costs and obstacles, to be consistent with its first principles, to help them take today's Bastilles.[34]

That evening well over one hundred thousand turned out for the concert on the place de la Bastille featuring, alongside Renaud, some of the top stars of the hour, including Johnny Clegg, the Négresses Vertes, Mano Negra, and Malavoi. Most of the crowd came from the capital and the suburbs, though there were highly motivated groups that took the trouble to come up from the provinces, including a chartered bus of Communists from Toulouse, another of ecologists from the Vienne, a band of lycéens from Besançon who earned their train fare selling sausage. The prime-time newscasts at 8:00 P.M. gave Attali a moment of illusory satisfaction in reporting a surprisingly low turnout. In fact the bulk of the audience did not arrive until later in the evening. They behaved remarkably well ("strangely peaceful," registered *Libération*, a bit disappointed that they so avidly ate bread when they were so cruelly denied cake), and they enjoyed themselves immensely. Arrayed as a sansculotte in tricolor trousers and a Phrygian cap, Renaud welcomed protestors of all persuasions with warmth and wit: "Hi there, pals. Hi there, revolutionaries, anarchists, Trotskyites. Hi there, Communists. Hi there, Socialists, there are certainly some here tonight. Hi there, pals from SOS-Racisme, how could you not be here?"

And with what *Le Monde* called "a special tenderness," he greeted "les anarcho-Mitterrandists—there is at least one among us." Introducing Gilles Perrault, the only speaker of the evening, whose presence on the program may have accounted for the many late arrivals, Renaud set the theme that was supposed to distinguish this counterbicentennial from the official commemoration: "It's good to celebrate the Revolution, but it's better to make one."

Perrault made an impassioned plea for the forces of good against the forces of evil, for the people crushed by neocolonialist debt and tortured in colonialist jails, against "les sept riches" ("Bush, the emperor of the dollar, Kohl, the kaiser of the mark," and so on). He exhorted the world to realize that the debt was a bloodier mass murderer than the Stalinist machine or the Chinese tank brigades. And he asked how anyone could allow forty thousand children to die of hunger every day in the Third World. For Perrault, the bicentennial commemoration was shockingly estranged from the sordid realities of the world, willfully insulated from the true fields of revolutionary engagement. The official Revolution was carefully "cadaverized, mummified." Perrault could not conceal his disgust for the phoney bicentennial of the Tuileries and the Champs-Elysées, "a bicentennial of bucks, junk, tricks."[35]

By and large, the press judged that Renaud had "won his bet," to borrow the phrase of the *Dépêche du Midi*. From this "popular success" *Libération* drew a lesson for Mitterrand on the communication gap that had flared between the Elysée and "his" generation of more or less young voters. More alienated from the official celebration than enamored of Renaud, André Fontaine, director of *Le Monde*, interpreted "the success of the counterdemonstration" as proof that "the people have trouble identifying in the expensive splendors monitored by a huge barrier of police the principles of Liberty, Equality, Fraternity—and frugality—for which the Grand Ancestors fought."

More sympathetic with the official commemoration, colleague Bruno Frappat acidly disparaged Renaud's supposed success: "No fête, and a smaller crowd than one expected, given the allure of the free concert so widely announced." Moreover, Renaud's stock in trade, the youth whom he helped transform into Mitterrand's fan club, were less evident at the Bastille than nostalgic *soixante-huitards* gorging themselves on sausages and Coca-Cola. Frappat's verdict: "Renaud's soirée was a semi-failure." The Communists and Trotskyites regarded this view as pure calumny.

They reveled in a sweet victory that they advertised with exaggeration far outstripping Frappat's as "a more and more massive questioning of the policies of those in power."

Significantly, to the detriment of Perrault's desperate summons for solidarity with the Third World, these postmortems focused almost exclusively on internal political repercussions. The seminar organized the day after the concert at the Mutualité by Perrault and Krivine garnered little attention. Nor did an appeal signed by over a hundred "personalities" including Abbé Pierre, René Dumont, and six Nobel laureates criticizing the official commemoration's alleged indifference to the truly urgent problems of the globe, among them the nuclear menace, ecological degradation, and "the social question: in the Third World misery, hunger, and epidemics afflict hundreds of millions of men, women, and children." While the G-7 made ready to convene in the majestic Arche de la Défense the following week, delegates from seven of the poorest African, Asian, and American countries, "which symbolize the exclusion and oblivion to which are relegated two-thirds of humanity," gathered on a theatre barge docked along the Canal Saint-Martin to prepare a countersummit inspired, the participants underlined, by the true principles of 1789.[36]

Goude's Opera
The *Marseillaise* Revisited

R enaud's counterbicentennial merely enhanced the burgeoning pressure on Goude, on the Mission, and on the government. The closer one approached to the fourteenth, the more immense seemed the stakes. With the world's leaders in the choice seats, with the world's eyes riveted on Paris, and, at least insofar as the domestic audience was concerned, in light of the perceived unevenness of the commemorative effort during the first half of the year and of the vigor of "a [public] opinion said to be hesitant, even hostile," *everything* suddenly lay in the hands of the busy little man with his baseball cap on backward. "Rarely has a political climate," remarked an insightful commentator, "so completely depended on a man and an event so utterly foreign to the [ordinary] political logic."

The Pressure Peaks

It seems astonishing that the Mission's Herculean year-long labors should abruptly be reduced to a test of two and a half hours on the Champs-Elysées. Jean-Noël Jeanneney, who liked to project an aura of always being in control, conceded: "this was wholly beyond us." In safe retrospect, he could argue, with understandable self-regard, that "the fourteenth of July was a success because it was preceded by many months of intensive effort of collective memory that [ultimately] bore fruit." But on the morning of the fourteenth the president of the Mission had absolutely no idea of just what claims he would be able to make for his stewardship. The uncertainty agitated everyone at the Mission. Monique Sauvage's assurance that even if the "symbolism" of the parade lacked powerful clarity, "the showy side" would surely compensate did not allay apprehensions. "We are scared to death," avowed a staff member.

Goude traversed "a crisis of doubt." The penultimate rehearsal had been "disastrous." That must have been the one that ignited Attali's anger and frustration as he watched it from the roof of the Hôtel de la Marine. "It's worthless," he erupted in Dupavillon's face. During the whole week before the fourteenth, Goude had not been able to sleep, despite the pills he ingested for that purpose. "I came to the starting line in utter despair," he told an interviewer. "Never in my life had I been under such pressure." Nor could he count on the upbeat, expectant mood of Parisians to raise his spirits. For them too, it had been "a hellish week": there were vexing restrictions on parking and traffic circulation imposed on the bicentennial by the parasitical summit, more police than the capital had known since the Occupation, and twice the normal density of tourists to further aggravate the situation.[1]

The summit-linked bicentennial ceremonies began the day before the national holiday (a.k.a. G-Day). Presided over and in part designed by Mitterrand, the inaugural event, an apotheosis of the Declaration of the Rights of Man, was meant to remind the world of France's proudest and least controversial Revolutionary achievement. A little past noon, on the space before the Trocadéro aptly named Square of Freedoms and Human Rights, the president greeted some thirty heads of state and government. North and South were treated with conspicuous equality, Mitterrand seating himself between George Bush and the Ivory Coast's Félix Houphouet-Boigny. On a background framed by a vividly blue sky interrupted only by the soaring Eiffel Tower, emblem of the first centennial, and the gigantic white dirigible constantly aloft to direct security arrangements for the second centennial's summit, the Orchestre de Paris played the *Requiem* that François-Joseph Gossec, friend of Rameau and Mirabeau, had composed for the Revolution's own pageants. Actors and actresses, led by André Dussolier, recited the articles of the Declaration interspersed with texts by Condorcet, Emmanuel Sieyès, and other leading revolutionaries. A band of white-garbed children drawn from races and ethnic groups representing the five continents placed flowers and tropical fruits before the guests. A miniature blue montgolfier, followed by scores of birds (witnesses describe them either as doves or wood pigeons), took to the air. This lean, sober ceremony lasted barely half an hour, thwarting predictions, primarily English, that these would be days of unremitting and overweening grandiloquence.

While Mitterrand received most of this company for lunch at the Elysée, Jack Lang hosted 120 ministers and other high officials from the national delegations. (Summing up his bicentennial experience, a top aide to the Uruguayan president remarked: "Montesquieu, Molière, they are nothing next to camembert," a product, he would have been delighted to learn, that, according to its Norman producers, had been invented in 1789.) At the end of the day the dignitaries rejoined Mitterrand to inaugurate the Opéra de la Bastille, the French president's so-called popular opera, an immense undertaking of urban renewal and architecture whose construction had begun in 1985. Many of the opera world's leading performers, including Placido Domingo, Barbara Hendricks, Shirley Verrett, and Ruggiero Raimondi, put on a concert drawn from French masterpieces. The masses were invited not to their opera house but to the traditional street balls in the different quarters. The Mission and the Ministry of Culture jointly sponsored what they insipidly baptized "the biggest dance in the world" at the place de la République. Till early morning, a crowd of several thousand danced to the music of the Garçons Bouchers, Zouk Machine, Les Satellites, and Manu Dibango.[2]

Fourteen July: The *Marseillaise* on Parade

The weather augured well at daybreak on the fourteenth: the morning clouds were sure to burn off, and they promised an afternoon that would not be scorching. The day began with the usual military swagger, another side of the complex Revolutionary heritage, the pendant to, yet in some ways the continuation of, the *bals populaires* of the night before. What did the observers from the other old-time Western democracies as well as the newer ones the world over make of this French tradition, and its relation to the paramount theme of human rights? France, grumbled journalist-philosopher Jean-François Revel, "is alone among the great democracies to celebrate its national holiday with a massive display of its armed might." The bicentennial incentive perhaps injected a note of rigor into the march, but aside from the fact, trumpeted by the military press office, that it was 40 percent bigger than its predecessors (among other elements: more women, more helicopters, more high-tech gadgets), it seemed very much like it had always been. Substantial numbers of spectators seemed determined to camp out on the Champs-Elysées the whole day, a long picnic bridging the gap between the tanks and the floats.

Before the military parade had ended, hundreds of theatre lovers were lined up outside the Comédie-Française for the annual free matinée, which in normal years required a wait of several hours. Happily, the senior national theatre company programmed *Le Mariage de Figaro*, an exuberant and poignant play replete with Enlightenment-Revolution motifs. Figaro was masterfully played by Richard Fontana, who reappeared after the final curtain to recite the entire *Marseillaise* with a subdued but urgent passion that deeply moved the audience.

Even as Figaro was still negotiating the terms of his triumph, more manifestly political theatre broke out in the streets. Chanting the somewhat worn "let's not celebrate the Revolution, let's make one," extreme leftists outside the Santé prison on the Left Bank demonstrated in favor of the hunger strikers of the Action directe terrorist movement. From two bridges near Notre-Dame, groups protesting lack of government aid to "creators" hurled six hundred decapitated heads made of a buoyant material congealed in strikingly expressive molds into the Seine, whence the police fished them out to avoid alarming the citizenry downriver. By the end of the afternoon, crowds were thick everywhere in the center of town. Without a carefully verified ticket to the bleachers constructed for the elite at the Concorde, it was difficult to get anywhere near the Champs-Elysées.[3]

The show began shortly after 10:00 P.M. before an immense crowd, distributed according to several different criteria, including age, athletic disposition, and wealth/influence. Children and old persons were allowed to sit on the street in front of the metal barriers. Adventurers climbed lampposts and perched on the top of bus shelters and press kiosks. They might very well have scaled the buildings along the avenue to reach the superb balconies, had the latter not been occupied by the happy few: businesses of all sorts, which used the occasion to flatter clients, luxury apartment dwellers, and so on. President Mitterrand and the thirty-three heads of state or government, and their families, were installed on the balcony of the Hôtel de la Marine on the place de la Concorde, around which some seventeen thousand members of the paying and invited elect sat in stands erected around the obelisk. Accompanied by forty drummers, whose throbbing beat set the tone for the whole evening, sixty Italians, painted in yellowface and wearing bouffant red trousers and white gloves, opened the show with a display of (tricolor) flag manipulation in the manner of the lancers of the Palio of Siena. In stark contrast to their kinetic energy came the solemn cortege of Chinese students, masked to conceal their identity, following an immense red drum that loomed like a derelict ship on a morose sea.[4]

Next marched three hundred professional drummers, attired in tuxedos bound with the tricolor sash worn by French mayors, who announced the arrival of fifteen hundred amateur drummers, recruited from every part of France, including Corsica and Guadeloupe, dressed in black, bearing lamps that illuminated their faces and their blue, white, and red drums. They were complemented by a mixed corps of more than one thousand amateur and professional musicians, similarly recruited in all the regions of France (represented by thirty-eight flag bearers flourishing their historic colors). On their traditional instruments (violins, oboes, fifes, bagpipes, hurdy-gurdies, accordians) they played Badarou's *Marche des Mille* in symphonic formation, a feat that required them to learn new habits and whose arrangement demanded a complicated collaboration between musicians and computers. Preceded by a ballet of some thirty dancers that further embroidered the regional/federationist theme, the drummers and the instrumentalists, fortified by a chorus of six hundred and a brass and percussion ensemble, entered the place de la Concorde in two lines, left and right, to execute Badarou's *Prélude à la Marseillaise*.

At the end of this piece, transported from below by a hidden elevator, Jessye Norman, larger than life, bedecked in a flowing gown in the French national colors fashioned by a designer of Maghrébin origin, surged onto the stage built around the obelisk. (Stunningly regal, exotically beautiful, dark ebony in color, and immense in size, Norman loomed as an upscale version of all of Goude's fantasies.) As the audience on the bleachers rose, the distinguished African American opera singer intoned the sixth and first couplets of the *Marseillaise* with great verve and emotion as she circled the monument, seconded by the other participants in the parade, singing in French or in their native languages. A vast wall of water, seventeen meters high and 210 meters wide, served as a backdrop on the Tuileries side of the square.[5]

Goude's parade on the Champs-
Elysées on 14 July 1989, the bicentennial climax. (Photo by Raphael
Gaillarde. Reproduced by permission
of Liaison International.)

During the rendition of the *Marseillaise,* the float of master Senegalese musician
Doudou N'Diaye Rose, a huge staircase that he mounted and descended in order to
direct the drummers, halted at the foot of the Champs-Elysées. Surrounded by 292
torchbearers in colonial outfit, the top of the float spotlighted six African women
percussionists in flowing native attire, two each in blue, white, and red, while the
back of the float served as a stage for dancers. Fifteen black-draped waltzing couples
followed, striking black and Maghrébin women set in giant gowns propelled by
hidden motorized carts embraced by little boys costumed to represent diverse
cultures and ethnic groups. They moved gracefully to a funk rhythm incorporating
bits and pieces of music from around the world, reinforcing the impact of Goude's
tableau métissé.

The Royal Tattoo inaugurated the British sketch, leading the way for 150 dancers
reflecting London's ethnic mix who performed their ballet on the theme of the
head cold while gently being sprayed by genuine English firemen from hose-and-
ladder trucks on both sides. The British exited on the wrong side of the Concorde,
infuriating Goude. The inclement weather continued as the Soviet troop marched
and danced under a thick flow of confetti imitating snow emanating from fourteen
trucks driven by babushka-clad women. On a plastic ice-skating rink, a bear and a
woman danced. The music seemed to link the Russian past with the Soviet future.
Conveying the constructivist vision through a series of multicolor geometric forms,

a float served as a stage for men and women dressed in sculptured outfits who moved with machinelike motions. Traditional folk dancers and guards from Lenin's tomb completed the eclectic tableau.

The parade took a tropical turn with an African float, a great pyramid of drum-cans played by ninety-one Guinean percussionists, who were were ringed on the ground by almost four hundred Africans impersonating Senegalese soldiers and flag bearers. Bare-chested women drummers, drawn by electronic trolleys, were arrayed on either side, while the rear was held by twelve ponies painted to look like zebras that pulled canons firing salvos even though they were mounted by trum-peters who played popular songs between shots. Still more drummers, this time on foot, the Tambours du Bronx, who in fact were descendants of railway workers from the central French town of Nevers ("It's still something of a ghetto," noted the CGT's *La Vie ouvrière* in reference to the SNCF's cultural and physical enclave in the city called the Bronx), announced the life-size locomotive, puffing and whis-tling, driven by a Jean Gabin look-alike in a scene inspired by Jean Renoir's version of *La Bête humaine*.[6]

America closed the show, represented by the 250-member, all-black marching band from Florida A & M University. Moonwalking backward part of the way in the manner of Michael Jackson, the student-musicians were wildly applauded from accompanying bleacher-floats by blond cheerleaders, pom-pom girls, and a diverse crew of adoring fans. On a mobile stage on the other side of the avenue Chinese break-dancers performed a hip-hop show. As if drawn magically by the Pied Piper music of James Brown, tens of thousands of spectators peacefully invaded the Champs-Elysées even before the band had left the avenue.[7] While the young musicians from Tallahassee took several enthusiastic and unsanctioned laps of honor around the obelisk, a stunning fireworks, incorporating effects produced in China, Italy, and the United States, illuminated the midnight sky.

Reading Goude

Many readings of the Gouderie competed for attention during the days of bicentennial decompression that followed. Goude himself cautioned against overly rapacious intellectual games. I am to be relished, I am to be devoured impulsively and viscerally, not pedantically decoded, not even pondered, he seemed to say. If he evoked the aesthetic of *La Bête humaine*, it was above all because "I adore locomo-tives: there is no need to search for a meaning in the form." Most critics were likely to regard this ingenuousness as a ploy, part of Goude's ludic, masking strategy, perhaps even a symptom of latent modesty. In any event, at the current moment in critical time, authorial intention does not carry much weight. Goude's ultimate apotheosis, once the object cools, will be the doctoral dissertations to be written about him. In the heat of (re)action, however, there were few elaborate attempts to textualize the parade. Most commentators in the press seemed to operate within a gentle tautology: this is what the parade was supposed to have done normatively, therefore this is indeed what it did. Like Goude, they deployed clichés, but without the refraction of *décalage* or a slight waft of irony.

Thus a garrulous television newsman, with an instinctive sense for risk-averse (no-lose), world-historical punditry, exuded: "Goude stands for liberty, equality, fraternity." Liberty: Goude's total freedom, his delicious craziness; equality: everyone was there, the USSR and Guinea, the big and the little; fraternity: the congenial promiscuity of all races and colors. The Revolution that fit the needs of 1989 was pacific and consensual: this then, was the message that *Le Provençal* read into the show, a show vaguely and wishfully portrayed as the celebration of "the values of the Revolution" and its ideal of liberty and peace.

Historian Michel Winock proposed a more robust interpretation, balancing the imperatives of the outer- and inner-directed selves. The Gouderie bespoke three themes: (1) "solidarity with the oppressed"; (2) "the pride of being French (that's what I said!)"; (3) "fraternity without borders." Even before the actual parade, Jeanneney was at pains to reassure the hundreds of historians gathered at the Sorbonne for the world congress that it would be about the Revolution despite its extreme modernity—"I believe that something will take place there that is close to a certain truth of the Revolution"—particularly in its emphasis on multiculturalism in both French and international arenas.

Mitterrand's first prime minister, subsequently the head of the Socialist party, Pierre Mauroy, accentuated the universalism of a Revolution that was not meant exclusively for French men and women, a theme that he felt Goude had brilliantly conveyed. Journalist Bruno Frappat emphasized the cultural anti-Lepénisme of Goude's "affirmation of the closeness [of peoples], the proclamation of the melting pot as a value," a perspective of acute relevance in a nation increasingly worried about the problem of reconciling the right to difference with the need for coherence and integration. Yet he overlooked the torrent of counterpoints by which Goude rejected racial amalgamation and sociocultural assimilation and gave voice to the persistence of strong ethnic, racial and cultural identities. Surely one of the chief merits of the parade was its decentering of Paris on the Champs-Elysées itself. Its cosmopolitanism reinforced its hardy Girondism. Fulfilling his contract to honor the Festival of the Federation, Goude portrayed the provinces without provincialism, the regions-constituting-the-nation without treacly sentiment.[8]

There were, of course, myriad ambiguities in the parade that invited less heroic constructions. At certain junctures pride in France seemed to turn imperceptibly into nostalgia for influence if not hegemony. The "power of the drum" seemed to be French rather than African. Some of the sketches underlined the indebtedness of the nations and cultures represented to France and not, more chastely, to ideals that happened to flower in French space. On the one hand, France reaffirmed her place among the five permanent members of the UN Security Council, the world's preeminent powers (perhaps power bloc?), the five nations whose identities were clearly defined in the parade and linked by revolutionary traditions of one sort or another. On the other, as illuminator and purveyor of human values to the world, France appeared to surpass the others, escaping caricature (the sneezing English, the Russian circus and cartoon characters, the equivocal use of marching, uniformed black youth to represent the United States) and militarization (the soldiers of the United Kingdom, the goose-stepping Soviets, the regimentlike Americans). The spots that transformed the white robes of the six African dancers atop the float into an undulating flag of blue, white, and red described a yoke even as they traced a homage. The French flag flying over the world, in particular the Third World, echoed a neocolonial theme that seemed to be the other side of the coin of *métissage*.

Beyond Goude's idiosyncratic involvement in black culture, there was something disquieting in his rampant Africanization, something that seemed subversive of the one-world fraternity that it was said to proclaim. Philippe Meyer articulated it in these terms:

> The cortege of Jean-Paul Goude brought back my childhood: the stories from *Tintin au Congo*, in which the Negroes speak Banania, and the huge wall maps at school, where French West Africa figured in pink alongside Equatorial Africa in green. At bottom, from the boxes of the famous chocolate breakfast drink [Banania] to the bicentennial parade, it is hereafter proven that the essence of the Negro, his earthly vocation, is to be an image—social, entertaining, of little consequence. The next day the press celebrates the mix of crossing cultures: this *métissage* is the new name of the sauce with that we serve to our former colonies.[9]

Triumphalism

From the perspective of the commemorators, the important thing was not what the Gouderie meant but how it fared. The almost universal judgment of the press was that it was a stupendous success. "The Triumph of Goude," headlined Limoges's *Populaire du Centre*. Concurring that the parade was "a triumph," the *Dépêche du Midi* suggested that, under the Old Regime, Goude would have been rewarded with "a lifetime pension." *Vendredi* hailed "a grandiose show." "So it was a triumph," wrote Bruno Frappat in *Le Monde*. Even the parsimonious *Canard enchaîné* conceded that "it [la fête] was worth the trouble." Part of that success resided in the routing of the meanspirited faultfinders, the savant cavilers, and the devout prophets of doom. The joyous crowds, contended *L'Evénement du Jeudi*, "drowned a partisan grumpiness under the flood of a genuine delight." The pageant's "success has swept away its critics," in the view of the *Canard;* "the 'Fronde' of the Third Worlders, the sulking of the right, the reticence of many people were forgotten [or] overcome." "The grousers, the wet blankets, the small-minded, the *ronchonopolémiquants*, suffered that night a Homeric defeat," esteemed an elated Frappat.

Those who expected and/or hoped for "a phenomenal flop" avowed their defeat by joining in the praise. "The Triumph of the Revolution," titled *Le Figaro*. "It's thanks to Jean-Paul Goude that the bicentennial was finally a triumph," wrote its coeditor-in-chief Franz-Olivier Giesbert in a front-page editorial, despite his misgivings about the style of manipulation—Mitterrandian to the core—the show betrayed. Referring to its own constituents in the third person, commented *Nice Matin:* "The grumpy felt terribly isolated yesterday in the midst of the praise generally triggered by the *Marseillaise.*"

This "complete turnaround," this "sudden reversal" meant sweet revenge for Jean-Noël Jeanneney, who had suffered for months "in the midst of a din of loud outcries predicting the worst." As stunned as he was gratified ("I found this sudden enthusiasm almost excessive"), the president of the Mission was content to observe that the success of this pinnacle of the bicentennial was incontrovertible even if it was beyond real measure: "The fact that people, in France and abroad, had the sense that things went well, that's what really counted." Happily conflating being and appearance, the evangelist of authentic Revolutionary values all too readily internalized the Goudean calculus: "The image of success is more important than success itself."[10]

With much perspicacity and perhaps a zest of whimsicality, André Fontaine, director of *Le Monde,* characterized the Gouderie as "too cerebral to unleash real enthusiasm." Yet the eruption of joyous enthusiasm betokened not only by the massive presence on the Champs-Elysées but also by the seismic spasm of the crowd at the end, whereby it seemed to fuse with and appropriate the pageant, proved to be the chief litmus of "success," success causally bound up with but somehow superior to the intrinsic merit of Goude's production. "On Friday the crowd on the Champs-Elysées rendered a verdict without appeal," declared the *Dépêche du Midi,* echoed by the *Centre Presse.* "Immense crowds become the heroes of their own fête," noted *L'Evénement du Jeudi.* Ironically, given its heavy handed conjuring, the opposition had made the magnitude of the crowd and its enthusiasm more significant and more charged than it might otherwise have been. The crowd was said to respond as much to the naysayers as to Goude: "The Parisian riposte," wrote Frappat, "was immense, riverlike—no, Amazonian." Even at some distance, the *Nouvel Observateur*'s Restif, Alain Schifres, recalled the Gouderie as above all a "formidable pop success," placing it in a section of his book called "tabacs."

Populism

This putatively "popular" dimension of the fête provided Jeanneney with the only quasi-argument he could marshal to explain the brusque change in bicentennial fortunes. (No one considered the possibility that the change in tone of the Hersant press and the others might have translated a patriotic tropism, a reluctance to embarrass France, whatever the partisan stakes, with the eyes of the world fastened on the Champs-Elysées.) Reasoned the president of the Mission: "The movement of popular support was so manifest that the turnabout was irresistible, with the readers sweeping along their newspapers. To fathom this, it is enough to have in the mind's eye the unforgettable image of the immense, joyous and fraternal crowd that brusquely invaded the Champs-Elysées, in the soft light, behind the last of Goude's floats."[11]

The idea that the fête was popular seemed equally important to commemorators and commentators. Mitterrand set the tone by promising "an astonishing popular fête" by which he meant primarily two things: huge numbers of people and no cumbersome message ("neither speeches nor protocolary ceremonies nor incense nor choir boys").[12] While the question of content provoked some interest (*Réforme* praised Goude for refusing to play to "either the intellectuals, the historians, or the in-people"), most attention bore on the issue of numbers. Would it be a genuine "popular fête," *Libération* asked Attali? "We will see how many hundreds of thousands will participate in Paris." For *Le Provençal*, it was the force of the "rassemblement" itself—the greatest since the Liberation—that sanctified the event as popular. Proposing a distinction between "the public" and "the people," Régis Debray and Gérard Fromanger were almost alone in contesting what they scornfully called "the proof of success by the million."[13]

In fact, over a million people attended the show. Everyone agreed that it was a heterogeneous group, as *métissé* as the parade itself, though no one seemed concerned that its "popular" nature, in the idiom of French domestic politics, could be thought to vary inversely with the number of foreign tourists present. (Remember Mona Ozouf's sally, probably targeting the military parade but suggestive nevertheless: "'89 or not, for the parade on 14 July there are very likely to be, as usual, only Swedish tourists.") Though much of the crowd could not see well and the acoustics were uneven at best, and though people were packed tightly and sometimes uncomfortably, observers commented with a certain awe on their good behavior, indeed their veritable discipline—a decent, even sympathetic crowd of the sort that George Rudé, the pioneer historian-rehabilitator of crowds, liked to describe.[14]

It was hard to resist the temptation to idealize the crowd, to infuse it with Micheletian magic, even to construe it as an oracle of Western civilization. Thus wrote *L'Evénement:* "When Paris gathers together in such a spectacular way, without the prod of a victory or a death or a revolution to justify these colossal movements of the crowd, then something significant must be happening in the collective unconscious of the French. It seems that the people, drugged and anesthetized by the [prolonged economic] crisis, is waking up. With the return of prosperity and East-West détente, they sense the dawning of new times." Less given to this genre of apocalyptic journalism, *Le Monde* nevertheless detected in the crowd a reassuring counterweight to the lamentable indifference that citizens had shown by record abstentions in the spate of recent elections and their reluctance to engage themselves in the public sphere.

For Laurent Joffrin of the *Nouvel Observateur,* the "bi-summit" owed its success in large part to "this old entity which one no longer invokes for fear of appearing corny but which was nevertheless the decisive actor of the commemoration: the people, Diable!" Joffrin dared see in the latterday people the reincarnation of the courageous Parisians who made history in 1789: "at two centuries' distance," he concluded breathlessly, "it's the same people." Not to be outdone in populist rhapsody, Bruno Frappat discerned something resembling a spiritual metamorphosis and displacement, a sacralization of the transposed people. As for "that other parade," which Olivier Mongin of *Esprit* also discovered, that parade of the people, "it signified: *we* are the event, *we* are the fête, *we* are the bicentennial. It announced this without shouting, without the slightest incident. [The people] slipped onto the Champs as had Jessye Norman, with the same imperious power inspiring the same respect. This crowd was no longer a crowd, it was the soul of the city, it was a mysterious 'we,' momentary of course, but sacred. [It was] the procession of an epoch that believes in itself." In this halcyon year of the political, Joffrin, Frappat, and Mongin seemed to be groping to restitute the social to a place of honor.[15]

Another so-called demonstration that the people were present massively and that the fête was quintessentially popular was the egregious absence of much of the sociopolitical elite, Parisian and national. This was the proof of revolution by emigration, the method of addition by subtraction. The people were the great residual that remained when the bulk of the others fled. So it seemed to follow that when the right decided to abandon the bicentennial vessel (in September 1988 Chirac petulantly counseled his fellow citizens "to go take the air outside the capital during that weekend"), followed by many centrists and a number of cultural stars who oscillated between left and right, the ship would automatically chart a more popular course. This emigration was hardly an unprecedented reflex. In the late nineteenth and early twentieth centuries, residents of the *beaux quartiers* closed their shutters and took to the countryside to avoid popular celebrations.

The *bouderie* of the Gouderie aroused sharp denunciation, reflecting civic indignation as well as partisan competition. For Noel Copin, writing in *La Croix*, the opposition's boycott was a "childish reaction" that bespoke deep flaws in the nature of the political debate. Jean-Jack Queyranne, spokesman for the Socialists, pointed to the emigration as evidence that the right "had never accepted the Revolution" and that it felt contempt for the people on its great day. The large numbers of persons attending the bicentennial events (habitually identified as members of the genus people) comforted the moral indignation of the left. *Esprit*'s latterday Louis-Sébastien Mercier, Olivier Mongin, wrote: "There could be no greater pleasure than to have the physical sensation that one's city was peopled on 13 and 14 July last. . . . [It was] a lovely and serene vengeance against all the cowards who deliberately went into exile. . . . Gang of imbeciles, you missed a moment in history."[16]

A handful of observers argued that, appearances aside, the (True) people were no less absent than the center-right elites. In the spirit of Debray, they contested the claim to a popular fête, which had jelled overnight into bicentennial doctrine and myth. In vague, albeit passionate, terms, literary scholar Robert Escarpit, most recently notorious for his defense of Albanian democracy, denounced the exclusion of the French people—"even the France of Paris"—from the "festivities of the rich and the privileged." "One should have in the first place gotten the people of France involved," he contended, "it is there that one discerns the profound meaning of the taking of the Bastille." Instead, the bicentennial program, shaped by the broader cultural policies of Mitterrand-Lang, issued in the confiscation of the Bastille, "stealing" it from its rightful trustees, the people. The *Canard enchaîné* developed the double paradox of the people, king of the Revolution, excluded from their commemoration by Mitterand, monarch of the bicentennial, who was himself committed to the prohibition of exclusion: "The king of the Revolution was the people, tumultuous and impassioned. The bicentennial has its king, sumptuous and solemn: that's Tonton. The people are asked to keep a bit back, well-behaved, behind the barriers."

For Marxists, the banishment of the people bespoke the abiding conservative dream-fantasy: "Ah! What a beautiful Revolution it would have been without the people." The Communist historian Maurice Genty embroidered the theme of an orchestrated and symbolically transparent passivity. Save in certain [read Communist?] localities, the people were "kept at a distance, if not entirely absent, at best simple spectators and not actors, contrary to the spirit of the revolutionary festivals." "The people were invited to be spectators at the commemoration, not actors," complained ultraleftist author Gilles Perrault, for whom the Revolution, by definition, was precisely the moment when the people decided to be actors once and for all. "My name is the indignation, the disgust, and the nausea of the French people, excluded from the celebration of 14 July," declared the idiosyncratic author Jean-Edern Hallier. The ostracism of the people was symbolized by the seating arrangements for the elites. "I would have been ashamed," said Hallier, with his usual blend of jocularity and outrage," to sit on the blasphemous bleachers of these blackguards [les gradins dégradants des gredins] who dare to remain seated while the people stand."

Filmmaker Serge Moati, a friend of the Socialists who traveled throughout the country capturing the bicentennial on tape, registered a quasi-universal complaint: "All the other 14 Julys, until this one, had been popular." Serge July, director of *Libération,* deplored the failure of the commemorators "to get the anonymous people to participate. As if they, too, had ceased being the subject of the history." In the eyes of the leftist cartoonist and social critic Wolinski, the commemorators had forgotten "the popular meaning of this fête." The Gouderie, he suggested, was geared to American tourists. Condemning the show as a "grotesque celebration, elitist and cosmopolitan," a provincial reader of *Minute,* his racism and politics aside, may have betrayed a genuine feeling of exclusion in his attack on what André Fontaine had called the cerebral nature of the pageant, what this alienated reader dubbed "an egghead-esoteric-idiotic revolutionary show." If it was un-French and inaccessible, then how could it be popular?[17]

Goude in the Cross Fire between Right and Left

The widespread acclaim for Goude's show did not stifle all criticism, especially on the far right, on the Jacobino–Marxist left, and among certain intellectuals here and there. Goude offered the extreme right a field day, for he transgressed all their taboos concerning race, cosmopolitanism, un- and anti-Frenchness, morality and values, and the Revolutionary legacy. "In homage to 'the glory of France' we were regaled with China, Africa, and Islam accompanied by a few bearded and dirty Western Zulus contorting themselves to the beat of Arab music in a spate of frenzied clowning of the most perfect bad taste," editorialized *National hebdo*. The "commotion and the cacophony of the cultural crossbreeding," featuring "the Negresses of Senegal and the half-naked women of Brittany," were sure signs of French decadence, accelerated by the hypocritical Socialists who banned the Germans ("not cleansed of the Holocaust") but welcomed the goose-stepping Soviets, whose gulags killed many more millions than the Nazis. Despite its profoundly counterrevolutionary stance, *National hebdo* did not shrink from expressing indignation over the outrage Goude committed against French national honor on this solemn occasion: "but as a homage to and in memory of France, one can merely take note of a stupid, insulting, and grotesque presentation."

The *Anti-89* associated Goude's "worldism" with classically Jewish and antinational influences. Perhaps there was a dose of admiration in *Minute*'s dismissal of the Gouderie as the work of an artist "having abused LSD." For the Lepéniste daily *Présent* the "sick minds" were those who had hired Goude for the job and who had to bear full responsibility for the "mascarade on the Champs-Elysées." Scrupulously respectful of the "exotic" populations of the world as well as the ignominious Soviets, Goude shamefully subjected the French provinces to harsh ridicule. And on what grounds did he impose as symbol of the United States the moonwalk of a Michael Jackson, the consummate hybrid, "neither black nor white, man nor woman, meat nor fish"? *Rivarol* took issue with the choice of another black American, the "mammothesque" Jessye Norman. There was no legitimate rationale for choosing "a black from the other side of the Atlantic to personify France." Even as the Catholic paper *La Croix* felt "all the humanity chanting the song of freedom" through the person of a woman, a foreigner, a black, and a descendant of slaves, so Bruno Mégret, a European deputy and a major figure in the Front national, felt obliged to "recall to M. Goude that 14 July is the national holiday and that the French nation is not black."[18]

One of the most strident excoriations of the Gouderie-as-decadence came from a member of the mainstream right, Olivier Passelecq, formerly an aide to Edgar Faure and more recently Chirac's bicentennial counselor. His critique testifies to the permeation of far-right discourse into, and its increasingly eager appropriation by, the RPR. The ethnicolor drums of the bicentennial fourteenth of July set off the tocsin in Passelecq's mind, sounding the alarm for an imperiled and a diminished France: "The tam-tams that resounded from the beginning to the end of the parade are in the last analysis nothing other than the drums of decadence!" They cast into relief the decadence "of a culture incapable of showing off to advantage its original creations, its specific values." Passelecq's anxiety-ridden parochialims and his stifling xenophobia reach a climax in his denunciation of "the decadence of a nation that loses its identity under the continual assaults of the partisans of a multiracial and multireligious society." Goude sullied the national holiday by casting the dark African shadow across the Champs-Elysées, thereby denying the France of the Declaration of the Rights of Man its unyielding Frenchness. Goude was apparently incapable of "original creation"; even if he were, his creations would not be fully national because he was "deeply marked . . . by American influence," an observation that offered nuance little purchase, right or left, in bicentennial France.[19]

Upstart Gaullists, like certain self-styled Jacobins, nourish the bittersweet myth of a pristine France, either lagging behind America in both creation and corruption or morally incapable on its own of either. But this is wishful thinking, and a dangerous and self-indulgent illusion. France does not need America any longer; the America in France is fully homegrown. Not every adman in France had an American dancer for a mother and Grace Jones, hardly an American, as lover and toy. Another adman on Dupavillon's short list, with parents from Châteauroux, would have put on as disconcerting and as striking a show as Goude. No American could have envisaged the sort of pageant that Goude imagined. It was as profoundly French as Orangina, Banania, and the scientific journal of the Pasteur Institute.

On the left the reproaches were considerably less vituperative but deeply felt and in certain ways resonant with those from the right. The left, too, detected signs of decadence, but of a different genre, and of excessive and perfidious foreign influence. Decadence for *L'Humanité* meant the lack of a serious message in Goude's pageant, his self-proclaimed ignorance of the Revolution he was supposed to commemorate, and his narcissistic advertising style. Similarly, Jules Gritti in *La Croix* contrasted the festive success with the distressing lack of context for reflection.

"The Gouderie was bereft of a strong message," echoed the Trotskyite philosopher Daniel Bensaïd, who decried the advertising axiom that "the enormity of the image would compensate for the vacuity of the words." Writer Claude Arnaud faulted Goude's Orangina-*lite* style: "the substance disappeared, the taste remains." Another intellectual, Philippe Genestier, exposed the adman's overwhelming philosophical and sociological weaknesses—they were not, after all, his areas of expertise—which led him to conflate the truly universal with "a kaleidoscope of some local colors," to fail to grasp that world music was an expression of current hegemonies rather than of unvarnished humanity, and, more generally, to trivialize a solemn and important occasion.[20]

In a searing and sanctimonious critique, one that paid unwitting homage to Goude's art of caricature, Debray and Fromanger mercilessly exposed Goude's intellectual infirmities, themselves a reflection of the image ("seller of nothing"), clip, and cliché world that engendered him. Under the slogan "the manner swallows up the matter," Goude managed to evacuate any serious historical referent from the bicentennial pageant ("Goude freed himself from the 'pretext' of '89 . . . as the Socialist government freed itself from the pretext of socialism") and at the same time to stifle any deep feelings. Cognitively and viscerally, the experience was utterly barren, the result of a "series of static scenes without a single idea concerning the whole [Revolutionary] enterprise," of a *mise-en-scène* without a text. There was one word that described all of this artificial, cathodic mediocrity, this postmodern *métissage:* America.

It was Goude *l'Américain* who contrived the show, Goude the Madison Avenue mesmerist who seduced the rulers and fooled the people, Goude the democrat who traduced the republican ethos that incarnated the best in the Revolutionary legacy. "They preferred to finish on the U.S. model," hardly an innocent choice. The debonaire haughtiness of the Florida A & M contingent troubled Debray and Fromanger. Composed of "Michael Jackson and James Brown look-alikes" (apparently, if all blacks don't look alike, they all look like Jackson and Brown), the all-black band, largely recruited in the rural Deep South, a region finally unmasked as the true bastion of American capitalism and the seedbed of democracy, was viewed as having flexed the imperial muscles of America B.D. (Before the Decline). They were the only group that dared "take several turns around the obeslisk of the Concorde." In this revealing gesture—no more adventitious than the placement of the marching band in the grand finale position—the Debray-Fromanger diagnostic team decrypted the symbolic essence of the Gouderie and expressed it in the *normalien* analogue of the clip, the quip: "the planetary gathering of the united nations finds its climax in the United States standing by itself." France sold out to the usurping tyranny of rampant America: "The republic of values gives in to the stock exchange of values; 1789 cedes to 1776. . . . We celebrated that night the bicentennial of America."[21]

This cheap, oblique scapegoating, undertaken perhaps for its (auto)therapeutic value, should not obscure Debray's far more compelling cultural criticism, criticism voiced by many other commentators. Characteristically, this critique acknowledged France's full creative autonomy and world leadership in the domain of culture commodification and image making and manipulation. No one was more caustic and morally outraged than François Gèze, whose description of the show, though not his reasoning, was redolent of François Brigneau's: "On the fourteenth of July we watched a farce at once sinister and grotesque." Gèze impugned not Goude's particular talent "but the idea of having chosen an adman to organize the festivities." The result was an affront to the rights of man and a caricature of the Revolutionary engagement of the French people. Following the egalitarian logic of "our civilization of the image," everything is reduced to an image of the same value: "the homage to the massacred Chinese is put on the same plane as the cortege of phoney, electrified Bretons." The sole unifying chord of the whole show was sham: false zebras, false snow, false rain, a false Gabin, false Senegalese, "and even true-false Negresses recolored in a uniform black so that the variety of the natural nuance of their skin 'does not shock.'"

Le Monde's Bruno Frappat found ample elements of redemption in the Gouderie, but he acknowledged a certain anxiety that anticipated Gèze's diatribe: "Doesn't the imperialism of the advertising art, whose goal is to sell anything and everything, result in flattening the hierarchies of values and placing on the same plane, for instance, Orangina and the repression in China, the gadget and the opera, the trivial and the sacred?" In his critique of Jack Lang, "an all-category champion lyrical demagogue, a veritable Sully-Prudhomme of the hip-hop culture," philosopher Alain Finkielkraut made some of the same points.[22]

Without Gèze's Jansenistic asperities, in his delightfully irreverent manner, the journalist Alain Schifres made the same case. He had nothing against Goude, who merely did his job. Rather, he was taking aim at the *Iznogoud*—a play on words drawn from a well-known comic strip—"who have been manipulating us for the past three years, at this machination that presented us with the news that *only* an adman could still save this fête, which was civic, to be sure, but continued to divide the French and to cause havoc for motorists." Spared the heavy didacticism so feared by Jeanneney, the people got the adman's soft message: "the Revolution is dead. In its place here is the New. The new Citroën, the new Pampers, the New Wave, the people who parade in reverse gear." In the same spirit, Cardinal Lustiger held no grudge against Jean-Paul II, as Schifres baptized Goude. "But advertising in the service of the Revolution, no. This is the zero degree of memory."

Like the archbishop of Paris, *Le Canard enchaîné* admired the show, but worried about its underlying significance—a bicentennial remembered as "the fête of Supreme Appearance [Paraître Sûpreme]" and "the triumph of ad-think." The historian Philippe Minard found a revealing and damning concordance between the creation and the reception of the event, seeing both as governed by the self-fulfilling manipulative prophecies that characterize media civilization: "Since the Parisian press, until then extremely skeptical, suddenly changed its mind and pronounced [the parade] formidable, it is agreed that it was indeed formidable. No: let us discuss it and interrogate it as a symptomatic fact. The choice of Goude is a terrible resumé of our epoch: the bicentennial was thus '*chic* and *choc*.'" Nor could the left decently cry foul when Gérard Spiteri, in a right-wing newspaper, dexterously reproached its hypocrisy in confiding the decisive bicentennial enterprise to an adman: "Not so long ago the left reviled showbiz society and the perversions of advertising as the vehicle of all modern frustrations."[23]

Carefully articulated before the event by the commemorators, the defense of Goude was rehearsed afterward in a rather halfhearted manner, largely because it seemed superfluous in the wake of his dithyrambic press. It went something like this: the critics are all "uptight" intellectuals; intellectuals are by nature cranky, rigid, moralizing, snobbish; they are allergic to having fun—or, rather, to other people having fun during their watch; they are so heavily invested in cultural *rentes de situation* that they refuse to recognize advertising as an art; they cling wistfully to the world of Rousseau, though they live in the age of Marshall McLuhan and the planetary village; they don't like to mix rock music with serious business; they are often exorbitantly chauvinistic; the management of French civilization is too important to be left in the hands of intellectuals.

"The attack of French intellectuals on the adverstising milieu is a very lazy cliché," protested Jean-Noel Jeanneney. Advertising was an art like any other, capable of "the best and the worst." The philistine was not the one who accorded artistic status to advertising but one who demonized and disqualified it on the basis of some moral litmus. Not only was advertising an art form in and of itself but given its inventiveness and alertness, it was particularly well equipped to "express the sensibilities of the time." As for the show itself, Jeanneney's assurance that he worked closely with Goude in its preparation—presumably to temper certain of his "artistic" inclinations?—was hardly likely to mollify the hard-core critics.

A number of prominent intellectuals, especially on the left, acclaimed Goude's achievement. It was a signal success in the eyes of sociologist-philosopher Edgar Morin, one that rescued the commemoration from the banal fireworks of anniversary celebrations. Though the historian Madeleine Rebérioux started out with a negative prejudice and a fear that Goude would disparage the sense of the event commemorated, she became an effusive fan: "I will defend this show before the entire world. I found it very beautiful, fundamentally antiracist. . . . I am a Goudian, and I did not expect to be."[24]

Without drawing universal lessons or soaring to Olympian heights of outrage, it was possible simply to dislike the Gouderie on its own terms. According to *Le Canard enchaîné,* employing quotation marks with the usual bravado of the French press, Mitterrand himself was not wholly enthralled: "It's very lovely, but it's a bit long and it lacks rhythm." Most of the grand dignitaries of the summit left after Jessye Norman's *Marseillaise.* Actor-director Roman Polanski likewise left early: he "was bored stiff."

Concurring with Mitterrand that the parade was too long, Jean Favier, the director of the French archival service and a member of the Institut de France, added that it was too Parisian, too remote from and inaccessible to *la France profonde.* "For once we are in agreement with *L'Humanité,*" wrote an editorialist in *Minute.* "We, too, were disappointed, by the slowness, the length of the parade." For the gigantic television audience in particular, complained the far-right weekly, Goude provoked no "epic inspiration." Another televiewer, François Furet, evinced similar disappointment. He approved the planetary concept but found that "my curiosity wearied before the cortege of tableaux. . . . and the camera work seemed to me to be very unimaginative."[25]

The View from Down Home

There is no doubt that most of France felt left out of the Gouderie. The provincials did not march or dance to the drumbeat of Goude's preparations. The idea that the whole bicentennial and the reputation of the nation lay in Goude's hands did not pervade middle France. Nor was this estrangement peculiar to the people as opposed to the cultural elite. Raymond Huard, a Marxist historian actively involved in commemorative activities in the Nimes and Montpellier areas, remarked that Goude's Parisian bicentennial "did not touch us especially." But, he added, "we had no reason to complain about what was done." Huard discerned in the parade "a certain grandeur." His accomplice in the Montpellier commemoration, fellow academic Guy Boisson, reported that his world felt the impact of Goude only "after the fact." He and his friends, many of them Communists, had been so disenchanted by what appeared to be the government's passivity and immobility vis-à-vis the Revolution that they were absolutely delighted by the volcanic jolt that Goude imparted. The parade was splendid not for its intrinsic aesthetic but because it was immediately represented as a monumental triumph for the commemorators and thus implicitly for the Revolution. Thanks to Goude, Boisson had the impression far from the Champs-Elysées and the media machines that "the people reappropriated 'its revolution.'"[26]

Of 182 inhabitants of the village of Rézentières in the Cantal, thirty-three were interviewed on the phone concerning their reaction to the show. *Le Figaro* reported "a very blunted enthusiasm." According to Madame Grenier, an active farmer-housewife, who vibrated to the cadence of the harvest calendar rather than the drums of world music, what happened on the Champs-Elysées, even on a special fourteenth of July, was not a priority affair: "You know, we have other things to think about this time of year with the work on the farm. We cut hay all day long under a hot sun. So at night, after dinner, we took a walk in the cool evening." Her neighbor Lucienne Cambon contended, in the same vein, that working people had no time to think about far-off revolutions and commemorations, an attitude that certain peasants had shared at the outset of the French Revolution: "It's very nice what happens in Paris, but my livestock, who's going to feed them? If I spend my time in front of the TV, it's not your Mister Goude who will give them drink and food." (One can perhaps imagine Goude choreographing a ballet starring Marie Antoinette milking the cows at the Trianon; there was a certain poetry in those rhythmic movements.)

The cost of the Parisian show scandalized a number of villagers, for it seemed radically out of proportion with both modality and object. "Ten billion [centimes, or Fr 100 million] for a parade seems excessive to me," commented Madame Jarlier. "A price like that gets on my nerves," the wife of the service-station operator, Madame Guillin, opined; "too much money, it's shocking." But Goude was not without admirers in this enclave of middle France. Gérard Vainier, a retired worker, was truly dazzled: "It was grandiose. Even if I did not understand everything." What did he like in particular? "The singer in the blue, white. and red dress." Her color did not seem to matter. "That one, one can say that she sings damned well."[27]

One of the great ironies of Goude's show was that it was conceived particularly for television yet it left many televiewers—seven hundred million worldwide— cold. The commemorators had enjoined Goude to aim at the vast electronic audience, the logic of which strategy corresponded to his own talent and experience. "If I were you," he told everyone who would listen in the weeks preceding the show, "I would stay in front of my television set." He chose his own director, Jean-Paul Jaud, who had convinced him with his enthusiasm for the task and his esteem for and apparent familiarity with Goude's work. "We talked about the way to film the dance, I had the impression that we were in agreement." In the end Goude felt utterly betrayed by Jaud's work: "He was and is well-intentioned, but he understood nothing. I feel that he made a mess of something which was probably not a major work, far from it, but which at least had the merit of freshness and originality. It was something never before seen that should have been even better on TV than in the flesh. It was, however, the very opposite that took place."

Goude located the fault in Jaud's presumptuousness: "In a strong position as a result of his accomplishments as a sports director, he said to himeslf that he was going to show these advertising jerks what a *clip* really is." His arbitrary conception produced a fragmented, chaotic representation, a caricature of Goude's caricatures, a fleeting and distorted image of his images that the television commentators could not master and the audience could not fathom or enjoy. Christian Dupavillon felt it was unfair to lay so heavy a blame on Jaud. He assigned much of the responsibility to the producers who failed to organize the collaboration between Goude and Jaud. Curiously, the official program for the Gouderie promised "a grand moment of television" precisely because of "the complicity" between the two. But if Goude limited his instructions to an evocation of Leni Riefenstahl's manner of filming a parade at the mass Nazi rallies at Nuremberg (hardly an innocent model for a self-proclaimed antiracist, noted Alain Finkielkraut) and capturing a crowd "in playing with close-ups [and] cross-angle shots," perhaps Jaud had reason to venture on his own.

Goude also reproached Jaud for projecting a misleading impression of what he took to be "my multiracial philosophy." A pragmatist rather than an ideologue, Goude claimed he would have aimed at a balance between black and white to avoid exasperating "middle France [*la France profonde*]." Jaud "showed practically only people of color, which needlessly provoked a sizable number of televiewers," complained Goude, who took the occasion to reassure his offended countrymen that it was Jack Lang who had chosen Jessye Norman. (Dupavillon received about 200 two hundred excoriating the minister of culture for this choice.)

The issue of fault aside, Goude's devastating judgment of the television production seems right on the mark. With few exceptions, the press concurred. Jean-François Revel's reaction was just: "It was curious, [but] it was not enchanting." The television show was poorly lit, hard to follow, and often monotonous. On TF1, once it became clear to him that he was lost, Léon Zitrone, doyen of television anchors for solemn occasions, had the good sense to recede into quasi-permanent silence. The same was not true in the case of Antenne 2, where news star Claude Sérillon giggled tirelessly in response to the unctuous, sometimes fatuous ramblings of the president's showbiz nephew Frédéric Mitterrand, who will be best remembered by historians of French culture for this hometown pun: "Tu as vu la femme du président des Etats-Unis, le spectacle lui en Bush un coin."[28]

Winners

When all is said and done, the fourteenth of July remained a signal victory for Jeanneney, for Goude, and for Mitterrand. Jeanneney's richly earned sigh ["ouf"] echoed across the hexagon: "I am relieved and happy. Yes, we pulled it off, we won!" In the immediate glow of success he struck an uncharacteristically triumphalist note and made bloated claims: "The bicentennial surpassed everything that we had for the centennial." As a rule, however, he was modest and reflective, rightfully proud of a job extraordinarily well done under horrendously adverse circumstances; hopeful that "my fellow citizens might have learned to live together better, and that French influence swelled abroad"; and already curious to know, as the vocation of the historian dictates, "how the facts through which we have just lived will settle into memory." It seems fitting too that tensions persisted between the Mission and the rue de Valois, nominally its tutelary ministry. When Jack Lang learned that Jeanneney was planning to affix his name to full-page congratulatory ads in the major newspapers, "he blew up in anger" and insisted that he be a cosignatory.

Contested within the Mission, Jeanneney's reputation soared beyond its walls. Sensitive to the enormity of the challenge that the Mission president had faced, especially since he had arrived at the reins so late, informed observers agreed that he had acquitted himself admirably as organizer and spokesman of the commemoration. On the right, Jean Favier, himself a highly successful intellectual-administrator, commended him for the skill with which he handled a very difficult task. On the Communist left, Raymond Huard noted that he had projected a sympathetic image throughout the country and had played "a useful role" in effecting the rendezvous between France and the Revolution. Navigating between civic consensus and Jacobin exegesis, Maurice Agulhon welcomed in Jeanneney a kindred spirit. He praised him warmly for his commitment to the right values and for the robust yet restrained way in which he conveyed them, "with neither polemical spirit nor political excess, and with much nuance." Jeanneney's ultimate reward, after a brief return to writing and teaching at the Institut d'études politiques of Paris, was the junior ministry he received in the cabinet reshuffle that brought Edith Cresson to the premiership in May 1991.[29]

Goude the creator stayed away from the quarrel over who was the creator of Goude. Morbidly obsessed with the fear that the headlines in the *New York Post* and *Libération*—a strange pairing, but further evidence that Goude privileged form over content—might simultaneously read "Shame"/"Honte" on the morning of the fifteenth, Goude, like Jeanneney, felt immensely unburdened and vindicated. Virtually unknown outside his professional milieu before the bicentennial, the adman/artist was now a superstar. He had achieved overnight something of the immortality for which he had always yearned. ("Yes, it's true, I need to be sacralized," he had confided to *L'Express* in 1987, "advertising is so ephemeral.") One mark of his status: the word "Goude" entered the journalistic vocabulary as a proper noun to refer to a certain kind of public extravaganza. When asked, however, by the CSA poll in November 1989 what they most remembered about the celebration in Paris on the previous fourteenth of July, 54 percent of respondents cited the military parade and only 44 percent the Gouderie. Yet when the question was recast to ask which of the "fêtes and commemorations of the bicentennial . . . come to mind," Goude roundly trounced the military parade, 41 percent to 24 percent. And 78 percent, in response to another query, pronounced the Goude opera a success (79 percent said as much for the military parade). Success did not imply perennial desire. "Would you like to have in the future, on the evening of upcoming July fourteenths, parades of this sort on the Champs-Elysées?" asked the CSA. 39 percent replied yes and 47 percent said no, the remainder venturing no opinion. The institutional memory, however, did not wane. In the spring of 1991, France honored Goude, alongside Pierre Cardin, another celebrated creator, with the Legion of Honor.[30]

Arguably the biggest winner was President Mitterrand. "For Tonton [Mitterrand], the days of glory have arrived," mused *Le Canard*, playing on the words of the national hymn. "What sweet revenge for François Mitterrand," affirmed *Le Nouvel Observateur*. For weeks the president of the republic had been the target of relentless criticism, violent attacks from the right (for his alleged megalomania, "the folly of grandeur," prodigal waste of public funds, poisoning the daily lives of Parisians with his summit and its draconian security requirements), and sharp attacks from the left wing (the Renaud-Perrault-Krivine-Communist axis). But in the wake of the Gouderie, and three days of festivities without incident in a city free of automobiles and full of sympathetic revelers, "the polemic on the bicentennial of the Revolution," in the words of *Le Monde*, "ended with the defeat of those who set it off."

The president himself was surprised and deeply moved by the way in which the world resonated with the bicentennial: "There is a sort of religion, that we French, who are somewhat indifferent and overly skeptical, don't practice enough. Who will complain of this rendezvous of History with the calendar, which will cast France into the center of so many memories and hopes?" With evident pride, Mitterrand showed the elegant new jewels of Paris to the leaders of the world, and through them, to the people of the world: the Opéra de la Bastille, the Musée d'Orsay, the Pyramide du Louvre, and the Arche de la Défense.

The meetings seemed to go as well as the sight-seeing. One of Mitterrand's most vitriolic critics, Philippe Tesson, director of *Le Quotidien de Paris*, conceded that "in terms of image, the summit of the Arch is a success for him." Echoing Jean-Noël Jeanneney in another domain, André Fontaine, one of France's leading specialists on international affairs, commented: "Now, the image today counts more than anything else." Given his success in dealing with his own economy, and his international stature, Mitterrand may have succeeded in moving the G-7 out of the tight grip of Reagano-Thatcherism. Mitterrand apparently achieved general agreement on a collective effort to integrate the USSR into the world economy and to revive the North-South dialogue in one form or another. While the president could not wholly conceal "his aura of self satisfaction," his sherpa Attali, for whom this was the most arduous of summits, breathed a great sigh of relief in unison with Jean-neney and Goude: "It's fabulous, everything happened the way I have been dreaming for a year."[31]

Let us not, furthermore, overlook the lucrative commercial side of the bicentennial balance sheet. The commemoration gave an enormous boost to tourism. The experts called it "an exceptional year," "one heck of a vintage year." Worldwide attention focused on the anniversary of the Revolution afforded France a vast amount of free publicity (estimated to be worth Fr 10 billion). With forty-three million tourists (over three million visiting Paris during July), France narrowed the gap on Spain and the United States as the world's leaders in the travel/hospitality field. The French tourist office in New York reported that Americans had never been so eager to visit the hexagon: "Ah, if only we had a bicentennial every year," dreamed its director. At least 20 percent more Americans than usual visited France (including some who paid Air France $1,789 for an "aristocratic" package at the Hôtel Crillon). The Japanese (up 26 percent, and spending on the average between forty-five hundred and eighty-five hundred francs a day, depending on the source consulted) and the Italians (up from 3.5 to 4 million visitors) registered similarly impressive increases. The results must have been particularly gratifying to the government in the wake of harsh strictures and bleak prophecies from the right—both politicians and the press—that inadequate planning would produce a mediocre yield.[32]

Beyond but through Goude: Assessing the Bicentennial Enterprise as a Whole

Will Goude, in the years to come, be the official synecdoche for the entire bicentennial celebration? To a considerable extent, observers, professional and amateur, tended to conflate bicentennial and parade, to reduce the one to the other, to measure the former by the latter. Even in general discussions of the commemoration, the Gouderie was often the implicit referent. Thus it seems appropriate to address the broad lines of criticism of the bicentennial experience in the penumbra of the treatment of the fourteenth of July.

Certainly one of the most frequent and vehement reproaches against the festivities concerned their allegedly extravagant cost. With characteristic myopia, the opposition made this charge the leitmotif of its bicentennial discourse. Founded on a purely political—that is, contrived and partisan—baseline of justifiable expenditure, this critique was usually predicated on one of two overlapping assumptions:

that the event was literally not worth celebrating, and thus any significant disbursement was abusive; and that any celebration would perforce redound to the advantage of the Socialists and therefore should not drain public funds. (Feeling both anomic and cuckolded in a commemoration that intrinsically they felt belonged to them, the Communist opposition underwrote the latter rather than the former premise: "the bill for the sumptuous festivities that have been programmed," complained *L'Humanité*, "will be particularly elevated.")

Rejecting the symbolic idiom of the bicentennial, the right painted itself into a narrow corner where money became the only language it could speak in dealing with the organization of the commemoration. That left little room for nuance or discrimination or substantive evaluation. According to the right's wishful thinking, what was conceptually a "failure" (to use journalist Henri Amouroux's unequivocal term) was bound to be commensurately a financial fiasco. In unison the rightist press "railed against the bottomless pit of the bicentennial." *Le Quotidien de Paris* denounced "the opulent excesses" it predicted Lang would further multiply now that his voracious ministry had got its hand on the commemoration. *Figaro-Magazine* tirelessly inveighed against festive extravagance, waste, and incompetence. The daily *Figaro* marveled at the millions upon millions depleted for unwarranted and/or merely ostentatious purposes, including such items as Fr 7.5 million just for erecting security barriers and temporary no-parking signs. Even as *Rivarol* on the far right assailed "the astronomical bill" that unconsulted taxpayers would have to bear, so did the self-consciously moderate centrist leader Pierre Méhaignerie call for the creation of a parliamentary watchdog commission to oversee the way the state spent money on the bicentennial.[33]

Many voices arose to rebut the charges of extravagance. *L'Evénement du Jeudi* mocked the horror of the upscale neighborhoods for "these popular feasts." "Do they want us, like Harpagon, to eat for very little money?" asked Jacques Julliard. Mitterrand's "taste for magnificence" notwithstanding, "who would have the nerve, being at the head of a country that believes itself to be a 'great power,'" asked *Le Monde* rhetorically, "not to commemorate the Revolution with luster?" Petty carping over costs must not be allowed to distract attention from the world-historical significance of the event commemorated, insisted the *Dépêche du Midi*. Scandalized by the distorted figures flourished by the right, Matignon published a careful enumeration of expenditures, which it characterized as modest and necessary, and reminded skeptics of the enormous gains France stood to make in terms of prestige and tourism. Jack Lang chided the "grousers" who would smother the fête. If anything, the state spent much less than it should appropriately have invested in an occasion of such importance. "What extravagance? Where are the extravagances?" queried the minister of culture.

Mitterrand himself vigorously rebuffed accusations of "gigantism." France spent less than the United States devoted to the celebration of the Statue of Liberty or the Australians invested in their national anniversary. Save for abject partisan reasons, how could one question the importance of organizing a celebration commensurate with France's European and international responsibilities and ambitions, and with the intrinsic significance of the event? asked Mitterrand: "it's the birth of the republic; it's the birth of modern times; it's the advent of democracy; and it's France that embodies this battle for the liberation of mankind."

The president, moreover, was not comforted exclusively by those of his ideological family. Political commentator Alain Duhamel, frequently an acerbic critic of Socialist management of public affairs, turned his venom against the opposition for its claim that the festive costs were exorbitant, calling it "the most hypocritical, the most pharisaical [of reproaches]." Whatever one thinks of the Revolution, whatever its crimes and errors, it was the "founding actor of modern history, on the scale not of the hexagon but of the Western world." It was inconceivable to minimize it. "Do they think that a Gaullist, liberal, or centrist chief of state would have been less ambitious than François Mitterrand?" asked Duhamel. "In these groundless accusations, there is a textbook example of the practice of a Pavlovian, knee-jerk politics that is fundamentally anachronistic."[34]

Both on the left and on the right, the reproach of prodigality was frequently linked to the accusation that the money was being spent less to fulfill a historic and civic obligation than to gratify Mitterrand's insatiable lust for self-aggrandizing magnificence and renown. Max Clos, retained by *Le Figaro* for precisely this sort of moralizing, stigmatized "this pharaohlike superproduction to the glory of François Mitterrand." Others preferred the Bourbon analogy: "the pomp of the bicentennial was worthy of the Sun King" or "would have amused Louis Capet more than Danton." Clos, like Renaud on the other side of the political spectrum, tried to identify his cause with that of the aggrieved Third Estate over against "the privileged" and "the court." For the far-left *Rouge*, Mitterrand revealed his true colors in orchestrating "opulent ceremonies befitting Versailles in the age when absolutism crushed France." It was a familiar charge, voiced against every president of the Fifth Republic, a residual allergy to the Gaullist fusion of monarchical and democratic regimes, but sharpened in the case of a Socialist chief who had allegedly forsaken his own origins.

This line enabled the right, opportunistically, to obscure its hostility to the Revolutionary heritage by focusing on Mitterrand portrayed as part Mirabeau, part Talleyrand, part Babeuf. Why all the pomp, the traffic jams, and "the idiotic propaganda"? asked right-Wing journalist Georges Suffert. "Quite simply, for the pleasure of the king. François Mitterrand is a Socialist who adores pomp and circumstance." It thus followed for Suffert that "for him the Revolution is a pretext, on top of all that a décor." For the RPR's organ, *La Lettre de la nation*, Mitterrand was a "megalomaniac," "a republican monarch" for whom the bicentennial was another opportunity for "self-celebration." Should not God, as Mitterrand was sometimes called, inquired *Minute*, be entitled to a "Corpus Christi"? The *Quotidien de Paris* did not know which aspect of the president to admire most.

The Mother Teresa side, François the Just (like Louis XIII) subduing the Brahmapoutre and forgiving the debt? The Mausoleum side, François the Great (like Louis XIV) builder of the Pyramid, of the Arch, and the Opera? The regilded statues, the bridges protected by the army, everything that shines, everything that is lovely and expensive reminds us that, unlike a dictatorship or monarchy, the republic is not stingy. Its simplicity costs a fortune, but it is never lacking in money.[35]

On the left there were milder echoes of the same theme. *L'Evénement du Jeudi* conceded that the commemoration had perhaps an excessive cast of "Tonton's fête." *Libération*'s Serge July detected something close to megalomania in the "dazzling hour" of which the president had dreamed. The contradiction between Mitterrand's presidential "cult" and the republican tradition made the philosopher Marcel Gauchet uneasy. The president himself responded, in Gaullist but also Jaurèsian terms, not to the charges of princely narcissism or institutional pollution but to the more instrumental hint that he sought to leverage the commemoration to gain something more for himself politically: "What did I have to gain from it? I will never again be a candidate for any post. I am a free man, without obligations. I do not need to please anyone. I have [in mind] only the love of France, of its history, of its message."[36]

Another line of bicentennial criticism nourished by the right concerned the intolerable burdens that the logistical and security arrangements placed on Parisians. Large areas of central Paris were to be closed off to traffic for almost a week. To facilitate circulation, parking restrictions encompassed an even wider band. Further interruptions would be caused by careening corteges of dignitaries for whom prestige was measured on the basis of speed and according to the magnitude and effrontery of motorcycle escorts. Even as Parisians of 1789 had marched on Versailles for bread, their descendants of 1989 were said to be ready to march on the Elysée to reclaim their inviolable rights. The fit between their local concerns and the larger issues of the age seemed almost perfect. While their ancestors had demanded regulation in the name of equality, today's Parisians denounced regulation in the name of liberty.

Since the automobile was one of the major vehicles of twentieth-century popular culture, numerous journalists and politicians of the right sensed that they had found their "popular" bicentennial issue. Several arrondissement mayors, Chiraquians, spoke darkly of the capital as a "stricken city." The academician Jean d'Ormesson, one of the voices on the right usually able to distinguish between genuinely compelling and purely specious issues, fell into the Poujadiste trap with the following strained effort at dialogic wit. Candide asks Pangloss how the essential matters of liberty and equality will be celebrated at the bicentennial climax:

Pangloss: With splendor, of course. Paris will be emptied of its cars, the highways will be purged of those engines which disfigure them day and night. In the streets without cars the cars of the powerful will sing, as they must, of the conquests of liberty and equality.

Le Figaro cited the outrage of the Chamber of Commerce and Industry, for whom the "asphyxia of the capital" entailed "dramatic" economic consequences. The *Quotidien* added the testimony of a right-leaning police union whose leaders expressed their "inquietude" over the "anarchic" organization of the bi-summit. Nor should *L'Humanité*'s solicitude for its now motorized constituents be overlooked. It deplored the cascading "vexations" to citizen-drivers, sacrificed to "the ballet of limousines." *L'Express* wrote ironically about the "unpredictable French, who bickered over traffic jams" when they were supposed to be debating "the virtues and the excesses of the Revolution." In the same vein, *L'Evénement* reported on the wave of fear that the ban on parking presaged a new September massacre.

Once again Alain Duhamel assessed the controversy with astringent common sense. This complaint was "the most small-minded and mediocre" of all the bicentennial protests. "Once a century for three days a few uncomfortable restrictions are imposed on Parisians, and its the call to battle stations." Given the occasion, this whining was not merely "derisory" but also "somewhat humiliating" before the eyes of six thousand journalists from around the world.[37]

The substantive criticism of the bicentennial celebration, beyond the epithets of animadversion, emanated largely, though by no means exclusively, from the left. To some extent, this discourse merely rehearsed the earlier debates over the proper commemorative style and the perils and advantages of a consensual approach. Probably the most widely voiced reproach, spilling over from far and mainstream left toward the center, was that the commemoration was morally and symbolically incommensurate with the event memorialized. Replete with gadgets, it lacked heart. Despite Jeanneney's vigorous reassurances, it constantly verged on "the derisory and the frivolous."

Regretting the dearth of surging "republican fervor," *La Croix* sadly noted that the bicentennial "arouses no sentiment of communion." Compared to the centennial "overinvestment of republican spirituality," the historian Eric Walter esteemed that the bicentennial suffered an egregious lack of civic sacredness. Thinking as much of the Exposition universelle and the Eiffel Tower as of the emotion of transcendence that marked the centennial, historian Claude Mazauric bemoaned the material as well as the spiritual deficit of the bicentennial. The ethnologist Pierre Sansot deplored the "faking without scruples" of an "obscene" festival inspired by "a caricatural vision, . . . anesthetized, embalmed." Historian Louis Oury reproved the official ceremonies, which "sank into triviality and folklore." Addressing the Revolution, the poet Pierre Garnier felt obliged to relay the embarrassing truth: "You are going to live the sad days of your celebration, the folklore! Even majorettes!" Instead of recalling "the spirit and the contribution of the Great Revolution," the government served up a "postmodern commemoration—that is to say, junk," according to philospher Cornélius Castoriadès.

Concomitantly, Gilles Perrault, seconded by Daniel Bensaïd, condemned the "mercantilization," the excessive role of money and publicity, emblem of the primacy of "the faithful management of the interests of the bourgeoisie" over the emphasis on what the Revolution "might offer today's world." "By refusing to recall either the fact or the program of the Revolution, by reducing its memory to a shop of accessories and an impoverished game of images," remarked philosopher Odile Marcel, avid to repoliticize French life, "the left will have relieved the right of its anxiety over the celebration of this once significant anniversary."[38]

One did not, moreover, need to be Marxist to deplore the bicentennial's pervasive "penury of meaning," to use the phrase of Pierre Billard, a moderate writing in the *Le Point*. Circumspection triumphed over daring, "showbiz" eclipsed pedagogy, a merchandised hollowness obscured the thick richness of the Revolutionary legacy. "The laic mass of the republic," concluded Billard, "was transformed into a cathodic mass of political showbiz." For the novelist Philippe Sollers, the "pure show" of the bicentennial precluded any serious reflection: "never has charlatanism been as developed as it is today." The commemorators reduced the Revolution "to the folklore of the spots of a media civilization," wrote Frédéric Lazorthes in *Le Quotidien de Paris;* this "spectacular" diminution of the significance of the Revolutionary event guaranteed the "failure" of the celebration. Gérard Spiteri of *Le Quotidien* joined historian Jean Tulard in regretting the lack of a grand project, a new idea directed toward the future with the illuminating power of the centennial's electricity.

Obviously, Jeanneney's tireless evangelism did not convince *Libération*'s François Reynaert any more than it had the other critics. Overwhelmed by the burdens of "prestige operations" and sundry diplomatic, touristic and commercial obligations, the commemoration "projects no light either on the Revolution or on its ongoing relevance," concluded this reporter. Generally sympathetic with the bicentennial, the sociologist-philosopher Edgar Morin nevertheless criticized its failure to engage in a profound reflection on the meaning of democracy, "the greatest shortcoming of the commemoration." With a different inflection and another agenda in mind, this was also the reproach of François Furet, Marcel Gauchet, and others in Furet's orbit, dubbed "the galaxy." Mona Ozouf reproached Jeanneney and other bicentennial organizers with a failure to draw the nation together in lucid commemoration for lack of forthright intellectual and moral leadership. She would have required of them a ticket of confession, in the manner of the eighteenth-century Jesuits, testifying to their frank adherence to the revisionist catechism, which featured a public denunciation of the Terror and an acknowledgment of its organic relation to '89.[39]

Critics on the far left would have endorsed Morin's judgment provided he gave the notion of democracy Michel Vovelle's social rather than François Furet's political vocation. Soboul's successor in the chair of the History of the Revolution at the Sorbonne found the commemorative pedagogy sadly lacking, in large measure because it failed to instill the "will to change" that he located at the core of the Revolutionary legacy. The gaping social deficiency, which rendered the commemoration frankly reactionary, was a major refrain of Daniel Bensaïd's commentary. "The sacred Thermidorean union," a sort of cumulative cohabitation where Mitterrand sat alongside de Gaulle, Mirabeau, Lafayette, Fouché, and Thiers, among others, espoused "'89 and the truncated rights of man against '93 and the rights of man in society."

Since he sold out to the party of meek reform, following his president's lead, it is no wonder that Michel Rocard—"Riquiqui," a.k.a. Turgot-Roland—was hostile to a genuinely social commemoration, argued Bensaïd. The crushing of the social by the political seemed to be reflected in the state's confiscation of the commemoration in conjunction with the monied interests that controlled the private sector (the equivalent of the union of crown and the mixed aristocracy of nobles and wealthy bourgeois) to the detriment of the bone and sinew of the Third Estate, the little people who more or less constituted society. In terms redolent of Pierre Chaunu, the object of his strictures on so many accounts, Bensaïd decried the "grand statist ceremony" and the "swallowing up" of civil society by the state. (Compare the appreciation of the Communist Claude Mazauric, who regretted the state's low profile and decentralizing spirit in the conduct of the commemoration, and conservative journalist Alain-Gérard Slama's alarmist apprehension of a hyper-Jacobin commemoration resulting in a Furet "circumvented" and a Soboul "almost rehabilitated.")[40]

Stifled in the "cathedral of good thought," where the rights of man were the only hymn intoned, Odile Marcel yearned for the time when "the project of transforming society had united men." The historian Madeleine Rebérioux made the same point more gently when she remonstrated that "the republic was absent from this commemoration." In a complaint symmetrical to the one Philippe de Villiers formulated for the Vendée, numerous Communists denounced a history that was "truncated" and "falsified" by the official commemorators. The exclusion of the social dimension, of the "second revolution" and Year II (a euphemistic rendering of what its partisans might have called the *versant lumineux* of the Terror) was tantamount to the exclusion of "millions of the poor [*va-nu-pieds*]." Hypersensitive to the stench of class collaboration, collaboration fostered in this case by "big capital," *Révolution* saw the bicentennial as a campaign of mystification and demobilization, the aim of which was to "to string up the very idea of Revolution."

What Furet welcomed and merchandised—a "France reconciled with itself, thanks to the values of the republic [around which that reconciliation is articulated], . . . finally [leading] a normal political life, pacified, adult, . . . with the Revolution accomplished"—the philosopher Concorcet [François Ewald] contested as a worthy and fruitful bicentennial theme. For it smothered the germs of division that were at once the legacy of the Revolution and the antitoxins of the body social. Instead of faithfully commemorating "the Revolution in its struggles and battles," the government preferred to invent "a clean Revolution to be used to clean up the revolutionary events, to clean away everything that made for a revolution and not simply a soft, tranquil, and pacific evolution toward happiness."[41]

Youthful idealists such as François Baroin, politically moderate yet morally exigent, drew great spiritual strength from the rights hymn stigmatized by Odile Marcel as a thrall of conservatism. Their voice is worth recording, if only because they worked so tirelessly to get young people involved in the public sphere. Globally, given the Herculean difficulties, the bicentennial was "not so bad" in Baroin's estimation. But he would have turned it much more resolutely toward the future. The leftist wistfulness for insurgency and a certain social violence struck him as obsolete; their discourse was the real folklore to be deplored in the commemoration. Like his father, Baroin felt it was futile and in a sense merely self-indulgent to make fetishes of heroic struggles and cleavages of the past. The intense historical preoccupation of the bicentennial had drained it of its vital energy. Baroin would have mobilized civil society not to rush the barricades, or the archives, but to enter into a permanent colloquy on the means of assuring justice and mastering progress. He shared the naïveté and the optimism of many of the newly aroused citizens of 1789. By making lists of grievances, by discussing the philosophical as well as the pragmatic grounds for dealing with them, and by writing down the rights to which people were entitled and the obligations they owed each other, he thought it possible to reconcile the political with the social, the demands of liberty with those of equality.[42]

Anticlimax, Zenith, and Finale

After the extraordinary élan of the fourteenth, everything that ensued was bound to be anticlimactic. Yet, in symbolic terms, the remaining events were not without genuine significance.[1] Given the enormous emphasis that Jean-Noël Jeanneney and François Mitterrand had placed on 1989 as the year of the rights of man, the anniversary of the promulgation of the Declaration on 26 August had to be commemorated with energy, even if the bodies and minds of vast numbers of their countrymen were located elsewhere. Held at the Arche de la Défense, the ceremonies included a number of interrelated events that pivoted around the inauguration of the Arch of Fraternity, the lyrical name of the International Foundation of Human Rights and Human Sciences. The theme of the day was the unrelenting relevance and necessity of a vigorous rights campaign two hundred years after the Declaration in a worldwide arena with special emphasis on the responsibility of the youth of all countries to confront "the rights that remain to be conquered."

Remembering and Recasting the Rights of Man (and Woman and . . .

The youth of eighty nations, making up the Association pour la Déclaration du 26 août 1989 (AD 89), among whose leaders were the son of Michel Baroin and the nephew of the African statesman-poet Léopold Senghor, presented the fruit of several years' toil: an updated version of the Declaration of Rights relative to the needs of the late twentieth century on a planetary scale. Imbued with the generous humanism of the Revolutionaries of '89, it addressed quite specifically issues of pressing concern today such as the protection of the environment, including outer space, and the circumspect utilization of the earth's resources, as a civic duty;

guarantees against the abuse of individual rights by computer technology; the imperious need to honor differences within the context of a commitment to equality; the affirmation of the inalienable rights of women (including the "free disposition of their bodies"), of children (claims to proper food, shelter, clothing, care, juridical aid), and of the handicapped, the unemployed, the ill, political refugees, and cultural, ethnic, and religious minorities; the abolition of capital punishnment; the freedom of each nation to determine the character of its economic development, a freedom viewed as intimately linked to its democratic prospects.

Another initiative, inspired by Bernard Kouchner, a physician and a junior minister for humanitarian action, involved the presentation of a petition signed by people around the world calling for the recognition of a right to intervene anyplace for the sake of humanitarian assistance. In the same spirit three humanitarian associations working for the welfare of children received Fr 250,000 each from the funds that had been raised with the launching of the hot-air balloons at the opening of the bicentennial. The Arch was also the site of a UN-sponsored exhibition dealing with the rights of refugees. As part of its introduction, Antenne 2 presented a sort of catalogue of some of the major rights arenas, ranging from China and eastern Europe to the Third World to the homeless and hungry of the so-called advanced Western countries.[2]

The Presidential Exegesis: A Reply to Maggie and Beyond

To mark the induction of his former minister of foreign affairs, Claude Cheysson, as president of the Arch Foundation, François Mitterrand delivered a spirited, wide-ranging speech. He argued that the Declaration of Rights had truly changed the course of history, despite its cobbled and incomplete nature and its practical weaknesses. Responding to Margaret Thatcher's cranky irritation over French claims to rights progenitorship, the president readily acknowledged the English and American contributions but contended that the French document distinguished itself by transcending the largely parochial focus of the latter in order to plead for the universality of the rights of man, rights applicable to all peoples and in all times. It was not mere "national vanity" to contend that France contracted in 1789 an eternal moral obligation to be in the first ranks of those struggling to preserve and extend human rights. Nor did Mitterrand avert his eyes from the Revolution's own inconsistency in prosecuting the rights philosophy. Women, the poor, and servants were denied full citizenly status; the forces of wealth frustrated the aspirations of blacks; "the absence of a social doctrine" impoverished the Declaration, and, even today, the social requirements were but halfway filled.

Despite the centrality of the Declaration in the Revolutionary arena, "crimes" were committed in contravention of its letter and spirit. Throughout the bicentennial Mitterrand had made a point of owning up to the Revolution's failures and its barbarities, not merely as a matter of intellectual rigor, but in order to reach out to those French citizens who felt victimized, through their families or in their values, by the Revolution's course. He condemned the "extermination" of the Carmelite priests, punished for service to their faith; whatever the injustices of the old order they embodied, it was profoundly unjust to wreak cruel vengeance on them. Citing his longtime intellectual companion Jean Jaurès, Mitterrand reminded his audience that fear was not a revolutionary force and that abuses must always be denounced, whatever their political fidelity. Like François Furet, following a legion of nineteenth-century critics, the president declared that the Terror no longer had the justification of the "necessity of circumstances" after the military victories of the spring of 1794.

Even as it was crucial to make these avowals, it was equally important not to allow the aberrations—for Mitterrand refused to follow Furet's tendency to regard the violations of rights as intrinsic to an underlying Revolutionary logic operative from the beginning—to obscure the deep impact and tenacity of the Declaration. Somehow, at least when viewed in long retrospect, its principles, Mitterrand would have us believe, were neither "affected" nor "weakened." The Declaration "announced the dawn of new times, whatever were the ulterior deviations, oppressions, and lapses. It remained inalterably engraved in our memories, and the message that it bears lost nothing of its force—on the contrary, it continues to inspire numerous international conventions and agreements." Mitterrand exhorted his hearers to be intransigent in the pursuit of rights and the combat for the liberation of the whole human race.

The president rehearsed another of his bicentennial leitmotifs: the refusal of exclusion of any sort. The struggle can never end: there will always be evil forces seeking to "hamper the march of free men," and new challenges generated by technological development (biotechnology, information systems, ecological transformations). Mitterrand ended as he began, with a word surely meant for Renaud, as much wounded as embittered. As part of his personal war against exclusion on the international plane, the president recalled that he had invited twenty-five heads of state and government from the Third World to the bicentennial-summit, that he had inserted a specific reference to the Declaration of Rights in the final summit communiqué, and that he had devoted much of his public career to attempting to attenuate the abyss between rich and poor, at home and abroad.[3]

The Checkered Fête: Parable of Fraternity and Exclusion

A nationally televised concert, using the sumptuous Arch as stage and backdrop, followed the inauguration of the Foundation. It replaced a more ambitious plan to hold a giant concert in Montpellier that the Mission had to abandon for logistical and financial reasons. Structured around the "I had a dream" refrain of Martin Luther King, Jr., the concert featured statements by persons associated with the human-rights campaign interspersed with music and song from a wide array of artists from the world over. Thus, for instance, Nobel laureate Wole Soyinka, an African playwright-essayist, read a text exalting difference and diversities as the crux of the Declaration as it applied to today's world, a perspective that was evincing increasing concern in French domestic politics. Abbé Pierre enunciated one of the Declaration's articles and then discussed the invidious ways in which misery undermined humanity, demanding that persons of good faith struggle against it. "What an idea can do against an army" was the poignant topic of an exiled Chinese student, who reasoned that the Declaration made dictators tremble more than tanks made insurgents lose courage. The presence of several children of the victims of dictatorship, including the daughters of Chilean Salvador Allende and Romanian Doina Cornea, underlined the bicentennial commitment to political democracy. In addition to a French troupe led by Maxime Leforestier, Claude Nougaro and Nicole Croizille, Senegalese, Chinese, and Bulgarian choral groups, and Kurdish, Maghrébin, and African singers and instrumentalists entertained the crowd.

The theme of exclusion took on a concrete and nasty immediacy when the police charged into hundreds of Fourth Estate spectators who invaded the stands reserved for those with tickets and the spaces closed off for so-called security reasons. At least fourteen people were wounded, four of them seriously enough to warrant hospitalization. The Mission had formally invited five thousand guests and allotted another seven thousand seats to the "Young Europeans," who were holding a congress in the capital to coincide with the bicentennial event. Large numbers of the "excluded"—according to *Libération*, "young hoods, students from proper families, executives, blacks, whites, and Beurs [North Africans born in France of immigrnt parents] mixed together"—showed up, many of them in response to television host Claude Sérillon's ill-considered summons to join the fun. Shouting "Liberty, equality, no to privileges," and "We want to get in—this is a celebration of human rights, isn't it?" they could not understand why they were denied access to the large open areas above the subway and the underground garage, areas closed off for fear that they could not support the weight of the crowd. Nor had the producer afforded ersatz access through giant screens on the aesthetically frail and impudent grounds that such broadcasts "would have shattered the emotional relation between the artists and the public."[4]

The Valmy Scenario: Aestheticizing the Bivouac

"The rule of law is nothing if it is not upheld by force," observed the once very social, now very military, always very Gaullist Jean-Pierre Chevènement, minister of defense. This view, echoed by Mitterrand ("in order to remain sovereign, a nation must be strong"), surely informed the Mission's choice of Valmy as the next great event of the bicentennial, a celebration of the nation-in-arms, of the role of a citizen army in a democracy, of the advent of the republic under extremely adverse circumstances. "A lovely site to triumph or to die," wrote Michelet of the hill set in a humid fog on which the motley French forces repulsed the Prussian invaders in September 1792, shortly after the "second revolution" and the deposition of the king, when the nation was particularly vulnerable.

The commemorators chose to focus not on the battle, whose authenticity as a military engagement the experts continue to dispute, but on its implications: "The birth of the nation" was the title chosen for the festivities of 16-17 and 23-24 September. Valmy interested Jeanneney because it was the first and only occasion to move beyond 1789 and face some of the issues and promises of the changing, struggling, unfolding Revolution. It appears, however, that it was largely Chevène-ment's show, two-thirds of whose budget of Fr 15 million he assumed. He decided how the space would be used—other concerns aside, the peculiarities of the site and the difficulties of access precluded a historical reconstitution—and, in consultation with Jack Lang, he chose the talent. The selection of the director, Patrick Bouchain, an ex-counselor to Jack Lang and the architect-builder of Daniel Buren's controversial black-and-white-striped columns in the cour d'honneur of the Palais-Royal, seemed to determine all the rest.

Bouchain invited a group of well-known artists ranging from architects and sculptors to a theatrical horse-trainer to develop projects that would constitute an itinerary ("a promenade") through which spectators could walk. Unconstrained by any narrow thematic injunction, these creators were expected to evoke in some way or another "the alliance between the army and the nation." Instead of imposing "a fixed and predigested vision" through the banal "subterfuges" of historical reconstitution, Bouchain hoped that "each work, each contribution, would arouse—or reawaken—in the spectators emotions and questions concerning this episode of our past." The plan was extremely vague. Though willing to court controversy over the aesthetics, Bouchain shied away from taking risks with the history. He avoided any hint about the Revolution's "anticipations," the radical social and economic measures that flowered in the second year of the new republic. As it turned out, the spectacle might have confused but would not have alienated Msgr. d'Hulst, rector of the Institut catholique of Paris in 1892, who saw Valmy as the very emblem of consensus, "a pure and honorable recollection."[5]

One wonders whether Chevènement really fathomed what he was getting into, and how his own officers and soldiers as well as a largely non-Parisian public would react. Rather than a Gouderie-II or a military Woodstock, it was a sort of open-air, partly hands-on, museofair, of a somewhat arcane and emphatically eclectic nature. A vast course was laid out, onto which the visitor was led by two powerful oxen, chosen, *Libération* assured its readers, "not for any obscure castration-related symbolism ('we aren't oxen,' as one said in the army) but because the animal is perfect to regulate man's step."

The first creation belonged to Sarkis, who contrived twelve stations in the woods to represent some of the great battles or popular struggles in history, including Tiananmen, Stalingrad, Budapest, and Vercors in addition to Valmy, each distinguished by sounds and songs of its time. (Brazen and perhaps naive, Sarkis would have liked to include Dien Bien Phu, a prospect that would not have enchanted the military professionals.) Next Daniel Buren constructed a tent-corridor of white-and-red striped cloth through whose apertures of different sizes and positions spectators could behold various vistas and objects on the Valmy landscape. At the end a red curtain theatrically opened on the reconstituted windmill that marked the Revolutionary battleground. Then Bartabas, of the Zingaro circus, unleashed one hundred wild horses, which dashed to freedom, one supposes, before the spectators (they were "beautiful, like an ad for Citroën," allowed the enthusiastic *Libération*). Finally, as the crowd headed for the cabbage soup and bread offered as a collation, the Garde républicaine serenaded them, and a "ballet" of twenty old Alouette helicopters framed in a pyrotechnic display performed above the bleachers where the public ended its visit ("It was Coppola without his means," noted a patriotic reporter from *Le Monde*).

The most astonishing thing about this perplexing array of images was the Gongoristic gloss, perhaps drafted by a conscripted *normalien* with a wry sense of the burlesque, that Chevènement conferred on it. Hailing the idea that "men of culture and men of war agree once more to look at each other, to listen and to understand each other, perhaps to admire each other," the minister gave full vent to his lyrical inclination: "I would like to see here the beginning of a new era: one in which would be reborn . . . a true culture of the nation-in-arms, one in which the army would deepen its reflection [concerning]. . . . how to refresh, vivify, consolidate, resuscitate the old marriage consummated at Valmy between the republic and its soldiers."[6]

The press evinced little enthusiasm for the Valmy show. Most observers agreed that, all in all, it was rather bewildering. No one was struck by moments of galvanizing emotion or unforgettable beauty. If there were any lessons to draw, they were more or less inscrutable. The presentation seemed gratuitously "intello" and "pretentious," entailing a sort of provocation to the audience in general and to the military personnel in particular, who were said to be "irritated" by the overrefined *décalage*. What passed for an encomium on the boulevard Raspail or the rue de Valois—"this highly conceptual walk"—bespoke deep reproach in *la France profonde*.

Le Monde tried to put the best face on it by styling it as inchoate, as the rough beginnings of what might have matured into a well-articulated idea. A commentator in *Le Monde de la Révolution française* regretted the politico-ideological timidity of the commemoration, the absence of reflection on the new situation created by the emergence of the nation-republic. Predictably, *Figaro-Magazine* deplored the extravagant sums spent on the event; yet even *Le Monde* suggested that the funds could have been better spent. *L'Humanité* disliked the ambient militarism; Chevènement did not shrink from using Valmy to extract more money to finance nuclear gadgets and to prevent a real debate on the military policy of the future.

One of the few organs to praise the "soft" evocation of the Valmy show was a left-royalist paper.[7]

The Republic and the Nation-in-Arms

President Mitterrand delivered his final address of the bicentennial season at Valmy. Though his performance could do little to rescue the event from its muddy mediocrity, it was an effective speech. He had two overlapping tasks. The primary one was to commemorate Valmy, but the particular inflection he gave it derived from the secondary mission, to assuage a burgeoning malaise in the professional military corps. The military "Fronde" had surfaced in July with the publication of a series of anonymous letters portraying strain and alienation in the services. The president used the stage and symbol of Valmy to buoy the morale of the military by acknowledging his awareness of the need for change and improvement on the concrete plane of daily military existence and by affirming the nation's gratitude to and continuing need of the armed forces to preserve its values. You emanate from us and we appreciate you, he told soldiers and officers: "today as much as yesterday, the army needs to feel that it is one with the nation."

Paying homage to "the exceptional quality of the army," demonstrated recently in Chad and Lebanon as it had been long ago at Valmy, the president of the republic did not shy away from a certain mea culpa. If abnegation and discipline were necessarily the army's credo and obligation, it was up to the government, and the society to assure better communication and dialogue, adequate (that is, better) financing, and a persistent effort toward adapting the military institution and condition to the requirements of its time. Mitterrand recalled the "radiant energy" (Jaurès's phrase) that forged the victory at Valmy for the nascent republic, and he argued, in terms that neither de Gaulle nor Reagan would have found uncongenial, that one must be strong in order to remain free. The strength of the French armed services lay in their special and intimate relation with the nation. The army was "the people in its truth." In its originary diversity, the republican army epitomized the sort of pluralistic society that France would later become. As sketched by the president, the army of Valmy was composed of noble officers, veteran troops, volunteers, federalists, and foreign patriots. They spoke different languages as well as different dialects, and they wore different uniforms. Responding to the peril to the nation, the army made of that cacophony a viable community.

Citizen soldiers were no less important to the nation at peace than to the nation in danger. Mitterrand argued that the system of mandatory national service had to be improved, the need for it more cogently formulated, and its universal and egalitarian character protected. The defense of the nation was no less a civic matter at heart today than it had been two hundred years earlier, the president argued. Neither nuclear arms nor advanced technology nor intensified specialization "could replace the collective effort outside of which national defense would lose its true meaning."[8]

The Pantheon: Candidates for Apotheosis

The bicentennial season fittingly closed with the induction of three Revolutionary figures into the Panthéon, the French national hall of honor. The choice of honorees was meant as a final expression of the government's view of the Revolution, and the value and relevance of its legacy. Unlike the centennial commemorators, who opted for the political and military heroes needed to help mobilize the republican and national will, those of the bicentennial selected men whose engagement highlighted today's concerns about public education, civic instruction, scientific progress, and the fight against racism. Closely associated with the Socialist-Mitterrandian agenda, these issues were sufficiently broad-based and consensual as to forestall any boisterous discordance.

The nation would not pay homage to the great and controversial protagonists of the Revolution. Mitterrand had clearly voiced the bicentennial *"ni-ni"*: neither Robespierre nor Danton. The choice fell on three relative unknowns: the philosophe and Girondin deputy Condorcet, the mathematician and minister Monge, and the cleric and Montagnard Grégoire. They constituted, in Mona Ozouf's words, "a balanced ticket that should defuse the chronic suspicion which poisons France's Pantheonizations."

These were not the only candidates considered, nor was it initally envisaged to close the bicentennial year on the rue Soufflot. Edgar Faure had pressed the case of Rouget de Lisle, a native of Lons-le-Saunier, located in Faure's political bailiwick. Apparently, the author of the *Marseillaise* had hovered on the brink of induction in 1915. Still awaiting reception, he has been languishing "temporarily" in the Invalides ever since. At the outbreak of World War I, his candidacy seemed perfectly geared "to revive the patriotic flame of the nation." Though France was today at peace, Faure considered the rationale of 1915 still applied now, for he saw love of country as a precondition of rather than an obstacle to love of the Other.

Jeanneney argued against Rouget on conceptual and strategic grounds. Rouget lacked not the resonance but the surface of other candidates. Jeanneney preferred to pay homage to "a lifetime's work" rather than to "a specific act"—in this instance, the writing of the national hymn. Moreover, the choice of Rouget, implicitly seconded by Goude's *Marseillaise*, risked downgrading "to a secondary level the universalist, humanistic, and scientific message" that Mitterrand favored. Strongly approving Grégoire, Monge, and Condorcet, the third president of the Mission proposed as alternate possibilities Lakanal, the legislator of educational reform, and Bichat, the renowned physician.

Commemorators accorded fleeting attention to the prospect of a woman candidate. A double impediment foreclosed this option, according to Jeanneney. First,

The French nation of 1989 recognizes and thanks the great men of the Revolution. The bicentennial season closed with the "pantheonization" of three more or less moderate heroes, acceptable to the majority of today's French women and men. (Photo: Bicentennial Mission.)

"no sufficiently eminent revolutionary [female] personality compelled recognition," a judgment with which not all historians would now agree. Second, if one chose a figure external to the Revolution, such as a Louise Michel or a Marie Curie, "the symbolism of the transfer of the first woman to the Panthéon threatened to obscure the message of the celebration of the Revolution itself."

On the matter of the calendar, Jeanneney came full circle. Shortly after he assumed office, he calculated that an early Pantheonization would powerfully marshal public opinion and lubricate the commemorative machine. Then Mitterrand made it known that he wanted to associate this most solemn of national acts with the convocation of the G-7 summit. With Lang's support, Jeanneney argued strenuously against this notion. Despite its (profanely) sacred nature for the French, the Panthéon was an affair of strictly national concern that commanded no international interest. Already too many events were scheduled for the thirteenth and fourteenth of July. Together they would "drown" the Pantheonization, thus devaluing the ceremony for the French people. Finally, Jeanneney worried about the institutional, logistical, and psychological carrying capacity of Paris, whose resources and tolerance would be strained to the limit without imposing a further burden during the same week. Since there was no longer time to inaugurate the bicentennial at the Panthéon by the time this issue was resolved, the ceremony transferring the remains of the inductees was scheduled as grand finale.[9]

Jack Lang took pains to underline the placatory and moderate nature of the triple selection, an important concession to the majority of French men and women who approved the Revolution, provided it was purged of its bloody violence, and a decision bound to disappoint the Jacobin faithful. Eliding the differences and tensions between liberty and equality as the left had to learn to do in the liberal climate of the late 1980s, the minister of culture justified the designation of "these three intellectuals in revolution through their thought, their words, their acts—but never with blood."[10]

These three contrapuntal Revolutionaries eddied against certain of the tides of their turbulent time but presciently addressed the needs of today's France, a France at peace with her neighbors and herself, whose "new frontier" is "the equality of rights and of knowledge." The candidates represented the three estates: a curate, Grégoire, of modest origins who entertained sweeping philosophical and reformist interests that antedated the Revolution and transcended the boundaries of his modest parish; Condorcet, the scion of a venerable noble family who refused the army in favor of studies in mathematics, and the intimate friend of the Old-Regime's reformist elite; Monge, the simple son of an itinerant merchant, who proved that "intelligence is not the privilege of birth" and who was the first to forge close ties among science, republic, and patriotism.

Though surely no less merited than the other two, Monge's induction was less replete with ideological significance. We have seen how contentious Grégoire's selection was for many Catholics and for numerous Jews as well. These Catholics regarded the abbé as an apostate for his adherence to the Civil Constitution, despite the fact that he tenaciously clung to his faith and eschewed violence; and these Jews read in Grégoire's famous essay on regeneration a deep strain of anti-Semitism, manifested in his characterization of Jewish degeneration, physiognomic as well as moral, and his threat to the survival of their group identity. In September 1988 Jeanneney had warned the president of the republic of ecclesiastical hostility to the "laic glorification of a dissident cleric." Publicly and privately, the commemorators had pressed the church to embrace Grégoire as a way of giving ritual closure to two hundred years' strife over the Revolution. There were even reports of something resembling (failed) negotiations between the president of the republic and the archbishop of Paris. In choosing a liturgical term to describe the induction of these insufficiently celebrated Revolutionaries into the Panthéon—"it is thus an act of reparation"—Lang thrust into relief the missed opportunity in the dialogue between church and state.

A victim of Revolutionary repression, sentenced to the guillotine but found dead in his cell, Condorcet entered the Panthéon in 1989 seeming to confirm the government's distancing from the Terror, its acceptance of the existence of fundamental divergences between Terror and democracy, and its rejection of any crude amalgamations in the name of the once inviolable bloc. Together, Condorcet, Grégoire, and Monge embodied the moral values and civic ambitions with which the Socialist government wanted to associate itself: education, "the priority of priorities," and human rights: the need for universal emancipation, the defense and integration of minorities of religion, race, gender. Education and equality were the themes that best responded to Mitterrand's commitment to the end of exclusions.

Induction: The Bicentennial Finale

The Pantheonization took place on 12 December, a gray but dry Tuesday, at the end of the afternoon. Christian Dupavillon, a veteran of the solemnities of the rue Soufflot, organized the ceremonies. The central figure in the austere choreography of the dusk was François Mitterrand, whose presidency and person had become intimately associated with the Panthéon. To mark—sacralize?—his ascension to power in 1981, "he had surveyed the Panthéon, passing in review the heroic dead of the nation." Subsequently, he returned to install Jean Monnet. On this bicentennial occasion, at 7:00 P.M., the president entered the rue Soufflot, greeted by the prime minister, and mounted toward the esplanade, where he was awaited by the rest of the government, the descendants of Condorcet, and the papal nuncio, the sole official representative of the church. Mitterrand took his place on the top step in front of the Pantheon in a glass shelter erected to protect him from the elements.

Preceded by a hundred drummers from all the armed services, a cortege bearing an enormous banner marched up the rue Soufflot. Painted by Dorothée Grosland, it recited the names of the inductees, decorated in blue, white, and red, surrounded by the inscription engraved on the facade of the monument: "To the Great Men, from the Grateful Homeland." The painted banner was carried by an honor guard of four distinct groups: in front, by students from the capital's Lycée Condorcet, on the sides by students from the Ecole normale and the Ecole polytechnique, the elite institutions with which Monge was associated, and in the rear by African women representing the island of Gorée in Senegal, one of the most important and hideous entrepôts of the international slave trade, object of the tireless criticism of both Grégoire and Condorcet. After the escort deposed the banner at the foot of the Panthéon, extracts of texts of each of the inductees were read, stressing their convergent preoccupation with developing the "republic of knowledge" with which Mitterrand identified his presidency.

Then Jack Lang delivered a wonderful speech, without the usual artifices and affectations. Sober but poignant, generous but without equivocation, Lang made the case for Condorcet, Grégoire, and Monge, both in terms of their intrinsic achievements and in terms of their relevance to the France of 1989. An evocation of the "values of the Mitterrand administration," it was also an exegesis of the good

Revolution: the Revolution of passionate engagement but unflinching commitment to inviolable humanistic principles, an equality that did not stifle liberty but made it credible and useful, an implacable hatred for all tyrannies, a respect for the national patrimony whatever its taint, a belief in something resembling perfectibility through education, a love of *patrie,* and an admiration for Michelet's people. Condorcet, Grégoire, and Monge were irresistibly attractive to a Mitterrandist minister of culture because "they were not afraid of grand projects, of grand building sites" and because they believed "beautiful things and advanced knowledge were the shortest path to reach the people."

Lang showed how they were united in "their sad deaths" as well as in their life struggles. "A man without hatred who believes more than ever in this revolution which pronounces his execution," Condorcet wrote his hymn to human progress while awaiting his death and his burial in an anonymous common grave. In the Restoration climate of hostility to Jacobins and Bonapartists and disdain for scientific genius, Monge had a clandestine funeral. Upon his death a half century after the Revolution, Grégoire was denied last sacraments by the archbishop of Paris.

The minister of culture hailed the foresight and the dynamism of these pioneers of human rights and democratic reform, whose thought was young and sparkling, whose manner was intrepid, and whose intuition about the difficulty of changing the world was a lesson still relevant today, even to Socialists, perhaps especially to those in the process of taking leave of Socialism: "We do not wish to embalm you, we do not wish to erect you into statues, because your treasure is precisely to have been sensitive to the complexity of a radically disrupted world. Every revolution is an inferno of contradictions. It is a glittering forge at which amateurs play with fire. It is a hammer without a master in the hands of millions of providential men who seek out harmony in the disorder." It was especially appropriate for Condorcet, Grégoire and Monge to receive their national immortality in this "unparalleled year" in which "1789 is reborn in Prague in 1989, in Berlin in 1989, in Moscow in 1989, in Budapest, in Sofia, in Santiago, in Peking in 1989." With the national trio Lang associated Vaclav Havel and Andrey Sakharov, with whom "returns the time of the intellectuals in the forefront of the action, the time of the men of the Enlightenment."

Upon the conclusion of the speech, the *Marseillaise* was sung and the honor guard brought the banner into the interior of the Panthéon, eerily illuminated by candles, to cover the three catafalques. On each was inscribed the epitaph that epitomized the inductee's life. For Condorcet, his celebrated formula "What is the first rule of politics? It is to be just. The second? To be just. The third? To be just." For Monge, the motto of the Polytechnique, "For the homeland, science, and glory." Rebuffed by his church, the abbé requested this prayer, along with a cross on his tomb: "O God, have mercy for me and pardon my enemies." Mitterrand alone followed the cortege inside the monument. The Orchestre de Paris played Mozart's Masonic funeral music, reinforcing the mood of republican and pacific sacrality. In the temple of national honor, the bicentennial came to a close.[11]

Counterpoint

Speaking in the name of the Catholic counterrevolution, the Lepéniste organ *Présent* deplored the ceremony, which it regarded as perfectly typical of the perfidious spirit of the bicentennial. It assailed Jack Lang for having attacked "the church yesterday and today" by criticizing its "inflexible severity" vis-à-vis an "oath-taking, schismatic bishop." Thanks to the vigilance and militant devotion of the Centre Charlier, the traditionalist think tank animated by Romain Marie, a European deputy and fervent nonschismatic *intégriste*, noted the newspaper with relief, "this new act of official impiety" by "the clerics of the new human-rights religion" would not go unanswered. The Charlier intellectuals recalled the true Grégoire, a Mason, a de facto regicide, and accomplice in the massacres of his diocese of Blois. To mark its indignation, the Centre Charlier called on like-minded associations and individuals to join together in "a gathering of atonement" to be held on 20 December at 9:00 P.M. "in front of the Church of Sainte-Geneviève, provisionally known as the Panthéon." After evoking the Revolution's martyrology, the demonstrators/congregation would proceed to the nearby Convent of the Carmes "where by the hundreds priests and monks had their throats slit and were torn limb from limb by the revolutionaries," friends and admirers of Abbé Grégoire.[12]

BOOK THREE

THE BICENTENNIAL
AND THE NATION

Mobilization for Commemoration

W hen Jean-Noël Jeanneney acceded to the Mission presidency, none of the major bicentennial events had yet been put together. It was not clear then how to mark the great moments: with popular mobilizations, show-business extravaganza, monuments of diverse sorts, activities mixing people and things, and so on. Nor was there yet a plan for filling up the time and space between the grand festivities with undertakings that would engage, entertain and educate. By itself, the Mission was not equipped to conceive and organize a year's worth of projects, large and small in design, central and peripheral in locus. In response to recurrent reproaches that it failed to "see things on a grand enough scale," in addition to requesting indulgence on account of the organization's tragic and dislocating leadership turnover and uncertainties attendant on cohabitation, it could only point to its official charge, which was to serve as midwife and broker rather than creator and executor, save on an extremely limited basis. The business of the Mission was to incite imagination in both public and private sectors and to coordinate the multifarious projects that were expected to pullulate.

The Avant-Première

Edgar Faure had taken the first steps toward the crystallization of the mar-ketplace of bicentennial culture with the preparation of the massive exposition at the Grande Halle de la Villette called 89, Avant-Première. Almost two hundred exhibitors, individual and collective, public and private, filled 10,000 square meters between 3 and 12 June 1988, barely a week after Jeanneney took office. It was organized by Didier Hamon, the Mission's director of programs, without whose "dynamism," staff members agreed, it would never have gotten off the ground. The

Paris municipality was a cosponsor, and Hamon skillfully won city cooperation and goodwill. Just before the opening, Hamon announced that he was leaving the Mission to become Jack Lang's chef de cabinet, though he agreed to stay on as general commissioner of the exposition. For Hamon, it was a logical return to an earlier career trajectory, for he had worked before in the Ministry of Culture. In the eyes of Chirac's cabinet, however, it was nothing less than a plot by the ministry to squeeze the capital out of the bicentennial action, as well as the credit it deserved, for Lang was Chirac's mortal enemy. For the moment, Jeanneney had confidence in Hamon. But when Lang shortly thereafter obtained the title of minister of the bicentennial, he, too, regarded Hamon as something of a turncoat.[1]

In the first instance, the Avant-Première aimed to attract sponsors and financiers for the myriad projects that aspired to bicentennial life. At the same time it served as a showcase, a harbinger of what the public could expect. A salon for bicentennial "products" ranging from architectural designs and monumental sculptures to books and plays to more ordinary consumer fare, the Avant-Première was also a forum for ideas—the occasion for a number of debates and colloquia dealing with the Revolutionary legacy. Faure had hoped that the display of creativity would attract investors and sponsors; when Jack Lang inaugurated it, he seemed most concerned with firing the interest of a lethargic and apathetic public and, almost as important, buoying the morale of commemorators everywhere. ("In a few months," he said, but with less conviction than he usually manifested when he believed in something, "we are going to try to build a grand bicentennial.")

Broad thematic rubrics articulated the presentation. There were categories for human rights and youth, for science and the Revolution, for the educational and publishing sectors, for arts and creation, for images and communication, for international affairs. A special slot was reserved for municipalities and departmental/regional councils to sketch out their commemorative designs. The exposition allocated a large space to "Invent 89," an international competition launched in March 1987 involving all modes of art (plastic, performance, etc.) appropriate for the urban, public sphere. Entrants were invited to contrive "rituals and expressions" that celebrated and and updated the legacy of the Revolution. An international jury selected 136 projects (of 772 submitted) representing sixteen countries (of thirty-four in the running).

Among the exhibits that attracted the most attention were a project for the construction of a mini-Bastille in bricks that would be delivered to the crowd for instant dismantling on 14 July; a plan to paint the base of the July column on the place de la Bastille in blue, white, and red; a model of a vast "Temple of the Nation" built of triangulated columns representing the republican motto; the design for an "Observatory of Ruman Rights" to be lodged in a vast crater illuminated with powerful beacons; a vision of a colossal "Chair of Uranus," 150 meters high, meant to symbolize the modern world and human consciousness, containing a terrace, a large auditorium, and panoramic galleries for celebrating the rights of man; a Dutch "revolutionary current," a happening on the Seine composed of 500,000 red balloons that would gradually rise from the water as the decomposing salt that held them there evaporated; a giant "wandering turtle" of uncertain relevance to the themes of the hour; a grandiose project by French architects Jean-Marie Hennin and Nicolas Normier entitled "Paths of Liberty" that envisoned the metaphorical linking of the Concorde to the Bastille by means of the actual connecting of the Pont Neuf to the Pont du Carrousel by a 900-meter footbridge complemented by eleven towers, each thirty meters tall and each devoted to exploring the theme of liberty from a different perspective.

Few of the projects displayed at the Villette were realized during the bicentennial year. In a mood of watchful waiting, the bulk of the press wondered to what extent, if any, the Avant-Première would shape commemorative events. A convergent signal of alarm emerged from the Communist left and the far right. Even as *Aspects de la France* characterized the salon as divided between two equally unappealing tendencies represented by "the Ideologues and the Merchants," so Michel Vovelle told *Révolution* that it bespoke "the spiritual landscape of a shattered celebration" wanting in leadership and focus and likely to see the triumph of a "rampant commercialization" over the realm of ideas.[2]

The Practice of Decentralization: Necessity, Advantages, and Costs

Though Jeanneney had more money and a stronger mandate than his predecessor, with very few exceptions he shifted the "project" focus from Paris to the provinces. It would be easier to make up time with a multiplicity of small enterprises, each autonomously driven, and the Mission would be less vulnerable without huge individual targets on the horizon. Quickly disgusted by the hostile attitude of much of the Paris press, Jeanneney was happy to aim at the more hospitable moral clime of *la France profonde*. Aside from these strategic considerations, this policy coincided with the decentralizing ethos of the Mitterrand regime and the specific charge of the Mission. If the name of the game was balance, then Jeanneney would offset his Jacobin civic message with a Girondin choreography of commemorative enterprise. Fruits of the Revolution, the "local collectivities," beginning with the communes, would serve as "foot soldiers of the bicentennial."

In return for exercising initiative and responsibility, however, the agencies of local life would also have to pay for the realization of their ideas. This was the less congenial aspect of decentralization that, the Mission conceded, "our interlocutors in the regions did not always understand right away." While the Mission provided partial funding to local projects only in rare cases, it did help to find sponsorship, put potential partners in contact, and proffer substantive suggestions aimed at making a given enterprise more attractive. Mona Ozouf insightfully noted how the decentralizing mode "contributed to the calming of the debate." The leitmotif (and in some ways the catharsis) of much of the bicentennial commemoration at the grass roots was simply, "this took place in our own backyard." Tragedies and confrontations "disappear, then, in the acceptance of a collective destiny: probably less because they are seen through the embellishing veil of past time than because they are confined to the reassuring intimacy of a space traversed and shared a hundred times over."[3]

The fact that seven different types of elections took place in a period of sixteen months in 1988–89, renewing the recruitment of all representative institutions except the regional councils, did not facilitate sustained and confident contact between the Mission and local governments. Electoral vicissitudes gutted projects long in gestation and generated others rather hastily. Christian de Montrichard's ardent courtship of the leading organization of mayors, the Association des maires de France (AMF), presided by a rightist from the Ile-de-France, did not yield any useful results in terms of cooperation or coordination. The recalcitrance of the AMF sapped one of Faure's wistful commemorative dreams, a banquet of all the mayors of the republic in emulation of the grand assembly of 1889. Unable to reach the mayors collectively, the Mission faced the daunting prospect of having to deal (potentially) with almost 40,000 individuals, each of whose "personality," observed Montrichard, would likely be the decisive variable in determining local commemorative parameters.

Edgar Faure failed to realize a critical organizational ambition: to create a "club of bicentennial clubs" in order to coordinate the multiple activities of voluntary bicentennial associations that operated outside government structures. Nor did the association of presidents or the Conseils généraux respond to Montrichard's entreaties. Three quarters of the Conseils were dominated by the right, and they demonstrated very little appetite for collaborating with the Mission. Montrichard felt grateful for more fruitful relations with numerous offices of the Direction régionale des affaires culturelles, the regional cultural institutions.[4]

Some continuity of exchange was assured by the departmental correspondents, designated by the prefects beginning in the late fall of 1987. Given the lack of fervor for promoting the Revolution evinced by Charles Pasqua, minister of the interior, the prefects were disinclined to demonstrate too much enthusiasm for their bicentennial role, regardless of their personal disposition. Left or right, it was after all still a Jacobin system.

One prefect, Alain Jezequel of the Deux-Sèvres, expressed sharp reservations about the wisdom of vigorous commemoration, first in a report to Pasqua, and then in the form of a history lesson administered to Faure that the academician did not appreciate. While much would depend on "the political hue of the local elected officials who will be in place in 1989," the prefect warned that for the north of his department and the neighboring departments that constituted the "military Vendée," the bicentennial would pose "a number of delicate problems." Jezequel went on to describe the "slaughter" of the Bocage, in which twenty localities lost 75 percent of their population and fifty-two others suffered mutilation by half, most of the massacres occurring after the blue armies had decisively defeated the whites on the battlefield.

"The Bocage retained in its collective memory the recollection of these atrocities which one barely dares to evoke, so much does their barbarity defy human reason and shock the national sentiment," wrote the prefect, who had rapidly espoused the regional ethos and found nothing problematic in the regional reading of the counterrevolutionary experience. In fact, Jezequel avowed his consternation that the true story had never been told in the public school textbooks and applauded the efforts of Philippe de Villiers at le Puy-du-Fou, and of Reynald Secher, René Sédillot, and Pierre Chaunu to set the record straight in their writings. Any strong commemorative impulsion from Paris or Niort could issue in "a violent clash of opposing ideologies that had gradually melded into a general consensus for the management of local business, but remain liable to brutal reawakenings."[5]

There were almost a hundred departmental correspondents, a number of whom served simultaneously as regional coordinators. Twenty-four were directeurs de cabinet of their prefects—either a sign of the latter's interest in the commemoration and desire to monitor its unfolding or a mark of indifference, given the vast number of tasks assigned to the directeurs. Four other correspondents were chefs du bureau of the prefectoral cabinet, and thus in a similar relation to the prefect. Ten correspondents were subprefects, theoretically in close touch with public opinion. More than a quarter of the corps came from the departmental archives, bearing the title of director or head curator. They were chosen ostensibly because of their historical training, and perhaps also their links with local and regional educational institutions. Numerous archivists subscribed to the conservatism traditionally associated with their Chartiste formation. Among the others were three university professors, four school teachers (one of whom, who taught high school history at Challans in the Vendée, met considerable resistance in his role), three presidents of local societies of erudition, one mayor (a former history teacher from the town of La Flèche in the Sarthe, described by his prefect as "close to the majority"), and a dozen civil servants of various sorts.[6]

The Mission framed the responsibilities of the correspondents in extremely general terms. Their chief task was informational: to diffuse data and instructions emanating from the center to the periphery and to furnish the center with intelligence on the preparation of the bicentennial locally, including an "evaluation" of the situation in addition to the raw news. (Not very many were sufficiently motivated—or naive?—to take the latter invitation seriously.) They were told that they would serve as counselors to the Mission to assist it in acting on requests for patronage, a function they were requested to perform much less often than many would have liked. The correspondents had an active hortatory/documentary/propagandistic role to play in their circumscriptions: to "sensitize opinion" to the significance and the opportunities presented by the bicentennial. The Mission provided them with hints as to substance rather than a script and left the critical question of harnessing the apposite media to their discretion. Only a handful of correspondents attempted to go directly to the people, although some made efforts to co-opt local press and radio.

The correspondents had more success in fulfilling another, more specific instruction: to make contact with the major promoters of commemorative activities (departmental committees, municipalities, associations, individuals) in order to encourage and orient them, and, where possible, "harmonize" their projects in order to avoid redundancy of effort and calendar overlap. The Mission reminded correspondents repeatedly that they must not play impresario or creator (in general its negative injunctions were much less vague than its positive ones): they were to "elicit and support initiatives," not to undertake any on their own. Given the fact that they disposed of absolutely no money, it was unlikely that they could venture into show business of any sort. The closest the Mission came to an overtly ideological command was the recommendation that correspondents encourage the formation of commemorative committees "broadly recruited to favor consensus" and that they maintain a posture of "neutrality" vis-à-vis these groups.[7]

A number of correspondents expressed discontent with the manner in which the Mission used them, a dissatisfaction that was probably widely shared. The complaint refrain was that "there was a lack of concrete follow-up support." It was widely agreed that Montrichard was a solicitous and knowledgeable interlocutor, but that he could not deliver: "the Mission was overwhelmed." It failed to keep correspondents sufficiently informed, or it informed them after the fact. Worse, it cut them out of the loop on issues that mattered to them, both in terms of their sense of authority and their quest for efficacity.

Patronage was the crux of the problem. After having assured the correspondents that all requests for support would have to pass through them and that they would be asked to offer an assessment and a recommendation, the Mission accepted scores of projects directly, and acted on them without obtaining the correspondents' views. To their mortification, correspondents frequently learned about the result from the supplicant, or from the press. "I had the impression that I was bypassed on each occasion," protested a subprefect, who decried "the complete dysfunctionality" of the Mission. Having visited the Mission—the correspondents were invited to Paris for several meetings—a prefectoral directeur de cabinet, favorably disposed to the bicentennial and the Revolution, characterized the Mission as a constant improvisational "cobbling," by which he meant to convey admiration in light of the penury of resources with which it operated.

The fact that they had no money at all (not even for stamps, lamented a correspondent from eastern France) frustrated the correspondents, who felt that this impotence crippled their ability to make a difference locally. Several felt especially bitter, because they felt Montrichard had led them to believe that in the end, once the Mission's budget was fully worked out, they would have some means at their disposal. Perhaps because they had so little to offer, the correspondents were also bypassed by the Conseils régionaux and généraux which decided to engage significantly in bicentennial festivities. Unhappy with the lack of funds and with the Mission's manner of disposing of subsidies and its labeling cachet, the correspondent for the Vaucluse quit in anger shortly after he took office. A former mayor of Cadenet (population 2,400) and an amateur historian, his brusque departure provoked "a big stir" locally and complicated the task of mobilization.[8]

An archival director criticized the recruitment of his fellow correspondents. Many of them knew absolutely nothing about the Revolution. Some of them even boasted of their indifference for the subject. Others were not convinced of the need to celebrate. An outsider, professionally removed from the prefectoral world, denounced the conservative climate fostered by these republican *commissaires*. The only thing they seemed to care about, he grumbled, was that the correspondents "avoid making waves." Viewing the same phenomenom from a different vantage point, a subprefect pronounced everything political—"all the initiatives were more or less political." There were no "pure" bicentennial operations, but "always various ulterior motives."

Nor was the Mission satisfied with the performance of all the correspondents, whose nomination had been wholly out of its hands. Perhaps overgenerously, it estimated that about a quarter of its correspondents were "very active" while 50 percent did an adequate job. "The correspondence network of the Jeanneney Mission did not exist in the Hérault as far as I know—I could not tell you the name of the official delegate," wrote Raymond Huard, an alert university professor and the president of a local bicentennial association. The torpor of certain correspondents as well as their own feeling of disconnectedness from the center contributed to the sense of estrangement and isolation that scores of local officials felt. The CSA pollster-analysts recorded "the admission by everyone of an absence of information on the program of events organized by the Mission, associated with a lack of concertation and the perception of a great disorder in the official preparation of the bicentennial on the national scale."[9]

Labeling: A Plethora of Encouragement and a Dribble of Subvention

Given its limited resources, the Mission's primary form of intervention in the field took the form of labeling. By according its imprimatur to a project, the Mission hoped to enhance its allure vis-à-vis potential sponsors as well as vis-à-vis its future clientele or audience. Even more immediately, it was a formal acknowledgment of the merit of the enterprise meant to buoy the morale of its author. Besides general boasting rights, the label enabled the beneficiary to use the Mission logo on all its advertising and to profit from the publicity that the Mission might be able to afford it. A label also conveyed the opportunity to participate in the Avant-Première. In Montrichard's words, the label represented the Mission's "moral sponsorship and scholarly guarantee," though the Jeanneney administration backed off somewhat from this maximalist definition. In the early days, before the Mission was inundated with requests, it attempted to scrutinize them carefully by requesting the appraisals of the pertinent member of the advisory committee. This vetting proved to be too cumbersome and costly; save in special cases, the in-house staff conducted the evaluation on its own. In the end, the label testified less to the quality of a project than to its likely interest.[10]

At its weekly sessions, the Mission's projects cell examined more than 3,000 proposals, slightly fewer than half of which received its warrant. As a rule, it favored the projects that were the most imaginative, the most civically ardent, the most likely to enjoy healthy media impact. Occasionally it succumbed to political or patronage pressure of one sort or another. To shelter itself from precisely this sort of influence, the Mission emphasized that it awarded labels to projects, not persons; the merit of the latter did not compensate for the defects of the former. It also found it necessary to remind prospective candidates that their ideas had to bear some strong relationship to the commemorative object. Ideally the projects were supposed to reveal "a real mooring in the events of the Revolutionary period." It would be even better if they managed to "place graphically into relief the relevant parts of the Revolution's fundamental achievements."

The Mission pledged to refuse its cachet not only to projects that were frankly "antirépublican" but also to those that framed the issues in excessively "manichaean" terms, which presumably excluded exorbitant Jacobins as well as zealous counterrevolutionaries. This consensual logic, which governed Mission decisions only in the extreme breach, required "political, social, and intellectual balance." Nor was the Mission indifferent to a certain minimal equity of geographical distribution or to an equilibrium of big city/small town, urban/rural, urbane/folkloric, professional/amateur, aesthetically impressive/morally worthy. (One of these considerations probably acounts for the label accorded to a village in the Vaucluse that organized a rooster-calling contest: the *coq* was after all one of the symbols of the republic.)[11]

Beyond the staggering number of projects submitted, one is struck by the extraordinary quality of the presentation (regardless of the substance) of many of them. High motivation and personal-computer high technology combined to produce dossiers with superb graphics, color illustrations, elaborate cross-referencing, and easy legibility. Two decades ago, perhaps even ten years ago, one would never have encountered this sophistication of marketing strategy in Landerneau, for example, to say nothing of more obscure and cramped places. Many of these associations, enterprises, and individuals knew how to compete. This professionalism rendered the task of the Mission more difficult.

On a given day, the Mission labeling committee examined scores of dossiers. It had to work rapidly, and depended heavily on the triage performed by the counselor in whose sector the project fell. Unless the project was particularly controversial, or aroused presidential concern, the committee generally followed the counselor's recommendation. There was an unspoken competition among the counselors, who imperceptibly became the advocates or adversaries of certain projects. Prudence induced the more enterprising members of the committee to lobby their colleagues before the meetings. Each project had its own particular trajectory. Some arrived laden with recommendations from local notables, Parisian power brokers who owned vacation homes in the place from which the project emanated and intellectuals advancing the benefit of their expertise. Barren of endorsement, others depended on their enthusiasm, their originality, or the level of mobilization implied by the project.

Still others followed the path initially envisaged by the Mission. Thus did the subprefect of Montluçon send a preliminary inquiry to Jeanneney to sound him out about a local theatrical project whose promoters had contacted him in the hope of finding sponsorship. In reply, the Mission president encouraged the group to apply, laying out the ground rules and the usual caveats. The Compagnie du Cerf volant of Cusset in the Allier (population 14,000) followed up with a rich dossier, including a detailed scenario outline for a play dealing with the kidnapping of Louis XVII from the Temple. The allure of the project resided in large measure in the way it involved a considerable number of children aged nine to twelve in the elaboration of the dialogue, the creation of the décor, the design of the costumes, and the acting. For its *Graines de Carmagnole,* the Cerf volant obtained the label but not the subsidy for which it yearned. On other days the committee approved projects described as "the organized labor movement looks at the Revolution," "Barnave and the Revolution," and "the Club des femmes of Besançon," all in Claire Andrieu's bailiwick; "Le Cannet during the Revolution," "Rouget de Lisle," and "the Revolution in the Bourbonnais," presented by Christian de Montrichard; and a number of concerts, expositions, and plays, including *Le Mariage de Figaro* and *Le Barbier de Séville,* that Elie Schulman reported.[12]

The labeling process was not always a smooth and straightforward affair. It was bound to generate frictions, for it involved losers as well as winners, and nominal winners who felt nevertheless like losers. Moreover, there were problems regarding the delivery of promises, and rancor born of misunderstandings. One of the few cases of such troubles that has surfaced concerns Anne Seurat, author of a performance piece on the Revolution for the Théâtre de l'Impromptu. Rebuffed at first in March 1988, she obtained a label of approval and a subvention the following August. Seurat complained that she had to wait over nine months before she finally received the grant, the amount of which was arbitrarily and gradually reduced from the initial pledge of Fr 500,000 to 250,000 (October 1988), then to 100,000 (January 1989), and finally, on the eve of opening night, to Fr 40,000. Understandably, she was enraged and disappointed, and her group suffered grave penalties, including the loss of prospective cosponsors as a result of the Mission's dilatoriness, and the embarrassment of hiring actors it could not pay. Yet there is a good bit in her story that is hardly plausible, especially her lack of documentary proof of claims ("But the Mission never commits itself on paper. Everything took place orally"). Without enumerating concrete instances, it was irresponsible for the (short-lived) newsweekly *Politis* to conclude: "Numerous others were swallowed up in the same morass."[13]

In a limited number of projects, generally with translocal cultural significance, the Mission became directly involved, sometimes with financial as well as promotional assistance. The audiovisual sphere was a privileged domain, given Jeanneney's professional experience and passion for it and his well-founded conviction that it was the crucible in which public opinion was largely wrought. The Mission directly funded a number of television series dealing with the Old Regime and the Revolution. It helped to launch major retrospectives of television and cinematic treatments of Revolutionary subjects. It aided numerous theatrical, musical, and dance projects. The Mission advised hundreds of museums, archives, libraries, and other institutions on various sorts of exhibitions of documents, historical artifacts, and artworks. It granted labels to 169 colloquia and provided financial aid totaling almost Fr 2 million to fifty-six of them. While the Mission failed to launch the publication (or continuation) of a great documentary series in the tradition of the centennial, it enabled many commercially unviable colloquium volumes to see the light of day, and through the Librairie du Bicentenaire it subsidized the publication of several score books. It participated materially in one splendid innovation, the publication of a sprightly monthly devoted to the Revolution in all its ramifications, *Le Monde de la Révolution française*, a subsidiary of the daily newspaper.[14]

CLEF 89

About half the projects examined by the Mission emanated from associations, a substantial number of which belonged to the "CLEF 89" network (Comités Liberté, Egalité, Fraternité) created in the spring of 1987 by a joint effort of the Ligue française de l'enseignement (LFE, already militantly engaged in the republican cause at the time of the first centennial) and the Ligue des droits de l'homme (LDH, of more recent vintage). Historian Madeleine Rebérioux, then the vice president of the LDH—and since, its first woman president—depicted her organization as the moving force in this civic marriage. Yet on the ground the midwifely (or infrastructural) contribution of the Fédération des oeuvres laïques (FOL), the secular arm of the other league, proved decisive in the birth and nurturing of many of the eighty departmental branches, a few of which also enjoyed municipal patronage. Though of marked leftist sensibility, neither of the leagues was organically connected with a political party, unlike the Vive 89 organization launched by the PCF, the only grassroots rival to the CLEF. Thus the boast of the CLEF national newsletter that it constituted "the only pluralist and decentralized network of voluntary associations put into place for the bicentennial."[15]

Its ideological pluralism, however, was stringently framed by its exuberantly Jacobinorepublican reading of the Revolutionary legacy. The leagues felt that it was urgent to reflect on the nation's debt to the Revolution, and on its obligation to complete the task that the Revolution had begun. Even as the future citizens of the republic made radical demands beginning in 1789 in order to obtain their liberty and open the way toward democracy, so citizens today had to make radical demands in order to extend the benefits of citizenship to the excluded, particularly to immigrants and the poor. The CLEF espoused a new vision of citizenship that implied not merely integration in a juridical sense but some form of social and economic empowerment. Though their language was different, their demands for a citizenship founded on equality as well as on liberty converged with those of the Communists and with the more Jacobin elements of the PS.

The CLEF grew out of left-republican alarm at the resurgence of the forces of counterrevolution, dissatisfaction with the tepid attitude of the Mission in its early incarnation, and frustration with the "blasé Parisian microcosm." ("Having rejected the option of doing nothing at all, we preferred to try to produce better-founded readings of the Revolution than the right-thinking porridge, for heretical diners, that the media, in particular the television, chose to serve us in 1987, 1988, 1989.") The offensive of the "conservative forces" worried the two leagues because those forces attained such a wide hearing in the media and because they sapped the will of the official commemorators. The national organization summoned its field leaders to "a heightened vigilance and a more resolute commitment." The greatest danger was the sort of complacency encouraged by Furetian appeasement. It was not sufficient to deride and dismiss as mere folkloric remnants those who denounced the Revolution as "the Absolute Evil." The CLEF believed that counterrevolutionaries had much more widespread, subtle, and corrosive influence than their extremist tribunes might lead skeptics to conclude. Education, and its attendant mobilization, remained the primary tools of the leagues.

In the view of the CLEF, the Revolution had to be defended; its defense was wholly coterminous with the defense of human rights. Far from being the source of modern evil, the Revolution was "the source of rights and liberties." Without ever directly making the connection, CLEF doctrine hinted that those who reviled the Revolution were themselves threats to the rights it had engendered. "Today the values espoused by the French Revolution are still often subjected to rough treatment," read a brochure for a colloquium on "citizenship" cosponsored by the CLEF. "The promise of 1789 must still flower in our country." With a certain Jacobin inquietude (which critics decried as either demagogic politics or paranoia), the CLEF reminded the citizenry that Revolutionary gains were never fully secure. There was something of both Saint-Just and Régis Debray in the discourse of Michel Morineau, the president of the Ligue de l'enseignement, who warned that "democracies are fragile when buffeted by passions, the citizen disappears too frequently behind the [self-regarding] individual, and the public good is forgotten in favor of private interests." The antidote/prophylactic was a relentless "republican practice," not a mere rite but a way of everyday civic life. That practice supposed that the best way to safeguard Revolutionary gains was to expand them.[16]

The CLEF idea took form in an operating system of coordination and support in the wake of the failure of the Association pour le Bicentenaire de la Révolution française (ABRF) to get off the ground. Initially, in 1986, representatives of both leagues had responded favorably to the enthusiastic overtures of Daniel Perissini, a geyser of ideas warmly recommended by Madeleine Rebérioux, who founded the ABRF with the objective of leading ordinary French men and women into the commemoration. He emerged at a propitious moment. The Ligue d'enseignement had begun to shift from a prudent, Baroinesque, neomasonic attitude toward the bicentennial to a more militant one, partly under the prod of the return of the right to government, and it was looking for both vehicle and projects. Suspicious of the Baroin-Faure line from the outset, the LDH also worried about the direction of commemoration, or rather its lack of direction, particularly in light of Mitterrand's procrastination. For both leagues, the ABRF seemed a potentially excellent solution: a structure outside the government closely linked with the civic base, capable of providing the audience as well as the show and committed to "progressive" ideals.

Perissini did not lack either ambition or connections: he talked of a vast scheme of television programs, and he promoted as future president of his association Jacques Pomateau, leader of the (then) huge and powerful union of teachers, the FEN, who had just been named to the Conseil d'état. From the beginning, however, the ABRF lacked a clearcut financial plan, though it spent money quite freely on a variety of administrative tasks. Even before a terrible automobile accident sidelined Perissini, the two leagues had begun to doubt his capacity to manage and to produce. (They also feared the hegemonic specter of the FEN.) Led by Bernard Wallon of the LDH, a convinced "localist," and Michel Morineau of the LFE, an adept administrator with great evangelistic talent, the leagues moved toward the CLEF model.

The two leagues collaborated quite effectively, in part because each understood its particular vocation and its potential contribution. The LDH was a small operation (between five and seven thousand members) with incommensurately strong moral influence. The LFE federated thirty-five thousand local associations, only a fifth of which were narrowly "teaching" organizations. More deeply and widely implanted, it was more comfortable with structure and logistics. Though the Masonic bent of the LFE caused some frictions with the LDH, the leagues found ample ideological grounds on which to coalesce, at least in terms of the Revolutionary legacy and the problems of citizenship and injustice that faced contemporary France. The LFE provided the infrastructure for many committees through the FOL, yet in the end a dozen CLEF groups transformed themselves into new-born sections of the LDH.

While decentralization and grassroots initiatives were the watchwords, the central or national CLEF organization provided numerous services to the departmental committees. It organized intensive three-day orientation programs to train the local leaders. In addition to furnishing a capsule survey of the history of the French Revolution, it rehearsed ideological themes, discussed communications

A publication of one of the departmental associations of the national bicentennial organization called CLEF 89, the acronym (literally "key") standing for Committee for Liberty, Equality, and Fraternity. The liberty tree, grand symbol for the revolutionaries themselves, flowered as an emblem of commemoration in 1989. (Photo: CLEF, Maine-et-Loire.)

strategies, and suggested the sorts of activities that might fill the commemorative/ festive calendar. In coordination with the central office, the FOL of the Loir-et-Cher was one of a number of provincial organizations to offer more specialized workshops, in this instance three- and five-day sessions on how to organize a citizens' ball, including instructions on music, dance, costuming, decorations, and so on. Through its *Lettre CLEF*, the national committee emitted a constant stream of exhortation and information. Introduced by muscular editorials, this bulletin was not timid about broadcasting the organizational line. It reprinted articles from the general press that it deemed relevant to its constituency—for example, François Dosse's slashing attack on Furet from *Politis*. Central headquarters made available a wide range of publications (generated by the two leagues as well as from the outside), lists of bibliography, audio- and videocassettes, and materials for expositions. The newsletter advertised items produced by departmental groups, such as T-shirts, sweatshirts, posters, and diverse educational tools, including full-scale dramatic performances (e.g., a life of Saint-Just offered by the FOL of the Oise for 13,200 francs plus transport fees for a single performance).

The national CLEF operated a lecture bureau that dispatched to middle France some of the finest historians of the nation, including Maurice Agulhon, François Lebrun, Maurice Garden, Roger Dupuy, Dominique Julia, Jean Ehrard, Jean-Paul Bertaud, and Jacques Guilhaumou, in addition to the ubiquitous Madeleine Rebérioux. The CLEF cosponsored the publication of the thoughtful and splendidly wrought monthly, *Le Monde de la Révolution française*. While the CLEF was primarily a coordinating vehicle, it was hard to separate it from the militant lives of its sponsors. Thus it was present when the LDH called a demonstration in front of the Bouffes du Nord theatre in Paris to protest the right/royalist hate attack on Hélène Delavault.[17]

The national CLEF launched a number of major projects on its own initiative. Two were stillborn: a costly plan for a "Pacquebot 89" pressed by the Ligue de l'enseignement and another for a "Train of the Revolution" proposed by the Ligue des droits de l'homme. The third project, though hardly a smashing success, got off the ground in a number of localities. Called "Traces," it aimed at fostering a consciousness of the experience of the Revolution and the impact of its legacy at the local level. The CLEF Jacobins had a decided Girondin bent: they resented Parisian bicentennial cynicism and they criticized the Parisian tendency to hoard the Revolution in historiography. Pitched at schools and associations, the program invited young people in particular to unearth the traces of the Revolution—not just 1789 but the period 1789–99—and at the same time to reflect on their implications for their lives today. The CLEF envisaged two genres of trace: more or less material remainders (archeological remnants, contemporary iconography, architecture) and testimonies of all sorts that nourished the memory, individual and collective. The ideal, never fully attained, was to constitute a cumulative exposition within each department, with each locality adding a distillation of its "traces" to the burgeoning whole as it traveled from place to place.[18]

In the judgment of the national organizers, about a third of the departmental committees were rather dormant, another third moderately active, especially in relation to activities in the schools, and the final third, widely dispersed in the north, east, center, and southwest, proved to be exceptionally dynamic and productive. Extensively implanted throughout the nation, the FOL frequently served as the fulcrum of organization for the departmental committees. The FOL at Blois,

With support from the Mission and the bicentennial network called the CLEF, *Le Monde* put out a very successful monthly newspaper devoted to both the history of the Revolution and the activities of the commemoration. Adopting twentieth-century size and format, *Le Monde de la Révolution française* attracted readers to eighteenth-century issues with very modern headlines, such as this: "Riots in Paris. 300 DEAD."

for example, published a newsletter, produced a play, and promoted the laic ritual of "republican baptism," a legacy of the Robespierrist phase of the Revolution. In the Haute-Garonne, the CLEF met in the offices of the FOL but set out self-consciously to create "a movement and not an [administrative] entity." This group reached widely into the community, stimulated local research and historical self-consciousness, lobbied for human rights, and toiled to disseminate "republicasn values." Other department committees sponsored exhibitions, solicited grievances, or *doléances*, in the Revolutionary manner, orchestrated "mass events," reconstituted Revolutionary moments, and organized popular festivals, parades, and dances. Nationally and locally, the CLEF network (CLEF also stood for "Commémorer, Lire, Enseigner, Fêter"—"Commemorate, Read, Teach, Celebrate") invested heavily in the schools, their natural constituency. Given the relative prudence of the ministry in engaging itself in the bicentennial, they filled a major gap by inspiring and framing educational action projects and providing technical expertise.[19]

As the bicentennial year came to an end, the organizers of the national CLEF gave their undertaking a mixed review. Despite many brilliant successes here and there, they wrote, "it is not certain that the CLEF were always able to play the federating role in the realm of voluntary associations which was one of their chief objectives or that the two founding leagues were always marching hand in hand." Doubts about their efficacy in the field seemed less decisive than ideological and personal tensions at the summit. Although the CLEF charter had specifically envisaged the prolongation of the enterprise beyond the inadmissibly narrow confines of the official bicentennial season in order to mark the other grand moments of the Revolution, the leagues now decided that it would be fruitless and "artifical" to continue the CLEF collaboration.

"Henceforth it is up to each of our organizations, concretely and in the ways most appropriate to the character of each," wrote the leaders, "to nourish the ideals of Liberty, Equality, and Fraternity that we have celebrated." *Le Monde de la Révolution française* predicted that "the most dynamic committees will transform themselves into Cercles Condorcet, those crucibles in which the intellectual destiny of laicity is forged." On the eve of her installation as president of the LDH, Madeleine Rebérioux pledged to make every effort to relaunch a commemorative project for the anniversary of the founding of the republic and the social "anticipations" of Year II.[20]

The "Social Demand" for Commemoration

Globally, 7,500 sundry events occurred during the bicentennial season, a third of which obtained Mission "patronage." In all, 5,000 cities and villages participated along with 2,000 associations of diverse parentage. In a CSA poll conducted in November 1989, 27 percent of those consulted claimed to have attended in person a fête, an exhibition, an entertainment, or some other sort of commemorative event (as opposed to 51 percent who did not). Only 7 percent, however, participated directly in the preparation and realization of such an activity. On both questions, there was relatively little disparity between respondents on the left and the right.[21]

On the basis of these crude quantitative indicators, it is impossible to say whether the claims for an "intense social demand" for commemoration and/or celebration are confirmed or impugned. Nor is there some sort of universal norm that one can apply in order to decide whether the French were more or less active than they *ought* to have been. Impressionistic evidence suggests that the bicentennial of 1789 in France had at least as much resonance in the nation as had the bicentennial of 1776 in the United States. But even were this comparison verifiable, it is not clear how much significance it would have, for Americans are increasingly inclined to spectate passively rather than to participate actively, and in any case, the two commemorative objects occupy very different places in the national consciousness and memory. All that one can say with confidence is that tens, perhaps even hundreds, of thousands of persons joined in some sort of hometown bicentennial undertaking. Reports suggest that a large number enjoyed themselves and will probably remember the experience. But that says nothing about how they will interpret it.

The activities ran a vast gamut of forms: highbrow and low, high tech and artisanal, brash and discreet, austere and festive, sectorial and mass, political and nonpartisan, professionally staged and more or less improvised, amply financed and more or less impecunious. Scholars will need to look carefully at what transpired within each municipal council in order to draw a convincing and comprehensive map of "official" or public bicentennial engagement (keeping in mind that official indifference or hostility did not preclude organized fervor within civil society on one scale or another).[22] Right-left polarities cannot by themselves account for the different models of behavior at the local level. Indeed, many communes quite self-consciously refuse to operate on the manichaean political logic of the macrocosm. Managed by good-government fusion tickets, these municipalities often opted for silence or neutrality or some other antiseptic solution on ideological grounds wholly foreign to the Revolutionary legacy.

Nor did municipalities dominated by the right or left automatically embrace or reject commemorative activism, though an inquiry among thousands of mayors, conducted by the Groupe sociologique de recherches de Nanterre, suggests that leftist municipalities have a significantly higher participation rating than rightist ones. The dominant groups tended to devise strategies that served their interests, but those interests were not easily reducible along binary lines. Certain Socialists, for instance, were no longer sure that revolution was in their interest in any sense. Rightist municipalities could not overlook the national and republican dimension of the anniversary. No less than the Socialists, the members of the opposition did not speak about the bicentennial in a single voice. Thus apparent anomalies abound. Habitually governed on the right, Saint-Genis, a commune near Lyon, actively commemorated the Revolutionary anniversary in large measure because of its historic hostility to Lyon, perceived as the center of the regional Counterrevolution. In the Var, the "political criterion" proved to be a seriously deficient predictor of commemorative energy: certain rightist towns put on lively celebrations while numerous leftist communes vegetated. If the map of bicentennial enthusiasm at the regional level is likely to conform by and large to traditional patterns of electoral sociology, it is worth remembering that those patterns have evolved considerably during the Fifth Republic, and that there is often dissonance within regions that could once be confidently stereotyped as white, blue, red, and so on. Moreover, "local logics" often operated wholly outside the national commemorative framework, endowing local events and rituals with meanings that are virtually impossible to decode from above and at the center.[23]

Long dominated by the left, the Nord was one of France's most energetic commemorative regions. Its Conseil général sponsored the most ambitious project that emanated from the periphery rather than the center. It was literally built around the reconstruction of the first monument that marked the hallowed ground of the demolished Bastille, a giant wooden elephant, proposed initially in 1808 by

Napoléon, ever the fervent Orientalist. The Conseil général counted on the power of attraction of its high-tech version of the mammoth to compensate for its lack of symbolic pertinence ("sort of an emblem of popular power," its promoters sheepishly advanced; or, alternatively and incongruously, the mightiest of animals summoned to recall the fragility of Revolutionary gains that "must be defended and enriched every day"). But architects, computer engineers, ironworkers, and casting specialists combined to make the "Elephant of Memory" an imposing sight, and a site for an imaginative array of games and lessons dealing with the Revolutionary experience and the relevance of its themes in the world today. The elephant traveled throughout the mother region during the bicentennial. It was dispatched to the Tuileries bicentennial park to help in the rescue operation, and it spread the good word in Belgium as well.[24]

In 1986 the Socialist mayor of Riom, Jean Ehrard, a leading historian of the Enlightenment, created the Association riomoise du Bicentenaire to prepare a huge costumed popular festival on the theme of the spirit of the federation not only as it found expression in 1790 but as a metaphor for the needs of a "living democracy, predicated, at the local level, on urban solidarity." Rebuffed by a hostile Conseil général and an impecunious Mission, the city managed nevertheless to put on an impressive show during three days in June 1989. It was the fruit of scores of convergent initiatives undertaken by some forty local groups (including the archers of Riom, the Accordeon Club, the Equestrian Club, a dance troup) and hundreds of schoolchildren. On 23 June hundreds of schoolchildren retraced the history of the Declaration in a series of tableaux. The next day began with a colorful street market, followed by a parade, an evening concert, and all-night balls in several locations. A children's chorale inaugurated the final day, highlighted by a costumed reenactment of the arrival of the deputies from Paris, the presentation of *cahiers de doléances,* and a patriotic repast.[25]

Another Socialist mayor and historian (economic rather than literary), Georges Frêche of Montpellier, talked boldly at a session of the municipal council about taking a strong bicentennial stand, not only to propel his city into the commemorative forefront as part of his endless task of hometown promotion but also to repel the counterrevolutionary onslaught. Montpellier, celebrating the *Marseillaise,* which one of its own medical school students had learned from Rouget de Lisle at Strasbourg and transmitted to the volunteers gathering at Marseille to march to Paris, would be a sort of anti-Puy-du-Fou. "If M. de Villiers comes here to sing his song," pledged a combative Frêche, exasperated by Vendée apologetics, "that very day we shall inaugurate the rue Hoche, because Hoche is a hero of the republic and a pacifier of the Vendée."

Inverting the doomsday thesis of the counterrevolutionaries, the mayor of Montpellier argued that, if the Vendéens had won, "France would have fallen back into the most total obscurantism." Hoche was no angel, but the Vendée meant regression, whereas the *Marseillaise* represented a great leap forward, the conquest of rights, the extension of French influence throughout the world as a beacon for liberty and model for sociopolitical change. Montpellier would not sanction "a bicentennial celebration in which everyone is lovely and kind and in which Larochejaquelein will be the equal of Hoche." Frêche wanted Michel Baroin to know that if the Mission agreed to support his idea for a series of expositions on the role of the *Marseillaise* in the world and the way in which it fostered the effulgence of France, "it will be to sing not the praises of the whites but those of the French Revolution of the central government."

The mayor's tirade jolted the meeting; a rightist councillor, M. Giffone, walked out in a huff. But Frêche himself backed away from such an aggressive commemorative posture, doubtless in part because he failed to obtain Mission financial support, perhaps also because his muscular discourse had little resonance at home. Montpellier celebrated the bicentennial more or less sedately. Its major programs aimed at the children of the community, its future citizens and leaders. The centerpiece, articulated around the consensual rights theme, mobilized 4,000 children in a series of athletic, artistic, and intellectual competitions.[26]

Impelled by a deep leftist tradition, the Drôme was the site of intense commemorative activity. Despite the official distaste for it at the national commemorative level, historical reconstitution elicited real enthusiasm at the grass roots. A half-dozen communes built and ritually razed a model Bastille, now a delocalized synecdoche that stood for everyperson's struggle for liberation. Beausemblant erected a guillotine alongside its Bastille, while Séderon made a replica of its village square at the time of the Revolution. Other communes relived the taking of châteaux and the Festival of the Supreme Being. Dieulefit and Le Poet-Laval atoned for national remissness by commemorating the abolition of privileges on 4 August. Thirty-five thousand people joined for the climactic celebration called "Voices in Liberty" at Valence on 8 July. All the communes in the department were invited to join in the processions and in the planting of a liberty tree. Animations took place on the squares throughout the city—theatre, music, dance, poetry. The municipal theatre company put on a special play about the Revolution. At nightfall, against the soaring towers that framed the cityscape, an immense sound, light, and music show took place, followed by dancing till dawn.[27]

Cherbourg served as the theatre of a department-wide festival that drew fifty thousand spectators on 11 June 1989. It was the culmination of a commemoration that worked through two hundred schools and local committees in order to uncover local Revolutionary experience and to connect it to the larger picture through historical research, the drafting of *cahiers*, and the reading of the great texts not only of '89 but also of '93. Roger Le Coz, president of the FOL and head of the CLEF, infused a certain ideological edge into the commemoration in the Manche, which he characterized as "a [collective] work of civism vis-à-vis [reawakened currents] of intolerance and obscurantism." It found expression in the historical reconstitution around which the June celebration was organized: five thousand costumed children acting out the diverse aspects of the Revolution in a series of twenty-five floats constructed by the students and their parents and teachers.

Fête de la Drôme / Valence 8 Juillet 1989
EVENEMENT SPECTACLE "VOIX EN LIBERTE"

Thousands of citizens of the Drôme gathered at Valence in July 1989 to celebrate the Revolution's anniversary in a sound, light, and music show devoted to the consensual theme of liberty. (Photo courtesy R. Léron.)

Among the themes they represented were the end of privileges (4 August), the Terror, the metric system, freedom of the press, the Festival of the Supreme Being, the *Marseillaise,* and Valmy. A mammoth popular banquet ended the day.

This sort of story can be told again and again throughout the nation. The Socialist mayor of Besançon commissioned a grand musical fresco on the origin of the R/revolutionary ideals and their impact on the world, a more durable yet more elitist mode of commemoration. The whole citizenry of Neuilly-Plaisance (Seine-Saint-Denis) had the opportunity, in a questionnaire-referendum, to decide exactly how to invest the festive budget of Fr 200,000 (historical theatre, costumed parade, ball and fireworks, exhibition, etc.). Meaux, run by a leftist municipality, proposed some form of bicentennial activity once or twice a week for almost two years. Villeurbanne conducted a yearlong celebration. Operating out of what was called the "House of the Bicentennial," the organizing committee of Montgeron, a small town in the Paris suburbs, engineered theatre-parades featuring thousands of local citizens, exhibitions, a school opera, the projection of films. It published a Revolutionary comic book and put out a record and cassette of Revolutionary songs.

Singing and dancing, the sansculottes take the city in the name of the Revolution. At Cherbourg, as in many other commemorative sites, children were at the center of the bicentennial festivities. (Photo courtesy of the Fédération des Oeuvres laiques de la Manche.)

"From the high schoolers to the senior citizens, from the practitioners of judo to the stamp collectors, the population in its entirety celebrated the bicentennial virtually without stopping from January onward," wrote a reporter for *Le Monde* in an uncharacteristic burst of enthusiasm.

Lavelanet, a town of about 10,000 in the Ariège, undertook an ambitious bicentennial program: liberty tree planting, expositions, essay competition, sporting events, and a historical procession on 14 July. The overriding goal was to make the citizens aware of their *own* past, to show them how they were implicated in the Revolutionary legacy. Saint-Genis-Laval, a slightly larger town in the Rhône valley, framed its commemoration around the poles of 1789 and 2089, a blend of history and futurology, of reconstitution and science fiction. To fund the exhibitions, dramatizations, and concerts, the commemorative committee sold "bicentennial stock shares" for fifty and one hundred francs to the public.

There was an active commemoration in the troubled territory of Nouvelle Calédonie, though it is difficult to estimate what proportion of the population was reached. The celebration could not fully escape the problematic relationship between the territory and metropolitan France. The dilemma was exemplified in a poem composed by a fourteen-year-old white female student:

> This liberty that we possess
> France gave it to us
> And we are France.

Students created an itinerant exhibition on the theme "there was once upon a time a Revolution." Youngsters aged ten to sixteen years competed in a series of competitions (history-geography, art-poetry, sports, and, specifically for the Melanesian population, "traditional" singing and dancing) for places in a group of a few hundred that would spend several weeks in France during the summer.[28]

Commemorative Frictions, Hesitations, and Compromises

Enthusiasm at the local level was not universally of the same order. Extremely sensitive to what he called the "ambivalence" of local feelings, Francisque Collomb, the centrist mayor of Lyon, France's second city, moved very cautiously in the direction of commemoration. After sometimes harsh internal debate, the municipality decided to devote Fr 2 million to bicentennial activities, a relatively paltry sum for a big city in the judgment of one of Lyon's leading papers, Le Progrès. Following the Baroin-Fauriste line, Collomb promised to "commemorate that which unites the French people—and not what divides them." Yet the mayor had to resist the wish of numerous city fathers to place a guillotine on the place des Terreaux as a reminder of the fate of many of their counterrevolutionary forbears. Some of these same councillors, closely linked with the association called Lyon 93, pushed to put up a plaque commemorating the "martyrs" killed by the Terror. Bitterly divided during the Revolution, France's second city remained sundered by the heritage, its "memory [still] unhealed" and in many ways clouded in ambiguity as well as anguish. "Can one commemorate the Revolution at Lyon?" asked more than one local historian. A determined group of notables more or less subtly blocked several attempts to induce the Lyonnais to confront their memory (and the posture of victimization) critically.

The city committed itself to sponsor several expositions, public lectures, and roundtables, to subsidize an opera and commission a piano concerto. Several of the city's institutions of higher education, notably the Centre de politologie historique, conducted significant scholarly programs. Impressed by Lyon's bicentennial timorousness, Le Monde awarded it "the phrygian donkey's cap" for commemoration. The city's torpor contrasted with the vivacity of celebration and/or commemoration in many of the communes surrounding it, not all of which gravitated to the left. They organized expositions, lectures, concerts, film showings, educational projects, and myriad symbolical events such as tree plantings, parades, banquets, civic/popular balls, and presentation of grievance lists.[29]

Another centrist mayor, Jean Bousquet of Nîmes, showed similar circumspection, though he was one of the first big-city heads in France to found a bicentennial planning commission. He forthrightly tried to stake out a consensual position. His hand was strengthened by the visit in June 1987 of Olivier Passelecq, chef de cabinet of Edgar Faure. Addressing a meeting on bicentennial plans at the city hall, he transmitted Faure's rights-republican message. "He insisted," reported the *Midi-Libre,* "on the necessity for an ecumenical vision—evolutionary, objective, consensual, free of political preoccupations." Local Communists complained bitterly of Bousquet's aseptic view of the Revolution, reduced to a lowest common ideological denominator (the rights of man) and purged of its decisive social dimension. Yet the mayor was not wholly unaccommodating. When Alain Clary, a Communist councillor and historian, denounced the city's failure to envision a bicentennial homage to its illustrious native son Albert Soboul, Bousquet calmly replied that he had been in dialogue with the Comité Albert Soboul, chaired by a former Communist elected official. Not only did he invite the Soboul group to participate in the commemorative commission, but he also pledged to support the naming of a building or street in honor of the celebrated historian of the Revolution and Communist militant. Among the rigorously conventional projects that the Bousquet commission envisaged for 1989 were a colloquium on Rabaut Saint-Etienne, a Protestant leader and revolutionary from Nîmes; public lectures; expositions; an opera, concerts, and a theatrical program; a series of school projects; and a summer university devoted to the Revolution.[30]

A group of energetic citizens in Viroflay (near Versailles) bypassed their centrist mayor who saw the Revolution in despairingly stereotypical terms of guillotines and massacres. Organized in a neighborhood-block association (the Association de la rue du Colonel Fabien—nothing at all to do with the PCF!), the members decided to "sing the rights of man" in period costumes to the accompaniment of drummers. Politically and culturally of diverse orientations, these women and men celebrated that part of their heritage that they believed was truly universal.[31]

The bicentennial community of Bressuire in the Deux-Sèvres had two strikes against it from the very beginning. First, the town had been devastated by the infernal columns of 1794, and, second, the president of the local organizing committee was named Bourreau. The citizens of the tiny rural commune of Piencourt near Bernay in the Eure refused to subscribe Fr 250 (collectively) toward the cantonal bicentennial festive fund. The merchants of Alençon, capital of another Norman department, did not betray a real passion for commemoration. Ostensibly in honor of the bicentennial, they organized a contest to choose the person who could consume the most herrings.[32]

Ideological reckoning (and reproduction) topped the bicentennial agenda of Count Hubert d'Andigné (RPR), president of the Conseil général of the Orne. "If it were strictly up to me," he volunteered, "I would celebrate the Revolution by setting up a guillotine in the courtyard of the prefecture and cutting off the heads of all the bearded ones"—that is to say, the Socialists. But the Poniatowskis, father and son, showed that it was possible for the right to handle the bicentennial with dignity and discrimination rather than vituperation. The father, Michel, Giscard's confidant and former minister, a gifted amateur historian whose cultivation did not inhibit the emergence of a xenophobic Lepéniste disposition, served as senator-mayor of L'Isle-Adam in the Val d'Oise. To structure an evening of music, fireworks, and a Franco-French rendition of the national anthem by popular singer Mireille Mathieu, Poniatowski wrote a six-page text entitled "En écoutant la *Marseillaise*," treating the Revolutionary period from the end of the Old Regime to the empire.

Avoiding the classical tropism of the unregenerate right, the senator-mayor told a core republican story, with only muted nostalgia for the old days and the good monarch. He felt comfortable with the early Revolution, which realized some of the reforms that Louis XVI had proven too weak to accomplish on his own: the end of privileges, equality of taxation, the abolition of feudalism, and the promulgation of the Declaration of Rights. But the spirit of the Festival of the Federation, with which Poniatowksi resonated, dissolved rapidly as the anarchic and antiparliamentary elements of the Parisian sections and clubs propelled the new nation toward Terror. "Blind and furious," the Terror was inexcusable: it murdered thousands of innocent people by guillotine and tens of thousands, including children, in the killing fields of counterrevolutionary repression. The author depicted Robespierre as a bloodthirsty tyrant, the Thermidoreans as self-serving opportunists, and the Directorials as weak, corrupt, and arbitrary governors. Even after this decade of turmoil and suffering, however, Michel Poniatowksi recognized and saluted "a grand and beautiful message"—the affirmation of liberty, equality, and fraternity. His bicentennial was monarcho-feuillant rather than counterrevolutionary.[33]

Ladislas Poniatowski, who has recently distanced himself from his father's extremist position on immigration and his skepticism about integration, was in any event by nature more pragmatic and less elitist. Spokesman of the Parti républicain in the Palais-Bourbon, he was also the vice president of the Conseil général of the Eure (population 500,000) and mayor of the hamlet of Quillebeuf-sur-Seine (population 1,100). Though he lacked his father's literary talent, he shared his passion for history. He construed historical consciousness as both an aesthetic pleasure and a powerful didactic tool, an endless source of civism and local/regional/national pride. Poniatowski the younger talked history the way he worked the marketplaces of his electoral district: with energy, enthusiasm, and no more nuance than the public could easily digest.

While on the departmental level the leaders turned to a professional company to mount an exposition, at the grass roots Poniatowski drew on the skill and drive of two members of his municipal council, a schoolteacher on the left and a retiree on the right, to organize an exhibition of local history. Combined with the annual town festival, it would show, in the words of the mayor, that, "right or left, we are all children of the republic." But Poniatowski was both a shrewd and a circumspect consensualist. He managed to decenter the Revolution, and implicitly deflate its central engendering claims, by casting the exposition in a long-run historical vein, reaching back to the early seventeenth century. The bicentennial would be an occasion for the citizens of Quillebeuf to remember that they had once been Henriqueville, that the hamlet had been razed for its fidelity to Henri IV, and that this populist monarch remained eternally grateful for their fidelity.

The deputy mayor's message was that local history was a bloc, and that it was tonic and necessary to embrace it all. He made no effort to draw connections, or contrasts, between the worlds of Henri and the last Capet, or to evaluate, in his father's manner, the positive and negative parts of the legacy. He felt that it was the responsibility of politicians to help their constituents understand that the past shaped the present and the future, but he wanted to pitch the issue on a plane of relative generality, where contentiousness could be avoided. While the Declaration spoke to the liberal's instincts, the rupture of 89–91 appealed to the regional and local governor's fascination for the details of public affairs. For Ladislas Poniatowski, the Revolution represented above all the drastic and necessary modernization of the system of administration.[34]

Deeply divided in their memories and fidelities, the 1,500 inhabitants of Bédoin in the Vaucluse conducted two very different sorts of bicentennial exercises, the preparations for which generated months of friction and animosity. The blues, now the majority, formed a "republican committee," planted a liberty tree, read the Declaration of Rights, and prepared for a gala fourteenth of July. The whites, led by the mayor and a handful of royalist-leaning aldermen, organized a "pilgrimage" for the planting of sixty-three cypress trees in commemoration of sixty-three villagers executed in 1794 in a brutal purge of counterrevolutionary influence.[35]

The Ministry of Education and the Schools

For the commemorators, the schools provided a captive (and potentially captivated) audience as well as a fertile supply of creators and actors. Shortly after assuming office Jeanneney concluded that the government had not seriously mined this vein. Despite myriad signs of an intense interest in the Revolution at all levels, the minister of education during the cohabitation period, centrist René Monory, complained Jeanneney, "had displayed a clear-cut repugnance toward everything that might appear as a warm celebration of the bicentennial in the schools." Jeanneney sought not central ministerial orchestration of a lock-step celebration but an articulated encouragement to local-level initiative, logistical assistance, and rewards of distinction and honor.

This approach corresponded with the temperament and the ambitions of the new education minister, Lionel Jospin, erstwhile professor and former head of the Socialist party. "What I wish," he told the press, "is a commemoration quickened by inspiration but shorn of puffery." This "mezza voce mobilization," as one journalist styled it, was meant to defuse and belie the reflexive torrent of accusations from the right of Jacobin indoctrination and manipulation.

Several counselors at the Mission deplored Jospin's prudence. "The teaching corps expected him to speak of the French Revolution with a bit of ardor," commented one of them. Another surmised that the minister refused to seize the will of the teachers to engage headlong in a vigorous commemoration for fear of a resurgence of the sort of bitter conflict that had marked the debate over private (notably Catholic) schooling early in Mitterrand's first term. In his dealings with the Mission, Jospin delegated to represent him Gérard Debry, a right-leaning *énarque* who proposed no significant ministerial initiatives and offered no supplementary financial aid for school-based undertakings.

The ministry published a superb anthology of texts dealing with the Revolutionary legacy and its connection to education, which it distributed to thousands of classes. In his preface Jospin energetically pressed the case for the school as the offspring of the republic, and thus a "child of the values of liberty and equality." The minister recalled that the Declaration of 1789 denounced ignorance as a major cause of public misfortune and that the Declaration of 1793 committed the state to providing education for everyone.

While Jospin construed the school's fundamental mission as the transmission of values and the national patrimony (in the abstract, a position more hospitable to the conservative than to the reformer), Yves Martin, the doyen of the ministry's inspectoral corps, cautioned in his introduction to the same volume that all the values of the Revolution were not worth transmitting, and that Revolution and patrimony were not interchangeable entities. Not only did he point out that the Revolution itself transgressed many of the rights it proclaimed, but he contested the left-bicentennial piety that the Revolution begot twentieth-century democracy ("it could not be reduced to [the fruit of] the thought of 1789"). More subtly, Martin suggested that the principles of '89 had to be "developed and enriched"—in a word, corrected—in order to constitute, with other currents of thought, the bases of "our democratic exigencies of today." The subtext of Martin's message to the teachers seemed to be, "be calm and judicious."[36]

Beyond this sturdy anthology, the ministry consecrated officially a national day for reflection on the bicentennial (to coincide with the liberty tree plantings), organized another day devoted to the theme of democracy and public finance (which led Prime Minister Rocard, a specialist in financial affairs, to explain taxation to elementary school children in the fourteenth arrondissement of Paris), and sponsored essay competitions on such subjects as the rights of man. But the focus of national policy was to promote and facilitate initiatives from below. Toward this end the ministry asked each rector to name an academic correspondent to stimulate and coordinate bicentennial projects in the schools. The correspondent chaired a commission that examined proposals submitted by teachers and students, disbursing funds and according curricular derogations to facilitate the realization of the most compelling ideas. The institutional vehicle was called a Projet d'action éducative (PAE), a collective undertaking organized by a teacher or teachers during school hours and dedicated to a theme likely to enrich the minds of the students.[37]

Over 2,500 PAEs dealt with the Revolution. The French and history classes at the fourth level of a *collège* at Evry outside of Paris wrote together a historical novel set in their region based on research in the *cahiers*, in local and national political deliberations, in memoirs and the press, and other relevant texts. Twenty-one classes in a lycée situated in what used to be the Faubourg Saint-Antoine developed a project, which took the form of musical theatre and historical exhibition, focused on the daily life of the common people of Paris during the Revolution. Another Paris-area *collège*, linked with a school in the Isère, put on plays, debates, and exhibitions treating the Revolution and the rights of man. The *collège* of Puylaurens worked on a shoemaker-poet who introduced Marianne into his songs. Focusing on the themes of civism, solidarity, and the impact of war, the students of the *collège* of Quissac conducted firsthand research in communal deliberations. Similarly, at the lycée of Sète, students researched many of the aspects of the local Revolutionary experience. The Ecole de Rosemont in Besançon conducted one of the most interesting PAEs, initiating young children into the practice of historical research and theatrical play.[38]

Poitiers and the Poitou-Charentes
A Descent into *la France Profonde*

onsisting of the Charente, the Charente-Maritime, the Deux-Sèvres, and
the Vienne, the Poitou-Charentes affords an interesting vantage point for
observing the bicentennial from below. Much of the region lived the Revolution very intensely, from the time the three Poitevin clerics providentially united
with the Third Estate, thereby permitting it to proclaim itself the National Assembly in June 1789. This was a region of violent extremes, from place to place and time
to time, and of extreme violence, rhetorical and physical. Of the cities, between
ardently republican Niort, directly faced with the Vendéen threat, and moderate
Angoulême, stood a deeply divided Poitiers, oscillating between Jacobin and counterrevolutionary poles. If the urban spaces were far more deeply politicized than the
countryside, the rural areas were much less passive than often supposed. The
peasants gravitated from advanced revolutionary positions (vis-à-vis the National
Assembly) on such issues as the disposition of "feudal" remnants to passionately
antirevolutionary postures when the Revolution seemed to infringe on their cultural and spiritual autonomy.

This was a region of martyrs, blue and white. It was in the Deux-Sèvres that the
Vendéens slew the boy-hero Bara, who quickly became a republican icon. The
marquis de Roux, writing during the first half of this century about revolution and
religion in the Vienne, envisaged his work, devoted to "the Poitevin martyrs," as "a
contribution to the glory of the saints of France." How would a region of scalded
memory, of deep historical cleavages, and of divergent political allegiances respond
to the call to commemorate?[1]

A Descent into *la France Profonde*

The Mission's Man in Poitiers

In some sense the story officially begins on 12 November 1987 with the appointment of Jean-Marc Roger, director of the Archives départementales de la Vienne, as
the Mission's correspondent for both the region and the department. For those who
believe nothing is coincidental, he must have seemed destined for the post. He had
served at Troyes, whence he had the opportunity to observe Michel Baroin at close
range, and he had personal ties with Yann Gaillard, Edgar Faure's right-hand man.
Yet in terms of background and inclination, he was not a likely choice (he was not a
"fanatic of the Revolution," he confided, with a straight face), though he was
genuinely "very sensitive" to what he reasonably perceived as a mark of honor
according to the regnant calculus of such things.

Roger resembled a great many other correspondents, subprefects as well as
archivists, whom he described collectively as politically conservative ("center-
right") and somewhat ill at ease in the bicentennial role ("in an awkward position
vis-à-vis ourselves"). Jean-Noël Jeanneney's arrival heightened his malaise, for he
found the new president "too engaged," rehearsing a "Jacobin" or "republican"
message—Roger used the terms interchangeably—from which he dissented. Nor
was he comfortable with the Mission's self-appointed secular arm, the local CLEF,
also too republican in ideology.

Now Roger was a professional who took his responsibilities seriously and fulfilled
his functions honorably, albeit without torrents of enthusiasm. Yet his family paid a
certain price, for the bicentennial connection caused strains in their daily life. His
daughter was maliciously teased in class as a result of her father's engagement, and
his wife would have preferred that he desist. The Rogers had only recently arrived
in Poitiers. That made his task extremely difficult, for he had not yet mastered the
workings of the local social and political system. The community to which he
naturally gravitated was the old ruling elite, or rather its remnants, the vestiges of a
world of intense social and moral stratification. He and his family were in some
sense still on probation and under the scrutiny of this frayed but still proud and
censorious milieu.

The material conditions in which the archivist had to work aggravated the stress.
The Mission did not subsidize the activities of the correspondent; it did not even
reimburse him for travel costs for meetings in Paris or expenses of sojourn (since
half the correspondents were subprefects with chauffeurs, Roger admitted that this
was an unevenly distributed hardship). Nor at the end did the Mission think to
reward the correspondents for their efforts, either with a specially cast medal of
recognition or with nomination to the Ordre de la mérite (the only correspondent
who received this accolade, Roger noted impishly, came from Jeanneney's ancestral
home base in the Haute-Saône).

On balance, Roger gave more than he received from the Mission. He did not
derive a great deal from the meetings held in Paris. Often vague in agenda and
wearily wordy in execution, they aimed more to buoy morale and to convey the

broad rhythms of the commmemorative calendar rather than to provide concrete orientation and tools. Like his colleagues, Roger felt frustrated by the lack of means at his disposition. Without funds to allocate on his own, he was a mere conduit for individuals and organizations seeking assistance or patronage from the Mission. Given his temperament and ideology, he was not inclined to serve as an inspirational fulcrum or to ferret out bicentennial projects through an aggressive campaign of canvasing and propagandizing. Sincerely pluralistic, his approach was also largely passive. The tree planting at Saint-Gaudent was one of the few undertakings that fully mobilized him, especially once he learned that the president of the republic would attend.

Roger was prepared to accommodate diverse local solicitations, but he conformed to the prefect's instructions to make no waves ("avoid confrontations"). He helped organize Christian de Montrichard's visit to Poitiers in late June 1988, which provided the occasion for several meetings presided by the prefect, Jean Coussiron, to discuss regional bicentennial activities with representatives of the various public administrations, local collectivities, and sundry associations and interest groups. As a result of Coussiron's transfer in the middle of the bicentennial year, Roger had to abandon at least one major project, a weeklong program focusing on the major branches of the bureaucracy, which he considered the finest part of the Revolutionary patrimony. (At the reception marking the changing of the guard on 13 July 1989, the new prefect had the good sense—taste is a wholly different matter—to serve Canard Duchêne, the official, albeit alienated, bicentennial champagne.)

The Physician-Notable Performs a Revolutionary Postmortem

At least one critical figure on the political landscape, Louis Fruchard, the head of the regional government, did not attend the the Coussiron-Montrichard gathering. He claimed not to have received an invitation, an unthinkable protocolary slight. A retired physician from Mauléon, the "Vendéen" part of the Deux-Sèvres, Fruchard had opened a practice in this area, the home of his great-grandparents, at twenty-six years of age in 1947. Like so many rural physicians, located at the very center of local life and death, exercising enormous power at the grass roots, he slid imperceptibly into electoral politics. The "system," as he calls it, led him from the municipal council in 1953 to the mayoralty several years later in a hamlet that fused with others under the aegis of Mauléon in 1965.

Already serving in the Conseil général, Fruchard received the mandate of the citizens of the enlarged agglomeration (population today under 3,000) to govern their affairs. Later he entered the Conseil régional, participated actively in the construction of the region, and rose finally to its presidency. With this veteran leader, a staunch political conservative, all the regional ambivalence over the Revolution surged to the surface. Fruchard found himself in the eye of a maelstrom when he told a reporter who inquired about his bicentennial plans that he would not "dance on the corpses." Given his official position in the tissue of republican institutions, many observers, including colleagues on the right, regarded his remarks as imprudent and inappropriate.

Fruchard was a counterrevolutionary, but not without nuance. He was not a royalist: he dreamed of no "chimerical resoration." He was a republican, primarily because he was a realist: there was no credible alternative in contemporary France. If he denounced the Revolution, he nevertheless recognized it as "a necessary evil." He was not wholly convinced that the monarchical regime had been capable of evolving on its own, as it had in England, a country whose history he knew only superficially but evoked repeatedly. But if certain changes had been imperative, "all the excesses were not at all required," Fruchard averred with conviction. That included the murder of the king ("they could simply have thrown him out") and the tens of thousands who were "exterminated."

Religious persecution drove the Vendéens into revolt, not fidelity to prince or lord, Fruchard contended. In his home region the rebels were defeated; they suffered massacre, not genocide, largely because the fall of Robespierre interrupted the process. But Fruchard detected unequivocally "a will to commit genocide." All the houses in his *pays* save three were burned; two-thirds of the population was wiped out. There was no need for these deaths, he stated, with deep feeling. He deplored the deaths of the blues at Machecoul as well as the slaughter of the whites throughout the Vendée to underline his sense of balance.

Against this cognitive and emotional background, it is hardly surprising that the bicentennial "deeply shocked" Fruchard, that the idea of "making merry" made him sick. Fruchard complained that many elements in the press and public did not understand his "malaise," or the specific context from which it issued. Perhaps backtracking somewhat in retrospect, the president of the region explained that his allergy to celebration was primordially a local matter, in deference to the scarred citizenry of the area. He claimed that he never intended to conflate the local and the regional dimensions. (He rarely addressed the national arena, from which he heard stentorian calls for celebration "without a word of regret," perhaps because he was not listening carefully enough.) He was falsely portrayed as against the Declaration of Rights, he protested. He warmly approved the principles but remarked that they were originally Christian precepts adopted opportunistically by the Revolution and then systematically violated by it. Fruchard looked forward to commemorating, in both liturgical and civic ways, in 1993. He planned to write a history of his home region in the context of the larger experience, in part because he observed that "young people today are forgetting the Vendéen tradition."

Louis Fruchard will not lack for assistance in his historical/pedagogical project. He will always be able to turn to Reynald Secher, his closest adviser in the period preceding the bicentennial. As a historian and polemicist, Secher had already devoted a substantial portion of his young life to the crusade for the rehabilitation of the martyred Vendée and for the acknowledgment of the real character and magnitude of its martyrdom. Genocide was the word Secher preferred. While there is no doubt about the organic (Burkean?) roots of Fruchard's position, his mind seemed to be infested with Secher's formulations, and his documentary claims bore Secher's imprint. Like his patron, Secher was scandalized by a state that "obliges young Vendéens to denounce their memory and to dance on the tombs of their ancestors in the name of 'founding principles.'"[2]

On 6 December 1987, at the last session of the Conseil régional for the year, the president of the Communist group (consisting of three members), brandishing a copy of *Le Monde*, which had picked up Fruchard's provocative antibicentennial statement, demanded that the president of the body explain himself. Surprise and consternation buffeted the assembly from the left across to the right. The physician explained that he had spoken as mayor of Mauléon and as a simple citizen, not as the president of the region, whose position he had not thus entailed. Critics rejoined that such a distinction was illusory, that Fruchard's words cast a shadow over the region, and that as "republican elected officials" they could not turn their back on "the gains of the Revolution." Moderates and certain conservatives concurred with the left that the region could not afford to be drastically out of step with the nation. Fruchard agreed to appoint a commission to study the question of how the region should participate in the commemoration. When the Communist group asked for an accounting in early June 1988, it was clear that the commission had only existed on paper. Cornered by a large majority of councillors, many of whom worried about the conspicuous presence of Secher in the presidential entourage, Fruchard had no choice but to honor his pledge.

Resolving the Dilemma: The Regional Commission

Fruchard was willing to "meet [his critics] halfway," but not to cede to the unseemly demands of those who wanted unvarnished celebration. To chair the commission he sought a moderate who was not deeply marked politically on the combustible issues that surrounded the bicentennial and whose hand was free for lack of a constraining local mandate as mayor or conseiller général. The pool of candidates was extremely confined; Claude Moreau, the former owner of a textbook publishing house purchased by Hachette, an easygoing and accessible man with the profile of a technocrat rather than a politician, received the call. Generally welcomed at the outset, the choice of Moreau proved to be a brilliant stroke. He managed the commision with considerable skill and expanded his own horizons substantially. He found the experience "enthralling," made new friends, and ended up joining the Cercle Condorcet, a discussion circle frequented habitually by those on the left with whom he had had few instinctive affinities in the past.

Delicately balanced, the commission consisted of the correct doses according to political current (the right dominated, reflecting the fact that it held thirty of the fifty-three seats in the Conseil) and territorial representation. In addition to the regional councillors and elected officials who formed the majority, three "experts" joined the group as scientific counselors: Jean-Marc Roger and two historians, both of marked republican sympathies, Jacques Péret of the faculty of letters of the University of Poitiers and Jean-Marie Augustin of its law school. The two professors were both active members of the Poitevin Comité Liberté, Egalite, Fraternité, part of the national CLEF network, sponsored locally by the very enterprising Fédération des oeuvres laïques based in Poitiers. Naturally allergic to what he perceived as CLEF's extremism, Roger reported that he had received instructions from the Mission, via the prefect, to keep his distance from their undertakings. The challenge for Moreau was to build confidence by unearthing a "unifying subjet" and, by so doing, to "avoid accentuating the cleavages."

Still under pressure from Secher, who elicited some sympathy on the commission, Moreau needed to find a way to circumnavigate the Revolution without overtly contesting the bicentennial pretext for the enterprise. Determined to marshal "regional unity," he proposed an exposition that celebrated regional progress by tracing the construction of the Poitou-Charentes from antiquity to the present. (Numerous local and regional leaders on the right used this strategy of the grand fresco to dilute the prominence of the Revolution without abjuring the republican responsibility to commemorate the common past.) Roger warmly supported Moreau's desire to blunt the conspicuousness of the Revolution. His preference for using maps as the chief tool of expression for charting change across time would have further obscured the explosive power of the Revolution. Initially only six of a projected forty-one panels were to treat the Revolution. The CLEF group vigorously opposed this "recentering." Moreau portrays himself in retrospect as extremely obdurate, perhaps excessively so. Since the region had suffered so much from division in the past, he was determined to "hide" and "erase" all the remnants of dissension.

His "obsession to impose unity" naturally squired the commission to the brink of rupture. Memories diverge on the precise chronology of events that ensued. Moreau compromised with the CLEF group, according the Revolution—the occasion was, after all, its bicentennial—about half the panels in the exhibition. Augustin, today the president of the Cercle Condorcet, apparently missed a critical meeting during this period. He argued with Moreau about the kind of portrayal that would be accorded to the Vendée. Behind Moreau's rigid embrace of what he called "the facts," Augustin detected the hand of Secher, whom he considered a dangerous man who used history for nefarious revisionist ends. At about this time, Fruchard vacated the presidency of the region; according to Roger, whose view is not shared by others closer to the president, he owed his fall in part to the scandal over the bicentennial, which had embarrassed the moderate right even as it had enraged the opposition. Shortly before he ceded his office on 19 December 1988 to a more temperate rightist, Jean-Pierre Raffarin, Fruchard apparently spoke up again in the name of the victims and martyrs of the Revolution.

Fiery in his republican conviction and offended by Fruchard's outbursts, Augustin wrote a letter that he himself qualified as "incendiary" to Raffarin demanding a public disavowal of his predecessor's positions on the grounds that the president of a region could harbor no hostility to republican institutions. What he wanted was tantamount to a relaunching of the bicentennial effort under more loyal auspices. Refusing to become ensnared in an argument he had not provoked, and anxious above all to avoid becoming tainted in any way by this volatile affair, the new president refused to respond to the indignant professor. He understood, however, that an anti-Revolutionary campaign would be counterproductive (nor did he retain the services of Secher in the presidential cabinet). This was the context in which Augustin stormed out the door of a meeting of the regional commission, after a particularly harsh exchange with one of its "political members," Armelle Guinebertière, who happened to be from Fruchard's home region. She did not relish Augustin's view that the real martyrs were the people who died for the republic throughout its existence.[3]

The Exhibition and Its Accompaniment

Augustin's bilious departure jolted the commission but did not derail it. Péret continued to collaborate and assumed the major responsibility, along with a retired schoolteacher, Robert Petit, secretary of the departmental CLEF, and another historian, Dominique Guillemet, for preparing the sections of the exposition dealing with the Revolution. Moreau must have given them full latitude, for they did not conceal the passions, the cleavages, or the violence. For compelling reasons, the Poitevins and Charentais of 1789 "challenged every aspect of the society of the Old Regime." Apocalyptic for the nobility and gratifying for the bourgeoisie, the night of 4 August did not satisfy many peasants, who continued to press for the end of all the remnants of what they called feudalism. The exposition offered a capsule prosopography of the region's deputies to the Estates General, placed in relief the "decisive gesture" of the three priest-deputies of Poitou, recounted the formation of departments, and, in an important and original panel, recounted the bitter local disputes ["querelles de clochers"] that pitted town against town in the contest to claim central-place status in the new administrative universe. One panel explored the affirmation of national unity in the Festivals of the Federation of 1790, while another looked at the Revolutionary symbols (national altars, liberty trees) and values (patriotism). Four panels treated the events of 1793–94 with sobriety and candor. Seventeen ninety-three inaugurated "the laceration of the whites and the blues." As the Bocage moved into opposition, prodded by the rupture in the church, "the revolutionary measures appear[ed] to be nothing less than attacks on this traditional rural world," whose authenticity is underlined. "A popular revolt at the outset," the uprising acquired a marked royalist and Catholic tonality as the nobility assumed direction. Neither Secher nor Fruchard could have appreciated this effort at evenhandedness: "To the violence of insurrection replies the violence of repression, the exactions of the infernal columns, which manage only to fortify the Vendéens in their alienation." The Vendée terrified the blues, who saw it as a menace to their Revolution and responded with "a veritable patriotic eruption" in the two Charentes, in the southern Deux-Sèvres, and in the Vienne. This "merciless civil war" persisted in the politics of the nineteenth century and remained "still quite relevant today."

The Terror "in the region," which Péret had carefully studied, was described as basically the product of circumstances, in particular the need to contain the nearby Vendée. The Terror meant administrative purges, the unmasking of suspects, and "a justice that had become political." Neither blood nor bloodthirstiness was a leitmotif of the panels, though the one devoted to "a unifying cultural Revolution" evoked "a policy of the tabula rasa requiring the elimination of the priests and a campaign against 'fanaticism,' that is, religion."

Under the title "From the Provinces to the Region," the "before" and "after" panels conveyed information of a largely technical and/or picturesque sort, with no conflictual coloring. The "before" panels dealt with geography, "our ancestors the Gauls," feudalism, Romanesque architecture, the provinces in the Old Regime, Protestants and Catholics, and the Atlantic window of prosperity. The "after" panels looked at administrative reorganization, political life, modernization, the World Wars, the new regionalization, the institutions and vocation of the region (five panels), and the dynamism and ambitions of the Poitou-Charentes.

Claude Moreau, vice-president of the Conseil régional as well as president of the bicentennial commission, avenged himself against the CLEF clique in subtle fashion. In the slick brochure announcing the exposition—there was no catalogue, only a mimeographed summary of the panels—he explained the undertaking in a full (and fulsome) page without once mentioning the Revolution. He adverted to it elliptically through the refrain of unity in diversity, unity requiring the respect of differences, diversity as the guarantee of authenticity, and so on. His aim was to elicit regional pride and to appropriate for the regional government the major credit for leading the Poitou-Charentes "to the top group among the French regions."

The son of a radical, trained in a business school, a former leader of the Young Giscardians and a future national spokesman of the UDF, allegedly a Mason (but of which obedience?), Jean-Pierre Raffarin contributed an introductory text to Moreau's brochure that comforted his image as an "man of communication." (Communications and public relations had been his profession before he became a full-time politician.) He uttered the "R" word, but he was happy to identify it as part of the historic experience of the west and not peculiarly French (not to mention Picton). The French revolutions, like the American Revolution and the European revolutions of 1848, shared one glorious feature: a preoccupation with liberty. Liberty was both safe and sacred ground for the liberal Raffarin, who associated its affirmation and dissemination with the Declaration of the Rights of Man. "In celebrating the bicentennial"—he did not fear the "c" word either—"the Conseil régional of the Poitou-Charentes wished to place itself in the most republican of traditions," Raffarin proclaimed (incidentally furnishing Augustin the reply and engagement he had demanded months earlier).

Inaugurated on 5 June 1989 in Poitiers, the exhibit remained for three weeks in each of the four departmental capitals. A historian named by the commission introduced it at each opening. Thousands of people visited it, many of them through organized school excursions. Two complementary actions completed the regional bicentennial triptych. In September the region hosted a colloquium, once again focused on regional identity rather than the Revolutionary past and heritage. Still, '89 claimed a place of honor, as hundreds of municipal councillors, mayors, and other elected officials witnessed the unveiling of a plaque commemorating the Declaration of Rights. Before the republican buffet, Raffarin made the sort of pithy, zesty speech one would expect from a communications man, more comfortable with popular singers Bernard Lavilliers and Yves Dutheil than with Voltaire or Danton (though it is only fair to note that he cited smidgens from Kant, Tocqueville, and Michelet to prove that he was not merely running for office). The Poitou-Charentes pledged its attachment to the Good Revolution, "to the ideals of 1789, to the republican ideal." It remembered the Other Revolution, that of the Terror. And it averred that "one can celebrate liberty without forgetting the Vendée." Liberty constituted Raffarin's refrain—the liberty that blew across the Atlantic on which the region faced, the liberty for which the students at Tiananmen died, the liberty that would flourish in the new Europe if it managed to liberate itself from its technocracy. The Declaration celebrated liberty and pointed toward the only way to assure its reproduction, Raffarin suggested, through education, which he construed as the chief mission of the region.

The third and final installment in the regional commemoration was the publication in October of a four-page color comic book—the comic strip is a regional specialty, the showcase art of Angoulême—distributed to all students in the secondary school system. Within the framework of the exhibition theme, "The Poitou-Charentes, from the Provinces to the Région," the story focused on interesting but noncontroversial aspects of the early Revolution. Aside from a passing allusion to misery, attributed in part to provincial rivalries, the cartoon avoided social, economic, and ideological questions. It examined the administrative reorganization of the nation, in particular on the levels of the commune and the department. Making the case for unity following Claude Moreau's holistic logic, it emphasized an issue to which too few historians have paid attention: the avid competition among departments and among towns for territorial, political, and economic advantages. Worried that the exposition might be "a bit too intellectual," Claude Moreau took special satisfaction from the cartoon strip, which was accessible to all and symbolized the priority the region accorded to education.[4]

Jean-Marc Roger agreed with Moreau that the region's efforts were intrinsically worthwhile and well received. "Very few people, at the beginning of 1988," wrote the director of the archives, "would have hoped for as much." Roger vigorously defended his region's bicentennial commitment against the charges, first of treason, then of tepidness, that had filtered up to Montrichard. His report bespeaks his own rapid acculturation in a region to which he was a stranger and the anguish of the provincial agent over the misapprehensions and the disapprobation of the Parisian mentors (one almost imagines a représentant en mission writing to justify himself as well as to educate the Committee of Public Safety). Roger had established a warm personal relationship with Fruchard, whose execrable press he felt was wholly exaggerated. "I protest vigorously against the criticisms whose essence your collaborators conveyed to me," he protested to the Mission, to whom he administered a brief history lesson. They had to undertsand that the Vendée was historically a part of Poitou, and that in the Poitou-Charentes today "opinion remains very much divided concerning the Revolution." As mayor of a town in the midst of the Vendée militaire, Fruchard could hardly have done otherwise than to "commemorate the martyrs of 1793, and not those who slaughtered them." Roger claimed credit ("on my initiative . . .") for gently bringing the president of the region to a more flexible position, in accordance with which he agreed to a regional role in the bicentennial.

Roger ascribed the success of the bicentennial undertaking in large part to Moreau's singular "dexterity." He was to be commended for holding together the fragile coalition that constituted the commission after "Monsieur J.-M. Augustin dramatically withdrew." Neither the opposition officials nor Péret followed suit, much to Roger's surprise and delight. The Mission's correspondent also found cause for satisfaction in the way in which Fruchard's successor, Raffarin, "made repeated public declarations, solemn and eloquent"—Roger obviously did not use the same standard as Augustin—"of attachment to the grand principles of the French Revolution." As if one required a genealogical explanation for all complex things, Roger informed the Mission that the new president's father, Jean Raffarin, had served as a junior minister in the Mendès-France cabinet of 1954–55.[5]

From Indifference to Circumspection: The Vienne and Its Capital

If the regional government ultimately acquitted itself respectably in terms of the bicentennial enterprise, the same cannot be said of the departmental government in the Vienne. Led by the centrist former minister René Monory, whose passion was the Futuroscope outside Poitiers, the Conseil général "was not warmly disposed." Still, it was careful not to "show hostility." It remained discreetly absent during the entire commemorative season, save for a single event. It helped to finance a film on Claude Chappe and the telegraph—in a double sense a revolutionary creation. Projected before an elite audience at its premiere at the Futuroscope, according to Jean-Marc Roger, it turned out to be "a total fiasco," eliciting literally no applause. Roger lobbied unsuccessfully to involve the department in a reflection on its own genesis. He proved unable to generate any support for a commemoration of the radical and decisive administrative reforms of 1790, a relatively "neutral" subject, which he plausibly considered as one of the most important legacies of the Revolution.[6]

The municipality of Poitiers, so long a conservative bastion, was now in the hands of the Socialists, but the latter evinced the same sort of reticence vis-à-vis the Revolution that marked many of their fellow militants in other parts of France. It was not clear, after so many false starts, that the bicentennial would be a winning issue. Though a Socialist, mayor Jacques Santrot had to worry about the diverse clienteles that constituted his electorate, many of which were not ideologically attuned to R/revolutionary themes. According to Jean-Marie Augustin, who sat on the municipal commission formed to consider the city's bicentennial engagement, the city government "was not very keen." Constrained to participate, once the mayor saw the scale of popular interest, he tried to "harness it [*récupérer*]" in the classical political manner.

The commission proposed a "festival of the people" in which the city agreed to invest five hundred thousand francs. (According to Roger, the municipal financial contribution turned out to be much larger: four hundred thousand francs directly for the festival, five hundred thousand francs in subventions to various participating associations, and a vast amount of nonmonetized aid through municipal services.) Augustin supplied the historical context of commemoration: it would take place on 13 June 1989 in order to honor the three Poitevin priests, deputies of the clergy to the Estates General, whose decision to join forces with the Third Estate enabled it to declare itself rapidly the National Assembly representing the entire nation.[7]

A critical organizing decision was to hold the festival not in the vast, charmless, asphalted spaces on the periphery but in the very center of town in the magnificent Blossac Park, named for the "improving" eighteenth-century intendant who embellished and modernized the provincial capital in numerous ways. Unwilling to assume the animating and orchestrating role itself, and unable to afford the cost of farming it out to professional festival makers, city hall turned reluctantly to the CLEF, with its base of permanent logistical support, the Fédération des oeuvres laïques (FOL). The municipality feared that the CLEF-FOL might imbue the festival with an excessively ideological hue or prove incommensurate with the organizing task. In fact, the passion of the CLEF militants and the considerable practical expertise of the FOL in providing a vast array of services for public meetings and mass activities of all sorts complemented each other perfectly. It is true that the CLEF group wanted to structure the festive events around historical themes in order to dramatize the Revolutionary connection. Like many other cultural professionals, Marc Bordier, the deputy mayor for cultural affairs, had little interest in history. History was dead and, by and large, it was dull. To turn the people on, he promised, rather, not without a patina of superfluous demagogy, that "Poitiers Rev en fête" would be "a modern fête, and not one turned toward the past."[8]

The sansculotte Santrot, as one journalist dubbed the mayor, echoed the same theme of the "striking modernity" of the Revolution as he received the *cahiers de doléances* of the youth of Poitiers on the place d'Armes in the early evening of 13 July. Six groups of marchers, led by cavaliers, converged on the square from the different quarters of the city. After a reading of the Declaration of the Rights of Man, an orchestra led the entire cortege to Blossac Park, transformed into a Revolutionary agora. Shortly after 7:00 P.M., a choir of twelve hundred school-children and several hundred adults presented a concert of Revolutionary songs from the Condorcet circle, located across the fountain from the CLEF crossroads. At various other stands and stages, actors presented extracts of plays, swordsmen dueled (somewhat incongruously evoking "the battles of the Revolution for more justice and liberty"), acrobats and mimes performed, and children took part in diverse games.

A dinner of country fare began around eight-thirty. For those preferring more exotic fare, the "foreign communities," emblem of the cosmopolitanism of the Revolution, served menus from their homelands along the street of the Cuisines of the World. The pastry artisans of Poitiers baked a huge bicentennial cake measuring six meters by six meters. Those who had purchased a tricolor bouquet for ten francs, the proceeds of which were used to finance the various exhibits, could claim a slice. Circus acts entertained during and after dinner. From Montgolfière avenue ensued the launching of balloons bearing souvenir postcards of the festival ("carrying with them messages of liberty, equality, and fraternity from the Poitevins"). The Robes et Pierres square was the site of a dance recital celebrating African American music followed by a Revolutionary fashion show. At around eleven a symbolic Bastille went up in flames, inaugurating a fireworks display at the circle of 14 July.

Two rock bands and the Revoswing jazz ensemble played music as many of the fifteen thousand guests danced late into the night and early into the next morning. Superb weather had favored a huge turnout—"more popular than bourgeois," noted Jean-Marie Augustin, who knew the local social structure. Without disrupting the lighthearted, festive mood, the CLEF organizers had deftly succeeded in incorporating many didactic elements. Poitevins celebrated with a convivial exuberance what Jeanneney liked to call the "luminous side" of the Revolution. Local observers and the press on the right as well as the left concurred that the evening was a smashing success.[9]

The CLEF, Key to Poitevin Bicentennial Success

The CLEF, the critical player in "Poitiers Rev en fête," was the most active force in the Poitevin bicentennial field. Summoned to life by the FOL, representing the Ligue française de l'enseignemnt et de l'éducation permanente, the local CLEF became one of the most productive units in all of France. The FOL sought out Jacques Péret and offered to provide a dense network of support if he agreed to lead the departmental committee. The aim of the FOL, an aim in consonance with the national CLEF manifesto, was to "celebrate the Revolutionary values." This implied a militant engagement that initially worried Péret, an intensely earnest scholar who was unwilling to be the instrument of anyone's propaganda, despite his leftward leanings. Still, the educational opportunity attracted him mightily, the chance to reach beyond his narrow university audience to the universe of ordinary citizens. After assuring himself that he would have a free hand to make policy decisions, Péret agreed to serve as the anchor for the operation. He recruited a half-dozen others (sometimes a few more, sometimes a few less), including historians such as Jean-Marie Augustin and retired schoolteacher Robert Petit, who became one of the committee's most indefatigable workers. Divergent in their politics, the members of the CLEF united around a common civic conviction that inspired and informed their program.

Given the stakes involved, Péret believed that the bicentennial must become "the affair not of a small number but of all the citizens." An understanding of the Revolution he viewed as a prerequisite for the practice of an enlightened and active citizenship. To know the Revolution and its legacy was to be in a position to "defend its gains, gains contested today by certain elements." A vivid historical memory would arm the citizen against the sort of self-indulgent complacency and/or withdrawal that worried many teachers, politicians, and other shapers of opinion. The bicentennial was an occasion for "all the people of France to discover," as the CLEF collective of the Vienne noted in the preface to its publication of local *cahiers*, "that the beautiful republican formula 'Liberty, Equality, Fraternity' could never have become the foundation of our society without the resolute and enthusiastic action of our ancestors of 1789." The French today had to learn their moral and political genealogy; this would show them that history was not merely an antiquarian affectation. A closer familiarity with the historical struggle to end privilege, obtain equality of rights, and found the republican nation would make French men and women more sensitive to the "extensions" of the Revolution today: the challenge to combat totalitarianism, which Péret regarded as the antithesis of the Revolutionary ethic, and to fight all forms of exclusion, including racism and excessive social inequality.

If such rhetoric situated him clearly on the left, the history professor pledged to honor a pluralistic approach to historical research. He would "recall the facts in their entirety," which he believed, perhaps with an overdose of positivistic optimism, would foreclose tendentiousness. The rejuvenated attack against the Revolution and its principles troubled him, in both scientific and civic terms. Like Augustin, he regarded the Chaunu-Secher invocation of "the so-called Franco-French Vendéen genocide" as fundamentally dishonest because it advanced political ends at the expense of "the historical truth." Despite his demonstrable scholarly scrupulousness, Péret left himself vulnerable because his own discourse took on a sharp ideological edge.[10]

The first operational goal of the CLEF was to involve as many citizens (and future citizens) as possible in commemorative endeavors, preferably as producers,

Lady Liberty leads the Poitevins to speak out. One of the most active of the CLEF associations, the group based in Poitiers produced several books, including this publication of the grievance lists composed by the three orders of the Poitou prior to the meeting of the Estates General in May 1789. (Photo: CLEF of the department of the Vienne.)

but if not, then as informed consumers. The committee met with numerous local and departmental associations to encourage their participation ("share our experience" was the strategic watchword). Through the FOL, and with the help of the national CLEF, it organized training sessions to show teachers and association leaders how to plan bicentennial events around song, dance, theatrical presentation, and local research. The CLEF argued for the commingling of the festive and the pedagogical in school projects (PAEs) and extracurricular events. Students could embark on adventures such as creating Revolutionary-style newspapers that would combine investigation with fun. Research into the daily life of local ancestors who walked and worked in the same streets and buildings could produce the same motivating dynamic. Projections of the great films on the Revolution (e.g., Renoir, Gance) could be accompanied by debates. Lectures could be illustrated with slides and music that would entertain as well as teach.

The CLEF both encouraged individuals to discover the archives (and uncover hidden archives) and undertook research on its own account. One major project, coordinated by Robert Petit, concerned the systematic study of tree-planting ceremonies during the Revolutionary period. He sent a questionnaire to a large number of teachers in the Vienne to solicit their help. He himself initiated people into firsthand historical research. The product was a book rich in both commentary and documents called *Les Arbres de la liberté*. Another group launched an inquiry into the preparation of the *cahiers* that mobilized many students. They learned how the *cahiers* were constructed, how to "read" their expression of needs and of anguish, and how to connect local with national concerns. This research produced the book called *Les Poitevins prennent la parole*. Other books followed, with astonishing celerity, most of them materializing between October 1988 and the end of 1989. Philippe Marchandion led a group studying the origins and trajectories of "les hommes de la Révolution dans la Vienne," which later became the title of a book. François Rieupeyroux published a book of engravings drawn from the *Journal de Paris* in order to present materials for a juxtaposition of the national to the local/provincial perspective. Along with Robert Petit, Rieupeyroux put togther a brochure, illustrated by twenty-four color slides, concentrating on the local side of the equation. *Révolution et révolutionnaires au quotidien* furnished clues for an understanding of how different sorts of people lived the Revolutionary experience. Products of the CLEF didactic strategy, these books in turn became instruments of emulation and pedagogy, drawing more students and amateurs into the historical tantalus.[11]

Péret, a specialist in the local and regional history of the eighteenth century, was elated to see the extent to which the interest in local roots motivated citizens young and old. He found a veritable "bulimia" to learn about one's ancestors; in retrospect, he regretted not having made an even more systematic and sweeping effort to open the gates to local research. Péret himself gave some fifty public lectures throughout the region on the occasion of the publication of his book *Histoire de la Révolution française en Poitou-Charentes, 1789–1799*. In small communities aloof from "the ruling citadels of provincial culture," he was astonished to encounter beckoning audiences of up to two hundred people, passionately attentive and avid to pose questions about the local dimension in particular. Towns such as Civray (population circa 3,300) organized a series of "chats" concerning the Revolution, to which they invited Péret and others. Jean-Marie Augustin, whose *La Révolution française en Haut-Poitou et pays charentais* appeared several months later, enjoyed similar success in his lecture itinerary. CLEF members participated in talks devised for the university of continuing education.[12]

The Schools

Given its particular interest in reaching future citizens, the CLEF had paid special attention to children and had reached into the schools through many of its programs. Apart from his collaboration with the CLEF, Jean-Marie Augustin served as the academic correspondent of the Mission for the rectorate of Poitiers, whose jurisdiction covered a large part of the region. His task was to encourage bicentennial consciousness and commemorative action in the schools and universities. In addition to providing technical advice and helping teachers (for whom the rectorate sponsored special training programs in conducting historical research and developing commemorative plans) and students make connections with resources, he disposed of a fund supplied by the Ministry of Education to subsidize Projets d'action éducative (PAEs). Seconded by a commission, he evaluated dossiers of candidacy according to their "pedagogical and scholarly merit." Given Augustin's republican ardor, it is hard to imagine that civic heedfulness played no role.

Students in this region engaged in the same wide range of activities that one found elsewhere in France: local history studies, dramatizations, historical reconstitutions, and so on. At the Collège Renaudot of Saint-Benoît, a culinary PAE incited students to recover and reproduce Revolutionary recipes, including such plates as *côtes de porc sauce Robert*, requiring six hours preparation. Their aim was to combine aristocratic and sansculotte foodways into a history cum recipe booklet. A lycée and two *collèges* in Poitiers produced student newspapers devoted to Revolutionary themes. A team at the Lycée professionnel du Verger at Châtellerault made a video on the life of the common people.

Augustin evinced special interest in a PAE called "Poitiers Sings," because it would be presented at the grand bicentennial fête on 13 June. Involving hundreds of children singing a battery of Revolutionary songs that marked European history from the Revolution to the twentieth century, it was the only PAE that stirred controversy. With a repertoire including the carmagnole, the song of the insurgent Lyonnais silkworkers, chants of Italian partisans, and the *International*, the project demonstrated that, albeit rooted in 1789, the Revolution was in certain ways permanent. The leading conservative association of parents of schoolchildren, the PEEP, sharply criticized the program's ideological inflection (anticlerical, pro-Revolutionary). Unyielding, Augustin defended the musical selection as diverse and representative, and he was deeply moved by the concert at the municipal festival. He regretted that he had not succeeded in promoting more PAEs, for he considered them to be of immense significance in attuning the children to commemorative issues. His efforts to penetrate the University of Poitiers were abortive, in large part because its president was indifferent to the bicentennial.[13]

Elsewhere in the Region: The Forest and the Tree

In the regional capital and beyond, there were scores of other imaginative bicentennial programs that have not been surveyed here. "Liberty" was the theme of the annual musical festival of Poitiers. Theatre companies put on *Marat/Sade* and the *Dialogues des Carmélites*. The future prime minister Edith Cresson, mayor of Châtellerault, inaugurated an exhibition on women in the Revolution and another, celebrating human rights and the city's tradition of high-quality craftsmanship, on the local experience of the Revolution. The Association rochelaise pour le Bicentenaire de la Révolution française published several anthologies of monographs on local historical topics. Supported by several municipalities, the association sold 844 copies of the first issue and planned to continue publishing after the end of the commemorative season. It also supported PAEs in nearby schools. The Association départementale des maires de la Charente-Maritime subsidized the publication of *1789–1792: De la paroisse à la commune, la naissance des municipalités en Aunis et Saintonge*. Written by V. Collette and F. Echard, this study focused on "the progressive implantation of democracy" in an administrative context rather than from the more contentious political, social, and economic perspectives. Projets Éditions published a series of studies on the local histories of Angoulême, Bressuire, Niort, Saintes and Rochefort, among others. Virtually all the local learned societies put out special issues on themes dealing with the Revolution.[14]

The prodigal (then Socialist) city of Angoulême, not yet teetering on official bankruptcy, put on a rich program. It welcomed exhibitions on human rights, Angoulême from 1789 to 1799, women in the Revolution, and scientists during the epoch. The theatres and cinemas played Revolutionary themes. "Rock and Roll and Revolution" was one of a number of musical events. Children presented their *cahiers de doléances*, while families gathered for republican banquets. The double climax was the "Grand Festival of the Bicentennial," marked by a series of historical tableaux, on the night of 13 July, and "Angoulême en fête" the following day—parades, music, a bonfire, and dancing.[15]

The major regional event of the bicentennial outside Poitiers was probably the tree planting at Saint-Gaudent. The initiative came from the commune itself (population 350). The idea was to build the local bicentennial celebration around the gesture of Norbert Pressac, the village's priest during the Revolution. Born in 1751, the first of eleven children whose father was a petty judge in a nearby town, Pressac responded warmly to the Revolution. Beyond his call for the planting of a tree signifying the hope of the nation, he was noteworthy for his political engagement. He served as procurator of the commune in 1790, and later as municipal agent under the Directory, and took a keen interest in promoting agricultural innovation.

In between, he unhesitatingly took all the oaths asked of him in the 1790s (which may explain why Msgr. Claude Dagens, auxiliary bishop of Poitiers and a brilliant historian on his own, would not commit himself to participating when Jean-Marc Roger initially contacted him). Decried as "impious and without faith" by his refractory brethren, he nevertheless managed to revert to royalism toward the end of his life, composing a panegyric entitled "Eulogy to Louis XVI" and receiving a decoration during the Restoration for fidelity to the Bourbons!

The town council knew that Saint-Gaudent would attract a certain amount of attention during the bicentennial, but it is doubtful that even M. Vaillé, the enthusiastic town father who had pressed the case for Norbert Pressac most vigorously, dared to imagine that the eyes of all France would turn to his commune. In order to provide a fitting cadre for the replanting of the famous tree, the council voted a number of improvements, with the hope of obtaining financial support from the department, the region, and perhaps the central government. Pressac's gravesite was to be refurbished, and a monument marking it erected. Another stela would designate the spot where the original tree stood until it was uprooted by a squall in 1961. The portal of the fifteenth-century Gothic church, in front of which Pressac planted his oak, would be installed on the side of the new, neo-Gothic church.

The council planned to publish a brochure evoking Pressac's story and to commission a historical reconstitution of the original planting ceremony, as well as to sponsor a reading of the Declaration of Rights by a cast of professional actors surrounded by townsfolk attired in period costume. It finalized its plans for a "grandiose" day during a meeting in early January attended by the local subprefect, a representative of the Direction régionale des affaires culturelles, and Jean-Marc Roger. Not long afterward, probably at Roger's behest, the mayor wrote to Jean-neney outlining the Saint-Gaudent project and soliciting both a label and unspecified "aid."

Not long afterward, on 24 January, Christian de Montrichard telephoned Roger to inform him that there was some chance that President Mitterrand would attend the Saint-Gaudent event to signal his interest in the "roots" idea and in the unfolding bicentennial program. To guide the decision makers, Roger hastily drew up a report on Saint-Gaudent and its project, which he dispatched to Montrichard and to Christian Dupavillon, whose surveillance thickened whenever the president was implicated. Subsequent research happily enabled him to correct the assumption of the Saint-Gaudent leaders that Pressac planted the tree on 13 May. The true date was 10 May, which also happened to be the anniversary of Mitterrand's first election to the presidency, a mythopoeic moment in the Socialo-Revolutionary consciousness, a day that sat well with the image of the liberty tree. So excited was Roger with this news that he called Montrichard at midnight to convey it. He also noted a possible genealogical linkage between Mitterrand and the seigneur of Saint-Gaudent at the time of the Revolution, Pierre Charles Gabriel Dexmier du Roc, through his cousin Dexmier d'Olbreuse. Whether or not Roger's diligence clinched the presidential visit, it was officially confirmed several weeks later.

Cultivating the commemorative spirit: in the Poitevin village where Father Norbert Pressac allegedly planted the Revolution's first liberty tree two hundred years before, President Mitterrand, Minister of Culture Jack Lang, and other dignitaries recalled this event by placing a sapling in the ground. (Photo courtesy of the Service Photographique of the Présidence de la République Française.)

Formal confirmation of the presidential visit thrust the commune into a state of intense excitement. Aided by the technical services of the nearby town of Civray, Saint-Gaudent undertook a "vast and impressive sprucing-up." While the authorities tended to the public spaces and monuments, the citizens washed (some even painted) their facades and set flowers wherever they could. The children in the single class of the communal school redoubled their efforts to learn their role in the reconstitution and complete their historical panel, which would be placed along with the documents Roger lent from the departmental archives in the exposition on the Revolution, human rights, and Pressac's tree set up in the Foyer rural. Observed the *Centre Presse:* "It's effervescence, not to say euphoria."

Save for the short address that the president would pronounce, the program remained unchanged. On 21 March, President Mitterrand swept in and out rapidly. Among those in attendance was the bishop of Poitiers, Msgr. Joseph Rozier. The president put a shovel to the ground where the robust American oak would take root, and he glossed the historical and contemporary significance of the liberty-tree-planting rite. Jean-Marie Augustin observed acidly that the multitude of national and regional notables who flocked to Saint-Gaudent to attend the president rather than to honor Pressac's tree fled as soon as Mitterrand left, disdaining the cocktail party and the country-style dinner that the citizens had so meticulously prepared. Perhaps the local folk took some consolation in the news transmitted by Roger, through Mitterrand's niece, that the president had enjoyed his fleeting embrace of Saint-Gaudent more than any other bicentennial moment.[16]

Counterrevolutionary Spasms

The tree symbol appeared to galvanize the relatively small dose of counter-revolutionary energy that erupted during the bicentennial. The now even more sacred than before tree at Saint-Gaudent, doubly tainted by a veritable priest and a political *Dieu,* was cut down not long after it was planted. Somehow the story was kept quiet, and a new tree rapidly and discreetly took its place. Apparently there was some discursive evidence linking the vandalism to the higher motives of the Counterrevolution. Poitiers experienced the same aggression. Leaving royalist propaganda, one night in late April mutilators uprooted the liberty tree in Blossac Park and broke the plaque dedicating it. The *Centre Presse* insisted on "the gravity of such an act," one tantamount to "a blow against the foundations of our democracy."[17]

No one was really surprised to witness counterrevolutionary sentiment surfacing in Poitiers. Republican during the Revolution, with a strong hostile undercurrent, Poitiers became fertile ground for counterrevolutionary politics, often linked with a militant piety, in the nineteenth century. The vestigial Poitevin nobility, for example, expiated for the Commune through the cult of the sacred heart. Through much of the twentieth century the city was in markedly conservative hands. Given the fund of counterrevolutionary fervor that still existed, it is surprising not that it manifested itself occasionally but that it did not intrude more frequently and vociferously. A rightist-*intégriste* group ran a cycle of lectures that were more or less confidential. Advertising a Poitiers postal box number, in reaction to the "excesses of Revolutionary proselytism," a "group of the friends of historical truth" announced in April 1989 the formation of the Comité Vérité 89. Among its leaders were François Legriel, the retired president of the Chambre syndicale de la métallurgie, who was passionately interested in history and in politics, and one of the descendants of the marquis de Roux, the eminent conservative historian of the Revolution in the Vienne. "By the distribution of tracts, the organization of colloquia, visits to the monuments of Vendée martyrdom, and, in the immediate, the publication of articles," this truth squad "plan[ned] to react against historical ravings." Either the committee died rapidly of inanition, or it operated with counterproductive discretion, for it generated no further attention in the public sphere.[18]

One of the very few overt counterrevolutionary manifestations during the bicentennial season memorialized the guillotining of thirty Poitevins in 1793, including priests, a noble, peasants, and lackeys. Organized by François Legriel and his friends, it was a solemn and simple ceremony that took place on the place de la Liberté. Between one hundred and 150 persons, according to the organizers (fewer than fifty, if one prefers the count of unengaged observers), listened to a reading of the names of the "martyrs" and then intoned songs from the Vendéen wars. Himself descended from participants on both blue and white sides, Legriel felt a deep sense of horror for the bloodthirstiness of the Revolutionaries and a profound resentment for the ruination that the Revolution wreaked on France. He described his group as emanating largely from the "old families of Poitou" who loved history and detested the legacy of the Revolution. The "noise" of the bicentennial shocked them and energized them to take collective action to express their "disgust." Legriel himself supported Le Pen, and suggested that the bulk of his (anti)commemorative circle sympathized with the Front National. Legriel shared an *intégriste* antipathy for the post–Vatican II church, whose local representatives refused to associate themselves with his demonstration. In his view the bishop and the bulk of the church had embraced the evil doctrines of the Revolution.[19]

To Be Continued

On the whole, the Revolution fared surprisingly well in "the city of all ages," of Hilary and Radegonde, of magnificent Romanesque churches and aristocratic private mansions. It was similarly well received in much of the Vienne and the two Charentes; the Deux-Sèvres, in the penumbra of the Vendée, manifested more reserve. A prefect apprised Louis Fruchard, to his delight, that the bicentennial was "a flop, the people did not respond." But this idea of failure was wishful thinking. Given his integrity and lucidity, it is unlikely that Jean-Marc Roger, Fruchard's friend and defender, would have framed his appreciation merely to please the Parisian hierarchy and flatter his own standing. He characterized the bicentennial as an unequivocal "success," capturing "a very widespread popular support" and eliciting "an extraordinary profusion of ideas, initiatives, good will . . . in the most varied milieux." From a very different ideological vantage point, Jean-Marie Augustin concurred: "it was very successful at the local level." If Augustin and Fruchard have their way, they will confront one another again on the commemorative battleground, the professor to hail the republic, the physician to honor its victims.[20]

The Bicentennial from Below
In the Communist Penumbra

Historiographically, ideologically, and strategically, the Communist bicentennial had to be both popular and populist. This was the space where mythology and electoral sociology commingled, the space that Communists believed was rightfully theirs, a *chasse gardée* that poachers from left and right transgressed with impunity. The party's patrimonial claims to control this social and moral space increased almost directly in proportion to its real loss of influence therein. Given its shrinking institutional hold in the public sphere, symbolically and practically the popular/populist card was the only one that the PCF had to play in the bicentennial. It still packed a powerful emotional charge. The problem was to convert this energy to political advantage rather than merely to folkloric gratification.

Objectively bourgeois (primarily), the Revolution was subjectively popular (primarily): this was the Communist credo in its bicentennial inflection. In a word, just as the Revolution was properly the People's, so should be the commemoration. Just as the bourgeoisie wrenched the Revolution from popular hands, so the state and its class allies sought to exclude "the people-actor," in the words of *L'Humanité*, from the anniversary celebration. In honor of the originary Bastille that the people took in 1789, the Communists would lead them in their assault on the bicentennial Bastille erected to keep them out. In a double sense, then, the commemoration was a reminder that "the struggle is permanent" and that nothing of fundamental importance can be achieved without "the intervention of the popular masses," "these demands that surge from the grass roots."

The Revolution remained the allegorical guide for the present and future; that is why the defense of the Jacobino–Marxist exegesis was not merely a matter of academic vanity. "It was the little people of the cities and the countryside, people like all of us, . . . who decided, together, to construct their own future on their own terms, and toward this end to change the society," wrote historian and Communist militant Roger Bourderon. "All the great conquests—let us insist: all of them—are associated with the development of the popular movement [*mouvement populaire*]." It was imperative, then, at the bicentennial moment, to remind the People of their strength and their vocation, to reappropriate the commemoration in order to make this case graphically and passionately, and to prepare them to take the many Bastilles that remained, none of which was "untakable, provided that men join hands to pull them down."

Concretely, this required a double campaign from above and from below. First, to fight tirelessly in the media for the recognition of the central and decisive (and positive rather than deleterious) role played by the People in the Revolution. Second, to reach the people themselves at the grass roots: to educate them and, ideally, to involve them actively in the celebration of their own heroism. While it was easy to wax lyrical about the intense social demand for R/revolutionary commemoration that, normatively, *had* to be there, waiting to burst forth like a latent geyser, it was far more difficult to locate it precisely and tap its power. Lucid Communists oscillated between the enthusiasm of the self-fulfilling prophecy and the realization that their potential clientele, especially its critically significant youthful component, was as inclined to civic indifference and the "individualist retreat" as the rest of the population.[1]

To mobilize the people, the party counted first on its elected officials, who were in regular contact with their constituents; then on the party apparatus, including its media, its research groups, and its federal structure, and on the ability of the militants to forge links with the population at large; and finally on new organizations especially created to manage commemorative affairs. Speaking for the central committee, Gaston Plissonnier urged mayors of Communist municipalities to devise programs likely to appeal to all sectors of their communities. He exhorted leaders at the federation levels to form collectives to plan activities in the vast majority of places where the Communists exercised marginal political authority. Roger Lejeune, secretary of the federation of the Seine-Maritime, responded by convoking meetings to "make an inventory of the diverse events projected for the bicentennial, in particular in the city halls run by Communists." Mayors of Communist cities such as Montreuil instructed their deputies for cultural affairs to aim at attracting "a maximum of citizens" to bicentennial events.[2]

The Association nationale des élus communistes et républicains organized training meetings for local officials on the theme "local government and the commemoration of the bicentennial." The Centre d'information et d'étude de formation des élus published lectures given by Michel Vovelle and Claude Mazauric at one such session. Both historians emphasized the enormous stakes of the commemoration yet at the same time admonished against the temptation to withdraw into a narrow, defensive position. Though they faced "an intense ideological battle," Vovelle counseled them to embrace the Revolution "in its diversity, without presenting an idealized image, because the balance sheet is sufficiently positive that we have nothing of which to be ashamed." Given the cumulative density of the crisis in which France was mired, and the salvo of elections at various levels that marked the prebicentennial calendar, Mazauric foresaw an "intense political confrontation, the most tense probably since the Liberation." The bicentennial was the occasion to show that "a popular solution" was no less the way out of today's crisis than it had been for the crisis of the Old Regime. To fortify our argument, however, Mazauric insisted, we need to gather "all the vital forces of the commune, the department, and the canton"—not just Communists but "all the people of progress." In taking initiatives to organize bicentennial associations, the Communists had to strike the right balance: "it is necessary to be watchful regarding their composition and especially their sense of the pluralism of sensibilities and their sense of measure; they must not be committees of agitators, preaching a unilateral discourse on the French Revolution that would upset a segment of opinion; nor must they fail to portray the Revolution in its popular and transformative dimension." Mazauric went on to suggest specific sorts of activities that could be undertaken at the local level: historical research on the roots of the community, film festivals, lecture-debates, contests geared for students, concerts, and plays. Vovelle and Mazauric each served as advisers to entrepreneurial groups that proposed "packages" for local celebrations, including historical exhibitions and a kit for music, dance, dramatic presentations, and costumes.[3]

Vive 89: The National Organization

No organization, with the possible exception of the CLEF, coordinated a more active and effective bicentennial network than Vive 89. It operated wholly outside the orbit of the Mission. Jeanneney complained that, with one exception, the association did not bother to stay in touch with his team. In his final report, he wrongly dismissed it for having enjoyed limited efficacy in the field. Vive 89 served as a fount of inspiration and resources, and as a clearinghouse, for scores of highly decentralized and self-propelling operations at the local and regional levels. Originally christened with the cumbersome title "Association of the Friends of the French Revolution for the Celebration of the Bicentennial," it was created in 1987 by the PCF, though Claude Mazauric, its indefatigable president, insisted, quite legitimately, that "Vive 89 transcended the Communist reference" in many of its local undertakings. Still, there is no contesting Georges Marchais's statement that "we founded an association, Vive 89, whose mission is to assist in the celebration [of the bicentennial]." The secretary of the central committee, Gaston Plissonnier, dispatched instructions to the party federations to establish branches. Mazauric himself assessed the map of implantation in terms of the strengths and weaknesses of the various *fédés,* or department-level units. Where the "comrades" were enterprising, Vive 89 got off the ground, even in such areas as the Ille-et-Vilaine, where "we are in charge of no municipalities." While a handful of committees took a self-consciously ecumenical public posture, others, such as the deliciously dubbed Mille Sète Cent Quatre-Vingt-Neuf of the Mediterranean city of Sète, merely scavenged Guy Hermier's bicentennial manifesto in order to describe its objectives.[4]

Incorporated according to the law of 1901 on nonprofit organizations, Vive 89 had a Paris address, which it shared with other party business, an accountant, Marcel Maréchal, assigned by the party to keep the books, and access to the considerable logistical infrastructure of the party and the Communist-dominated labor union, the CGT. Its most precious asset was Claude Mazauric, a battle-scarred veteran of the historiographical wars of the Soboul period, a ferocious debater, a passionate believer in the R/revolutionary vision, and an increasingly skeptical party militant (who did not let his political disaffection undermine his bicentennial engagement). Mazauric accepted the assignment after Michel Vovelle refused it because he felt that it might prove to be incompatible with his official commemorative assignment. That the PCF obstinately recruited a historian and a professor suggests the sort of inflection that it wanted to give the undertaking. Unlike many commemorators, who wanted the future to eclipse the past on the bicentennial horizon, the Communists intended to root themselves firmly in history, and emphasize the logic that bound past, present, and future. They had an enormous stake in both the historical legacy and the historiographical tradition of the Revolution—a stake that they were determined to exploit and protect.

Mazauric felt that the PCF was particularly well placed to benefit from the neglect with which he charged the ministry in terms of its flaccid bicentennial planning. Given their tradition of grassroots militancy and their institutional strengths, the Communists rushed to fill the vacuum left by an indifferent, slow-starting, or abjuring government. With Soboul and Vovelle as early as 1979, re-counted Mazauric, in concertation with the mayor of Vizille, site of one of the pre-Revolution's most significant political gatherings, he helped to launch the project for a museum of the Revolution to mark the bicentennial. "Those who were in the field and who had a coherent idea about the French Revolution," he continued, "were able to play a much larger role than would have been left them had the state taken charge of everything." Insufficiently Jacobin, the state did not co-opt or restrain the Jacobins: "we were not conscripted by the prefects, for instance, or by the rectors, the general inspectors, the police commissioners, and so on." The professor from Rouen had been utterly free to say and do what he wished, whether on the occasion of an invitation abroad organized by the Ministry of Foreign Affairs or with regard to the formulation of PAEs at home, to which he gave a spin that the government would not have solicited. In launching Vive 89, Mazauric was determined to turn the "state's inadequacy" once again to his advantage: "may the best [team] win, and we are among the best in the field."[5]

From the outset, Mazauric set up a tension between a demanding ideological line on the one hand and a desire to open and reach out on the other. For him the bicentennial crystallized a stark choice that could not be evaded, though he chose to phrase it in an ambiguous and highly charged way likely to generate anxieties for those not socialized into the Jacobino–Marxist ethos: "bury the Revolution or make it live again." The Revolution produced cleavages that persist, indeed that have deepened, contrary to Furet's contentions and Mitterrand's wishes. Given the nature of the Revolution and its legacy, "it cannot therefore be celebrated through a consensus." The consensus marketed by today's social controllers was a trap geared to confine the women and men of France in "these so-called rules of the game, which are unbearable to the oppressed and the exploited." Their recourse was the memory of *their* Revolution, the vision of people like themselves—"the people victorious"—rising up to affirm their right to real equality and social justice. Mazauric stressed the Revolution as the source of hope and the model for action, both of which were necessary and germane in today's society, "all of whose structures are in crisis." The Revolution pointed the way out through the voluntarism that Furet had warned led inexorably to tyranny: "the will and the capacity of a great people to take its destiny in hand." Mazauric wanted Vive 89 to convey this message, and to use it to protect the popular memory and the history that informed it "in order to salvage the people's chances for the future."6

If "struggle" and "relevance today" were the leitmotifs of Mazauric's manifesto for Vive 89, so was the appeal to all "progressive forces" to join regardless of political engagement. He conceived of the national association as nothing more than "a coordinating tourist agency." It attracted only a limited number of "direct subscribers, a few thousand drawn from employee-elected councils (*comités d'entreprise*), elected officials, labor unions, Communist cells." (The national organization placed advertisements in the bulletins of the myriad local Vive 89 branches proposing direct membership for one hundred francs.) A substantial part of its clientele consisted of people it reached indirectly, through committees bearing various names, "keeping their autonomy and deciding on their own action." With results that are very difficult to measure, Vive 89 sought to recruit "people of very different horizons, Communists, non-Communists, union members, priests, local historians, other figures."7

Fête, Truths, and Videotape

A training video, devised to teach local organizers how to present—"package" is the less squeamish word—the Revolution, betrayed the same tensions betwen openness and closedness, between sectarian militancy and generic fervor. Despite certain technical flaws, the charms of residual amateurism, the cassette was cleverly and effectively fashioned. Using a wide array of cinematographic, documentary, and interview footage, it inventoried the major R/revolutionary themes, suggested modalities for conveying them, proposed strategies for mobilization, and pointed emphatically to connections between the Revolutionary legacy and the persistence of injustice everywhere. The trick was not merely to inform would-be mediators but also to motivate them to urgent and passionate action in a spirit that blended sermon and song.

The video began logically with an evocation of the *cahiers de doléances:* the bicentennial was the time for French women and men to voice their grievances. Michel Vovelle, captured outside the classroom at the annual festival of the PCF, stressed the need to reach the (ordinary and true) people with a complex yet timeless R/revolutionary message in order to help them "reappropirate their Revolution." There followed an interview with a peasant, an endangered species on the European horizon of the 1990s that still commanded disproportionate political clout and continued to symbolize one of the two archetypal faces of the world-historical people. Against a background that shifted from a modern dairy farm to Old Regime tableaux, the peasant explained how he still felt exploited in the manner of his eighteenth-century forebears, who included both *chouans* and re-publicans. Though he was grateful for the rights the Revolution accorded him as a legal and economic agent to operate his farm, he resented the capitalist irrationality that left a world hungry even as it restricted agricultural production.

The camera panned across the panels of the exposition created by Vive 89, its main "product," whose origin and character we shall discuss shortly. As he toured it, a leading Communist intellectual, the mathematician J.-P. Kahane, declaimed the standard Communist view of the bourgeois Revolution opening the way for the efflorescence of capitalism, implicitly linking the "global crisis" of the late 1780s with the "global crisis" of the late 1980s. This sectarian moment gave way to a more universal note with a discussion of the Declaration of Rights. Without reproaching the Declaration for privileging formal rights as opposed to real ones, as Communists had often done, Vovelle and Mazauric suggested much more subtly that the nature of the R/revolutionary dynamic was permanently to beget new rights. Like the Revolution, the Declaration was still alive, "making demands on us in our current struggles."

The appearance of Georges Séguy in splendid hunting regalia, as if he had just stepped out of a National Rifle Association/Neiman Marcus promotional catalogue, augured the return of the pendulum to the party line. The former head of the CGT and Communist leader reminded viewers that the monopoly exercised by the nobility would have prevented him from hunting, even to satisfy his family's hunger, under the Old Regime. The people obtained the right of hunting along with their fundamental human rights as a result of "social pressure." That was the core of his message, as relevant today as it was in 1789: "nothing in society can advance without a powerful social movement." Séguy's reflections were interspersed with the angry and poignant complaints of workers in troubled industries, such as the coal miners of the CGT.

The next segment dealt again with class, contrasting the social immolation of the post-Revolutionary proletariat with the deficit of social rights briefly glimpsed in 1793. But it also addressed race and gender: the incomplete efforts to free women and blacks from their status of stigmatization and subordination. The grand "anticipations" of '93—laws guaranteeing social justice—have yet to be fully realized. Séguy's refrain applied more than ever: "we must continue the struggle." Rendering homage to the "immense action" of the peasantry and the sansculottes, Antoine Casanova bestowed the historian's unction on Séguy's visceral rendition of the argument.

Utilizing a scene from Renoir's *Marseillaise,* the video next turned to the vexed question of war. The Communists hated war and somehow wished to believe that war and Revolution were not merely separable but in some sense antagonistic. They were also fervent patriots, however, and believed deeply in the notion and the destiny of the nation. The portrayal of Europe as hostile to the Revolution from the beginning tempered the guilt of the self-seeking Girondins and incidentally bore the trace of the PCF's deep mistrust of the impending reinvention of Europe in 1993. The exemplar of Vive 89, Mazauric's personal hero, was Robespierre, who was a great patriot because he knew when to oppose war and when to prosecute it pitilessly. Without agonizing over a transition, the video switched easily from conflict to comity, highlighting the universal resonance of the Revolution by interviewing German students, a Hungarian intellectual, an Irish Communist, a Cuban working woman, and so on. They all testified to the centrality of the Revolutionary trinity to their lives; curiously, several associated the Revolution with the (ultimate?) onset of peace in the world.

If the Revolution carried universal significance, that meant that France still had "things to say to the world," as Yves Mourousi put it. A capitalist communicator par excellence, in his own way no less a populist than Georges Séguy, Mourousi proved that the Communists were not the only group in the country that believed this. He urged his fellow citizens to remember that the eyes of the world would fix on France during the bicentennial and that it was not the moment to succumb to subaltern quarrels, whether over history or politics—advice that was not easy to reconcile with the ideological thrust of Vive 89, which was not likely to agree on the application of the word "subaltern" to matters it deemed crucial.

The film ended on themes that Mourousi would have found gratuitously provocative. Mazauric denounced the black legend that blemished the image of Robespierre. Despite his passionate rehabilitation of the Incorruptible as a great democrat, discerning, restrained, and committed to humanistic values, it is doubtful that Robespierre was the right icon for rallying national enthusiasm. But Mazauric was no more interested in consensus than the central committee. He wanted to reach out to nonbelievers, but not without conditions. Nor was Casanova's attack on capitalist exploitation designed to lure the profane. "We revolutionaries today," the historian contended, must press our struggle in emulation of our R/revolutionary forebears. Vive 89 hinted that "a better world," freer and more equitable, allowing autonomy to individuals, could not be obtained outside the R/revolutionary path. Despite its occasional sanctimoniousness and certain recurrent ideological rigidities, the video was rife with practical ideas that an imaginative would-be local commemorator not of the Communist persuasion could put to good use.

The Revolution in Exposition

Vive 89 offered a medley of concrete products that would help launch a bicentennial campaign. Adroitly used, these consumer goods could be transformed into producer goods, thus permitting citizen-users to move from a passive to an active relation to the object of commemoration. They included tapes of Revolutionary songs, reproductions of the Declaration of the Rights of Man, multiposter sets devoted to such themes as the liberty tree, as well as board games and playing cards. Nor did the association scorn the more vulgar souvenir items such as T-shirts, sweatshirts, handkerchieves, and key chains, commodities identified with the "merchants of the temple" vehemently denounced by many purists, often members of the PCF.

The most significant product, however, was wholesomely pedagogical in nature, and sufficiently dense and coherent to constitute by itself the central instrument for a local committee's mobilizing strategy. It was an entire exhibition on the Revolution, fully wrought, comprising seventeen large color panels (60 by 80 cm) available either on high-quality poster paper (Fr 2,100) or under a thick plastic protection that would guarantee their longevity (Fr 3,500). It could also be rented for Fr 350 a week, a price that made it accessible to organizations of all sizes. Despite its strikingly Jacobin tonality, the exposition and the *Petit Guide d'une grande Révolution* that accompanied it, obtained the label of the Mission.[8]

An atelier of graphic artists, Grapus, headed by a German designer who was also a Communist, proposed the idea of an exposition. In collaboration with those artists, in particular with a Swiss designer who avowed an utter ignorance of the Revolution, Claude Mazauric devised the exposition, selecting the rich, sometimes swarming iconography and composing the texts with the help of his daughter. Each of the tableaux corresponded to a moment in the Revolution, designated by a title, symbolized by a principal illustration and a series of ancillary images, along with texts drawn from contemporary discourse or venturing historical narration and/or analysis. The introductory panel, a striking sea of coagulating red, which might have represented a thick and sensual curtain rising on the drama, announced the colors of Vive 89. Framing the aims of the exhibition, it emphasized the "contemporary relevance of the message of emancipation" of the Revolution but promised not to obfuscate its shortcomings. It construed the Revolution not as the beginning of time, in emulation of the perfervid actors themselves, but as a critical moment in the nation's development. At the outset it insisted not on the Revolution's bourgeois cast but on its profoundly democratic and popular dimension. Finally, Mazauric imprinted the exhibition with one of his major bicentennial concerns: the defense of the memory of the "calumnied" patriots who incarnated the democratic and/or popular spheres: Robespierre, Saint-Just, Marat, and Babeuf.[9]

Colorful, busy, and, like the bulk of the panels, offering multiple points of entry, the second panel, "Misery or Prosperity," reconciled the divergent emphases of Michelet and Jaurès in a tacit encomium to Ernest Labrousse. The central images portray the tension that informs the panel: a vignette of the monarch distributing alms to the despairing poor and a lush portrait of the thriving port of Marseille by Vernet. In a way that might be construed as gratuitously tendentious, the authors characterize the eighteenth century as "a period of economic growth and enrichment of the bourgeoisie," as if it did not simultaneously enrich a large segment of the nobility and the peasant elite. Inset images and text recall the taint of slavery on the commercial affluence of the Atlantic ports; the relative stagnation of agricultural technology; the curves of the two major economic indicators, wheat prices and textile production; the demographic and social structures; all the events relevant to the major theme in a time line that snaked across the century; and the lurching toward crisis after 1776.

On a stunning green background under the invocations of Figaro's jeremiad against the arrogance of so-called noble birthright, the third panel, "Privileges and Injustice," presents the classical view of the clergy and the nobility trampling the Third Estate embodied by the peasantry. A Rigaudlike portrait of the king weighing on top of the peasant suggests the alliance between aristocracy and crown, a sort of feudal front that again evokes familiar Marxist landmarks. Though the evidence suggests that the nobility continued to replenish its ranks from the Third Estate, the panel defines it as evolving toward hereditary cast status. "A lucid bourgeoisie," poised for opportunity, is implicitly associated with the Enlightenment, defined as essentially concerned with the philosophy of natural rights/natural law, and represented by inserts depicting Montesquieu, Diderot, Voltaire, and Rousseau. The time line ranges from the introduction of the potato to the century's major military reforms to the amelioration of the condition of Protestants.

Devoted to the political crisis, which it interprets as part of a global crisis, the fourth panel is very readable. The picture of the Day of Tiles, complemented by an insert evoking the allegory of the triumph of Jacques Necker, suggests both the alternatives and the strategies available to the various players as the nation moves closer to the convocation of the Estates General. The fifth tableau features David's *Tennis Court Oath* announcing "the good news of '89" to an eagerly expectant and increasingly politicized (popular) public. On the imposing background of a massive Bastille in dialogue with a smaller image of a municipal rising in the provinces and with an insert on the Great Fear burning over the rural expanses, panel six, "A Whole People in Revolution," shows the convergence of popular amd bourgeois insurgencies. The seventh panel is entirely devoted to the momentous Declaration of the Rights of Man, whose full text beckons the spectator to civic meditation.

Even as the nation is celebrated in an eruption of powerful colors—an unintended parable of the soon to be stifled potential for revolutionary multiculturalism and pluralism?—the contrapuntal concept/practice of class affirms itself. Entitled "Laissez-faire, Laissez-passer," this eighth panel features the Festival of the Federation, whose unifying vocation is sapped by the corrosive application of "economic liberalism" in the form of the Allarde and Le Chapelier Laws abolishing the guild system and prohibiting collective association in the world of work. The swirl of colors mobilizes the crowd and transforms it from spectators into actors by melding it into the festival. A blend of melancholic populism and romanticism infuses the tableau, reflected in the triumph of Harsh Reality (inexorably inscribed in the unfolding of history) over Communitarian Idealism.

War is another harsh reality that dominates the very crowded ninth panel. As France prepares to go to war in scenes on the top and the bottom, in the middle, in an iconographical mode common at least since the Reformation, the bare-bottomed National Assembly—sansculottes of a displaced genre—defecate in artillery trajectories on the monarchs of Europe, including the pope, over whom towers a bare-breasted Catherine of Russia. A cannon aimed up the behind of Louis XVI presages an "emetic violence."

A striping technique superimposed on a neoclassical picture of the taking of the Tuileries on 10 August 1792 serves as an imaginative ersatz for italicization in "The Fall of the Monarchy." The famous image of Louis Capet's severed head surmounts the scene, as the sansculottes and the *fédérés* combine to overthrow him and set the stage for the proclamation of the republic. The next panel, featuring Robespierre in massive profile and Marat in the foreground, is perhaps the centerpiece of the entire exhibition. Embroidering the theme adumbrated in the first tableau and echoed in several others, Mazauric portrays the two heroes as the artisans of the popular and democratic Revolution, the catalysts of the alliance of peasants and sansculottes against all manner of aristocrats, new and old, counterrevolutionaries of one sort or another. Just as the PCF contends that only the intervention of the people can decisively reshape the course of France in today's quasi-permanent crisis, so too do "the Friend of the People and the Incorruptible judge that France and the Revolution can be saved only by the intervention of the people."

The most conventionally pedagogical panel uses a map of revolts, invasions, and other disorders to convey the dire situation of "the republic in a desperate plight" in the spring of 1793. With admirable subtlety, this tableau makes the positivist case for the thesis of circumstances as condition and overriding rationale of the Terror. But the Terror would not be fully comprehensible without the social program— "the time of economic, political, and social anticipations"—highlighted in panel thirteen, "Terror and Virtue." A winged Virtue interposes himself between Justice and the Grim Reaper in a painting glossing the staple theme of liberty or death. But the text suggests that liberty unalloyed and unaccompanied is an insufficient ideal. Citing the stillborn Declaration of Rights of 1793, the panel reminds the visitor that "the goal of society is shared happiness." That happiness meant a cultural revolution driven by a comprehensive system of education for all, a moral revolution marked by the abolition of slavery, and a social revolution augured by the re-distribution of the confiscated property of enemies of the Revolution (émigrés and suspects).

Panel fourteen, "Thermidor: The Tragedy," is probably the most conflicted and least coherent. The top depicts the tragedy in question, Robespierre's execution. It evokes the steps leading to the end: the execution of the Hébertistes and the Dantonists, the promulgation of the laws of the Grand Terror, and the Festival of the Supreme Being. The bottom half of the tableau consists of a robust painting of the victory of Fleurus, whose impact is heightened by the deep red color given to the puffs of gunfire. Fleurus doubtless contributed to the overthrow of Robespierre, but it is difficult to view it as a tragedy from the perspective of the Revolution's survival. Perhaps saved, the Revolution is despairingly "frozen," and it begins to unravel. The "contradictions" between sansculottes and bourgeoisie become more pronounced; sated by the quasi-definitive end of feudalism, the peasantry devolves into conservative torpor. Yet the only evocation of the Thermidorean regime is contained in the censorious observation that "class society supplants the dream of a social order regenerated by Virtue."

Voluntaristic militancy transforms the tragedy of the next panel, "Babeuf's Combat," into millennial hopefulness. The image of a desperately hungry people dominates the tableau. Famished, in torn clothing, downtrodden, they grope for the charity food that is dispensed to them. The dearth is partly the product of the insidious economic liberalism that the Revolution spawned and persistently rebelled against. At the confluence of populism and miserabilism, Babeuf incarnates the Revolution's future, and the people's redemption. The people's presence—that is to say, its absence—is embodied in the next-to-last panel entitled "The Bourgeois Republic." It is a somberly joyful, exquisitely Augustinian moment, captured by Boilly's painting of the arrival of a stagecoach. It projects a solid, confident, well-to-do air. It connotes the stability of the Revolution, heralded by the Thermidorean confirmation of civil equality, freedom of enterprise, and the end of both feudalism and the corporate system. Insets of Toussaint-L'Ouverture and Napoleon seem to suggest two moral poles in the (post)Revolutionary field of expansion, conquest, and consolidation.

The exhibition closes with aesthetic flare in a panel symmetrical to the first tableau. It portrays an extremely engaging and somewhat troubling sky (or heaven?), at once gentle and explosive. The text, swamped in the cascading blue and difficult to discern, is the most stridently Communist of the show. It recounts how the people chose in 1789 between the conservative route of limited reforms and "the path of democratic radicality." Faced with "the crisis," the PCF's shorthand for the congeries of ills associated with capitalism in its current state, how would the French people respond today? "How will they reject the road of decline and national eclipse?" The only compelling answer to the rhetorical question was of course through renewed commitment to the R/revolutionary ideal. Jean Jaurès, the patron saint of the exhibition, emerged from the blue to remind his fellow citizens that the French Revolution was not the definitive revolution, and to remind historians that it was at bottom a bourgeois phenomenon.

The *Guide*, drafted by two Marxist historians under Mazauric's aegis, presented the standard "classical" exegesis in a relatively temperate fashion. (The "list of indispensable works" is massively dominated by the Marxist school: Jaurès, Mathiez, Lefebvre, Soboul, Mazauric, Vovelle, a colloquium sponsored by the Institut de recherches marxistes.) There is no ideological bludgeoning despite the strongly populist tone. There is didactic simplification, necessary to render the booklet accessible and lively. Occasionally the results are needlessly reductive (e.g., "the king and the state in the service of the aristocracy" and the physiocrats stereotyped as "spokesmen of the bourgeoisie and the landed proprietors"). The idea of complexity tends to prevail over a narrowly bourgeois-revolution interpretation, at least until the end when Jaurès is summoned to insist on the class limits of the Revolution and its essential character as a political triumph of the bourgeoisie. Robespierre is rehabilitated (along with Marat), the Terror is ascribed to circumstances, driven by both war and social pressure. The latter endowed the Jacobin republic with its democratic and popular character, creating a regime doped by "anticipations" of social justice in which the first of all rights was the one guaranteeing existence.

Mazauric himself took responsibility for drafting two dense pages on the Declaration of the Rights of Man. The issue was extremely delicate in light of the traditional Communist strictures against its inadequacies on the one hand and the enormous prestige it enjoyed in France and the rest of the world, especially in the late 1980s, on the other. Mazauric navigated a cautious course. Following Lefebvre, he recognized the Declaration as a "war machine" against the Old Regime and an expression of the Enlightenment struggle for natural rights and a humanitarian political logic. Far from dismissing the rights enumerated in the Declaration as purely formal and in some sense tainted by their bourgeois genesis, Mazauric celebrated liberty as the keystone in terms that Chaunu or Villiers (not to mention Furet) could have endorsed: "Among the rights the most important is the one that constitutes the essence of all the others: liberty." Despite its confinement to the juridical terrain, the proclamation of the right of equality had a volcanic impact, spreading "subversion in all the aristocratic societies of Europe." Instead of unleashing "an exacerbated individualism," it set up a permanent tension between the demands of the collectivity and the exigencies of individual autonomy.

The Declaration failed in one domain, according to Mazauric, whose critique echoed the older Communist line but in a context of much more generosity and nuance. To the extent that the Declaration "implies no obligation for the national collectivity to reduce the social disparities or the inequality of economic and cultural perspectives, its promise to establish the equality of conditions remains formal." Thus, "in the first instance," the Declaration favored the efflorescence of bourgeois society. But Mazauric was quick to acknowledge its broader, more diffuse yet decisive ideological impact. It framed the struggles that ventured to extend and deepen its implications; in this sense, it inspired its own revision. An international model, "a part of the Patrimony of Humanity," as the bicentennial season opened it stood as "a formidable reference in the real combat, which is aquiring a universal dimension, against [all forms of] discrimination: racist, sexist, economic, political." It was a thoughtful as well as an adroit text that enabled Mazauric to remain faithful to certain deeply held notions and at the same time to reach beyond his earlier positions in search of himself as well as of non-Communist supporters.

For local organizers and visitors, Vive 89's exhibition had several advantages. It was easy to transport, handle, and repack. It could be used rapidly and repeatedly in different places. It could be adapted to large and small spaces. Visitors could engage it at multiple levels. Composed of striking images, it was accessible on a viscerally aesthetic level to spectators who were very young, impatient, or unmotivated to explore and reflect. Those with more time and interest could excavate more deeply. The cunning of the conception was that it had an Alice-in-Wonderland quality of successive doors through which one could choose to pass (or which one could bypass). The exhibit lent itself very well to group visits under the guidance of a historically knowledgeable teacher. While some of the panels presented an intellectually constrictive perspective on a Revolutionary moment or problem, others offered enough play for diverse interpretation that would not put off "readers" who did not subscribe to the Jacobino-Marxizing view.

By November 1989, Vive 89 had sold 439 exhibits and given away four. At the same time it sold 267 videocassettes and made gifts of fourteen. According to the final report of the association, "not all" were purchased by the party federations, but it is not clear how many filtered beyond the Communist institutional net. Nor can one determine how many times each was used, in how many different places, or for how long. Theoretically, tens of thousands of people could have been marshaled, especially when schoolteachers and administrators organized mass visits. The geography of distribution reveals a thick concentration in the Parisian area: thirty-seven expositions circulated in Paris, thirty-two in the still densely Communist Seine-Saint-Denis, eighteen in the Val-de-Marne, seventeen in the Hauts-de-Seine, ten in the Val-de-Oise, and nine in the Essonne. Without a closer examination from the field one cannot determine the relation between the sale of these potentially powerful tools and local organizational dynamism. For instance, the Meurthe-et-Moselle bought thirteen expositions and nine cassettes, but "the association never held a meeting."[10]

Pastoral Activities

As Mazauric had promised, the national association purveyed a multitude of ideas in its bulletin, in a vast correspondence by letter and especially by phone, through the more or less subterranean vector of the party offices in the departments, and through the much more visible avenue of personal contacts, site visits, and public lectures. Michel Vovelle boasted that he was the international *commis-voyageur* of the bicentennial; in many ways, Mazauric was his domestic counterpart. He received an infinity of invitations, for large and small occasions, and he traveled widely and tirelessly. After one evening in a large urban center in the north, he spent the next day at the fourth annual Foire du livre of Le Breuil in the arrondissement of Autun (Saône-et-Loire) in response to the pressing demand of Claude

Thomas, an official "in charge of youth and culture" and, not incidentally, "the only mayor's deputy representing the PCF."

Thirteen other historians (of some fifty who were solicited) joined the professor from Rouen on the Vive 89 campaign trail. (This number apparently does not include lecturers commissioned on the initiative of departmental and local committees—for example, the association of the Loire-Atlantique, which dispatched Alain Bergerat, Emilienne Leroux, and Louis Oury, among others, to conduct a dozen lecture-debates within its bailiwick; or the association in the Loire, which called upon a regional historian of the working-class movement and an advanced graduate student completing a thesis on Saint-Etienne in the Revolution.) The national association claims they attracted thirty thousand people at three hundred separate lectures.

The grassroots results varied enormously according to the venue, the occasion, and the investment of local organizers. Operating largely in the Paris area, Maurice Genty drew twelve to twenty listeners at ten lectures, and almost one hundred for two others. In thirty appearances, Raymond Huard averaged fifty-six hearers. Working the Savoy and the Dauphiné, Michel Etiévant attracted over seventy-five persons in thirty-three lectures (including over 150 in eleven of these). Jean Michaud voyaged all over France, encountering his nadirs at *comités d'enterprise* of the EDF at Beaune and at Cergy-Pontoise (five in each of the audiences) and his zenith, over a hundred, at Marly. He hailed the role of a "young comrade" at Charlieu (Loire, population 4,500), where he spoke twice to enthusiastic audiences of a hundred, the second time in direct competition with the televised France-Scotland rugby match. This local militant "was not content to hang a poster or distribute a lecture announcement; he personally contacted the bulk of the audience." Only one historian suffered the mortification of finding no one present when she arrived to deliver her talk.

Lectures associated with the projection of films or the performance of plays or with musical soirées or rock operas or tree plantings or evenings of folklore or openings of exhibitions allured a larger turnout than the straightforward lecture-debates. Certain places offered large captive audiences, such as school assemblies or vacation centers. The presence of political leaders amplified the demand, such as when Charles Fiterman and Anicet Le Pors (both ex-ministers and Communist insurgent-reformers joined Mazauric at Vénissieux (Rhône).

The subjects of the lectures varied widely. Some focused on general themes of the Revolution: the *cahiers*, the peasant movement, the sansculottes, the Rights of Man, the three orders, the flight of the king, the battle of Valmy, federalism, censorship in the Revolution, the schools and the Revolution. Others addressed issues of local or regional concern: the Jews and the linguistic question in Alsace, hunger in Lyon, the Revolution in Haute-Normandie, Limoges in revolution, the Convention members in the Marne, Javogues in the Loire, the popular and patriotic societies in this or that locality. Lectures on Robespierre, Marat, Saint-Just, and Babeuf involved a rehabilitative and evangelical dimension. Still others blended

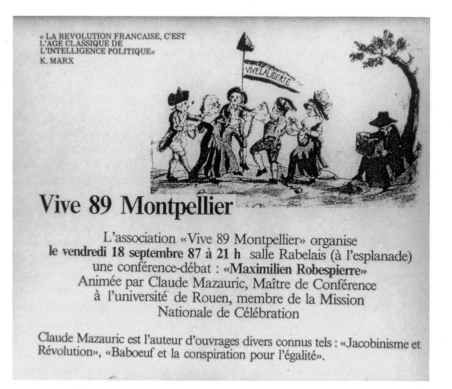

« LA REVOLUTION FRANCAISE, C'EST L'AGE CLASSIQUE DE L'INTELLIGENCE POLITIQUE»
K. MARX

Vive 89 Montpellier

L'association «Vive 89 Montpellier» organise
le vendredi 18 septembre 87 à 21 h salle Rabelais (à l'esplanade)
une conférence-débat : «Maximilien Robespierre»
Animée par Claude Mazauric, Maître de Conférence
à l'université de Rouen, membre de la Mission
Nationale de Célébration

Claude Mazauric est l'auteur d'ouvrages divers connus tels : «Jacobinisme et
Révolution», «Baboeuf et la conspiration pour l'égalité».

Announcement for a public lecture on Robespierre organized by the Montpellier branch of the national bicentennial association called Vive 89, animated by Communists who sought to attract all others committed to the ideals of 1789 and preferably also of 1793. (Photo: Vive 89 Montpellier.)

contemporary and historical issues, such as the bicentennial celebration and its stakes, the PCF and the Revolution, the Revolution and the Resistance.[11]

The partial balance sheet of activities drawn up by the national Vive 89 toward the end of the bicentennial year emphasized the dominant institutional role of the PCF in each branch-by-branch accounting. It was by no means triumphalist. On the contrary, it was a prudent overview that did not neglect widespread areas of weakness. The various Vive 89 organizations launched over a thousand "initiatives," including the utilization of the exhibit (with its unknown multiplier effect), the hosting of a lecture, or the production of a grand bicentennial festival, almost always in tandem with the annual fête of the PCF or the CGT. Many local associations launched their own newsletters, usually dubbed *Bulletin de l'Association Vive 89* of such and such place, or sometimes more exotically or historically christened, as in the case of *L'Ami du peuple* of the Association savoyarde pour la célébration du Bicentenaire de la Révolution—Vive 89–92. Vive 89 was associated with the massive "Invent Happiness" project that elicited *cahiers de doléances* from over twenty thousand children from 160 vacation centers.

The good news concerned "the federations which took this commemoration truly to heart and which fathomed the political aspect." Of these, twelve obtained "excellent results" and over twenty enjoyed "good results." They planned to pursue their activities in 1990 and perhaps through 1992–93, "consistently in this perspective of political and ideological struggle." Given their size, other federations presented "relatively weak results" (e.g., Nord, Aisne, Sarthe) or "very weak results" (e.g., Ain, Gard, Haute-Garonne). Election reverses hampered undertakings. For instance, when the PCF lost the municipality of Amiens during the March 1989 elections, it proved unable to transfer its energizing will from the city to the party institutions, perhaps because they were so intertwined. To the astonishment and the ill-concealed annoyance of Vive 89, certain federations with no compelling excuses managed to take "no initiative" during the whole year. The leaders found some consolation in the multiple successes at the local level of associations without any ties to the PCF and without any preexisting structures on which to build. They evinced a real measure of "revolutionary voluntarism." Though it ended the season with a debt of Fr 120 million that obliged it to declare bankruptcy, the national association, given its extraordinarily thin structure, paucity of means, and limited time, did a more than creditable job of stimulation and coordination.[12]

Vive 89 at the Grass Roots

In the Allier, where the PCF still wielded considerable influence, a small but vigorous Vive 89 took root. Seven persons attended the founding meeting in March 1987 at Moulins and elected as president Jean-Claude Mairal, a teacher and member of the Conseil régional. The three others selected as officers were all historians and professors. The group asked André Lajoinie, an amateur historian, a deputy from the Allier, and the Communist candidate for the presidency of the republic in 1988, to assume an honorary leadership role. Their association espoused a classically Jacobin ideological line with little sign of opening to the (less intrepid) progressive forces outside the Communist sphere of influence whom Mazauric envisaged recruiting. This Vive 89 detested Faurist consensus: elitist, antiseptic, and devoted to the interests of the dominant class, the Mission evicted the people from the celebration ("the People have the right to the Revolution"). Rebuffed in its quest for aid by the Conseil général, the association behaved aggressively toward a potential ally in the field, the CLEF, denounced for ideological timidity if not treason. Isolated, the group achieved only a small portion of the ambitious program it had envisaged, including the publication of a *Bulletin*, a historical anthology treating regional and local themes, and a self-help guide to local commemoration.[13]

The collective of ten persons who created and governed the association at Montpellier consisted of teachers and union militants, most if not all of whom were

Communists. The president and secretary were respectively Raymond Huard, a well-known historian of the nineteenth century serving as professor at the university, and Guy Boisson, a professor of philosophy, who was also a municipal councillor. They were well equipped to conduct a campaign of "popular education" which they viewed as their primary mission. Less strident than their colleagues in the Allier, the Montpellier group remained committed to the same general ideological goals: to celebrate the Revolution as "the decisive intervention of the French people in their own history" and to seek out "the fecund links that can be established between the action of the Revolutionaries and the present struggles of our people." The membership cards of the 130 adherents of Vive 89 bore the aphorism drawn from Marx that "the French Revolution is the classical age of political intelligence."

The association organized activities that blended entertainment and sociability with learning. "A fraternal drink" habitually followed a historical debate—on the role of women in the Revolution, on Condorcet's contribution, and on other Revolutionary issues and figures. It (co)sponsored several theatrical representations, including *Le Vigan fait la Révolution,* which drew eight hundred spectators in two performances. Vive 89 recounted the Revolution to hundreds of children through songs and skits. Almost five hundred persons attended a projection of Ariane Mnouchkine's film, which was followed by a debate. Huard led another discussion after the showing of *La Nuit de Varennes.* Claude Mazauric hailed the virtues of Robespierre before 125 listeners. Vive 89 also spread the bicentennial word to diverse *comités d'entreprise,* to the Caisse d'allocation familiale, to the Electricité de France, and to the annual festival of the PCF.[14]

Locally run and financed and "totally autonomous," Vive 89 Montpellier nevertheless suffered on occasion from the "advanced coloration of the movement," as Huard phrased it elliptically. In fact, according to Guy Boisson, "Vive 89 was at the outset the expression of the thinking of the PCF about the bicentennial. (E. Macia, the federal secretary, expressly asked me to organize the association at Montpellier at the end of 1987.)" The party wanted Vive 89 to diffuse "a few convictions deeply anchored among us," including the decisive role of popular intervention, the importance of '93 and its social contents, and the connection between the memory of the Revolution and today's revolutionary exigencies ("For French Communists," remarked Boisson, "'93 has become a better reference than 1917!"). Then a member of the Comité fédéral, Boisson presented the report to the party on the formation of the bicentennial association. Huard esteemed that the identification with the PCF was not particularly bothersome, save in terms of the systematic animosity of the major daily paper, *Le Midi libre.*

Boisson was more sensitive to "resistances associated with the situation of the party." The "bad image of the Communists" dissuaded potential partners from joining the initiatives that seemed to emanate from a party-dominated organization. "When we said 'democracy,' 'change of society,' etc.," Boisson related, "we heard in response 'utopia,' 'terror,' etc." Moreover, in Languedoc, Jacobinism did not have a

good reputation among those persons, infused with an occitan regional consciousness, who could have found common ground with Vive 89 on other aspects of the
Revolution. Ironically, the relations between Vive 89 and the PCF, in the local
arena, gradually deteriorated during the bicentennial campaign.[15]

The driving force of Vive 89 in the Lot-et-Garonne was local historian Hubert
Delpont, who situated himself "in the wake of the great historical school of the
Revolution (Michelet, Jaurès, Mathiez, Soboul)." He tried to imbue his press
releases and fliers with a tone that was at once progressive and pluralistic. Yet he
had no more use for Faure's mutilating line than his comrades in the Allier. In the
spirit of the PCF, Vive 89 refused to divorce past and present, history and politics.
In the interest of the masses today, Vive 89 pledged to defend the R/revolutionary
ideals not just of '89 but also of '93 and of Babouvisme. It would promote the most
wonderful and timeless lesson of the Revolution: "the possibility of changing the
world when it becomes too oppressive."

Vive 89 aroused some resentment around Agen, ostensibly for its alleged pretension to celebrate without any particular mandate, but probably also for its pugnacious ideological line. "There are some in the department who were taken aback
by this somewhat parallel enterprise," commented a local paper on 27 February
1988, "since a departmental committee was created precisely for the purpose of
bringing together all those who were interested in this question [of commemora-
tion]." Hubert Delpont replied mordantly in a letter to the editor that he was
"amazed at their amazement." Vive 89, he reassured them, drew its inspiration
from the article of the Declaration of the Rights of Man that authorized anyone,
under the title of liberty, to undertake anything that did not harm anyone else.
"Those who fear that Vive 89 will cast a shadow over the departmental committee
flatter us inordinately," he allowed, "and betray a deplorable tendency to consider
the event as their exclusive property, a quasi monopoly, which brings to mind the
time before the Revolution." He concluded modestly that Vive 89 sought only to
make a contribution to the bicentennial effort.

The association made a substantial contribution on the commemorative stage. It
exposed the Vive 89 exhibit in the hall of the CGT at Agen and in twenty other
places, mostly schools. It drew substantial crowds to showings of *1788* and *La
Marseillaise*. Delpont gave over twenty lectures to audiences varying in magnitude
from thirty to two hundred in various towns, villages, associations, schools, and
comités d'entreprise. Finally, Vive 89 helped to put on the festivals of the local PCF
and the CGT. Delpont took particular pride in advancing the cause of local historical self-consciousness. It was this evocation of the ancestors rather than the appeal
to progressive values that permitted Vive 89 to penetrate to the local level. "We
were the only ones to take [the memory of the Revolution] so close to the people,"
boasted Delpont.[16]

The association in Haute-Alsace projected at least two images. The first was
moderate and ecumenical; it was reflected in the introduction of Vive 89 by the
newspaper *L'Alsace* as an organization seeking to unite "those who are concerned

Conducting their own archival research, sewing their costumes, and orchestrating their two-day event, hundreds of citizen-actors from sixteen communes in the upper Maconnais reenacted the uprisings and castle-burnings of the Great Fear of the summer of 1789. (Photo courtesy Vive 89.)

with the notions of liberty, democracy, amd humanism." The second image, conveyed in the prose of André Leroy, a retired teacher and secretary of the association, was far more strident and denominational. Like militant colleagues elsewhere in the Vive 89 network, he insisted on the intimate linkage between past and present/future. Leroy juxtaposed the economic and social injustice of the oppressive Old

Regime, which issued in a popular revolution affirming dignity and liberty, to the capitalist oppression of 1989. The bicentennial injustices were Madame Bettencourt's obscenely bloated fortune, the scandalously huge profits of many companies, the proliferation of unemployment, and the deepening of the new poverty. Implicitly Leroy suggested that "the intervention of the people" was again required, for "our liberty is never to accept injustice."[17]

Vive 89 in Haute-Alsace boasted that its activists and adherents came from "all the points of the vast democratic horizon." Clearly, they shared both a deep regional pride and a keen interest in exploring the eighteenth-century origins of "the attachment of the Alsatian people to social justice" and the trajectory that led the people of Alsace to enter into the "marriage of love" that united them with the people of France. The regional theme shaped most of the association's initiatives. To the seventeen panels of the Mazauric exposition, which toured the region during the bicentennial year, they added twenty-six "local" panels. Vive 89 presented lectures in schools, cultural centers, and *comités d'entreprise*, and it prepared programs for two local radio stations. With sponsorship from the very mainstream Caisses d'Épargne Écureuil du Haut-Rhin, the association published two splendid anthologies of regional history.[18]

In part because they encountered aggressive counterrevolutionary currents on the ground, activists in Brittany were highly motivated to forge a sustained and coherent alternative. The Vive 89 of Saint-Brieuc, built around a nucleus of Communist militants, framed their objectives partly in negative terms. It resolved "to oppose any attempt to defame the Revolutionary period."[19]

Fired by similar passions, the Breton compatriots (and largely comrades) at Rennes conducted a vociferous campaign under the Vive 89 banner. They founded their own organ, *Vive 89 en Ille-et-Vilaine*, a substantial quarterly that contained up to thirty pages of bicentennial news, rich historical documentation, and ideological exhortation. Though the bulletin reached over five hundred subscribers, the work of the association reposed "on an (excessively) small team," wrote the secretary. Beyond the hub of militants, the association consisted of a relatively diverse membership, extremely uneven in their participatory vigor, including "wage earners from the public and private sectors, retired persons, housewives, students, and teachers." Nor did their activities elicit any cooperation from the official institutions of commemoration, which responded to their overtures with "a disdainful silence." Vive 89 presented the national exhibition, "eagerly sought after" by various groups. Its members organized public meetings, lectures (rather poorly attended), and debates, and they visited schools, youth clubs, and *comités d'entreprise*.

In a country of *chouans*, it seemed especially important to the Rennes militants (as it had to Marcel Alory and his friends at Saint-Brieuc) to insist on the popular character of the Revolution. The idea was to teach the people that the Revolution was theirs in the hope that this knowledge would stimulate them to assume responsibility collectively for their destiny today. The Revolution was the People's affair:

"the decisive actor in 1789, they must not be reduced to the rank of spectator in 1989."[20]

The Bretons were angry with the state and its timorous Mission—angry that they abandoned the world's fair, that they did not put Robespierre, Marat, or Saint-Just on their commemorative postage stamps, that they created a moral and political ambience which gave rise to Philippe de Broca's "huge cinematic flop" on the *chouans* rather than Jean Renoir's "magnificent" *Marseillaise*. Like the central committee, they held Mitterrand directly responsible for "the philosophical orientation given to the official celebrations," that is, for the sell-out of the Revolution and the People. "Poor Bicentennial," lamented these hard-liners, "how many outrages to the Revolutionary ideal are committed in your name!" This blend of fierce idealism and intransigence guaranteed their isolation in the commemorative field, cutting them off from many of the prospective players with whom Mazauric hoped they would connect.[21]

Founded by a group of Communists, the Association rochelaise pour le Bicentenaire suffered from the same paucity of critical self-consciousness that strained the credibility of sister Vive 89 organizations elsewhere. On the one hand, it affirmed its commitment to pluralism and the open mind ("without any a priori stand, without any sectarianism"). On the other, it avowed its utter intolerance for anything that smacked of the Revolution-libel ("sullying this prodigious epic of the people of France"). This tension easily took on the appearance of a lack of candor. After endorsing a Jacobino–Marxist exegesis of the Revolution as a bourgeois and popular undertaking, acknowledging their close ties with Michel Vovelle's Institute at the Sorbonne, and affirming their commitment to the abiding progressive ideals of the Revolution, the Association rochelaise insisted that "we are not the bearers of an ideology."[22]

This tension surely accounted in part for the sometimes stormy relations the association entertained with city hall. The municipality, run by a leftist coalition led by former minister Michel Crépeau, appointed a commission to direct La Rochelle's commemorative efforts. Presided by Claude Latrille, a Socialist city councillor, it promised to work with all interested agencies, associations, and individuals. Chaired by a Communist deputy to the mayor, a professor named Henry Moulinier ("citizen-president"), the Vive 89 group had a different conception of how to celebrate. The council majority regarded the very existence of Vive 89 as a sort of provocation; it was denounced by one official as "unfair competition." The city commission invited Vive 89 to work under its coordinating aegis, like all other citizen associations, following the rules and the calendar established by the mayor. Replaying the scene from the municipal revolutions of 1789, Vive 89 refused the bridle of subordination. Bad feeling peaked at the time of municipal elections in the spring of 1988, a year after the incorporation of the Association rochelaise. Crépeau reminded the press pointedly that his commission was "the only institution officially representing the city." On numerous concrete projects, however, the municipality and the Vive 89 group ended up by collaborating fruitfully. Partly thanks to municipal funds, Vive 89 mounted several exhibitions, sponsored lectures and PAEs, and launched a series called *Cahiers d'histoire de La Rochelle et de la Révolution*, which may very well become a permanent feature of local intellectual life.[23]

Commemoration in a Red Bastion: 89 en 93

One of the most vigorous and coherent commemorative efforts at the local and supralocal levels took place in the Seine-Saint-Denis, the department that hugged the capital on the north and east. Wholly independent of the Mission and contingent on the participation of organizations and individuals at the grass roots, it was in several ways an undertaking from below. Yet it was driven and orchestrated by the political will manifested first in the Conseil général and then in many of the municipalities. The Seine-Saint-Denis was one of the two remaining departmental bastions of the Communist party. The bicentennial provided an occasion for the PCF to exploit its historical and moral identification with the Revolution in order to reaffirm its mobilizing capacity. Party and elected officeholders rightly understood that they would be expected to set the example for celebratory fervor and imagination in a context of dilatoriness and indecisiveness at the national commemorative level. In order to profit politically, the PCF had to satisfy its own clienteles. If it failed to nourish an energetic bicentennial program, it would implicitly undermine its own claim to the intensity of the social demand for R/revolutionary commemoration.

Inhabited by 1.3 million people, 16 percent of whom were foreigners, the Seine-Saint-Denis still had many of the traits that distinguished the old Red belt despite the economic transformations of recent years. Workers still represented more than a third of households, and some seventy thousand people were unemployed. Nineteen municipalities (twenty until March 1989) remained in the hands of the PCF. Significant gains by the extreme right and an alarmingly high level of abstention worried the party and doubtless quickened its desire to use the bicentennial as an educational and civic instrument. The place du Colonel Fabien must also have been concerned that six mayors in the department were insurgent *refondateurs* of one sort or another, though their alienation from party line and leadership did not seem to affect their enthusiasm for the R/revolution or their commitment to the idea of a robust commemoration. Under the aegis of two prominent Communists, Georges Valbon, president of the Conseil général, and Jean-Claude Gayssot, parliamentary deputy and son-in-law of Georges Marchais, a coordinating committee took form in the late spring of 1987 under the intriguing label 89 en 93.[24]

Ninety-three was the department's identification number, the number that appeared, for example, on the license plates of all automobiles registered in its territory. Beyond proclaiming the collective name of its constituents, 93 evoked the ideology of the committee and the bicentennial line it intended to follow. 89 en 93 announced its intention to inject a serious dose of 1793 into 1789 and into 1989.

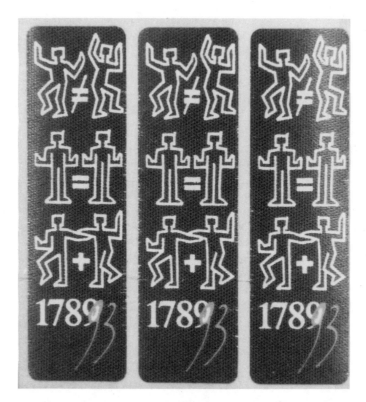

Graffiti-style logo of the extremely imaginative Comité 89 en 93, the emanation of the Communist government of the Seine-St.-Denis (number 93 in
the list of departments), which put together a rich commemorative program
geared especially toward the youth of the department, a large proportion of
whom were "beurs" and "blacks," of Arab and African origin. (Photo: The
"89 en 93" association.)

Even as the state made clear its intention to focus on the more or less consensual
Revolution of 1789, the Seine-Saint-Denis argued implicitly that 89 without 93
despoiled the Revolution of a fundamental part of its very meaning. Though the
Revolution was arguably "popular" and "social" from the very beginning, in the
eyes of the Communists, among others, 93 embodied its richest popular and social
veins. By popular they understood, in idealized terms, the People taking control of
its own destiny through interventions that were decisive if not always massive. By
social they construed policies that "anticipated" the concrete forms of democratization for which the People would struggle during the next two centuries.

This notion of the social found expression in the Constitution of 1793, the
Jacobino-Robespierrist testament promulgated as the legal and moral framework of
the republic in June but suspended before it could be applied until the termination

of hostilities. Its detractors contend that it was a demagogic text never meant to be executed but merely to allay fears concerning the intentions of the Convention, while its admirers see it as a veritable charter for popular sovereignty and democratic practice, including referendal control over legislation. Its institutional features interest its partisans less than its recasting of the relation of state to society in order to enable the people to attain happiness ("the goal of society is common happiness"). The artisans of commemoration in the Seine-Saint-Denis appreciated in particular what they considered to be the progressive character of the Constitution of 1793: its proclamation of basic rights to employment, to assistance, to education, and to the legitimate recourse to insurrection in case of violation of the rights of the people; its "generous and humanistic definition of citizenship, offered to all those who were denied rights in their country; and its abolition of slavery.[25]

The 89 en 93 committee portrayed '93 as both a complement to and a revenge upon '89. With the Constitution of 1793, it maintained, "for the first time, equality becomes the first of the rights." Equality, the product of a militant "social movement," was what was missing in '89, eclipsed by a triumphant liberty. They did not denigrate liberty, which, in any event, the nation owed, in Marat's words, to "popular risings," not to the bourgeoisie that appropriated it. Rather, invoking the double authority of Rousseau and Robespierre, they contended that liberty without equality was a vain word. Seventeen ninety-three was complicated terrain, for it seemed to mark both the culmination and the rupture of the alliance between (elements of) the bourgeoisie and the People incarnated by the sansculottes. Ninety-three usefully forced French citizens today to reexamine the relationship between the political and the social, between liberty and equality ("Are they complementary or antithetical, as is often suggested these days?" asked historian Roger Bourderon, vice president of the committee).

For the overriding objective of 89 en 93 was to make the case for the relevance of the R/revolutionary legacy in the world of the late twentieth century. "No, the Revolution is not dead!" was a leitmotif in its literature. It was a reminder of both the necessity and the possibility of radical social transformation. Not without a certain demagogic conceit, it affirmed that "in Seine-Saint-Denis, we are not celebrating past events." Presumably, a mere historical regard on the Revolution would be a waste of time and in any event would not resonate with the needs and aptitudes of a large part of the population. So the committee emphasized the Revolution's quintessential "modernity," its invasive "pertinence," and, in an effort to rivet the attention of the young people in whose hands the future lay, its "astonishing youthfulness."

Thus, for example, the Constitution of 1793 stressed the primacy of education as a public, collective goal, an issue that remained pertinent and controversial to the nation two hundred years later, since questions still persisted about the extent to which education could even the playing field by affording equal opportunity to all, about the availability of quality education to all, about the ways to achieve it, and about the relation between education and the job market (which, for many in the

Seine-Saint-Denis, had to begin with the learning of French). The Constitution's embrace of diversity in its liberal conception of citizenship spoke directly to the multicultural character of the Seine-Saint-Denis, where common first names among schoolchildren included Karam, Chafika, Samia, Nassim, Amar, Ahmed, Azzedine, Cherif, and Nabil. Since certain Communist mayors were among those who had lost their nerve in dealing with immigration issues, the citizenship question had political as well as moral pertinence.[26]

89 en 93 did not veer from the classical Marxist exegesis pivoting on "the historical necessity" of the Revolution as the vehicle of the transition from feudalism to capitalism. But in place of abstract and theoretical formulas, it sought to put the case in local and familiar terms accessible to its constituents. An exposition entitled "Modernity and Revolution" traced in linear terms the development from the realm of the sansculottes through the world of the proletariat. In the eighteenth century, "men already knew the new forms of work and of exploitation, and wish to see economic and social relations transformed." The northern suburbs of the capital began to industrialize early in the next century. "Today scientific and economic progress cast into relief the question of democracy in the workplace."

Another exhibition, "1789–1989, Let Us Pick Up Where They Stopped," rehearsed the same connections between social transformation then and now, crisis in the late eighteenth century and crisis in the late twentieth century. The recognition that the appeal for democratization had to be accompanied today by a call for "economic efficacy" served as proof that the working classes were realistic and advanced in their thinking. This exposition cast the Revolution as centrally bourgeois in its focus, with certain achievements of universal benefit to mankind. The nineteenth century witnessed workers struggling for rights against the bourgeois occlusions. Examples drawn from the Seine-Saint-Denis illustrated the movement for the right to organize and to strike, and for limitations on hours worked. The "power of money" enhanced its dominion and its techniques of control in the twentieth century. The exhibit ended with testimonies of today's workers frustrated by blockages, exclusions, and oppressive conditions, redolent of the voices of the *cahiers*.[27]

The coordinating committee provided a wide range of services to its constituents. A sleek monthly bulletin, blending information, indoctrination, and games, introduced 6,000 subscribers to the Revolution and to the commemorative calendar of events. Like the Mission, 89 en 93 accorded its label of patronage to projects deemed worthy ("those which appear to correspond best to the objectives set by the committee"), which were announced in the bulletin. Though it avowed an ideological test, the committee showed considerable suppleness, especially with regard to aesthetic innovation. It furnished pedagogical tools to teachers and association leaders. Roger Bourderon and his colleagues compiled a very usable kit for non-specialists on the theme "Revolution and popular movement," including a historical guide, slides, and a cassette. Historian Madia Tovar gathered *cahiers* from thirty-four of thirty-six possible communes in a book that offered readers a

An ordinary woman of the Revolution hands its legacy to the T-shirt-and-sneakers generation. The programs of the department of the Seine-St.-Denis emphasized the theme of continuity of responsiblity and aspiration between 1789 and 1989. (Photo: The "89 en 93" association.)

cushioned and instructive voyage back into their towns and villages at the end of the Old Regime. Various writers and artists illustrated a day in the Revolution in the almanac entitled *93 écrit 89*. Carefully prepared (and often quite stunning) dossiers for the press on specific activities supplied historical context and orientation.

89 en 93 organized numerous commemorative/celebratory activities, including a mass contest (focused for the older children on the significance of the Constitution

of 1793) pitched to mobilize as many young people as possible through the school and associative networks, a huge outdoor festival at Bobigny held on the anniversary of the adoption of the Constitution of 1793, a rally and walk set to the theme of "hunting for the king" ("le Gros Louis"—the managers of 89 en 93 evinced none of the compassion for the monarch that Yves Mourousi and others attempted to foment), and the planting of a "liberty forest." 89 en 93 put on a festival of fourteen films on R/revolutionary themes. it supported two major colloquia, one concerning slavery, colonization, and national liberation, the other dealing with how the French Revolution has been taught to children in textbooks in countries around the world. It helped to fashion and to place several exhibitions on R/revolutionary topics, and in coordination with the Vive 89 network, it arranged lectures throughout the department.[28]

Proud of the committee's "uncontestable success," the Conseil général asked the organizers to prolong its existence beyond 1989. Rebaptized Idéaux de 89 en 93, it pledged to continue inculcating the R/revolutionary message, aiming especially at youth. Broadening its purview, it organized programs commemorating the one hundred twentieth anniversary of the Commune and the fiftieth anniversary of the Second World War, the latter enabling the Communists to dramatize their vision of the intimate connections between their R/revolutionary and Resistance legacies. Among future projects the committee envisaged a rehabilitation/celebration of Robespierre and a climactic commemoration of '93 in '93.[29]

The Bicentennial and the Labor Unions: The CGT

The posture of the CGT vis-à-vis the Revolution was virtually indistinguishable from the standard line of the PCF. Especially in light of the counterrevolutionary resurgence and the hesitations among the Socialists, the CGT wanted to make its adherence to the Revolution unequivocally clear. It was important to reiterate, in the words of the syndical organ La Vie ouvrière, that "the Revolution is not dead." The CGT appeared less inclined than the CFDT or Force ouvrière to puzzle over the relation between the Revolutionary project and the Le Chapelier Law (June 1791), which banned associations and effectively stifled overt labor organization for almost a century. More than their sister/rival unions on the left, the CGT was disposed to embrace the Revolution en bloc, even if it avoided that term.[30]

A "progressive celebration" of the bicentennial for the CGT implied an emphasis on both the radicality of the event and on its ongoing character. Even more than the leaders of the PCF, the CGT focused on the class struggle as the engine of R/revolutionary advance. Without impugning the "bourgeois" character of the Revolution, necessary albeit unjust, it dramatized the decisive and autonomous popular role. This militant-voluntarist view, in the judgment of Georges Pruvost, secretary-general of the Institut CGT d'histoire sociale, set them apart from the "reformist" unions. Pruvost chided Marc Blondel, leader of the Force ouvrière, for espousing a fashionable preference for liberty over equality, while Blondel denounced both those who conflated liberty with liberalism ("the reason of the strongest") and those who coupled equality with egalitarianism. The CGT reproached the CFDT with following a Furetian neoliberal line, a charge that seemed plausible in light of the collaboration of two of Furet's close intellectual accomplices, Pierre Rosanvallon (the former editor of a CFDT periodical) and Jacques Julliard (a former member of the CFDT national bureau) in the preparation of the CFDT's bicentennial album, *Libertés, Liberté*.[31]

Tepid and timid, following the mark of "the smallest consensual common denominator," the official commemoration left the CGT cold and resentful. Former secretary-general Georges Séguy complained that the government associated no syndicalists in its bicentennial preparations. In his mind, this snub was an emblem of the official desire to conceal the popular nature of the Revolution and its living, intrusive legacy. Indeed, the government's "grand parade of liberties" seemed decidedly cruel and ironic in light of the recent "multiplication of attacks on liberty" in the workplace. Citing Renault in particular, where the "ten" CGTists continued their struggle for reinstatement and vindication, but also Peugeot, Nestlé, Philips, and Air France, *La Vie ouvrière* asked: "How indeed can one speak of the rights of man when the workplace/place of business, where everyone passes the most substantial part of his/her life, remains the site of the arbitrary action of the bosses?" Mitterrand and others—"the camp of the Versaillais and the privileged"—estranged from the real world, spoke of the rights of man as axioms of public law "and not as a living and daily reality." Meanwhile workers suffered lockouts, beatings, and a host of more subtle forms of tyranny. Nothing seemed more symbolic of the government's indifference to the suffering of unemployed and immiserated workers at home and abroad than the decision to transform "the bicentennial into a banquet for the seven great capitalist countries." The CGT warmly supported Renaud's boycott and counterdemonstration.[32]

The Bicentennial in the Workplace: The *Comités d'Entreprise*

The story of the *comités d'entreprise,* worker-run associations within the business establishment/workplace mandated by law, is by no means coterminous with Communist influence. While many committees are dominated by the CGT, intimately tied to the PCF, others operate under the auspices of the CFDT, the FO, autonomous unions, or coalitions of unions. For evident ideological reasons, the CGT was particularly motivated to appropriate the Revolution and celebrate it in terms resonant with its interests and its memory. Claude Mazauric claimed that "militants of the CGT and sympathizers of other class organizations in the labor movement" showed much more energy in bicentennial actions than the members of "organizations of reformist tradition."[33]

The national organization made a studied effort to capture the multiplicity of grassroots activities in a bicentennial working-class coffee-table book, beautifully produced, replete with striking photos in color and black and white, and cast in a boldly iconoclastic graphic design. Entitled *Comités d'entreprises en Révolutions*, it was prefaced by the secretary-general of the CGT, Henri Krasucki, who had no trouble, instinctively, making the connection between the "authors" of the book and their subject. The working class was "the most logical and dynamic continuator" of the Revolution. In the twentieth century no less than in the eighteenth, the people have to struggle to impose their democratic ambitions. Krasucki depicted the *comités d'entreprise* as revolutionary conquests that issued from the combat of the Resistance. Like other popular victories, this one was pitilessly contested by counter-revolutionaries of various sorts. For the labor leader, these committees represent a possible road toward the "democratization of management." He hailed the role they have played in the classical socioeconomic struggles (for the guarantee of workers' rights, improved work conditions, and job security) and the pioneering steps they have taken to establish grounds for social and cultural autonomy in the workplace, thus freeing workers from the subtle tyranny and mortification of paternalism.[34]

Krasucki saw proof of the militant and creative energies of the committees in their bicentennial projects. The Caisse d'action sociale of the electric and gas company (EDG-GDF) in Bordeaux put on a light-and-sound show featuring three hundred volunteer actors. The *comité d'entreprise* (CE) of the Parisian subway system commemorated the Tennis Court Oath with music, dance, exhibitions, dramatic skits, and a liberty-tree planting.

Workers in the Staubli enterprise located in Faverges, a town of 1,200 in the Haute-Savoie, put on a street play evoking the Revolution as their ancestors lived it. The library group of the CE of Sextant at Châtellerault mounted an exhibition on the Revolution that traveled widely in the region. In collaboration with local students, the CE of the national railway company (SNCF) used railroad cars to present two exhibitions on the Revolution. Worried by the gradual amputation of their work force, employees at the Norsolor plant in the Moselle town of Dieuze erected a bronze statue in the "Alley of Liberty" whereby they wanted to stress the human, visceral, and concrete dimension of the rights of man. It seemed both tragic and fitting that the workers should be fighting for their jobs in this year of Revolutionary commemoration.

The CE of the Nouvelles Messageries de la Presse Parisienne was one of thirty-one workplace organizations to show the exposition put together by Vive 89. Presented at different work sites of the NMPP, it was usually accompanied by a discussion led by a historian. One such meeting, held during "the union hour of information," ran substantially over into work time. When a manager appeared to summon the workers to return to the job, he met this "Revolutionary" rebuke, one cheered by his colleagues and reported with a muscular swagger by the union: "We just learned that there are two distinct periods in the Revolution: the Convention and the Terror. If you insist, we shall pass directly to the second."[35]

Paris

Bicentennial Accommodation and Resistance

hough he sported the Phrygian cap of the RPR, and in many ways remained a Jacobin in liberal's clothing, Jacques Chirac, mayor of Paris,
never felt comfortable presiding over Paris-as-world-capital-of-revolution.
On the one hand, it was true that his party ceded to no other in its republican ardor,
and it located itself squarely within the Revolutionary lineage, albeit exclusively in
that branch that descended from 1789. On the other hand, Chirac and his party had
tacked with the international wind, renouncing or repressing their centralizing-
dirigiste proclivities in favor of a Reagano-Thatcherite orientation. The prestige of
revolution had declined precipitously in the 1980s. Whatever residual benefits to be
wrenched from it would naturally accrue to the Socialists, who paradoxically acceded to power just when their ideological patrimony and legitimacy were crum-
bling everywhere.

In this context, on the morrow of Mitterrand's conquest of power, when partisan
feelings and mutual suspicion ran deep, powerfully reinforced by the entry of the
Communists into the government, the idea of celebrating the anniversary of the
Revolution exercised little allure on the retrenched denizens of the state-within-
the-state at city hall. A commemoration might be good for France in commercial
and international terms, but in the eyes of Chirac and his counselors its advantages
would redound in particular to their political adversaries. Certainly this sort of
calculation counted heavily in Chirac's decision to torpedo the plans for a world's
fair in the tradition of 1889. Yet it was inconceivable for the city of Paris to turn its
back flatly on the Revolution, whose primary seat was Paris, whose heroic reputation still resounded loudly throughout the world (beyond ideological nuance and
ephemeral political maneuvering), and whose legacy included many ideas that
Chirac and his friends held dear.

The View from Matignon

As mayor of Paris, Chirac had to find a way to commemorate that would salvage face without compromising interest. His return to the premiership in 1986 significantly compounded the problem. He then had to factor in national and international requirements and a blunt daily confrontation with the Elysée, which turned into something resembling an extended presidential campaign. He had to reckon with two bicentennial scenarios, one which saw him ensconced in the royal presidential palace and another which banished him once again to the baronial-*frondeur* Hôtel de Ville.

"There is a trap in this damned bicentennial," Chirac the mayor had mused aloud to his close associates. He had encouraged his staff to begin planning in 1985, though the state's own lack of zeal took some of the pressure off the city. The mayor's idea was to "do a bit of everything," to showcase the city and its riches, to fortify its claim to European cultural and economic leadership. His instructions were: "do not forget the Revolutionaries" in our prudence, but "do not underestimate the tragic side" in our enthusiasm to put on a good performance.

Even before the municipal commemorative operation got off the ground, however, the mayor found himself in Matignon. Under his impulsion, in consultation with Mitterrand, the national Mission finally began to function under the direction of his old friend Michel Baroin. As long as Chirac remained in the premiership, it was easy enough for his municipal team to align itself ideologically more or less on the moderate mark fixed by Baroin and the slightly sharpened version of it crafted by Edgar Faure. Even if some conceptual dissonance emerged between the Mission and the more conservative voices at the Hôtel de Ville (notably historian Yves Durand, representing "the right wing of the right wing"), there were no problems in coordination, since both groups answered ultimately to the same boss. The situation changed when Chirac left the government a defeated, shaken, and occasionally rancorous man.

Chirac's Bicentennial Discourse:
Reconciliation through Relativization and Resignation

In a press conference dealing with the bicentennial shortly before the presidential elections, Chirac struck an exremely cautious pose. Intent on portraying himself as a sober statesman utterly devoted to the national interest, he wanted to stress themes that comforted this image. A man likely to become the steward of French destiny had to situate himself in an all-embracing perspective, in the historical long run. Just as certain German conservatives ventured to "historicize" Nazism in order to free their country from the stranglehold of culpable memory, so did Chirac, under Durand's tutelage, attempt to historicize the Revolution by reinserting it into the long narrative in order to liberate France from the tyrannical grip of its originary pretensions.

"France did not begin in 987 at the coronation of Hugues Capet," affirmed the mayor, and "the modern epoch was not opened by the Revolution of 1789." Modernization was a long, cumulative process. Contemporary France was the product of *all* its history, not just of relatively recent spasms. Continuity was a more powerful force, in Chirac's reckoning, than rupture. Beyond the paroxysms on which one was inclined to dwell, the patient construction of continuity engendered the unity of France, the unity Chirac yearned to symbolize.

The process of forging French national identity began at Bouvines (the decisive victory of Philippe Auguste in 1214 said to mark the first glimmerings of French national sentiment) and culminated in the Festival of the Federation, which sealed, "with a unanimous surge, the unity of our country." This was the 14 July that Chirac preferred to commemorate, the one which would project him as the leader of all the French. This was the Revolution of the Declaration of the Rights of Man, which made of France a model emulated the world over (even if its values were in gestation long before 1789). What interested Chirac the unifier in the Revolution were "the values best suited to bring together the French people." He would not focus on the "sometimes devastating energy" unleashed by the Revolution.[1] France had since overcome most of the handicaps that had crippled it economically and destabilized it politically. As it steadfastly confronted the challenge of the new Europe and the highly competitive world, France could thank the Revolution for its major positive contribution: propelling France into the forefront in the realm of ideas. ("France has no oil, but it has ideas," one hears oneself piously rehearsing in response to Chirac's oblique encomium.) In a follow-up news conference a week later, Chirac's chief deputy, Jean Tibéri, underscored the theme not of the bicentennial but of the anniversary "crossroads" linking the Capetian millennium and the Revolution.[2]

The defeated presidential candidate was hardly more voluble about the Revolution, which somehow seemed to bear some responsibility for his rout, than the prime minister had been. The preface signed by the mayor in the catalogue of the Avant-Première once again stressed the themes of unity and of international reverberation. Unity implied reconciliation, even if Chirac did not spell it out in pastoral terms. The notion of a united, free, creative, and independent France, to which all French women and men were now so deeply attached, emerged from the Revolution. At the same time the Revolution had endowed the nation with "an unprecedented intellectual and moral primacy," whose momentum France needed to summon as it entered the next century.

Now that the bicentennial season was in full swing, Chirac dropped the awkward Capetian linkage. If the shadow of Durand still lingered in the mayor's presentation of the city's commemorative program to the press, there was nevertheless a more therapeutic tone. "The time has come for France to accept the totality of its past and to consider all the events, all the dramas that compose it, as if they were so many strophes of an epic poem, the poem of the identity of our nation." Denied paternal exercise, Chirac still spoke of France in avuncular terms as a single family whose kinship the (early/good) Revolution reinforced. "It is clear that we are the children of the great moment of 1789, if only because we are the heirs and the trustees of the Declaration of the Rights of Man."[3]

The mayor made his most effective bicentennial statement, and the one with which he felt most at home, in his welcoming talk to the hundreds of descendants of Revolutionaries who gathered at city hall in May 1989. Addressing the Robespierres as well as the Charlotte Cordays, Chirac once again worked the theme of unity through totality, lucidity, and toleration. It was the sort of speech that Michel Baroin might have given, evenhanded but upbeat, positive but realistic, didactic but not overbearing. It was as if the presence of the descendants enabled Chirac to see the Revolution in flesh-and-blood rather than abstract terms. "Glorious when it unites, painful when it divides"—unity still remained the supreme test and the all-purpose euphemism for the mayor—the Revolution was born of and engendered contradictions that all French people today had to acknowledge and to assume.

"Let us avoid blindness, let us avoid caricature," he proposed. The incapacity of the Old Regime to realize urgently needed reforms condemned it. Some of the Revolution's results were truly and durably admirable: the abolition of privileges and the articulation of human rights, the affirmation of national sovereignty, the reorganization of the territory and the administration, the introduction of the metric system, the creation of the *grandes écoles*. Some of the consequences of the Revolution were frankly abominable—the vandalism, the "irremediable damage," the "crimes committed in the name of liberty." Without asking anyone to renounce his or her freedom of moral judgment, Chirac reminded his audience of monarchists, moderates, Jacobins, and others that "each one of us bears equally the historical and even the genetic memory of everything that made up the history of our country." For the mayor of Paris, who was also the head of the major opposition party and a likely candidate for the presidential elections of 1995, this was as big a step as he could allow himself toward making peace with the Revolution.[4]

The Municipal Mission

There was more clarity in municipal bicentennial discourse than in municipal commemorative organization. City hall was a sprawling administration, in which rival claimants competed for control of tasks, and funds, that did not fall unequivocally in one sector or another. Part of the bicentennial pie—but how much?—gravitated naturally into the hands of Françoise de Panafieu, parliamentary deputy and head of the Parisian office of cultural affairs, daughter of a former minister, classical *héritière*, but with taste and a sense of humor. Yet Jean Tibéri, the first deputy to the mayor, could not allow an issue with such political ramifications to pass wholly out of his grasp. He became president of a transdepartmental commission, ardently sought by Panafieu, who hoped that it would reduce subterranean frictions and allow services of a very different order (public works, traffic control, accounting, contracting, etc.) to collaborate efficiently.[5]

Christened the "Commission municipale du Bicentenaire de la Révolution francise," Tibéri's committee had a professional/administrative/political component (directors of municipal services, city councillors, etc.) and a scientific/"civil-society" branch consisting of museum directors and academics (the conservative tandem of Michel Fleury, a municipal monarchist, archaeologist, and historian of early Paris, and Jean Tulard, a specialist in the Revolutionary-Napoleonic era). The commission did not meet very often and, according to insiders, achieved very little of substance. It is interesting to observe how it gradually metamorphosed from a "commission du Bicentenaire" into the "Association pour l'information et l'animation pour les célébrations de 1989," purged of any direct reference to the Revolutionary object.

The commission boasted an inner cabinet, to deal with ostensibly urgent matters between formal sessions, headed by Guy Longueville, a municipal councillor and delegate for human rights. Meanwhile the mayor named another municipal councillor, an old friend and political intimate, Jean de Préaumont, as "general commissioner for the organization of the Grand Days of the Bicentennial." Worried that planning was advancing too slowly and in fragmented fashion, Tibéri subcontracted the task of commemorative conceptualization to a public relations/creative events firm headed by Jean Saint-Bris, whose kinship with brother Gonzague, a literary and television critic for *Le Figaro*, guaranteed his ideological pedigree. He planned to frame the municipal bicentennial around the theme of unification, a focus fully congenial with Chirac's instincts.

Viewed disdainfully by a number of key players in the city hall hierarchy, Saint-Bris was dismissed after many months of toil. "The graft did not take," remarked Thierry Aumonier, the euphemism concealing his own role in Saint-Bris' defenestration, for he had never relished the presence of this talked-about outsider. An *énarque*, a former cultural affairs specialist, and now secretary-general both of the city hall administration, a position of immense power, and of Tibéri's commission, Aumonier was a politically adroit operator with an elegant Machiavellian strain who had ready access to the mayor. Bypassing regular channels, increasingly yet somewhat furtively, he took command of the bicentennial vessel, which was off course and perilously behind schedule if not precisely derelict.

Bright, energetic, and manifestly ambitious, more or less of the same generation, Françoise de Panafieu and Thierry Aumonier emerged as the municipal shakers and doers. Panafieu concentrated on the less spectacular but more durable projects that drew heavily on the city's existing resources or were geared to enrich its cultural patrimony, though she was not devoid of more general ideas, which she had been discussing directly with Chirac since the early 1980s. Aumonier became the strategic coordinator, serving as both a conceptualizer (but through a shrewd sort of synthetic parasitism rather than a gift for creation) and an executor. He focused on the grand and evanescent events that would have immediate media and political impact.

Panafieu Deploys and Fattens the Patrimony

Françoise de Panafieu began with the reasonable working premise that the bicentennial was a "minefield." Her engagement with the Revolution was not deeply ideological. Clearly there was much in it that she found detestable. But she was decidedly more interested in the opportunities that the commemoration proffered than in the moral imperatives to settle world-historical scores. For her the Revolution elicited not "rancor" but "pain." Yet the Revolution loomed large in the shaping of France's physiognomy and soul. It was time to "look at it as adults" and to seize this "unique opportunity to reconnect the broken threads." Baroin's discourse put her at ease; she liked the idea of targeting the future rather than exhuming the past.

Given Panafieu's moderate pragmatism, one grand scheme that she proposed to Chirac in the spring of 1985 seems somewhat outlandish. There was one dynamic young man who had already proven himself in the domain of historical festival making, she told the mayor, who could organize a truly memorable event that would please Parisians and tourists. He was sufficiently "cunning," she assured Chirac, "to "treat tactfully the diverse currents of feeling." The name of this creative pacifier was Philippe de Villiers. Known by insiders and locals for his Puy-du-Fou triumph and his pioneering efforts at regional radio, he had not yet become a controversial national personality. Still, it is hard to imagine how he could have been entrusted with a task that required judiciousness, loyalty, and self-effacing discretion. The idea was to give him the Champ-de-Mars, consecrated Revolutionary space, on which he could orchestrate a pageant—"folkoric" was the irenic word promisingly flourished—centered around the arrival of the representatives of all the provinces in the spirit of the Federation. Once Villiers joined the new cohabitationist government the following year, the project fell by the wayside, much to the chagrin of the (future) ethnographers and historians of the bicentennial.

The postcohabitationist period Panafieu recalls as replete with tension and bitterness around city hall. "We were walking on eggs," and no one was much interested in talking celebration. But she pursued numerous projects that she had launched in 1986 and '87. Despite the moroseness, she had ample funding. She boasted that Chirac never refused her money for an exciting idea. Directly and indirectly, Panafieu was responsible for many of the city's most substantial bicentennial achievements. Her inclination to focus on the future led her to commission a number of contemporary artists to express themselves in reference to the anniversary but in giving free rein to their imaginations to "go beyond the strict framework of the Revolution."

The most important creation was Yvan Theimer's powerful sculptural monu-

The city of Paris launched a vast hunt for the descendants of men and women who participated in any way in the Revolution, bringing together relatives of terrorists and émigrés, deputies and shoemakers. (Photo: Cultural Service, City of Paris.)

ment to human rights, a marriage of limestone and bronze, of classical architecture and Egyptian obelisks. Before the mayors of the twelve capital cities of the European Community, Chirac inaugurated the monument on the Champ-de-Mars on 24 June, insisting in terms that would have pleased Mrs. Thatcher on the European and long-run historical context of the construction of rights doctrine, in which Joan of Arc, Thomas Moore, Jan Hus, and others played a decisive part long before the Enlightenment began to shine.[6]

As she watched "the state lapse into tawdriness"—she was thinking in particular of the Tuileries—Panafieu took pride in her commitment to "things of substance." She asked the curators of the city museums to excavate in their collections for forgotten or unexposed pieces concerning the Revolution. She encouraged and in some cases helped to develop exhibitions on themes drawn from the Revolution: the experience of the first centennial ("When Paris danced with Marianne" at the Petit-Palais), eighteenth-century costumes ("Modes and Revolutions" at the Musée de la Mode et du Costume), the constitution of the patrimony during the Revolution (at the Bibliothèque Historique de la Ville de Paris), the events for which the city hall served as fulcrum ("The City Hall and the Revolution" at the city hall); and a rich series of expositions on such themes as the fête, the signs of liberty, the Tuileries Palace, and the career of Talleyrand held in the city halls of the arrondissements. The municipal museums marketed a collection of beautifully reproduced facsimiles of Revolutionary objects and contemporary creations inspired by Revolutionary designs and images (porcelain, crystal, jewelry, foulards, games, the key to the Bastille, decorative pieces), accompanied by explanations of their genesis and significance.

Panafieu managed the huge restoration project of the statues of the major cities of France at the Concorde, to which the city and a private bank each contributed Fr 5 million. The inauguration, at the beginning of the year, marked the city's opening of the commemorative season. The bicentennial witnessed the opening of the splendid Le Peletier-Saint-Fargeau wing of the Carnavalet Museum. Containing the entire Revolutionary collection, constituting a breathtaking itinerary through Paris from the late eighteenth through the early nineteenth centuries, the new wing made Carnavalet the largest museum in the world devoted to the history of a capital city. Counseled by Jean Tulard, one of France's most knowledgeable historians of cinema, Panafieu organized a film festival of the Revolution ("89 sur Grand Ecran"). Up to 2,800 persons at each showing watched Renoir, Rappeneau, Delannoy, Scola, Wajda, and Gance under a giant tent raised in front of the Hôtel de Ville.

Panafieu had the most fun, and the greatest media success, with the project called "Paris Writes Its History." Launching "an appeal to memory" on hundreds of billboards in the subway, on buses, and in the streets, the city summoned descendants of actors at all levels of the Revolution to make themselves known. To Panafieu's astonishment, the city was inundated with a cathartic geyser of testimonies of greater or lesser plausibility. As many as fifty thousand persons contacted the city, by letter, telephone, or minitel. A team of genealogists and historians assembled to sift through the candidacies. The organizers sought representatives from the ranks of national political leaders as well as ordinary artisans and workers, aristocrats and takers of the Bastille.

The somewhat blasé Furetians of the municipality were surprised to encounter the "extreme passions" of many of the descendants. To the "true sentiment of Revolutionary pride" was joined "a violent anti-Revolutionary reaction," in the words of Jean-Jacques Aillagon, one of Panafieu's collaborators. He detected "a new snobbism"—a reflection of the times—of hatred for the Revolution among "people of still modest condition." The sociological stereotypes were only partially impugned, for many royalists, scions of royalist families, boycotted this convocation on the ground that it was "unworthy" of their heritage and vocation.

A little under a thousand descendants were fully authenticated. Given the acuity of feelings, one wonders how they and their families responded to Chirac's efforts to "cool down" the mood in his speech at the reception held in their honor. The partisans of Louis XVI could not bring themselves to be photographed with the survivors of the (ritually polluted) executioner family named Sanson. Robespierre suffered denunciation at the hands of one of his heirs, a rightist journalist. Danton's offshoot, a Peruvian national, also situated himself on the right. The Incorruptible's lodger and friend, the carpenter-builder Duplay, found favor in the heart of a pro-Revolutionary career military officer. Charlotte Corday's distant offspring refused to consider her forebear a murderess.[7]

Downgrading the Bicentennial: The City Cuts Back

While Françoise de Panafieu oversaw enterprises which were esteemed to be intrinsically justifiable and which had for the most part been in gestation for some time, Thierry Aumonier turned his attention to the more volatile calendar of *grandes journées*. In March 1988 Jean Tibéri had announced a dense and ambitious program, the bulk of which the municipality ultimately renounced. The project conceived with Antenne 2 for the mayor to address his New Year's greetings to the foreign capitals of the world and thus give an international impulsion to the start of the bicentennial was abandoned. The same fate befell the proposed gathering of the mayors of France to celebrate the "advent of the municipal fact" in 1789. The plan to set up a vast "historical itinerary" of Revolutionary sites, with restored or reconstituted eighteenth-century points of interest, beautification efforts, the erection of signs, street theatre for ambience, and trained guides for explanation never saw the light of day.

Another abortive scheme involved Yves Mourousi, who was to have recruited the much sought-after Quincy Jones to put on a concert for the youth of the world at the Champ-de-Mars on the anniversary of the Declaration of the Rights of Man in collaboration with François Baroin's association. Nor was a Bastille of two thousand square meters constructed "of stones made of poplar wood, subscribed by citizen-purchasers in early '89, to be returned to them after the dismantling." This modernized Bastille, light and transparent, "leaving the visitor the choice of construing it as either half built or half demolished," was supposed to house a wide range of cultural activities for most of the year. (A Bastille of 180,000 unsealed clay bricks was "taken" at La Villette in early July, a happening sponsored in part by Danièle Mitterrand's foundation, which had nothing to do with the city's very different idea.) "Twelve Hours for a Revolution," a high-tech light show, never illuminated the night sky above the Etoile. Mireille Mathieu, a Chirac favorite, did not do a bicentennial performance at Bercy, the Parisian Madison Square Garden, as announced.

Successive versions of a grandiose project proposed by Philippe Vilamitjana were stillborn. Focused on the universality of the ideals of liberty, equality, and fraternity, none was ideologically risky, and each struck some of the multicultural and ritually harmonious tones of Jean-Paul Goude. The "Carnival of the Worlds" was a parade, geared for world television and for several hundred thousand spectators and scaled down to cover only a small half of the Champs-Elysées, that involved two hundred to four hundred performers from each of seventeen nations. The "Colors of Liberty" followed the same basic scenario, with the addition of a Christolike carpet to be laid across the whole route on Paris's most renowned thoroughfare.

These projects failed for many of the usual reasons, including prohibitive cost (the Vilamitjana parades, for instance, were priced at between Fr 70 and 100 million), redundancy (Goude sealed Vilamitjana's fate), calendar encumbrance, conceptual flaws, and so on. But a number of them were sacrificed on the altar of state-city discord, and still others, including several not cited above, were stifled as a result of calculated political decision. Obviously, the critical moment after Tibéri heralded the city program was Jacques Chirac's loss to Mitterrand. Defeat inclined him to disengage. That inclination, however, was dramatically quickened by what he regarded, not implausibly, as unseemly and triumphalist/vindictive behavior by the state, incarnated by old enemy Jack Lang and upstart adversary Jean-Noël Jeanneney.

The state seemed intent on displacing the city, confiscating the entire festive calendar and space, and strutting before the public. Since Chirac's electoral clientele was hardly in the R/revolutionary orbit, he had little to gain from investing heavily in the bicentennial. Since Paris was the site of the state's major celebratory gestures, it was likely that the state could claim credit in the public's mind for *everything* that took place in the streets and edifices of the capital. Articulated cogently by Thierry Aumonier, this analysis corresponded with the mayor's state of mind. Chirac thus ordered a general retrenchment. In addition to several of the projects that Tibéri had announced, he squelched a number of Jean de Préaumont's plans for concerts, fireworks, and sound-and-light shows. For Chirac this decision was dictated by "reasons of principle" that he considered imperious.

Thierry Aumonier and the Eiffel Tower Caper

Aumonier argued, at the end of 1988, that the city ought to strike one major media blow. Since the Mission was still floundering, it could turn out to be the highlight of the bicentennial, a well-deserved vengeance for the city. This event would have a distinctive municipal signature, Aumonier suggested, because it would avoid any overt association with the Revolution. Nothing was more Parisian, symbolically and juridically, than the Eiffel Tower. Even as 1989 struck the two hundredth anniversary of the Revolution, it also marked the centennial of the Tower. And even as the Tower had been distanced in 1889, for political/international reasons, from the commemoration of the Revolution per se, so it would be legitimate to proceed in the same fashion in 1989. There had been vague and modest plans for an Eiffel birthday party. With Chirac's warm endorsement, Aumonier appropriated the commemorative license for the Eiffel monument, and planned to build around it an extravaganza of towering proportions.

Framed by the Eiffel show, the city's revised bicentennial calendar, issued at the end of 1988, was staunchly defended by the conservative press. "The accusations of tepidness lodged by certain Socialists against the mayor of Paris concerning the celebration of the bicentennial," affirmed *Le Quotidien de Paris*, "are the product of groundless imputations of a sort that the state is curiously spared."[8]

It is hard to imagine a better fall-back position than the Eiffel Tower. Arguably France's best-known monument around the world, it was a wonderful vehicle for Parisian promotion, an emblem of precocious technological prowess and a promise of continued innovation in the third millennium. As the beacon of the City of Lights, it also cast Paris in the romantic aura that appealed to tourists. The Tower's historical association with the French Revolution was relatively esoteric knowledge. Implicitly, a celebration of the Tower could be interpreted as an indirect homage to 1789.[9] But the municipality was not obliged to underscore or even articulate the connection. The public would revel in a megashow that had nothing to do with guillotines and everything to do with the post-Revolutionary development Paris strained to project. Nor would the city have to worry about the Ministry of Culture or the Mission usurping credit for the production.[10]

Yves Mourousi had already generated some plans for integrating the Eiffel Tower into the bicentennial festivities, but Aumonier turned instead to Olivier Massart, an experienced producer who had used the site before and appeared sufficiently dynamic to put together a star-studded, technically dazzling spectacle in a few months. (Aumonier briefly entertained the sweetly vengeful idea of integrating Jean-Michel Jarre into the Eiffel show; the notion was dropped perhaps in part to avoid inscribing a link with the bicentennial.) Massart was no Goude, but he did not come to the advertising world in the normally pedestrian way. He had been a sort of professional adventurer in photojournalism before he became "the adventurer of the ephemeral," a virtuoso-specialist in grandiose fashion shows and other one-shot publicity galas.

"Something of a technological genius," Olivier Massart marshaled six thousand projectors, eighteen hundred square meters of netting woven through the pillars of the Tower to serve as reflectors, thirty-one water cannons to create liquid walls on which to project images, fifteen tons of powder for fireworks, forty-four mini-towers of sound equipment, and twenty-five kilometers of cable to power everything. He could not have Jarre, but he hired his lighting engineer, Jacques Rouveyrolles, who performed admirably. He entrusted the choreography to Dee Dee Wood, Michael Jackson's dance master. And, in addition to hiring camels, elephants, circus acrobats, four hundred actors, a thousand dancers, eight hundred musicians, and three thousand extras, he contracted with some twenty international stars in order to enhance his prospects for success.

Massart began with a budget of about Fr 60 million, which soon swelled to Fr 80 million. The Hôtel de Ville contributed Fr 30 million, and the company that held the operating concession on the Tower added another ten. Television rights, purchased by fifty-six countries, were supposed to account for over Fr 15 million. Aumonier looked to private sponsors for the rest. Citroën, for instance, had a historic interest in renewing with its early-twentieth-century practice of advertising directly on the Tower. Béghin-Say Sugar and Bouygues Construction were among the other sponsors, a number of whom Chirac personally prodded into commitment, who shared six thousand reserved bleacher seats for friends and clients on the Pont d'Iéna and enjoyed a sumptuous reception in a tent pitched near the Tower. Only forty guests, including the Reagans, received a mayoral invitation to dine in the Tower's gastronomic Jules Verne restaurant before the show.[11]

L'Humanité did not miss the occasion to excoriate the elitism of "Monseigneur Chirac, duc de Paris." "In the eighteenth century at Versailles villeins could at least approach the gate of the royal castle while the nobles feasted inside," the newspaper commented. "Two hundred years after 1789, the privileged of this century realized that, to be left in peace, it was best to keep the plebeians very far away from their royal personnages." In fact almost a half a million people thronged to the magnificent show site, and for the most part were unable to see anything. The failure to anticipate a logistical strategy commensurate with the appetite of the spectators was one of Aumonier's two regrets. The other was the camera style of the American crew responsible for the images. (Aumonier criticized them almost as vehemently as Goude would rail against his television director.) Oblivious to their surroundings, as if the stage were a set in a Hollywood backlot, the Americans failed to incorporate the Tower itself and the ambient nocturnal beauty of Paris.[12]

Show Time

Without once evoking 1789, Chirac displaced his bicentennial discourse onto the Eiffel Tower in his introduction to the program for the show. "A sign of rallying together," the Tower was "a symbol of communication among men" and a summons to "the spirit of fraternity." Scheduled for 17 June 1989, the anniversary of the proclamation of the National Assembly, the Eiffel Tower show became the mayor's personal Festival of the Federation. Still, the show opened with a striking sketch devoted to the Revolution entitled "The Hymn of Liberty." In an eerie blend of antiquity and outer space, hundreds of white-garbed Revolutionaries bearing torches marched double-time to take the Bastille (without bloodying their robes) and then dedicated themselves to the peaceful commemoration of 14 July 1790. As the Tambours de Bâle beat out the powerful yet ambiguous stroke of the people oscillating between mob and congregation, Placido Domingo delivered a robust *Marseillaise* backed by the London Symphony Orchestra.[13]

The succeeding scenes focused on the building of the Tower and on the changing rhythms of Parisian life. "The Grand Mechanic" represented energy as fire and light. Under a sky of bursting fireworks, it featured a ballet of construction with dancers wearing flashlights on their heads, shoulders, and knees; tightrope walkers; and a human pyramid mimicking the Tower. "Noah's Ark" portrayed the Exposition of 1889, an exotic colonial reminiscence, showing the animals of the future Third World and the pavilions of the fair. Léger-motifs framed a riveting tableau of men with giant wrenches and hammers adjusting the gear systems that announced the nascent age of the automobile and the accelerating second age of industrialization.

The show then descended into a more hackneyed Hollywoodish mode, with a peppy retrospective of Paris through the songs of Josephine Baker, Maurice Chevalier, and Edith Piaf. Wonderful visual effects and the charm of Charles Trenet salvaged "Paris-Paname." The numbers by Mireille Mathieu, Claude Nougaro, and Charles Aznavour were neither witty nor moving. The program announced "the joy of a liberated people," but Johnny Hallyday croaked a somewhat anguished ballad on the high price of freedom that seemed inconsonant with the motorcycle and leather décor.

The scene shifted brusquely and felicitously to 2089, the Tower serving as a rocket-vector into the future and a bridge between familiar and strange peoples, extraterrestrials on stilts. Opening with a prayer for the students at Tiananmen, Stevie Wonder had less difficulty than Johnny in transmitting the felt emotion of liberty in his "Song on Freedom." A song-and-dance finale performed by the entire cast (which, including the crew, numbered around five thousand), along with yet another magnificent explosion of fireworks, set the stage for official birthday wishes. Chirac beamed his approbation, followed by an ever-boyish Ronald Reagan, dazzled by the show, struggling to read a few words from one of his ever-present notecards. Stevie Wonder closed with a thumping rendition of "Happy Birthday" before "the world's biggest cake." The only mention of the word "bicentennial" the entire evening was an invitation to return to celebrate the two hundredth birthday of the Tower in 2089.

Festering Wound: The Jarre Affair

Despite the acrimony that attended the outcome of the presidential election, it might have been possible for the Hôtel de Ville to maintain correct if not cordial diplomatic relations with the Mission had it not been for the Jarre affair. The mayor's office claimed at least copaternity for the Jarre concert idea. It had agreed first with Baroin and then with Faure to participate in the financing of what would have been a joint municipal-national project. The negative press that Jarre harvested following the London Docklands concert worried Aumonier a bit, but he believed that the Jarre organization was capable of a world-class show and that Jarre's perspective on the bicentennial guaranteed against "any ideological deviations in the subject matter." In the summer of 1988 Aumonier's major anxiety seemed to find a way to prevent the concert from becoming "a Festival of the Ministry of Culture." Given the warm relations that existed between Jean-Michel Jarre and Jacques Chirac, Aumonier felt that the city would have sufficient leverage over the artist. To make sure that the public understood that it was not strictly a state affair, one member of the city's bicentennial team reports that Aumonier wanted the thousands of people who would be setting up and rehearsing the concert during the first two weeks of July 1989 to wear T-shirts emblazoned "Office of the Mayor of Paris—14 July."

Jean-Noël Jeanneney gave every indication when he succeeded Faure in late May 1988 that he counted on the Jarre concert as the climactic point in the popular festive calendar. Apparently in response to the thickened density of events, Jarre cut back his scenario from a two-day happening to the afternoon and evening of the fourteenth. Until late in the summer, neither Thierry Aumonier nor his friend and former schoolmate André de Margerie, Jeanneney's right-hand man, the natural bridge between municipality and Mission, suspected that Jarre's star was imperiled.

On 16 September 1988 Jack Lang and Jean-Noël Jeanneney convoked Jarre to a meeting at the Ministry of Culture. The fact that it was chaired by Jacques Attali, Mitterrand's chief counselor, signaled some sort of crisis. The municipality, although a partner of the state in the enterprise, was not asked to participate, or even informed of the impending meeting. Attali solemnly explained to Jarre that security requirements for the G-7 summit would make it impossible for him to present the sort of concert that he had planned for Bastille Day. Attali apparently did not tell Jarre that the president of the republic wanted something fresher than he (and especially Lang) thought Jarre could achieve. Invoking *raison d'état* with great aplomb, and flattering Jarre with the assurance that the Elysée held him in high esteem, Attali offered him the night of 16 July as an alternative date for his show. Jarre seemed (provisionally) willing to accede to this arrangement; at least this is the reading that de Margerie transmitted to Aumonier.

The state's decision, and especially its manner of reaching that decision, shocked and infuriated the Hôtel de Ville. From the vantage point of the mayor's cabinet, it was tantamount to the unilateral rupture of a contract that bound not merely a musician and public authorities but, more important, the state and the city-state. The soothing assurances about a will to cooperate mouthed by Jack Lang when he assumed the bicentennial mantle now took on an odiously hypocritical edge. Aumonier viewed the state's action as a crude maneuver to monopolize the bicentennial. Livid, Chirac virtually called for a citizens' boycott of the climactic bicentennial moment.[14]

The security pretext tied to the summit was both plausible and casuistic. Surely Jarre could have modified his logistics to accommodate the needs of the police. De Margerie conveyed to Aumonier a second reason: Mitterrand wanted a ceremony more thematically commensurate with the commemorative object. Apparently the Elysée had settled on a specific motif: *La Marseillaise*. This rationale also seemed duplicitous to Chirac's counselors in retrospect, for there was no historical rootedness in Goude's parade, and the very title *La Marseillaise* was obscured by millions spent puffing the adroitly/scandalously personalized "Opéra Goude."

Jean-Michel Jarre was doubly victimized by political Machiavellianism. Though he was treated abusively by the state, the compensation it proposed him was not a poisoned gift. There was enough festive energy in France, and around the world, to assure him an ample audience on the sixteenth; and the state would have been obliged to guarantee the funding. Under no circumstance, however, was Chirac willing to accept this solution. Hoping till the end to find some honorable accommodation, Jarre did not announce his definitive withdrawal till mid-December. In light of his manifest desire to put on his show, the city's posture was no less cynical than the state's. Aumonier and Chirac vigorously pressed Jarre to renounce. They hinted that to be in "the very end of the pack" was nothing less than a public humiliation.[15] Once it mastered its bile, the Hôtel de Ville savored the Jarre affair. It was the perfect occasion to extricate the city at very low political cost from an uncomfortable situation. With righteous indignation, it distanced itself from any further involvement with the perfidious commemorators.[16]

The Mission and the Municipality

Between the Mission and the municipality, there was no further collaboration on major projects ("Complicity cannot be fabricated," philosophized Françoise de Panafieu). There were no more sustained exchanges as there had been during the Baroin-Faure tenures. The joint-venture rhetoric of Jean Tibéri's news conference of 22 March 1988 found no further echo. Jeanneney's affirmation, after visiting with Tibéri in late September, that "no bridge had been burned between the city and the state" did not ring true. The public assurance that Chirac gave in mid-December that the Mission and the Hôtel de Ville would continue to work "hand in hand" seemed utterly hollow if not sardonic. Accompanied by Monique Sauvage and André de Margerie, Goude visited Aumonier in early January to expose his project. But this placatory gesture did not improve the climate. On the contrary, confirmation of the nature of Goude's design reinforced Chirac's conviction that the Jarre affair was a personal "snub" joyfully administered by Jack Lang.[17]

The rupture between the municipality and the Mission was acted out on the podium at the dedication of the famous statues at the Concorde at the beginning of the bicentennial year. Both camps agree that the mayor castigated the president of the Mission and predicted in colloquial terms that he would fall flat on his face in the coming months. In the days of Richelieu, or of Guizot, the encounter would have provoked a duel. (The scenario is irresistible: school chums de Margerie and Aumonier as seconds, negotiating first the place of battle, for one would have had to find ground belonging neither to state nor to city . . .)

Eminently civilized (in Norbert Elias's terms), Jeanneney responded to the insult with an irate and censorious epistle. "On the dais at the ceremony for the unveiling of the statues of the place de la Concorde, where I was your guest last Tuesday," wrote the Mission president, "before I had fully seated myself, you conveyed to me vigorously your indignation and reprobation concerning the current state of the projects for the festivities the night of 14 July, next." Shocked by "the tone of your remarks in such a place and in such circumstances," Jeanneney told Chirac, he nevertheless wanted to address the issues raised. He questioned the basis of Chirac's "stupefaction" at having learned "very recently" that a replacement show was in gestation for 14 July since security imperatives had seemed to preclude any such endeavor. "Permit me, Mr. Mayor, to express astonishment in turn at your astonishment."

In considerable detail Jeanneney set out to prove that Chirac had been well informed, beginning in early October, by the Mission. Strategically, it was wise for Jeanneney to take Chirac literally. In fact he must have understood that the mayor's smoldering anger had little to do with recent information and much to do, by contrast, with the manner in which the state made its decision. The Mission president berated Chirac for "unilaterally" foreclosing the possibility of rescheduling the Jarre concert. Jeanneney's evocation of the Goude project as "a more historical and more strictly commemorative show than the concert of Jean-Michel Jarre" seems rather strained in retrospect, though it is possible that Jeanneney at the time expected that Goude would in fact instill his parade with convincingly historical and commemorative dimensions. The security differential was real, the Mission president contended, because the Goude parade would not result in "a dense concentration of people fixed in one spot in the sensitive zone of the place de la Concorde."

While the information on the evolving Goude project that the Mission furnished the Hôtel de Ville was "inveterately rich," Jeanneney complained, "I cannot, unfortunately, say the same in reference to the information furnished the Mission on the celebration of the centennial of the Eiffel Tower on 17 June, despite our recent and repeated requests for details." He concluded on a swollen note, calling on the mayor to "confirm the efficacy of the sincere relations" that had ostensibly been forged between his team and Chirac's "in the service of a national success."

Chirac justified his wrath in his response to Jeanneney. "The terms in which I expressed to you my indignation were probably a bit sharp," the mayor conceded, "but, at bottom, the manner in which the city of Paris was treated in this affair fully merits my condemnation." That was indeed *the* issue, though Chirac made a point of stressing the enormous prejudice suffered by his friend Jarre, an international star, treated "cavalierly," who had devoted a large part of two years in laboring for his country and its bicentennial. The state's rationale for replacing Jarre with Goude struck him as patently hypocritical. From what Goude himself had indicated, his itinerant publicity vignettes would have little to do with commemoration, and the enormous magnitude of his preparations and of the parade itself would generate far more horrendous problems of logistical and spatial management than Jarre's enterprise.

In Chirac's view, then, this was a political execution, a day of dupes, in which one artist was substituted for another, arbitrarily, without discussion among the contracting parties. "The constraints of security and traffic were thus merely a pretext, destined to free the terrain gently, in order to occupy it subsequently in force according to a schema wholly defined by the state without any concertation with the city," concluded the mayor, plausibly demonstrating in this way that his "good faith was betrayed."[18]

The Bicentennial Destiny
of Robespierre

Emile Fournier-Elipot, laureate of the Rosati, the Artesian literary society of which Robespierre had been a member, imagined a bicentennial scenario in which the leader of the Committee of Public Safety returns to France ("God resuscitated me," volunteered the Incorruptible, still on the side of Providence and eternal life) to see "how [his] name has been treated since [the Revolution]." History had no shortage either of heroes or villains, revered and reviled.

> Et parmi tous ces noms, oui! le mien Robespierre,
> Peut encore diviser la France toute entière.
>
> And among all these names, yes! Mine, Robespierre,
> Can still divide France in its entirety.

Though he admitted that objectivity in these matters was hard to attain, the ambivalence that engulfed his posterity troubled him, for he had fought for the same values of happiness, peace, and liberty for which the people have always risen.

> J'ai vécu pour servir la Révolution
> Et pour le bien du peuple et de la Nation.
> En toute honnêteté, jusqu'au bout inflexible;
> C'est pour cette raison qu'on dit "l'Incorruptible."[1]
>
> I lived to serve the Revolution
> And for the good of the people and the nation
> In all honesty, [I was] to the end inflexible.
> That is why they call me "the Incorruptible."

441

Robespierre's Reputation

It is hardly surprising that a man who became a dramatic, albeit never unequivocal, marker of political position in his own time should have remained an object of intense controversy. Nor has he served simply as a litmus of Revolutionary versus counterrevolutionary persuasion. While counterrevolutionaries have always clustered around a common horror/hatred of Robespierre, Revolutionaries have been divided among themselves in their appreciation of him since well before his fall on the ninth of Thermidor. In different ways reflecting their different ambitions and ideological inflections, the Thermidoreans themselves began systematically to show that one could be a more or less fervent Revolutionary despite Robespierre. While the left/liberal nineteenth-century historiography of the French Revolution cannot be reduced to the debate over Robespierre, he loomed inordinately large, not only in the discussion of the Terror but in the very way one framed one's global reckoning of things.

Robespierre was not riveting merely because of the bloodshed with which he was intimately associated. He fascinated because he disconcerted; kneaded of contradictions, he was not easy to fathom. Pilloried for his alleged indifference to human life, he had forthrightly opposed the death penalty and the war. Aloof and elitist in manner, he was the defender of the pariahs. He identified with the People—provided the People obeyed certain norms that he had envisaged for their conduct. He toiled for a more robust conception (and application) of equality, yet he rebuffed the proponents of the "agrarian law" with as much determination as he repudiated the dechristianizers.

Robespierre defended liberty passionately, and the suspension of liberty, putatively in order to save it, with no less vehemence. He wielded the sword of rationality in the battle for liberation, yet he defended the shroud of religion, which many of his friends perceived as incapacitating superstition. Beyond the concrete issues, his self-abnegating/self-righteous posture and his moralizing political signature exasperated would-be allies as well as outright enemies, neither of whom escaped their strangely charismatic impact.

Alphonse Aulard and his renegade student Albert Mathiez crystallized the modern left-left debate at the beginning of this century. A radical republican, Aulard found reason to suspect Robespierre on multiple grounds: political, personal, religious, and more generally ideological. To seal the historico-historiographical consolidation of the republic, he preferred Danton, the earthy and truculent man of audacity, of the defense of the nation, of the prosecution of a vigorous but intelligent, demystified, and in some ways measured Revolution.

Danton disgusted Mathiez; he embodied everything dubious and contestable in the accelerating experience of Revolution. On the basis of searching archival research, Mathiez believed that he had established Danton's gross avidity and venality, his opportunism, and his flirtation with the enemy in several different avatars. Danton's scabrousness triggered a chiaroscuro that set into relief the irresistible

Two hundred years after his death, Robespierre continues to embody the fundamental controversy between partisans and enemies of the Revolution. In a laser sculpture in acrylic crystal, Ana Rosa Richardson explores "le Mythe Maximilien Robespierre" (Paris, 1988). (Photo courtesy of the artist.)

allure of the Incorruptible. Mathiez deeply admired Robespierre, not only for his purity but also for what we have since been taught to call his progressiveness. Mathiez's Robespierre unsparingly fought for the oppressed, and chastened their class oppressors. He embodied the ideals of the Revolution in the correct proportions and relations.

Mathiez founded the Société des études robespierristes and pressed hard for the full rehabilitation of his hero. Implicitly, he argued that the scientific study of the Revolution in some sense required a Robespierrist orientation. Mathiez died at age fifty-eight in 1932. By assuming the Robespierrist mantle even as he obtained the titled chair of the Revolution that Mathiez never enjoyed, his exact contemporary, Georges Lefebvre, embalmed the Incorruptible in the Sorbonne, investing him with an academic unction that took him literally as well as figuratively one step closer to the Panthéon. The Société des études robespierristes shared the same address as the Institut d'histoire de la Révolution française.

More judicious and temperamentally sober than Mathiez, Lefebvre tried to defuse the captious and increasingly sterile scholarly confrontation. After scrutinizing the evidence, he agreed that Danton was almost certainly tainted, but he emphasized his positive contributions and he demonstrated that an obsessively sustained Danton-Robespierre bipolarity would not yield historiographical dividends. Still, Lefebvre presided over the Robespierrists, and made a ritual pilgrimage to Arras to further the cause of rehabilitation, as we shall see below. His immediate successors did not assume the Robespierrist stewardship. But with the advent of the Communist historians to the chair, first Albert Soboul and then Michel Vovelle, Robespierre recovered his talismanic status in the university.

Happy Anniversary to You?

The (prosaic) experts confirmed the bicentennial Robespierre's lyric intuition: he continued to divide France deeply. The Incorruptible remained Inco-optable. The Revolution-is-over consensus reserved no place for him. Selected in the bicentennial surveys of public opinion as the most important personnage in the Revolution, Robespierre repelled an imposing segment of respondents for his fanaticism and cruelty. He was admired in substantially smaller numbers for his leadership and progressivism. On a Sofres–*Nouvel Observateur* poll, Robespierre headed the list of those who evinced "negative" feelings and was third, after Lafayette and Danton, for positive resonance. The same question in a Sofres–*Figaro-Magazine* study found the Incorruptible in first place for antipathy and seventh place for sympathy, trailing Lafayette, Marie Antoinette, Mirabeau, Danton, Carnot, and Louis XVI. While the Communists still manifested staunch devotion for Robespierre, the majority of the rest of political France, from left to right, entertained serious reservations about him.[2]

One critically situated group, high school history professors, was largely pro-Robespierre. According to a Sofres-*Express* poll, almost two-thirds judged his role in the Revolution as "rather positive." Only 16 percent esteemed that he bore chief responsibility for the Terror; almost four-fifths believed that he was merely one of many who forged it. In any event, almost twice as many (61 percent) viewed the Terror as the product of the assaults of the Revolution's internal and external enemies rather than the consequence of Revolutionary excesses themselves or of Revolutionary doctrine (33 percent). This sounding comforted the belief of the right that de-Robespierrization in the school system had hardly begun. A survey of textbooks deeply worried *Figaro-Magazine.* Hachette published a manual that portrayed Robespierre as "concerned not to move beyond republican legality," while Belin's Robespierre dreamed "of inaugurating a fraternal society," statements with which the vast majority of professional historians of all stripes would agree. The magazine reproached the amoralists at Hatier for allowing readers to choose between flattering and sinister images. Yet a commission that examined textbooks in the third from last year of lycée was struck by "the deliberately negative image given to Robespierre."[3]

Like all other R/revolutionary icons, Robespierre suffered in the counterrevolutionary resurgence of the 1980s. His name served as a shorthand for epitomizing every deviation, an alibi for the indolence of those who ached to excoriate, but not at the cost of elaborating a real argument. To prove that Robespierre still mattered to his enemies as well as his friends, the former were no longer content to identify him with the Terror, or even the Enlightenment-run-amok. In his anniversary aggiornamento more than ever before, Robespierre was Modern Evil, Totalitarianism, Stalin, Hitler, Pol Pot. In unconscious mimesis of the worst brand of Jacobin scapegoating by association and anachronism, *Le Figaro* resolved the issue expeditiously: "Lenin pronounced himself a Robespierrist." With the Revolutionary leader thus idealized, it was not necessary to have recourse to the historical record, whose inherent complexity/ambiguity risked attenuating or somehow clouding the case against Robespierre. During the bicentennial period Robespierre suffered the inexorable fate of the *arroseur arrosé:* he was lynched by the media in the name of human rights.[4]

Scholars on the right tended to follow François Crouzet, the excellent historian of French economic development. His public lecture at University College, Swansea, dealing with the historiographical treatment of Robespierre was predicated on the impervious conviction that no reasonable case could be made for Robespierre. One had only to remember that in Brazil a "Robespierre" signified an undercooked piece of beef, "très saignant," or very rare. Though he did not stop there: to avenge colleagues on the extreme and moderate right, from Pierre Chaunu to François Furet, Crouzet assimilated Michel Vovelle to Robespierre. The holder of the chair of the French Revolution at the Sorbonne was an ayatollah, a "Tartuffian" manipulator, an "unashamed apologist" of Revolutionary violence.[5]

Furet discredited Robespierre far more artfully. The Incorruptible understood the benefits of giving expression to Revolutionary policy in moralizing terms. He knew how to play rough politics, how to use principles as cudgels, how to cover a purge with "the intelligent use of quasi-puritanical intolerance." For Furet, Robespierre's passion for the abolition of slavery was also a wedge to liquidate Barnave, just as his opposition to the war was geared to ruin Brissot. Robespierre's "maneuvering genius" enabled him to cast opprobrium on those who resisted the move to bar the reelection of incumbents to the next legislature, thus weakening the parliament vis-à-vis the clubs in the same measure that it strengthened him vis-à-vis ostensibly less high-minded adversaries. His opportunism led him to favor alternately the claims of the parliament to exercise a represented sovereignty and the argument for direct democracy that precluded representation.[6] Furet's Robespierre is neither mad nor macabre. He is diabolical in his cunning and rapacious in his appetite for the right exercise of power. His is a wholly plausible if unattractive Robespierre.

To the Panthéon

On the national scene, the Communists were the driving force behind efforts to rehabilitate Robespierre. If Mathiez, fugitively a Communist, inaugurated the romance early in the century, Maurice Thorez made Robespierrism official party doctrine in a speech delivered at Arras in the sesquicentennial year. The party "recognized in Robespierre a true defender of the people, of peace, and of democracy." On the occasion of the two hundredth anniversary of Robespierre's birth in 1958, a year redolent in (neo)Robespierrist political imagery, the Communist group in the National Assembly proposed the edification of a national monument in his honor. In the 1970s, as the PCF launched its campaign for "a Socialism in French garb," Communist troubadour Jean Ferrat sang "it answers still to the name of Robespierre, my France."[7]

There was nothing fatal about the Communist embrace of the Incorruptible. Even when violence was still considered by many an acceptable weapon in the world-historical struggle against oppression, there were perfectly good grounds to reject Robespierre as a role model; Trotskyite Daniel Guérin explored many of them in his *Bras nus*, a study of the so-called proletariat during the Revolution that the party guardians vilified. According to this view, while Robespierre had defended many lofty causes, he had, after all, struck the gravest blow against the "popular movement" in his campaign to extirpate Hébertistes and *enragés*. His social policy was more Bismarckian than Babouviste. He repeatedly compromised himself with interests that the Communists would call bourgeois in both analytical and pejorative inflections. Babeuf himself indulged briefly in harsh strictures against Robespierre, who struck him before Thermidor as more an overbearing despot than a servant of social revolution. There is some reason to believe that Robespierre's interest in religion was not purely functionalist but that it bespoke a mystical current incompatible with Communist scientology.

Still, there were more or less compelling reasons to gravitate to Robespierre. Soviet fascination with Robespierre surely helped some Communists to overcome their doubts. The limited choices the Communists faced in their efforts to insinuate themselves into the management of the national memory induced them to regard him indulgently. The Revolution afforded them few alternatives around which to build a cult. Marat did not last long enough, and he carried some questionable psychological and political baggage. Babeuf lacked stature and a certain stability of R/revolutionary purpose—unless he stood on someone else's shoulders.

Robespierre offered many inherently attractive traits. The Incorruptible's incontrovertible honesty, and perhaps also his moralizing discourse, appealed to the Communists, who so deeply abhorred the corruption of bourgeois society and politics. So did his willingness to be merciless in the name of Grand Principles, his ferocious patriotism wrought in the pacifist crucible, and his espousal of advanced/progressive/"anticipatory" positions associated (correctly) with the Constitution of 1793 and (incorrectly) with the Laws of Ventôse. The Communists found it easy to identify with Robespierre's martyrdom and to empathize with him for both the myopia and the cynicism to which he fell victim. Like them, Robespierre seemed to be made of the stuff of a Resistance Fighter.[8]

Throughout the bicentennial period, the Communists hailed the Incorruptible and railed against the attacks of which he was incessantly the object. Before the party central committee, Guy Hermier denounced the calumnies that stained the honor of Robespierre, on whom he bestowed the title "sansculotte." Economist Philippe Herzog, the leader of the Communist ticket for the elections to the European Parliament in the spring of 1989 (and a *refondateur* in the making), quite self-consciously took Robespierre as a model, a philosophical and moral guide to follow in navigating the treacherous shoals of European integration. *L'Humanité* and *Révolution* echoed party indignation at the Socialist refusal to accord a proper place to the Incorruptible in the commemoration. If he had been president of the Mission, wrote historian Claude Mazauric, "I would have placed the figure of Robespierre at the heart of the celebration" as the peerless devotee of "the grand human causes." In the same spirit, the organ of the CGT proclaimed: "More than ever, the philosophy of Robespierre is ours."[9]

No one worked harder for the rehabilitation-cum-apotheosis of Robespierre than Claude Mazauric. Given his evangelical commitment and his relentless combativeness, "crusade" is the proper word to describe his efforts. He took his campaign around the world, summoning all those who loved the principles of democracy to support the cause. Scores of times he crisscrossed the hexagon to inform and to harangue groups large and small. A powerful speaker who fed on his own enthusiasm, the professor from Rouen was capable of holding an audience captive for over two hours at a time with his mixture of vignette, exhortation, and lesson. He was at his best when he told the story of Robespierre, read extracts from his masterly speeches, and commented on them in the context of unfolding events. While he was viscerally incapable of avoiding the pitfalls of hagiography, he managed to articulate the dense complexity and extremely uneven topography of Robespierre's political landscape, in which problems always outstripped solutions. Mazauric was at his worst when his tone soured and hardened, his passion congealed into polemic, and his political agenda undercut (and corrupted) his pedagogical one. This is what happened, for instance, when he crudely harnessed the Incorruptible to the party line in order to discredit the forces of consensus—the anti-Robespierrists from the PS through the RPR-UDF—who "are motivated by narrow and self-regarding ambitions, and sacrifice everything to the single European market of 1992!"

For Mazauric, the creation and nurture of the black legend of Robespierre was a permanent means of rejecting those parts of the Revolution that he considered most decisive for the future of humanity. The historian vigorously contested the sinister bicentennial version that portrayed Robespierre as a Stalin. This amalgam was not a mere intellectual construct to a militant who had for so long remained faithful to a party whose Stalinism he openly acknowledges. "Robespierre is at antipodes from Stalin," he affirmed. The "carnivorous shamelessness of a dictator like Stalin, who utilizes a social transformation to constitute a completely aberrant political system that contradicts the social system," had nothing at all in common with Robespierre's mission. Barely in power for ten months, the latter sought to govern rather than to rule. Always subordinating "political interest to morality," even as he exercised the dictatorship of the committee, he remained (somehow) "the man of antiterrorism."

Mazauric played out the paradox in the classical terms of Jacobino-Marxist historiography. He rationalized Robespierre's failure to condemn the ravages of Revolutionary violence on the grounds that he could not make such an enormous "gift" to the forces of Counterrevolution. Though Mazauric placed Robespierre in direct intellectual descendance from Rousseau, he preferred not to see the Terror in ideological terms (just as he contended that "the essence of Robespierrism is not in the Terror"). A "concrete" history of the Terror, privileging the imperious constraint of circumstance, would show that the Counterrevolution at home and abroad menaced France with "decomposition." Public safety was not the moral equivalent of cynical reasons of state. Faced with survival or annihilation, Mazauric's Robespierre turned to "the legal Terror," a belated response to four years of remorseless counterrevolutionary violence. Fully aware of the perils of becoming entrapped in the Terror, Robespierre reached for constitutional ways out, Mazauric argued nebulously and evasively, but found himself locked in by the persistent gravity of the threat to the Revolution.

Obviously, the professor from Rouen could not ignore the Terror, but he sought to shift the ground to the whole breadth of Robespierre's career: the early struggle for constitutional compromise, "with the king if necessary"; the campaign for the abolition of the death penalty and the emancipation of the slaves; the fight against "the partisan bellicosity of the court and the adventurism of the Brissotins"; and his unwavering moral incorruptibility. Not least important was the social dimension in Robespierre's thought and action. In Mazauric's opinion, nothing better underscored the relevance of Robespierrism today than his hero's intransigent dissatisfaction with an abstract conception of human rights and human dignity. Despite his apparently ethereal temperament, Robespierre espoused a worldview firmly rooted in social life, daily life. Democracy required the social application of the lofty principles proclaimed in the declarations. Mazauric did not use Robespierre to demean the political rights (liberty in particular) that the Communists had been in the habit of excoriating as formalistic duperies. He stressed Robespierre's conviction, however, that without social rights political rights remained unequally useful and usable by the mass of citizens. Nor did the historian espy in the Incorruptible a harbinger of Socialism: "Robespierre is far away from a vision of the restructuring of society." But Mazauric deeply admired the measures by which he anticipated "social security" in the modern sense, notably the guaranteed "right to existence," the assurance of an opportunity to work, the promise of public assistance, and the opportunity/obligation to acquire a free education. These were the ideas and the projects that made Robespierre one of the greatest democrats and humanists of all time in Mazauric's eyes.[10]

For Mazauric and fellow Robespierrists, not all of whom were Communists, it was time to end "the ostracism," to repudiate the use of Robespierre as "the scapegoat of all conservative fears." This "sifting in the heritage" they felt as an "unbearable injustice," an offense against "all historical equity." In a speech to the Association "Paris-Révolution" (part of the Vive 89 network) just a few days after the bicentennial-closing apotheosis of Condorcet, Grégoire, and Monge, Mazauric declared: "We will never be able to rest until Maximilien receives the national and republican honor that is due him." Or, as he put it less obliquely in an interview with a local radio station in the provinces, "we will never stop talking of Robespierre until he is in the Panthéon."[11]

Inclined to joke only about very serious matters, *L'Humanité* had already anticipated his installation in its April Fool Day issue. Under a front-page photo of the
Incorruptible, it announced that the president of the republic had finally decided to
transfer Robespierre's remains to the Panthéon. It playfully credited *Figaro-
Magazine*, through its letters-to-the-editor column, with helping to locate
Robespierre's ashes. Persuaded to act by a "blue-ribbon panel of historians" con-
vened at the Elysée, a hesitant Mitterrand drew his justification from his one-time
mentor Jaurès, who had pledged that "I am with Robespierre, and it is next to him
that I am going to sit at the Panthéon."[12]

The Robespierrists could not count on much support from governing quarters.
Individual Socialists such as party spokesperson Jean-Jack Queyranne felt a strong
bond with the legacy of the Incorruptible, for whom he named his son Maximilien.
(According to *L'Evénement du Jeudi*, when little Max pulled his sister Julie's hair,
she cried out: "Maximilien, he was horrid, he cut off people's heads.") A native of
Arras, Louis Mexandeau, a minister with a degree in history, energetically supported efforts to honor his fellow hometownsman. Senator Jean-Luc Mélenchon,
one of the principal spokespersons for the party's left wing, deplored the bicentennial "caricature" of Robespierre. "Without question Robespierre was the major
forgotten figure of 1989, which is regrettable," editorialized *L'Ours*, generally
known as a moderate voice in the PS. But, by and large, Max Gallo correctly noted
that "in the Socialist orbit it is clear that one does not dare declare oneself
Robespierrist, in fact one does not even dare to confront the personage." In distancing himself from a Robespierre whom he represented in stereotypical terms, earthy
Marcel Debarge, a national secretary of the party, probably spoke for a large number
of Socialists: "I like Danton because I have always had a weakness for the people
who live, who screw, who know how to ally an idealist commitment to a sense of the
realities. The visionary side of Robespierre sends shivers down my spine. Danton at
least was not too much of a killer."[13]

It was hardly a surprise that Mitterrand failed to follow *L'Humanité*'s script.
Though he regarded Robespierre as "a key figure in our history," the president felt
that "he inspired too many bloody events" to merit immortalization in the national
shrine of the Panthéon. Consonant with Mitterrand's presidential temperament,
this assessment also bespoke a political determination to conduct a judicious bicentennial commemoration. The president's friend and former minister of justice
Robert Badinter concurred. Despite Robespierre's political talent and his lucid
historical vision, he tainted himself irretrievably in the spring of 1794. Badinter the
lawyer thought first of the Laws of Prairial radically abridging the rights of the
suspected and accused. Following the canonical liberal line, he esteemed that republican military advances at home and abroad no longer justified extraordinary
measures of administration and repression. "Robespierre symbolizes the Terror,"
concluded the president of the Conseil constitutionnel, and "one cannot put the
Terror in the Panthéon."

Given the range of Robespierre's accomplishments, Jean-Noël Jeanneney conceded that his stigmatization was partly unjust. But because he was so intimately identified with the systematic violation of human rights, the president of the Mission did not believe that the Incorruptible "embodies for our time the qualities that the majority of the French people desire to choose first in the Revolution." Thus Robespierre did not fit into a strategy for the celebration of the "luminous side" of the Revolution.[14]

Alternative Sites of Apotheosis:
Hometown Rejection; or, Moral Arras-ment

Arras has never felt comfortable with its most illustrious native son. The dominant voices in the local public sphere rejected him throughout the nineteenth century as a "hateful monster" and "bloodthirsty." Profiting from the renewed revolutionary climate of the 1840s, *Le Progrès*, a regional paper inspired by Lamartine's favorable portrait of the Incorruptible, vainly sought to overcome the black legend. Around midcentury local historians developed the damning thesis that Robespierre bore direct responsibility not only for horrors committed elsewhere in France but also for the human depredations wrought in his own town of Arras. If the representative-on-mission Le Bon had been the hand, Robespierre had been the head. Hippolyte Taine's writing on the national scene reinforced the demonized local portrait. The call to erect a statue in his honor, vigorously formulated in 1848 and reiterated by Louis Blanc in the 1870s, fell on deaf ears. There was little evocation of the Incorruptible at Arras during the centennial.

Albert Mathiez spearheaded the drive for rehabilitation in the early years of the next century. With Charles Vellay, he founded the Société des études robespierristes, the frankly partisan objective of which was to render Robespierre "the justice that is due him" by publishing his corpus and launching scholarly studies of his career, thereby permitting historians and other commentators to make the right judgment. *Le Réveil du Nord* reported that the society's civic goal was to erect a statue of Robespierre through a national subscription. The clerical journal *La Croix* launched a vicious counteroffensive, heaping bloody obloquy on the man of the Terror. "Never will the said statue be erected in Arras," it warned, for "an army of honest persons" was prepared to prevent "by force" this "glorification of crime" and "insult to our ancestors."

After sixteen years of indefatigable lobbying, the Robespierrists earned their first victory in October 1923. In a ceremony presided by the mayor, Gustave Lemelle, a leftist lawyer, and attended by Mathiez and other members of the society, a plaque commemorating a great son of Arras was installed on the house in which he had lived in the late 1780s. Five hundred persons attended, according to newspapers favorable to the rehabilitation; fifty "drinkers of blood," mostly "foreigners," outside agitators, said the anti-Robespierrist press. Frightened by the prospect that the project for a monument would now move rapidly toward fruition, the editor of *Le*

Beffroi sounded the alarm against this Red plot: "The Russia of the Soviets, of Tyrants and torturers is going to raise a statue to Maximilien Robespierre, nothing more chic could be found." (In fact, the Soviet leaders, shortly after their revolution, erected two of the rare monuments known to exist in Robespierre's honor; one at Moscow prophetically collapsed as a result of defective materials, while the other at Leningrad/Saint Petersburg apparently survives—at last report.) To fortify its view, the paper published a stinging attack on the "most criminal of the Terrorists of your community" by a professor at the Institut catholique of Paris. Mathiez responded in kind in *L'Avenir,* a leftist paper in the area. The *Beffroi* rejoined with an open letter to Mathiez: "Do like Le Bon, embrace him if you love him, but do not undertake to install his effigy in the place that he depopulated."

After intense negotiations with the mayor over the emplacement of a bust, Mathiez believed that he was on the brink of success in 1925. But discussions collapsed at about the same time that the plaque on the Incorruptible's house was vandalized and removed. Regional Socialists pressed for the restoration of the plaque and subsequently offered to support a statue in honor of Joan of Arc in return for a monument to Robespierre. The municipal council agreed with this Solomonesque solution, but the populace remained deeply divided. Georges Lefebvre, a Lillois with many connections in the north, succeeded Mathiez as president of the society. Controlled by a Radical Socialist majority, the municipal council announced a solemn ceremony to dedicate the monument to Robespierre to be furnished by the Société des études robespierristes on 15 October 1933. Meanwhile, it baptized rue Maximilien Robespierre the street on which the Incorruptible's house sat.

The polemic quickened in tone. Opponents organized a "an anti-Robespierrist committee." The mayor's pacifying claims that it was not at all a political affair but a local honor to a native son who was a distinguished lawyer, academician, and Rosati were immediately contested by a series of spectacular refusals to attend the ceremonies by distinguished Arrageois, including the head of the order of lawyers and the president of the Académie des sciences, des lettres et des arts. When the Rosati agreed to be present, several prominent members, led by their rightist president, Emile Poiteau, resigned. For days on end *Le Courrier* published lists of local prisoners, suspects, and victims of the guillotine—1,675 names in all. The affair was complicated by an unseemly brawl between the current mayor, Désiré Delansorne, and his predecessor Lemelle. The former imputed the responsibility for the statue project to Lemelle. The latter, perhaps because he had since entered national politics and sought to secure a wider appeal, distanced himself more and more emphatically from the Revolutionary whom he had once effusively praised.

Author of six anti-Robespierrist poems ("Es-tu content, maudit, d'avoir ton effigie / Dans la ville d'Arras que ton règne a rougi / Du sang de trop de gens dont nous portons les noms?" [Are you satisfied, cursed one, to have your effigy / In the city of Arras that your reign turned red / With the blood of too many people whose names we bear?"]) published in the press and in a brochure financed by the anti-statue committee, Emile Poiteau asked the prefect five days before the ceremony to ban it in deference to the memory of the dead of Revolutionary Arras and in order to prevent the disorders that a promised counterdemonstration would provoke. A member of the robespierrist committee, the prefect refused. Poiteau embroidered the theme that the statue was the product of foreign intrusion. *La Croix* affirmed that no donor came from Arras, save "the wogs." Historian Robert Schnerb, a member of the Société des études robespierristes, criticized in temperate tones the refusal of Maître Dhôtel, head of the local bar, to attend the ceremonies honoring one of his professional forebears. In response, Dhôtel scurrilously questioned the right of an outsider, who was also a Jew, to take part in a debate concerning Arrageois.

On the eve of the ceremonies, Poiteau exhorted his fellow citizens to stay away in order to avert violence. The bishop of Arras seconded the call for a boycott. Ready for trouble, the local police had obtained prefectoral reinforcements. On the morning of the dedication, the anti-Robespierrists set up three model wooden guillotines, filled with cement and weighing two hundred kilograms each, at the site of the Revolutionary executions and at two other major squares. Claiming to have boobytrapped the guillotines with bombs that would explode if the authorities tried to remove them, the militants hung cardboard heads on the lampposts, poured red paint in the streets to simulate blood and plastered the walls with shrill denunciations of the Incorruptible and his band of foreign admirers. Undeterred, the police removed the guillotines without incident, took down the heads, and covered the bloodlike paint with sand. They arrested a royalist lawyer who tried to paint the mayor's house red.

Three Socialist deputies of the region greeted Georges Lefebvre, president of the Société des études robespierristes, and a substantial delegation of members and supporters (including historians Philippe Sagnac, who had sat on the board of Aulard's journal, Ernest Labrousse, and Louis Jacob) at the train station. The cortege was insulted on its route to the monument to the dead where Lefebvre placed a wreath, but the rest of the day's activities transpired in relative tranquillity. Apparently very few local people attended the various events. Most of the elected officials of the Arras left avoided attending the luncheon banquet. But the Société des études robespierristes reported that many regional mayors, highly placed public servants, representatives of the unions and the Ligue des droits de l'homme, and teachers were present. In officially proferring the bust to the mayor, Lefebvre recounted the long and obstinate ordeal of Mathiez. He hailed the courage of the Robespierrists throughout France who resisted "the incredible heap of tales and accusations wherein ignorance and bad faith joined with secret political, philosophical, and social hostilities to damn the the vanquished man of Thermidor."

Mayor Delansorne welcomed this reparation of a "great injustice," a gesture delayed by the "opportunistic and self-seeking policy" of his predecessor, he did not miss the occasion to remark. He painted a picture of Robespierre as a man of balance, navigating between extremes of terroristic Hébertiste and Dantonist defeatists—Mathiez's ultras and citras. "We do not have to be ashamed of Robespierre," he concluded, citing a recent piece in *Les Nouvelles littéraires*, for he was "a reasonable and proper bourgeois." Delansorne did not ask himself whether every such bourgeois would have joined the Incorruptible in rushing to the defense of those the orator called "the little people, the humble, the oppressed." The great-grandson of a deputy and physician who tended to Robespierre's wounds after he was shot by the gendarme Merda on 8 Thermidor, Paul Feuillette, also chancellor of the Rosati, delivered a moving eulogy to the Revolutionary leader, unjustly assigned the role of historical scapegoat.

Before six hundred to eight hundred persons in a packed municipal theatre, Georges Lefebvre delivered the keynote speech, in which he spoke less as a historian ("as such we have neither to praise nor to blame," thus distancing himself somewhat from Mathiez) than as a citizen and republican (in which capacity he energetically endorsed the core of the Mathiez thesis). A theorist of modern political democracy, Robespierre espoused universal suffrage and fought against barriers to the right to vote and to run for office. "An apostle of social democracy," he understood that without social rights the people could not exercise their political rights. He favored the attenuation of excessive inequalities, aiming at a utopian middling society of small proprietors. A "social right" guaranteeing existence to the people and authorizing the state to limit the property rights of others served as the rampart of democracy and the ethical basis of social life. In Lefebvre's view, Robespierre's real religion was the nation.

A Gaullist long before the term was coined, the Incorruptible was "the unshakable defender of national independence." But since he vibrated with the spiritual as well as the material needs of the people, Robespierre favored the practice of a religion with which they could identify and which would comfort them. Far from a mystic, however, Lefebvre's Robespierre was above all a pragmatic politician. "In a word, he's the man who knew how to take account of circumstances," and circumstances largely accounted for the Terror, in Lefebvre's analysis. To Mathiez's Bolshevik parallels and Labrousse's "anticipations," Lefebvre more prudently preferred a series of analogies to the constraints imposed on the governments during the First World War.

Created by sculptor Maurice Cladel, the bust was supposed to be placed in the gardens of the Palais du Vast between statues honoring a military prefect and a Rosati. On the strength of an expert's report, however, the Committee of Monuments decided that white marble could not survive in the harsh outdoor weather. It is not clear to what extent this decision was shaped by political considerations. The committee decided that Robespierre would reside in the reception hall of the Hôtel de Ville, which would be named in his honor. Perhaps because local leaders feared exposing themselves to further risks, the bust was "temporarily" placed in a less prestigious and less accessible room, where it was to remain for many years.

The Arrageois seemed to want to forget the episode and heal their wounds as rapidly as possible. A sign that the bitterness withered quickly was the fact that

Delansorne remained mayor until his death in 1937, despite the strident pledges made by the anti-Robespierrists in 1933 to unseat him rapidly and ritually as a punishment for his apostasy. After the war passions over Robespierre mattered less and less, as Arras underwent a demographic renewal and a pervasive modernization that blunted the collective consciousness of and interest in the past.[15]

The friends of Robespierre regarded 1933 as merely a first step. Indeed, the failure to accord the effigy of the Incorruptible the highly visible place of honor that had apparently been promised continued to distress them. They elaborated a series of projects for the bicentennial of Robespierre's birth in 1958, including a film scenario, dramatic texts for the theatre, an exposition for the Archives nationales, and a pedagogical brochure to be distributed in the schools. At the last minute, however, the Bidault government vetoed the commemoration for fear that it would provoke too much controversy. Socialist leader Guy Mollet, who was also mayor of Arras, supported the anniversary homage, but with restrained public enthusiasm. Rumor had it that Mollet kept a portrait of the "plague-stricken"—the Incorruptible's other sobriquet—in his Paris office at the party headquarters of the SFIO— the socialist party of the time—but not in his municipal office at Arras.[16]

For decades the Robespierrists, led by local history teachers, campaigned to have a lycée named for their hero. At the beginning of 1968, they obtained a provisional accord to name the boys' high school the Lycée Robespierre. They encountered resistance from the administrative hierarchy. "You are not going to bestow the name of a victim of the guillotine on a lycée located on the avenue des Fusillés [the Avenue of the Executed]!" complained the school's principal. As if it somehow mitigated the ignominy, the regional academy's inspector proposed the name Maximilien *de* Robespierre. The process was accelerated when the students, caught up in the Revolutionary élan of the moment, formed an action committee to demand the change during the demonstrations of May 1968. Although the ministry granted approval in 1969, the official inauguration of the rechristened high school never took place.[17]

On the eve of the bicentennial, the Robespierrist glass was half full and half empty. The vandalized and defiled plaque on Robespierre's house had been restored, but placed so high on the building, in order to shelter it from further insult, that no one could read it. The bust of the Incorruptible existed, but it remained concealed in the Salle du conseil des prudhommes in the city hall—or, as the local Association des amis de Robespierre pour le Bicentenaire de la Révolution (ARBR) put it more dramatically, "scellé dans une salle privée de l'Hôtel de Ville." The ARBR helped arrange for the casting of two copies of the Cladel sculpture. Pressed by his Communist deputy Marcel Roger, a leading member of the ARBR, the Socialist mayor Léon Fatous, the onetime assistant to Guy Mollet, agreed to preside over a ceremony to unveil and install the new busts.

As president of the Société des études robespierristes, Michel Vovelle traveled to Arras in June 1988 in support of the ARBR bicentennial campaign. In the municipal theatre where Lefebvre had passionately defended Robespierre in 1933, he gave an address called "Why we are *still* Robespierrists," evoking the title used by Mathiez in his talk at Arras in 1920. He celebrated the Incorruptible in terms that his predecessors would have warmly approved. Vovelle's Robespierre was above all the "defender of the people," especially the little people who were most exposed, and the social pariahs who suffered indignities that linked them to the purgatory of the people: slaves, Jews, actors, the disinherited, and so on. Vovelle resonated with Robespierre's denunciation not only of the fact of misery but of the authors who created and profited from that misery. A prophet of social democracy, Robespierre understood the primacy of education but realized that other equalizers were necessary to make its effects work.

The professor at the Sorbonne loved Robespierre for the very reasons that François Furet feared and disliked him: because he wanted "to construct a happy society." What for one led down the road to emancipation for the other leads down the road to totalitarianism. Like Lefebvre, Vovelle interpreted the Terror as "this necessity" that imperiously constrained Robespierre to act, for there was "nothing bloodthirsty" in his character or in his ideology. "Are we the last Robespierrists?" asked Vovelle in his conclusion, therapeutic/cathartic variations of which marked the finale of many of his bicentennial talks (Are we the last Marxists? the last Jacobins? the last social historians?). "Are we this last generation, the last batch of shameful Robespierrists, who still dare, but not without embarrassment, to affirm this quality of fidelity, and even more this quality of hope? I don't believe it for a moment, and it is precisely that hope which I find once again in assembly."[18]

The totemic Robespierre did not arouse molten passions in the Arras of 1989. Yet there were still voices hostile to any further gesture in his honor. "Even in the exercise of his liberal profession, he was not sympathetic," charged Michel Beyls, an accountant and rightist municipal councillor, "because it is said that his famous brief defending Franklin's lightning rod was plagiarized from a colleague." Miller Charles Gheerbrant, president of the chamber of commerce, whose father had sold the red paint that had cascaded down the streets in 1933, could not swallow the "abnormal ascetic aspect [of his personality], having no relation with women." He was the sort of political figure who "would have fired on the crowd in Tiananmen Square." Nor was *Nord matin*'s contribution toward rehabilitation very reassuring. "With the benefit of hindsight, those who were considered in their own time as bloodstained tyrants sometimes appear now as genuine statesmen," commented the paper. It grouped Robespierre in this category, along with Peter the Great and Oliver Cromwell. But it raised more doubts than it allayed by adding: "Will a Stalin be in this category in a century? Bets are open."

Optimistically Maître Fernand Bleitrach, the president of the ARBR, did not anticipate obstacles to the bicentennial inauguration of the monument. "A large public today shares the admiration of Jean Jaurès for the courageous democrat and patriot that Robespierre was," he observed. Risk-averse in the social-democratic tradition, however, Mayor Fatous opted for relative discretion given the persistently ambivalent climate of his constituency. "We thought that a public place in the heart of the city, near the most visited spots would be appropriate for the site of the bust," Bleitrach wrote the wary mayor. "The choice that you have made of the lycée courtyard leads our committee," the president of the ARBR continued, "to call to your attention that after forty-five years of waiting it is perhaps not suitable to present this bust to the public behind an iron gate." If we must have the lycée—an indirect opportunity to atone for the failure to inaugurate it—Bleitrach demanded at least that the mayor arrange for the monument to be placed in a vantage point that made it accessible both to the students in the school and to passersby on the avenue. In the militant rejectionist spirit of the 1930s, Gheerbrant urged Fatous "to have it insured adequately. There are many persons here ready to join in a commando attack."

The inaugural ceremony took place on 6 May 1990. A legion of ARBR, many Rosati, and a handful of distinguished guests such as Claude Mazauric joined a large part of the city council to pay homage to the Incorruptible in the courtyard of the Lycée Robespierre, where the bust was erected near the garden "well in sight." Observers were distressed that so few of the 150 guests were young people. Anxious to keep the event nonpolitical in tone, the notables were vexed that the only organized youth cadre unfurled a Young Communist banner proclaiming the (imminent) resurrection of their party. Even more laconic than his predecessors, Mayor Fatous acknowledged the implanting of the bust as yet another reparation that Arras owed its distinguished son. He pledged to attempt to place the second copy of the statue in Robespierre's house, which the city was negotiating to purchase as a municipal museum. Despite many auspicious signs, Maître Bleitrach wondered whether "the city of Arras is still ashamed of Robespierre, the key actor in the Revolution?" Speaking on behalf of the Société des études robespierristes, Mazauric expressed great satisfaction that the hopes of Mathiez were coming closer to full realization. In his characteristically robust fashion, the historian rehearsed the virtues of the politician of virtue and of progress, the defender of the people, the crusader for social justice who incarnated "the commoner essence of the Revolution.[19]

The ARBR

Founded in February 1987, the Amis de Robespierre pour le Bicentenaire de la Révolution vowed to "return Robespierre to the Artois and to the republic." Its president, Fernand Bleitrach, was a well-known local attorney. Its vice presidents included a deputy, Rémi Auchedé, an assistant to the mayor of Arras, Marcel Roger, and a director of the Rosati, J.-C. Vanfleteren. Christian Lescureux, a retired teacher, elected municipal official, and Communist militant, was the secretary. The ARBR positioned itself in ways that were not entirely coherent. On the one hand, it wanted to rescue its hero from ignorance and abuse, to "cleanse Robespierre of the calumnies." On the other hand, it articulated open-ended pedagogical and quasi-scholarly ambitions, not irrevocably entailed by ideological imperatives. "The ARBR does not wish to cast itself as the unconditional supporter of Robespierre; it introduces the debate and desires it to be as broad as possible."

The voice of zealotry, however, regularly superseded the cast of pious neutrality, in part as a function of the deep feelings of the leaders and in part because of the impact of the anti-Revolutionary mood of the national media. The least politically engaged members of the ARBR stressed Robespierre's place as an intellectual and political luminary of his region and town. While the Incorruptible loomed massively on the national landscape, these Robespierrists wanted to honor him first as a hometown boy made good, a legendary native figure; and they tended to focus on his achievements before 1789 and during the first few years of the Revolution. Given their localist perspective, one of the strictures they found most difficult to answer was Robespierre's apparent failure to discriminate in favor of his townsmen by modulating the ferocity of the Terror in Arras.

The dominant discourse of the ARBR energetically transcended this moral and political parochialism. Bleitrach assumed responsibility for Robespierre en bloc. Intellectually, he was the conscience of the Revolution; politically, he was the voice of the people. To the extent that the Revolution aspired to real democracy, it was Robespierrist. Lescureux added a sharp Vovello-Communist inflection to this blend of Rousseauian populism. He made it clear that the black legend was not merely—indeed not primarily—the fruit of ignorance. Rather, it was a politically orchestrated cabal that tarred Robespierre in order to defile certain contemporary/timeless political and moral options with which he was intimately coupled. Thus the Incorruptible's "generous ideas" were still "burning with contemporary relevance"; the work of the Revolution that he initiated "was not finished"; the Revolution was "still a hot object." For Lescureux bicentennial Robespierrism implied an unequivocal commitment to a certain brand of so-called progressive politics.

Yet the harder and softer lines coexisted more or less comfortably; and the ideologues did not underestimate the mobilizing capacity of the folkloric dimension. The ARBR recruitment included many persons who were not nostalgic for the barricades or acutely sensitive to the current political implications of the debate. By mid-1989 the association claimed between 420 and 450 members located in twenty-seven departments and several foreign countries. At least ten local committees throughout the region complemented the mother organization in Arras, and other associations based elsewhere in France affiliated with the ARBR in vaguely Jacobin style.

The central ARBR published a regular bulletin, rich in historical discussion, polemic, and a dense array of commemorative information concerning ongoing and future activities. Sister organizations put out their own variants. The thirty members of the association at Carvin, the home of much of the Robespierre family, issued *Ça ira! Gazette des sans-culottes de Carvin*. Another section of the ARBR

Bulletin du Comité Local d'Arras   novembre - décembre 1989

LA TERREUR DANS LA RÉGION :
Entre modération et excès

Comme promis dans notre bulletin de mai-juin 89, voici enfin une étude sérieuse sur les rapports de Robespierre et Lebon. Nous la devons à M. Arsene Duquesne, Membre du Comité Scientifique de l'ARBR, secrétaire du Comité Local de Meurchin et Directeur du journal "Le Ci-toyen" de cette même ville. L'intérêt de cet article suscitera, nous n'en doutons pas, réactions, commentaires et

LE BON, d'après une lithographie de Delpech (*Archives Nationales.*)

LA TERREUR DANS LA REGION	P.1
Joseph Lebon, l'homme du sursaut	p.2
Lebon choisit le patriotis-me exagéré	p.2
Robespierre fait mettre en li-berté les patriotes d'Arras arrêtés par Lebon	p.2
Les hésitations du Comité de Salut Public pour ap-précier l'activité de Jose-ph Lebon	p.2
Robespierre fait définiti-vement libérer les pa-triotes arrageois	
Menace de complot	p.3

The "Friends of Robespierre for the Bicentennial of the Revolution" (the ARBR) based in Arras fought "the black legend" that sullied the Incorruptible in a bimonthly publication which mixed historical evocations and commemorative news.

produced *Le Citoyen de Meurchin-en-Artois, journal des amis de Robespierre,* which traced Robespierre's career from his school days through the Revolution, and sold about one hundred copies of each issue, half to subscribers.

In addition to serving as a federal correspondence committee linking Arras and the rest of the world, the central ARBR proposed multiple ways in which to militate for Robespierre's rehabilitation and commemorate his achievements. It helped to coordinate a Robespierre lecture circuit throughout the country, the yeoman-voyagers of which included the novelist André Stil, a longtime member of the central committee of the PCF, and Claude Mazauric. It launched a national sub-scription for the construction of a monument to the Incorruptible to be erected in the Artois on 21 September 1992. It organized visits to Arras, and it dispatched its own members on excursions to Paris ("In Robespierre's tracks") to visit the school Robespierre attended, the house in which he lived, and other relevant sites under the beneficent direction of the sister Paris organization (Fr 190, restaurant included).

Keenly interested in promoting new scholarship, the ARBR helped to sponsor colloquia and seminar-style discussion meetings. To reach a larger audience, it arranged for dozens of showings of films such as Renoir's *Marseillaise* and Failevic's

1988, sometimes followed by debates. It mounted an exhibition called "Robespierre, the Unknown," which traveled around the region. It set up a library in Carvin that specialized in Robespierriana. To mobilize the living vestiges of the hero, and to generate beneficial publicity, the ARBR orchestrated a "Day of Reunion of the Cousins of Robespierre." One of the highlights in its bicentennial program was the "Robespierre Day," conjointly managed with the Société d'études robespierristes, which held an extraordinary assembly in Arras. On this day Vovelle delivered his torchbearing address, Vanfleteren put on his theatrical creation called *Les Robespierrots,* and the friends of the Incorruptible fraternally broke bread at a "republican banquet" held at the Lycée Robespierre.[20]

Given the motivation of the organizing nucleus, as well as the sharp focus and the hometown roots of the enterprise, the ARBR is more likely to survive the bicentennial than many of the commemorative organizations with earnest perennial wishes. The association hopes to increase substantially its cultural capital and ideological influence by developing closer ties with the schools in the region, adding to the stock of reading materials in the library at Carvin, working toward the foundation of a veritable museum in Robespierre's house, becoming a national resource for information concerning Robespierre, and making that information accessible to the general public. For the ARBR, the bicentennial commemoration will continue at least through the summer of 1994. It will organize lectures, debates, and exhibitions, and participate in colloquia such as the one planned for 1993 at the University of Lille III, whose organizers believe that Robespierre was insufficiently present in 1989 "owing in part to the desire to celebrate the Revolution in terms of its most consensual aspects" and because of the specious notion that "everything has [already] been said about him."[21]

Robespierrism beyond the Artois

A handful of other organizations toiled in defense of Robespierre's reputation and/or agenda. Marianne Becker, an astrophysicist from Oullins, fell under Robespierre's spell during a protracted illness. He has remained her steadfast companion, serving therapeutic as well as intellectual and aesthetic needs. Rapidly it became clear to her that History had maligned the Incorruptible, partly by ignoring his real story, partly by deforming it. "In order that the truth be reestablished in its entirety," Becker devoted years of research to her hero. She did not enhance her prospects of achieving credibility by choosing to present her findings in the genre she described as "romanticized biography [*biographie romancée*]."

Becker's grasp of the Robespierrist problematic was somewhat simplistic: "For goodness' sake, do not mix together Robespierre and the Terror," she pleaded. "They have only circumstances in common." She seemed more at ease with the Revolutionary's private life than with his public career. "I wanted to reveal it in his everyday life: he who loved milk, adored coffee, beautiful clothing, who was very

ÇA IRA !

GAZETTE DES SANS-CULOTTES DE CARVIN

Une publication des amis de Robespierre

UNE IDÉE NEUVE
EN EUROPE ...

1789-1794, les temps difficiles : il fallait vaincre la misère et l'ignorance, abattre les privilèges, rendre à chacun sa dignité, bâtir l'égalité, fonder la liberté.

"Comme les arbres dans la tempête", les gens vivaient au quotidien leur lutte dans les grands vents de l'histoire.

1789-1989, deux siècles plus tard, autour de nous aujourd'hui le vent siffle encore : la liberté, l'égalité, la fraternité sont à conquérir pleinement.

1789-1992, dans 3 ans donc, devrait être signé l'acte unique européen : la Révolution, comme le bonheur, reste une idée neuve en Europe, et qui est à construire. Robespierre l'a dit en 1792 : "le courage et la vérité peuvent seuls achever cette grande Révolution". Notre ÇA IRA ! se veut d'être une pierre dans un vaste édifice de courage et de vérité.

A tous et à toutes, citoyens et citoyennes de Carvin, d'Europe et d'ailleurs, salut et fraternité !

Carvin, duodi 12 Floréal de l'an 197 de la République

La République

Le Comité de Rédaction

JOURNAL DE L'A.R.B.R · n° 4 · Avril 1989

"Everything will be ok": this Revolutionary exhortation became the title of a bicentennial newsletter published by an association of "the friends of Robespierre" in Carvin, a town near Arras where many of the Incorruptible's relatives had lived. The paper was devoted to the rehabilitation of their hero and the celebration of his social and political objectives.

much surrounded by women, and who had only one mistress, whose identity he preferred to keep hidden." Rebuffed by countless publishers, Becker financed the publication of two volumes of her study at the cost of great personal sacrifice. Her conviction that she is heir to the injustices suffered by her protagonist has redoubled her determination to press forward.

In anticipation of the bicentennial, Becker founded around 1987 the "Association Maximilien Robespierre pour l'idéal démocratique," lodged juridically in Duplay's house on the rue Saint-Honoré where the Incorruptible lived the most turbulent moments of his Revolutionary life. Committed to the rehabilitation of Robespierre, the group planned to republish his works, to campaign for a revision of the school texts that presented him in a hostile light, and, more broadly, to reeducate the public in order to enable it to overcome its prejudices. Over a hundred sympathizers joined the association, whose vitality propelled Becker into the forefront of the national Robespierrist arena.

Several pilgrimages to Arras put her in touch with like-minded militants, who encouraged her to found "La Coordination des associations robespierristes," a clearinghouse and lobbying hub for the diverse efforts to advance the cause. Among other projects, the Coordination has embraced the struggle to have a street named for its champion. Becker continues to denounce imposture and falsification (for instance, the protrayal of Robespierre in two feature films supported by the Mission), she lectures at every opportunity, and she serves as unofficial curator of the Parisian itinerary of the Incorruptible, organizing visits by provincial militants.[22]

The writer Roger Caratini founded the "Association pour Robespierre," whose object was to celebrate the Incorruptible's memory within the context of a broader defense of the Revolution. "Resistance against revisionism" became its shibboleth. The organization included persons of diverse professional and political horizons, including lawyer Jacques Vergès, actress Charlotte Rampling (wife of bicentennial guillotiné Jean-Michel Jarre), singer Maxime Leforestier, physician and ephemeral minister Léon Schwartzenberg, and Georges Marchais. Another member, writer François Cavanna, explained that it was urgent to act collectively because "the bicentennial of the Revolution takes on more and more the air of a platform for counterrevolutionaries. . . . Reactionaries of all stripes succeeded in reducing the Revolution in the memory of the French people to a [single] sinister image: the guillotine. In the same way they imposed a simplified and fallacious image of a bloodthirsty Robespierre." The association called for the rechristening of the rue Saint-Honoré as the rue Robespierre, a gesture that would symbolically mark a profound change in the official management of Robespierre's memory. (Apparently the Paris city government had decided in 1946 to give the place du Marché-Saint-Honoré the name place Robespierre but retracted the rebaptism four years later.)

Caratini was also indignant that during the restoration of the cell that had housed Marie Antoinette in the Conciergerie, the architects, under the aegis of Jack Lang's ministry, literally destroyed the adjoining cell, in which Robespierre had spent several of his last hours. In the same gesture of official vandalism, the plaque placed in the Conciergerie in 1930 with the collaboration of the Société des études robespierristes, and renewed in 1983, was peremptorily removed. Citing Michel Vovelle, Caratini concluded that the destruction of this "symbolic site . . . cannot be innocent."[23]

Certain high-minded critics on the left wrongly dismissed Caratini's preoccupation with naming and marking as trivial, further proof of the vapidity of the bicentennial. Replete with symbolic significance, cognitively intrusive in everyday life, street and place signs were trophies worth fighting for—all the more so because the effort to obtain them was often so staunchly resisted. (One might locate the proof a contrario in the grandstanding efforts of Claude Pernes, president of the UDF in the heavily Communist Seine-Saint-Denis, to suppress the names of the scores of streets and squares in the department named for Marx, Lenin, and other Red heroes "at the moment when the peoples of the ex–Soviet Union sack the statues of their former official idols.")

Partisans of Robespierre throughout France used the commemoration as a lever to extract semiological concessions of this sort. Vowing to increase the ration in favor of the Incorruptible, the Association des amis de la Révolution française pour la célébration du Bicentenaire in the Allier discovered only two Robespierre streets in twenty-two communes surveyed, including the principal cities, as opposed to four Dantons, three Rouget de Lisles, three Diderots, and two Carnots. Friends of Robespierre in Dijon, Aix, Toulouse, and Limoges lobbied in vain for street consecrations. In the shadow of Versailles, in the Communist-run town of Les Clayes, the mayor planned to inaugurate an avenue Robespierre. The town of Romans took a step in the right direction by baptizing three streets in honor of the fervently Robespierrist historians Mathiez, Lefebvre, and Soboul. Alès, led by the Communist mayor Gilbert Millet, named a "Maison pour Tous" in honor of Robespierre and invited Michel Vovelle to help inaugurate it. (It was closed after the Communists lost control of the municipality in the March elections.)

The ARBR reported with consternation that prior to the bicentennial there were only nine Robespierre streets in the nine hundred communes of the Pas de Calais. Lens, Montigny, Billy, and Sallaumines were among the towns that rectified this lacuna. In the presence of Lionel Jospin, two other ministers, and Maître Bleitrach, Lens dedicated its high-tech Lycée Robespierre in 1990, whose library flaunted a bust of the Incorruptible, thus in part expiating for the shame that had swathed its counterpart at Arras for so many years. Bleitrach delivered a speech relating Robespierre's life at the christening of the school restaurant "Robespierre" in Sallaumines. Near its Nelson Mandela media library, the city of Grande-Synthe (Nord) dedicated a Galerie Robespierre.[24]

Robespierre's relatively dense presence on the dramatic stage reinforced the bicentennial drive for discussion and recognition. "In this year of the bicentennial, it is very important to hear on the stage Robespierre refuting the accusation of aspiring to a personal dictatorship," wrote the CGT's La Vie ouvrière, in reference to Romain Rolland's famous drama, on tour throughout France. Based on a book by J. P. Domecq, Un Robespierre de papier, presented by the Théâtre du Maquis of Aix, explored "by what chemistry of historical memory Robespierre has become today a globally monstrous figure, negative at best." Claude Vermoret, a Lyonnais writer and producer, sought support from the Ministry of Culture for a play called "Robespierre" with a view toward clarifying the story of "this very much calumnied statesman."

J.-C. Vanfleteren built his Les Robespierrots around the battle in Arras in 1933 over the famous statue. For lack of financial assistance from the municipality, ever a step behind the ardor of the Robespierre lobby, the angry playwright, leader of the Rosati, had to scale down his ambitions considerably. Another group at Arras commissioned Algerian author Kateb Yacine to write a play treating Robespierre and his persistent relevance. Moved especially by the Revolutionary who crusaded for the suppression of slavery, Yacine violated the unities of time and place to portray the Incorruptible in Indochina and Algeria as well as in the Revolution and alongside Toussaint-Louverture, leader of a black revolution against French colonialism. Several actors played Robespierre, this protean symbol of universal ideals, including a child who embodied him on the ninth of Thermidor, a turning point portrayed as a blow against youthful hope, not against stultifying tyranny. The immigrant workers in the play's final tableau represented the sansculottes of 1989 (in search of a Robespierre? Presumably Albert Mathiez's rather than Daniel Guérin's).

Robespierre was less present in other performance media. "The great absent protagonist in the television productions linked to the bicentennial," the Incorrupt-ible was nevertheless the object of a ninety-minute docudrama sponsored by the Sept, France's still very discreet cultural channel, and the Conseil général of the Pas de Calais. He attracted the director, Hervé Pernot, precisely because he was ex-cluded by the gluttonous consensus, because "today, more than ever, he troubles [us]." Despite a certain sympathy for the man, Pernot asked probing questions about his relationship with power, the corruption of his principles by his exercise of authority, and his inclination to apply political solutions to moral problems. In his film, the director alternated scenes of historical reconstitution and interviews with contemporary political figures, ranging from the royalist count of Paris to the Communist deputy André Lajoinie, asking them to comment on the issues embod-ied by Robespierre.

In a very different medium, in response to other concerns, choreographer Maurice Béjart made of Robespierre the "invisible guide" that his ballet *1789 et nous* had theretofore lacked. In Robespierre, Béjart discovered "a genius! Misun-derstood by the French, unrecognized by the whole world. All the things that I was saying, without knowing it, they were his ideas." The theme of Béjart's dance-spectacle became the timelessness and the immediate relevance of Robespierre's thought, which he apparently derived from the Incorruptible's printed speeches and the Jacobin biographies by Jean Massin and Henri Guillemin. Theatre of all sorts of drama, the Chancellory briefly became a bicentennial stage as the minister of justice, Pierre Arpaillange, organized a reading of Robespierre's speeches, in-cluding the oration against the death penalty.[25]

A Bicentennial Maelstrom: Thionville Attempts to Adopt Robespierre

It is not surprising that in a city with a Communist mayor, Senator Paul Souffrin, a highly respected physician, a branch of the Vive 89 network would thrive. Led by

Gaston Mertz, an erudite and eloquent real estate agent, "Vive 89–La Carmagnole" was born in the summer of 1987. Of the sixty who attended the organizing meeting, thirty became active, dues-paying members, joined by several dozen others in the following two years, "all of them on the left." The broad aim of the association was, following the line articulated by Claude Mazauric, "to assist in [acquiring] knowledge [and] thus understanding of the French Revolution, of its complex and contradictory process."

Mertz grafted onto this base a global-historical model of modernization, of which the Revolution was the fulcrum. Oversimplified and dependent on a Marxist exegesis that the specialists themselves have substantially nuanced, Mertz's Revolution marked a jarringly brusque discontinuity between the agricultural and industrial worlds, between the era of windmills and the era of steam mills. Mertz's materialism itself was less disturbing, though it was vulnerable to serious criticism, than his impatience to subsume a panoply of profound mutations directly under the Revolutionary banner. Out of tune with revisionist work within his own camp, Mertz portrayed an Old Regime economically dominated by "the rich *bourgeoisie industrieuse*," and a Revolution that profited largely if not exclusively this class.

Though in many ways quite learned, Mertz was not a historian, and it would be curmudgeonly to insist excessively on the flaws in his understanding. Still, it is revealing to note the historical culture that shaped and inspired his undertaking, that framed his enthusiasm and his goodwill, and that gave a gratuitously insular tone to his project. It undercut the force of his critique of the impoverishment of the teaching of history in the schools today and of the alleged alteration of the historical truth in the lessons children learned. It suggested that the "deep reality" of the Revolution to which he committed La Carmagnole was essentially telic and meta-historical: "combat those who distort the progressive and human meaning [of the Revolution] or exalt the retrograde forces which have taken up arms against it."[26]

La Carmagnole followed the pattern of most of the Vive 89 operations: lectures, debates, films, exhibitions, liaison with the schools, and so on. Rapidly, however, it became fixed on Robespierre, from whom it drew its mission, and its notoriety. It began modestly with a proposition to the city council, controlled by a coalition of Communists and Socialists, to rename two streets for the Convention and for Robespierre, and to rebaptize two schools in honor of Diderot and Rousseau. The opposition councillors were plainly hostile; the majority, which accorded La Carmagnole a subsidy of sixty thousand francs, was less troubled about the implications of rehabilitating the Incorruptible than about the idea "of giving to a preschool [*école maternelle*] the name of a father who abandons his children." Subsequently the association submitted a project to erect a bust of Robespierre on one of the city's major squares, which would be renamed for him. The left unanimously approved the idea, following its enthusiastic endorsement by Mayor Souffrin. Curiously, this time the right abstained. "Those who are against the project are the well-to-do of the city," contended the mayor. "I prefer a Robespierre Square to a Thiers Avenue honoring the butcher of the Commune."[27]

La Carmagnole announced the opening of a national subscription campaign, and a competition for the selection of the sculptor. A sectarian reflex impelled it to place advertisements uniquely in two Communist papers, the daily *L'Humanité* and the weekly *Révolution*. This marked the beginning of a stormy debate that jolted this rather tranquil town and brought it to the attention not only of French television and other national media but of the press of the entire world. *Time Magazine, Asahi Shimbun*, and British, Swedish, and American television journalists visited. Invited to lecture on Robespierre, Claude Mazauric was stupefied to encounter five hundred persons (other sources say three hundred) and to find himself engaged in "a fierce debate" until 2:00 A.M. A local judge assailed the historian for adulating the "first to perpetrate genocide." The controversy spilled over into such unlikely sites for ideological confrontation as the Rotary and Lions Clubs. Mertz worked the local scene relentlessly, giving talks in schools and cultural associations, organizing a projection of Pernot's documentary, and sponsoring Robespierrist drama.[28]

Local opponents of the Robespierre project protested increasingly vociferously even before they knew that the rest of the world was listening. "It's shameful!" declared rightist councillor Dr. André Lacroix. "Robespierre was a sort of Ayatollah Khomeini, a fanatical and narrow-minded person." Even in his hometown of Arras, added Lacroix, "nothing was done [in deference to him] except for a bust that was locked away in the cellar of the city hall." Thionville had already done its commemorative duty, in the councillor's view, for it had erected a statue at the entry to the town in honor of Merlin de Thionville, one of the men responsible for the Incorruptible's fall. "So, it's as if one were to erect a statue of Pétain directly opposite one of de Gaulle." Mertz might have been tempted to reverse the analogy, for he recalled Robespierre's suspicions that Merlin was sold to the Prussians; an "opportunist," Merlin was not worthy of Thionville.

The media helped to displace the center of opposition a few hundred meters from the Thionville city hall to the stately château of La Grange, situated in the adjacent commune of Manon. Its sixty-nine-year-old mayor, the chatelaine, was Sylvie de Selancy, née Berthier de Sauvigny. Her ancestor Berthier, intendant of Paris, and his father-in-law, a senior administrator named Foulon, both suspected of being implicated in the infamous famine plot, were brutally murdered in the days following the taking of the Bastille. Through a chain of reasoning that might charitably be called holistic, Madame de Selancy held Robespierre morally accountable for these "massacres." An "assassin" and a "sadist," he embodied the Revolution, and the Revolution slaughtered a welter of innocent people in its spasms of manic violence. To honor Robespierre was to "insult" the descendants of all the Revolution's martyrs. Beyond these deep objections, the mayor of Manon considered the monument project to be "idiotic and scandalous," for Robespierre had nothing whatever to do with Thionville.

Perhaps inspired by her feisty protests, an "Association pour la vérité historique" began to hound Mertz and other Robespierrists. As artisan of the Terror, Robespierre no more merited a statue than Amin-Dada or Khomeini deserved

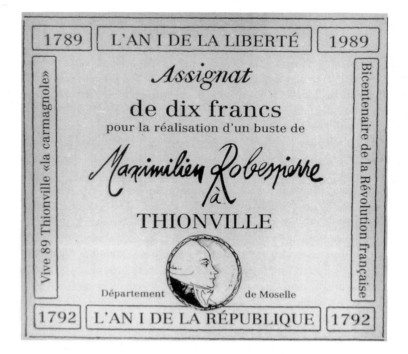

A reproduction of the Revolutionary paper money, the "assignat," inscribed with Robespierre's image, this commemorative currency advertised the fund-raising efforts of the Vive 89 association at Thionville in eastern France. It aimed to erect a statue of the Incorruptible. (Photo: Vive 89 Thionville.)

thoroughfares named for them. Since the French still pursued old Nazis, the association syllogized, there was no justification for absolving Robespierre. The leader of the Committee of Public Safety evinced violent feelings and feelings of violence. In Thionville, as in Arras, anti-Robespierrists promised to destroy any statue within twenty-four hours of its emplacement.[29]

Annette Scholtès, of the oven-fabricating family, denounced the Robespierrist fever in a letter to the regional newspaper and interviews with the national press. "Do you know that in Thionvillois patois, very close to the Luxembourgeois," she observed, "one calls a very little commendable person a 'roges pierre,' which became quite a while ago a 'robespierre'?" Solidly grounded, this distaste for Robespierre reflected revulsion for his pathological character: "this man was a slaughterer, a sick man." Madame Scholtès drew on the whole stock of Robespierrist demonology: he was effete, precious, and aristocratic in manner; he was hypocritical and opportunistic; "he wanted to add his version of the papacy to his dictatorship."[30]

In a letter to the *Républicain lorrain*, reader Bernadette Muller confided that "the guillotine gives me nightmares, nausea," and that it would be a "dishonor" to pay homage to the man whose "fanaticism" powered the killing machine. If he sensed that a monument to Robespierre might draw visitors to Thionville, R. Dreidmy, president of the tourist bureau, did not permit vulgar commercial concerns to supersede moral ones. He reminded the public that three nonjuring priests from Thionville perished at Rochefort in 1794. The bicentennial focus should be on these victims, not on their executioners. Dreidmy felt that Thionville had reason to be content with the crafty Merlin, whom he pictured as a moderate.[31]

Gaston Mertz led the chorus of rebuttal. The *Républican lorrain* refused to publish his text entitled "Violence in the Eighteenth Century" on the specious grounds that it had already treated the subject. The president of Vive 89-La Carmagnole rehearsed the standard arguments with intelligence and brio. The anti-Revolutionary offensive fed on self-serving selections and distortions of history. Otherwise it would be impossible to profess that "the terrorist storm broke out in a hitherto immaculate sky." Even as the Revolution exacted victims, so had the Old Regime, described as the "hideous face of suffering and death." But Mertz claimed that his point was not to attenuate responsibility by "the comparison of macabre scorekeeping" but to note that all history was rife with violence. "The Revolution did not break with this violence—which marks one of its limits," he readily conceded. In response to the brutal repression deployed by "the conservatives" to preserve the old order, "insurrection and terror were the means to which the people took recourse to construct a new social order."[32]

In Mertz's view, violence was a wholly secondary aspect of Robespierre's career. What distinguished him from the other Revolutionaries was his audacious and firm commitment to genuine democracy: "For me he remains the symbol of the struggle for social equality and human rights." It was the *social* banner flourished by the Incorruptible that still frightened his denigrators. If Robespierre had been "a good servant of the bourgeoisie—even of the Revolutionary bourgeoisie—he would be pardoned the deaths of the Terror, as one has done for Bonaparte and others." Following the bicentennial blueprint most closely associated with the PCF, Mertz linked Robespierre with the social and popular Revolution that the official com-memorators allegedly sought to snuff out.[33]

Letters to the *Républican lorrain* echoed many of Mertz's positions. Complaining that the rich hoarded the nation's honors, one reader contended that because the Incorruptible was close to the people and boldly raised "the great social question," he deserved recognition "despite the decapitations." If violence were the para-mount criterion, numerous streets in Thionville would have to be debaptized, suggested another correspondent, who pointed in particular to Napoléon and Foch. Several local citizens endorsed the thesis of circumstances: Robespierre turned to terror only in extremis to save the nascent republic. A history teacher hailed him for articulating a vision of social justice and for moving toward a democratization of society and of politics. Yet another writer praised him as an archetypal child of the Enlightenment who earnestly sought to realize "universal happiness."[34]

At the Lycée Hélène Boucher student opinion seemed squarely in the Incorruptible's corner. "He's the defender of the Revolution. It's true that he used extremist methods, but they were indispensable," proclaimed Vincent. For Pierre, Robespierre's bust at Thionville "honors the Revolution." Stéphane stood practically alone on the issue: "Robespierre, for the most part, an assassin!" Several *projets d'action éducative* in the Thionville school system dealt directly with the deputy from Arras. La Carmagnole provided teachers with documentation and lecturers. It was hard to argue with the idea that it was healthy to talk about the Revolution in the schools, especially after a professor of French asked the students in his class in *troisième* (first year of high school), "Who is Robespierre?" Half of the sixty-four respondents could not answer. Among the conjectures: a nineteenth-century writer, a royal counselor, a regional counselor, an author of encyclopedias. Among those who situated him more or less correctly, the lack of precision was often surprising: "a knight during the French Revolution" or "a man of the republic during the French Revolution."[35]

In the context of the public debate, with its media repercussions, the competition for the statue ran its course. Twenty artists submitted entries. A jury of twelve, chaired by the head of the Direction régionale des affaires culturelles (DRAC), unanimously rejected them all: "the competition is declared without a winner as a result of the insufficiency of artistic quality of the works proposed." Mertz apparently agreed that the deputy from Arras merited better, but declared that the decision was "badly digested by the rank and file of the association." For them—several dozen at most—the aesthetic criterion was "wholly secondary; what mattered was the political significance of the operation, even if the work chosen was intrinsically mediocre." Nor were the results of the fund-raising drive heartening: "the letters of encouragement are legion, the checks scarce." La Carmagnole received barely a tenth of the four hundred thousand francs required.

Demoralized, the association was divided in its attitude on the next step to take. Mertz, supported by the mayor, argued for soliciting state aid. A vocal minority feared that this would ensnare La Carmagnole and the project in "various manipulations." Non-Communist supporters seemed less and less avid to press the issue. Increasingly worried about the harshness of the polemic, a local Socialist leader, Robert Malgras, took what the Robespierrists could only consider a defeatist-citra (Dantonist) position: "I wish a general consensus on all the gains of the Revolution." The "old admirer of Robespierre," Mayor Souffrin, avowed that he could not remain indifferent to "resistance at all levels."

Through the DRAC, La Carmagnole submitted a request for a state grant for a scaled-down monument to be chosen from two projects presented by Colette Deblé, a French artist and the preferred candidate, and by Ana Richardson, an artist of double Argentine and French nationality, who had achieved considerable notoriety for a sculpture of Robespierre made of transparent material, designed by computer and cut by laser, that had been exposed at a bicentennial art show at the International Monetary Fund in Washington. ("The Incorruptible celebrated by the country that honors Lafayette!" enthused Mertz. "Now there is history treated with objectivity and not as a function of social affiliations and political opinions.")

The skeptics who had worried about foundering on the shoals of bicentennial problems must have derived some bitter satisfaction from the denouement of the affair. In May Dr. Souffrin wrote directly to Jack Lang to urge his support for a project that had elicited international attention and engaged the municipality to consecrate a "Robespierre Square" for the emplacement. According to Mertz, a representative of the Ministry of Culture, Catherine Bompuis, visited Thionville in June to announce that a large subsidy was forthcoming. But on 17 October, Dominique Bozo, a well-known figure in museum-curatorial circles and Lang's delegate for the plastic arts, expressed "artistic reservations" on the quality of the Deblé and Richardson entries. He was not against a public commission, he insisted, provided that his office was closely associated in the choice of the site and the artist. The head of the DRAC told a murkier story. Citing budgetary constraints as the basic reasons for rejection, he noted that the region had already superseded its share of public commissions for the year 1990–91. He added, however, that the ministry entertained grave reservations about the project and doubts about the site.

Gaston Mertz felt betrayed. He would have been happy to accept any artist of Bozo's choice: that was never an issue and indeed struck him as an ultimately shallow pretext. "The dominant feeling of the association," he concluded, "is that we had been duped by the state, which opted for a commemoration of consensus rather than of contradiction." As proof he referred to the admission of the DRAC that "in the current circumstances the public authorities preferred to celebrate what drew the French people together rather than what divided them." Mertz still hoped to realize a yet smaller version of the Deblé monument for September 1992, but the mayor no longer backed him in light of cumulative difficulties. The bicentennial left the hard-working president of La Carmagnole with a bitter taste. The official commemoration was "partisan," and the official portrait of Robespierre presented to the nation was a caricature: "in France the time of historical truth has not yet arrived."[36]

Farewell

No one imagined that it would be easy to commemorate the French Revolution. Even allowing for the attenuation of passions over time, it would have been unrealistic to think that the nation could celebrate with equanimity the greatest trauma in its history. The very act of resurrecting and paying homage to the event was sure to revivify, at least in the short run, feelings that had gradually lost their acuity and urgency over time. The Revolution carried such heavy tropological freight that it was bound to reopen or exacerbate painful wounds and old debates. All-purpose metonym, it seemed to stand, during those ritual moments when it resurged to public consciousness, for every disagreement that the French had ever had among themselves. Precisely because the Revolution had the unique capacity to epitomize all of French history in an irresistibly reductive way, and thus to renew itself opportunistically, it always administered a jolting blow of posttraumatic shock.

Save on the fringe, no one seriously imagined that it would be possible *not* to mark the two-hundredth anniversary in a more or less dramatic fashion. To deny the Revolution a central place in the French past required a truly perverse perspective. Even if one denied it any positive achievement, one could not overlook that a large segment of the French public *believed* that the Revolution accomplished much that was admirable, especially in its first year. Nor could one cavalierly dismiss the great esteem in which much of the world held the Revolution, regarding it as the source of the modern panoply of human rights. France's international image and prestige as well as its representation of itself hung in the bicentennial balance.

The debate of the 1980s turned for the most part not on whether there should be a commemoration but on the sort of commemoration that should be encouraged (or permitted). The very traumatic nature of the object of commemoration made it enticing to some and worrisome to others. For reasons that were not always symmetrical and rarely morally equivalent, elements on the left and right relished the prospect of replaying the Revolution as they saw it in order to right wrongs, settle scores, underline uncompleted business, ventilate critical ideas, proclaim/reaffirm putatively fundamental principles, and mobilize popular support. Because they regarded this infinite contentiousness as futile or exorbitantly costly, or because they wanted to build on common ground in order to forge a pragmatic and civically salutary consensus, other commentators preferred a more selective or muted approach to the bicentennial. In an arena midway between battleground and marketplace, a host of rival political, ideological, intellectual, and aesthetic interests scrambled to shape the bicentennial template.

There was nothing extravagant in the plans of the official commemorators, either during the boggy interlude of cohabitation or the triumphant phase of restoration socialism. They all betrayed a lucid sense of plausibility. Although they gave significantly different inflections to the mise-en-scène, they agreed on the scenario of the Revolution that the French wanted to remember and celebrate. "Remember" does not strike the right note, however, for it was much more a question of learning about the Revolution than recalling it. Broad-brush stereotypes guided the reckoning of individual citizens, but few knew enough history to fill in even the most basic details. For most of the French the Revolution had to be reinvented and re-implotted in a hospitable story-line, compatible with their current needs and expectations. All three Mission presidents understood that the commemoration would sustain interest and crystallize meaning only if it effected a dialogue between past and future, with a constant displacement in favor of the latter. The collective emotional deficit of the bicentennial probably resulted from their inability to calibrate this exchange optimally.

While intellectuals debated whether commemoration and history were compatible undertakings and what relation myth bore to each, the commemorators promised not to manage memory in a sectarian or partisan fashion. Jacobins and counter-revolutionaries complained that the state was unwilling to remember everything and thus was untrue to its moral trusteeship. Each contested the narrow commemorative focus, virtually confined to '89; each debunked the image of a clean (largely nonviolent and lyrical) '89; each demanded a spotlight on '93–'94, with very different ends in mind. Concerning the Vendée, whose memory had not been fully excavated, the right had a strong case. Yet it is clear that memory remains a profoundly political affair, despite the higher-order claims that the various plaintiffs invariably made.

The recent Touvier affair casts into stark relief the self-serving double standard that still marks the way in which certain French women and men deal with memory. A substantial part of the muscular right, which had been adamantly opposed to "truncated memory" during the bicentennial of the French Revolution, was delighted with the controversial decision of three Parisian magistrates not to indict the man who ran the Vichy militia in Lyon, charged with crimes against humanity for his role in torture and murder—that is, the decision not to unmask the workings of that other national revolution, not to permit France, as *Le Monde* put it, to "dig around in its past, at the risk of making disagreeable discoveries."[1] Thus, Alain Griotteray, a journalist and parliamentary deputy, fervently, and quite justifiably, supported Philippe de Villiers's refusal to "turn the page" on the Revolution's horrors. Yet he excoriated the critics of the Touvier judgment, hysterical haters who took pleasure in shaming France.

The Touvier judges, maintained Griotteray, evinced "a great independence of mind" because they resisted "a dominant historical school" (apparently exercising more of an "ideological hegemony" than had Vichy itself) whose paramount preoccupation was demonstrating French guilt. "To do this," wrote Griotteray, "Robert Paxton [an American historian, *encore un*] went about unearthing the Jewish Statute *that a healthy reflex for the preservation of national unity* had incited everyone to relegate to the depths of the collective memory."[2] Presumably it was not a healthy reflex that failed to denounce with sufficient vigor the Oradours of the Vendée. Too bad Paxton had not targeted the Revolution for his muckraking. The Vichy syndrome thus looms as the inverted expression of the Vendée syndrome.

In fact, the shift toward normalization and routinization that Griotteray wished for Vichy had begun to mark the view of the French Revolution well before the bicentennial. This nascent consensus was less the fruit of historiographical advances than the product of institutional changes and economic development that themselves both reflected and provoked a gradual tempering (some would contend modernization) of opinion. As more French women and men converged toward the center, their willingness to enter into quarrels over the Revolution diminished. The French by and large shared the widespread revulsion in the West for the violence and apparent futility of revolution and for its propensity to result in cruel despotism. If the French Revolution became increasingly suspect as the ideological progenitor and model of totalitarianism, arguably it also became more widely cherished, in its earliest moments, for having put an end to privilege and proclaimed individual freedom and equality before the law. These basic human rights constituted the symbolic and political nucleus around which consensus jelled. It was on these grounds, but on these grounds alone, that the Revolution could claim legitimate status as a founding instance and shed its chronically litigious nature.

While its proponents heralded consensus as proof (and further promise) of a growing maturity and stability, its critics denounced consensus as a sign of vacuity, indolence, timidity, abdication, gorged complacency, and so forth. (Sooner or later, consensus seems to bother everyone inclined to act in the public sphere: many of the commentators who had welcomed Revolutionary/bicentennial harmony now regard thickening consensus as a treacherous state of mind that seems to encourage apathy, withdrawal, the impoverishment of the public debate, and the attenuation of perceived ideological differences, thereby imperilling the vigorous interactions of party politics.) The most vitriolic assault against consensus emanated from the flanks of the left and right, uninhibited by responsibilities of or prospects for governance, intransigently invested in positions that morally and intellectually preclude compromise, and dependent for recognition and ultimately survival on their capacity to sharpen distinctions vis-à-vis the Other(s). For Jacobino-Marxists and anti-'89ers, the Revolution constituted the supreme test of true grit. Equally convinced, at antipodes from each other, that certain principles were timeless and immutable, they came closest to identifying themselves with their Revolutionary forbears, seeing themselves as "les mêmes." Even as they reviled consensus, they profited from it in their mobilization and pedagogy.

Players on the margins were not the only adversaries of consensus. Significant segments of the elites—teachers, clergy, intellectuals and cultural professionals of various sorts, higher civil servants, elements of the so-called political class—joined the resistance to consensus, some on grounds of strong positive conviction, others in order to promote a tonic and frank debate in place of an exorcism or obfuscation of the issues. Consensus was not a neutral, middling position. On the surface, the argument for consensus seemed to favor those who viewed the Revolution as at least partly commendable. In this light, the hostility of the counterrevolutionaries was perfectly coherent. Yet, many of the arguments for consensus were not based on Maurice Agulhon's fervent civic-republicanism, but derived instead from a deep suspicion of what the Revolution represented and a desire to strip it down and domesticate it once and for all. The lowest common denominator was meager consolation to those who believed that the Revolution had an incompressible central message. Product (in part) of years of incessant bickering, the emergent bicentennial consensus paradoxically (but not quite dialectically) generated a polymorphous movement to undermine it. These voices of critical diversity rescued the commemoration both from a stifling concord and a narrowly bipolar shouting match.

The bicentennial consensus-in-the-making seemed to be one of many signs that "the Revolution was over." This little phrase, at once trenchant and enigmatic, structured much of the bicentennial debate. Its rhetorical might resulted in large measure from the many ways in which it could be spun. Following the leanest definition, it connoted something like the true beginning of a scientific historiography of the Revolution and the true end of a turbulent, envenomed, unstable political-institutional system. It meant that the French Revolution was no longer a useful or reliable framework for understanding or practicing politics. The end of the Revolution announced and issued from an inversion: instead of reading the past into the present, the French would henceforth read the present into the past.

Of course there was the risk of succumbing to one's own febrile enthusiasm and pressing the case too far. Louis Pauwels best illustrated this genre of *dérapage*. "The French Revolution is finshed," he wrote. Ergo: "The left is dead." Following this logic, the right must also be dead, for it lived in symbiosis if not in synergy with the left; the one was no less nourished by the Revolution than the other. (More plausibly Pauwels might have contended: Socialism is dead. What will the future left look like?)[3] The problem was less that the right (via Pauwels) believed that the death of the left followed ineluctably from the end of the Revolution than that a substantial part of the left believed it. To be sure, many Socialists had tried to bail out, to distance themselves from the old guideposts. But the burial of the Revolution cast a pall even over these New Age apostates. The end of the Revolution seemed to threaten the very identity of the Jacobino-republicans; they fought to keep it alive in order to assure their own survival.[4] Yet this very *acharnement thérapeutique* probably sapped their capacity to adjust and renew. They would have been wise not to allow themselves be attached to the Revolution's life support system.

The "Revolution is over" fed on all the profound changes that preceded and followed the bicentennial. The new era was postrevolutionary, postideological, and posthistorical in addition to being postmodern. The international conjuncture, despite certain ambiguities, amplified the idea of the obsolescence as well as the stigma of Revolution. It was a cruel irony to watch the commemoration of a birth metamorphose into the commemoration of a death. If one accepted the claim that a world plebiscite was voting revolution more or less permanently out of existence, then the best possible gloss for the French seemed to be: thanks to our Revolution, we need no more revolutions. A slightly more portentous alternative might be: thanks to our deeply ambiguous experience and legacy of R/revolution, we have learned how (exorbitantly) perilous the revolutionary exercise is.

Distancing oneself from the Revolution was a luxury that not everyone could afford. With the best of intentions, Edgar Faure took it as an efficient way to address the needs and challenges of the future. But to many people, it seemed to say, in language not peculiar to punk nihilism: no future. For those who were left out, R/revolution was still the dream of last resort, the Land of Cockaigne and the way to get there, the rightful and righteous settling of scores, and the struggle for and the promise of social justice. This R/revolutionary vision, driven by a blend of romanticism, nostalgia, and rage, will find refuge in an abiding enclave of emotional extraterritoriality as France moves further away from the myths and practices that constituted its singularity.

With the end of R/revolution came the end of French exceptionalism (whether one construes it as a diffuse state of mind or as a specific historical trajectory). The French tended to take their singularity for granted, until they were told that they were dissipating it as they grew and ripened. The realization that they were joining the (now regnant) western mainstream relieved some and anguished others. The former took it as a reward for progress: purged of a poison, unburdened of an oppressive millstone, France would now be able to invest national energies in more productive directions. The latter bemoaned yet another blow against the integrity of the French self, a diminution of Frenchness. Ideologically and politically, with the triumph of the democratic idea over the revolutionary one, of liberty over equality, of private initiative over *volontarisme étatique*, France was no longer exceptional. Exceptionalism drew to a close in the economic domain as well, with the Socialists' recognition of the superiority of the market and their abjuration of the plan to abandon capitalism. Institutionally, with its supreme court, popularly elected presidency, and parliamentary stability, France was no longer exceptional. Internationally this evolution coincided with the end of the long Bolshevik interlude, the end of the Other Revolution, and the exceptionalism that linked 1793 and 1917 in the eyes of certain observers, both friendly and antagonistic.

Embroidering a distinction cast in language that was at once *rétro* and postmodern, many of those who clung most tenaciously to exceptionalism argued that it was "much more the Republic than democracy that founds French specificity."[5] Régis Debray provocatively articulated the argument for this quintessentially French psychological and practical bifurcation. Because his vision of the republican spirit seemed so intimately tied to the Revolution and its anniversary effusions, it stirred much less debate across the political spectrum than it might today in the fretful climate of Maastricht. Debray raised fundamental questions about many of the most cherished values associated with the putative national character, the role of the state and state-society relations, the limits of decentralization, the connections between the individual and the nation, the claims of religion and reason, the attributes of the marketplace and the power and prestige of money, the proper allocation of authority between the political sphere and the economic arena, the play between public and private, the influence of the media including show-business and publicity, and the place of multiculturalism and its institutional implications.

To be sure, Debray's binary categories evoked considerable caricature and hyperbole. One imagines the philosopher—not the social scientist, a creature of democracy—eating rillettes instead of hamburgers and drinking Sancerre instead of cola in old zinc bar rather than a fast-food emporium, which was located near a *mairie* or a school or an army post rather than a cathedral, a stock exchange, or a brothel; listening to 45s rather than CDs; reading (Michelet rather than Tocqueville) instead of watching television (if obliged to indulge in the latter, France2 rather than TF1); identifying himself with the state and the nation *une et indivisible* rather than with the ever-encroaching civil society; espousing patriotism rather than nationalism; praising institutions and execrating communications; practicing civism instead of moralism; and deferring to law in preference to contract. Yet Debray pointed to issues worth discussing, and he challenged an evolution whose consequences were surely not universally benign or ineluctable. What more appropriate time than the two hundredth anniversary of the birth of modern democracy to consider the ways in which democracy as it came to be understood and practiced undercut some of the principles with which it was initially linked in the pioneering days of the Republic? It made no difference that Debray's Republic, demystified and historicized, was much more democratic and less republican than he pretended. His questions were still heuristically valid, and the dilemma he posed merited discussion: "To oppose republic to democracy is to kill it. And to reduce republic to democracy, which carries within it the destruction of the commonweal, is also to kill it."[6]

For the Jacobino-republicans in particular, it was harrowing to mark a grandiose birthday party with a series of renunciations. "We are ashamed to be ourselves," grieved Régis Debray.[7] While his national republicanism propelled him in an increasingly Gaullist direction, culminating in a post-bicentennial encomium to the general, the Gaullists lay low. Traditionally exceptionalist to the core, more or less Jacobin on the rim, they had found that their rendez-vous with liberalism required major changes in the way in which they projected themselves. Once the bicentennial had past, it was no longer necessary to conceive of exceptionalism in terms of the Revolution. Under the prod of the treaty of Maastricht preparing the road for European union, Philippe Séguin, one of the leading figures in the RPR, echoed Debray's lament. In the breach, exceptionalism found a fleeting second chance in an unlikely alliance linking Jean-Pierre Chevènement, Philippe de Villiers, and Georges Marchais with the Séguins and the Debrays.[8] Albeit in many ways less radical than the accord of the late eighties setting up the single market, Maastricht emerged just at the right time to galvanize and symbolize an accumulation of postponed and displaced frustrations. Its critics regarded it as a blow against the sovereignty and thus the identity of France. Anxiety over identity had been rife in France for some time, though not all politicians and intellectuals were willing to admit it and attempt to deal with it. It had been Le Pen's signature issue, and it seemed tainted with various hues of xenophobia, racism, and retrograde populist-nationalism. In fact, the FN exploited the preoccupation with identity, but it did not invent or patent it.

There were numerous reasons for a diffuse but burgeoning inquietude about the nation's selfness (not all of which were peculiar to France, though they were refracted by French experience and memory). German unification, unexpected so soon, was emotionally fulfilling (the fall of the Berlin Wall seemed so much more *real* than the fall of the Bastille), but politically and economically alarming. The next stage in the evolution of the European community suddenly seemed more threatening because the internal balance had been rudely upset. With almost three million unemployed, almost a third of them long-term economic invalids, French society did not seem prepared to enter a world of harsher competition. Sectorial recession, high interest rates, and a tight job market caused despair among the young, the soon-to-be dismissed, and would-be entrepreneurs. The larger currents of globalization, some overweening and others quite subtle, further sapped confidence. France no longer seemed in control of its destiny, whether that signaled its environment, its culture, its companies, or its borders.

The immigration problem enhanced the growing sense of malaise. It mattered little that France had proportionately no more foreigners than it had had twenty years earlier: they appeared to be everywhere (Giscard's "invasion"), taking up precious resources (jobs, hospital beds, social allocations), while remaining indifferent or inimical to French customs and expectations (Chirac's "odors"). They wreaked havoc in the suburbs, swelled the ranks of *les classes dangereueses*, and demanded mosques in the shadow of cathedrals. The traditional antiracist nostrums no longer seemed to work vis-à-vis what the Commission national consultative des droits de l'homme styled "a mass xenophobia." In his vast field study the sociologist Michel Wieviorka described the deepening of a racism nourished both by social problems imputed to immigrants and "a feeling of a crisis of order, of institutions, and of national identity." Polls in 1991 and 1992 showed that over 40 percent of persons questioned admitted they were "rather" or "a little" racist. Antipathy to Arabs solidified: 70 percent of those surveyed believed "there are too many Arabs in France."[9]

A disenchantment with the nation's governors and its political class heightened this uneasiness. Instead of defining and defending national interests, they seemed more concerned with their own. Bitter internal squabbling raised questions about their capacity to lead. They appeared to devote more energy to the (illicit) financing of their parties (or their homes) than to the financing of economic growth. Scandals, convenient amnesties, and murky cover-ups amplified their discredit.

The commemorators could not have, in a magic stroke of the bicentennial wand, resolved the identity anxiety, stemmed the tide of increasingly virulent racism, or allayed the "new fears."[10] Yet they ought to have made an effort to address some of these questions directly in the context of their civic/pedagogic/historical discourse on the Revolution. They rarely talked about identity, as if it were a taboo subject. Yet they discussed legacy, patrimony, and tradition, all of which implied traits of identity. They insisted on the profound and lasting influence of the Revolution on every aspect of public and private life, a claim once again dealing obliquely with identity. Neither the commemorators nor the nation's leaders made the case lodging the core identity (moral, cultural, political) of their compatriots in 1789 (or 1789–92). They were of course right to stress the universal character of the human rights that the Revolution proclaimed. Yet with all the emphasis on their abstract, quasi-transcendental nature, they were not able to inculcate a sense that the failure to live up to the values of '89 amounted to a sort of *lèse*-Frenchness, an abnegation and betrayal of national identity. Similarly, the appeal to universal fraternity was too olympian and the call for justice for all, everywhere, too vague. The struggle against exclusion was not portrayed or perceived as a *requirement* rather than merely an ambition of citizenship.

It is not clear whether Monsieur Dupont (France's John Q. Public) saw the significance of nonexclusion in terms of his self-representation and self-interest. No wonder, given the ambiguity of the republican discourse on integration and its general uncertainty regarding identity. Until the chador affair, the right to be different seemed to be the standard line. This right, however, appeared utterly indifferent to identity, as if identity (unlike economic or social security) were fit to be worked out by the invisible hand in the marketplace of life. If integration were not the goal, then it must be in part for lack of a sufficiently compelling sense of identity, it might have been argued. Yet, to deny difference its claims was to do violence to individual liberty, the keystone in the bicentennial arch. Navigating among these shoals was a parlous task, but surely it was worth trying. As it turned out, given the hesitations and calculations, the "'*droit à la différence*,' preferred slogan of the antiracists of the seventies and eighties, was wholly turned around by the extreme right and put in the service of the thesis of the unassimilability of the foreigner, of the dread of crossbreeding, and the loss of identity."[11]

If the commemorators had trouble dealing with the identity question in the bicentennial context, it was not merely because of the Lepéniste specter. The Revolution itself did not offer an unequivocal set of cues. On the one hand, the Revolution seems to guarantee a primordial right to be different, at least at the individual level; on the other, the revolutionaries took measures of an authoritarian sort to quash differences judged prejudicial to the constitution of a single national community. If there is much in the Revolution that is threatening to the sense of bounded identity that many French people seek today, that part of the Revolution that insists on identity in narrower compass speaks in its least compassionate voice. One of the major failures of the Revolution, according to certain of its critics, was precisely its inability to incorporate a durable pluralism into its politics and its civic life. Forcing one to be French, like forcing one to be free, did not prove to be either a worthy or a workable strategy.

The Revolution did not seem to interest many of the targets of exclusion any more than it did those who yearned most for stark and easy answers to the identity question. Renaud's quasi-improvised anti-summit was one of the few mobilizations of the crazyquilt of *exclus*. The Revolution seemed to have almost no resonance among the *beurs*, and their organizations did little to kindle it through education. After its early summer concert, Harlem Désir's SOS-Racisme appeared to lose interest in the bicentennial scene. Arezki Dahmani, president of the rival France-Plus, whose desk faced a framed copy of the Declaration of the Rights of Man, acknowledged that "we missed a great opportunity" in 1989. He regretted his organization's failure to launch a major debate on the notion of citizenship, rights, and duties. Staunch critic of an untrammeled *droit à la différence* and its multicultural logic, which he believed led to the American ghetto of permanent exclusion, Dahmani favored an integration (economic as well as social, cultural, and political) based not on a "wild liberalism" that had already generated so much "tragedy," but on an ethos and practice of "new solidarities." It is too bad that Désir and Dahmani did not publicly debate their very different concepts of republicanism at a time when people's minds were focused on kindred matters. The grand plans of Mohsen Dridi's Conseil des associations d'immigrés en France for a bicentennial celebration organized around the theme of "Spaces for a new citizenship" and featuring François Mitterrand sputtered. Important colloquia such as the one at Amiens cosponsored by a university research center and the Groupement pour les droits des minorités remained virtually confidential happenings. Devoted to the Declaration and the minorities, this meeting asked critical questions about the attitude of the Declaration concerning differences, its assimilationist thrust, and the relation between the national and particular communities.[12]

The state's inability to solve the identity and immigration problems figured among the many reasons for its growing disrepute. In the wake of the commemoration, the political commentator Alain Duhamel detected "a contagious public disease that threatens the entire social body." Despite the bicentennial effort to resurrect civism and awaken citizens to assume their responsibilities, the far right continued its advance, "skepticism gained ground," public affairs turned people off, and anxiety found expression in irrationality as well as intolerance. The image of the political class had been sullied, the usual norms of vilainy surpassed. Citizens weren't voting, and they were rejecting card-carrying participation in the parties.

Institutionally, the governors reinforced the inclination of the citizenry to play a passive role by foreclosing direct access to the Conseil constitutionnel and recourse to an enlarged field for referenda. Meanwhile the parliament, while it maladroitly barred the route to greater popular democracy (in the best Revolutionary tradition), failed to defend its place and influence in the institutional balance, further accentuating what Duhamel called the "democratic deficit." A sterile political imagination and an ideological desert aggravated the illness by depriving the society of an exhilarating ideal and a collective objective (the famous *grand dessein*), thereby sapping its cohesion.[13]

In retrospect, the post-bicentennial summons to "rehabilitate politics" (the phrase belongs in this instance to Gérard Le Gall, electoral strategist of the PS) strikes a number of ironical chords.[14] First, one of the major themes that ran from Revolutionary historiographical revisionism to liberal political commentary was that the faith in the "omnipotence of politics" led ineluctably to disaster. The remedy for Revolutionary "overinvestment" in political voluntarism was clearly a disinvestment, a recognition that the major responsibility for (healthy) change had to reside in society itself rather than the state. If the bicentennial legitimately celebrated the founding of the modern institutions of governance, Napoleon's famous "blocks of granite," it was hard pressed to celebrate the state, whose despotic potential seemed undeniable. The revisionist assault on the hubris of the political resonated well with the debate that the liberals of the 1980s organized on "how much state?" and with the widespread sense that the state was not capable of dealing with the problems that worried the people (who wanted, as always, to pay less for more).

In counterpoint to this bicentennial critique of politics was the commemorative call to the citizenry to reenact symbolically the decisive role played by the People in the crafting of their own Revolution. Wistful for a return to the world of republican virtue (and discipline), countless commentators deplored the alienation and/or apathy of the public, its self-absorption, its spectator's role. Whereas liberal thinkers obliquely warned the People that the political arena was not the proper place for them to take their destiny in their hands, Jacobins exhorted them to extreme vigilance on the grounds that the great achievements [*acquis*] were never irretrievably achieved. Yet this was not a compelling mobilizing theme. The bulk of the public took their great achievements for granted, didn't believe they were menaced, and in any case relied on their institutions to protect them. Mitterrand's deeply felt Vichy scenario-specter had small effect.[15] What mattered more and more in the new international configuration was the economy, and the economy seemed more clearly than ever to be a post-revolutionary matter, beyond the competence of the state or the political process.

The triumph of liberty over equality, celebrated throughout the world and in the revisionist historiography of the Revolution, underlined the limits of the state and the peril of venturing to treat social problems through political means. To privilege equality, the liberals argued, was to risk tyranny. The only certain basis for human moral, social, and economic efflorescence was liberty, that is, a circumscription of the intrusive power of the state and a widening of the sway of the market as *idée-force* as well as institution. The liberals twitched with *schadenfreude* as they watched the Jacobins strain to account for the Terror's egalitarian brutality. The predicament posed by the horrendous Bolshevik experiment, portrayed as a remake of the original French script (1917 = 1793), heightened their pleasure. In this climate, it was impossible even for the most zealous (or the most reasonable) commemorators to prepare the (cyclical) revenge of equality upon liberty. The best that could be done was to argue that liberty, properly understood, implied equality or could not survive without a certain unspecified dose of equality. It was easy to forget the long history of state correctives—now lazily thought of as entitlements—to the perverse effects of unfettered liberty in social practice.

Liberty and equality, the left contended overtly; liberty or equality, the right intimated obliquely. But the major political parties, with the exception of the PCF and the FN, did not invest heavily in the bicentennial, though each used arguments shaped by a view of the Revolution and its legacy to favor its position. The PS and the mainstream right seemed torn between a conviction that it was time to look resolutely to the future (the Revolution no longer furnishing a plausible idiom or framework for politics) and a reflexive nostalgia for the old cleavages, reassuringly manichean and *ringard*, which obviated the need for searching self-analysis.

Potentially the PS had a great deal to gain from the bicentennial. But it was in too much institutional, ideological, and personal disarray to seize the opportunity: deeply divided into "currents" whose legitimacy the public did not fathom; increasingly mired in a sort of Dantonism that corroded its moral capital; searching for its fin-de-siècle soul and vocation. ("We have become a party of Mickey Mouses!" J.-P. Chevènement later wailed in his nationalist-republican-elitist manner.)[16] Mitterrand managed his bicentennial much better than did his fellow Socialists, though the president, in his sensitivity and moderation, never forgot that he was still the leader of a party that had passionate ties with the R/revolutionary heritage. His very real success on the commemorative stage compensated in part for his party's languor.

Arguably the church played the bicentennial as skillfully as the president. It had virtually as many "currents" to manage and assuage as had the PS. Historically, it had been as heavily engaged against the Revolution as the left had been in its favor. First the stabilization of republican institutions and later the conciliar movement spurred the church to soften considerably its adamantine opposition to the Revolution. It made several adroit decisions regarding the bicentennial: that it would cultivate a low profile; that it would not allow itself to be drawn into the debate in a defensive posture as if it had something to account or apologize for; that it would not take any provocative action that might revive the old confrontational roles.

In retrospect, and somewhat anachronistically, one could characterize the church's bicentennial attitude as "ni Grégoire ni Touvier." Committed to humanitarian ideals and a pluralistic society, the church was not interested in identifying itself with the forces of reaction. Yet it was not prepared for a reconciliation that blurred what it considered fundamental distinctions of principle (and that might alienate significant segments of its flock). The conjuncture seemed favorable to the church: there were signs worldwide of a rise in demand for transcendental points of reference and values rooted in spirituality. In the French context, traditional laicity was foundering on what it acknowledged as its own rigidities and archaisms.[17] By avoiding a bicentennial blowup, the church was positioning itself for the negotiation of a new deal in the public sphere of the spirit.

Despite the (official) church's circumspection, the Counterrevolution enjoyed an impressive rhetorical resurgence. In the middle or long term, it had few prospects. In the heat of the bicentennial, a motley array of voices briefly coalesced, but for the most part they had quite different agendas. In the short run, however, they articulated a powerful and passionate critique of the Revolution that flooded the media, dampened enthusiasm for and spread doubt about the Revolution beyond the confines of the traditionally anti-Revolutionary universe, and disconcerted the left.

If the counterrevolutionaries failed to obtain a retrial not just of the king, but of the whole Revolution, they nevertheless struck a telling blow in linking the Revolution in artful ways with the totalitarian horrors of modernity. If they failed in tarring the bicentennial-governing left as the party of Revolution (i.e., of moral decadence, economic decline, renunciation of identity, and despotic inclination), they succeeded in reinforcing that left's growing diffidence about its own symbolical past. If the Vendée failed to reduce the Revolution to an endless series of massacres culminating in a genocide, it managed to gain considerable sympathy as a (more or less compartmentalized) case of injustice and excess, of the Revolution run amok.

Although it could never attain the coherence of the church, the intelligentsia plays a quasi-institutional role in French life. Given its far more fragmented nature, generalizations concerning its role in the bicentennial are even more difficult to sustain. More so in France than in many other countries, the intelligentsia covers a sprawling socioprofessional space, including practitioners of the liberal professions, journalists and other media persons, creative and performing artists, teachers of all sorts, scholars, writers, and more. Probably only a small percentage actively participated in the bicentennial. Many intellectuals sat it out for reasons that were not always compelling: "I have no time"; "it's not my field"; "it's meretricious and/or superficial (show-biz, *toc,* etc.)"; "it's political manipulation"; "it's not a significant or worthy event."

Even more than politicians, the intellectuals who participated in the commemoration seemed riveted to the traditional template of right-left cleavage, reified and sanctified by the Revolution. Each side operated on the assumption that the other controlled the levers of cultural power. The right complained that the schools and universities were red (or blue/red), while the left contended that the right controlled the media, both print and electronic, which exercised the greatest hold on the massive yet elusive public-at-large.

Intellectuals on the right took the offensive early and vociferously, joined by many neocon *transfuges* from the left making the liberal pilgrimage-adjustment. The left, benumbed by a midterm stupor, was slow to respond and riven with divisions. Intellectuals on the right and center had an easier task than their counterparts on the left: save for a relatively small number of anathematists who reviled the Revolution indiscrimately, they could select parts to espouse and parts to assail, and project an image of critical spirit, sobriety, and wisdom. There was great pressure on intellectuals of the left to defend everything, more or less fiercely, or at least not to attack anything too sharply.

One of the salient traits of the intellectual community as it entered the bicentennial period remained the strong (albeit often furtive) residue of Communist influence. That influence must not be construed in narrowly institutional terms. Far more crucial intellectually than the desperate efforts of the PCF to survive or regroup was the lingering impact of the Communist experience on ex-Communists who lived it directly and on other intellectuals who lived it vicariously or suffered it resentfully. The debates occasioned by the commemoration revealed how deeply the protracted Communist moment (and more broadly its Marxist sequellae) shaped feeling as well as thinking. It would be simplistic to reduce those debates to a mere settling of Communist scores. Yet it is clear that much of the discussion, ostensibly about the Revolution, really concerned the gods that failed the twentieth century, not the gods athirst in the eighteenth.

Often displaced or partially repressed, the tensions generated by the Communist connection obstruct our clarity of vision. The intellectuals marked in one way or another by their involvement with the party have to come clean, with themselves and with each other. The experience of exit from (but also entry into) the PCF needs to be critically examined both by the actors (who must gaze more deeply) and by scholars (who must take stock of their own subject positions). The transferential aspects in the discourse on the Revolution of certain former Communists must be assessed. The Communist roots of (neo)liberal revanchism have to be scrutinized. The Leninist complex that continues to haunt the (largely non-Communist) left needs to be unmasked.

Theoretically, the intellectuals bespoke at least some of the concerns that affected ordinary citizens. In any case, intellectuals, like politicians and clerics, took extraordinary license in claiming to speak for the People. It became a widely held bicentennial conceit, most prominently on the far right and left, but present throughout the landscape, to conflate Revolution and People, and to talk of each in terms redolent of Michelet (and sometimes of Carlyle). It was hardly a new experience for the people to find themselves peremptorily amalgamated into a unitary lyrical category and appropriated for myriad purposes by various groups claiming stewardship of the mystical *vox populi*. This canonical manipulation took on a particularly machiavellian air, however, on the occasion of the anniversary of the People's violent assertion of their unmediated sovereignty.

Two (more or less equally exploitable and romantic) views concerning the role of the People in the bicentennial competed for attention. The first, associated with the official commemoration, portrayed the bicentennial as a quintessential popular festival—if not from beginning to end then at least at the high points. The Gouderie, despite its manifold ambiguities in representation and reception, was invoked as incontrovertible proof of this proposition. The second, associated with critics on both left and right, depicted the bicentennial as the ritual exclusion of the People, not a potentially glorious re-*embastillement*, but an ignominious sequestration. Precisely to dissuade them from taking charge of their fate, this line of reasoning went, the people were reduced to the secondary status of passive citizens. Once again, the Gouderie was invoked as incontrovertible proof of this proposition.

Despite our technological advantage, we in the twentieth century are not much more reliable in talking about the People with a capital P (probably because the People has a mythopeoic existence) than were the Michelets and the Voltaires. There is no doubt that significant segments of the people—in the Seine-Saint-Denis, at Lugny, at Lille, but not in the Vendée—actively and heartily participated in the celebration/commemoration. Yet, the polls to the contrary notwithstanding, it is really not clear to what extent the Revolution and its anniversary ramifications penetrated into the popular culture.

What did the people make of the cues broadcast by the intellectuals? Were there sufficient cues broadcast? Neither television nor cinema inundated the land with Revolutionary stories and histories; the Ministry of National Education was extremely cautious in the message it disseminated; the state's commemorators rarely found a direct channel to the citizens who qualified as People. Apart from those who had every ancestral reason to detest the Revolution, for many the Revolution remained remote, even forbidding—as far from the scenario of People-as-King as one can imagine. For others, who sported a Phrygian bonnet, it is hard to say what part was Festival of the Federation and what part Foire du Trône.

Like the citizens who lived the bicentennial, the scholars who study it are unlikely to take it en bloc. Some parts of the commemoration simply worked better than others. It is important to remember that the bicentennial and the Mission were not coterminous phenomena. Much of the bicentennial was far beyond the reach of the central coordinating office. Save for a handful of evanescent moments, the bicentennial was a profoundly local affair, undertaken without assistance or instructions from above. Ordinary citizens are likely to retain a durable memory of the bicentennial to the extent that it impinged directly on their daily lives, not through the intermediary of Léon Zitrone or Frédéric Mitterrand (or even François Mitterrand). The stories of these adventures have just begun to surface. It is too bad that every local group did not have the means to produce its own narrative (in the manner, say, of the brigands of the Maconnais) and thus immortalize its achievement, however modest.

Most attention is likely to concentrate on the operation of the Mission. There are at least two traps to avoid in appraising its work, very different in character but symmetrically seductive. The first is to slide into the Mission's own reductive idiom for taking its measure, which amounts to rehearsing degrees of "success," usually calculated with crude quantitative indexes of press approbation, audience in attendance, and electronic diaspora. Of course it was the business of the Mission to represent itself in this fashion; indeed, it might very well have foundered had it not combatted vigorously for the consecration of these successes. It is not the business of the historian, however, to take its press releases as his or her categories of analysis.

The other quasi-irresistible trap is to find fault with everything the Mission did. Nothing is easier than to compile an inventory of putative errors, missed opportunities, losses of nerve, and moral and ideological infirmities. To the extent that these flaws can be documented, they deserve to be discussed. But the point is to understand, not to scapegoat and discredit. Understanding entails a willingness to take stock of the serious difficulties and real possibilities that hedged the Mission's actions.

It may not be an entirely futile exercise to imagine how the bicentennial might have been, given other circumstances. (The members of the Mission were constantly second-guessing themselves and fantasizing "what-ifs.") Would a world's fair have constituted a more compelling symbol and crystallized a more imaginative, varied, and stimulating commemoration? Or would it have provoked a further displacement and semi-obfuscation of the Revolution's heritage? (How many people today identify the Eiffel tower with the Revolution's centennial?) With his tentacular connections, would Michel Baroin have succeeded in eliciting a greater effort from so-called civil society? With his gift for bridge-building and compromising, would Edgar Faure have transformed festive consensus into a permanent cultural and political capital paying regular dividends in the future?

Certainly it would have been a different bicentennial had there been more time and continuity in preparation. More players—sponsors, project makers, and simple doers—would have become involved. A far greater degree of integration of information and effort could have linked like-minded imaginations and organizations that operated in relative isolation, and spurred a fruitful spirit of emulation and competition as well as collaboration. Ideas could have been tested and refined. A better balance between the ephemeral and the durable might have been attained. The Mission would have been in a position to elaborate a sort of metanarrative, investing the festive calendar with a considerable degree of coherence. Fragmented, uneven, and lacking a unifying inspiration, the great moments produced, or elicited, no sustaining emotion, no binding sacrality, no cumulative sense of exaltation. The commemoration suffered from a permanent incongruity between Jean-Noël Jeanneney's pugnacious discourse and the motley character of the major events that were only nebulously related to it. There were too few national arenas for his *versant lumineux* and insufficient opportunity to play out the "living message" of the Revolution in unvarnished language.

It would be naive, or disingenuous, to think that more money would not have made a significant difference. Jeanneney's operation was pitifully understaffed and underequipped. Despite the tensions and problems that plagued the Mission, most of the members performed remarkably well under enormous pressure. With more help and more favorable working conditions, the Mission would have been more efficient, more exacting, and more enterprising. More money would have increased the number and enhanced the quality of projects, salvaged excellent ideas that languished for want of resources, and permitted whole new vistas of activity. It would have been extremely fruitful, for instance, to distribute a very large amount of seed money in small doses to thousands of grassroots undertakings.

More time and resources would have permitted the Mission to explain its mission more cogently to the women and men of France. Despite its more or less prodigious efforts, the public remained undereducated both about the history (the Revolution) and the commemoration (its opportunities, means, and objectives). There was an insufficient understanding of the ambitions and practices of the commemorators, which rendered the Mission vulnerable to misinformation and distortion as well as legitimate criticism in the media. It found itself on the defensive, which is not a good pedagogical or mobilizing posture. The Mission's failure to define itself compellingly issued in part from its internal flux. But had it deployed a dexterous communications strategy from the beginning, it could have attenuated the impact of its own disarray.

Manifestly Jeanneney did not succeed in getting the French to "live better together." They forgot the lessons of the bicentennial with stunning celerity.[18] That does not mean that Jeanneney was a bad teacher. On the contrary, he articulated those lessons with intelligence and brio. They carried conviction and passion, and they addressed issues in whose importance everyone instinctively concurred. But they were too general and too abstractly pious. They took too little concrete account of the psychological and material situation of the citizenry. They were too far estranged from everyday life despite their claims to matter urgently. The commemorators were right to aim high, but it was beyond their capacity not only to reach the bulk of the public (which they surely failed to do), but also to change the general way of thinking and behaving (which the appeal to the Revolution could hardly bring about).

There are very few things that Jeanneney could have done differently that might have made a serious difference in this domain where politicians, clergymen, and moralists have been failing for years (nay: for generations). Yet it may be that, paradoxically, the commemorators could have made their case for the present-future more tellingly had they made their case about the past more strikingly. Given the relatively little interest that historians themselves evinced for the Revolution-in-history (as opposed to the Revolution-as-instrument/emblem/alibi), it is perhaps curmudgeonly to reproach the commemorators (sometimes themselves historians) for failing to play the historical card. The conventional wisdom was that history would turn the people off, especially the young people (thus reinforcing their lack of historical literacy that the same conventional wisdom deplored).

Fulsomely historical events, especially reconstitutions, could not be popular, according to prevailing definitions and apprehensions. Apparently history was intractably dull (an implausibly defeatist presumption in a nation renown for its effervescent historical imagination), frustratingly complex, and potentially perilous (since it might sow doubt or discord were it fully aired). Instead of inviting, and then enabling, their fellow citizens to become intimately familiar with the Revolution, to make the imaginative leap, to develop a real feel for the world of the late eighteenth century and an empathetic identification with their forbears, the commemorators (save at the local level) furthered the tendency toward a moralizing, totemizing, folklorizing, and thus disfigured view, epitomized in stock phrases and simplistic images. Elaborated with the best of intentions, this strategy bespoke an unavowed paternalism and condescension that bore an Old Regime cast. Given the bent in the direction of a constant displacement toward the present and future, and the prudential inclination for a highly metaphorical (and thus modern) language rather than the historical idiom, Goude was the preferred choice for the climactic moment, and he acquitted himself whimsically and masterfully.

Notes

Book I / Chapter 1
Commemoration: Aporias, Dilemmas, and Opportunities

1. *Les Nouvelles calédoniennes*, 3 July 1989.

2. C. Manceron in *Le Monde*, 8 October 1986; A.-G. Slama in *Le Figaro*, 17 December 1984. The bicentennial, journalist Philippe Boucher later noted, "donne plutôt l'image d'une mise en accusation que d'une commémoration." *Le Monde*, 24 June 1989. Cf. *Le Canard enchaîné*, 12 July 1989: "Le Bicentenaire a ses Chouans, ses Feuillants, ses Jacobins, ses Indulgents, ses Enragés, comme autrefois, ce qui entretient la polémique. Heureusement, il n'y a pas la guillotine, ce qui épargne bien des têtes." Note also sociologist Alain Touraine's half-facetious, half-sincere one-liner: "J'ai participé à l'effort collectif pour ne pas commémorer la Révolution française." Film interview by Serge Moati, *Journal autour du 14 juillet*. For a suggestive piece on the ambiguities of memory, see Christian Ruby, "Commémorer la Révolution," *Regards sur l'actualité*, no. 155 (November 1989): 43–55.

3. Gérard Namer, *La Commémoration en France de 1945 à nos jours* (Paris: L'Harmattan, 1987), 143–44, 159–60; Namer, *Mémoire et société* (Paris: Meridiens-Klincksieck, 1987), 192–93, 238–39; M. Ozouf, "Célébrer, savoir, fêter," *Le Débat*, no. 57 (November-December 1989): 21; Ozouf, "Les Artifices de la fête," *Armées d'aujourd'hui*, March 1989, 159. On the gradual desacralization of the notion of commemoration, see Charles-O. Carbonell, "Commémoration, commémorer . . . Histoire de mots," in *Etudes du temps présent: Quel Avenir pour notre passé?*, ed. Y.-M. Le Bozec et al. (Office de Cliométrie Appliquée, 1990), 11–14. Maurice Agulhon considered Ozouf's "purisme" unrealistic and unobtainable. It was impossible, he maintained, to separate the historian-in-her-time from her historical gaze. Ultimately, he feared, the logic of Ozouf's position would make the teaching of history impossible. Interview with Agulhon, 11 April 1991.

4. M. Ozouf, *La Fête révolutionnaire* (Paris: Gallimard, 1976), 202; Ozouf, "Célébrer, savoir, fêter," *Le Débat* no. 57 (November-December 1989): 19; *Le Monde*, 24 November 1989; J.-D. Bredin filmed interview, S. Moati, *Autour du 14 juillet*; E. Borne, *La Croix*, 17–18

July 1989; P. de Villiers, *Le Nouvel Observateur,* 4–10 May 1989; F. Brigneau, *Le Choc du mois,* no. 10 (September 1988).

5. C. Manceron, *Le Monde,* 8 October 1986; J.-B. Morvan, *Aspects de la France,* 24 March 1988.

6. J.-M. Varaut, "La Déclaration des droits de l'homme et du citoyen de 1789: Généalogie, esprit et contradictions," *Libéralia,* no. 4 (winter 1989): 10; M. Rebérioux, "Un Processus qui s'étend sur deux siècles," *Revue politique et parlementaire,* July-August 1987, 12; M. Ozouf, "Célébrer, savoir, fêter," *Le Débat,* no. 57 (November-December 1989): 21; P. Garcia, "La Révolution momifiée," *EspacesTemps,* nos. 38–39 (1988): 4; P.-A. Taguieff, "La Révolution de gauche à droite," *Cahiers Bernard Lazare,* nos. 119–20 (1987): 24.

7. E. Morin, "L'Ere des ruptures," *EspacesTemps,* 38–39 (1988): 42–43; F. Furet, *Le Monde de la Révolution française,* no. 1 (January 1989); *Le Monde,* 8 October 1986; M. Ozouf, "Peut-on commémorer?" *Le Débat,* no. 26 (September 1983): 161; *Le Nouvel Observateur,* 4–10 May 1989. Cf. Emile Durkheim's precocious and inordinately sanguine revisionism: "Qu'on le regrette ou non, la Révolution française, d'objet de foi qu'elle était, devient de plus en plus un objet de science"; and "La doctrine révolutionnaire ne nous apparaît plus comme un exemple impeccable ni comme un tissu de monstrueuses aberrations, mais nous nous habituons peu à peu à n'y voir qu'un fait social de la plus haute importance, dont nous cherchons à connaître les origines et la portée." Durkheim, "Les Principes de 1789 et la sociologie," cited by P.-A. Taguieff, "La Révolution de gauche à droite," *Cahiers Bernard Lazare,* nos. 119–20 (1987): 18.

8. M. Ozouf, "Peut-on commémorer?" *Le Débat,* no. 26 (September 1983): 162, 165–70; Ozouf, "Célébrer, savoir, fêter," *Le Débat,* no. 57 (November-December 1989): 18, 24; Ozouf, *La Fête révolutionnaire,* 200, 201. Cf. Ozouf's lapidary analysis of the need to embrace the future in the logic of commemoration: "Tout souvenir qu'un projet ne soutient pas s'asphyxie.": The appeal to memory had to be matched, even governed by a vision of the future. Or, as she framed it elsewhere, "toute commémoration vit d'un équilibre délicat entre l'acquis et la promesse." Ozouf was more concerned than any of the official commemorators that the perspective on the future had to be hedged by the deference that the past demanded: "Il faut à la commémoration assez d'ouverture sur l'avenir pour respirer; mais pas trop non plus, car elle n'entend nullement se laisser aller à la dérive temporelle qui emporterait toute velléité de 'rester' les mêmes." Cf. "La commémoration est un message épique que l'on envoie vers le futur, vers des commémorations futures, vers des publics futurs": Gérard Namer, *La Commémoration,* 154.

9. R. Debray's contribution to "L'Actualité de la Révolution française," an international colloquium held on 5 December 1987, in *Bicentenaire 89, lettre de la Mission,* no. 3 (May 1988), and reutilized in Debray, "Diviser pour rassembler," *EspacesTemps,* nos. 38–39 (1988): 15; J.-N. Jeanneney, "L'Héritage de la Révolution française," *Revue des deux mondes,* December 1988, 56; M. Agulhon, "Pourquoi célébrer 1789?" *L'Histoire,* no. 113 (July-August 1988): 5; M. Ozouf, *La Fête révolutionnaire,* 209–10; *Le Quotidien de Paris,* 8 January 1988; *La Croix,* 21 June 1988.

10. Odile Rudelle, "Lieux de mémoire révolutionnaire et communion républicaine," *Vingtième Siècle,* no. 24 (October-December 1989): 4; J.-N. Jeanneney, "L'Héritage de la Révolution française," *Revue des deux mondes,* December 1988, 46–49, and *Concordance des temps* (Paris: Editions du Seuil, 1988), 322–32; J.-F. Revel, *Le Point,* 24 October 1988; Marc Angenot, *Le Centenaire de la Révolution* (Paris: La Documentation Française, 1989); P. Ory, "Etude comparée du centenaire et du cent-cinquantenaire de la Révolution française," in *L'Image de la Révolution française,* ed. M. Vovelle (Oxford and Paris: Pergamon Press, 1989) 3:2177–83, and *L'Exposition universelle 1889* (Brussels: Complexe, 1989); P. Garcia, "La

Révolution momifiée," *EspacesTemps*, nos. 38–39 (1988): 7, 8, 10; P. Ory, "La Commémoration révolutionnaire en 1939," in *La France et les Français en 1938–39*, ed. Janine Bourdin
and René Rémond (Paris: Presses de la Fondation Nationale des Sciences Politiques, 1978),
and "Le Centcinquantenaire, ou comment s'en débarrasser," in *La Légende de la Révolution
au vingtième siècle*, ed. Jean-Claude Bonnet and Philippe Roger (Paris: Flammarion, 1988),
139–56. For a vigorous rehabilitation of the festival making of 1939, especially on the local
level, obscured by the towering relics of 1889, see Patrick Garcia, Jacques Lévy, and Marie-
Flore Mattei, *Révolutions, fin et suite* (Paris: EspacesTemps-Centre Georges Pompidou/
Bibliothèque Publique d'Information, 1991), 179–80, 185.

11. Interview with M. Ozouf, *Le Nouvel Observateur*, 4–10 May 1989; Ozouf, "Célébrer,
savoir, fêter," *Le Débat*, no. 57 (November-December 1989): 19, 20; interview with Ozouf, *Le
Monde de la Révolution française*, no. 4 (April 1989); Ozouf, *La Fête révolutionnaire*, 201–2.
On the state's obsessive need to *trier*, see P. Garcia, "La Révolution momifiée," *EspacesTemps*,
no. 38–39 (1988): 5–6. Ozouf's Sorbonne *boutade* reminds one that Communist intellectuals
seem to have been much more inclined to follow the yellow brick road to the thesis "Oz"
much more frequently than the mavericks of Furet's galactic orbit.

12. J. Julliard in *Le Nouvel Observateur*, 19–25 January, 4–10 May, and 13–19 July 1989.
Julliard could also have taken his text from Edouard Herriot, for whom the Revolution
"comprend de l'excellent et de la détestable" and for whom "l'effusion de sang" had to be
harshly condemned. Herriot, *Aux sources de la liberté* (Paris: Gallimard, 1939), 31–32.

13. J. d'Ormesson on A. Sinclair's television show, *Sept sur sept*, and in *Figaro-Magazine*,
15 July 1989; *Le Figaro*, 15 May 1988; J.-F. Revel in *Le Point*, 24 October 1988; J.-C.
Casanova in *L'Express*, 25–31 December 1987; J.-M. Benoist in *Le Monde*, 19 January 1989
and *Le Quotidien de Paris*, 20 June 1989; *Le Monde*, 4 July 1989; interview with J.-N.
Jeanneney, *Vie publique*, October 1988.

14. P. Dujardin, director of the Centre de politologie historique of Lyon, interviewed in
Le Monde de la Révolution française, no. 6 (June 1989); E. Borne, "Réponse à J.-N. Jeanneney," in *Les Catholiques français et l'héritage de 1789*, ed. P. Colin (Paris: Beauchesne, 1989),
381; E. Morin, *Le Monde*, 9 June 1989.

15. R. Debray, "Diviser pour rassembler," *EspacesTemps*, no. 38–39 (1988): 14–15.

16. M. Rebérioux, "Un Processus qui s'étend sur deux siècles," *Revue politique et parlementaire*, July-August 1987, 13; Rebérioux, "Les Enjeux du Bicentenaire," *Politis*, 11 February 1988; *Nouvelle République du centre*, 12 January 1989.

17. M. Vovelle, "La Révolution, 'une et indivisible,'" *Revue politique et parlementaire*,
July-August 1987, 19; Vovelle, "L'Age de la prise de conscience," *EspacesTemps*, nos. 38–39
(1988): 36; M. Gallo, "La Révolution: Une Dynamique sociale et politique," *Revue politique
et parlementaire*, July-August 1987, 9.

18. Agulhon voiced the same patriotic test, predicated on an equivocal dose of tolerable
dissent, in an interview he accorded the weekly of the Socialist party: "A trop discréditer la
Révolution, c'est la France qu'on discrédite." *Vendredi*, 27 January 1989. The former defense
minister, Jean-Pierre Chevènement, a Marxo-Gaullist and Jacobino-republican, put it
slightly more sententiously: "La République est fille de la Révolution et l'amour de la
République est au principe même du patriotisme français moderne." Interview with J.-P.
Chevènement, *Armées d'aujourd'hui*, March 1989, 8–9.

19. M. Agulhon, "Faut-il avoir peur de 1989?" *Le Débat*, no. 30 (May 1984): 27, 29 ("Les
historiens sont maintenant les seuls à savoir que la Gauche est libérale et démocrate, républicaine pour tout dire, par essence et de fondation, alors que la Droite l'est par conversion et
accoutumance"); interview with Agulhon, *Vie publique* July-August 1989; Agulhon, "Pourquoi célébrer 1789?" *L'Histoire*, no. 113 (July-August 1988): 5; Agulhon, in *Magazine lit-*

téraire, March 1987; Agulhon, "En avant les idées," *Armées d'aujourd'hui*, March 1989, 18. Cf. the observations of Edgar Faure, surprisingly convergent in a number of ways with the neo-Jacobin analysis of Agulhon: "En réalité, le procès contre la Révolution est, dans une large mesure, factice. Il est, pour une part, alimenté par quelques ennemis résolus de la démocratie qui n'osent pas la combattre en visière, et qui saisissent l'occasion de compromettre la liberté à travers les crimes commis (indiscutablement) en son nom, mais (non moins indiscutablement) à son encontre et sous son désaveu. Il est, d'autre part, entretenu par certains esprits qui se disent démocrates et qui sont sincères, mais dont la conviction n'est pas très profonde. Le procès de la Révolution leur ouvre le cabinet du psychanalyste." E. Faure, "1789–1989: La Révolution française," *Revue des deux mondes*. July-September 1987, 286.

20. M. Agulhon, "Quelle stratégie pour le Bicentenaire?" *Revue politique et parlementaire*, July-August 1987, 15; Agulhon, "Faut-il avoir peur de 1989?" *Le Débat*, no. 30 (May 1984): 28–31, 36–37; Agulhon, "La Révolution française au banc des accusés," *Vingtième Siècle*, no. 5 (January-March 1985): 7–8. On the extraordinary ways in which preexisting, deeply hewn consensus (mystification or not) lubricated the gears of the American bicentennial celebration, see the three major programs (Heritage '76, Festival '76, and Horizon '76) discussed in American Revolution Bicentennial Administration, *A Final Report to the People: The Bicentennial of the U.S.A.* (Washington, D.C.: U.S. Government Printing Office, 1977), vol. 1.

21. *Le Point*, 10 July 1989, J.-D. Bredin, *Le Monde*, 3 January 1989; J.-P. Rioux, *Le Monde*, 26 August 1988; interview with R. Debray, *Le Monde de la Révolution française*, no. 3 (March 1989); S. July, *Libération*, 12 July 1989; Condorcet, *Lettre au président de la Mission du Bicentenaire*, 7, 9, 13, 31–33, 36–37. In his apocryphal letter inviting Condorcet to provide some understated pyrotechnics in an otherwise dull celebration, the president of the Mission pledges to substitute for the sanguinary apothegm "La liberté ou la mort" the more decorously consensual "Pour une vie libre, solidaire et heureuse." This is what Debray dubbed "la pudeur postmoderne." R. Debray, *Que vive la République* (Paris: O. Jacob, 1989), 87. Over the course of time various claimants have flourished Condorcet in the name of radicalism, socialism, anti-Bolshevism, anti-Nazi humanism, and—most recently, through the work of the Ligue de l'enseignement—democracy and civism. *Dépêche du Midi*, 3 July 1989. On the connections between the "cooling" of the Revolutionary object and the crystallization of consensus, see P. Garcia, "La Révolution momifiée," *EspacesTemps*, nos. 38–39 (1988): 4. For an incantatory treatment of consensus as a galacto-Tocquevillean triumph, see D. Pinto, "Autour du Bicentenaire de la Révolution française," *French Politics and Society* 7 (summer 1989): 141.

22. D. Bensaïd, *Moi, la Révolution* (Paris: Gallimard, 1989), 10, 17–18, 32. Cf. Bensaïd's continuing assault on the spirit of consensus in his *Walter Benjamin: Sentinelle messianique* (Paris: Plon, 1991). One of the saddest and most sordid bicentennial episodes concerned the efforts of a powerful and assiduous courtier to spare his prince the pain and embarrassment of Bensaïd's slings and arrows. The courtier was celebrated lawyer and future deputy minister of justice Georges Kiejman, perhaps best known as the crusading defender of Pierre Goldmann, a victim of injustice. Kiejman was also counsel to the venerable publishing house Gallimard. In that capacity this celebrated spokesman for individual rights did his best to prevent publication of Bensaïd's book, according to the investigative reporter Edwy Plenel, editor of the series in which the book was slated to appear. Alerted by a member of the Elysée staff, the prince himself let it be known that he had no objections to the publication of *Moi, la Révolution*. See Plenel, *La Part de l'ombre* (Paris: Stock, 1992).

23. R. Debray, *Que vive la République*, 15, 16, 40, 44, 87, 110, 115; M. Gallo, *Le Monde*, 28 January 1989. A psychologist and writer, Bernard Lhôte, used sepulchral images redolent of Debray. "Commémorer, comme mémoire, commémourir." Lhôte viewed the consensual

approach, a conservative, ultimately repressive undertaking, as "un acte d'exhumation aus-sitôt suivi de réinhumation afin de mater les dangereux démons des morts." How should one commemorate the Revolution? "En révolutionnant sa commémoration." B. Lhôte in *Lettres à la Révolution,* ed. Jean-Marie Lhôte (Amiens: Trois Cailloux for the Maison de la culture, 1989), 164, 167. For Communist strictures against a consensus geared to serve the interests of "big capital" and nostlagia for the rough music of revolutionary contestation, see Claude Gindin, "200 ans après, la Révolution," *La Pensée,* no. 267 (January-February 1989): 10, and interview with Georges Labica, *Raison présente,* no. 91 (1989), 23, 24, 29. A theme that carried beyond the bicentennial was the idea that consensus endangered the very practice of democracy. See J.-L. Martens and Olivier Ihl, "La Révolution française et le narcissisme idéologique," *La Revue Tocqueville,* no. 9 (1987–88), 132. See also the commentary by two political sociologists, F. Ivernet and N. Tenzer, in *Libération,* 30 May 1989. More super-ficially, without much concern for etiology, Jean-Pierre Chevènement, in his postministerial voice, avers that "la démocratie est malade de l'argent parce qu'elle est malade du con-sensus." *Figaro-Magazine,* 17 May 1991. The businessman and political commentator Alain Minc makes a general case against the political perils of consensus in *La Vengeance des nations* (Paris: Grasset, 1991).

24. A. Touraine interviewed on film by S. Moati, *Journal d'un bicentenaire.* Cf. Touraine, "Passé présent: Les Français et leur Révolution," *EspacesTemps,* nos. 38–39 (1988): 32; Y. Bosc and P. Garcia, "La Perception de la Révolution française à la veille du Bicentenaire," in Vovelle, *L'Image de la Révolution française,* 3: 2324.

25. *Révolution,* 6–12 February 1987 (one wonders whether the date of the polling, 21 January, consciously influenced pollsters or subjects); *L'Expansion,* 21 October-3 November 1988.

26. *Le Nouvel Observateur,* 5–11 January 1989; *L'Express,* 7 July 1989. The astringent commentary accompanying the Sofres-*Express* poll assails Michel Foucault and his "Maoist structuralism" for coming to the aid of an agonizing Soboulo-Bolshevik exegesis by lending his intellectual prestige to the apology for R/revolutionary bloodletting. On the growing divorce between attitudes toward the Revolution and political persuasion, see Garcia, et al., *Révolutions, fin et suite,* 284.

27. *Figaro-Magazine,* 23 January 1988; *L'Express,* 7 July 1989; *Le Monde,* 13 July 1989.

28. *Le Monde,* 4 January 1989; *Le Nouvel Observateur,* 5–11 January 1989. "S'il y a violence, elle n'excède pas la violence sportive: 'C'est pire que la mêlée du Quinze de France,' nous a confié un Toulousain en mal de métaphore." Y. Bosc and P. Garcia, "La Perception de la Révolution française à la veille du Bicentenaire," in Vovelle, *L'Image de la Révolution française,* 3:2322.

29. *Le Nouvel Observateur,* 5–11 January 1989; *Figaro-Magazine,* 23 January 1988. On the Lafayette-de Gaulle nexus, see Odile Rudelle, "Lieux de mémoire révolutionnaire et com-munion républicaine," *Vingtième Siècle,* no. 24 (October-December 1989): 6 ("La Fayette, l'homme de la guerre d'indépendance américaine et de la cocarde tricolore et du 14 juillet, donne la main à l'homme d'une Libération dont l'épopée vient désormais se superposer à celle de la Révolution").

30. *Pèlerin Magazine,* 14 July 1989; O. Duhamel, "Chronique de l'opinion: 'La Révolu-tion française est terminée,'" *Pouvoirs,* no. 50 (1989): 123–25.

31. G. Sorman, *La Lettre politique et parlementaire,* 12 July 1989; *L'Anti-89,* no. 11 (September 1988).

32. M. Ozouf, *Le Nouvel Observateur,* 4–10 May 1989, and interview in *Le Monde de la Révolution française,* no. 4 (April 1989); F. Furet, *Le Monde de la Révolution française,* no. 1 (January 1989); *Le Quotidien de Paris,* 14 July 1989; J.-F. Revel, *Le Point,* 24 October 1988; J. Daniel, *Le Nouvel Observateur,* 29 December 1988–4 January 1989; M. Bedjaoui cited in *Le*

Monde, Cf. the vigorously liberal phrasing of the Revolution's objectives articulated by the business-philanthropist wing of the bicentennial Mission, the Association d'entreprises pour le Bicentenaire, headed by J. Friedmann, the then chief executive officer of Air France: "Les entreprises participeront ainsi à la diffusion dans le monde du message universel de *liberté* qui est celui de la Révolution française et de la Déclaration de 1789." *Bicentenaire 89, lettre de la Mission,* no. 2 (March 1988).

33. *National hebdo,* 30 March–5 April 1989; *Libération,* 14 July 1989; interview with C. Manceron, *Bicentenaire 89, lettre de la Mission,* no. 1 (January 1988); J.-M. Benoist, *Le Monde,* 8 July 1989. Cf. Jacques Chirac's stress on the international vocation of the Declaration. *Le Monde,* 15 December 1988. The Communists sharply criticized the church's bicentennial opportunism and its efforts to put rights discourse in the service of capitalist exploitation: "A travers le texte des évêques de France, on voit se confirmer que le Bicentenaire pourrait bien être de moins en moins celui de la Révolution française, et de plus en plus celui de l'idéologie libérale, à travers la Déclaration des droits de l'homme." J. Lelong, *Bulletin de l'Association des amis de la Révolution française—Vive 89 en Allier,* no. 4. Cf. Jean Chaunu's strained effort to show that Pope Pius VI was not fundamentally hostile to the Declaration, "L'Etat, l'Eglise et la Révolution," *France catholique,* no. 2215 (14 July 1989). Playing, as he often did quite adroitly, on leftist themes for rightist ends, historian Jean Tulard felt that it was not historically honest to place rights in the center of the commemoration because the "bourgeois" [!!] Revolution excluded so many important groups from access to rights (women, workers, slaves). It was aberrant to celebrate a Declaration (that of 1789) that was repudiated in part by the Convention in 1793. Interview with Tulard, 10 April 1991.

34. *Le Monde,* 2 November, 9 December 1988, and 17 March, 23–24 April, 22, 26 August 1989; *La Lettre politique et parlementaire,* 6 January 1989; *Le Nouvel Observateur,* 26 August–1 September 1988 and 13–19 July 1989.

35. *Le Quotidien de Paris,* 30 June 1989; Condorcet, *Lettre au président de la Mission de Bicentenaire,* 19, 23, 28–30; F. Ewald, *Le Quotidien de Paris,* 21 June 1989; C. Ducol, in C. Mazauric and A. Casanova, *Vive la Révolution 1789–1989,* ed. C. Ducol (Paris: Messidor/Editions Sociales, 1989), 15; D/ Bensaïd, *Moi, la Révolution,* 54, 73, 290; P. Joxe interviewed by Marie-Laurence Netter, *La Révolution française n'est pas terminée,* (Paris: PUF, 1989), 131–33; G. Perrault, "Le Pamphlet au vitriol d'un sans-culotte," *Politis,* 21–27 April 1989; R. Debray, *Que vive la publique,* 171, 173;

36. A. Touraine, *Le Monde,* 23 January 1990; J.-D. Bredin, *Le Monde,* 3 January 1989; J.-N. Jeanneney, *Rapport du président de la Mission du Bicentenaire à Monsieur le président de la République* (Paris, 1989), 190–91. For a discerning treatment of both the risks and the opportunities of a rights discourse, see the discussion between J. Lévy and P. Garcia, "Les Chemins de la mémoire," *CLEF, la Lettre,* no. 12 (December 1988–January 1989).

37. J. Dumont, *Pourquoi nous ne célébrons pas 1789* (Bagneux: A.R.G.E., 1987); B. Pascal, *Aspects de la France,* 3 November 1988; F. Brigneau, *National hebdo,* 15–21 December 1988.

38. P. de Villiers interviewed in *Aspects de la France,* 13 July 1989; J.-M. Varaut, *Le Quotidien de Paris,* 20 June 1989; M. Thatcher interviewed in *Le Monde,* 13 July 1989; *Le Monde,* 11 July 1989.

39. *Ouest France,* 13–14 July 1989; *La Tribune de l'expansion,* 17 July 1989; *Le Figaro,* 17 July 1989; *Le Monde,* 11, 15, 29 July 1989; *Minute,* no. 1424 (19–25 July 1989); *Le Canard enchaîné,* 19 July 1989.

40. *Présent,* 13 July 1989; *La Croix,* 1 August 1989; J.-F. Revel, "Leur 14 Juillet," *Le Débat,* no. 57 (November–December 1989): 63–64; E. Herriot, *Aux sources de la liberté,* 9–13 (to help forge the alliance, Herriot reminds readers that "il y a eu constamment interpénétration de la pensée française et de la pensée anglaise"); interview with Jeanneney, *Magazine littéraire,* October 1988, 28. Cf. the strenuously Thatcherite position of Georges Gusdorf, *Les*

Révolutions de France et d'Amérique: La Violence et la sagesse (Paris: Perrin, 1988), 135. On the German reaction to Thatcher's strictures and claims, see J. von Uthmann, "Hat die Revolution stattgefunden?" *Frankfurter Allegemeine Zeitung*, 29 July 1989. Thatcher's depreciation of the Revolution doubtless comforted the far right; *intégristes* continued to hold the English partly responsible for its outbreak. The Revolution had its roots in the seven centuries of war waged by the English against the French and in the contamination "des loges maçonniques venues d'Angleterre," according to *Réparation de la France offerte au Christ Roi et à la Vierge Marie* (program of the procession/demonstration of 15 August 1989), 35.

41. *Bicentenaire 89, Lettre de la Mission*, no. 1 (October 1988): 2; "Entretien avec J.-N. Jeanneney," *Armées d'aujourd'hui*, March 1989, 183; J. Citron, "Premiers Regards sur le Bicentenaire," *Cercle Condorcet*, no. 11 (March 1990): 8. I think that it is fair to say that Jeanneney was at least partly successful in setting the example: the bicentennial celebration was less narcissistic than it might have been. Yet Mona Ozouf's assessment strikes me as excessively optimistic and not a little *cocardier*: "There was very little chauvinism in our Bicentennial." Ozouf, "Célébrer, savoir, fêter," *Le Débat*, no. 57 (November-December 1989): 33.

42. E. Morin, "Remarques brisées. Entretien," *Le Débat*, no. 57 (November-December 1989): 209–10 ("Mais la vraie, la grande commémoration de 1789 a été l'oeuvre d'un scénariste génial et invisible qui l'a mondialement organisée à Moscou, Pékin, Varsovie, Budapest et autres lieux"); D. Bensaïd, *Le Monde*, 8 December 1989 ("Indignée de cet anniversaire en forme d'obsèques nationales, la vieille dame est passée à l'Est"); *Le Monde*, 24 November 1989; *Libération*, 22 June 1989; *Le Sud Ouest*, 14 July 1989; Mitterrand's speech of 20 June 1989, *200e Anniversaire du Serment du Jeu de Paume*, (Paris: Présidence de la République, 1989), 8; interview with Mitterrand, *L'Express*, 14 July 1989; *Le Monde*, 23 May 1989; Gérard Leclerc in *Royaliste*, no. 518 (26 June-9 July 1989); *L'Alsace*, 16 July 1989.

43. A. Fontaine, *Le Monde*, 3 January 1989 ("A bien des égards, 1989 répète 1789: de Pékin à Santiago, un même amour de la liberté a jeté dans les rues des millions d'hommes et de femmes dont on avait trop vite admis qu'ils avaient pris à jamais leur parti de leur servitude"); *Libération*, 26 October 1989; J.-N. Jeanneney cited in *1789: Le Livre du Bicentenaire*, ed. Claire Andrieu (Paris: Le Chêne-Hachette, 1990), 173, 182–83; *Le Monde*, 25 November and 7, 8, 14 December 1989; *Vive 89 en Ille-et-Vilaine*, no. 7 (December 1989); interview with C. Mazauric, 14 April 1989; Mazauric to the author, 20 April 1989; Mazauric presentation for "Paris Révolution, Association Vive 89 à Paris," 14 December 1989; *Le Point*, 16 July 1990; *Le Figaro*, 5 January 1990; *Populaire du centre*, 26 August 1989; *New York Times*, 28 December 1989. Alain Touraine was pessimistic about the way in which his compatriots reacted to the new challenges: "Les bouleversements du monde, qui sont vécus ailleurs comme espoirs, apparaissent menaces aux Français . . . . au lieu de regarder banalement vers le présent et l'avenir, cherchons un nouveau bicentenaire pour nous convaincre une fois encore que nous ne sommes décidément pas comme les autres, empêtrés dans leurs particularismes et leurs croyances, puisque nous sommes la fille aînée de la Raison—ou peut-être même sa mère—après avoir été la fille aînée de l'Eglise." *Le Monde*, 23 November 1989.

Chapter 2
Resurgent Counterrevolutionaries and New Age Antirevolutionaries

1. See, among others, Max Gallo, "Le Nouveau Catéchisme," *Le Figaro*, 17 December 1984, and René Rémond, "La Tradition contre-révolutionnaire," *Projet*, no. 213 (September-October 1988).

2. M. Winock in *L'Evénement du Jeudi*, 24–30 November 1988; R. Debray, "Diviser pour rassembler," *EspacesTemps*, nos. 38–39 (1988): 14. Cf. *Aspects de la France*, 24 March 1988; D. Guérin, "Controverse sur la Révolution française," *Cahiers Bernard Lazare*, nos. 119–20 (1987): 81; M. Agulhon, "La Révolution française au banc des accusés," *Vingtième Siècle*, no. 5 (January-March 1987): 14–15; J.-C. Vanfleteren in *Bulletin de l'Association des amis de Robespierre pour le Bicentenaire de la Révolution*, no. 2; *Le Monde*, 8 October 1986; R. Rémond, "La Tradition contre-révolutionnaire," *Projet*, no. 213 (September-October 1988). There is a pressing need for a serious sociological study of the continuities and changes in counterrevolutionary recruitment, akin to Claude Grignon's brilliant examination of the changing nature of Catholic culture and social structure and their relation to the exercise of power. See Grignon, "Sur les relations entre les transformations du champ religieux et les transformations de l'espace politique," *Actes de la Recherche en sciences sociales*, no. 16 (1977): 3–34. Such an investigation would, for example, help situate a commentator like Jean d'Ormesson—*normalien*, academician, scion of a celebrated Old Regime family, columnist for *Figaro-Magazine*. Like Msgr. Gaillot, and unlike Pierre Chaunu, d'Ormesson regarded the Revolution as the most important event in French history, and perhaps the most important happening in the world since the birth of Christ. The Revolution was not, however, a bloc, and d'Ormesson felt comfortable endorsing certain of its features and criticizing others pitilessly. See his appearance on Anne Sinclair's television program, *Sept sur sept*, 20 June 1988.

3. *Libération*, 7 May 1987; *Le Quotidien de Paris*, 15 August 1989; *Le Figaro*, 20–21 February 1988; *Présent*, 6 December 1989.

4. *Aspects de la France*, 19 November 1987; *Le Choc du mois*, no. 14 (January 1989): 24; *National hebdo*, 27 April-1 March 1989; *Le Monde*, 12 July 1989; J. Eisenberg and T. Klein cited in Belloin, *Entendez-vous dans nos mémoires: Les Français et leur Révolution* (Paris: La Découverte, 1988): 82–83; *Figaro-Magazine*, 20 January, 4 February 1989. On the role that the Jewish community had taken in previous celebrations of the Revolution, and on the program envisaged for the bicentennial, see Roger Berg, "1839–1889–1939–1989: Le Judaïsme français commémore la Révolution," *La Tribune juive*, 23–29 September 1989, 15–18.

5. *Figaro-Magazine*, 3 December 1988; *Le Nouvel Observateur*, 15–21 December 1988.

6. *Le Choc du mois*, no. 14 (January 1989); *National hebdo*, 25–31 May, 7–13 September 1989; *Aspects de la France*, 24 March 1988; Michel de St.-Pierre cited by Christian Amalvi, *De l'art et la manière d'accommoder les héros de l'histoire de France* (Paris: Albin Michel, 1988), 333. Just as certain German conservatives ventured to "historicize" Nazism in order to free their country from the stranglehold of inculpating memory, so did Jacques Chirac, under the tutelage of historian Yves Durand, attempt to historicize the Revolution by inserting it into the long meta-Capetian narrative in order to liberate France from the tyrannical grip of its originary pretensions. See his news conferences of 18 and 22 March 1988, documentation of the Hôtel de Ville.

7. J. Dumont, *Pourquoi nous ne célébrons pas 1789* (Bagneux: A.R.G.E., 1987); *Aspects de la France*, 13 July 1989; J.-M. Varaut, "La Déclaration des droits de l'homme et du citoyen de 1789: Généalogie, esprit et contradictions," *Libéralia*, no. 4 (winter 1989): 10; *Le Matin*, 16 February 1987; *Minute*, no. 1372 (26 July 1988); *Le Choc du mois*, nos. 7 (June 1988) and 14 (January 1989); *Rivarol*, 14 July 1989. Always seeking to reconcile the traditional and modern vectors of counterrevolution, Philippe de Villiers oscillated between endogenous and exogenous reasons not to celebrate. If he could not impugn the rationale for honoring the Declaration, he could find external factors that militated against celebration. Thus, "avec ce qui se passe aujourd'hui en Chine, en Iran et en Pologne, faire une fête de la Révolution est impensable." Villiers in *Le Figaro*, 14 June 1989.

8. *Aspects de la France*, 3 November 1988; *Rivarol*, 14 July 1989; *Le Quotidien de Paris*, 19–20 August 1989; *Le Choc du mois*, no. 14 (January 1989); *Présent*, 14–15 July 1989.

9. F. Lazorthes in *Le Quotidien de Paris*, 31 July 1789; J.-M. Benoist, "La Révolution contre les droits de l'homme," *Libéralia*, no. 4 (winter 1989): 13.

10. L. Pauwels in *Figaro-Magazine*, 9 December 1989.

11. *Présent*, 23–24, 25, 26 October 1989. Cf. J.-Y. Camus in *Le Front national à découvert* ed. N. Mayer and P. Perrineau (Paris: Presses de la Fondation nationale des sciences politiques, 1989), 24.

12. *Présent*, 14–15 July 1989; *National hebdo*, 25–31 March 1989; Serge Moati's filmed interviews in *A propos de la Révolution française;* undated brochure of SOS-Identité. Cf. the postbicentennial boycott SOS-Identité proposed against the giant clothier Benetton because its multicultural and multiracial advertising campaign "tourne en dérision tout sentiment d'identité en faisant l'apologie du mélange des peuples." *La Lettre politique et parlementaire*, 26 July 1991. Concerning the far right's self-proclaimed stewardship of Catholicism, see the argument of Jean Boussinesq, who insists that "la recherche identitaire" connecting French selfhood with Christian origins is not an exclusively *intégriste* theme. Boussinesq, "Lectures catholiques de la Révolution française," *Raison présente*, no. 91 (1989): 88.

13. J. Dumont, *Pourquoi nous ne célébrons pas 1789*, 29–30, 54, 79, 92–93.

14. F. Léotard cited in *Le Monde*, 7 December 1989; *La Lettre politique et parlementaire*, 13 December 1989; Fernand Braudel, *L'Identité de la France*, 3 vols. (Paris: Flammarion, 1990); *Le Nouvel Observateur*, 8–14 February 1990, reports an angry confrontation at a preparatory meeting for the Estates General between Edmond Alphandéry of the Centre des démocrates sociaux (CDS) and Didier Bariani of the Parti radical:

Alphandéry: "Si on maintient l'amalgame entre identité nationale et immigration, je préfère m'en aller tout de suite."

Bariani: "Dans ce domaine, il faut être passionnel, je n'en ai pas honte de le dire. Soyons clairs: il faut savoir si on veut sauver ou non la race blanche."

Alphandéry: "Va-t-on aller jusqu'à proposer un statut des immigrés, comme il y a eu un statut des juifs? Un croissant à la place d'une étoile?"

At this juncture "hurlements" erupted as Bariani and his friends cried out "provocation" while others tried to calm the tone. Cf. centrist B. Stasi's anxiety that France was "le seul pays développé aussi où le patriotisme et l'affirmation de l'identité nationale soient si souvent assimilés au rejet de l'autre." *Le Monde*, 17 May 1990.

15. G. Sorman, "L'Identité nationale," *Vie publique*, January 1990.

16. *Libération*, 12 January 1990; *Figaro-Magazine*, 24 November 1990. Cf. the extreme reluctance of the FN to relinquish full control of the identity issue in the response of Jean-Yves Le Gallou, president of the FN's group in the Conseil régional of the Ile-de-France. V. Giscard d'Estaing, letter to *Figaro-Magazine*, 8 December 1990.

17. R. von Thadden, "Die Revolutionsfeiern ohne Botschaft," *Frankfurter Rundschau*, 15 July 1989; CSA poll, commissioned by the Mission, November 1989; *Libération*, 12 December 1989. In that poll, 36 percent believed that it was "important" to welcome immigrants while 11% believed it was not important. In response to a similar question, a slightly higher percentage took an enlightened attitude: 52 percent felt that it was important to combat racism, while 9 percent said it was not important and 32 percent said that the struggle against racism had nothing to do with the legacy of the Revolution. A month after his startling pronouncement that immigration had stepped beyond "the threshold of tolerance in France,", Mitterrand backed off and nuanced. He conceded that "ma réponse a été trop elliptique" and that the threshold concept was itself "une notion trop vague pour n'être pas suspect." Pleading for a focus on the integration of those immigrants with the legal right to

remain in France (they have "toute leur place parmi nous"), he added: "J'ai simplement constaté qu'en réalité le nombre d'immigrés en France disposant d'un titre de séjour était à peu près constant depuis quinze ans. Ce qui relativise les irritations d'une opinion chauffée à blanc par des campagnes démagogiques." *Le Monde*, 12 January 1990.

18. B. Renouvin in *Royaliste*, 10–17 September 1989.

19. G. Belloin interviewed by Patrick Garcia, "Les Chemins de la mémoire," in *CLEF la lettre*, no. 12 (December 1988-January 1989).

20. R. Debray, in *Le Nouvel Observateur*, 30 November-6 December; Debray, "L'Actualité de la Révolution française," in *Bicentenaire 89, lettre de la Mission*, no. 3 (May 1988); Debray, "Diviser pour rassembler," *EspacesTemps*, nos. 38–39 (1988): 19–20; S. Citron, "Premiers Regards sur le Bicentenaire," *Cercle Condorcet*, no. 11 (March 1990): 24. Cf. Jean-Louis Martens and Olivier Ihl, "La Révolution française et le narcissisme idéologique," *La Revue Tocqueville*, no. 9 (1987–88): 129–30, and Jean-Marie Domenach, "Identité culturelle française et identité européenne," *France-Forum*, nos. 252–53 (April-June 1989).

21. "Entretien avec J.-N. Jeanneney," *Armées d'aujourd'hui*, March 1989, 181; M. Gallo, "La Révolution: Une Dynamique sociale et politique," *Revue politique et parlementaire*, July-August 1987, 10; Gallo cited in *CLEF la lettre*, May 1988; D. Bensaïd, *Moi, la Révolution* (Paris: Gallimard, 1989), 102. Cf. Bensaïd's robust summons to fill "le vide identitaire de la gestion socialiste . . . . il fallait restaurer la ligne Maginot idéologique de la République et de la Nation, battue en brèche par la mondialisation de l'économie et de la culture." *Le Monde*, 8 December 1989. On the need to "resituer le débat [on immigration and nationality] dans une perspective historique" under the prod of the commemoration of the Revolution, see the brochure announcing a colloquium on "citoyenneté" sponsored by the Ligue des droits de l'homme (Lille, April 1989).

22. M. Agulhon, "Faut-il avoir peur de 1989?" *Le Débat*, no. 30 (May 1984), 367; J.-P. Chevènement in "Nationalité, citoyenneté, Europe," *Cahiers du Bicentenaire de Belfort*, no. 2 (October 1988): 22–23; *Socialisme et République*, no. 32 (15 November 1989); Chevènement in *Le Monde*, 9 November 1989; M. Rodinson in *Le Monde*, 1 December 1989. On the Jacobin roots of French identity, see William Safran, "The French and Their National Identity: The Quest for an Elusive Substance," *French Politics and Society* 8 (winter 1990): 56–67. While Thierry de Beaucé, the junior minister for international cultural relations, did not like the word "identity," "parce qu'il est réducteur, alors que la France se définit par des valeurs—les droits de l'homme—qu'elle veut universelles," Chevènement, despite his commitment to universality, believed strongly in a concept of national identity. Beaucé interviewed in *Le Point*, 16 July 1990; Chevènement, letter to the editor, *Le Nouvel Observateur*, 26 April-2 May 1990. François Furet diagnosed a French identity crisis, a weakening of the idea of nation and an eclipse of the image of the Revolution that had furnished for so long the "cement" for political unity. F. Furet, "La France unie," in *La République du centre* (Paris: Calmann Lévy, 1988), 52–53.

23. *Socialisme et République*, no. 33 (15 December 1989); *Synthèse Flash*, supplement to no. 418 (16 October 1989) and no. 420 (13 November 1989); *Le Point*, 18 June 1990; *PS Info*, no. 419 (4 November 1989); *Vendredi*, 27 October and 10 November 1989.

24. *Le Nouvel Observateur*, 14–20 December 1989. On the postbicentennial Socialist flight from multiculturalism, see Judith Vishniac, "French Socialists and the *Droit à la différence*: A Changing Dynamic," *French Politics and Society* 9 (winter 1991): 40–56. See the Masonic point of view, expressed by Christian Pozzo di Borgo, grand master of the Grand Orient de France, for whom *laicity* was one of the pillars of French identity, yet who felt that "parmi les reflexes que nous devons avoir à l'occasion du Bicentenaire, il y a celle qui consiste à repenser le concept de laïcité." *Le Quotidien de Paris*, 6 July 1989. Cf. the remarks made by

his successor, Jean-Robert Ragache, a year after "l'affaire mineure" of the veil, which led to the "flottement de la classe politique," in reference to the imperative of *laicity* and the dangers of "la communautarisation." *Le Monde,* 12 September 1990.

25. J.-N. Jeanneney interviewed in *France-Soir,* 29 November 1989; *Le Monde,* 10, 14 May 1990. See also sociologist Alain Touraine's reflections on the menace to national identity in a broader international framework, involving Americans and Germans more than Arabs, and "la culture de masse transnationale." *Le Monde,* 18 September 1990. During the postbicentennial year, Max Gallo called passionately for a frank rehabilitation of the idea of national identity in the context not of the recrudescence of French xenophobia but of the resuscitation of French exceptionalism. Gallo, "La Faute de J. Julliard," *Le Nouvel Observateur,* 2–8 August 1990, and interview with Gallo.

26. J. Dumont, *Pourquoi nous ne célébrons pas 1789,* 29–30, 54, 79, 92–93; *National hebdo,* 2–8 February 1989.

27. *National hebdo,* 6–12 April, 27 April–1 March, 8–14 June 1989; G. Millière, editorial in *Libéralia,* no. 4 (winter 1989); P. Chaunu, *Le Grand Déclassement: À propos d'une commémoration* (Paris: R. Laffont, 1989), 276; Jean-Louis Margolin, "Une Révolution, mais de longue durée," *EspacesTemps,* nos. 38–39 (1988): 89–90; *Le Choc du mois,* no. 7 (June 1988); Comité d'initiative des Cercles catholiques d'ouvriers, 1889, cited by B. Plongeron, "Conclusion de la table ronde," in *Les Catholiques français et l'héritage de 1789,* ed. P. Colin (Paris: Beauchesne, 1989), 64; Olivier Bétourné and Aglaia I. Hartig, *Penser l'histoire de la Révolution: Deux Siècles de passion française* (Paris:La Découverte, 1989), 153–60; R. Marie in *Le Matin,* 16 February 1987; *L'Express,* 25–31 December 1987; *Le Figaro,* 31 October 1988; *Le Choc du mois,* no. 14 (January 1989). Cf. Claude Sarraute's burlesque of the declinist thesis: "Vous avez vu, dans *Le Point,* le bilan qu'en dresse, après bien d'autres, René Sédillot? Il n'en reste rien. Si, quand même: le système métrique! A part ça, la *cata.* Elle a saigné le pays à blanc . . . . Pol Pot, c'est rien à côté . . . . elle a appauvri les pauvres . . . et enrichi les riches qui spéculaient . . . . Même la Déclaration des droits de l'homme, elle n'a pas été foutue de l'inventer. La Fayette l'a piquée aux Américains . . . . Je vous prie, messieurs, n'en jetez plus. Si ça continue, le 14 juillet, place de la Bastille, mon Mimi va prendre le bide de sa vie. A moins de se cacher sous la perruque poudrée de Louis XVI, le front ceint d'une couronne: regrets éternels." *Le Monde,* 23 March 1989. See also Edgar Faure's somewhat surprising argument against the "revolution-was-avoidable" thesis. Apparently, once Turgot failed, there was no nonrevolutionary passage from a closed to an open society. "1789–1989: La Révolution française," *Revue des deux mondes,* July–September 1987, 282-83.

28. R. Marie in *Le Matin,* 16 February 1987; P. de Villiers, *Lettre ouverte aux coupeurs de têtes et aux menteurs du Bicentenaire* (Paris: Albin Michel, 1989), 47, 51, 67–68, and *Le Nouvel Observateur,* 4–10 May 1989; *L'Anti-89,* no. 3 (December 1987); J.-M. Le Pen cited in *Le Monde,* 2 September 1989; *Minute,* no. 1422 (5–11 July 1989); J.-M. Benoist in *Le Figaro,* 13 July 1989; *Libération,* 7 May 1987; L. Pauwels in *Figaro-Magazine,* 11 October 1986; Georges Gusdorf, *Les Révolutions de France et d'Amérique: La Violence et la sagesse* (Paris: Perrin, 1988), 51, 58, 59; B. Gollnisch in *L'Anti-89,* no. 16 (January 1989). François Bédarida perceptively suggested that the antitotalitarian model reinvigorated the somewhat languid satanic reading of the Revolution. *La Croix,* 9 March 1989. Cf. Madeleine Rebérioux's comment on "l'air du temps" in "Un Processus qui s'étend sur deux siècles," *Revue politique et parlementaire* (July-August 1987), 11.

29. J.-M. Benoist, "La Révolution contre les droits de l'homme," *Libéralia,* no. 4 (winter 1989): 14; R. Pucheu, "Ceux qui crurent à la Révolution et ceux qui n'y crurent pas," in Colin, *Les Catholiques français et l'héritage de 1789;* A. Grosser in *Le Monde,* 9 March 1989; P. Lepape in *Le Monde,* 29 January 1988.

30. J.-E. Hallier in *L'Humanité*, 22 December 1988; M. Rebérioux, "Les Enjeux du bicentenaire," *Politis*, 11 February 1988; P. de Villiers, *Lettre ouverte*, 31, 41, 47, 70–71, 77, 110, 118; J.-N. Jeanneney, "Après coup: Réflexions d'un commémorateur," *Le Débat*, no. 57 (November-December 1989): 103; P. Nora cited by R. Bernstein, "The French Revolution: Right or Wrong," *New York Times Book Review*, 10 July 1988. There is no doubt that certain historians and commentators on the right misused Furet. Jean Dumont caricatured him by reducing his argument to the proposition that "la Révolution n'a servi à rien." ("Il rejoint Rivarol," exulted *Le Choc du mois*, the rightist periodical that interviewed Dumont.) Like Dumont, journalist Georges Suffert seemed interested only in finding in Furet what he wanted to believe. Thus he attributed to Furet a claim which the historian never formulated, that "la séquence 1789–1795 n'est plus la matrice de la nation française républicaine." Interview with J. Dumont, *Le Choc du mois*, January 1989; G. Suffert, "La Révolution n'est plus ce qu'elle était," *Le Point*, 8 July 1985.

31. C. Imbert in *Le Point*, 15–21 May 1989.

32. J.-M. Domenach, "Révolution et modernité," *Esprit*, no. 139 (June 1988): 32; J. Julliard in *Le Nouvel Observateur*, 4–10 May 1989.

33. F. Furet, *La Gauche et la Révolution*, 8, 89; interview with Furet, *Le Nouvel Observateur*, 28 February-6 March 1986; Furet, *Dictionnaire critique*, 1051; interview with Furet, *Libération*, 7 May 1987; M. Ozouf, "Célébrer, savoir, fêter," *Le Débat*, no. 57 (November-December 1989): 28. François Furet tends to exaggerate his persecution at the hands of the Jacobino-Marxists. After the bitter attack on him following the publication of the book he coauthored with Denis Richet in the 1960s, there was remarkably little fire from the enemy camp. To serve his polemical and psychological needs, Furet fantasizes an endless salvo and fabricates a sort of crossing of the desert that he never really had to undertake. In a very different context, where historical debate in the public sphere mattered enormously, see how neoconservative historians made it a lot easier for right-wing extremism to flourish. Richard J. Evans, in *Hitler's Shadow: West German Historians and the Attempt to Escape from the Nazi Past* (New York: Pantheon Books, 1989).

34. Interviews with F. Furet: *Libération*, 7 May 1987; *Le Figaro*, 20–21 February 1988; by author, 13 April 1991.

35. J.-N. Jeanneney, "Après coup: Réflexions d'un commémorateur," *Le Débat*, no. 57 (November-December 1989), 103.

36. P. Nora cited by Richard Bernstein, "The French Revolution: Right or Wrong," *New York Times Book Review*, 10 July 1988.

37. F. Furet in *Le Nouvel Observateur*, 28 February-6 March 1986; F. Ewald, "Histoire de l'idée révolutionnaire," *Magazine littéraire*, October 1988, 19; Furet, "Réponse à M. Agulhon," *Le Débat*, no. 30 (May 1984), 42; Furet, "1789–1917: Aller et retour," *Le Débat*, no. 57 (November-December 1989): 15–16; O. Giesbert, interview with Furet, *Le Figaro*, 17 July 1989; Furet in *Le Monde de la Révolution française*, no. 2 (February 1989); *New York Times*, 13 March 1989. On the question of the relation (harmony versus conflict) between 1789 and 1917, Achille Ochetto, leader of the Italian Communist party, had these enthusiastic words to say in 1989: "Nous, communistes, nous sommes plus les fils de la Révolution française que ceux de la Révolution d'Octobre." Cited by J.-R. Suratteau, "89 'régénéré,'" *Annales historiques de la Révolution française*, no. 277 (July-September 1989): 311

38. F. Furet, "Réponse à M. Agulhon," *Le Débat*, no. 30 (May 1984): 42; interview with Furet, *Le Nouvel Observateur*, 28 February-6 March 1986; interview with Furet, *Le Figaro*, 17 July 1989; Furet in *Le Monde de la Révolution française*, no. 2 (February 1989). See also D. Bensaïd's burlesque of Furet's "loi des séries totalitaires," *Moi, la Révolution*, 251–52. Cf. Furet's articulation of the "despotic drift" to an American audience in a lively piece in the

New York Times, 13 March 1989: "'Today when I write I try to see what was already there in 1789 that became incompatible with liberty in 1793,' said Mr. Furet, who terminates his most resounding pronouncements with a nervous, hissing laugh. 'The sovereignty of the people is not necessarily liberal—now there is a great idea!'" Though Furet is not responsible for marketing his books, he should not wonder about his intimate identification with the Counterrevolution in the United States when Harvard University Press advertises his *Critical Dictionary* with a single word inscribed in Gargantuan letters, "BLOODBATHS," followed by an ecstatic endorsement from the rabid antirevolutionary Simon Schama.

39. Madame Wajda filmed by Serge Moati, *Journal d'un bicentenaire* (1989); "L'Arrosoir thermidorien: Entretien avec Bronislaw Baczko," *Le Monde de la Révolution française*, no. 6 (June 1989); L. Karpinski interviewed in *Le Nouvel Observateur*, 25–31 May 1989; Odile Rudelle, "Lieux de mémoire révolutionnaire et communion républicaine," *Vingtième Siècle*, no. 24 (October-December 1989): 3–16; J.-L. Martens and O. Ihl, "La Révolution française et le narcissisme idéologique," *La Revue Tocqueville*, no. 9 (1987–88): 146–47. Cf. *Le Nouvel Observateur*, 4–10 May 1989 ("La violence fait-elle nécessairement partie du processus de changement?")

40. Mary-Emilie Crouzet-Guillou, "*Danton* de Wajda: Image, mythe, représentation," in *L'Image de la Révolution française*. ed. M. Vovelle (Oxford and Paris: Pergamon Press, 1989), 3:2100; M. Ozouf in *Le Monde de la Révolution française*, no. 4 (April 1989); *Le Point*, 10 July 1989; F. Lewis *New York Times*, 29 January 1989; T. Garton Ash, "Eastern Europe: The Year of Truth," *New York Review of Books*, 15 February 1989, 19 (cf. André Fontaine's "Jamais révolution n'aura été si pacifique," *Le Monde*, 11 November 1989); E. Faure, "1789–1989: La Révolution française," *Revue des deux mondes*, July-September 1987, 282–83; P. Lepape in *Le Monde*, 29 January 1988; A. Grosser in *Le Monde*, 9 March 1989; M. Rocard cited in a letter to the editor, radio-television supplement to *Le Monde*, 18–19 December 1988; D. Langlois in *Le Monde*, 22 September 1989; J. Lévy, "Révolution, fin et suite," *EspacesTemps*, nos. 38–39 (1988): 69; R. Debray cited in *L'Anti-89*, no. 5 (February 1988); Debray, "Diviser pour rassembler," *EspacesTemps*, nos. 38–39 (1988): 16; Debray, *Que vive la République* (Paris: O. Jacob, 1989), 71–73.

Chapter 3
Velvet Dreams and Satanic Nightmares:
The Range of Bicentennial Rejectionism

1. C. Andrieu, ed., *1789: Le Livre du Bicentenaire* (Paris: La Documentation Francaise, 1989), 118; *Le Monde*, 12 January, 30 June 1989; *Dépêche du Midi*, 28 April 1988; J.-P. Chevènement in *Armées d'aujourd'hui*, March 1989, 10; *Libération*, 24 December 1991; *La Lettre politique et parlementaire*, 6 March 1991; M. Gallo, "La Faute de J. Julliard," *Le Nouvel Observateur*, 2–8 August 1990. For a vigorous defense of the *Marseillaise* as a song of fraternity and cultural pluralism, see Chantal Georgel and Robert Delband, *Marseillaise et Marseillaises* (Paris: le Cherche-midi for the Ligue des droits de l'homme, 1992). A 1987 poll commissioned by *Figaro-Magazine* (10 July 1987) had revealed that only 60 percent of the public (dominated by older people) felt "very moved" or "quite moved" by the *Marseillaise*. Twenty-one percent were "not really moved" and 17 percent "not at all moved." Pierre Bourgeade, in his language column in the same weekly, wrote puckishly about the "coincidence" that the hymn was written by a man called Rouget (de L'isle), the name of a delectable Mediterranean fish, and that it was named for a prominent Mediterranean city, Marseille. As a revolutionary hymn, the *Marseillaise* was naturally Red (*rouge*). In Dutch, the word for

rouget was *zee naen*, or *coq de mer*, and the *coq* was the symbol for the Gallic people of France. The Italians called this fish *lucerna*, or *lumière*, another word for the Enlightenment which infused the *Marseillaise* and which it carried around the world. "On se demande aussi, parfois, ce qu'il serait advenu de notre hymne s'il avait été composé par un homme qui se fût appelé, par exemple, *Bleuet*, et s'il avait été chanté par les volontaires de Lyon." *Figaro-Magazine*, 7 October 1989.

2. S. July in *Libération*, 12 July 1989; M. Gallo in *Le Monde*, 26 July 1983.

3. M. Gallo, *Lettre ouverte à Maximilien Robespierre sur les nouveaux muscadins* (Paris: Albin Michel, 1986), 11–14, 23, 25–40, 42–44, 138, 162–63; Gallo, "Le Nouveau Catéchisme," *Le Figaro*, 17 December 1984.

4. R. Debray, *Que vive la république* (Paris: O. Jacob, 1989), 17, 24, 26–28, 57, 77.

5. M. Gallo, "La Révolution: Une Dynamique sociale et politique," *Revue politique et parlementaire*, July-August 1987, 10; R. Debray, "Diviser pour rassembler," *EspacesTemps*, nos. 38–39 (1988): 18; interview with J.-N. Jeanneney, *Le Monde*, 27–28 August 1989. Jean-Louis Margolin tried to rehistoricize the debate in order to take the Jacobins off the defensive. "Une Révolution, mais de longue durée," *EspacesTemps*, nos. 38–39 (1988): 97. Cf. *L'Humanité*, 14 July 1988; Florence Gauthier, "Guerre du blé, guerre du droit," *EspacesTemps*, nos. 38–39 (1988): 114; Yannick Bosc, "La Conspiration du droit," *EspacesTemps*, nos. 38–39 (1988): 101; Daniel Bensaïd, *Moi, la Révolution* (Paris: Gallimard, 1989), 221–22

6. M. Agulhon, "Faut-il avoir peur de 1989?" *Le Débat*, no. 30 (May 1984): 29, 35; Agulhon, "Quelle stratégie pour le Bicentenaire?" *Revue politique et parlementaire*, July-August 1987, 15; Agulhon in *Magazine littéraire*, March 1987; Agulhon, "La Révolution française au banc des accusés," *Vingtième Siècle*, no. 5 (January-March 1985).

7. E. Faure, "1789–1989: La Révolution française," *Revue des deux mondes* (July-September 1987), 281; M. Agulhon, "La Révolution française au banc des accusés," *Vingtième Siècle*, no. 5 (January-March 1985): 10–11; Odile Rudelle, "Lieux de mémoire, révolution et communion républicaine," *Vingtième Siècle*, no. 24 (October-December 1989): 10; D. Bensaïd, *Moi, la Révolution*, 155; Bensaïd in *Le Monde*, 7 July 1989; A. Laguiller filmed by S. Moati, *Journal d'un bicentenaire* (1989); C. Mazauric in Mazauric and A. Casanova, *Vive la Révolution 1789–1989*, ed. C. Ducol (Paris: Messidor/Editions Sociales, 1989), 108, 110–12; M. Vovelle in *Le Monde de la Révolution française*, no. 7 (July 1989); R. Debray, "Diviser pour rassembler," *EspacesTemps*, nos. 38–39 (1988): 18; M. Agulhon, "Quelle stratégie pour le Bicentenaire?" *Revue politique et parlementaire*, July-August 1987, 14; M. Gallo, *Lettre ouverte*, 19–20, 132–40, 150-51, 153–54, 160; A. Casonova in Mazauric and Casonova, *Vive la Révolution*, 25. See also Agulhon's tender exculpation of 1789 ("ce n'est pas ta faute si les choses ont mal tourné") in *Lettres à la Révolution*, ed. Jean-Marie Lhôte (Amiens: Trois Cailloux for the Maison de la culture, 1989), 10. S. Farandjus makes a vigorous case that the diffuse but terrible violence of which the anonymous masses are victim must be taken into account in any reckoning of costs. "1789: Le Monde entier est concerné," *Revue politique et parlementaire*, July-August 1987, 17.

8. M. Ozouf, "Célébrer, savoir, fêter," *Le Débat*, no. 57 (November-December 1989): 25; *Libération*, 7 May 1987. Cf. F. Crouzet's scorn for the left's classical relativization of violence. In particular he cites J. Massin, a worthy predecessor of C. Mazauric, who compared the numbers of the Revolution's killings "to the far more numerous victims of counterrevolutionary repression, for instance in 1848 and 1871." Citing French soldiers shot after the mutinies of 1917, he recalls that 2,700 of them were later rehabilitated, which corresponds to the number guillotined in Paris in 1793–94. "So, why so much fuss?" asks Crouzet rhetorically. "Possibly," writes Massin, "because the latter included royalty, prelates, bankers, and

landowners," and he suggests that they more or less got what they deserved. Crouzet, *Historians and the French Revolution: the Case of Maximilien Robespierre* (Swansea: University College, 1989), 16.

9. *La Croix*, 5 July 1989; *Le Sud Ouest*, 15 July 1989; *National hebdo*, 3–9 August 1989; *Journal des guillotinés*, no. 2 (August 1989). Cf. *Présent*, the far-right daily, 11–12 December 1989, on the bicentennial rehabilitation of guillotines and the commemorative fetish for violence: "Ils se sont gaillardement refamiliarisés avec la guillotine. Des cartes postales 'amusantes' ont plaisanté sur ce beau sujet, les enfants des écoles ont mimé des exécutions, etc. Rien de plus naturel chez des gens qui pour un oui ou un non se mettent à crier: 'le peuple aura ta peau' (l'humanisme de gauche aime ces délicatesses)."

10. *Le Monde*, 15 November 1988, 9 June 1990; *Libération*, 14 January 1989; *Le Soir*, 7 January 1989; *Dauphiné-Libéré*, 8 January 1989; *Républicain lorrain*, 8 January 1989; *Le Quotidien de Paris*, 9 January 1989; *La Croix*, 24 January 1989; *Vendredi*, 13 January 1989, where the Socialist party condemned the "agression indigne" upon Delavault; *Le Choc du mois*, no. 14 (January 1989), which announced that "le mouvement maurrassien entend lancer ses militants à l'assaut des divers spectacles ou cérémonies prévus pour célébrer le Bicentenaire"; *Cité*, no. 21 (Spring 1989): 4; *Figaro-Magazine*, 7 October 1989 and 5 July 1991; *Le Canard enchaîné*, 28 December 1988. The most characteristic form of counterrevolutionary assault seemed to be the rather innocuous gesture of royalists at Rueil-Malmaison who "bravent le drapeau tricolore en pavoisant leur domicile de linges blancs le 14 juillet." *Le Monde de la Révolution française*, no. 10 (October 1989).

11. Marc-André Vernes le Morvan, "Une Cité de la Révolution française: Versailles, 1789, 1889, 1939, et 1989," unpublished *mémoire* submitted to the Institut d'études politiques de Paris (1989), 97; *Bulletin de la Société historique de Vimoutiers*, no. 16 (March 1989): 21; Lévêque and Belot, *Guide de la Révolution française* (Guide Horay), cited by *Libération*, 3 July 1989; Dr. R. de la Querière, letter to the editor, *Le Figaro*, 5 July 1989; P. Chaunu, preface to J.-F. Fayard, *La Justice révolutionnaire, chronique de la Terreur* (Paris: R. Laffont, 1987), 12.

12. Interview with M. Debré, November 1983, in Marie-Laurence Netter, *La Révolution française n'est pas terminée* (Paris: PUF, 1989), 223–24.

13. *Figaro-Magazine*, 3, 10, 23 December 1988; *Le Monde*, 23 November 1988.

14. *Figaro-Magazine*, 17, 23 December 1988; *Le Figaro*, 27 December 1988; H. Bellamy to editor, *Figaro-Magazine*, 23 December 1988; *New York Times*, 19 December 1988; *Le Monde*, 14 December 1988. Cf. the Sofres–*Nouvel Observateur* poll showing that 59 percent of the French opposed the execution of Louis XVI. *Le Nouvel Observateur*, 5–11 January 1989. A royalist periodical remarked that the majority of the public only learned in 1989 that the king had not been guillotined in 1789. Editorial, *Cité*, no. 21 (spring 1989). Cf. the CSA poll commissioned by the Mission du Bicentenaire in November 1989, which found that Louis was both more and less popular toward the end of the commemorative year. 38 percent found him sympathetic in late 1989 as opposed to 33 percent in 1987 (in a Sofres poll); 40 percent found him antipathetic in November 1989 as opposed to 27 percent in 1987. The number of "no opinions" fell substantially from 40 percent to 22 percent. Those respondents identifying with the RPR liked Louis most, ahead of the partisans of the Front national by 56 percent to 54 percent. The PCF respondents disliked him most (53 percent). I am grateful to J.-N. Jeanneney for kindly making these results available.

15. *Le Monde*, 14 December 1988.

16. *Le Canard enchaîné*, 28 December 1991; *Le Nouvel Observateur*, 15–21 December 1988; *Le Monde*, 14 December 1988; *Le Tribun de Loir et Cher*, no. 3 (March 1989).

17. "Un Entretien avec J.-N. Jeanneney," *Historiens-Géographes*, no. 327 (May-June

1990): 157; Jeanneney, "Après coup: Réflexions d'un commémorateur," *Le Débat*, no. 57 (November–December 1989): 92. Cf. D. Bensaïd, *Moi, la Révolution*, 185.

18. *Libération*, 23 January 1989.

19. *Le Figaro*, 21–22 January 1989; *Libération*, 23 January 1989; G. Braud (Charente-Maritime) to the editor, *L'Evénement du Jeudi*, 14–20 July 1988. An Ipsos poll of January 1988 cited by *Le Figaro* claimed that 17 percent of the French coveted a reestablishment of the monarchy. Cf. the Marie Antoinette prize that the Communist weekly *Révolution* had established in 1987, in memory of the queen's contempt for the hunger of the people, to reward each Bastille Day "ceux qui, par leurs paroles et leurs actes, symbolisent cette dimension des affrontements sociaux." The prize was a brioche. *Révolution*, 6–12 February 1987.

20. *Point de vue*, 31 March 1989; *Le Figaro*, 21 January 1989; *Royaliste*, no. 511 (20 March–2 April 1989); J. Reglat (Bazas) to the editor of *Figaro-Magazine*, 1 July 1989. In the cause of the exoneration of the king, see the recent study of Paul and Pierrette Girault de Coursac, *Enquête sur le procès du Roi Louis XVI* (Paris: La Table Ronde, 1983). Note also in the cause of royal rehabilitation and the execration of the "crimes" of the Revolution the recent American production of *The Ghost of Versailles* at the Metropolitan Opera.

The trial and more generally the opinions elicited by the bicentennial underscored just how uninformed the bulk of the French public was about its history. Many frankly avowed their ignorance. In all the polls, the number of "no opinion" respondents was very high (over one-third, for instance, in an Ipsos survey commissioned jointly by *Le Monde* and TF1. *Le Monde*, 4 January 1989. In other cases, the public revealed its woeful lack of historical literacy inadvertently. See, for example, the Sofres poll for *Figaro-Magazine* (10 December 1988) in which 25 percent of respondents believed that Louis Capet was guillotined in 1789; 29 percent characterized Robespierre as a Girondin; 47 percent did not know who Saint-Just was (6 percent called him the archbishop of Paris). On this "ignorance," which "n'empêche cependant pas les jugements sur l'histoire," see Olivier Duhamel, "Chronique de l'opinion: 'La Révolution française est terminée,'" *Pouvoirs*, no. 50 (1989): 121. A royalist organization, the Institut de la maison de Bourbon, commissioned a "Requiem à la mémoire de Marie Antoinette," which has its première in 1993 in the Conciergerie, the prison from which the queen went to the guillotine. *Figaro-Magazine*, 9 October 1993.

21. *L'Anti-89*, no. 2 (November 1987).

22. *L'Anti-89*, nos. 7 (October 1987) and 11 (September 1988).

23. *Le Figaro*, 11 August 1989.

24. *Le Choc du mois*, no. 14 (January 1989). Cf. the Comité de propagande contre la célébration du centenaire révolutionnaire" evoked by Christian Amalvi, *De l'art et la manière d'accommoder les héros de l'histoire de France* (Paris: Albin Michel, 1988), 374.

25. *L'Anti-89*, nos. 1 (October 1987), 5 (February 1988), 16 (January 1989), and 18 (March 1989); *Le Monde*, 12 August 1989; *La Croix*, 24 January 1989. The sole member of the Dijon municipal council who represented the FN also served as president of the local Association of 15 August. See Philippe Poirrier, "Le Bicentenaire dans l'agglomération dijonnaise," in Institut d'histoire du temps présent, *Lettre d'information*, no. 8 (July 1993): 19.

26. *L'Anti-89*, nos. 3 (December 1987), 4 (January 1988), 7 (April 1988), 14 (November 1988), 17 (February 1989), 18 (March 1989), 24 (September 1989). Cf. the text of the program-souvenir of the gathering of 15 August 1989, *Réparation de la France offerte au Christ Roi et à la Vierge Marie*, 35.

27. *L'Anti-89*, nos. 1 (October 1987) and 2 (November 1987). Cf. the remarks of Bruno Gollnisch, ibid., no. 16 (January 1989).

28. *L'Anti-89*, no. 1 (October 1987), in which there are separate articles by Abbés Coache

and Aulagnier, the latter being a membre supérieur du district de France de la Fraternité sacerdotale Saint-Pie-X, created by Msgr. Lefebvre; *L'Anti-89;* nos. 2 (November 1987), 7 (April 1988), and 21 (June 1989), which all contain articles by Coache); Coache in *Réparation de la France* (15 August 1989); *Le Monde,* 24 January, 4 July 1989. Given Brigneau's track record, there is surprisingly little *overt* anti-Semitism in *L'Anti-89.* Elsewhere Brigneau frequently evokes the evil trinity of Masons, Protestants, and Jews who conspired to subvert society at multiple junctures; or the deicidal crimes of Jews, unfaithful to God and perfidious in their refusal to recognize Christ as the Messiah. The allusions to Jewish actions and mores in *L'Anti-89* are more muted, for example, "Nous ne serons pas comme les juifs qui vont partout se lamenter sur leurs malheurs sans reconnaître jamais qu'ils ont une part de responsabilité." No. 20 (May 1989). Cf. *National hebdo,* 16–22 February and 7–13 September 1989; *Minute,* 13–19 September 1989. Cf. Brigneau's recent conviction for racism, a verdict he appealed. *L'Anti-89,* no. 25 (October 1989).

29. *L'Anti-89,* nos. 1 (October 1987), 8 (May 1988).

30. *L'Anti-89,* nos. 17 (February 1989), 18 (March 1989), 20 (May 1989), 24 (September 1989).

31. *L'Anti-89,* nos. 3 (December 1987), 10–11 (July-August 1988), 17 (February 1989), 21 (June 1989).

32. *L'Anti-89,* nos. 2 (November 1987), 3 (December 1987), 4 (January 1988), 5 (February 1988), 8 (May 1988), 10–11 (July-August 1988), 13 (October 1988), 15 (December 1988), 24 (September 1989). Cf. Brigneau's acerbic attack on the moderate Catholic daily *La Croix,* "le journal de l'église conciliante à tout ce qui est de gauche, d'extrême-gauche, cosmopolite et de préférence anti-français." *L'Anti-89,* no. 25 (October 1989). See also Marc Dem's venemous onslaught, in lockstep with Brigneau, against the "ralliement sans réserves" of the church hierarchy, for whom "la Révolution française, anti-religieuse dans son essence, a été faite pour la plus grande gloire de Dieu." "La Danse macabre de l'épiscopat français," *Le Choc du mois,* no. 14 (January 1989).

33. *L'Anti-89,* nos. 13 (October 1988), 16 (January 1989), 19 (April 1989).

34. *L'Anti-89,* nos. 1 (October 1987), 2 (November 1987), 7 (April 1988), 11 (September 1988), 14 (November 1988), 15 (December 1988), 18 (March 1989), 17 (February 1989), 19 (April 1989). At the end of June Coache vaguely but hopefully envisioned "des centaines de milliers de catholiques." Ibid., no. 22 (July 1989).

35. *Le Monde,* 17 August 1989; *L'Anti-89,* no. 21 (June 1989); *Le Quoditien de Paris,* 15 August 1989. Cf. the reaction of one of the participants in the procession, a seventy-one-year-old jeweler from Nantes, a Pétainist, a *chouan,* and a member of the Front national: "Harlem Désir l'aurait eue, lui, la place de la Concorde!" This was another proof of the partiality of a government "vendu à la cause judéo-maçonnique, comme le dit Jean-Marie." *Le Nouvel Observateur,* 17–23 August 1989.

36. *L'Anti-89,* nos. 17 (February 1989), 24 (September 1989), 25 (October 1989); *L'Express,* 18–24 August 1989; *Le Nouvel Observateur,* 17–23 August 1989; *La Croix,* 17 August 1989; *National hebdo,* 17–23 August 1989; R. Debray, "Diviser pour rassembler," *EspacesTemps,* nos. 38–39 (1988): 14; J.-N. Jeanneney, "Intervention à la séance de clôture," in *Les Catholiques français et l'héritage de 1789,* ed. P. Colin (Paris: Beauchesne, 1989), 370; *France-Soir,* 29 November 1989; *Le Monde,* 12, 16 August 1989. If Brigneau was slightly deflated, Jean-Marie Le Pen was not. Allowing for the difficulties of an August mobilization, he declared the procession a frank success. But he avoided commenting on the Anti-89er view of the Revolution and on the matter of intratraditionalist frictions. *National hebdo,* 24–30 August 1989. Focusing narrowly on the Revolution rather than on the more diffuse issue of spiritual decadence, Pierre Chaunu was one of very few outside personalities who warmly

supported the demonstration: "Je suis tout à fait solidaire de ces gens parce qu'ils ont le droit le plus strict de manifester le plus violemment leur désaccord." *Le Quotidien de Paris*, 15 August 1989. An editorialist for the latter paper saw justification for the Anti-89er movement in the fact that recent university scholarship partially supported the satanic view of the Revolution. Ibid.

Chapter 4
The Vendée: Trope and *Idée-Force*

1. *Figaro-Magazine*, 1 July 1989; *Le Quotidien de Paris*, 30 June 1989; *Vendée matin*, 3 July 1989; Jean-Clément Martin, *La Vendée de la mémoire* (Paris: Editions du Seuil, 1989), 218–19; J.-C. Martin and Charles Suaud, "Le Puy du Fou: Histoire en revue et politique de la mémoire" (mimeographed monograph, Université de Nantes/Centre national de la recherche scientifique, September 1991), 6, 74, 105–8, 127, 138 (a perspicacious and thoughtful ethnography and analysis that merits much wider diffusion than it has received; for an abridged version that is readily accessible, see Martin and Suaud, "Le Puy du Fou, l'interminable réinvention du paysan vendéen," *Actes de la Recherche en sciences sociales* 92 (June 1992). I am grateful for the information kindly provided by Geoffroy Linyer, a member of Villiers's staff. Under the title "Gare au pis centenaire," *Le Canard enchaîné* ventured this unflattering appreciation of Villiers's theatre at Le Puy-du-Fou: "c'est lent, lourd, sans rythme, aussi authentique qu'une salle à manger Louis-XIII des Galeries Barbès." 20 July 1988. For a more sympathetic presentation of the show and a history of the site, see Gilbert Prouteau, *La Fabuleuse Histoire du Puy du Fou* (Paris: Albin Michel, 1990). The *Canard* also revealed that the Vendéen theme park, erected in the wake of the show's enormous success, was built without proper permits, in violation of the POS, or plan regulating the use of space. *Le Canard enchaîné*, 29 July 1992, and *Libération*, 3 August 1992. In the Villiers system, everyone was expected to respect the same values, but apparently not the same law.

2. *Le Monde*, 28 May 1991. A recent example of the cruel streak in Villiers's ambition was his characterization of a woman candidate for the presidency of the National Assembly following Laurent Fabius' resignation. He deplored the "choix pathétique entre deux personnages charismatiques de la République socialiste: M. Emmanuelli, trésorier du PS, personnage éminent qui est à la vertu ce que Mme Bouchardeau est aux nymphes, aux grâces de Boticelli." Is this the standard of decency and generosity to which this moral crusader wants to hold his fellow citizens and his fellow Christians? Another moralizing aesthete who relished the beauty of the spirit and the flesh, Jean-Marie Le Pen, had already compared Huguette Bouchardeau "à une véritable pollution de l'oeil" in a legislative campaign in 1983. Villiers resembles Le Pen in numerous ways. Along with Le Pen, he is one of the rare politicians today capable of filling an auditorium in virtually every town in France. François Léotard quite plausibly suggests that his former junior minister is preparing to capture the Lepéniste heritage. The leaders of Villiers' own parti républicain, and their counterparts in the RPR, now worry aloud about the costs of his self-regarding campaign against the ignominies of politics and politicians. See *Le Monde*, 21 January 1992.

3. *Le Figaro*, 20 February 1984; *Revue du souvenir vendéen*, February 1984, 29–32, and June 1984, 1–3; J.-M. de Montremy, "La Nouvelle 'Guerre' de Vendée," *Histoire*, no. 92 (September 1986): 77.

4. J.-C. Martin, "Histoire de la Vendée, histoire de la Révolution," in *L'Image de la Revolution française*, ed. M. Vovelle (Oxford and Paris: Pergamon Press, 1989), 2:1154, 1162; F. Lebrun, in *La Croix*, 29–30 June 1986; J.-C. Martin, *La Vendée de la mémoire*, 217–18;

Claude Langlois, "La Révolution malade de la Vendée," *Vingtième Siècle*, no. 14 (April-June 1987): 63–64, 69–70; J. Duquesne in *La Croix*, 11 July 1989; Hugh Goff, "Genocide and the Bicentenary: The French Revolution and the Revenge of the Vendée," *Historical Journal*, no. 30 (1987): 982–84 (among the defects Goff uncovers are: Reynald Secher's egregious bibliographical lapses, French and Anglo-American; failure to examine church doctrine and popular piety in the late eighteenth century; anachronistic usage of Revolutionary legislation for polemical purposes; sweeping ad hominem condemnation of all juring clergy; indifference to counterrevolutionary violence, one example being the massacre of Machecoul in 1793). Secher tried to reach a larger public by way of a cartoon book for which he drafted the text, "une bande dessinée de qualité montrant la tragique histoire et le martyr de ce malheureux pays." *National hebdo*, 24–30 August 1989.

Cf. Mona Ozouf's optimistic contention, uttered in the spirit of consensus, that "l'affrontement historiographique entre droite et gauche est, lui, largement épuisé. Il n'y a plus aujourd'hui, comme au siècle passé, *deux* histoires de la Vendée." *Le Nouvel Observateur*, 4–10 May 1989.

5. For the conception and style of the *Revue du souvenir vendéen*, see no. 146 (June 1984): 14–17; see also the interview with the secretary of the association, Simone Loidreau ("Je m'occupe personellement des colonnes infernales. . . . Je suis arrivée au chiffre . . . de 180,000 morts."), in G. Belloin, *Entendez-vous dans nos mémoires? Les Français et leur Révolution* (Paris: La Découverte, 1988), 37.

6. P. de Villiers, *Lettre ouverte aux coupeurs de têtes et aux menteurs du Bicentenaire* (Paris: Albin Michel, 1989), 16–17, 29, 30, 35, 37, 45–46; L. Oury, "Les Chapelets de Machecoul," *Révolution*, no. 487 (30 June-6 July 1989); *Aspects de la France*, 13 July 1789; *Presse-Océan* (Nantes), 13 June 1989; *Le Figaro*, 14 June 1989. Tensions between Jeanneney and Villiers dated from well before the bicentennial. See their clash over radio station France Culture's invitation to Villiers in Martin and Suaud, "Le Puy du Fou. Histoire en revue," 127.

7. F. Furet in *Le Nouvel Observateur*, 28 February-6 March 1986; P. Chaunu in *La Croix*, 29–30 June 1986; C. Nicolet in *Entretiens de la Fédération française des Maisons de la jeunesse et de la culture*, December 1988; R. Debray, intervention at the colloquium entitled "L'Actualité de la Révolution Française," 5 December 1987, in *Bicentenaire 89, lettre de la Mission*, no. 3 (May 1988); Guy Millière in *Libéralia*, no. 4 (winter 1989); J.-N. Jeanneney, "Premiers Regards sur le Bicentenaire," *Cercle Condorcet*, no. 11 (March 1990), p. 28; "Un Entretien avec J.-N. Jeanneney," *Historiens-Géographes*, no. 327 (May-June 1990): 154; *Lettre de la nation*, 6 July 1989; Serge Moati, *Journal d'un bicentenaire* (abridged film version); B. Guinoiseau to *Figaro-Magazine*, 24 June 1989; E. Borne in *La Croix*, 8 October 1988; J.-C. Martin, "1789–1989: Quelle Commémoration pour la Contre-Révolution?" *Le Débat*, no. 39 (March-May 1986): 187–90; R. Dupuy in *Le Figaro*, 20–21 February 1988. On Villiers's heavy dependence on Furet, see his performance on Bernard Pivot's *Apostrophes*, 30 June 1989. Cf. Aymar de La Rochefoucauld's indignation concerning the utter lack of any "cérémonie en souvenir du 'génocide' français" in his letter to *Le Figaro*, 5 July 1989. But it should not be thought that *Figaro-Magazine* was the unique sounding board for counterrevolutionary spleen. "Pourquoi la Mission du Bicentenaire veut-elle absolument occulter le génocide vendéen?" asked reader Guy Francheteau of *L'Evénement du Jeudi*. "Ce n'est pas en cachant la vérité que l'on obtiendra la paix et l'union des Français." 13–19 July 1989.

8. P. de Villiers, *Lettre ouverte*, 24, 25, 29, 123, 127–30; *Le Nouvel Observateur*, 4–10 May 1989. Cf. *Le Monde*, 23 June 1989, which questioned the precision of the comparison between Oradour, where the Nazis forced women and children into the church and then burned them alive in the building, and Les Lucs where the bulk of the victims "de cette journée parmi les plus sombres de la Terreur" were killed not in the church but on the nearby

roads. On the recycling of human skin, see the clinical citation by Brigneau, who compares "la peau des hommes [qui] avait une consistance et un degré de beauté supérieur à la peau de chamois" with "celle des femmes présentant moins de solidité à raison de la mollesse du tissu." This difference explains "sans doute le nombre moins élevé de femmes que d'hommes guillotinés." As a coming attraction, Brigneau the sociodemographer promises "bientôt une étude [consacrée] aux femmes enceintes exécutées par la Révolution des Droits de l'Homme." *L'Anti-89,* no. 8 (May 1988).

9. Jean Dumont, *Pourquoi nous ne célébrons pas 1789* (Bagneux: A.R.G.E., 1987), 62, 71; H. Amoureux in *Figaro-Magazine,* 23 January 1988; P. Mestre in March 1984 cited by Marie-Laurence Netter, *La Révolution française n'est pas terminée* (Paris: PUF, 1989), 253–54; Luc Baresta, "Sainte Guillotine," *France catholique,* no. 2215 (14 July 1989): 31; G. Belloin, *Entendez-vous dans nos mémoires?* 40, 42; *Midi-Libre* (Montpellier), 9 July 1989; *Figaro-Magazine,* 14 July 1989; *Rivarol,* 14 July 1989; R. Secher in *Figaro-Magazine,* 24 May 1986; *L'Anti-89,* no. 3 (December 1987); Madeleine Rebérioux, "Un Processus qui s'étend sur deux siècles," *Revue politique et parlementaire,* July-August 1987, 11; *Minute,* no. 1422 (5-11 July 1989); Madame Loidreau, secretary of Souvenir vendéen, cited by Belloin, *Entendez-vous dans nos mémoires?* 50.

10. J.-M. Benoist, "La Révolution contre les droits de l'homme," *Libéralia,* no. 4 (winter 1989): 14, and *Le Figaro,* 13 July 1989; J.-M. Lustiger in *Le Monde,* 29 August 1989; *L'Anti-89,* no. 16 (January 1989); L. Baresta, "Sainte Guillotine," *France catholique,* no. 2215 (14 July 1989); *Le Monde,* 12 July 1988. On the discussion of the Enlightenment and on the use of "other" genocidal analogies in the German *Historikerstreit,* or historians' controversy, of the 1980s, see Charles Maier, *The Unmasterable Past: History, Holocaust, and National Identity* (Cambridge: Harvard University Press, 1988), 54, 66. German historian Ernst Nolte extended the term "genocide" to cover American behavior in Vietnam and Soviet conduct in Afghanistan, as well as the Allied bombing of major German cities during the Second World War. See Richard J. Evans, *In Hitler's Shadow: West German Historians and the Attempt to Escape from the Nazi Past* (New York: Pantheon Books, 1989), 85–87. See also the sociologist of religion Gilles Kepel's characterization of the Catholic Church's return to a traditionalist theo-ideological line: "L'Eglise ne se cache plus pour tirer à bout portant sur les valeurs des Lumières. Chez Lustiger, elles sont l'abomination suprême. Il n'hésite pas, le cardinal: le nazisme, le stalinisme sont les conséquences directes de ce siècle où la raison s'est émancipée de la foi! C'est la faute à Voltaire, si on a pratiqué l'extermination de masse." Interview in *Le Nouvel Observateur,* 3–9 January 1991.

11. J.-M. Varaut, "La Déclaration des droits de l'homme: Généalogie, esprit et contradictions," and J.-M. Benoist, "La Révolution contre les droits de l'homme," *Libéralia,* no. 4 (winter 1989): 10–11, 15; J. Dumont, *Pourquoi nous ne célébrons pas 1789,* 66, 84; Madame Loidreau cited by G. Belloin, *Entendez-vous dans nos mémoires?* 51; *Rivarol,* 14 July 1989; *Présent,* 27–28 November 1989; P. de Villiers, *Lettre ouverte,* 29, 52–53, 55–56, 125; *L'Anti-89,* no. 8 (May 1988); M. Gallo, *Lettre ouverte à Maximilien Robespierre sur les nouveaux muscadins* (Paris: Albin Michel, 1986), 139. On the potential for "une compétition malsaine" among genocide claimants, see the piece on the Armenian genocide and the reluctance to engage in what Alfred Grosser called "une comparaison nécessaire et difficile." *Le Monde,* 4 January 1991. Cf. the rightist German historians and commentators who pressed the case for other genocides and crimes against humanity in order to relativize Nazism "by stressing in what respects other countries have undergone comparable experiences." C. Maier, *The Unmasterable Past,* 16–17. See also the postbicentennial book by Reynald Secher, an ambiguous attempt at recentering composed of old materials and fresh reflections in which the author seeks a new legitimacy and a wider audience by distancing himself sharply

from the Faurrisson school and playing a feebly Machiavellian philo-Semitic card. He insists on the structural identity of the crimes against Jews and Vendéens. He stresses the homologies of the engendering and the practice of the two genocides (evil ideology as cause and the tanning of skins as signature). The two horrors were fatally solidary, and the affirmation of the validity of the first would strengthen the capacity of the second to resist revisionist assault. Secher posited a direct causal relation between "the negation of the genocide committed in the Vendée" and "the negation of the Jewish Holocaust." Jacobins, yesterday and today, were the real collaborators of Nazi revisionism, argued the historian, for "the negation, the dissimulation, the relativization" they practiced would spread ineluctably to the Shoah as the Jews became Vendéenized. He imputed to Jacobins (in both ultrarepublican and Marxist inflections) an immense moral responsibility. Had they not suppressed the truth about the Vendéen genocide, perhaps the Shoah would not have occurred, or would have been much less catastrophic. Morally as well as strategically, it was wrong for the Jews to hoard the genocidal label. R. Secher, *Juifs et Vendéens, d'un génocide à l'autre* (Paris: Olivier Orban, 1991), 15, 17, 19, 82–85, 173, 196–99, 202–4, 207, 212, 217. Cf. Secher, introduction, in Secher and Jean-Joël Brégeon, *La Guerre de la Vendée et le système de dépopulation* (Paris: Tallandier, 1987), 40. In late 1993, Secher announced the creation of an association called "Mémoire du Futur." Its goal is to kindle the memory of the (regional) past by building monuments, undertaking restorations, and promoting research. *Figaro-Magazine,* 4 December 1993.

12. *La Croix,* 29–30 June 1986; *National hebdo,* 18–24 May 1989; *L'Anti-89,* no. 16 (January 1989); *Figaro-Magazine,* 11–17 October 1986; P. de Salagnac, "Les Vendéens victimes d'un crime contre l'humanité," *Le Choc du mois,* no. 14 (January 1989); *National hebdo,* 2–8 February 1989; *Le Monde,* 21 June 1986; Michel Winock, "La Gauche, la droite et la Révolution," *L'Histoire,* no. 113 (July-August 1988). Cf. the cavalier denigration of the number of victims in the Vendée, precisely the sort of attitude that fed counterrevolutionary wrath, by writer Roger Vrigny in *Lettres à la Révolution,* ed. J.-M. Lhôte (Amiens: Trois Cailloux for the Maison de la culture, 1989). For a scholarly treatment of this question, see Jean-Clément Martin, "Est-il possible de compter les morts de la Vendée?" *Revue d'histoire moderne et contemporaine,* no. 1 (1991): 105–21. See also the pastiche of Romain Marie by his fellow European deputy, the Socialist J.-P. Cot, "rappelant l'intolérable accès des juifs à la citoyenneté française sous la Révolution, et observant que ces mêmes juifs ont cherché à s'attribuer, au travers des incidents regrettables survenus en Allemagne de 1933 à 1945, le bénéfice du beau terme de génocide, qui ne sauraient [sic] s'appliquer qu'aux seuls Vendéens, comme le démontrent scientifiquement les articles d'éminents journalistes français contemporains."

Claude Autant-Lara, a filmmaker and former European deputy representing the Front national, burst on the bicentennial scene with virulent remarks bearing indirectly on the genocide/revisionist debate. Queried, provocatively, about the concentration-camp experience of Simone Veil, a former minister and leader in the European Parliament where he had served, Autant-Lara replied: "Oh! Elle joue de la mandoline avec ça. Mais elle en est revenue, hein? Et elle se porte bien. . . . Bon, alors quand on me parle de génocide, je dis: en tout cas, ils ont raté la mère Veil." Autant-Lara was indicted for inciting racial hatred. *Le Monde,* 31 October 1989.

13. F. Lebrun in *La Croix,* 29 June 1986; F. Bédarida, "Du bon usage des mots," *L'Histoire,* no. 92 (September 1986); J.-M. Montremy, "La Nouvelle 'Guerre' de Vendée," *L'Histoire,* no. 92 (September 1986); Henri Guillemin, *Silence aux pauvres!* (Paris: Arléa, 1989), 104; R. Dupuy in *L'Express,* 24–30 June 1988; M. Agulhon, "La Révolution française au banc des accusés," *Vingtième Siècle,* no. 5 (January-March 1985): 15; A. Grosser in *Le*

Monde, 9 March 1989; F. Furet in *Le Nouvel Observateur,* 28 February-6 March 1986; J. Meyer, preface, R. Secher, *Le Génocide franco-français: La Vendée-Vengé* (Paris: PUF, 1986), 15; J.-F. Revel, in *Le Point,* 18 August 1986; C. Nicolet, in *Entretiens de la Fédération des Maisons des jeunes et de la culture,* December 1988; C. Mazauric, "La Révolution dans les processus d'acculturation politique des Français contemporains: Quelques Données," in *L'Image de la Révolution française,* ed. M. Vovelle (Oxford and Paris: Pergamon Press, 1989), 3:2314; C. Mazauric and A. Casanova, *Vive la Révolution, 1789–1989,* ed. C. Ducol (Paris: Messidor/Editions Sociales, 1989), 34, 120–21. Nicolet was not the only commentator on the left to accord the status of genocide to the Vendée. "Je suis un homme de gauche, mais je dénonce le génocide vendéen," wrote Pierre Bernis, president of Nouveaux droits de l'homme, at one time closely linked with the PS, "et je pense que la gauche française s'honorerait en reconnaissant qu'il y a eu génocide, qui tache la Révolution." "Entretien avec P. Bernis," *L'Ours,* no. 197 (February 1989). See also the argument for the coherence and unity of the Catholic and Jewish spiritual selfhoods, and for the specificity and singularity of the "Jewish genocide," which cannot be reduced to another form of Stalinism (nor presumably to another form of Revolutionary republicanism): Yves Ternon, "L'Unicité du génocide juif," *Etudes,* October 1988, 359–70.

14. L. Oury, "Les Chapelets de Machecoul," *Révolution,* no. 487 (30 June-6 July 1989). Alain Touraine characterized the pro-Vendéen polemic as "tellement excessif et stupide." The same description fit the overdrawn rhetoric of the adversary camp. S. Moati's filmed interview, *A propos de la Révolution.*

15. *Figaro-Magazine,* 8 July 1989; J.-C. Martin, *La Vendée de la mémoire,* 213; P. de Villiers, *Lettre ouverte,* 136, 138; *Aspects de la France,* 13 July 1989; *Le Canard enchaîné,* 12 July 1989; *Le Figaro,* 10 July 1989; *Le Quotidien de Paris,* 11 July 1989; *La Croix,* 5 July 1989. Cf. Emmanuel Le Roy Ladurie's comparison of the Napoleonic Vendée to the Poland of today. Preface to Martin, *La Vendée de la mémoire,* iii. Several left-leaning Catholic organizations, along with the Communist party and at least one peasant association, denounced Glemp's visit as an ideological manipulation masquerading as a humanitarian gesture. Madeleine Lelièvre, whom Villiers had defeated in the parliamentary election, wrote to Glemp: "Beaucoup de chrétiens sont choqués que vous célébriez la messe à Puy-du-Fou car elle ne sera pas à la gloire de Dieu mais à celle de celui qui va vous payer pour cela." *Le Figaro,* 10 July 1989.

16. "L'Appel du Club conservateur à Lodz," manuscript in author's possession; *Le Figaro,* 10 July 1989; *Libération,* 10 July 1989.

17. *Le Provençal,* 16 July 1989; *The Christian Century,* no. 106 (13–20 September 1989): 808; *Time* 134 (11 September 1989): 77; *Newsweek* 114 (11 September 1989): 36; John T. Pawlikowski, "A Sign of Contradiction: Pain to Jews, Shame to Catholics," *Commonweal* 116 (22 September 1989): 485–88; Leon Klenicki and Elias Mallon, "Close Enough to Step on Toes: Tensions between Jews and Catholics," *Commonweal* 116 (6 October 1989): 521–22. For a warm defense and "reading" of the Carmelites' most recent saint, see Xavier Tilliette, "Edith Stein," *Etudes,* October 1988, 347–58 ("Elle est une martyre juive de confession chrétienne; elle n'a pas interprété son sort autrement"). Cf. several suggestive and sober pieces on Polish-Jewish historical and cultural intersection: Michael T. Kaufman, "Poland: The Ghosts of Jews," *Commonweal* 116 (14 July 1989): 439–32; Aleksander Smolar, "Les Juifs dans la mémoire polonaise," *Esprit,* June 1987, 1–31; and Paul Valadier (S.J.), "Juifs et chrétiens, indépassable rivalité?" *Etudes,* November 1989, 509–20. For a passionate critique of the church's position on the Carmelite convent, cast in the context of the Vatican's equivocal attitude toward Judaism and Israel, see Raphaël Drai, *Lettre ouverte au cardinal*

Lustiger: Sur l'autre révisionisme (Paris: Alinéa, 1989), 123–30. For recent studies of the Auschwitz controversy, see Wladyslaw Bartoszewski, *The Convent at Auschwitz* (New York: G. Braziller, 1991), and Carol Rittner and John K. Roth, eds., *Memory Offended: The Auschwitz Convent Controversy* (New York: Praeger, 1991).

18. *L'Anti-89*, no. 25 (October 1989); *National hebdo*, 3–9 August 1989; *Rivarol*, 28 July 1989; Guy Konopnicki in *Le Monde*, 5 September 1989.

19. P. de Villiers's performance on B. Pivot's *Apostrophes*, 30 June 1989; Villiers, *Lettre ouverte*, 81, 87, 90, 105; *Le Quotidien de Paris*, 16, 30 June 1989; *L'Express*, 7 July 1989; *Libération*, 14 July 1989; *Midi-Libre*, 9 July 1989; *Aspects de la France*, 13 July 1989; letters to the editor, *Figaro-Magazine*, 2 December 1989.

20. *Ouest-France*, 6 May 1989; *Presse-Océan*, 6 May 1989; *Vie publique*, July–August 1989; *Le Quotidien de 89*, 11 May 1989; Serge Moati's film, *Journal d'un bicentenaire;* letter to the editor by P.D. of Nantes, *Minute*, 9–13 August 1989; *Le Monde*, 7 July 1989; *La Croix*, 24 January 1989; *Le Quotidien de Paris*, 30 June 1989; *L'Anti-89*, no. 14 (November 1989); *Libération*, 3 July 1989. There was resistance to the bicentennial celebrations in the Vendée outside the Vendée. One example is the town of Bédoin in the Vaucluse, where sixty-three persons, aged sixteen through seventy-four, were executed in 1794 in reprisal for the uprooting of a liberty tree. *Le Choc du mois*, no. 22 (September 1989). See L. Coulommiers, "Petite Vendée briarde," *Figaro-Magazine*, 10 June 1989.

21. On the transformation of Villiers's "Combat" crusade into a veritable political movement "ayant pour mission de faire émerger une génération neuve de vérité de conviction," see *La Lettre politique et parlementaire*, 21 April 1992, and *Le Monde*, 25 April 1992. Even as he preached the incomparable merits of an open and liberal world, Philippe de Villiers tightened control of the public sphere in his appanage. Any criticism of the chief's position was considered an act of treason. Nicole Fontaine, a former executive of the Catholic school system, was the first figure to declare publicly that "le KGB n'avait pas complètement disparu. . . . il existe encore en Vendée." See the evocation of this political machine ("intimidation, paranoia, megalomania") in *L'Evénement du Jeudi*, 24–30 September 1992. On the burgeoning revolt against the heavy hand and narrow spirit of the local potentate, accelerated by the debate over the Maastricht treaty of Eurepean union, see *Le Monde*, 30 September 1992.

22. *Le Monde*, 22 November 1990, 28 May 1991; *Figaro-Magazine*, 24 November 1990; *La Lettre politique et parlementaire*, 28 November 1990, 10 October 1991; *Ouest-France*, 4 June 1991. Villiers had his work cut out for him if he hoped truly to mobilize a national interest in the Vendée. "Pour vous, quels sont les événements qui symbolisent le mieux la Révolution française?" a poll asked French women and men toward the end of the bicentennial year. For 89 percent, it was the Declaration of the Rights of Man (as opposed to 74 percent in June 1987 in a Sofres poll); for 54 percent, the taking of the Bastille (55 percent in 1987); for 12 percent, the Terror and the September massacres (6 percent in 1987). The uprising of the Vendée claimed only 4 percent, a point down from its score in 1987. Voters for the FN constituted the single largest component in this category, followed by the RPR and the UDF. The left was virtually absent. Religion did not appear to influence the choices of respondents. Those in the west and southwest were more likely to reveal a Vendée consciousness than others. CSA poll, commissioned by the Mission du Bicentenaire, November 1989.

23. *Le Monde*, 19-20, 25, 27, 28 September 1993; *Figaro-Magazine*, 25 September 2, 9 October 1993; letter to the editor of *Le Monde*, 2, 9 October. On the bicentennial Solzhenitsyn, see also David Remnick, "The Exile Returns," *The New Yorker*, 14 February 1994, and Jacques Almaric's remarks in *Libération*, 31 May 1994.

Chapter 5
The Church

1. J.-N. Jeanneney, "Après coup: Réflexions d'un commémorateur," *Le Débat,* no. 57 (November–December 1989): 78.

2. See B. Basdevant-Gaudemet, "L'Episcopat français et le centenaire de la Révolution," in *Les Catholiques français et l'héritage de 1789,* ed. P. Colin (Paris: Beauchesne, 1989), 29; M. Lagrée, "Le Clergé breton et le premier centenaire de la Révolution française," *Annales de Bretagne et des pays de l'Ouest,* no. 91 (1984): 249–68.

3. The preceding discussion draws heavily on the sanguine view of René Rémond and on the more reserved appreciation of Claude Langlois. Rémond, "Présentation de la problématique du colloque" and "Conclusion," in Colin, *Les Catholiques français et l'héritage de 1789,* 19, 21, 389–95; Langlois, "Le Ralliement des catholiqes," *L'Histoire,* no. 113 (July–August 1988), and his piece in *Le Monde de la Révolution française,* no. 11 (December 1989). See also Pierre Eyt, archbishop of Bordeaux, whose interpretation comforts Rémond's, "L'Eglise, la Révolution française et les révolutions," *Communio* 14 (May–August 1989); Jean Boussinesq, closer to Langlois than to Rémond, "Lectures catholiques de la Révolution française," *Raison présente,* no. 91 (1989): 93 "Après deux cents ans, la Révolution n'a pas fini d'embarrasser l'Eglise"; the cartoon placing the latter embarrassment in telling caricature in *Le Canard enchaîné,* 2 November 1988; on the vigor of the antirevolutionary line within the church today, Christian Amalvi, *De l'art et la manière d'accommoder les héros de l'histoire de France* (Paris: Albin Michel, 1988); and the intelligent fresco in *Le Monde,* 22 March 1989. Political commentators such as François Furet, Jean-Denis Bredin, and President Mitterrand agree that the church has accepted the republic and the idea of popular sovereignty but still has problems dealing with "des moeurs modernes" according to the spirit and code of democratic practice. After noting that it is of little importance that "quelques catholiques gardent au coeur la nostalgie d'un temps que rythmaient châteaux et presbytères," Bredin asks, quite pertinenetly, "Faut-il vraiment, en outre, que l'Eglise se décide à aimer la Révolution?" *Libération,* 4 August 1989. F. Furet in *Le Nouvel Observateur,* 5–11 October 1989; F. Mitterrand in *L'Express,* 14 July 1989.

4. *La Documentation catholique* 85, no. 1973 (4 December 1988): 1124; *Le Monde,* 31 October 1988.

5. *La Documentation catholique* 86, no. 1988 (16 July 1989): 707–10; *Figaro-Magazine,* 24 July 1989; *Rivarol,* 7 July 1989; *La Croix,* 22 June 1989; *Libération,* 22 June 1989; *Le Monde,* 22 June 1989; D. Julia, "L'Anathème," *Le Débat,* no. 57 (November–December 1989): 202–3. On the problematic relation of the church and the Revolution, see the somewhat timorous remarks of Claude Langlois, "Droits de l'homme, liberté religieuse et Révolution," *Études,* September 1989, 229.

6. R. Rémond, "Présentation de la problématique," in Colin, *Les Catholiques français et l'héritage de 1789,* 20; Marcel Merle, "Le Discours des catholiques français sur les droits de l'homme," ibid., 355; Gérard Leclerc, "Voyage contemporain dans la Révolution," *France catholique,* no. 2215 (14 July 1989).

7. Interview with Msgr Dagens, 12 April 1991; C. Dagens, "La Mission de l'Eglise dans l'épreuve de la Révolution," *Communio* 14 (May–August 1989): 113–14. Cf. Lustiger's claim that bicentennial fervor had aroused anticlericalism, reinforced by the "chador affair," which "a suscité d'étranges fantasmagories au sujet des religions, accusées d'être la cause de la tyrannie et de l'oppression." *Le Monde,* 8 December 1989.

8. *La Croix,* 1 August 1989, 20 October 1988; *Pèlerin Magazine,* 6 January 1989.

9. "L'Eglise et le Bicentenaire: Entretien avec Msgr Thomas, évêque de Versailles," *France catholique,* no. 2216 (28 July 1989).

10. *Le Monde,* 21 June, 15 July 1989.

11. The preceding paragraphs drew heavily on the superb portrait of Cardinal Lustiger by Laurent Greilsamer and Daniel Schneidermann in *Le Monde,* 29 March 1991. Cf. the stringent critique of Lustiger by a group of Belgian and Lyonnais "progressive" Catholics in *Golias* on the anniversary of his ten years as archbishop. They denounced his manner ("autocrate," "normalisateur," "cassant"), his method of governing (founded on "copinage" and/or "mépris"), and his "théologie conservatrice."

12. *L'Express,* 7 July 1989; *Le Monde,* 29 March 1991.

13. Jean-Marie Cardinal Lustiger, "L'Eglise, la Révolution et les droits de l'homme: entretien avec François Furet," *Le Débat,* no. 55 (May-August 1989): 3–21; *Le Monde,* 8 December 1989.

14. *Le Monde,* 8 May 1989; S. Moati's film, *Journal d'un bicentennaire;* "Un Entretien avec J.-N. Jeanneney," *Historiens-Géographes,* no. 327 (May-June 1990), 155; D. Julia, "L'Anathème," *Le Débat,* no. 57 (November-December 1989): 206–7. On Lustiger's "postmodern" evangelism, see M. Loriaux, "Prodigal Daughter: Karol Wojtyla and 'la fille ainée de l'Eglise,'" *French Politics and Society,* no. 9 (spring 1991): 61–74.

15. Interview with F. Furet, 13 April 1991; J.-M. Lustiger interviewed on film by S. Moati, *A propos de la Révolution.* According to a probing portrait in *Le Monde* (29 March 1991), "si Jean-Marie Lustiger fait parfois bon marché de la vérité historique, s'il tord ses souvenirs, . . . c'est pour les faire coller à sa vision permanente d'une chrétienté en butte à l'hostilité de l'univers." Thus the resoluteness with which he exonerated the Catholic Church of any form of anti-Semitism since the end of the Middle Ages and imputed the responsibility for the tragedies of the twentieth century to the Enlightenment.

16. *L'Express,* 11 August 1989. *Le Monde* (29 March 1991) subsequently reported that Lustiger had originally planned to be abroad during most of July, a convenient, temporary emigration. Jeanneney was scandalized by his absence on the fourteenth: "Je n'ai pas compris pourquoi. C'est la fête nationale!"

17. *Le Monde,* 8 December 1989; "Entretien Furet-Lustiger," *Le Débat,* no. 55 (May-August 1989): 3–21.

18. P. Eyt, "L'Eglise, la Révolution française et les révolutions," *Communio* (May-August 1989): 124–31.

19. M. Schumann cited by Marie-Laurence Netter, *La Révolution française n'est pas terminée* (Paris: PUF, 1989), 193; Joseph Vandrisse in *Le Figaro,* 15 August 1989; Jean Li Sen Lie, "Les Guillotinophiles," *France catholique,* no. 2217 (4 August 1989): 13.

20. R. Rémond, "L'Intégrisme catholique: Portrait intellectuel," *Etudes,* January 1989, 98–103. See also Rémond's "Présentation de la problématique," in Colin, *Les Catholiques français et l'héritage de 1789,* 21–23.

21. *Le Monde,* 27 March 1991; P. Lauguérie cited by G. Belloin, *Entendez-vous dans nos mémoires? Les Français et leur Révolution* (Paris: La Découverte, 1988), 61, 63, 65; J. Bacon, in *Pensée catholique,* nos. 234 (May-June 1988): 32–34; 238 (January-February 1989): 7–9, 241 (July-August 1989): 34–41. For the church's vantage point on Lefebvre's schism, see *La Documentation catholique,* nos. 1966 (17 July 1988): 733–41, 1969 (2 October 1988): 928–32. On the orthodox *intégristes,* see the stimulating article by Jean Boussinesq, "Lectures catholiques de la Révolution française," *Raison présente,* no. 91 (1989): 90–91.

22. Yves Daoudal, "La Révolution sacrilège," *Pensée catholique,* no. 241 (July-August 1989): 42–51.

23. J. Bacon, in *Pensée catholique,* nos. 234 (May-June 1988): 32–34, 238 (January-February 1989): 5–9, 241 (July-August 1989): 34–41. Paolo Calliari, *1789, Révolte contre Dieu* (Paris: Editions Dominique Martin Morin, n.d.), and his essay in *Pensée catholique,* no.

241 (July–August 1989): 5–11; *Figaro-Magazine,* 18 March 1989; Jean Dumont, *Pourquoi nous ne célébrons pas 1789* (Bagneux: A.R.G.E., 1987), 15, 89; *L'Anti-89,* no. 14 (November 1988); *Présent,* 14 June 1989; *Libération,* 23 January 1989; *L'Evénement du Jeudi,* 23 July-2 August 1989.

24. *Le Figaro,* 21 July 1988; *National hebdo,* 20–26 July 1989; *Le Canard enchaîné,* 7 December 1988; *Le Monde,* 9–10 July 1989; *Le Nouvel Observateur,* 13–19 July 1989; J. Comblin, "Révolution française, révolution bourgeoise," *Concilium,* no. 221 (1989): 67-68. Cf. *Présent's* attack on Jacques Gaillot as an all-out subversive, in the church and in the nation. 16–17 October 1989.

25. B. Plongeron, "L'Eglise et la Révolution," *Documents épiscopat. Bulletin du secrétariat de la conférence épiscopale française,* no. 8 (April 1988).

26. J. Marensin, "La Révolution française et l'Eglise," *Commentaire,* no. 47 (Fall 1989): 479–80, 483; D. Julia, "L'Anathème," *Le Débat,* no. 57 (November-December 1989): 205-6; P. Valadier, *Le Monde,* 21 June 1989; M. Clouet cited in *Le Figaro,* 8 March 1989.

27. *La Croix,* 13 September 1988, 11 July 1989; *Témoignage chrétien,* 10–16 July 1989; *Libération,* 24 July 1989. Cf. the somewhat more mitigated call for "reconciliation" in *Pèlerin Magazine,* 6 January 1989.

28. J.-N. Jeanneney, "L'Héritage de la Révolution française," *Revue des deux mondes,* December 1988, 50; *La Croix,* 20 January 1989; Jeanneney, "Intervention à la séance de clôture," in Colin, *Les Catholiques français et l'héritage de 1789,* 369–77; *La Lettre de la Mission,* no. 9 (June 1989); Jeanneney, *Le Bicentenaire de la Révolution française: Rapport du président de la Mission du Bicentenaire au président de la République sur les activités de cet organisme et les dimensions de la célébration,* March 1990 (typescript), 115; E. Borne in *La Croix,* 25 March 1989; D. Julia, "L'Anathème," *Le Débat,* no. 57 (November-December 1989): 200–201, 205. See Jeanneney's use of the same rationale in his interview with *Pèlerin Magazine* (6 January 1989): "Quatre-vingt-quatre ans après la séparation de l'Eglise et de l'Etat, je ne songerai pas un instant, en tant que chargé d'une mission officielle, à donner des conseils, encore moins des directives aux catholiques. Mais cela ne m'empêche pas, comme historien et comme citoyen, d'être très attentif aux choix qu'ils vont faire et à leur portée nationale." Cf. the remarks of Jean Boussinesq: "La Révolution est ainsi une sorte de révélateur, et le Bicentenaire a mis à jour et accusé les contradictions. Il a servi aussi de test pour mettre en question l'Eglise elle-même, car elle parle de démocratie, de droits de l'homme, elle s'affirme publiquement comme source de liberté et maîtresse d'éthique pour le monde moderne: mais elle-même est-elle démocratique? La question est posée, avec de plus en plus d'insistance, par les catholiques eux-mêmes." "Lectures catholiques de la Révolution française," *Raison présente,* no. 91 (1989): 91.

29. *National hebdo,* 4–10 August 1988.

30. D. Julia, "L'Anathème," *Le Débat,* no. 57 (November-December 1989): 199; J.-Y. Calvez, "Chantiers pour le Bicentenaire," *Projet,* September-October 1988, 18; "L'Eglise et le Bicentenaire: Entretien avec Msgr. Thomas, évêque de Versailles," *France catholique,* no. 2216 (28 July 1989).

Chapter 6
The Presidential Mode of Commemoration

1. See the combination of scorn and wishful thinking in Louis Pauwels's interpretation of the presidential trajectory from sectarian Jacobinism (Valence) to dreams of a monumental Socialist bicentennial to the presidential decentering of the Revolution by late 1986:

"Dans son Elysée où il trône à l'imitation d'un monarque constitutionnel, il voit plus d'urgence et de grandeur à célébrer, en accord avec les autres autorités de l'état, le millième anniversaire de la France capétienne, qui échoit en 1987." "Pour en finir avec la Révolution française, tout simplement," *Figaro-Magazine,* 11 October 1986. What a myopic view of Mitterrand's relation to history, of his political imagination, and of his practice of presidential politics.

2. *Le Canard enchaîné,* 28 December 1988. *Libération* (3 July 1989) proposed three political scenarios for 14 July 1989, each of which at one time had been plausible. With Chirac as president, Jean-Michel Jarre presents his megaconcert and Michel Baroin hails the coming age of fraternity (Dr. Schwartzenberg, ephemeral minister in the Socialist government, falling asleep next to Cardinal Lustiger). With a Mitterrand-Chirac cohabitation, Edgar Faure provides a "zézéyant cordon-sanitaire" between president and prime minister, Mireille Mathieu sings the *Marseillaise* from the turret of an AMX 30 tank, and the entrepreneurial Yves Mourousi does the commentary for the parade, sponsored by business interests willing to meet his inordinate salary demands. (Mourousi wears a banner proclaiming, "Robespierre, ça c'est du camembert.") The third scenario was the one that took place, Jean-Paul Goude serving the mass celebrated by "Tonton, dit Dieu, dit (pour les intimes) le chef de l'Etat."

3. *Le Point,* 8–14 August 1988.

4. The Tennis Court speech was one of the few bicentennial events about which the Communists were excited. *Libération,* 22 June 1989.

5. F. Mitterrand, "Allocution . . . à l'occasion de la présentation des archives de la Révolution française," Sorbonne, 15 January 1988; *Le Quotidien de Paris,* 16–17 January 1988; Mitterrand, *200e anniversaire du serment du Jeu de Paume* (Tennis Court speech) (20 June 1989) (Paris: Présidence de la République, 1989), 6. In the Sorbonne speech, Mitterrand made the connection between animosity to the Revolution and hostility to liberty a second time: "Depuis deux siècles, les divers régimes qui ont mis sous le boisseau le souvenir, les emblèmes et les principes de la Révolution sont aussi ceux qui ont mis sous séquestre les libertés publiques, les libertés individuelles."

6. Interview with Christian de Montrichard, 17 January 1991; interview with M. le Recteur Robert Mallet, 4 February 1991; F. Mitterrand, "Allocution au cours de la réception offerte en l'honneur du comité scientifique de la Mission," 24 June 1987; Mitterrand, "Allocution . . . à l'occasion de la présentation des archives de la Révolution," Sorbonne, 15 January 1988; Mitterrand's speech opening the World Congress entitled "Les Images de la Révolution," Sorbonne, 6 July 1989. For a perceptive treatment of Mitterrand's recentering and his talent for using allies to destroy allies, see F. Furet's analysis, in which he shows the primacy of "circonstances" and "la force des choses" over ideology. Furet's Mitterrand was no Robespierre. *Le Nouvel Observateur,* 2–8 May 1991.

7. Yet cf. Maurice Agulhon's argument that Mitterrand earnestly wanted a commemoration "au-dessus de la division droite-gauche." Toward this end, he waited until the right repossessed the government before (re)launching the bicentennial campaign. According to Agulhon, he (re)turned to a leftish orientation only after Edgar Faure failed to disarm the general hostility of rightist ideologues and overcome the general passivity of the citizenry. Interview with Agulhon, 11 April 1991. F. Furet suggests that Mitterrand was vexed with Régis Debray and Jean-Noël Jeanneney for pressing too far in the Jacobin direction, a claim that reinforces Agulhon's line of argument. Interview with Furet, 13 April 1991. Claude Mazauric proposes suggestively (but cryptically in terms of the unarticulated definition of revolution that frames his argument) that Mitterrand's centrist surfing foundered on exogenous rather than endogenous factors: the sociocivic explosions in East Germany and elsewhere in the Soviet bloc. Mitterrand's "pauvre dialectique" could not account for what

French women and men witnessed on television every night from the streets of Leipzig and elsewhere. Interview with Mazauric, 14 April 1991.

8. Interview with Edgar Faure, *Le Monde*, 12 March 1987; Mitterrand's speech to the comité scientifique, or advisory committee, 24 June 1987; *New York Times*, 15 September 1988. Cf. Alain Duhamel's admonition against transforming "l'histoire en machine de guerre contemporaine" and inevitably becoming its "première victime." *Le Point*, 8 August 1988. Was Mitterrand pressing consensus (which "invite à l'arrêt") or "la transaction" (which "invite à la marche")? See Mirabeau, *Qu'est-ce que le principe de gouvernement?* (Paris: Quai Voltaire 1989).

9. "Mais s'il y a débat, et il y a débat—et sur quel ton, comme si à distance égale les adversaires de la Révolution avaient repris espoir—occupons la place qui nous revient, celle d'héritiers fidèles et fiers, déployons le drapeau et donnons à la République l'élan auquel aspire notre peuple." F. Mitterrand, Tennis Court speech, 20 June 1989, 7.

10. Mitterrand's speech to the Mission's advisory committee, 24 June 1989.

11. Mitterrand's speech at the Sorbonne, 15 January 1988; *Le Quotidien de Paris*, 16–17 January 1988; *L'Express*, 24–30 June 1988.

12. In that famous Bulgarian toast, Mitterrand could not have more emphatically repudiated shopping in the storehouse of the heritage: "Puisse-t-on comprendre, à l'Est comme à l'Ouest, que cet héritage forme un bloc indissociable, que nul ne saurait y puiser à sa guise ce qui convient à ses thèses et rejeter ce qui les dérange sans dénaturer profondément l'esprit de la Révolution." Still, the history and the heritage were not coterminous. *Le Monde*, 20 January 1989. F. Mitterrand cited in *Le Nouvel Observateur*, 12–18 January 1989; Mitterrand's Tennis Court speech, 20 June 1989, 7.

13. D. Julia, "L'Anathème," *Le Débat*, no. 57 (November–December 1989): 197; interview with Mitterrand, *L'Express*, 14 July 1989; *Libération*, 28 August 1989.

14. P. Boucher in *Le Monde*, 29 June 1989; P. Guilbert in *Le Figaro*, 7 July 1989; Mitterrand's Tennis Court speech, 20 June 1989, 5. Cf. the Sorbonne speech of 15 January 1988 in which the president noted that by embracing the bloc, he included certain counterpoints that he listed without explicitly labeling them horrors or crimes: "Et quand je parle de la Révolution, je fais comme vous, enfin je le suppose: j'embrasse l'ensemble des événements des années qui vont de 1789 à 1800 . . . sans chasser de mon champ de vision les massacres de septembre, les colonnes infernales, la loi des suspects et la guillotine." Sorbonne speech, 15 January 1988.

15. Interview with Mitterrand, *L'Express*, 14 July 1989; *Le Monde*, 16–17 July, 29 August 1989; *Libération*, 28 August 1989; Mitterrand's speech of 26 August 1989 at the Arche de la Défense, provided on cassette by Antenne 2. Cf. Mitterrand's sympathy for Louis XVI (in contrast, say, to Chaunu's inclination to hold him at least partially responsible for the failure of a wholly viable social system). *Le Monde*, 16–17 July 1989.

16. Mitterrand's speeches at the Sorbonne, 15 January 1988, 6 July 1989; interview with C. Andrieu, 17 January 1991. Cf. R. Debray's intervention at the colloquium entitled "L'Actualité de la Révolution française," 5 December 1987: "Ne soyons pas positiviste. Ce qu'on s'accorde à tenir pour 'réel,' c'est ce qui définit une idéologie." Thus certain commentators held the Vendée uprising for "plus réelle" than, say, the battle of Valmy or the abolition of slavery. In *Bicentenaire 89, lettre de la Mission*, no. 3 (May 1988).

17. Interview with Mitterrand, *L'Express*, 14 July 1989; *Libération*, 15–16 July 1989; *Le Monde*, 16–17 July 1989.

18. Tirelessly, Mitterrand riveted his cost-benefit reckoning: "On a beau allier parfois ou encore l'image de la Révolution à celle du sang versé, il existe en fait une corrélation rigoureuse entre le respect des libertés et de la vie et l'espoir d'une Révolution dont la

Déclaration des droits de l'homme et du citoyen constitue l'incarnation la plus définitive." Speech at the Sorbonne, 15 January 1988.

19. Mitterrand's speech at the Sorbonne, 15 January 1988. Cf. the interview the president accorded *L'Express*, 14 July 1989:

Question: "Pensez-vous que la marche vers la démocratie soit, dans le monde, inéluctable?"

Answer: "Non! Tirons la leçon des aller et retour de l'Histoire. J'ai passé ma jeunesse dans un environnement d'où la liberté était proscrite. C'était l'époque de Staline, de Hitler, de Mussolini, de Franco, de Salazar, et de quelques autres en Europe. Autant de souvenirs qui incitent à la prudence . . . . La liberté est fragile. Je l'ai répété tout le long de ma vie politique: elle n'existe pas à l'état naturel, mais résulte d'une construction sociale."

20. Mitterrand speech, 26 August 1989; *Libération*, 28 August 1989; interview with Mitterrand, *L'Express*, 14 July 1989; Mitterrand's speech at the fortieth anniversary of the Déclaration universelle des droits de l'homme, Palais de Chaillot, 10 December 1988; Mitterrand, "Allocution prononcée à l'occasion de l'ouverture des assises des Nouvelles Solidaritées," 9 January 1989; *Le Monde*, 14 December 1988, 10–11 December 1989; Mitterrand's speech at New York University (28 September 1988), *New York Times*, 29 September 1988; *La Lettre politique et parlementaire*, 17 May, 12 July 1989; television interview with Mitterrand, *Sept sur sept*, reported in *Le Monde*, 27 March 1990; Mitterrand's Tennis Court speech, 20 June 1989, 7. Though Mitterrand was flattered by the Soviet homage to the French Revolution ("c'est pour un Français un sujet de fierté que cette référence à notre Révolution"), he rejected out of hand Gorbachev's contention that "en 1789, vous avez lancé des principes, vous ne les avez pas suivis; nous les avons suivis." *Le Nouvel Observateur*, 27 July–2 August 1989. *Le Monde* (28 April 1990) remarked on Mitterrand's shift from "I" to "II," but without Guy Sorman's causticity: "Depuis sa première élection à la tête de l'Etat, François Mitterrand s'est assagi. Le tribun qui promettait de 'changer la vie,' le prophète qui ambitionnait d'achever 1789 en prenant les Bastilles économiques est celui qui a rompu avec la matrice de la gauche progressiste (à savoir la recherche de la détention du pouvoir économique pour transformer les structures de la société); il est celui qui passe aujourd'hui un compromis historique avec le patronat. Il est aussi devenu celui qui refuse de 'déchirer le pays.' A la témérité du 'socle du changement' cher à Pierre Mauroy, il a substitué une prudence qu'apprécie Michel Rocard."

21. R. Debray, "Diviser pour rassembler," *EspacesTemps*, nos. 38–39 (1988): 20; P. Billard, *Le Point*, 10 July 1989; A. Duhamel, *Le Point*, 8 August 1988; J.-N. Jeanneney, "L'Héritage de la Révolution française," *Revue des deux mondes*, December 1988, 46–7; *Le Canard enchaîné*, 19 July 1989 ("On disait que de Gaulle, tout à ses rêves de grandeur, ne s'intéressait passionnément qu'aux grands problèmes planétaires. Le Tonton du Bicentenaire est son digne continuateur"); Mitterrand's speech at the Sorbonne, 6 July 1989; S. Moati's film, *Journal d'un bicentenaire;* Mitterrand's speech for the reception of the Mission's advisory committee, 24 June 1987; Mitterrand's Tennis Court speech, 20 June 1989, 7; television interview with Mitterrand, reported in *Le Monde*, 16–27 July 1989, and *Libération*, 16–26 July 1989.

22. *La Dépêche du Midi*, 15 July 1989; *La Lettre politique et parlementaire*, 12 July 1989; *Aspects de la France*, 13 July 1989; *Médias*, 1 September 1989; Mirabeau, *Qu'est-ce que le principe de gouvernement?* 21, 52; *L'Idiot international*, 19 July 1989. A poll conducted toward the end of 1989 asked whether respondents felt that the bicentennial "was excessively dominated" by Mitterrand or whether "it's normal" for the president of the republic to have been "very much present." Seventy-three percent (including almost 90 percent of those on the left) endorsed the latter, favorable view of Mitterrand's action; 19 percent (including

about 45 percent of those on the right) the former, critical appraisal. CSA poll, commissioned by the Mission du Bicentenaire, November 1989.

Chapter 7
The Political Parties: Managing Memory in the Microcosm and the Macrocosm

1. Marie-Laurence Netter, *La Révolution française n'est pas terminée* (Paris: PUF, 1989), 9–14; Netter, "Le Rôle de la référence à la Révolution française dans le discours de la gauche au pouvoir, 1981–89" *Communisme*, nos. 20–21 (1988–89): 143–51; *Le Monde*, 9–10 April 1989; L. Pauwels in *Figaro-Magazine*, 11 October 1986; H. Amouroux, *Figaro-Magazine*, 23 January 1988. "Le P.S. était alors un parti révolutionnaire," noted the conservative *Lettre politique et parlementaire* in reference to 1981. "Souvenez-vous des harangues de Max Gallo et du Congrès de Valence, mini-Convention robespierriste." 12 July 1989. Cf. the way in which the French Communist party in 1939 likened the fascists to the émigrés of Koblenz.

2. Netter, *La Révolution française n'est pas terminée*, 151.

3. *Le Monde*, 16 January 1983, 8 October 1986; G. Suffert in *Le Point*, 8 July 1985; J.-F. Revel in *Le Point*, 24 October 1988; Netter, *La Révolution française n'est pas terminée*, 44, 62–63, 129, 150.

4. Interview with L. Mexandeau, September 1993; *La Lettre politique et parlementaire*, 17–24 March 1988; *Libération*, 12 July 1989.

5. Filmed interviews by S. Moati, *Journal d'un bicentenaire;* Netter, *La Révolution française n'est pas terminée*, 118–20, 130, 137–40, 160, 163; *Le Quotidien de Paris*, 8 January 1988.

6. *Vie publique*, June 1988; *Le Monde*, 27 February 1988, 1–2 October 1989. Cf. Laurent Fabius's postbicentennial and post-Rennes mea culpa-cum-project, *C'est en allant vers la mer* (Paris: Editions du Seuil, 1990).

7. *Le Monde*, 12 July 1989; Jack Lang's speech at the Pantheon, 12 December 1989, in *Supplément à la Lettre d'information* [du Ministère de la culture], no. 273 (25 December 1989); J.-F. Revel, "Leur 14 Juillet," *Le Débat*, no. 57 (November-December 1989): 64.

8. Interview with R. Léron, 10 April 1991.

9. *Le Monde*, 7 November 1988; *L'Humanité*, 31 October 1988.

10. *L'Ours*, no. 197 (February 1989); article by Patrick Kessel in *Renouveau socialiste*, no. 16 (June-July 1989); *PS Info*, no. 411 (24 June 1989).

11. *PS Info*, no. 411 (24 June 1989).

12. *L'Evénement du Jeudi*, 20–26 July 1989; *Le Militant de Paris*, (Fédération de Paris), special issue on the Congrès de Rennes, n. d. (1991), 16.

13. *Le Militant de Paris*, n.d. (1991); *Militant 13*, May 1989 supplement and no. 4 (June 1989); *L'Espoir de la Corrèze*, no. 256 (15–30 June 1989); Philippe Bonnard, Christophe Dubois, and Isabelle Gourdon, "Les Spectacles du Bicentenaire à Lyon et dans le Rhône," mémoire for the Institut d'études politiques de Lyon (1992).

14. *Vendredi*, 3, 10, 17, 24 February, 3, 24, 31 March, 21, 28 April, 12 May, 2, 16 June, 7 July, 3 November 1989; *Le Poing et la rose*, no. 124 (January 1990): 19; interview with L. Mexandeau, September 1993; the following materials from the Vive la Liberté (VLL) archives, kindly made available to me by Mexandeau's resourceful parliamentary assistant, Mme Chantal Grimal: P. Rouyer of VLL, Gironde, to Mexandeau, 25 September 1988; Mexandeau to G. Grandjacques, VLL, Haute-Savoie, 13 April 1988; D. Pilon of the VLL national committee to N. Morichaud, VLL, Essonne, 24 November 1988; J.-C. Gegot, VLL, Hérault, to Mexandeau, n.d.; M. Godzik, VLL, Saint-Etienne, to Mexandeau, 21 March

1988; Mexandeau to F. Triquet, Chanteloup, 24 March 1988; open letter from the VLL, Dauphiné (Saint-Egrève), 20 April 1988, and the statutes and rules of the association and the minutes of the board, 4 March 1988; Association dauphinoise pour le Bicentenaire–Vive la Liberté, *Bulletin*, no. 1 (June 1988); Gironde, Association départementale pour la commémoration du Bicentenaire de la Révolution française, *Bulletin*, nos. 1 (November 1988), 2 (December 1988), and 4 (February 1989); R. la Borderie to Mexandeau, 29 November 1988; Mexandeau to Vive la Liberté 33, 6 October 1988; Mexandeau to Théâtre de l'Impromptu, 10 January 1989; Mexandeau to Pégase Productions, 6 December 1988; national committee VLL broadside on tree plantings ca. mid-1988, and Mexandeau to all federal and local associations, 24 February 1989. According to a close observer of the bicentennial at the local level, himself a Socialist partisan, Vive la Liberté, conceived as the grassroots engine of Socialist commemoration, lapsed rapidly into inanition—"demobilization"—once Mitterrand was reelected and the party restored to its governing status. Interview with C. de Montrichard, 18 January 1991.

15. The connections in Communist writing between the Revolution and the Resistance merit systematic scrutiny. One encounters allusion to the linkage throughout the bicentennial. See, for instance, the lecture announced by G. Krivopisko of the Musée de la Résistance nationale, in Val de Marne, *Bulletin de l'Association départementale pour le Bicentenaire*, no. 2 (June 1988). An exhibition at Montreuil commented: "Le peuple souverain s'avance. Les idéaux de la Révolution, de la Résistance au nazisme." *93 prépare 89. Ephéméride pour la Seine-St.-Denis*. See also the parallels developed between the Revolution and the Resistance in Jean Matifas (a Dachau survivor and secretary of the Section rochelaise de la Fédération nationale des déportés, internés, résistants, patriotes), "De l'influence des idéaux de la Révolution française sur la Résistance," *Les Cahiers d'histoire de la Rochelle et de la Révolution*, no. 1 (1988): 119–22.

16. On the Communist interest in memory in the wake of World war II, see Gérard Namer, *La Commémoration en France de 1945 à nos jours* (Paris: L'Harmattan, 1987), 91–92, 97. On the Communist organization of the fête for the sesquicentennial, see Jean-Marie Goulemot and Jean-Jacques Tatin, "Le Parti communiste et le 150e anniversaire de la Révolution française: L'Année 1939," *Communisme*, nos. 20–21 (1988–89): 88–100. Achille Ocheto, secretary-general of the Italian Communist party (henceforth the Democratic Party of the Left, the Communists having renounced the now ignoble and irrelevant label), told a bicentennial audience that "sans aucun doute [son parti] se sent fils de la Révolution française." His political rival Bettino Craxi, head of the Socialist party, commented ironically on the comrade's repudiation of the heritage of October 1917. *Le Monde,*, 23 June 1989.

17. C. Mazauric in *L'Humanité*, 2 January 1989; P. Garcia, "La Révolution momifiée," *EspacesTemps*, nos. 38–39 (1988): 11–12; L. Viannet in *Le Journal des amis du cinéma*, no. 4 (August-September 1988); A. Lajoinie, preface, to E. Liris et al., *L'Allier révolutionnaire: Contributions à la connaissance de la Révolution française* (Moulins: Les Amis de la Révolution Française pour la Célébration du Bicentenaire, 1989); *Ah, ça ira*, Bulletin du comité d'établissement, Cléon-Renault, no. 1; *L'Ami du peuple*, June 1989 (published by "les communistes et sympathisants du service Information Communication de la mairie de Montluçon); G. Séguy in *Bulletin national, Vive 89*, no. 1; Séguy in *Bourbonnais hebdo*, 25–31 May 1988; interview with Séguy in the training video of the Association Vive 89; G. Marchais in *Les Nouvelles de la Nièvre*, 7 July 1989; Marchais, "La Révolution française et le parti communiste," in *Vive la Révolution française: Documents édités par le PCF*, 4–5; municipality of Montreuil in *93 prépare 89: Ephéméride pour la Seine-St.-Denis; Regards sur l'Eure*, 20 June 1989; A. Casanova, "D'hier à aujourd'hui," in *Vive la Révolution française*, 18–20.

18. G. Hermier, cited in *Libération*, 7 May 1988; G. Marchais in *L'Humanité*, 21 April

1989; *Le Monde*, 17 January 1989. Cf. Elisabeth G. Sledziewski, "Dans nos mémoires la Révolution," *La Quinzaine littéraire*, no. 526 (16–28 February 1989): 23 ("Le PCF fait du Bicentenaire le fleuron de sa politique de reconquête, tout en renouant avec la stratégie [classe contre classe des années 1920–34]").

19. *93 prépare 89. Ephéméride pour la Seine-St.-Denis; La Marseillaise*, 17 May 1987; C. Mazauric, *Conférences pour le Bicentenaire, 1789–1989* (C.I.D.E.F.E.); Mazauric, editorial, *Les Cahiers d'histoire de la Rochelle et de la Révolution*, no. 2 (1990).

20. *L'Humanité*, 12 July 1989; Roger Bourderon, vice president of the Comité 89 en 93, conseiller général of the Seine-Saint-Denis, in *Révolution*, 8–14 July 1988; interview with C. Mazauric, *Révolution*, 2–8 December 1988. Cf. Mazauric's denunciation of truncation and triage in the *Conférences pour le Bicentenaire* of the C.I.D.E.F.E., 6, 13: "Face à ces données de fait, on comprend très bien que les forces de conservation sociale, ou celles qui ont peur de la transformation sociale, celles qui la craignent ou qui n'en veulent pas, essaient de 'trier' dans la Révolution française ce qui est honorable et utile et essaient de rejeter ce qui est 'déplorable,' c'est-à-dire le mouvement populaire lui-même."

21. *L'Evénement du Jeudi*, 20–16 July 1989.

22. *Le Monde*, 18 November 1988; G. Marchais, "La Révolution française et le parti communiste," in *Vive la Révolution française*, 4–5.

23. *Le Monde*, 23 November 1988; *Le Nouvel Observateur*, 13–19 July 1989; *L'Humanité*, 16, 29 June, 13 July 1989. Summoning me to read his *Flight from Truth*, J.-F. Revel insists that Mitterrand had very little to do with the decline of the PCF, already in a state of irreversible decadence in 1980. Personal communication, 4 May 1993.

24. *Le Figaro*, 8–9 July 1989; *La Dépêche du Midi*, 11 July 1989; *L'Express*, 14 July 1989; *Le Monde*, 13 July 1989; *L'Evénement du Jeudi*, 20–16 July 1989; *L'Humanité*, 13 July 1989; *L'Humanité 7 Jours-Alsace-Lorraine*, 14–20 July 1989; *La Vie ouvrière*, 10–16 July 1989. A party newspaper published in Limoges, *L'Echo du centre*, 13 July 1989, claimed that over forty thousand demonstrators thronged to the place de la République on 12 July, five to ten times as many as other observers estimated. Several years after the bicentennial the PCF relaunched its campaign against the Conseil constitutionnel, "chapeau dérisoire d'une dérisoire démocratie," in the words of Jean-Paul Jouary, a philosopher and member of the central committee. The idea that the court could annul laws without appeal struck the Communists as a travesty of the notion of a government of, by, and for the people. *La Lettre politique et parlementaire*, 10 December 1991.

25. G. Marchais in *L'Humanité*, 14 July 1989. Cf. this autocriticism in the words of Claude Mazauric, one of the party's leading historical theoreticians, who acknowledged the grave Communist error of "la critique sociale faite de l'humanisme théorique chez les penseurs de la lutte des classes, cette conclusion donc, que la conquête des droits 'réels' pour les dominés passe par la suppression des libertés 'formelles' de l'individu: l'urgence de classe contre les idéaux civilisateurs." Preface, *Comités d'entreprises en révolutions* (Paris: Messidor, 1990), 53.

26. J. Roux cited in Comité 89 en 93, *Bulletin*, no. 1, (November 1988); G. Marchais in *L'Humanité*, 14 July 1989; *Révolution*, 4–20 July, 4–10 August 1989.

27. Editorials in Comité 89 en 93, *Bulletin*, no. 4 (February 1989); Bulletin Vive 89 en Ille-et-Vilaine, n.d. (1988); C. Mazauric, in *Profession politique*, 15 January 1990; Mazauric, in *Entretiens de la Fédération française des Maisons des jeunes et de la culture*, April 1989; Ligue des droits de l'homme, brochure for a colloquium on "citoyenneté," Lille, April 1989. The Communist preference for the rights of '93 over those of '89 remained undiminished during the bicentennial. See G. Marchais, "La Révolution française et le parti communiste," in *Vive la Révolution française*, 6–7.

28. *Révolution*, 8–14 July 1988; M.-L. Netter, *La Révolution française n'est pas terminée*, 183–84, 190; *Libération*, 7 May 1987; *Le Monde*, 5 May 1990; *L'Humanité*, 14 July 1988.

29. This paragraph and the following ones derive from G. Hermier's report to the central committee, "Les Communistes dans la préparation du Bicentenaire," 6–7 April 1987. On the history of communist attitudes toward the Revolution and the reorientation of the PCF in the 1930s, see C. Mazauric, *Jacobinisme et Révolution: Autour du bicentenaire de quatre-vingt-neuf* (Paris: Editions Sociales, 1984), 30–36.

30. Minutes of Vive 89 Allier, Association des amis de la Révolution française, 16 March 1987 (kindly communicated by J.-C. Mairal).

31. *L'Humanité*, 15 July 1988. See the chapter in Book Three entitled "The Bicentennial from Below: In the Communist Penumbra" for a full treatment of Vive 89 and other Communist-inspired activities at the grass roots.

32. G. Plissonnier to leadership of the federations, 5 May 1988, Vive 89 Archives; *L'Humanité*, 9, 10, 12 September 1988; "Vive la Révolution," unsigned commentary celebrating Editions Messidor in *Vive la Révolution française*, 9.

33. *L'Humanité*, 21 April 1989; *Le Monde*, 23–24 April, 10–11 September 1989.

34. *Libération*, 14 July 1988, 18 July 1989; *L'Evénement du Jeudi*, 26 February–4 March 1987; A. Juppé interviewed in S. Moati's film, *Journal d'un bicentenaire; La Lettre de la nation*, 6 July 1989; *Le Monde*, 8 July 1989; M.-L. Netter, *La Révolution française n'est pas terminée*, 223, 244.

35. With genuine regret for the missed opportunity, M. Winock deplored the opposition's lack of imagination, intellectual courage, and lucidity: "il est désolant de considérer à quel point la droite modérée ou gaulliste"—a rather idealized equivalency!—"a du mal à assumer l'héritage de notre Révolution. Elle s'imagine sans doute qu'en lui faisant quelques signes de gratitude elle ferait le jeu de ses adversaires de gauche. Elle devrait relire certains discours du général de Gaulle . . . les hommages qu'il rendait à Danton, Hoche, Carnot ou Kléber. L'instinct 'national,' que l'on dit être à droite depuis Boulanger, devrait inspirer aux têtes pensantes de l'opposition une certaine admiration rétrospective pour les volontaires nationaux, pour l'élan patriotique extraordinaire qui a soulevé une armée de traîne-savates contre l'envahisseur. Et s'ils n'aiment pas le principe d'égalité, qu'ils aient du moins de la reconnaissance pour ceux qui ont célébré et mis dans la loi les principes de liberté!" "Mais où est passée la droite républicaine?" *L'Evénement du Jeudi*, 20–26 April 1989. An unlikely bellwether, Giscard pointed in the right direction by dedicating his *Démocratie française* (1976) to Marianne and Gavroche. J.-N. Jeanneney, *Concordances des temps* (Paris: Le Seuil, 1988), 330.

36. *Libération*, 18 July 1989; M.-L. Netter, *La Révolution française n'est pas terminée*, 208, 215, 252, 260; *Le Figaro*, 7 July 1989; *Le Quotidien de Paris*, 20 June 1989; *Le Canard enchaîné*, 12 July 1989; *L'Evénement du Jeudi*, 26 February–4 March 1987; M. Poniatowski, "En écoutant *la Marseillaise*," text prepared for the celebration at L'Isle-Adam on 14 July 1989 (kindly communicated by the author).

37. *Le Monde*, 15 December 1988, 19 July 1989; *Libération*, 3 July 1989; *Le Canard enchaîné*, 12, 20 July 1989; *L'Evénement du Jeudi*, 13–19 and 20–26 July 1989. For a more detailed discussion of the Parisian bicentennial strategy and the relations between Jacques Chirac and the Mission, see the chapter entitled "Paris: Bicentennial Accommodation and Resistance" in Book Three below.

38. G. Belloin, *Entendez-vous dans nos mémoires? Les Français et leur Révolution* (Paris: La Découverte, 1988), 259–66; Y. Blot, "Le Marxisme et la Révolution française," *Contrepoint*, no. 40 (winter 1982): 9–10, 16–18; P.-A. Taguieff, "Un Programme révolutionnaire," in *Le*

Front national à découvert, ed. Nona Mayer and Pascal Perrineau, (Paris: Fondation nationale des sciences politiques, 1989), 197–99.

39. F. Furet, "La France unie," in *La République du centre* (Paris: Calmann-Lévy, 1988), 24; *Le Monde,* 27 April, 2 September 1989; *National hebdo,* 25–31 March 1989; filmed interview with J.-M. Le Pen, S. Moati, *A propos de la Révolution* and *Journal d'un bicentenaire.*

40. *Le Figaro,* 27 December 1988; *Le Monde,* 29 December 1988; *Politis,* 20–26 January 1989.

41. *National hebdo,* 15 February 1989; *Le Monde,* 2 February 1989.

42. *L'Express,* 27 January 1989; *Le Monde,* 17–18 December 1989, 3 April, 3 May 1990. It is interesting to note that Le Pen continued to draw on the imagery of the Revolution long after most other players on the political landscape, left and right, had put it to rest. Fouquier-Tinville was still on his lips at the end of 1991, as he vigorously pressed the constituencies of the civilized right for a recognition of legitimacy. Like certain anti-Lepénistes, "à partir d'un mot seul, Fouquier-Tinville se faisait fort de faire condamner un homme; mais il fut le précurseur de la Terreur, l'ancêtre des Beria, Himmler ou Pol Pot." Le Pen consoled himself with the warming thought that "après les hivers de la Terreur et les raids des colonnes infernales, refleurissent toujours les haies des chemins creux de la liberté." *Figaro-Magazine,* 23 November 1991.

Book II / Chapter 1
Toward a Bicentennial Project:
From the World's Fair to the Grand Orient

1. *Le Monde,* 26 September 1981; *L'Est républicain,* 12 June 1988; Max Gallo, "La Révolution: Une Dynamique sociale et politique," *Revue politique et parlementaire,* July-August 1987, 9.

2. Claire Andrieu, ed., *1789: Le Livre du Bicentennaire* (Paris: Le Chêne-Hachette, 1990), 9; interview with Robert Bordaz, September 1993; R. Bordaz, *Pour donner à voir* (Paris: Diagonales, 1987), pp. 244–77; *Livre blanc: Projets pour l'exposition universelle de 1989 à Paris* (Paris: Flammarion, 1985), 11–23, 30–35, 83–89, 142–45; interview with Jean Favier, July 1991.

3. *Le Monde,* 7 July 1983; *Le Figaro,* 6 July 1983; interview with Bordaz, September 1993. "Hard times" was one of the reasons that American bicentennial planners cited for rejecting the idea of imitating the international exhibition of 1876. American Revolution Bicentennial Administration, *A Final Report to the People: The Bicentennial of the U.S.A.* (Washington, D.C.: U.S. Government Printing Office, 1977), 1:57.

4. *Le Figaro,* 6 July 1983.

5. *Le Monde,* 7 July 1983; *L'Humanité,* 6, 7 July 1983; interview with J. Favier, July 1991.

6. Interview with Bordaz, September 1993; Bordaz, *Pour donner,* 265–77; *Livre blanc,* 112–22, 131–32. Putting a positive spin on the outcome, Trigano hoped that it would result in a more "national" focus on the Revolution and its legacy. *Livre blanc,* 149–60. *Le Monde,* 7 July 1983; *Le Figaro,* 6 July 1983; *Libération,* 7 July 1983.

7. René Blanchez, *Bonchamps et l'insurrection vendéenne* (Paris: Perrin, 1902), 287–312; P. M. Chauveau, *Vie de Charles-Melchior-Artus, marquis de Bonchamps, général vendéen* (Paris: Bleuct et Lenormand, 1817), 219, 220–21, 228–29, 248, 268–70; A. Joubert, "Bonchamps," in *Généraux et chefs de la Vendée militaire,* ed. Alexis de Nouhes (Cholet: Editions du Choletais, 1987), 12.

8. Interview with R. Mallet, 4 February 1991; interview with C. de Montrichard, January 1990.

9. For the record it should be noted that the formal title cited here aroused the purist ire of a number of citizens. Denouncing this "véritable défi à la langue française," a reader of *Le Monde* protested that "on 'célèbre' un bicentennaire, on ne le commémore pas. On peut 'commémorer' la Révolution française ou la Déclaration des droits de l'homme, mais pas leur anniversaire." The issue could not be overlooked by Baroin's successor as Mission chief, Edgar Faure, a member of the Académie française. To the rescue he dispatched his one-time intimate collaborator Gérard Antoine, professor emeritus of the history of the French language. Antoine unearthed at least three usages of the verb *commémorer,* one of which was "célébrer," as in "commémorer un anniversaire"—precisely the Mission's role. But in Cartesian deference to clarity and concision, Antoine, Solomonlike, suggested rejecting both *commémorer* and *célébrer* by shortening the administrative title to "Mission du Bicentenaire de la Révolution française." J. Lebar to the editor, *Le Monde,* 16 April 1987; G. Antoine's response, 12 May 1987.

The extreme counterrevolutionaries of *L'Anti-89* protested against the usage—the misappropriation—of the word "mission," defined in the *Robert* as "un ordre divin donné à un fidèle d'accomplir quelque chose." The government named its mission "pour organiser la fête de la décatholisation." No. 8 (May 1988). Yet these same counterrevolutionaries did not hesitate to adopt Revolutionary language. Abbé Coache, for instance, envisioned the antibicentennial ceremonies of 15 August as "cette levée en masse." *L'Anti-89,* nos. 10–11 (July–August 1988).

10. *Le Quotidien de Paris,* 17 September 1986; *Le Monde,* 8 October 1986 and 15 December 1988; M. Baroin, *La Force de l'amour* (Paris: Odile Jacob, 1987), 57, 58; interview with M. Rebérioux, 11 April 1991.

11. *Michel Baroin: Un Homme, une voix,* interview by Michel Baron (Paris: Editions C.I.E.M., 1985), 15–33; M. Baroin, *La Force de l'amour,* 39.

12. *Michel Baroin: Un Homme, une voix,* 10, 34; Baroin, *La Force de l'amour,* 44.

13. M. Baroin, *La Force de l'amour,* 56–57, 76–77.

14. *Michel Baroin: Un Homme, une voix,* 10–12.

15. *Michel Baroin: Un homme, une voix,* pp.21, 33, 38, 40, 44, 71–73, 78, 80–81, 85, 87, 89, 90, 97; M. Baroin, *La Force de l'amour,* 101, 155–56, 218, 242–43; *Le Quotidien de Paris,* 17 September 1986; *Le Monde,* 8 October 1986; *Libération,* 3 July 1989; *L'Anti-89,* nos. 1 (October 1987) and 7 (April 1988). Chirac underlined his desire to distance the bicentennial from the Revolution in his speech installing the Mission. Its leitmotif was a decentering of the Revolution, whose anniversary he construed as not intrinsically more important than the thousandth anniversary of the election of Hugues Capet in 987. Louis and Hugues, *même combat!* "Discours de Monsieur le premier ministre, installation de la Mission," kindly communicated to me by François Baroin. See also the excerpts in Andrieu, *1789: Le Livre du Bicentenaire,* 11.

To help move toward "objectivity" and "serenity," Chirac discreetly purged the memory managers of the left. Thus he replaced the leftist historian Madeleine Rebérioux as president of the Association pour les célébrations nationales with Jean Leclant, "un égyptologue peu remuant." *Le Monde,* 24 November 1989.

16. I am grateful, first, to Ambassador Cabouat and later to François Baroin for procuring me copies of the Baroin charter. I also drew on Baroin's inaugural address to the cabinet; "Une Déclaration pour le troisième millénaire," a bulletin produced by AD 89 (1988); and that association's *Manifeste pour 89,* all of which François Baroin graciously supplied me. See also M. Baroin, *La Force de l'amour,* 151–53, and *Le Quotidien de Paris,* 17 September 1986.

17. J. Mullender and A. Gally (Inspection générale de l'administration), "Les Associations" (June 1989), 3; M. Baroin's inaugural address to the cabinet; interview with F. Baroin, 11 April 1991; interviews with two Mission collaborators who demanded anonymity; interview with C. Andrieu, 4 February 1990.

18. Interview with F. Baroin, 11 April 1991; M. Baroin's inaugural address to the cabinet; C. Manceron to M. Baroin, 15 December 1986, Mission papers, Archives nationales (AN), carton 1.

19. Interview with F. Baroin, 11 April 1991; "Compte rendu de la réunion interministérielle," 31 October 1986; M. Baroin's inaugural address to the cabinet.

20. *Stratégies*, no. 633 (12 December 1988); interview with F. Baroin, 11 April 1991; *France-Soir*, 28 October 1988.

21. Interview with F. Baroin, August 1991; *Le Point*, 24–30 June 1990; *Le Nouvel Observateur*, 18–24 July 1991; Raingear to M. Vovelle, 18 March 1987, Mission papers, AN, 900506/937.

22. Interview with C. Andrieu, 4 February 1990; interview with J. Favier, July 1991.

23. Interview with F. Baroin, 11 April 1991; interview with J.-N. Jeanneney, January 1990; interview with C. de Montrichard, January 1990; interviews with several sources in the civil service and in politics who demanded anonymity; *Le Nouvel Observateur*, 8–14 August 1991. The new president of GMF is said to have removed the company's desktop computers before the personnel of the Mission could drain them of the data bases lodged in their memories. P.S.: In 1991 François Baroin, not yet thirty years old, won election to the National Assembly on the RPR ticket. In 1994 J.-L. Pétriat abandoned the presidency of GMF and was indicted for misuse of letters of credit. *Le Monde*, 21 May, 15 June 1994.

Chapter 2
A Man for All Seasons: Edgar Faure as Bicentennial Missionary

1. *Libération*, 7 May 1987; *Le Monde*, 12 March 1987, 29 January and 31 March 1988. In the last issue of *Le Monde* just cited, Plantu has a marvelous cartoon depicting de Gaulle sitting on a celestial cloud between Mendès-France and Faure. To the latter the general intones: "Tu vas voir. Ils vont tous dire que tu étais un rassembleur." De Gaulle described Faure as "un homme de juste milieu, expert dans l'art de tenter de concilier les inconciliables." Cited in *Bicentenaire 89, lettre de la Mission*, no. 7 (April 1989): 15. I don't believe that Professor Schwartzenberg's outspoken hostility to the Faure selection was widely shared among his Socialist friends. See Serge Moati's film *Journal d'un bicentenaire*.

2. Undated communiqué of the Mission. In a more academic version, redolent of the rhetoric of Reformation colloquies, Faure ended his sentence with the formula "asymptote à l'unanimisme." "1789–1989: La Révolution française," *Revue des deux mondes*, August 1987, 280. See also *Le Figaro*, 20–21 February 1988 and *Bicentenaire 89, lettre de la Mission*, no. 1 (January 1988).

3. On this major effort to reknit the sundered American fabric, see Paul H. Buck, *Road to Reunion, 1865–1900* (Boston: Little, Brown, 1937). See also Cathérine Nay's interview with E. Faure, 9 March 1987: "une occasion de réconciliation nationale, que des hommes qui se sont opposés souvent violemment, mais qui étaient tous des hommes de bonne volonté, qui ont été victimes des malentendus de l'histoire, se réconcilient dans le vaste élan de l'identité nationale." Cited in *Bicentenaire 89, lettre de la Mission*, no. 7 (April 1989).

4. E. Faure cited by L. Lemire, "Bicentenaire, mode d'emploi," *L'Histoire*, no. 113 (July-August 1989): 125.

5. *Figaro-Magazine*, 21 November 1987. I generally concur with J.-N Jeanneney that Faure felt a deep antipathy to the "fait révolutionnaire." See his interview in Serge Moati's film *Journal d'un bicentenaire*.

6. E. Faure, address to the advisory committee, 26 May 1987, Mission papers, AN, 1035; interviews with C. de Montrichard, January 1990.

7. Undated public letter by Edgar Faure, Mission; Faure, "1789–1989: La Révolution française," *Revue des deux mondes*, October 1987, 19, and *Revue des deus mondes*, July 1987, 15–23.

8. "Projet de création de la Fondation internationale des droits de l'homme et des sciences de l'humain," 25 August 1987, Mission papers, AN, 900506/666; draft statutes for the Foundation, 900506/4; minutes of the advisory committee, 26 May, 14 December 1987 and 12 January 1988, respectively 900506/1035 and 1033; *Libération*, 27 August 1987; *Bulletin de la Mission*, 25 February 1988.

9. Mission press release, March 1987; E. Faure, "1789–1989 La Révolution française," *Revue des deux mondes*, July 1987, 15–23, and *Revue des deux mondes*, August 1987, 280–89; minutes of the advisory committee, 26 May and 14 December 1987, Mission papers, AN, 900506/1035 and 1037. Cf. Faure's idea of a "commémoration tournée vers l'avenir"; in Faure's view it was the proper task of "la philosophie de la célébration de regarder vers l'avenir." Undated public letter, Mission.

10. Mission du Bicentenaire, *Guide du Bicentenaire des élus*, May 1988; Mission press release, March 1988; *Bulletin de la Mission*, February 1988; *Figaro-Magazine*, 10 July 1987; *Libération*, 3 July 1989; minutes of the advisory committee, 26 May 1987, Mission papers, AN, 900506/1533; interview with F. Baroin, 11 April 1991; *Bicentenaire 89, lettre de la Mission*, no. 1 (January 1988). Baroin's chief collaborators in AD 89 were two fellow students, Jean-Michel Blanquer and Richard Senghor, nephew of the academician and former president of Senegal.

11. Faure circular to deputies, December 1987, Mission papers, AN, 900506/815; minutes of the advisory committee, 14 December 1987, ibid., 1035.

12. Minutes of the advisory committee, 14 December 1987, Mission papers, AN, 900506/1535; Mourousi projects, compte rendu, 10 November 1987, ibid., carton 41; Jarre contract proposal, 5 October 1987, ibid., carton 42.

13. Undated memo, probably C. de Montrichard, Mission papers, AN, 900506/815; compte rendu, 1 March 1988, ibid., carton 41.

14. *France-Soir*, 28 October 1988; interview with Ambassador Cabouat, January 1990; *La Lettre politique et parlementaire*, 25 February-3 March 1988; interview with Monique Sauvage, January 1990; interview with Louis Mexandeau, a Socialist deputy, *Vie publique*, August 1988; Mission press release, January 1988; *Le Canard enchaîné*, 20 July and 28 September 1988; Y. Gaillard, "Idées," *La Lettre de la rue St.-Guillaume* (1989), 3–4.

15. Faure address to the advisory committee, 26 May 1987, Mission papers, AN, 900506/1035; interview with F. Baroin, 11 April 1991; interview with C. de Montrichard, 15 January 1991. My portraits of the personnel of the Mission in the following pages derive from my study of archival material and from over a dozen interviews I conducted with Mission members. The bulk of the latter requested that I not cite them directly. Much of their testimony was strikingly convergent. I have been careful to sift out personal animosity and to seek corroboration for specific characterizations and accusations. In no case have I depended on the exclusive testimony of Jean-Jacques Lubrina, one of the Mission counselors, for reasons I explain below.

16. Interview with C. de Montrichard, 17 January 1991; interview with F. Baroin, 11 April 1991; Cabouat memo, 2 December 1987, Mission papers, AN, 900506/42.

17. J.-J. Lubrina, *Une Ménagère était attelée au carrosse du Bicentenaire* (Paris: L'Harmattan, 1991), 15, 30, 84, passim.

18. Faure's address to the advisory committee, 26 May 1987, Mission papers, AN, 900506/1035; minutes of the meeting of 12 January 1988, ibid., 1033; Faure's editorial in *Bicentenaire 89, lettre de la Mission*, no. 1 (January 1988) interview with J. Favier, July 1991.

19. Minutes of meetings of the advisory committee of 26 May and 14 December 1987, and staff memos prepared for E. Faure, Mission papers, AN, 900506/1533 and 1535; minutes of subsection meetings, ibid., 1534; interview with C. Andrieu, 17 January 1991. Cf. Montrichard's suggestions on the efficient usage of the subsections (memo, 21 September 1987), and the minutes of the meeting of the "cultural" subsection the same day (AN, 900506/1035.

20. "Organigrammes provisoires," 17 August and 23 October 1987, Mission papers, AN, 900506/4; interview with C. de Montrichard, January 1991; interview with F. Furet, 13 April 1991.

21. Outside the Mission orbit—even among those persons who monitored its activities with keen interest—the organizational structure was not well understood. Addressing a bicentennial training meeting of local Communist officials, historian and party member Claude Mazauric inveighed against the Mission's alleged partisanship in highly partisan and hyperbolic terms—"c'est de bonne guerre"—but at the cost of conflating the two commissions and misconstruing the nature of their recruitment: "Il y a tout d'abord cette grande Commission interministérielle qui tient lieu de conseil 'scientifique' et de syndicat d'initiative pour la mise en oeuvre des objectifs de 14 ministères rassemblés dans la mission ex-Baroin, actuellement Edgar Faure, composée de telle sorte que tout le monde s'y trouve, sauf des communistes en tant que tels! [The formula warrants deconstruction.] Beaucoup de gens d'extrême droite et aussi beaucoup de socialistes et d'amis du président de la République." C. Mazauric, *Conférences pour le Bicentenaire, 1789–1989*, (C.I.D.E.F.E.), 23.

22. Interviews with C. Andrieu (17 January 1991), J. Tulard (10 April 1991), and M. Agulhon (11 April 1991).

23. Interviews with C. Andrieu (15 January and 2 June 1991), C. de Montrichard (17 January 1991), and J. Tulard (10 April 1991); letter of the "twelve" to Faure, 3 December 1987, Mission papers, AN, 900506/1033. According to my notes, Favier signed the letter. According to Favier, in an interview in July 1991, he did not. Since he has easier access to the archives than I, I invite him to verify; and I apologize in advance if I erred.

24. E. Faure to the "twelve," 8 December 1987, Mission papers, AN, 900506/1033; minutes of the meeting of the advisory committee, 12 January 1987, ibid. J. Chailley to Faure, 27 January 1987, and Faure's reply, 27 January 1988, ibid., 1034.

25. Interviews with C. Andrieu, 17 January and 2 June 1991. Cf. *Bicentenaire 89, lettre de la Mission*, no. 1 (January 1988). Officially, J.-N. Jeanneney, when he assumed the Mission presidency, reduced the periodicity of advisory committee meetings from monthly to trimestrial. In practice, the few assemblies that were held were of no interest. Mission papers, AN, 900506/1533.

26. C. Manceron to M. Baroin, 22 December 1986, and confidential memo, 5 February 1987, Mission papers, AN, 900506/666; interviews with C. de Montrichard, 15 and 17 January 1991, and C. Andrieu, 2 June 1991; dialogue between R. Debray and F. Dosse, *Politis*, 3–9 February 1989.

27. *Le Progrès*, 25 June 1987; interviews with C. de Montrichard, 15 and 17 July 1991; interview with J. Favier, July 1991.

28. Minutes of the advisory committee, 26 May 1987, and undated memoranda (circa April-June 1987), Mission papers, AN, 900506/1035; J.-J. Lubrina, *Une Ménagère*, 19, 30; interview with C. de Montrichard, 17 January 1991; text promoting the Association d'en-

treprises pour le Bicentenaire in the catalogue *89 Avant-Première*. Cf. Pierre Lunel's some-what precious contempt for the (over)preoccupation with money ("un complexe inavoué devant le faste des commémorations américaines"). Lunel, "Note sur le Bicentenaire," AN, 900506/4.

29. My discussion of the Faure Mission's finances is drawn from J. Mullender and A. Gally (Inspection générale de l'administration), "Les Associations" (June 1989), 13–17, 20–38, 46, 48–49. Montrichard's comments emanate from the interview of 17 January 1991. This episode was by no means unique in Faure's public career. His financial administration and management practices had been questioned numerous times—a further reason for Jeanneney's circumspection. His death did not halt the investigatory process. On 16 July 1991 *Libération* reported that "the Chambre des comptes of Besançon denounces the malver-sations which occurred during the tenure of Edgar Faure." The court found "stupefying promotions" for a secretary, who obtained seven raises in a short period; "exorbitant claims for expense accounts," and "unjustified bonuses"; and "false billings" ostensibly aimed at raising money for Faure's campaigns involving a public relations company now indicted for trafficking in influence. A propos what the French call a *série noire*, or chain of disasters: a government audit in 1993 exposed "a large number of irregularities" in the financial manage-ment of the Arche de la Fraternité to which Faure had been so attached. It was presided over by former French foreign minister Claude Cheysson until March 1993 and then by former secretary-general of the United Nations J. Perez de Cuellar. *Le Monde*, 9 December 1993.

30. See sundry proposals for projects and for timing in Mission papers, AN, 900506/815; P. Lunel, "Note sur le Bicentenaire," ibid., carton 4; the memoranda of Didier Hamon, the commissaire-général of 89 Avant-Première, as well as his published solicitation letter, ibid., 815; *Bicentenaire 89, lettre de la Mission*, no. 3 (May 1988).

31. Interview with Thierry Collard, 6 August 1991; interview with C. Andrieu, 18 July 1991; interview with F. Baroin, 6 August 1991; interview with C. de Montrichard, 17 January 1991.

32. The subhead quotation is from J.-J. Lubrina, *Une Ménagère*, 49; *Aspects de la France*, 9 June 1988; *National hebdo*, 13–19 July 1989; *Minute*, (12–18 March 1987); *L'Anti-89*, nos. 7 (April 1988) and 9 (June 1988); *Le Canard enchaîné*, 20 April 1988. Brigneau's portrait of Faure is at once odious and scintillating: "Le *frère* Baroin, à peine enterré (à l'église), fut remplacé par Edgar Faure. Le choix fut trouvé pertinent et approuvé par tous. Edgar c'était une vieille ficelle; un vieux roublard; malin comme un singe; mi-chèvre, mi-chou; le cham-pion des formules reversibles et des majorités de rechange; capable de rouler tout le monde dans la farine, lui compris. A près de quatre-vingts ans, il était en parfait état de marche. Jeune marié, porté sur le Chivas et le Caporal ordinaire qu'il fumait à la pipe, comme un sapeur, le crâne rose, l'oeil vif, jamais un rhume, jamais un bouton, il pétait le feu. Avec lui, ça allait ronfler. Hélas. A peine nommé, il déclina. Son teint jaunit. Ses épaules se voûtèrent. Il se plaignit des reins, entra à l'hôpital, fut opéré et mourut. Et de deux. Deux cents ans après, le massacre continuait." See the warm homages to Faure from *Le Courrier de Saône-et-Loire*, *Ouest-France*, and *L'Yonne républicaine*, all from 31 March 1988, in Mission papers, AN, 900506/4.

Chapter 3
Alle Guten Dinge Sind Drei:
Jean-Noël Jeanneney and the Mission Impossible

1. Interviews with J.-N. Jeanneney, January 1990 and 4 January 1991; Jules Jeanneney, *Journal politique, septembre 1939-juillet 1942*, ed. Jean-Noël Jeanneney (Paris: A. Colin, 1972), p. 231; *Le Canard enchaîné*, 28 December 1988; *Libération*, 3 July 1989; *L'Express*, 22

July 1988; *Le Monde*, 26 May 1988 and 20 May 1991; *Who's Who in France, 1988–89* (Paris: Editions Lafitte, 1989), 872; F. Bédarida, "Le Tournant des années 40: De la guerre à l'après-guerre," in *Les Catholiques français et l'héritage de 1789*, ed. P. Colin (Paris: Beauchesne, 1989), 383; *Minute*, (13 April 1988); interview with F. Baroin, 11 April 1991. Among Jeanneney's most important works are: *François de Wendel en république: L'Argent et le pouvoir, 1914–40* (Paris: du Seuil, 1976); *Leçon d'histoire pour une gauche au pouvoir: La Faillite du Cartel, 1924–1926* (Paris: du Seuil, 1977); *L'Argent caché: Milieux d'affaires et pouvoirs politiques dans la France du XXᵉ siècle* (Paris: Fayard, 1981); *Echec à Panurge: L'Audiovisuel public au service de la différence* (Paris: du Seuil, 1986).

2. Interviews with J.-N. Jeanneney, January 1990; Jeanneney interviewed by Anne Sinclair on the television show *Sept sur sept*, 20 June 1988; Jeanneney, "Après coup: Réflexions d'un commémorateur," *Le Débat*, no. 57 (November-December 1989): 75–76; Jeanneney, "L'Héritage de la Révolution française," *Revue des deux mondes*, December 1988, 45. Cf. "Un Entretien avec J.-N. Jeanneney," *Historiens-Géographes*, no. 327 (1990): 156 ("J'appartiens à une catégorie d'historiens qui n'a jamais eu peur des médias").

3. *La République du Centre*, 26 May 1988; *Le Quotidien de la Réunion*, 26 May 1988; *France-Soir*, 1 September 1988; "Entretien avec François Furet," *L'Histoire*, no. 52 (January 1983); *Le Figaro*, 22 September 1986; Claire Andrieu, ed., *1789: Le Livre du Bicentenaire* (Paris: Le Chêne-Hachette, 1990), 14; *Le Point*, 6–12 June 1988; *Le Quotidien de Paris*, 24 May 1988; *Le Canard enchaîné*, 8 June 1988; *Le Monde*, 25 May 1988.

4. *Nord Matin*, 26 May 1988; *Charente libre*, 26 May 1988; *Aspects de la France*, 2 June 1988; *L'Anti-89*, no. 7 (April 1988); *Le Choc du mois*, no. 14 (January 1989); *Le Quotidien de la Réunion*, 26 May 1988; *L'Est républicain*, 12 June 1988; *Actualité rurale*, July 1988; *La Presse française*, 10 June 1988; *L'Express*, 18 November 1988; interviews with J.-N. Jeanneney, January 1990; *CFDT Magazine*, no. 140 (July 1989).

5. J.-N. Jeanneney, *Rapport du président de la Mission du Bicentenaire à Monsieur le président de la République*, (Paris, 1989) 33–34, 299, 318; Mission papers, AN, 900506/42; "Entretien avec J.-N. Jeanneney," *L'Histoire*, no. 113 (July-August 1988): 122–23; Jeanneney, "Après coup: Réflexions d'un commémorateur," *Le Débat*, no. 57 (November-December 1989): 81; *Libération*, 3 July 1989; *Le Canard enchaîné*, 20 July 1988; *Le Quotidien de Paris*, 24 May 1988.

6. Interview with C. Andrieu, 18 July 1991; J.-J. Lubrina, *Une Ménagère était attelée au carrosse du Bicentenaire* (Paris: L'Harmattan, 1991), 14, 22.

7. J.-N. Jeanneney, *Rapport du président de la Mission du Bicentenaire*, 30–38, 49–52; Jeanneney, "Après coup: Réflexions d'un commémorateur," *Le Débat*, no. 57 (November-December 1989): 81–82; interviews with J.-N. Jeanneney, A. de Margerie, and J. P. Cabouat, January 1990; *Profession politique*, no. 26 (26 October 1990); interview with C. Andrieu, 4 February 1991; interview with F. Baroin, 11 April 1991; Mission papers, AN, 900506/4, 20, 42, 1533; interview with C. de Montrichard, 15 January 1991. Jean-Jacques Lubrina hinted that the young Baroin was in some sense vindicated by the antibicentennial/summit demonstration led by the singer Renaud, who spoke for Baroin's commitment to youth and to the cause of the excluded. *Une Ménagère*, 142.

8. Minutes, staff meetings, 15 December 1989, Mission papers, AN, 900506/41; interview with C. de Montrichard, 15 January 1991; interview with J.-N. Jeanneney in *Phosphore*, July 1988, AN, 900506/24; Jean Mendelson, personal communication, 7 July 1993. On the ascensions of El'brus, Mont Blanc, the Grand Teton, and so on, see AN, 900506/8. On Jeanneney's interest in contemporary rights issues, see L.-E. Petiti to Jeanneney, 1 July 1988, AN, 900506/24.

9. J.-J. Lubrina, "*Une Ménagère*, 75, 107, 109, 112–23, 116–17; interview with C. de

Montrichard, 17 January 1991. The rights issue was also the proxy for a more diffuse yet deep resentment to which Jeanneney appeared utterly oblivious: his failure to acknowledge the depth of the cumulative contribution of the first two Missions. We had prepared "the soup he spat in," fretted a bruised counselor.

10. Interview with C. Andrieu, 18 July 1991.

11. "Comment imaginer un seul instant que des personnalités comme Baroin ou Faure aient accepté qu'on leur impose un tuteur en la personne d'un ministre du Bicentenaire? Quand Jack Lang fut nommé ministre du Bicentenaire on ne prévint même pas Jeanneney. On ne songea même pas à lui présenter quelques semblants d'excuses. On peut même penser pire. A peine Jeanneney nommé, on ne pensa plus à lui." J.-J. Lubrina, *Une Ménagère*, 108.

12. J.-N. Jeanneney, *Rapport du président de la Mission du Bicentenaire*, 338; Jeanneney, "Après coup: Réflexions d'un commémorateur," *Le Débat*, no. 57 (November-December 1989): 84; *L'Oreille en coin*, radio program, 25 June 1989; *Le Canard enchaîné*, 23 November 1988; interviews with Jeanneney and A. de Margerie, January 1990; interview with C. Dupavillon, January 1991; interviews with C. de Montrichard, 15 and 17 January 1991; interview with F. Baroin, 11 April 1991; interview with J. Favier, 30 July 1991; J. Lang to the president of La Carmagnole-Vive 89, 7 February 1989 (kindly communicated by the association); minutes of staff meeting, 22 March 1989, Mission papers, AN, 900506/41.

13. *Jours de France*, 6 August 1988; *Libération*, 3 July 1989; J.-N. Jeanneney, "Après coup: Réflexions d'un commémorateur," *Le Débat*, no. 57 (November-December 1989): 85; interviews with Jeanneney and A. de Margerie, January 1990. For more on the frictions between Mission and Parisian municipality, see the chapter on Paris in Book Three below.

14. J.-N. Jeanneney, *Rapport du président de la Mission du Bicentenaire*, 24–28, 42; interview with Philippe Blondel, secretary-general of the Mission, January 1990.

15. J.-N. Jeanneney, *Rapport du président de la Mission du Bicentenaire*, 28, 44–47, 85–86, 92; *Stratégies*, no. 633 (12 December 1988); *Le Quotidien de Paris*, 14 June 1989; Jeanneney, "Premiers Regards sur le Bicentenaire," *Cercle Condorcet*, no. 11 (March 1990): 34.

16. Interviews with J.-N. Jeanneney, J.-P. Cabouat, and P. Blondel, January 1990; Jeanneney *Rapport du président de la Mission du Bicentenaire*, 30–32, 41; *Le Parisien*, 17 May 1989; *France-Soir*, 29 November 1989; Jeanneney, "Après coup: Réflexions d'un commémorateur," *Le Débat*, no. 57 (November-December 1989): 83. In his official report (p. 30), Jeanneney claimed that the Australians spent four times the Mission budget (Fr 1.2 billion), but on a radio program he used the coefficient of three. *L'Oreille en coin*, 25 June 1989.

17. Interview with P. Blondel, January 1990; J.-N. Jeanneney, *Rapport du président de la mission du Bicentenaire*, 314–17; *L'Ardennais*, 13 October 1988); *Bicentenaire 89, lettre de la Mission*, no. 2 (November 1988); *Vins et gastronomie*, December 1988.

18. *Le Nouvel Observateur*, 23-29 March 1989; *Figaro-Magazine*, 8 July 1989; interview with P. Blondel, January 1990; Pascal Andriveau to Mission, 2 May 1989, Mission papers, AN, 900506/180.

19. J. Veillon in *Le Quotidien de Paris*, 12 May 1989; *Le Figaro*, 13 May 1989; interview with P. Blondel, January 1990; J.-N. Jeanneney, *Rapport du président de la Mission du Bicentenaire*, 315–16.

20. *Le Canard enchaîné*, 20 July 1988 and 19 July 198; *Le Choc du mois*, Janaury 1988; *Le Courrier de Saône-et-Loire*, 29 January 1989; *La Croix*, 27 December 1988; *Le Figaro*, 15 May and 8–9 July 1989; *L'Evénement du Jeudi*, 14–20 July 1988; *Figaro-Magazine*, 7 January 1989; *Le Monde*, 15 April 1989; *Minute*, nos. 1396 (4–10 January 1989) and 1423 (12–18 July 1989); *National hebdo*, 30 August 1989; *L'Anti-89*, no. 18 (March 1988).

21. *Libération*, 14 July 1989; *Le Quotidien de Paris*, 29–30 July 1989; *Le Monde*, 15 July 1989.

22. Though it was not ready until late in the year, the Mission president could draw on a study by CSA, a public opinion research institute, to steer him in his ongoing choices. The report first took stock of attitudes and expectations and then composed policy recommendations, most of which stressed the need for consensus building on clear and simple foundations, the strict avoidance of the Revolution's negative or conflictual dimensions, avoiding politicization, and the development of an effective communications strategy for the Mission. CSA, *Images de la Révolution: Attentes par rapport au Bicentenaire, synthèse des principaux résultats* (Paris, 1988), 23–26, 34–36, 38–42.

23. Interview with J.-N. Jeanneney, January 1990; Jeanneney interviewed in S. Moati's film *Journal d'un bicentenaire* (1989); Jeanneney, "Après coup: Réflexions d'un commémorateur," *Le Débat*, no. 57 (November-December 1989): 80; Jeanneney, "Premiers Regards sur le Bicentenaire," *Cercle Condorcet*, no. 11 (March 1990): p. 6.

24. J.-N. Jeanneney, "L'Héritage de la Révolution française," *Revue des deux mondes*, December 1988, 51; Jeanneney, "Intervention à la séance de clôture," in *Les Catholiques français et l'héritage de 1789*, ed. P. Colin (Paris: Beauchesne, 1989), 371; Jeanneney, "Après coup: Réflexions d'un commémorateur," *Le Débat*, no. 57 (November-December 1989): 78; *La Voix du Nord*, 26 November 1988; "Entretien avec J.-N. Jeanneney," *L'Histoire*, no. 113 (July-August 1988): 123–24; *Le Quotidien de Paris*, 13 July 1988; *Le Nouvel Observateur*, 15–21 July 1988; Jeanneney, "L'Héritage après 200 ans," *Projet*, September-October 1988, 180; *Pèlerin Magazine*, 6 January 1989.

25. J.-N. Jeanneney, "L'Héritage de la Révolution française," *Revue des deux mondes*, December 1988, 51–52; "Vive le Bicentenaire: Entretien avec J.-N. Jeanneney," *Armées d'aujourd'hui*, March 1989, 182; Jeanneney, "Après coup: Réflexions d'un commémorateur," *Le Débat*, no. 57 (November-December 1989): 78; television interview of Jeanneney by Anne Sinclair, *Sept sur sept*, 20 June 1988; Jeanneney, "L'Héritage après 200 ans," *Projet*, September-October 1988, 179–80; *Ouest-France*, 6 May 1989; Jeanneney in *Bicentenaire 89, lettre de la Mission*, no. 1 (October 1988): 2; Jeanneney in staff meeting, 31 May 1988, Mission papers, AN, 900506/41; Jeanneney, "Allocution d'ouverture," Colloque international de Belfort, *Cahiers du Bicentenaire*, no. 4 (October 1988): 12; Jeanneney interviewed by S. Martin, *Vie publique*, no. 184 (October 1988).

26. "Un Entretien avec J.-N. Jeanneney," *Historiens-Géographes*, no. 327 (1990): 151, 156; Jeanneney *Rapport du président de la Mission du Bicentenaire*, 14, 78, 126, 300; interview with Jeanneney, *La Croix*, 20 January 1989; *Bicentenaire 89, lettre de la Mission*, nos. 1 (October 1988), 3 (December 1988), 7 (April 1989); interviews with Jeanneney, *Le Nouvel Observateur*, 15–21 July 1988 and 4 May 1989; interviews with Jeanneney, *Le Monde*, 27–28 August 1989; interview with Jeanneney, *L'Histoire*, no. 113 (July-August 1988): 123–24; Martha Zuber, "*Les Enjeux de la mémoire:* An Interview with J.-N. Jeanneney," *French Politics and Society*, no. 7 (spring 1989): 32; Jeanneney, "Premiers Regards sur le Bicentenaire," *Cercle Condorcet*, no. 11 (March 1990): 4, 6; Jeanneney, "Après coup: Réflexions d'un commémorateur," *Le Débat*, no. 57 (November-December 1989): 77, 79–80; *Convergence Secours*, May 1989; *Ouest-France*, 6 May 1989; *Le Quotidien de 89*, no. 55 (20 March 1989); Jeanneney, "L'Héritage de la Révolution française," *Revue des deux mondes*, December 1988; C. Andrieu, *Le Livre du Bicentenaire*, 103 (on the SOS-Racisme concert, sponsored by the Mission, which honored Toussaint L'Ouverture and was dedicated to the people of China). Cf. philosopher-jurist F. Ewald's characterization of the Mission as "un ministère de l'Idéologie." *Le Quotidien de Paris*, 21 June 1989. On the social demand for bicentennial relevance, see Y. Déloye and O. Ihl, "Chronique d'une commémoration," *Le Monde de la Révolution française*, no. 12 (December 1989).

27. "Premiers Regards sur le Bicentenaire," *Cercle Condorcet*, no. 11 (March 1990): 24, 31.

28. *Le Nouvel Observateur*, 15–21 July 1988; televison interview with J.-N. Jeanneney by Anne Sinclair, *Sept sur Sept*, 20 June 1988; Jeanneney's editorials in *Bicentenaire 89, lettre de la Mission*, nos. 1 (October 1988): 2, 2 (November 1988): 2, and 5 (February 1989): 2; Jeanneney, *Rapport du président de la Mission du Bicentenaire*, 17, 131–32; Jeanneney, "Premiers Regards sur le Bicentenaire," *Cercle Condorcet*, no. 11 (March 1990): 6, 7, 9. On the criticism of those in Furet's orbit, see "Entretien avec Marcel Gauchet," *France catholique*, no. 2215 (14 July 1989), and M. Ozouf, "Célébrer, savoir, fêter," *Le Débat*, no. 57 (November-December 1989): 17–33. On the refusal to sponsor antirevolutionary events in the name of a "pluralism" that had a deep blue hue, see the interview of Mission historian Claire Andrieu regarding an overly "manichaean" project from Nantes in Serge Moati's bicentennial film entitled *Autour du 14 juillet*.

29. *Japan Times*, 14 July 1989; *Pèlerin Magazine*, 6 January 1989; *Phosphore*, September 1988; J.-N. Jeanneney, address at Perpignan, 25 March 1989, Mission papers, AN, 900506/8; Jeanneney's editorials, *Bicentenaire 89, lettre de la Mission*, nos. 6 (March 1989) and 9 (June 1989); *Le Figaro*, 13 July 1989; Jeanneney, "L'Héritage de la Révolution française," *Revue des deux mondes*, December 1988, 52; Jeanneney, "Après coup: Réflexions d'un commémorateur," *Le Débat*, no. 57 (November-December 1989): 89; Jeanneney, "Intervention à la séance de clôture," in Colin, *Les Catholiques français et l'héritage de 1789*, 272–73; *L'Humanité*, 6 January 1989; *Le Nouvel Observateur*, 15–21 July 1988; M. Zuber, *"Les Enjeux de la mémoire:* An Interview with J.-N. Jeanneney," *French Politics and Society*, no. 7 (spring 1989): 27, 30–31.

Chapter 4
The Opening of the Bicentennial Season

1. J.-N. Jeanneney, "Intervention à la séance de clôture," in *Les Catholiques français et l'héritage de 1789*, ed. P. Colin (Paris: Beauchesne, 1989), 373; Jeanneney, *Rapport du président de la Mission du Bicentenaire à Monsieur le président de la République* (Paris: Beauchesne, 1989), 17, 101; *Jeune Afrique*, 19 July 1989; *Bicentenaire 89, Lettre de la Mission*, no. 1 (October 1988); "Un Entretien avec J.-N. Jeanneney," *Historiens-Géographes*, no. 327 (1990): 156; *Le Quotidien de Paris*, 24 September 1988; *Le Nouvel Observateur*, 5–11 January 1989; *Libération*, 4 August 1989; *Le Calendrier du Bicentenaire* (Paris: Mission release, 1989).

2. J.-N. Jeanneney, *Rapport du président de la Mission du Bicentenaire*, 55–57; *Nouvelle République*, 2 Janaury 1989; *L'Eveil de Haute-Loire*, 2 January 1989; *Le Monde*, 3 January 1989; C. Andrieu, ed, *1789: Le Livre du Bicentenaire* (Paris: Le Chêne-Hachette, 1990), 26–28.

3. C. Manceron to M. Baroin, 24 December 1986, Mission papers, AN, 900506/666; Mission du Bicentenaire, *36,000 Arbres pour la liberté* (Paris: Mission, 1989), 8. Cf. the qualification adduced by the historian Andrée Corvol concerning the Revolution and the liberty tree: "The Convention's first decree regarding liberty trees dates only from 3 Pluviose in year II (22 January 1794). On a close reading, it does not appear as a fundamental document, demanding that every commune should plant one, as was hastily asserted during the Bicentennial of the French Revolution. It was not a question of planting trees but of replacing them, a very different proposition." "The Transformation of a Political Symbol:

Tree Festivals in France from the Eighteenth to the Twentieth Centuries," *French History*, no. 4 (December 1990): 455–86. On the ceremony at Saint-Gaudent, see Book Three below, the chapter entitled "A Descent into *la France Profonde.*"

4. Mission du Bicentenaire, *Les Arbres de la liberté;* Mission du Bicentenaire, *36,000 Arbres pour la liberté;* Mission press kit; *Rapport d'activité, bilan de la commémoration du Bicentenaire dans la Drôme* (kindly communicated by R. Léron, a deputy from Valence); J.-P. Donnadieu, "Perception cartographique du Bicentenaire dans l'Hérault," in *Etudes du temps présent: Quel Avenir pour notre passé?* Y.-M. Le Bozec et al., eds. (Office de Cliométrie appliquée, 1990), 18; interview with C. de Montrichard, 18 January 1991. The *Méridional*, 25 February 1989, stressed the utter preoccupation with municipal elections.

5. *Bicentenaire 89, lettre de la Mission*, no. 4 (January 1989): 14; J.-N. Jeanneney, *Rapport du président de la Mission du Bicentenaire*, 58–61; *Le Monde*, 25 February, 17 and 23 March 1989; *Le Figaro*, 8 March 1989; city of Montreuil, *Projets Bicentenaire*, 1–2; *Ouest-France*, 23 March 1989; *Presse de la Manche*, 25 March and 17 April 1989; *La Montagne-Riom*, 24 March 1989; *La Montagne*, 24 March 1989; *Dernières Nouvelles d'Alsace*, 22 March 1989; *Le Pays de la Franche-Comté*, 24 March 1989; *L'Est républicain*, 29 March 1989; *Pays d'Auge*, 24 March 1989; Mission papers, AN, 900506/845; *La Lettre du maire*, 7 September 1988 and 22 March 1989; C. Andrieu, *Le Livre du Bicentenaire*, 55–60. Anxious to remind the public, at a time when liberty seemed to be much more cherished around the world than equality, that "liberalism is also a legacy of the Revolution in the same sense that socialism is," an association of Socialist politicians (imaginatively baptized "Vive la Liberté") had already begun a tree-planting drive through the municipalities in 1988. *Vie publique*, April 1988. At Nantes the "Amis de Varlet" (Varlet having been the leader of the leftist group of Year II called the *enragés*) disrupted the tree-planting ceremonies. *Le Monde de la Révolution française*, no. 10 (October 1989). Cf. the central role played by liberty-tree imagery in the American centennial. David B. Little, *America's First Centennial Celebration* (Boston: Houghton Mifflin, 1974).

6. J.-N. Jeanneney, *Rapport du président de la Mission du bicentenaire*, 63–65; *Valeurs actuelles*, 2 May 1989; *Le Monde*, 20 January, 15 April, and 6 May 1989; interview with T. Collard (who stresses Jeanneney's unhappiness with the pedagogical and media aspects of the Versailles reconstitution), 6 August 1991; Marc-André Vernes le Morvan, "Une Cité et la Révolution française: Versailles 1789, 1889, 1939, 1989," unpublished *mémoire*, Institut d'études politiques de Paris (1989), 80–83, 138–40, passim; *Figaro-Magazine*, 10 June 1989.

7. Interview with André de Margerie, January 1990; *Libération*, 11 May 1989; *Paris-Capitale*, November 1989; *Figaro-Magazine*, 8 July 1989; interview with J.-N. Jeanneney, *Le Nouvel Observateur*, 15–21 July 1988. Among the unfulfilled projects of the same order was an installation "au Palais-Royal [où] on restituera l'atmosphère." Jeanneney, "L'Héritage de la Révolution française," *Revue des deux mondes*, December 1988, 56.

8. "Projet Révoparc," 30 October 1987, Mission papers, AN, 900506/4; F. Bauer to (?), circa August 1988, ibid., unclassified.

9. J.-N. Jeanneney to G. Alexandroff, 1 August 1988, Mission papers, AN, 900506/163.

10. All the above-mentioned projects are from Mission papers, AN, 900506/163 and 168.

11. Interview with A. de Margerie, January 1990; J.-N. Jeanneney, *Rapport du président de la Mission du Bicentenaire*, 67–88; *Le Monde*, 29 September and 9–10 October 1990; GRAHAL to J.-N. Jeanneney, 1 February 1989, and Yves Jouen to Jeanneney, 7 November 1988, Mission papers, AN, 900506/163. In the context of Jeanneney's defense of the jury, it is ironic that the jury asked the winning architects to use materials that conceded "une part plus importante à la transparence." Jeanneney, *Rapport du président de la Mission du Bicentenaire*, 69.

12. J.-N. Jeanneney to Hennin and Normier, 19 September 1988, AN, Mission papers, 900506/163.

13. Interview with A. de Margerie, January 1990; interview with T. Collard, 6 August 1991; *Stratégies*, no. 633 (12 December 1988); J.-N. Jeanneney, *Rapport du président de la Mission du Bicentenaire*, 69; *Le Choc du mois*, no. 14 (January 1989).

14. J.-N. Jeanneney, *Rapport du président de la Mission du Bicentenaire*, 69; *Le Monde*, 26 October and 2 November 1988; minutes of Mission staff meeting, 26 October 1988, Mission papers, AN, 900506/41; *Le Canard enchaîné*, 23 November 1988; interview with T. Collard, 6 August 1991.

15. Interview with A. de Margerie, January 1990; J.-N. Jeanneney, *Rapport du président de la Mission du Bicentenaire*, 69–72; *Le Monde*, 10 February (letter from Claude Saintenay to editor), 11 February (op-ed column by G. Alexandroff and M. Zoratto), 15 February 1989.

16. *Bicentenaire 89, lettre de la Mission*, nos. 3 (December 1988) and 8 (May 1989); press kit for Tuileries 89; M. Rocard, inaugural remarks, Mission papers, AN, 900506/180; *L'Humanité*, 15 May 1989; *Le Monde*, 15 February, 2 March, 15 June 1989; *Figaro-Magazine*, 8 July 1989. Cf. Jeanneney's inaugural remarks, which have a sharply ironic ring, concerning the full agreement between the Mission and the Ministry of Culture that resulted in the necessary crystallization of energies. Mission papers, AN, 900506/180.

17. *Libération*, 11 May 1989; *Le Monde*, 25 March 1989; C. Andrieu, *Le Livre du Bicentenaire*, 83.

18. *Paris-Capitale*, November 1989; F. Edelmann in *Le Monde*, 20 May 1989; *Vie publique*, July-August 1989; *L'Humanité*, 15 May 1989; *Le Quotidien de Paris*, 13 and 30 June 1989; *Figaro-Magazine*, 8 July 1989; P. Andriveau, 2 May 1989, Mission papers, AN, 900506/180; *Le Canard enchaîné*, 12 July 1989, described the "shipwreck" of Tuileries 89, where "more than eighty actors play every day to empty seats." Olivier Passelecq, former chef de cabinet of Edgar Faure, saw "a fiasco in every way." *Le Quotidien de Paris*, 10 November 1989.

19. Minutes of staff meetings, 10, 31 May 1989, Mission papers, AN, 900506/41; meetings of the oversight panel, AN, 900506/173; interview with T. Collard, 6 August 1991.

20. Letter from the actors and technicians to M. Zulberty, 9 June 1989, Mission papers, AN, 900506/180; minutes of Mission staff meeting, 14 June 1989, AN, ibid., 41; *Paris-Capitale*, November 1989; J.-N. Jeanneney, *Rapport du président de la Mission du Bicentenaire*, 72–74, 76; *Le Monde*, 15 June and 28 September 1989; *Figaro-Magazine*, 8 July 1989. Cf. the scorn for the Tuileries-new-and-improved-model by a consumer-visitor who complained about persistent organizational and technical problems (for example, a concert that was "totally inaudible for half the audience"). Alain Couzinet of the rue Pigalle to the Tuileries management, Mission papers, AN, 900506/180.

21. J.-N. Jeanneney, *Rapport du président de la Mission du Bicentenaire*, 74–76; interview with Jeanneney in S. Moati's bicentennial film, *Autour du 14 juillet*. André de Margerie had special responsibility for overseeing the Tuileries operations. He was genuinely forlorn about the negative press, less for himself than for the way it tainted Jeanneney, his friend and mentor. It was not fair, he repeatedly said, for Jeanneney to "absorb all the blows." Interview with de Margerie, January 1990.

22. On Jeanneney's extensive travels, see Mission papers, AN, 900506/8.

23. Interview with A. Oussedik, January 1990; *La Croix*, 13 September 1988 and 20 January 1989; *Révolution*, 2–8 December 1988; *L'Humanité*, 31 October 1988; *Figaro-Magazine*, 28 October 1988 and 8 April 1989; *Nouvelle République du Centre-Ouest*, 12 January 1989; *Le Monde*, 2 November 1988; *Libération*, 3 May 1989; *Historama*, special issue on the bicentennial, July 1989. Cf. the far right's evaluation: "chaque jour qui passe donne à cette commémoration des allures de peau de chagrin" (*Le Choc du mois*, no. 14 [January

1989]); "le Bicentenaire patauge déjà dans le fiasco" (Brigneau in *L'Anti-89*, no. 17 [February 1989]); "le troisième, M. Jeanneney, un insignifiant supérieur, bien causant, propre sur lui, la potiche qui fait honneur à toutes les étagères a, pour l'instant, été épargné, sauf dans sa tâche. Il n'a connu que des déboires. . . . La kermesse des Tuileries est un bide tricolore. . . . Les Mouettes de Folon sont devenues des pigeons" (Brigneau in *National hebdo* [13–19 July 1989]). Patrick Garcia asks a question that is worth first verifying and then reflecting upon: Why were "presque tous les grands médias" persuaded "un an, 2 ans auparavant, que la commémoration ne serait qu'un non-événement"? "Premiers Regards sur le Bicentenaire," *Cercle Condorcet*, no. 11 (March 1990): 29.

24. Intervew with A. Oussedik, January 1990; *Bicentenaire 89, lettre de la Mission*, no. 2 (November 1988); interview with J.-N. Jeanneney, *La Croix*, 20 January 1989; Jeanneney, "Après coup: Réflexions d'un commémorateur," *Le Débat*, no. 57 (November-December 1989): 92–94; Jeanneney, "Premiers Regards sur le Bicentenaire," *Cercle Condorcet*, no. 11 (March 1990): 26–27; Jeanneney, "L'Héritage de la Révolution française," *Revue des deux mondes*, December 1988, 56; "Vive le Bicentenaire: Entretien avec J.-N. Jeanneney," *Armées d'aujourd'hui*, March 1989, 180–81; Jeanneney, *Rapport du président de la Mission du Bicentenaire*, 61, 75, 95, 321–23; interview with Jeanneney, *Le Quotidien de Paris*, 13 July 1988; minutes of staff meeting, 21 June 1989, Mission papers, AN, 900506/41; interview with C. de Montrichard, 15 January 1991; G. Philip to Jeanneney, n.d., AN, 900506/24; interview with C. Andrieu, 18 July 1991.

Chapter 5
Preparing the Climax: From Jungle Fever to Summit Fever

1. J.-N. Jeanneney, *Rapport du président de la Mission du Bicentenaire à Monsieur le président de la République* (Paris, 1989), 83; *Bicentenaire 89, lettre de la Mission*, no. 1 (October 1988): 5; interview with M. Sauvage, January 1990; interview with C. de Montrichard, 15 January 1991; interview with François Baroin, August 1991; interview with Thierry Collard, August 1991; interview with T. Aumonier, 2 December 1991; *Libération*, 10 October 1988; *France-Soir*, 13 June 1988; *L'Humanité*, 16 December 1988; *Le Quotidien de Paris*, 24 September 1988; *Show Magazine*, 28 October 1988; Bulletin of the Association Vive 89 en Ille-et-Vilaine.

2. Interview with M. Sauvage, January 1990; interview with C. Dupavillon, 3 January 1991; interview with C. Dupavillon, *Le Quotidien de Paris*, 12 July 1989; *Libération*, 14 July 1989; *Le Monde*, 15 June 1989 and 14 July 1990. Born in 1940, Dupavillon became Lang's principal collaborator in the Festival of the Théâtre de Nancy in 1967 . In 1973 he assumed the artistic directorship of the Théâtre national de Chaillot. After a brief journalistic stint, he joined Lang's cabinet in 1981, and returned to it again in 1988.

3. Interview with C. Dupavillon, 3 January 1991; *Le Figaro*, 10 July 1989.

4. Interview with C. Dupavillon, 3 January 1991; interview with Dupavillon, *Le Quotidien de Paris*, 12 July 1989; *Libération*, 14 July 1989; *Le Monde*, 15 and 16–17 July 1989.

5. *Los Angeles Times*, 5 December 1982; *Punch*, 27 October 1982; interview with Goude, *Le Nouvel Observateur*, 14–20 February 1991. Against the strictures of racism in his talk with the *Nouvel Observateur*, Goude defended himself passionately but rather feebly, in a self-indulgently naive and tautological manner: "J'ai repris cette expression, 'la fièvre de la jungle,' inventée par les noirs dans les années 20 pour décrire les riches Blancs qui montaient s'encanailler à Harlem, dans un tout autre esprit. Non pas, comme le croit Spike Lee [whose own *Jungle Fever*, a love story involving a black man and a white woman, Lee felt should have

won the Cannes Film Festival's highest prize in 1991], pour raviver la haine raciale mais parce qu'elle me suggère quelque chose de très vaste: l'ailleurs. Du temps de l'esclavage, les plus ignobles maîtres s'accordaient à louer la beauté, la force de leurs nègres qui savaient si bien danser. Mais moi, je ne suis pas un négrier, je ne suis qu'un dessinateur béat d'admiration devant cette beauté et ce talent. Est-ce une raison pour me suspecter et me reprocher de toucher à des sujets tabous?" Goude's inability to undertake his own analysis may reinforce the skepticism of those critics who question the putatively antiracist character of his bicentennial parade. "Je voudrais rappeler, par surcroît," wrote the philosopher Alain Finkielkraut. "qu'on a célébré à son propos l'émergence d'une France antiraciste, alors que, comme le dit le réalisateur de son défilé du 14 juillet 1989, le premier film que Goude lui a montré, en guise d'exemple, c'est *Le Triomphe de la volonté* de Leni Riefenstahl sur le rassemblement nazi de Nuremberg en 1934, 'pour sa façon de filmer une parade.'" *L'Evénement du Jeudi*, 20–26 December 1990.

6. The above treatment of Goude's life is drawn from his *Jungle Fever*, ed. Harold Hayes (New York: Xavier Moreau, 1982). It seems to have been a vanity-press publication. The text appears to be in Goude's own words. The idiom is Franco-American, and the style redolent of what Goude has said in other contexts. The photos and drawings are invariably striking, often beautiful, and sometimes quite erotic. The book was very hard to find. In light of the cultural stereotypes regarding the allegedly censorious American heartland, I am pleased to acknowledge that my copy came from the library of the University of Iowa. I have also drawn on Goude's interview with *Le Nouvel Observateur*, 14–20 February 1991.

7. Interview with C. Dupavillon, *Le Quotidien de Paris*, 12 July 1989; *Libération*, 14 July 1989; *Le Monde*, 15 June and 16–17 July 1989; *Le Nouvel Observateur*, 1–7 December 1988 and 6–12 July 1989; *L'Express*, 10 July 1987 and 30 June 1989. According to the last-named source, Goude was approaching fifty years old.

8. *Le Nouvel Observateur*, 6–12 July 1989; *Libération*, 14 July 1989; O. Salvatori, "Bricolo-les-belles-images," *Le Débat*, no. 57 (November-December 1989): 69; *Le Figaro-Magazine*, 28 October 1988; interview with C. de Montrichard, 15 January 1991; *Le Monde*, 15 June 1989; interview with M. Sauvage, January 1990; interview with C. Dupavillon, *Le Quotidien de Paris*, 12 July 1989. Money seemed to be Goude's ultimate litmus of judgment, no matter what the object/subject. "Quand j'étais môme, j'adorais me faire passer pour un gosse de riches," he confessed. "Aujourd'hui encore, je garde le même émerveillement pour les milliardaires de Saint-Tropez et les symboles de la réussite." *L'Express*, 10 July 1987.

9. Interview with C. Dupavillon, *Le Quotidien de Paris*, 12 July 1989; *Libération*, 14 July 1989; *Communication et business*, 24 October 1988; interview with M. Sauvage, January 1990; *Point de vue*, 31 March 1989; *Le Provençal*, 14 July 1989; *Le Nouvel Observateur*, 6–12 July 1989; *Le Monde*, 15 June 1989; interview with J.-P. Goude, *Le Figaro*, 10 July 1989.

10. Jeanneney television interview, *Sept sur sept*, 20 June 1988; *La Voix du Nord*, 26 November 1988; Jeanneney radio interview, *L'Oreille en coin*, 25 June 1989; *VSD*, 9 June 1988; *Le Quotidien de Paris*, 13 July 1988; Jeanneney, "L'Héritage de la Révolution Française," *Revue des deux mondes*, December 1988, 55; *Libération Champagne*, 28 May 1899; interview with A. Finkielkraut in *L'Evénement du Jeudi*, 20–26 December 1990.

11. Interview with J.-N. Jeanneney, *Le Monde*, 27–28 August 1989; *La Croix*, 5 July 1989; *Libération*, 14 July 1989; "Un Entretien avec J.-N. Jeanneney," *Historiens-Géographes*, no. 327 (1990); interviews with Jeanneney in S. Moati's films, *Journal d'un bicentenaire* and *Autour du 14 juillet;* Jeanneney, "Après coup: Réflexions d'un commémorateur," *Le Débat*, no. 57 (November-December 1989): 94–95; Jeanneney, "Premiers Regards sur le Bicentenaire," *Cercle Condorcet*, no. 11 (March 1990): 9; *Le Quotidien de la Réunion*, 26 May 1989; *L'Eveil de Haute-Loire*, 27 March 1989. Cf. Mona Ozouf's eloquent argument for "la fête d'un côté, la

pédagogie et le civisme de l'autre" in "Peut-on commémorer la Révolution française?" *Le Débat*, no. 26 (September 1983): 164, and *Le Monde de la Révolution Française*, April 1989, 4. See also a sharp critique of historical reconstitutions—"qui, voulant rejouer le passé, lui ôtent toute proximité et donnent à voir le musée Grévin"—in Patrick Garcia, Jacques Lévy, and Marie-Flore Mattei, *Révolutions, fin et suite* (Paris: EspacesTemps–Centre Georges Pompidou Bibliothèque Publique d'Information, 1990), 230. The same authors nevertheless note the taste, both on the left and on the right, for the cognitive equivalent of a rigorous reconstitution, the "rêve d'une histoire neutre." Ibid., 209.

12. Interview with C. Dupavillon, 3 January 1991; interview with T. Collard, 6 August 1991.

13. Interviews with M. Sauvage and P. Blondel, January 1990; J.-N. Jeanneney, *Rapport du président de la Mission du Bicentenaire*, 84–87. For fragmentary hints concerning Goude's multiple scenarios, see his *Bleu, blanc, Goude: La Marseillaise* (Paris: Nathan Images, 1989). Across several sketches—for instance, "Le Soleil d'Afrique"—he scrawls "Annulé, trop cher" or "Non, trop cher!" In recounting (smugly—an accomplished Don Juan) his seduction of Mitterrand, Goude explained that he had shown the president in March during the audience of a quarter hour that swelled into an hour "un projet relativement abouti. Enfin, abouti sur le papier. Quand on commence à le concrétiser, on s'aperçoit que ce n'est pas possible, qu'il faut passer du plan A au plan B, quelquefois au plan C, D . . ." *Le Figaro*, 10 July 1989.

14. On Goude's lifelong fascination with parades, see his filmed interview with S. Moati, *Journal d'un bicentenaire*, and Goude's *Jungle Fever*, 8 ("Cocteau had dancers move to noises, to the sound of typewriters"). In an earlier version of the parade, Goude envisioned beginning at the Porte de Maillot and adding several hours to the procession. Compte rendu (Sauvage), 1 December 1988, Mission papers, AN, 900506/41.

15. Goude's comments in *Opéra Goude: L'Aventure de 'la Marseillaise'* (1989), inspired and choreographed by Goude, produced by C. Gassot, and filmed by Gérard Stérin; Goude, "Ce que j'ai voulu faire," *Le Débat*, no. 57 (November-December 1989): 35; *L'Express*, 30 June 1989; interview with Goude, *Le Figaro*, 10 July 1989.

16. The Boy Scout persona was of considerable importance to Goude. He called upon it as a sort of counterpoise to his bohemian, socially iconoclastic side. The Boy Scout was the eternal youth in him, the assurance of a certain purity, but also the reminder of a permanent diminutiveness, a partially arrested growth. Even as a Boy Scout, however, Goude was special, self-consciously out of line with the standard, yet something of a leader. At age twelve, he started the first "free Boy Scout company" in Paris "because I didn't like the regular outfits. . . . I arranged for us to look like paratroopers." *Jungle Fever*, 7.

17. Interview with Goude, *Le Monde*, 15 June 1989; J.-N. Jeanneney, "Après coup: Réflexions d'un commémorateur," *Le Débat*, no. 57 (November-December 1989): 96; *L'Express*, 30 June 1989.

18. *Opéra Goude.*

19. Interview with J.-N. Jeanneney, *Le Monde*, 27–28 August 1989; Jeanneney, "Après coup: Réflexions d'un commémorateur," *Le Débat*, no. 57 (November-December 1989): 95; J.-P. Goude, "Ce que j'ai voulu faire," ibid., 35–45; *Politis*, 9–15 June and 7–12 July 1989. In the weeks before the fourteenth, there was a welling anxiety that Goude would somehow embarrass France with a self-parody of sorts. Having monitored Goude rather tightly, Jeanneney was serene on this point. Goude, he assured, will be joyous, jaunty, perhaps a bit fanciful, but "très républicain." Filmed interview with S. Moati, *Autour du 14 juillet.*

20. J.-P. Goude, "Ce que j'ai voulu faire," *Le Débat*, no. 57 (November-December 1989): 41; Goude, *Jungle Fever*, 107. Cf. Dominique de Saint Pern's query about Goude's "a

contrario racism" and Goude's double response focusing on his celebration of the "aesthetic qualities" of blacks and on their imperative need for integration. *L'Express*, 10 July 1987. On hip-hop culture, see the *New York Times*, 18 November 1991, and *La Lettre politique et parlementaire*, 5 November 1991.

21. J.-P. Goude, "Ce que j'ai voulu faire," *Le Débat*, no. 57 (November-December 1989): 36–37, 42; *Opéra Goude; Le Canard enchaîné*, 21 June 1989; *Le Monde*, 15 June, 15 July 1989; *Libération*, 11–12 February 1989; *Politis*, 9–15 June 1989; interview with Goude, *Le Figaro*, 10 July 1989. Cf. "Je suis allé à Bombay, au Brésil, à Moscou, à Hongkong. J'ai constaté que la jeunesse avait adopté un rhythme afro-occidental. Le hip hop anglais, le piliwu chinois, le breakdance américain: tout ça, c'est la même chose. Le 14 Juillet sera la consécration de cette rhythmique universelle." *L'Express*, 30 June 1989.

22. J.-P. Goude, "Ce que j'ai voulu faire," *Le Débat*, no. 57 (November-December 1989); interview with M. Sauvage, January 1990; *Le Monde*, 15 July 1989; *Politis*, 9–15 July 1989.

23. J.-P. Goude, "Ce que j'ai voulu faire," *Le Débat*, no. 57 (November-December 1989): 45–47; J.-N. Jeanneney, *Rapport du président de la Mission du Bicentenaire*, 88; *Le Monde*, 14 July 1989.

24. J.-P. Goude, "Ce que j'ai voulu faire," *Le Débat*, no. 57 (November-December 1989): 45; *Politis*, 9–15 June, 7–13 July 1989; *L'Express*, 30 June 1989.

25. J.-P. Goude, "Ce que j'ai voulu faire," *Le Débat*, no. 57 (November-December 1989): 40–41; *L'Express*, 30 June 1989.

26. Interview with Dr. W. P. Foster, director of bands, Florida A & M University, 15 February 1991. Cf. *Libération*, 11–12 February 1989.

27. *Opéra Goude;* Goude's journal-story board, *Bleu, blanc, Goude;* Goude, "Ce que j'ai voulu faire," *Le Débat*, no. 57 (November-December 1989): 41–42; *L'Express*, 30 June 1989; *Libération*, 3 July 1989. One hopes that the large legend that Goude drew above one of his sketches for the Chinese tableau bespoke irony rather than political analysis: "Those who follow the principles of democracy will be rewarded. Those who go against it will be destroyed." *Bleu, blanc, Goude.*

28. *Le Monde*, 15 July 1989.

29. J.-N. Jeanneney, *Rapport du président de la Mission du Bicentenaire*, 88–91; Claire Andrieu, ed., *1789: Le Livre du Bicentenaire* (Paris: Le Chêne-Hachette, 1990), 117; interview with P. Blondel, January 1990; *L'Express*, 30 June 1989.

30. Dialogue between R. Debray and F. Dosse, *Politis*, 3–9 February 1989; J. Julliard in *Le Nouvel Observateur*, 13–19 July 1989; Attali interview in S. Moati's film *Journal d'un bicentenaire; Le Monde*, 13 July 1989; *Libération*, 10, 12 July 1989.

31. *Le Monde*, 13, 15 July 1989; *Libération*, 12, 14 July 1989; *Le Nouvel Observateur*, 13–19 July 1989; *Le Canard enchaîné*, 19 July 1989.

32. *Le Figaro*, 5 July 1989; *Le Monde*, 9–10 July 1989; for J.-L. Mélenchon's attack on "l'hypocrisie ambiante du discours sur le tiers monde" and the ignobly meretricious character of the commemoration of the Great Revolution, see *A gauche* (Nouvelle Ecole socialiste), no. 318 (15 June 1989); minutes of Mission staff meeting, 7 June 1989, Mission papers, AN, 900506/41; *Libération*, 18 July 1989; *Le Quotidien de Paris*, 30 June 1989.

33. *L'Evénement du Jeudi*, 13–19 July 1989; interview with Renaud, *Le Quotidien de Paris*, 16 June 1989; interview with Renaud in *Révolution*, no. 487 (30 June-7 July 1989); *Dépêche du Midi*, 8 July 1989; *Rouge*, 13–19 July 1989; *L'Humanité*, 29 June, 13 July 1989; *Vendredi*, 14 July 1989; *PS Info*, no. 413 (15 July 1989); *Le Nouvel Observateur*, 13–19 July 1989; *L'Express*, 30 June 1989; *Vive 89 en Ille-et-Vilaine*, bulletin no. 6 (September 1989). Cf. the stinging portrait of Krivine by *L'Evénement du Jeudi* (20–26 July 1989): "L'inévitable Krivine, qui est à la Révolution ce que Line Renaud est à la chanson, et à Trotski ce que celle-ci

est à Chirac, et qui mourra à 95 ans toujours chef d'un mouvement de jeunesse." Fellow Trotskyite Daniel Bensaïd considered Renaud's undertaking "la seule initiative populaire" of the bicentennial season. *Le Monde,* 8 December 1989. Renaud received encouragement from certain Catholic quarters, which expressed deep solidarity with the Third World-as-heirs-to-the-Revolution, but which had no interest in furthering the "manoeuvre trotskysto-stalinienne." See *Témoignage chrétien,* 10–16 July 1989

34. S. Moati, *Journal d'un bicentenaire; Libération,* 10 July 1989; *Dépêche du Midi,* 9 July 1989; *Le Monde,* 13 June 1989; *Le Figaro,* 8–9 July 1989.

35. *Libération,* 10 July 1989; *Le Monde,* 11 July 1989.

36. *Dépêche du Midi,* 10 July 1989; *Le Monde,* 13, 15, 16–17 July 1989; *Libération,* 11 July 1989; *L'Humanité,* 13 July 1989; open letter to the G-7 heads of state, *Témoignage chrétien,* 10–16 July 1989. Toward the end of the bicentennial year, a CSA poll asked respondents with which of the following propositions they agreed: (1) "C'est dommage qu'il y ait eu, en même temps, le 14 juillet, la fête du Bicentenaire et le Sommet des pays les plus riches"; (2) "C'est une bonne chose que les dirigeants des grandes démocraties du monde [the allusion to wealth is eschewed] se soient retrouvés à Paris pour la fête du Bicentenaire." Twenty-eight percent endorsed the first proposition, while 58 percent preferred the second. Almost two-thirds of those identifying themselves with the left opted for the second statement, which also attracted slightly more than half the right. CSA poll, commissioned by the Mission, November 1989.

Chapter 6
Goude's Opera: The *Marseillaise* Revisited

1. Interview with J.-N. Jeanneney, January 1990; Olivier Salvatori, "Bricolo-les-belles-images," *Le Débat,* no. 57 (November-December 1989): 67; M. Dupont, "Le Défilé, couronnement de l'art mitterrandien," *Esprit,* September 1989, 127–28; minutes of staff meeting, 5 July 1989, Mission papers, AN, 900506/41; interview with Jeanneney, *France-Soir,* 29 November 1989; J.-P. Goude, "Ce que j'ai voulu faire," *Le Débat,* no. 57 (November-December 1989): 44; *Le Monde,* 8, 13, 14 July 1989; *Le Quotidien de Paris,* 14 June 1989. In the weeks preceding the show, the Mission indulged in an extraordinary rhetoric of puffery to build anticipation. It was hinted that the Gouderie would be a distillation of Hollywood studios and Soviet realism—superpower balance?—along with a melange of African tribal spirit and Latin American delirium. "Et tout sera décalé au point qu'il en surgira autre chose." Fearing no cliché, the Mission promised "Du jamais vu." *Bicentenaire 89, lettre de la Mission,* no. 10 (July 1989).

2. Personal observation, 13 July 1989; *Libération,* 14 July 1989; *Le Monde,* 14, 15 July 1989; J.-N. Jeanneney, *Rapport du président de la Mission du Bicentenaire à Monsieur le président de la République* (Paris, 1989), 97–99; Claire Andrieu, ed., *1789: Le Livre du Bicentenaire* (Paris: Le Chêne-Hachette, 1990), 127–29.

3. Street interviews and personal observations, 14 July 1989; J.-F. Revel, "Leur 14 Juillet," *Le Débat,* no. 57 (November-December 1989): 60; *Le Monde,* 16–17 July 1989.

4. The Chinese government strenuously protested against the presence of "its" students in the offensive parade. The Chinese Ministry of Foreign Affairs convoked the French ambassador at Beijing to denounce "l'attaque insidieuse contre l'écrasement de la rébellion contre-révolutionnaire à Pékin par le gouvernement chinois" qui "constitue une ingérance grossière dans les affaires intérieures du pays." *Le Monde,* 19 July 1989.

5. In his sketchbook, Goude referred to the scene in which the wall of water serves as backdrop to the singing of the *Marseillaise* as a "Rideau d'eau [qui] s'ouvre devant Jessie [*sic*], comme la mer rouge devant Moise." *Bleu, blanc, Goude: La Marseillaise* (Paris: Nathan Images, 1989). Cf. the lyric description of Ms. Norman by the awestruck reporter of *L'Humanité:* "Nimbée de soie tricolore cousue main par Azzedine Alaia, émergeant de la mer nocturne comme une caravelle toutes voiles dehors, orgueilleuse nef voguant à la crête des flots de musique, semblant voler comme une Junon tutélaire sur l'histoire de France, semant à gorge déployée le chant fier des sans-culottes, pythie en majesté, maman enceinte de tous les espoirs du monde, noire effigie de tous les damnés: Jessye, *la Marseillaise* en un final sublime." 17 July 1989.

6. On the Tambours du Bronx, see *La Vie ouvrière,* 17–23 July 1989, on the whole rather content with this "Red" moment in the parade evoking the industrial revolution from below.

7. Goude, as we have seen, had felt a strong attraction for James Brown's soul music from his youth in Paris. He would have liked to incorporate a filmed interview of Brown in his prison cell into the televised version of the parade. See his wonderful *croquis* of King James wearing a crown, a long cape, and high heels and bearing a scepter, juxtaposed to a melancholic James Brown behind bars saying "Ain't it funny now?" *Bleu, blanc, Goude.* See also Goude's *Jungle Fever,* ed. Harold Hayes (New York: Xavier Moreau, 1982), 31.

8. Interview with Claude Serillon in S. Moati's film, *Journal d'un bicentenaire; Le Provençal,* 15, 16 July 1989; M. Winock in *La Vie,* 20 July 1989; J.-N. Jeanneney's closing talk to M. Vovelle's Congrès mondial, in Mission papers, AN, 900506/81; P. Mauroy interviewed in S. Moati's film, *Autour du 14 juillet;* B. Frappat in *Le Monde,* 23–24 July 1989. *L'Humanité* caustically reproached Sérillon for his biases as well as his silliness. "Il ne faut pas oublier que l'U.R.S.S. est une menace pour la démocratie," the journalist is said to have commented as the goose-stepping Russians paraded by. The Communist daily remarked—incongruously, given its standard Orwellian version of newspeak: "Et Sérillon une menace pour l'éthique de son métier qui est d'informer et non de lécher les bottes au Pentagon." 17 July 1989.

9. M. Dupont, "Le Défilé, couronnement de l'art mitterrandien," *Esprit,* September 1989, 128 (for the Security Council image); P. Meyer, "Leur 14 Juillet," *Le Débat,* no. 57 (November-December 1989): 60. A CSA poll interrogating 1,004 persons aged eighteen and older asked an open-ended question inviting respondents to indicate what the Goude parade evoked for them in retrospect. The answers follow: (1) universality, the mix of peoples, races, and cultures: 15 percent; (2) waste, too much money spent, grandiose means incommensurate with the product (and implicitly with the referent?): 15 percent; (3) the fête, carnival, joie de vivre: 13 percent; (4) the Revolutionary idea, liberty, equality, fraternity: 11 percent; (5) the rights of man: 5 percent; (6) great prestige for France: 5 percent; (7) an excessively modern and commercial spectacle of buffoonery: 5 percent; (8) political propaganda: 3 percent; (9) a very Parisian event, not made for the people at large: 2 percent. (Multiple responses result in a total over 100 percent.) J.-N. Jeanneney, *Rapport du président de la Mission du Bicentenaire,* 357.

10. *Populaire du Centre,* 17 July 1989; *Dépêche du Midi,* 17 July 1989; *Vendredi,* 14 July 1989; *Le Canard enchaîné,* 19 July 1989; *L'Evénement du Jeudi,* 20–26 July 1989; *Le Monde,* 23–24 July 1989; *Le Figaro,* 15–16 July 1989; *Nice Matin,* 16 July 1989; J.-N. Jeanneney, "Après coup: Réflexions d'un commémorateur," *Le Débat,* no. 57 (November-December 1989): 90–91; interview with Jeanneney, *Le Monde,* 27–28 August 1989. See also *Réforme,* 29 July 1989. On the basis of a number of interviews, Patrick Garcia concludes that the sentiment of bicentennial saturation [*ras-le-bol*] diminished considerably. "Premiers Regards sur le Bicentenaire," *Cercle Condorcet,* no. 11 (March 1990): 29. The shift in opinion that gratified and puzzled Jeanneney was arguably only skin deep. It is worth noting that the

right-wing press, while it acknowledged the perceived/proclaimed success, still entertained grave reservations about the character of the Gouderie. See Renaud Matignon in *Le Figaro*, 17 July 1989, and Gérard Spiteri in *Le Quotidien de Paris*, 17 July 1989.

11. *Le Monde*, 19 (A. Fontaine) and 23–24 (B. Frappat) July 1989; *Dépêche du Midi*, 17 July 1989; *Centre Presse*, 17 July 1989; A. Schifres, *Les Parisiens* (Paris: J. C. Lattès, 1990), 335; J.-N. Jeanneney, "Après coup: Réflexions d'un commémorateur," *Le Débat*, no. 57 (November-December 1989): 94. Cf. Jeanneney's remarks on the strange alchemy of a commemoration, where everything turns on "joining in," a phenomenon of mass, however subterranean and difficult to measure: "C'est l'adhésion ou la non-adhésion qui fait le succès ou l'échec." *Le Monde*, 27–28 August 1989.

12. Cf. the scintillating exchange between the bicentennial commemorators and an imaginary Condorcet. The philosophe is told that the intellectual approach, including elitist speeches, is no longer appropriate: "nous tenons à intéresser le peuple." Thus the idea for a show in which Condorcet would appear in the illuminated sky over Paris: "Votre apparition . . . serait si stupéfiante, elle étourdirait si fort le peuple qu'il ne songerait plus à demander combien coûtent les festivités qu'on lui prépare. Vous comprendrez aussi aisément qu'un tel miracle, qui ne manquerait d'être mis au compte de la puissance de nos actuels gouvernants, leur assurerait à eux-mêmes l'éternité." Condorcet agrees that the recipe "en matière de fêtes populaires" must be changed: "Il me semble qu'un concert rock retransmis en mondovision, qu'il serait d'ailleurs facile d'organiser dans le nouvel Opéra de la Bastille, inoccupé et désert, remplirait beaucoup plus efficacement la fonction que vous voulez me faire jouer. Les articles de la Déclaration des droits de l'homme et du citoyen pourraient être chantés dans toutes les langues sur tous les rythmes par des chanteurs de tous les pays." This scenario, and perhaps this reckoning, were not far off the mark. Condorcet [F. Ewald], *Lettre au président de la Mission du Bicentenaire*, 9–10, 17.

13. Interview with F. Mitterrand, *L'Express*, 14 July 1989; *Réforme*, 15 July 1989; *Libération*, 10 July 1989; *Le Provençal*, 15, 16 July 1989; R. Debray and G. Fromanger, "Leur 14 Juillet," *Le Débat*, no. 57 (November-December 1989): 56–57. Cf. *Figaro-Magazine*'s prediction that Chirac's Eiffel Tower centennial celebration would be "la plus grande fête populaire parisienne depuis la Libération." 10 June 1989. On the social demand for a popular fête, see the result of a poll of one hundred persons reported in "Passé présent: Les Français et leur Révolution. Une Enquête qualitative," *EspacesTemps*, nos. 38–39 (1988): 29.

14. *Le Monde*, 16–17 July 1989; *L'Evénement du Jeudi*, 20–26 July 1989; M. Ozouf cited by L. Lemire, "Bicentenaire, mode d'emploi," *L'Histoire*, no. 113 (July-August 1989): 127. Cf. the self-protective prediction of *Figaro-Magazine* that "la foule ne sera pas française." Commentators on the right in particular were inclined to diminish the potential numbers of French citizens in the Goude crowd. Thus wrote Xavier Beguin-Billecoq: "Un succès considérable, mais plus auprès des touristes étrangers que des Parisiens qui ont boudé les fêtes." *Sud-Ouest*, 17 July 1989.

15. *L'Evénement du Jeudi*, 20–26 July 1989; *Le Monde*, 18, 23–24 (B. Frappat) July 1989; L. Joffrin in *Le Nouvel Observateur*, 20–26 July 1989; O. Mongin, "Le Paris de Goude," *Esprit*, no. 154 (September 1989): 126–27. Cf. the remarks of Jules Gritti, *La Croix*, 9 August 1989. Cf. Joël Roman's juxtaposition of a "bicentenaire de la foule" and a "bicentenaire des clercs." "Commémorer la Révolution française?" *Esprit* (September 1989): 87.

16. *Le Quotidien de Paris*, 24 September 1988 and 12 July 1989; Christian Amalvi, *De l'Art et la manière d'accommoder les héros de l'histoire de France* (Paris: Albin Michel, 1988), 376; *La Croix*, 13 July 1989; *Dépêche du Midi*, 18 July 1989; O. Mongin, "Le Paris de Goude," *Esprit*, no. 154 (September 1989): 126. A poll conducted by the CSA in November 1989 reported that 54 percent of French persons esteemed that Jacques Chirac was wrong not to

attend Goude's show. J.-N. Jeanneney, *Rapport du président de la Mission du Bicentenaire*, 356. Under the exultant title "Le Tout-Paris émigre," *Figaro-Magazine* (8 July 1989) asked a number of prominent Parisians where they would be on 14 July. Here are two exemplary responses. The celebrated defense attorney Jacques Vergès: "Le 14 juillet? Parlons-en, de cette fête indécente! On a interdit Paris aux Parisiens. Le 14 juillet et le Bicentenaire se devaient d'être une fête populaire. On en a fait un délire, avec la volonté de se célébrer soi-même. Oui, je serai à Paris, mais surtout pas dans ces manifestations grotesques. J'ai du travail." The macho crime-and-thrill novelist and popular-culture commodifier Gérard de Villiers: "Je serai à Saint-Tropez. Je ne passe jamais le 14 juillet à Paris. Et cette année, je n'ai pas envie de fêter des massacres qui n'ont rien apporté de bon à notre pays. Les autres pays d'Europe ont fait l'économie d'une révolution. Au lieu de crier haro sur les communistes chinois, on ferait mieux de regarder de notre côté."

17. R. Escarpit in *Le Monde*, 15 July 1989; *Le Canard enchaîné*, 12 July 1989; M. Genty, "1789, une Révolution sans le peuple," *Cahiers d'histoire de l'Institut de recherches marxistes*, no. 40 (1990): 47; G. Perrault, "Premiers Regards sur le Bicentenaire," *Cercle Condorcet*, no. 11 (March 1990): 31; J.-E. Hallier in *L'Idiot international*, 13 juillet 1989; S. Moati in minutes of a staff meeting, 5 July 1989, Mission papers, AN, 900506/41; S. July in *Libération*, 12 July 1989; Wolinski in S. Moati's film, *Journal d'un bicentenaire;* reader from Apt to *Minute*, no. 1427 (9–13 August 1989). On the exclusion of the people in a broader sociopolitical sense, see the piece by J.-D. Bredin, *Le Monde*, 3 January 1989 ("Et la République elle-même ne cesse de rappeler la supériorité des détenteurs du pouvoir, riches de passedroits"). With a dash of demagogy, *Figaro-Magazine* (8 July 1989) had suggested before the show that the sort of product endorsed by Lang would not be the sort of product that popular France would consider comestible. Mona Ozouf recalled that Festivals of the Federation were moments of exclusion: "Car le spectacle a été octroyé au peuple, le banquet était fermé à la foule, le serment réservé aux notables, se mêler à la procession n'allait de soi ni pour le menu peuple ni pour les femmes." *Le Monde*, 8–9 July 1990.

18. *National hebdo*, 10–16, 20–26 July 1989; *L'Anti-89*, no. 25 (October 1989); *Minute*, no. 1415 (17–23 May 1989); *Présent*, 14–15 July 1989; *Rivarol*, 9 July 1989; *La Croix*, 17–18 July 1989. *Présent* returned to the treason-miscegenation theme later in the year: "Cela s'est bien marqué au défilé du 14 juillet, beaucoup plus africano-américain que français." 11–12 December 1989. Cf. *Le Monde*'s comment on Bruno Mégret's purge of blacks: "Merci pour les Antillais, les Réunionnais, les Canaques et tous les métissés. Vive la nation blanche." 23–24 July 1989. On the distaste of ordinary traditionalists for the "ignoble" and "decadent" parade showcasing blacks and Communists, see the interview with the elderly woman from the west in S. Moati's film *Journal d'un bicentenaire* and the interview with Alexandre of Nantes in *Le Nouvel Observateur*, 17–23 August 1989.

19. *Le Quotidien de Paris*, 10 November 1989. Cf. Jean-Christophe Averty's ambiguous and overrefined appraisal: "C'est normal qu'il y ait un grand foutoir au moment de la célébration du plus grand foutoir français." *Le Figaro*, 15–16 July 1989.

20. *L'Humanité*, 16 June 1989; *La Croix*, 9 August 1989; D. Bensaïd in *Le Monde*, 8 December 1989; C. Arnaud, "Leur 14 juillet" *Le Débat*, no. 57 (November-December 1989): 49; P. Genestier, "Par-delà fête et cérémonie ou contre la gaie commémoration," ibid., 73–74. François Léotard, one of the leaders of the liberal right, felt embarrassed by the vacuity of the Goude show, which was "à la mesure de notre traditionnelle légèreté." For him and for many other critics, left and right, the real bicentennial in 1989 was celebrated in Leipzig, Budapest, Warsaw, Berlin, and the other old cities of Eastern Europe. *Le Monde*, 7 December 1989.

21. R. Debray and G. Fromanger, "Leur 14 juillet" *Le Débat*, no. 57 (November-

December 1989): 54–57. Cf. a slightly milder version of the jeremiad in *Le Nouvel Obser-vateur*, 30 November 1989. The right also castigated Goude for leaving out all of the history. On "l'absence de la Révolution française," see Renaud Matignon in *Le Figaro*, 15–16 July 1989.

22. S. Moati's filmed interview with R. Debray, *Journal d'un bicentenaire;* F. Gèze, "Vive la Ringardise," *Esprit*, September 1989, 128–29; *Le Monde*, 23–24 July 1989; interview with A. Finkielkraut, *L'Evénement du Jeudi*, 20–26 December 1990.

23. A. Schifres in *Le Nouvel Observateur*, 13–19 July 1989; S. Moati's filmed interview with Cardinal Lustiger, *Journal d'un bicentenaire;* Lustiger in *Le Monde*, 8 December 1989; *Le Canard enchaîné*, 21 June 1989; P. Minard, "Premiers Regards sur le Bicentenaire," *Cercle Condorcet*, no. 11 (March 1990): 33; G. Spiteri in *Le Quotidien de Paris*, 13 June 1989.

24. Emmanuel de Roux in *Le Monde*, 16–17 July 1989; J.-N. Jeanneney, "Premiers Regards sur le Bicentenaire," *Cercle Condorcet*, no. 11 (March 1990): 35; E. Morin inter-viewed in S. Moati's film, *Autour du 14 juillet;* M. Rebérioux, "Premiers Regards sur le Bicentenaire," *Cercle Condorcet*, no. 11 (March 1990): 35. Cf. Goude's acknowledgment of the influence of Marshall McLuhan. *Elle*, 10 July 1989.

25. *Le Canard enchaîné*, 19 July 1989; *Le Monde*, 16–17 July 1989; interview with J. Favier, July 1991; *Minute*, no. 1424, 19–25 July 1989; *Le Figaro*, 17 July 1989.

26. R. Huard to the author, 19 May 1991; Guy Boisson to the author, 7 July 1991.

27. *Le Figaro*, 17 July 1989.

28. *L'Express*, 30 June 1989; *Le Monde*, 8, 16–17, 18 July 1989; J.-N. Jeanneney, *Rapport du président de la Mission du Bicentenaire;* J.-P. Goude, "Ce que j'ai voulu faire," *Le Débat*, no. 57 (November-December 1989): 47–48; interview with C. Dupavillon, 3 January 1991; *La Marseillaise*, the official program of the parade; J.-P. Jaud cited in *Télérama*, 5 July 1989, cited in turn by A. Finkielkraut, "L'Esprit du temps par lui-même," *Le Messager européen*, no. 4 (1990): 100; J.-F. Revel, "Leur 14 Juillet," *Le Débat*, no. 57 (November-December 1989): 62; *L'Evénement du Jeudi*, 20–16 July 1989. André Fontaine and Emmanuel de Roux in *Le Monde* (16–17, 19 July 1989) shared a positive view of the television impact. The *Quotidien de Paris* took pleasure in underlining the fact that only a quarter of French televiewers (9.3 million) were tuned to the Gouderie, fewer than watched a vulgar film like *Les Bronzés. Le Canard enchaîné*, 19 July 1989. In an interesting argument that it would have worked better had Jaud cooperated more fully, M. Dupont claimed that the television broadcast was the real venue of the popular fête, with a veritable carnivalesque dimension. "Le Défilé, couronne-ment de l'art mitterrandien," *Esprit*, September 1989, 128. On the plan for using four sopranos to sing the *Marseillaise*, and on Goude's own enthusiastic announcement of Nor-man's collaboration, see *Libération*, 11–12 February 1989.

29. *Le Monde*, 18 July, 24 November, 12 December 1989; interview with J. Favier, July 1991; R. Huard to the author, 19 May 1991; interview with M. Agulhon, 11 April 1991; *Nice Matin*, 16 July 1989; *La Vie*, 20 July 1989; *L'Express*, 25–31 August 1989; J.-N. Jeanneney, *Rapport du président de la Mission du Bicentenaire*, 20; *Le Canard enchaîné*, 19 July 1989.

30. *Le Monde*, 16–17 July 1989; *L'Express*, 30 June 1987; *Figaro-Magazine*, 10 March 1990; CSA poll commissioned by the Mission, 17–24 November 1989, Mission papers, AN, 900506/84; *Le Monde*, 2 April 1991.

31. *Le Canard enchaîné*, 19 July 1989; *Le Monde*, 18, 19 July 1989; *Le Nouvel Observateur*, 20–26 July 1989; *L'Express*, 14 July 1989; *Ouest-France*, 17 July 1989. Cf. *Minute*'s scornful assessment of the summit, no. 1424 (19–25 July 1989).

32. Mission papers, AN, 900506/42; *Le Monde*, 28 September, 6 December 1989 and 7 May 1990; *Figaro-Magazine*, 29 September 1989; *Libération*, 3 July 1989; *Le Quotidien de Paris*, 30 June 1989; X. Beguin-Billecoq, bicentennial coordinator of the Maison de la

France, appendix to J.-N. Jeanneney, *Rapport du président de la Mission du Bicentenaire*, 364–65.

33. *L'Humanité*, 12 July 1989; *Le Quotidien de Paris*, 11 August 1988; *Figaro-Magazine*, 26 November 1988 and 8 July 1989; *La Lettre politique et parlementaire*, 31 August 1988 and 12 July 1989; *Rivarol*, 9 June 1989.

34. *L'Evénement du Jeudi*, 20–26 July 1989; *Le Nouvel Observateur*, 13–19 July 1989; *Le Monde*, 10, 13, 14, 19 July 1989; *Dépêche du Midi*, 13 July 1989; interview with F. Mitterrand, *L'Express*, 14 July 1989; Mitterrand's television interview reported in *Le Monde*, 16–17 July 1989 and *Libération*, 15–16 July; A. Duhamel in *Le Quotidien de Paris*, 14 July 1989. While *L'Humanité* railed against costly pomp, a Communist writer contended that the commemoration was substantially underfunded—they looked not to the United States and Australia as a yardstick but to nearby Spain on the forthcoming celebration of the five hundredth anniversary of Columbus's voyage—apparently as a result of the government's tepid feeling for the Revolutionary heritage. Claudine Ducol, in *Vive la Révolution, 1789–1989*, ed. C. Mazauric and A. Casanova, (Paris: Messidor/Editions sociales, 1989), 7. François Furet agreed with the view of the mainstream left that the government had not engaged in inordinate expense for "a great anniversary." *Le Figaro*, 17 July 1989. In support of its line, *Figaro-Magazine* cited a Sofres poll conducted in late June 1989 in which 44 percent of respondents felt that the celebration was "a bad idea" (as opposed to 39 percent who considered it "a good idea") and 62 percent regarded the expenditures as "shocking" (as opposed to 29 percent who saw them as "justified"). 8 July 1989.

35. M. Clos in *Le Figaro*, 7 July 1989; *Libération*, 18 July 1989; *Rouge*, 13–19 July 1989; G. Suffert in *Le Figaro*, 10 July 1989; *La Lettre de la Nation*, 6, 11 July 1989; *Minute*, no. 1424 (19–25 July 1989); *Le Quotidien de Paris*, 29 June 1989.

36. *L'Evénement du Jeudi*, 20–26 July 1989; S. July in *Libération*, 12 July 1989; "Entretien avec Marcel Gauchet," *France catholique*, no. 2215 (14 July 1989); interview with F. Mitterrand, *L'Express*, 14 July 1989.

37. *Le Monde*, 13 June 1989; J. d'Ormesson in *Figaro-Magazine*, 8 July 1989; *Le Figaro*, 3 June 1989; *Le Quotidien de Paris*, 30 June 1989; *L'Humanité*, 16 June 1989; *L'Express*, 14 July 1989; *L'Evénement du Jeudi*, 20–26 July 1989; A. Duhamel in *Le Quotidien de Paris*, 14 July 1989. While Pierre Joxe predicted that a vehicle-free core city—a pedestrian's paradise—would favor "popular revelry," Georges Suffert tried to elevate the inconvenience argument to a loftier plane in a contrary sense. The people "value their Revolution." With thirty thousand police on the streets and "ground-air missile batteries hidden God knows where," the effect will be to "exclude the people from this new '89." *Le Monde*, 13 June 1989 and *Le Figaro*, 10 July 1989.

38. *La Croix*, 11 July 1989; Eric Walter, "Avec Marianne," in *Lettres à la Révolution*, ed. Jean-Marie Lhôte (Amiens: trois Cailloux pour la Maison de la culture, 1989), 273; C. Mazauric, "La Révolution dans les processus d'acculturation politique des Français contemporains: Quelques Données," in *L'Image de la Révolution française*, ed. M. Vovelle (Oxford and Paris: Pergamon Press, 1989), 3:2315–16; P. Sansot, "Du bon et moins bon usage de la commémoration," in *Mythe et révolutions* (Grenoble: Presses Universitaires de Grenoble, 1990), 306–10; L. Oury, "Les Chapelets de Machecoul," *Révolution*, no. 487 (30 June–6 July 1989); P. Garnier in Lhôte, *Lettres à la Révolution*, 103; G. Perrault, "Premiers Regards sur le Bicentenaire," *Cercle Condorcet*, no. 11 (March 1990): 33; D. Bensaïd, in *Rouge*, 13–19 July 1989; C. Castoriadès, "L'Auto-constituante," *EspacesTemps*, nos. 38–39 (1988): 550. O. Marcel, *Libération*, 24–25 June 1989. Cf. *L'Idiot international*, 5 July 1989, which refers to the "bide-centenaire de la Vérolution française.")

39. P. Billard, in *Le Point*, 10 July 1989; P. Sollers in *Le Quotidien de Paris*, 21 June 1989;

F. Lazorthes, in *Le Quotidien de Paris*, 31 July 1989; G. Spiteri in *Le Quotidien de Paris*, 15 December 1988; interview with J. Tulard, 10 April 1991; F. Reynaert, in *Libération*, 3 July 1989; E. Morin, "Remarques brisées: Entretien," *Le Débat*, no. 57 (November-December 1989): 212; "Entretien avec Marcel Gauchet," *France catholique*, no. 2215 (14 July 1989); M. Ozouf, "Célébrer, savoir, fêter," *Le Débat*, no. 57 (November-December 1989): 25. Apparently Ozouf regarded Furet as a mere figurehead monarch, for at the end of his bicentennial reign she detected the toxic persistence of "a reverence for a conventional history, in a strong position because of a power of intimidation that is still at work among those who learned history between [Albert] Mathiez and [Albert] Soboul." Ibid.

40. M. Vovelle, "L'Age de la prise de conscience," *EspacesTemps*, nos. 38-39 (1988): 37; D. Bensaïd, *Moi, la Révolution* (Paris: Gallimard, 1989) 146–47, 290; Bensaïd in *Rouge*, 13–19 July 1989, and in *Le Monde*, 8 December 1989; C. Mazauric, "La Révolution dans les processus d'acculturation politique des français contemporains," in Vovelle, *L'Image de la Révolution française*, 3:2315–16; A.-G. Slama in *Le Figaro*, 14 July 1989.

41. O. Marcel, *Libération*, 24–25 June 1989; M. Rebérioux, "Premiers Regards sur le Bicentenaire," *Cercle Condorcet*, no. 11 (March 1990): p. 23; C. Ducol in Mazauric and Casanova, *Vive la Révolution*, 7–16; *L'Humanité*, 16 June 1989; *Révolution*, 2–8 December 1988 and 14 June 1989; Condorcet [F. Ewald], *Lettre au président de la Mission du Bicentenaire*, 26–27. Citizens writing to the editors of the leftist press often complained of the failure of the commemoration to connect the Revolutionary legacy with the harsh contemporary problems of unemployment, poverty, homelessness, and the persistence of privileges for a narrow elite. See, for instance, the letters of Y. Lanos (Le Havre) and A. Voegelé in *L'Evénement du Jeudi*, 13–19 July 1989. Cf. the peculiar fashion of criticizing the commemoration—"pantalonnades révolutionnaires"—adopted by the so-called Amis du chevalier de la Barre. *Le Monde*, 29 August 1989. François Furet was skeptical of the call for a Relevant Revolution. He disliked the appeals to Revolutionary remedy and aggiornamento implicit in the formula "Bastilles à prendre." The Bastille evoked the idea of a revolutionary rupture that virtually no one believed in or associated concretely with the reforms that were in fact necessary. F. Furet, "1989–1917: Aller et retour," *Le Débat*, no. 57 (November-December 1989): 5.

42. Interview with F. Baroin, 11 April 1991. See the similar views expressed by his colleague at the Mission Thierry Collard, interview of 11 April 1991 and "Note à l'attention de M. le Président," n.d., Mission papers, AN, 900506/102.

Chapter 7
Anticlimax, Zenith, and Finale

1. Though beautiful, the fireworks at Chaillot on the night following the Gouderie have no special claims on the bicentennial calendar. For a report on the event, see *Le Monde*, 18 July 1989.

2. *Le Monde*, 19, 27–28, 29 August 1989; cassettes of the coverage of the Arch ceremonies by Antenne 2, to whose staff I am indebted.

3. Mitterrand speech carried on Antenne 2.

4. Coverage by Antenne 2; *Libération*, 28 August 1989; Mission papers, AN, 900506/41; J.-N. Jeanneney, *Rapport du président de la Mission à Monsieur le président de la République* (Paris, 1989), 600–01; J. Mendelson, personal communication, 7 July 1993. The Mission denounced the Foundation for "deficiencies of organization," the prefect of police for

gratuitous and perilous prudence, and the television commentators for presumably inadvertent provocation.

5. Claire Andrieu, ed., *1789: Le Livre du Bicentenaire* (Paris: Le Chêne-Hachette, 1990), 151, 153; Patrick Bouchain, ed., *Valmy 20 September 1792* (Macon, 1989), 35–42; *Pèlerin Magazine*, 15 September 1989; *Le Monde*, 27 April 1989; J.-N. Jeanneney, *Rapport du président de la Mission du Bicentenaire*, 107–9; Paul Guiberteau, "Ouverture du colloque," in *Les Catholiques français et l'héritage de 1789*, ed. P. Colin (Paris: Beauchesne, 1989), 16.

6. Coverage by Antenne 2; *Libération*, 16 September 1989; *L'Express*, 8 September 1989; Andrieu, ed., *Le Livre du Bicentenaire*, 152–53.

7. *Le Monde*, 17–18 September 1989; *L'Ardennais*, 18 September 1989; *Le Populaire du Centre*, 18 September 1989; N. Weill in *Le Monde de la Révolution française*, no. 11 (December 1989); *L'Humanité*, 14, 18 September 1989; *Figaro-Magazine*, 24 September 1989; *Royaliste*, no. 521 (1989).

8. Coverage by Antenne 2; *Le Populaire du Centre*, 18 September 1989; *Le Monde*, 19 September 1989; *L'Humanité*, 18 September 1989.

9. *Le Monde*, 15 April, 14 December, and supplement 18–24 December 1989; M. Ozouf, "A ses grands hommes, la patrie reconnaissante," *Le Monde de la Révolution française*, no. 12 (December 1989); E. Faure to J. Chirac, 19 February 1988, Mission papers, AN, 900506/6; J.-N. Jeanneney to F. Mitterrand, 20 November 1988 and 14 April 1989, ibid., 900506/24.

10. Cf. the remarks uttered by Abbé Gregoire in 1794 and later regretted concerning the patriots who "will plant upon the bloody cadavers of tyranny the tree of liberty which can flourish only if it is watered with the blood of kings." Mission du Bicentenaire, *Les Arbres de la liberté* (1989), 7. Jean Mendelson, a Mission staff member who today directs the press service at the French embassy in Washington, reminds me that the choice of Monge was not as ideologically neutral as was generally believed. After all, he had been vice president of the Paris Jacobin Club a month before Thermidor, and he later served Napoleon with utter fidelity, even beyond Waterloo. Personal communication, 7 July 1993.

11. "Discours de Jack Lang à l'occasion de l'hommage solonnel à Condorcet, l'abbé Grégoire, Monge au Panthéon, mardi, 12 décembre 1989," in Ministry of Culture, *Supplément à la Lettre d'information*, no. 273 (25 December 1989); J.-N. Jeanneney to F. Mitterrand, 13 September 1988, Mission papers, AN, 900506/24; *Royaliste*, no. 526 (11–25 December 1989); D. Julia, "Commémoration et histoire: Aux origines de l'instruction publique," *Histoire de l'éducation*, no. 42 (May 1989): 8–9; Julia, "L'Anathème," *Le Débat*, no. 57 (November-December 1989): p. 197; *Libération*, 12 December 1989; Jeanneney, *Rapport du président de la Mission du Bicentenaire*, 113–15; television coverage, Antenne 2, 12 December 1989. Cf. the harsh words expressed by the Socialists regarding Lustiger's unwillingness to attend the Panthéon ceremony: "Must one conclude that our Fifth Republic still lacks a little something in order to win the support of the Catholic Church?" *Synthèse-Flash*, no. 422 (18 December 1989). The PS was extremely content with the balanced Panthéon ticket. *Vendredi*, 8 December 1989.

12. *Présent*, 14 December 1989.

Book III / Chapter 1
Mobilization for Commemoration

1. Interview with T. Collard, 6 August 1991.

2. J.-N. Jeanneney, editorial, *Bicentenaire 89, lettre de la Mission*, 6 October 1988, 2; Jeanneney, "L'Héritage de la Révolution française," *Revue des deux mondes*, December 1988,

46; Jeanneney interview, *La Croix,* 20 January 1989; *VSD,* special number on the Avant-Première, June 1988; catalogue entitled *89 Avant-Première; Le Monde,* 5 June 1988; *Minute,* no. 1372 (20–26 July 1988); *Stratégies,* no. 633 (12 December 1988); *Aspects de la France,* 16 June 1988; *Révolution,* 2–8 December 1988.

3. *Le Quotidien du maire,* 3 November 1988; *La Voix du Nord,* 26 November 1988; J.-N. Jeanneney, "Premiers Regards sur le Bicentenaire," *Cercle Condorcet,* no. 11 (March 1990): 7; *Le Guide du Bicentenaire des élus,* May 1988 and January 1989; M. Ozouf, "Célébrer, savoir, fêter," *Le Débat,* no. 57 (November–December 1989): 32–33.

4. Memo by C. de Montrichard, n.d., Mission papers, AN, 900506/664; memo by Faure, 25 May 1987, AN, 900506/4; interview with Montrichard, 17 January 1991. The politics of commemorative organization will have to be studied on the local level. Experiences differed dramatically from place to place, largely as a function of existing relations of power. For instance, while the PS and the PCF brawled on the national scene, locally they practiced fruitful cooperation at Vizille, site of the early evocation of the pre-Revolution and of the establishment of the Museum of the French Revolution. As long as the PC controlled the municipality and the PS headed the Conseil général, things worked well. When the Conseil fell to the right, the left resigned from the board of trustees of the museum over both budget and political conflicts with the Conseil. Interview with Montrichard, 21 January 1991. The CSA, a public opinion research institute, argued that commemorative enthusiasm followed very strictly the right-left cleavage at the local level. *Images de la Révolution: Attentes par rapport au Bicentenaire, synthèse des principaux résultats* (Paris, 1988), 31.

5. A. Jezequel to E. Faure, 13 November 1987, Mission papers, AN, 900506/817.

6. Mission papers, AN, 900506/42 and 817.

7. Note by C. de Montrichard, circa late 1987, Mission papers, AN, 900506/815.

8. Mission papers, AN, 900506/817. On the limited means and weak influence of the Dijon area correspondent, a retired jurist, see Philippe Poirrier, "Le Bicentenaire dans l'agglomération dijonnaise," in Institut d'histoire du temps présent, *Lettre d'information,* no. 8 (July 1993):10–11.

9. R. Huard to author, 17 May 1991; CSA, *Images de la Révolution,* 32.

10. Meeting of the group "Manifestations culturelles," 21 September 1987, Mission papers, AN, 900506/1035; note by J.-P. Cabouat, circa October 1987, AN, 900506/665.

11. Mission papers, AN, 900506/41; interview with C. de Montrichard, 21 January 1991.

12. Meetings of 6 and 13 April and 18 August 1988, Mission papers, AN, 900506/665; M. Soulignac to J.-N. Jeanneney, 30 November 1988, and dossier by Daniel Mauberty of the Cerf volant, AN, 900506/673.

13. *Politis,* 7–12 July 1989.

14. J.-N. Jeanneney, *Rapport du président de la Mission du Bicentenaire à Monsieur le président de la République* (Paris, 1989), 129–40, 162–87, 196–220; *Bicentenaire 89, lettre de la Mission,* no. 1 (October 1988); *Le Monde,* 14 December 1988 and 17 July 1989; *L'Evénement du Jeudi,* 14–20 July 1988; Philippe Minard, "Premiers Regards sur le Bicentenaire," *Cercle Condorcet,* no. 11 (March 1990): 33. Michel Vovelle was more optimistic in his assessment than Minard. See his foreword in *Préfaces: Les Livres de la Révolution française* (numéro hors série), 5.

15. Interview with M. Rebérioux, 11 April 1991; *La Lettre CLEF,* no. 13 (March–April 1989). According to *La Lettre CLEF,* no. 9 (June–July 1988), in July 1988 there were CLEF committees already established in sixty-nine departments and eleven others that were in the process of constitution. There were no committees in eleven other departments, but the national CLEF instituted contacts with local commemorative committees in a number of them. Cf. the May issue, no. 9, which claimed CLEF committees in eighty-five departments. R. Huard informs me (letter of 17 May 1991) that the CLEF was "inexistent" in the Hérault.

16. Ligue française de l'enseignement and Ligue des droits de l'homme, *1989* (Paris, 1990); editorial by B. Wallon, *La Lettre CLEF*, no. 13 (March-April 1989); editorial by H. Leclerc, *La Lettre CLEF*, no. 12 (December 1988-January 1989); brochure for the colloquium entitled "Citoyenneté" (April 1989); editorial by M. Morineau, *La Lettre CLEF*, no. 11 (November 1988); editorial by M. Rebérioux, *La Lettre CLEF*, no. 10 (August-October 1988); editorial by M. Morineau, *La Lettre CLEF*, no. 14 (March 1989); editorial by B. Main, *La Lettre CLEF*, no. 7 (April 1988); B. Wallon cited in *Le Monde*, 27 May 1989; *La Dépêche du midi*, 2 April 1988; *Echo républicain*, 14 November 1988; *Ouest-France*, 14 February 1988; *Le Populaire du centre*, 16 March 1988; *La Montagne*, 3 April 1988.

17. Interviews with Michel Morineau and Bernard Wallon, September 1993; interview with M. Rebérioux, 11 April 1991; *La Lettre CLEF*, nos. 10 (August-October 1989), 12 (December 1988-January 1989), 13 (March-April 1989), and 15 (June 1989); the list of lecturers and of other services in Ligue française de l'enseignement and Ligue des droits de l'homme, *1989*.

18. *Le Monde de la Révolution française*, no. 10 (October 1989); interview with M. Rebérioux, 11 April 1991; interview with C. de Montrichard, 17 January 1991; minutes of staff meeting, 9 February 1989, Mission papers, AN, 900506/41; M. Bacot and J. Dubuis to C. de Montrichard, 24 February 1989, AN, 900506/805; instructions received in the Aveyron, AN, 900506/750.

19. M. Rebérioux, "Premiers Regards sur le Bicentenaire," *Cercle Condorcet*, no. 11 (March 1990): 20–21; *Le Tribun de Loir-et-Cher*, no. 2 (November 1988); Mission papers, AN, 900506/750 (Aveyron); *La Lettre CLEF*, nos. 2 (December 1987), 5 (February 1988), and 16 (July-December 1989). *Le Monde*, 27 May 1989; Ligue française de l'enseignement and Ligue des droits de l'homme, *1989; La Lettre CLEF*, nos. 2 (December 1987), 14 (March 1989), and 16 (July-December 1989); M. Rebérioux, "Premiers Regards sur le Bicentenaire," *Cercle Condorcet*, no. 11 (March 1990): 22; Ligue française de l'enseignement, *Catalogue des réalisations CLEF 89* (Paris: n.p., n.d.).

20. *La Lettre CLEF*, no. 16 (July-December 1989); *Le Monde de la Révolution française*, no. 10 (October 1989); interview with M. Rebérioux, 11 April 1991.

21. CSA poll, commissioned by the Mission, November 1989. Concerning Dijon, site of a prudent celebration that avoided controversial veins of the regional memory, Philippe Poirrier noted that "all the actors concur in underlining the feeble mark on posterity of the commemoration of 1989." "Le Bicentenaire dans l'agglomération dijonnaise," in Institut d'histoire du temps présent, *Lettre d'information*, no. 8 (July 1993):24.

22. Thierry Collard, who worked on a variety of programs for the Mission, deplored "les carences de la société civile et du partenariat privé." Whereas myriad collectivities, especially in the provinces, played a vigorous role in the commemoration, Collard esteemed that "les structures composantes de la société civile (associations, syndicats, organisations professionnelles, chambres de commerce et d'industrie . . .) n'ont pas toujours été en mesure de relayer ces initiatives." He attributed this failure to the inherent limits of volunteer work and to "un manque d'imagination flagrant, voire un certain conservatisme."

As for the private sector, "ses potentialités semblent avoir été largement surestimées." Beyond the problem of time that bedeviled the Mission, the major obstacle was the lack of a developed philanthropic practice in the French business community. T. Collard, "Note à l'attention de M. le président," Mission papers, AN, 900506/102.

23. *Bilan de la Mission* (December 1989); raw data kindly supplied by the Groupe sociologique de recherches de Nanterre through the good offices of Patrick Garcia; Bruno Benoist, "Spectacles et Bicentenaire à Lyon et autour de Lyon," in Institut d'histoire du temps présent, *Lettre d'information*, no. 9 (October 1993):24; Jean-Marie Guillon, "Le Bicentenaire dans les Bouches-du-Rhône et dans le Var," ibid., no. 8 (July 1993):25–32. Cf. Jean-

Clément Martin's salutary warning against viewing the "local logics" through a "national" prism. Ibid., p. 43. Two scholarly assessments of the local bicentennial illustrate some of the difficulties of measuring fervor, amplitude, penetration, mobilization, and so on. Both cynical and moralizing, Pierre Sansot, a professor of ethnology at Montpellier, went after an easy mark, deriding the administrative and journalistic habit of denoting "success" through crude quantitative measures. "Au château de Bidasse, on dénombre 1500 costumes, cousus main, 300 chapeaux également cousus main, 80 perruques et croix de pèlerin," he ironized with a heavy hand that cut to the quick of the souls of the hundreds of cultural associations and their volunteer worker-participants. "Rocamadour se vante de compter 300 acteurs dont 100 handicapés!" P. Sansot, "Du bon et moins bon usage de la commémoration," in *Mythe et révolutions* (Grenoble: Presses Universitaires de Grenoble, 1990), 307. Sociologist Jean-Pierre Donnadieu was neither carping nor judgmental, perhaps because he actually did some of the work on the bicentennial. He wrote to 360 mayors of communes in the Hérault to inquire whether or not they planned any types of commemoration/celebration ("manifestation"). The overwhelming majority did not bother to reply, a fact on which Donnadieu astonishingly does not comment. Twenty-six communes said no while thirty-six replied in the affirmative (plus six others that planned tree plantings). Donnadieu was particularly struck by the quiescence of the western section called the Minervois, an area steeped in Catharist tradition, resolutely committed to the Revolution, and marked by a Red-Socialist inclination throughout the nineteenth century: "The Minervois should have celebrated the Revolution." "Perception cartographique du Bicentenaire dans l'Hérault," in *Etudes du temps présent: Quel Avenir pour notre passé?* ed. Y. M. Le Bozec et al. (Office de Cliométrie appliquée, 1990), 20.

24. Mission papers, AN, 900506/827.

25. Ibid., 900506/673.

26. Extract of the minutes of the municipal council meeting of 27 October 1988, graciously communicated by Guy Boisson; *Montpellier votre ville*, nos. 117 (February 1989) and 122 (July-August 1989); program for the "Parcours des droits de l'homme," 12–16 June 1989; C. Lazerges to professors of classes participating in the Parcours, 29 May 1981; Ville de Montpellier, *10 Ans de Révolution à Montpellier* (Montpellier: Bicentenaire de la Révolution Française, 1989). Pragmatic rather than ideological, the artisans of this pedagogical dossier published at the end of the volume a chronology of Revolutionary events drawn from the work of the ultraliberal Florian Aftalion, much of whose economic analysis had to be anathema to Frêche, despite his own hard-nosed entrepreneurial bent. I am indebted to Christine Lazerges for furnishing me this documentation.

27. *Bilan de la commémoration du Bicentenaire dans la Drôme* (kindly communicated by the deputy of Valence, Roger Léron).

28. Ligue française de l'enseignement and Ligue des droits de l'homme, *1989;* Ville de Besançon, *Besançon, 1789–1989* (Besançon, 1989); interview with C. de Montrichard, 21 January 1991; Mission papers, AN, 900506/805, 750, and 808; *Le Monde*, 13 July 1989; *Bicentenaire 89, lettre de la Mission*, no. 9 (June 1989); *La Lettre du maire*, 14 September 1988; Drancy, press dossier, "Les Enfants de la Révolution"; Nouvelle Calédonie, "Le Livre du Bicentenaire" (manuscript scrapbook).

29. *National hebdo*, 13–19 July 1989; *Lyon Figaro*, 5 October 1899; *Lyon Libération*, 5 October 1988; *Le Progrès*, 5 October 1988; Philippe Dujardin, "Lyon 1989: Un 14 juillet en décembre," *Mots*, no. 31 (June 1992); Dujardin, "Politique du deuil, politique de la perplexité," *Cahiers d'histoire* (1993): 6, 14, 17; Dujardin's moving account of the "failure" of his major bicentennial project: "Réflexions d'un commémorateur sur un geste commémoratif: Le Parcours-spectacle," in Institut d'histoire du temps présent, *Lettre d'information*, no. 9 (October 1993); Bruno Benoist, "Spectacles et Bicentenaire à Lyon et autour de Lyon," ibid.

18–20; Benoist, "Peut-on commémorer la Révolution à Lyon?" in Jean Duvallon, Philippe Dujardin and Gérard Sabatier, eds., *Politique de la mémoire: Commémorer la Révolution* (Lyon: Presses Universitaires de Lyon, 1993), 93–104; Brigitte Abdelmajid, Sandra Perrot, and Florence Rodin, "La Commémoration du Bicentenaire à Lyon et dans son agglomération," unpublished memoir, Institut d'études politiques of Lyon (1992), 53, 83–107, 128–29, appendix 1 (this and the following two items were kindly communicated by Bruno Benoist); Karine Gonsse, Laurence Marlier, and Anne Moreau, "La Commémoration du Bicentenaire de la Révolution française dans les bulletins municipaux de la communauté urbaine de Lyon," unpublished memoir, Institut d'études politiques of Lyon (1992); Philippe Bonnard, Christophe Dubois, and Isabelle Gourdan, "Les Spectacles du Bicentenaire à Lyon et dans le Rhône," unpublished memoire, Institut d'études politiques of Lyon (1992).

30. *Midi-Libre*, 11, 13, 14, 16 June 1987 and 20 February 1988; *La Marseillaise*, 20 February 1987 and 18 February 1988; minutes of the second meeting of the Comité d'organisation du Bicentenaire de la Révolution française à Nîmes, 23 April 1987.

31. Interview with Dr. and Mrs. P. Luxereau, 1 January 1992.

32. Mission papers, AN, 900506/805; *La Lettre du maire*, 28 February 1989.

33. *Le Canard enchaîné*, 19 July 1989; M. Poniatowski, "En écoutant *La Marseillaise*," 14 July 1989, at l'Isle-Adam, kindly communicated, along with additional commentary, by the author through the good offices of Guy Sorman. Cf. the similar tone that the Gaullist mayor, Robert Poujade, imprinted upon Dijon's commemoration. Philippe Poirrier, "Le Bicentenaire dans l'agglomération dijonnaise," in Institut d'histoire du temps présent, *Lettre d'information*, no. 8 (July 1993): 16.

34. Interview with L. Poniatowksi, 10 April 1991.

35. *L'Evénement du Jeudi*, 27 July–2 August 1989.

36. *1789: Recueil de textes et de documents du 18e siècle à nos jours* (Paris: Centre National de Documentation Pédagogique, 1989).

37. On the institution of the academic correspondent, see *Centre-Ouest*, 17 April 1988.

38. "Un Entretien avec J.-N. Jeanneney," *Historiens-Géographes*, no. 327 (1990): 152; *Le Quotidien de Paris*, 8 March 1989; *Libération*, 12 May 1989; *Bicentenaire 89, lettre de la Mission*, no. 5 (February 1989), 14; Colette Darmagnac and Denise Le Guelte, "Si la Révolution nous était contée," *Historiens-Géographes*, no. 324 (August–September 1989): 93–94; Phryné Pigenet, "Un P.A.E. sans tambours ni trompettes: Sur la vie quotidienne de Paris pendant la Révolution française," ibid., 90–91; Marie-Claude Angot, "Un P.A.E. sur la Révolution française et les Droits de l'homme," ibid., 95–97; Ecole de Rosemont, *1789–1989* (Besançon: L'A.S.C.R. de l'Ecole, 1989). The Ministry of Culture, which boasted "bicentennial" in its official title, also promoted reflection on the Revolution in the schools. See, for instance, the essay competition stressing regional experiences. *Figaro-Magazine*, 14 January 1989. The city of Paris provided its schoolchildren with revolutionary documentation (e.g., the *Cartable 89*, a packet of brochures) and organized festive and commemorative activities (e.g., the *grand spectacle* in the Arènes de Lutèce in June). *Le Monde*, 1 June 1989.

Chapter 2
Poitiers and the Poitou-Charentes:
A Descent into *la France Profonde*

1. On the Revolution in the Poitou-Charentes, see the excellent studies by two authorities deeply implicated in the bicentennial experience and profoundly rooted in Poitiers: Jean-Marie Augustin, *La Révolution française en Haut-Poitou et pays charentais* (Toulouse: Bibliothèque Historique Privat, 1989), and Jacques Péret, *Histoire de la Révolution française en Poitou-Charentes, 1789–1799* (Poitiers: Projets Editions, 1988). The citation from Roux is

from my own copy of his *Histoire religieuse de la Révolution à Poitiers et dans la Vienne* (Lyon, 1952), 11–12, purchased from the Société des Antiquaires de l'Ouest. As I write these lines about the Poitou, I think fondly of my teachers at Poitiers in 1964, the late historians Jean Egret and Jacques Roger.

2. Interview with L. Fruchard, April 1991; R. Secher, *Juifs et Vendéens, d'un génocide à l'autre* (Paris: Olivier Orban, 1991), 266. As part of its investigation of bicentennial public opinion, the *EspacesTemps* team led by P. Garcia interviewed an anonymous "agriculteur" from Mauléon, born in 1939, a "catholique non pratiquant, ancien responsable syndical et politique, extrême gauche," who described himself as the son of the mayor. Given the temporal and political context, one is tempted to infer that his father was Fruchard, whom he denounced for having "laisser délabrer l'école publique, parce que c'était l'école *laïque*, c'était vraiment la saloperie des saloperies qui arrivait," for it was one of the few sources of enlightenment/demystification in the area. Dr. Fruchard informs me that this "son" is an impostor—neither his progeny nor that of his predecessor. The former mayor also notes that there is a thriving public school in his commune, expanded during his tenure. The farm worker is cited in Patrick Garcia, Jacques Lévy, and Marie-Flore Mattei, *Révolutions, fin et suite* (Paris: EspacesTemps Centre Georges Pompidou/Bibliothèque Publique d'Information, 1991), 150–51; Louis Fruchard, personal communication, 16 August 1993.

3. Interview with L. Fruchard, July 1991; C. Moreau, July 1991; interview with J.-M. Roger, 12 April 1991; interview with J. Péret, 12 April 1991; interview with J.-M. Augustin, July 1991.

4. *Poitou-Charentes: Des provinces à la région* (the regional program for the bicentennial); *Poitou-Charentes: Des provinces à la région* (commentaire de l'exposition); D. Guillemet and Frenel, *B.D.: Poitou-Charentes, des provinces à la région;* J.-P. Raffarin, "La Liberté est un cri, qui vient de l'intérieur."

5. J.-M. Roger, undated report to the Mission, unclassified bicentennial papers, Archives départementales de la Vienne, hereafter AD Vienne (kindly communicated by Monsieur Roger).

6. Interview with J.-M. Roger, 12 April 1991; interview with J. Péret, 4 April 1991.

7. Interview with J.-M. Augustin, July 1991; interview with J. Péret, 12 April 1991; undated draft report by Roger to the Mission, unclassified papers, AD Vienne; *Charente libre,* 6 January 1989 ("Chaque jour je reçois trois ou quatre lettres de gens qui veulent faire quelque chose pour le bicentenaire," Santrot declared, anxious to keep up with the burgeoning level of public interest).

8. Interview with J.-M. Augustin, July 1991; interview with J. Péret, 12 April 1991; J.-M. Roger's draft report, AD Vienne; *Nouvelle République du Centre-Ouest,* 7 June 1989.

9. Interview with J. Péret, 12 April 1991; interview with J.-M. Augustin, July 1991; J.-M. Roger's report to the Mission, AD Vienne; *Poitiers Magazine,* no. 14 (April 1989); *Nouvelle République du Centre-Ouest,* 13 April and 7, 13, 15 June 1989; *Centre Presse,* 13, 14, 15 June 1989; *Charente libre,* 15 June 1989.

10. Interview with J. Péret in the bulletin of the FOL, n.d; interview with Péret, July 1991; interview with J.-M. Augustin, July 1991; preface to *Les Poitevins prennent la parole: Cahiers de doléances de la Vienne* (Poitiers, 1989); *Nouvelle République du Centre-Ouest,* 27 January, 17 December 1988; *Charente libre,* 6 January 1989.

11. For documentation of the books mentioned here, see the CLEF catalogue, *La CLEF 89 de la Vienne: Un Centre de ressources.* The books were published by the FOL; some were subsidizied by the Conseil régional among other public institutions. See also *Nouvelle République du Centre-Ouest,* 28 June, 14, 27 October 1988, and 1 March 1989; *Centre Presse,* 26 October 1988 and 30 May 1989.

12. Interviews with J. Péret and J.-M. Augustin, July 1991; interview with J.-M. Roger, 12

April 1991; *Centre Presse,* 1 March 1989. Nor was the CLEF the sole impresario for bicentennial lectures. The Association des juristes catholiques also put together a program of public
lectures that Jean-Marc Roger regarded as a sort of ideological counterpoise to the CLEF
machine, and the Masons organized their own cycle of talks.

13. J.-M. Roger, "Situation au 1er mai 1988," draft report to the Mission, AD Vienne;
Centre Presse, 7 March 1989; *Charente libre,* 6 January 1989; interview with J.-M. Augustin,
July 1991.

14. J.-M. Roger, draft reports to Mission, AD Vienne; interview with J. Péret, July 1991;
La Révolution française en pays châtelleraudais (Châtellerault, 1989); Claudy Valin et al., *Les
Cahiers d'histoire de La Rochelle et de la Révolution,* nos. 1 (1989) and 2 (1990).

15. Mission papers, AN, 900506/779.

16. *Exposition de documents d'archives sur Norbert Pressac,* catalogue of the AD Vienne
(Mairie de Saint-Gaudent, 1989); *Le Journal de Civray,* 12 January 1989; P. Barrusseau,
mayor of Saint-Gaudent, to J.-N. Jeanneney, circa mid-January 1989, Mission papers, AN,
900506/782, 841, 845; J.-M. Roger to J.-N. Jeanneney, 24 January 1989; *Nouvelle République
du Centre-Ouest,* 20 March 1989; *Charente libre,* 21 March 1989; *Centre Presse,* 1, 3, 14, 16, 21
March 1989; interview with J.-M. Roger, 12 April 1991; interview with J.-M. Augustin, July
1991.

17. Interview with J. Péret, 12 April 1991; *Centre Presse,* 27 April 1989. Liberty trees were
also cut down in Dijon and Le Muy (Var). Philippe Poirrier, "Le Bicentenaire dans l'agglomération dijonnaise," in Institut d'histoire du temps présent, *Lettre d'information,* no. 8
(July 1993):19; Jean-Marie Guillon, "Le Bicentenaire dans les Bouches-du-Rhône et dans le
Var," ibid., p. 27.

18. Interview with J. Péret, 12 April 1991; interview with J.-M. Augustin, July 1991;
Nouvelle République du Centre-Ouest, 23 April 1989; interview with Philippe Desmarest, local
historian and official of the Conseil régional, 4 November 1991.

19. Interview with M. Legriel, 9 August 1991; interview with J.-M. Roger, 12 April 1991.
One of Legriel's ancestors was Jean-Joseph Laurence (1745–1803), who was elected to the
Estates General by the Third Estate of Poitiers. A publication entitled *Journal des guillotinés*
appeared during the bicentennial, enumerating the names of all the victims and placing the
danse macabre of the Revolution in stark relief. *Jours de France* published a call by Jacqueline
de Bouet du Portal, in the spirit of Legriel, for "cérémonies expiatoires" in memory of all the
victims. "Je suis scandalisée par tout ce qui se prépare pour ce Bicentenaire. . . . en tant que
descendante de victime, je ne fêterai certes pas cet anniversaire."

20. Interview with Fruchard, 12 April 1991; J.-M. Roger, draft report to the Mission,
n.d., AD Vienne; interview with J.-M. Augustin, July 1991. Fruchard's book on the wars in
the Vendée (focusing on Mauléon) appeared in 1992. During that same year, he became
entangled in a conflict over a project to build a memorial to the fallen troops of the Vendée,
denounced by critics as an anti-republican and anti-Vatican II enterprise. In 1993, Fruchard
grappled with scholars participating in a colloquium at Mauléon who described his views as
tainted for lack of documentary rigor and scholarly method. He dismissed them as petty and
partisan. *Courrier de l'Ouest,* 3, 5 March, 16 June, 21 July, 11 October, and 18 November
1992, and 22, 23, 24 May 1793; *Nouvelle République du Centre-Ouest,* 18, 22, 23 May 1993; *Le
Grand Mauléon,* no. 1 (December 1992). I am grateful to Claudy Valin for his assistance.

Chapter 3
The Bicentennial from Below: In the Communist Penumbra

1. *L'Humanité,* 9 September 1988; *93 prépare '89: Ephémérides pour la Seine-St.-Denis;* R.
Bourderon, "Aujourd'hui la Révolution," *Le Journal des amis du cinéma populaire* ("Spécial

89"), no. 4 (August-September 1988); C. Mazauric, "Conférences pour le Bicentenaire," in Centre d'information et d'étude de formation des élus, *1789–1989: Bicentenaire de la Révolution française* (Paris: Messidor, 1987); M. Vovelle in *Entretiens de la Fédération française des Maisons de la jeunesse et de la culture,* December 1988. Cf. an interview with Mazauric by Radio Bessèges (Gard) in which he marvels over the interest of electrical and gas workers in a Revolution that was so remote from them professionally and chronologically.

2. G. Plissonnier to federal directorates of the PCF, 5 May 1988, and R. Lejeune "aux camarades membres du collectif 'Bicentenaire,'" 27 December 1988 (correspondence kindly furnished by C. Mazauric); *93 prépare 89: Ephéméride pour la Seine-St.-Denis.*

3. Centre d'information et d'étude de formation des élus, *1789–1989: Bicentenaire de la Révolution française,* 16, 19–20, 30, 32–33, 35–36, 52; *Le Tribun de Loir-et-Cher,* no. 2 (November 1988).

4. G. Marchais, "La Révolution française et le parti communiste," in *Vive la Révolution française: Documents édités par le PCF,* 4; G. Plissonnier to directors of the federations, 5 May 1988, Archives of Vive 89 (which C. Mazauric very kindly put at my disposition); J.-N. Jeanneney, *Rapport du président de la Mission du Bicentenaire à Monsieur le président de la République* (Paris, 1989), 242; Mazauric to author, 12 March 1991; "Bilan Vive 89," Archives of Vive 89 (see, inter alia, the entries for 16 and 31 March and 16 April 1989); *Bulletin de l'Association Vive 89,* no. 1; *La Marseillaise,* 7 and 11 May 1987. Cf. Guy Hermier's reference to "le collectif national que la direction du parti a mis en place et qu'anime Claude Mazauric." Report to central committee, 6–7 April 1987, Archives of Vive 89.

5. C. Mazauric, *Entretiens de la Fédération française des Maisons de la jeunesse et de la culture.*

6. Mazauric cited in *Vive 89 en Ille-et-Vilaine,* no. 2; *Bulletin de l'Association Vive 89 en Somme,* no. 1; *Bulletin de l'Association Vive 89* (national organ), nos. 1 and 2.

7. Mazauric to author, 12 March 1991; interview with Mazauric in *Bourbonnais hebdo* (organ of the Fédé PCF of the Allier), 25–31 March 1987; *Association des amis de la Révolution française pour la célébration du Bicentenaire,* no. 2; *Vive la Révolution: Association pour la célébration de la Révolution en Sarthe,* no. 1 (n.d., circa December 1987-January 1988).

8. *Bulletin de l'Association Vive 89,* no. 3.

9. Interview with C. Mazauric, 14 April 1991.

10. Vive 89, Association nationale, "Bicentenaire de la Révolution française: Bilan provisoire de la commémoration," 29 November 1989, Archives of Vive 89.

11. Ibid.

12. Ibid.

13. *Bulletin de l'Association des amis de la Révolution française pour la célébration du Bicentenaire (Allier),* nos. 2 and 4, and minutes of the founding meeting, 16 March 1987, and of 29 April, 23 September, and 9 December 1987 (kindly communicated along with other precious documentation by the president, J.-C. Mairal); *Bulletin de l'Association Vive 89,* nos. 3 and 4; André Sérézat et al., *L'Allier révolutionnaire: Contributions à la connaissance de la Révolution française* (Amis de la Révolution Française pour la Célébration du Bicentenaire de 1789, n.d.); unsigned article contributed by Vive 89, *Bourbonnais hebdo,* no. 488 (30 March-5 April 1988); Vive 89, "Comment célébrer le Bicentenaire de la Révolution française dans nos communes."

14. R. Huard to author, 29 April 1991; publicity for C. Mazauric's visit and related documents kindly provided by R. Huard and G. Boisson.

15. R. Huard to author, 29 April and 17 May 1991; G. Boisson to author, July 1991.

16. H. Delpont to author, 5 April 1991, and a dossier of fliers and press clippings generously communicated by Delpont.

17. A. Leroy, "200 ans après: Des réalités d'hier à celles d'aujourd'hui," in *La Révolution française et l'Alsace: Particularités alsaciennes,* ed. Charles Kieffer (Cernay: Vive 89 en Haute-Alsace, 1989), 147–49; *L'Alsace,* 20 July 1988 and 13 January 1989.

18. C. Kieffer, *La Révolution française et l'Alsace: Particularités alsaciennes,* 5–6; Charles Kieffer, ed., *La Révolution française et l'Alsace: Révolutionnaires et contre-révolutionnaires en Alsace* (Cernay: Vive 89 en Haute-Alsace, 1990); *L'Alsace,* 22 January 1990. André Leroy graciously furnished the publications of the association as well as other useful documentation.

19. *Le Télégramme* (Saint-Brieuc), 7 November, 12 December 1988; *Ouest-France,* 4 January and 7 October 1990; M. Alory to author, 12 April 1991. I am grateful to M. Alory for his kind assistance.

20. J. Roquier to author, 12 April 1991; *Vive 89 en Ille-et-Vilaine,* nos. 1 (March-July 1988), 2 (September 1988), 3 (December 1988), and 5 (n.d.); J. Roquier to author, 12 April 1991. I am indebted to J. Roquier for precious information and documentation.

21. *Vive 89 en Ille-et-Vilaine,* nos. 1 (May-July 1988), 2 (September 1988), and 4 (March 1989).

22. *Bulletin de l'Association rochelaise pour le Bicentenaire de la Révolution française,* no. 1; *La Nouvelle République,* 26 April 1988.

23. Statutes of the Association rochelaise, prefectoral receipt no. 1930–87; *La Nouvelle République,* 26 April 1988; *Sud-Ouest,* 13 February, 4 March 1987; C. Valin to author, 3 May 1991; *Les Cahiers d'histoire de La Rochelle et de la Révolution,* no. 1: 5–8, 151–56; and no. 2: 7–9, 12–15; carte d'invitation, "La Révolution au quotidien," 13 January 1990. I am grateful to Mr. Valin for providing helpful documentation.

24. R. Bourderon (vice president of 89 en 93), "89 en 93: Le Bicentenaire de la Révolution française," typescript essay (circa 1990) kindly communicated to me by its author; *Bulletin 89 en 93,* December 1989; *Le Monde,* 16 April 1991.

25. For differing views of the Constitution of 1793, see J. Tulard, J.-F. Fayard, and Alfred Fierro, eds., *Histoire et dictionnaire de la Révolution française* (Paris: Robert Laffont, 1987), 694; and A. Soboul, in *Dictionnaire historique de la Révolution française,* ed. J.-R. Suratteau and F. Gendron (Paris: Presses Universitaires de France, 1989), 283–84.

26. Conseil général, *Programme: 89 en 93; Bulletin 89 en 93,* November and December 1989; notice of Aubervilliers in *93 prépare 89: Ephéméride pour la Seine-St.-Denis;* M. Tovar and R. Bourderon, *Révolution française et mouvement populaire* (Conseil Général de Seine-Saint-Denis, 1989).

27. *93 prépare 89: Ephéméride pour la Seine-St.-Denis; Bulletin 89 en 93,* November 1988; R. Bourderon et al., catalogue for *1789–1989, Prenons le relais.*

28. M. Tovar, *Cahiers de doléances* (Bobigny, 1989); Conseil général, *Programme: 89 en 93;* press release, "Je fête la Révolution à Bobigny," 23 May 1989; R. Bourderon, "89 en 93: Le Bicentenaire de la Révolution française"; press release, "Le Roi par ici, le roi par là, cherchons-le," 14 April 1989; *93 prépare 89: Ephéméride pour la Seine-St.-Denis.*

29. *Bulletin 89 en 93,* December 1989; R. Bourderon, "89 en 93: Le Bicentenaire de la Révolution française"; Bourderon to C. Mazauric, 10 April 1991 (kindly furnished by C. Mazauric); committee press packets for "Les Appels de l'été 1940" and "Ralliez la commune."

30. For the reservations of the two other syndical centrals, see *FO: Hebdomadaire,* 12 April 1989, and *CFDT Magazine,* no. 140 (July 1989).

31. G. Pruvost, "La CGT, le courant syndical réformiste et la Révolution française," *Institut CGT Cahiers d'histoire sociale,* November 1989, 72–80; *FO hebdomadaire,* 22 March 1989; *CFDT Magazine,* no. 139 (June 1989). *FO hebdomadaire* tirelessly lambasted the "esprit

de dénigrement" of the Revolution during the bicentennial season and argued, in terms less shrill but no less persuasive than the CGT, that "les droits de l'homme passent par les droits des travailleurs." *FO hebdomadaire*, 12, 28 April and 7, 28 June 1989.

32. G. Séguy cited in the national *Bulletin Vive 89*, no. 1; *La Vie ouvrière*, 2–8 January, 29 May–4 June, 10–16 June, 26 June–2 July 1989.

33. *Comités d'entreprise en révolutions* (Paris: Messidor, 1990), 19.

34. Henri Krasucki, preface to C. Mazauric, *Comités d'entreprise en révolutions*, 9–11.

35. C. Mazauric, *Comités d'entreprise en révolutions*, 74–75, 78–79, 84, 86, 88, 94–95, 112, 120–21. Cf. the example of the CE of the SNCF at Nancy, embracing over six thousand railroad workers, which refused, for unspecified reasons, "the ambitious project" put forth by the CGT delegates, who wanted to spend Fr 110,000 on the bicentennial. Ibid., 118.

Chapter 4
Paris: Bicentennial Accommodation and Resistance

1. "La Révolution fut l'occasion de destructions," noted the mayor at the unveiling of the refurbished and partially replaced statues of the major cities of France at the Concorde, "il est juste que le Bicentenaire soit l'occasion d'un effet de restauration." *Libération*, 15 December 1988. Beyond the Capetian linkage, Chirac could have drawn on an array of anniversaries that fell in 1989: the Treaty of Azay-le-Rideau (1189), marking Philippe-Auguste's affirmation of French identity vis-à-vis the English; the birth of Guillaume Farel, a humanist and reformer (1489); the Edict of Villers-Cotterêts (1539), establishing the basis of an administrative record in the French language; the accession of Henri IV (1589); the birth of Montesquieu (1689); and so on.

2. Press conferences of 18 and 22 March 1988, documentation of the Hôtel de Ville.

3. Preface to *89 Avant-Première*, catalogue of the exposition; Chirac's presentation of the Paris bicentennial program, documentation of the Hôtel de Ville, n.d.

4. J. Chirac's welcome at the reception of 26 May 1989 in Hôtel de Ville, *Paris, 1789–1989* (Paris: Christian, 1990).

5. What follows is based heavily on the convergent testimony of two municipal figures involved in bicentennial planning who asked not to be identified. It also draws on printed documentation provided by the Hôtel de Ville and on interviews with F. de Panafieu, July 1991 (for whose generosity I am especially grateful); T. Aumonier, 2 December 1991; T. Collard, 3 August 1991; and J. Tulard, 10 April 1991.

6. *Le Monde*, 27 June 1989.

7. Interview with F. de Panafieu, July 1991; *Le Parisien*, 21, 25 November and 3–4 December 1988; *Le Journal de Dimanche*, 27 November 1988; *Le Monde*, 27 November 1988; *L'Express*, 3 December 1988; *Le Figaro*, 15 December 1988; Reuters dispatch, 7 March 1989; *Le Nouvel Observateur*, 2–8 February 1989; Hôtel de Ville, *Paris, 1789–1989*.

8. *Le Quotidien de Paris*, 15 December 1988. Cf. *Le Figaro*, 15 December 1988, and *Le Figaroscope*, 21 December 1988.

9. "Figure mythique et emblème populaire, la Dame de fer, qui fut élévée à la gloire de la Révolution," conceded a journalist for *Le Figaro*, 16 June 1989.

10. "La Ville de Paris, pas mécontente de faire un pied de nez à la gauche, à la Mission du Bicentenaire de la Révolution, au président de la République, et aux sans-culottes," observed *Le Monde* (20 June 1989), "avait choisi de célébrer 1789 en exaltant 1889." In a similar vein, *L'Humanité* (17 June 1989) wrote: "Les sommes engagées sont telles qu'on peut se demander

si la Mairie de Paris n'a pas trouvé là une sorte de substitut à la célébration du Bicentenaire de la Révolution française."

11. *Le Figaro*, 16 June 1989; *Le Monde*, 20 June 1989.

12. *L'Humanité*, 19 June 1989; interview with T. Aumonier, 2 December 1991.

13. *Paris 89. Programme officiel, 17 June 1989.*

14. *Le Quotidien de Paris*, 26 September 1988. In a poll conducted by CSA for the Mission in November 1989, 54 percent of respondents esteemed that the mayor was wrong not to attend the Gouderie (almost two-thirds of those on the left and 43 percent of those on the right fell into this category). CSA poll, November 1989.

15. Remarks attributed to J.-N. Jeanneney did not help to reassure Jarre that he was genuinely wanted. The president of the Mission promised the public imminent news of the "exceptional" July fourteenth that the state had decided to substitute for Jarre's concert, which was thus implicitly stigmatized as less than exceptional. *Le Quotidien de Paris*, 26 September 1988.

16. Georges Sarre, president of the Socialist group in the municipal council, railed against the mayor's decision to back out of the Jarre concert, assimilating it to his alleged sabotaging of the international exposition and the Parisian candidacy for the Olympic Games. The lack of attention that the PS gave this affair on the national stage suggests how little political benefit it could yield.

17. J. Tibéri, "Conférence de presse," 22 March 1988, documentation Hôtel de Ville; *Le Parisien*, 26 September 1988; *Libération*, 15 December 1988; *Le Quotidien de Paris*, 15 December 1988.

18. J.-N. Jeanneney to J. Chirac, 30 January 1989; Chirac to Jeanneney, early February 1989. Privately communicated.

Chapter 5
The Bicentennial Destiny of Robespierre

1. E. Fournier-Elipot, "Robespierre m'a dit," *Bulletin de l'Association des amis de Robespierre pour le Bicentenaire de la Révolution française* (hereafter *Bulletin ARBR*), no. 8.

2. *Le Nouvel Observateur*, 5–11 January 1989; *Figaro-Magazine*, 23 January 1988. "Despite the disparagement and the repression," noted philosopher Daniel Bensaïd, with 38 percent of respondents expressing a rather positive opinion of Robespierre, he was "well above [Georges] Marchais." *Moi, la Révolution* (Paris: Gallimard, 1989), 270. A CSA poll, commissioned by the Mission toward the end of the bicentennial year, suggests the need for some nuancing. In November 1989 more people liked Robespierre than had done so two and a half years earlier (37 percent vs. 32 percent), *and* more people disliked him than had before (40 percent vs. 34 percent). Substantially fewer people were without an opinion in November 1989 than in June 1987 (23 percent vs. 34 percent). The CSA poll revealed considerable antipathy for Robespierre on the left as well as sympathy for him on the right, though the classical lines of cleavage remained the same. Around 30 percent of the right had a favorable view of him, while about 40 percent of the left had a negative perception. Among the avowed Communists (n = 42), 39.5 percent found Robespierre sympathetic, while almost the same number, 38.6 percent, found him antipathetic (22 percent not expressing an opinion). Among the PS–MRG (Mouvement des radicaux de gauche) voters (n = 277), 47 percent had a favorable opinion of Robespierre and 40.2 percent an unfavorable one, with the remainder abstaining. Respondents declaring to be without religion were much more inclined than conventional Catholics to esteem Robespierre (43 percent vs. 24 percent). He was by far most

popular in the north (51 percent sympathetic vs. 21 percent antipathetic) and least popular in the west (24 percent favorable vs. 52 percent hostile). Though the French public clearly learned a considerable amount about Robespierre during the bicentennial season, a substantial number of respondents (over a third) could not respond to a question asking them to situate him politically on a spectrum from extreme left to extreme right.

3. The Sofres-*Express* poll, *L'Express*, 7 July 1989, reproduced in *La Voix du Nord*, 22 November 1989 and the *Bulletin ARBR*, no. 7; *Figaro-Magazine*, 28 October 1988; J.-Y. Mollier, rapport introductif, *Manuels scolaires et Révolution française*, colloquium at Créteil, June 1989 (Association départementale pour le Bicentenaire/Editions Messidor, 1990), 25–27.

4. *Le Figaro*, 14 July 1989; Charles Josquin, "Robespierre en 1989," *Raison présente*, no. 41 (1991): 36. Those who see Dominique Jamet, once a rightist journalist and now custodian of France's embryonic new national library, as a Mitterrandian terrorist may find some solace in the knowledge that he, too, viewed Robespierre as the direct ancestor of Stalin and Pol Pot.

5. F. Crouzet, *Historians and the French Revolution: The Case of Maximilien Robespierre* (Swansea: University College, 1989), 23–24, 26. Cf. M. Vovelle's complaint, drafted long before the publication of Crouzet's lecture: "Without being singled out as archaic or perhaps shamefully bloodthirsty, could one speak openly today in the name of the Société des études robespierristes?" Editorial, *Annales historiques de la Révolution française*, no. 263 (January-March 1986): 5.

6. F. Furet, "Est-il coupable?" *L'Express*, 7 July 1989.

7. M. Thorez cited in *Libération*, 23 April 1989; J. Ferrat quoted by Patrick Garcia, Jacques Lévy, and Marie-Flore Mattei, *Révolutions, fin et suite* (Paris: *EspacesTemps*–Centre Georges Pompidou/Bibliothèque Publique d'Information, 1991), 70.

8. Georges Lefebvre, who shared many positions with the PCF, described Robespierre as "the immovable and incorruptible head of revolutionary Resistance." Cited by F. Crouzet, *Historians*, 17. Crouzet also notes that "Lefebvre's brother, a professor of geography, had been beheaded by the Nazis during the Occupation. Ibid.

9. G. Hermier, report to the central committee of the PCF, 6–7 April 1987; P. Herzog cited in *Le Monde*, 3 May 1989; *L'Humanité*, 13 July 1989; *Révolution*, 2–8 December 1988; C. Mazauric, in Mazauric and A. Casanova, *Vive la Révolution, 1789–1989*, ed. C. Ducol (Paris: Messidor/Editions Sociales, 1989), 57; *La Vie ouvrière*, 29 May-4 June 1989.

10. C. Mazauric, *Entretiens de la Fédération française des Maisons des jeunes et de la culture*, April 1989; Mazauric in Mazauric and Casanova, *Vive la Révolution*, 132–42; Mazauric interview on the radio, France Culture, 24 July 1980; Mazauric, *Jacobinisme et Révolution: Autour du Bicentenaire de quatre-vingt-neuf* (Paris: Editions Sociales, 1984), 62–63; *Vive la Révolution*, bulletin of the Association "Vive la Révolution, 1789–1989," no. 2 (February 1988); *Balistica*, special bicentennial issue (1989): 17–19. Cf. philosopher Jean-Pierre Faye's moderate and discriminating defense of Robespierre before the audience of the enemy, *Le Quotidien de Paris*, 15 July 1983.

11. C. Mazauric cited in *La Lettre du comité* of the Caisse d'action sociale of the EDF, no. 16 (December 1989); Mazauric address to the Association "Paris-Révolution," 14 December 1989; Mazauric, interview, Radio Bessèges, July 1989.

12. *L'Humanité*, 1 April 1989.

13. *L'Evénement du Jeudi*, 26 February-4 March 1987; *À gauche*, no. 318 (15 June 1989); *L'Ours*, no. 204 (November 1989); M. Gallo, *Entretiens de la Fédération française des Maisons des jeunes et de la culture* (February 1989).

14. Interview with F. Mitterrand, *L'Express*, 14 July 1989; interview with R. Badinter, *Libération*, 12 December 1989; "Vive le Bicentenaire, entretien avec J.-N. Jeanneney," *Armées d'aujourd'hui* (March 1989): 183.

15. The bulk of the preceding discussion of the history of Robespierre in Arras is derived from the very informative master's thesis of Anne Gillion, "La Mémoire de Robespierre à Arras," submitted to the Université de Lille III in 1987 and kindly communicated to me by the ARBR. See also *Le Monde*, 13 July 1989; interview with C. Mazauric, 13 July 1989; F. Crouzet, *Historians*, 33–34; E. J. Hobsbawm, *Echoes of the Marseillaise: Two Centuries Look Back on the French Revolution* (New Brunswick, N.J.: Rutgers University Press, 1990), 68–69; speech of Mayor Delansorne at the 1933 dedication, *Bulletin ARBR*, no. 2; report of the ceremonies and speeches at the dedication, *Annales historiques de la Révolution française*, November–December 1933), 481–510.

16. Undated letter from retired historian Marc Bouloiseau, long active in the affairs of the Société des études robespierristes, to the editors of the *Bulletin ARBR*, no. 6. *Le Monde*, 13 July 1989.

17. Interview with C. Mazauric, 14 April 1991; *Le Monde*, 13 July 1989; *Bulletin ARBR*, no. 4.

18. M. Vovelle, *Aventures de la raison* (Paris: Belfond, 1989), 153–55. Cf. his editorial in the *Annales historiques de la Révolution française*, no. 263 (January–March 1986): 5.

19. *Le Monde*, 13 July 1989; *Nord matin*, 7 February 1988; F. Bleitrach to L. Fatous, 26 January 1990, in *Bulletin ARBR*, no. 8; ARBR to C. Mazauric (as vice president of the Société des études robespierristes), 1 February 1990; minutes of assembly of the ARBR, 12 April 1990 (graciously conveyed by an officer of the ARBR, C. Lescureux); *La Voix du Nord*, 9 May 1990; interview with Mazauric, 14 April 1991; Mazauric to author, 19 May 1991. Again, feelings healed rapidly in Arras, especially under the prod of collective self-interest. Gheerbrant, as head of the chamber of commerce, warmly collaborated with Mayor Fatous in a campaign to make the city more attractive to investors/employers. *Le Monde*, 12–13 January 1992.

20. *La Voix du Nord*, 20 February, 8 May and 6 June 1987, 24 May, 9 and 12 June 1988, and 12 May, 22 June, and 22 November 1989; *Nord matin*, 4 April 1987 and 12 June 1990; *Liberté*, 5 April 1987 and 19 February 1989; *Bulletin ARBR* (which was apparently briefly called *L'Incorruptible*), nos. 4, 5, 7, 10; minutes of the board of the ARBR, 17 April 1990; G. Sentis to C. Mazauric, 7 September 1989 (an invitation on behalf of the ARBR to a colloquium entitled "L'Image de Robespierre dans les manuels scolaires"); *Ça ira! Gazette des sans-culottes de Carvin*, nos. 1 through 5 (June 1988 through July 1989); *Le Citoyen de Meurchin en Artois, journal des amis de Robespierre*, nos. 1–6 (dated 1779 through Year II).

21. *Bulletin ARBR*, no. 10.

22. *Bulletin ARBR*, nos. 7, 8; *La Voix du Nord*, 22 October 1989; *Le Figaro*, 28 September 1988; M. Becker to author, 15 July 1992. I am grateful to Mme Becker for contacting me and supplying me with precious information as well as copies of her work.

23. R. Caratini in *Le Monde de la Révolution française*, no. 4 (April 1989); C. Josquin, "Robespierre en 1989," 33–34; *Raison présente*, no. 41 (1991): *Le Parisien*, 26 May 1989. Jacques Charrier, a historian from Paris, informed *Le Monde* (6 December 1988) of the fleeting existence of a square in Paris named for Robespierre. He also called attention to "a large-scale bust by Séraphim" that the municipality of Saint-Denis erected "in a square in the center of town" in 1949. This statue, near the Théâtre Gérard Philippe, is apparently the only such monument to Robespierre outside Arras. *Dialogues-Sevran*, no. 25 (April 1989).

24. *Le Monde*, 9–10 September 1990 and 28 August 1991; *Bulletin de l'Association des amis pour la célébration du Bicentenaire de la Révolution française (Allier)*, no. 2; "Clayes en fêtes,"

bicentennial program; *Rapport d'activité, bilan de la commémoration du Bicentenaire dans la Drôme;* interviews with Gilbert Millet and his staff, October 1992; *La Marseillaise,* 19 and 28 February 1988; *Bulletin ARBR,* nos. 7 and 8; *La Voix du Nord,* 9 September 1990; *Nord matin,* 19 April 1988. On the failure of Dijon to concede a street to Robespierre, see Philippe Poirrier, "Le Bicentenaire dans l'agglomération dijonnaise," in Institut d'histoire du temps présent, *Lettre d'information,* no. 8 (July 1993): 15.

25. *La Vie ouvrière,* 1–7 May 1989; C. Vermoret to C. Dupavillon, 26 September 1988, Mission papers, AN, 900506/805; *La Voix du Nord,* 16 October 1989; Patrick Berthier, "Kateb Yacine et la Révolution française," *Études,* September 1989, 242–45; *Le Monde,* 27 April, 24 June, and 2–8 December (television supplement) 1989.

26. "Rapport moral de l'assemblée générale constituante de l'Association Vive 89," 26 September 1987 (graciously communicated by G. Mertz).

27. Documentation furnished by G. Mertz; P. Souffrin to author 2 July 1989; C. Mazauric to author, 19 May 1991.

28. *Républicain lorrain,* 2 December 1988 and 1 February 1989; *Le Monde,* 18 November 1988; *La Lettre du maire,* 23 November 1988; Mazauric to author, 26 April 1991; *Time,* 9 January 1989.

29. *Républicain lorrain,* 20 January and 28 October 1989; *Le Figaro,* 7 January 1989; *Time,* 9 January 1989.

30. A. Scholtès to *Républicain lorrain,* 1 November 1988; *Le Figaro,* 7 January 1989.

31. B. Muller to *Républicain lorrain,* 1 November 1988; R. Dreidmy to *Républicain lorrain,* 28 October 1988.

32. G. Mertz, "La Violence au 18e siècle," manuscript essay amiably furnished by its author.

33. *Le Figaro,* 7 January 1989; *Le Monde,* 18 November 1988; interviews obligingly provided by G. Mertz.

34. Letters of D. Cuny, A. Baur, D. Graziani de Terville, B. Tarillon, and J.-C. Magrinelli to the *Républicain lorrain,* 1, 4, and 13 November 1988.

35. *Républicain lorrain,* 12 December 1988 and 7 January 1989.

36. *Républican lorrain,* 6 and 20 November 1988, 21 and 28 January 1989; P. Souffrin to author, 2 July 1991; *Time,* 9 January 1989; G. Mertz to director of the DRAC, 17 May 1989; Souffrin to J. Lang, 23 May 1989; D. Bozo to [?], 17 October 1989; Beauvralot (DRAC) to Mertz, n.d.; Mertz to author, 31 July 1991. In the margin of the statue saga, Charles Tordjman, director of the Théâtre populaire de Lorraine, planned to stage a play in the Robespierre square of Thionville entitled *La Guillotine.* The assembled crowd would be asked to decide whether the blade should remove . . . the head of a pig. "We can't just do pretty spectacles with blue, white, and red sansculottes," argued the director. "We have to provoke people. History has to wake up." *Time,* 9 January 1989.

Farewell

1. *Le Monde,* 16 April 1992 (from an excellent piece by Thomas Ferenczi).

2. *Figaro-Magazine,* 25 April 1992. The fact that Griotteray served in the Resistance has no bearing on the odious causes he often espouses.

3. *Figaro-Magazine,* 25 January 1992. The pretext for Pauwels's remarks was a new book published by the former socialist minister of defense Jean-Pierre Chevènement ("Ah! quel admirable homme de droite serait M. Chevènement s'il ne se croyait pas à gauche!").

4. One imagines the Jacobino-republicans chanting Clemenceau's refrain as prayer-pledge-mantra: "C'est que cette admirable Révolution, par qui nous sommes, n'est pas finie. C'est qu'elle dure encore. C'est que nous en sommes encore les acteurs, aux prises avec les mêmes ennemis." Cited in *Le Monde*, 8 October 1986.

5. Franck Lepage, organizer of the *Entretiens de le Fédération française des Maisons des jeunes et de la culture*, in the introduction (May 1989).

6. R. Debray in *Le Nouvel Observateur*, 30 November–6 December 1989 and, in abridged form, *Que vive la République* (Paris: O. Jacob, 1989), pp. 26–28, 81–82. Jacques Julliard rebuffed and debunked Debray's argument. In mourning for the passing of "une conception volontariste de l'Histoire," the elitist philosopher could not bring himself to accept the idea of the nation freeing itself from tutelage in order to assume its own responsibilities. Presciently, the historian-journalist detected and denounced in the republican credo the pretext for a rejection of the new Europe. *Le Nouvel Observateur*, 7–13 December 1989. Max Gallo used the republican-democratic dichotomy in a manner quite similar to Debray's. See his contribution to the *Entretiens de la Fédération française des Maisons des jeunes et de la culture* (February 1989). In her satiric piece in *Le Monde* (31 January 1991), Claude Sarraute had J.-P. Chevènement defending his conduct during the war against Iraq in these terms: "Je suis un républicain, pas un démocrate, moi, M'sieur le Président, et ils me courent sur le haricot, ces intégristes saoudiens."

7. R. Debray interviewed by S. Moati in his film *A propos de la Révolution française*. On Debray's ever-deepening pessimism, see "'République', un mot 'ringard'! Entretien avec Régis Debray," *L'Histoire*, no. 155 (May 1992): 42–43.

8. "La France est en péril," announced two Gaullist barons, former premier Michel Debré and former justice minister Jean Foyer, in a declaration reminiscent of the style of 1793. *Le Monde*, 29 April 1992.

9. *Le Monde*, 31 March 1992.

10. On the "nouvelles peurs," see the recent reflections of a Socialist minister, Paul Quilès, *Nous vivons une époque intéressante* (Paris: Gauche Contrat, 1992).

11. *Le Monde*, 31 March 1992.

12. Interview with A. Dahmani, 10 April 1991; M. Dridi to C. Mazauric, 22 June 1989, Vive 89 papers; extract of *La Lettre du Groupement pour les droits des minorités* published in the *Lettre CLEF*, 7 April 1988.

13. *Le Monde*, 5 June 1990. Duhamel's regret about the absence of hopefulness brings to mind Babeuf's "Peuple, réveille-toi à l'espérance." Writing a year after Duhamel in the same newspaper (17 September 1991), the journalist Jean-Yves Lhomeau struck the same theme of "l'usure de la démocratie" and pathology in the public sphere: "La France a bonne mine! Au moment où la démocratie submerge la 'nouvelle Europe', 2 ans après les célébrations en grande pompe du Bicentenaire de la Révolution, elle boude un système offert en exemple au monde entier."

14. *Le Point*, 18 June 1990. Cf. Thierry de Beaucé, a junior minister for international cultural affairs, quoted on the need to incite the intellectuals to return to the political domain. Ibid., 16 July 1990.

15. To measure the extent to which this memory of the rapid reversal of *acquis* continues to weigh upon Mitterrand's mind, see, beyond his bicentennial speeches, his press conference following the failed Soviet coup. *Le Monde*, 13 September 1991. Mitterrand's jolting Vichy memory/prod takes on a somewhat (tragically) ironical air in light of certain "memory holes" in his mind revealed by Pierre Péan, *Une Jeunesse française: François Mitterrand, 1934–1947* (Paris: Fayard, 1994) and the president's commentary on his own behavior and Péan's portrayal of it.

16. *Le Monde,* 14 April 1992.

17. For an interesting discussion of the reorientation of laicity, see "Quelle laïcité au-jourd'hui?," *L'Evénement du Jeudi,* supplement to no. 297 (1990).

18. A poll commissioned by the Mission toward the end of the bicentennial season showed that the public then had a more positive attitude toward the Revolution and a better understanding of what the Revolution meant to France than it had expressed in earlier polls. The Mission attributed this evolution to the educative aspects of the commemoration, in which it had played a paramount role. For almost three-quarters of all respondents, the word "revolution" evoked a positive image; fifteen months earlier, only 38 percent had viewed it this way. About three-quarters of those surveyed were also "proud to be a citizen of the country that made the Revolution of 1789 [and presumably not that of 1793–94?]." No huge gap separated respondents on the right and left. Eighty-five percent thought that it was a good thing that the Revolution occurred, up from 77 percent two years earlier. Eighty-seven percent (with only a relatively small disparity between left and right) believed that the ideas of '89 had either a "very positive" or "rather positive" impact on bicentennial France. Whereas only 44 percent of persons queried in June 1987 considered the Revolution of '89 a source of international prestige for France, almost two-thirds espoused this view toward the end of 1989.

As for the celebration/commemoration, while 48 percent esteemed that the scale of festivities was not justified (down from 59 percent in June 1989), and 60 percent felt that the expenses were excessive (the right embracing this view much more heavily than the left), 65 percent appraised the "ceremonies of the bicentennial" as "rather a success." (Barely a month earlier, in a BVA poll, only 50 percent endorsed this judgment—a puzzling incongruity in such a short period of time.) A slight majority (51 percent vs. 43) agreed with the statement: "Fortunately the year 1989 is coming to an end—we won't hear any more about the Revolution." CSA poll, November 1989 (1,004 persons aged eighteen years or more).

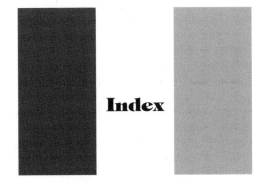

Index

Index